An Introduction to Film Studies

'The first edition went a long way to meeting the need for an introductory text accessible to A level, further education and beginning higher education students of film. The second edition builds on the success of the first, reflecting some of the newer emphases in the subject in revised or rewritten chapters, and incorporating more cross-referencing, useful 'think points' and new material on areas such as spectatorship. Overall, *An Introduction to Film Studies* is now an even more valuable resource.'
Jim Hillier, *Senior Lecturer in Film Studies, University of Reading*

'Probably the clearest, most comprehensive and accessible introduction to film studies available.'
Martin Price, *Stratford-upon-Avon Sixth Form College*

'I highly recommend this text to any student embarking on the study of film.... An admirable synthesis of historical, social and theoretical considerations of cinema, presented in an engaging and accessible manner.'
Alan Burton, *De Montfort University*

This completely revised and updated second edition provides a guide to key issues and concepts in film studies, and traces the historical development of film, while introducing some of the world's key national cinemas. Written by experienced teachers in the field and lavishly illustrated with over 160 film stills and production shots, it will be essential introductory reading for any student new to film studies.

Key features of the second edition include:

- updated coverage of a wide range of concepts, theories and issues in film studies
- in-depth discussion of the contemporary film industry
- a new chapter on spectatorship in the cinema
- marginal key terms, notes and cross-referencing
- new case studies and examples, review questions and follow-up activities, website resources and a glossary of terms
- suggestions for further reading, further viewing and a comprehensive bibliography

Contributors: Lez Cooke, Chris Jones, Mark Joyce, Asha Kasbekar, Julia Knight, Searle Kochberg, Jill Nelmes, Patrick Phillips, Allan Rowe, Chris Webster, Paul Wells

Editor: **Jill Nelmes** is Senior Lecturer in Film Studies at the University of East London.

Comments on the first edition:

'Indispensable for the A level, degree student or lay reader in film communications or media courses … will indisputably be the standard text for many years to come…. If I had to unreservedly tell a student at any level to buy one book, this is it: as close to the perfect film studies textbook as you're likely to see.'
John Lough, *Senior Lecturer in Media Theory, University of Humberside*

'To me it is simply the best introductory volume in the field so far.'
Jesus B. Sanchez, *Castilla La Mongha University, Ciudad Real, Spain*

'A new perspective joining different categories such as nation/genre/gender/technology/cinema as an institution. A wonderful final index.'
G. Elisa Bussi, *University of Bologna, Forli, Italy*

'I loved the book. High readability of layout, excellent quality of images, wide range of case studies and topics…. Also, a wide range of theory, debates and concepts covered in depth using accessible language. Terminology is clearly explained.'
Elaine Scarratt, *Christ the King Sixth Form College, Lewisham*

'This book is a treasure. Clear and well presented. I shall recommend it.'
Francine Wetherill, *Manchester University Institute of Science and Technology*

'An indispensable text for any student of film or media theory. The book logically and coherently addresses the main concepts relating to the film industry and its texts, defining key terms along the way. The case studies are illuminating and wide ranging in their concerns.'
N.R. Corran, *Edge Hill HE College*

'The source book for all introductory level. It provides a pathway to more advanced levels of reading, viewing and research, depending on the interests, either academic or otherwise, of reader level.'
J.E. Mair, *Edge Hill HE College*

'An excellent book within which students will encounter not only descriptions of the media and culture industries, but also the relationship between them and the structural practices affecting textual production.'
A. Thew, *Edge Hill HE College*

'It is stylishly written, handles contemporary theory cleverly, draws on a wide range of films and approaches to film and features a generous selection of stills. It will be the set text for my course on A level film studies.'
Nicholas Freeman, *Care and Early Education College, Lawrence Weston, Bristol*

An Introduction to Film Studies

Second edition

Edited by Jill Nelmes

London and New York

First published 1996

Second edition first published 1999
by Routledge
11 New Fetter Lane, London EC4P 4EE

Simultaneously published in the USA and Canada
by Routledge
29 West 35th Street, New York, NY 10001

Routledge is an imprint of the Taylor & Francis Group

Reprinted 2000 and 2001

Selection and editorial matter © 1996, 1999 Jill Nelmes
Individual chapters © 1996, 1999 individual contributors

Typeset in Monotype Neue Helvetica by Routledge
Printed and bound in Great Britain by Butler and Tanner Ltd, Frome
and London

British Library Cataloguing in Publication Data
A catalogue record for this book is available from the British Library

Library of Congress Cataloguing in Publication Data
An introduction to film studies / edited by Jill Nelmes – 2nd ed.
Includes bibliographical references and index.
1. Motion pictures.   I. Nelmes, Jill
PN1994.1537   1999
791.43–dc21

ISBN 0–415–17309–4 (hbk)
        0–415–17310–8 (pbk)

Contents

Illustrations   xi
Notes on contributors   xvii
Preface to the second edition   xix
Acknowledgements   xx

■ **1 Introduction**   1
JILL NELMES

**PART ONE: INSTITUTIONS, AUDIENCES
AND TECHNOLOGY**   11

■ **2 Cinema as institution**   13
SEARLE KOCHBERG
Introduction   14
The origins of the American film industry (1900–15)   14
The studio era of American film (1930–49)   17
CASE STUDY 1: WARNER BROS.   21
The contemporary film industry (1949 onwards)   26
CASE STUDY 2: A MAJOR US PRODUCTION, JAWS (1975)   34
CASE STUDY 3: A MEDIUM-BUDGET UK PRODUCTION, THE CRYING GAME (1992)   37
CASE STUDY 4: A LOW- TO MEDIUM-BUDGET UK PRODUCTION, FELLOW
    TRAVELLER (1989)   39
Film audiences   44
Censorship and classification   48
CASE STUDY 5: US – THE HAYS CODE   49
CASE STUDY 6: UK CENSORSHIP – INTERWAR AND SECOND WORLD WAR   51
CASE STUDY 7: UK CONTEMPORARY – PLATOON (1986)   52
'Cinema as institution' – summary   53
Notes   53
Further reading   57
Further viewing   57
Resource centres   58

■ **3 Film and technology**   59
CHRIS WEBSTER
Introduction   60

Film and the technology of illusion 62
In the beginning 64
From toys to Tinseltown 66
Somewhere between then and now 69
Computer-generated imagery 73
CASE STUDY 1: MARS ATTACKS! (1996) 77
Other ways of seeing 79
World economics and new technologies 84
Final frame: conclusion 85
Further reading 86
Further viewing 87
Resource centres 87

PART TWO: APPROACHES TO STUDYING FILM TEXTS 89

■ **4 Film form and narrative** 91
ALLAN ROWE
Introduction: the act of viewing 92
CASE STUDY 1: ROBOCOP (1987) 92
CASE STUDY 2: BEGINNING OF KEATON'S THE GENERAL (1925) 95
Cinematic codes 98
Narrative 115
Alternative narratives 121
CASE STUDY 3: IF... – AN ALTERNATIVE TEXT (1968) 124
Notes 127
Further reading 127
Further viewing 128
Resource centres 128

■ **5 The film spectator** 129
PATRICK PHILLIPS
Introduction: spectators, audiences, screenings 130
What we can learn from Early Cinema 132
Some characteristics of the spectator of film and cultural theory 136
More on the spectator as 'subject' 143
More on communication models and response 147
CASE STUDY 1: PULP FICTION (1994) 148
Some notes on spectatorship and regulation 157
Notes 159
Further reading 160

■ **6 Genre, star and auteur – critical approaches to Hollywood cinema** 161
PATRICK PHILLIPS
Introduction 162
CASE STUDY PART 1: GENRE, STAR AND AUTEUR – CRITICAL APPROACHES TO NEW YORK, NEW YORK 164
Genre 166
CASE STUDY PART 2: NEW YORK, NEW YORK AS PROBLEMATIC MUSICAL 178
Stars 181
CASE STUDY PART 3: NEW YORK, NEW YORK AS CLASH OF THE STARS 193
Auteurs 195

CASE STUDY PART 4: SCORSESE AND NEW YORK, NEW YORK   202
Beyond a structuralist critical approach to Hollywood cinema   204
Notes   207
Further viewing   207

PART THREE: GENRE FORMS – REALISM AND ILLUSION 209

■ 7 The documentary form: personal and social 'realities' 211

PAUL WELLS

Introduction   212
What is documentary?   213
Some developments in non-fiction film   215
From travelogue to authored documentary   216
CASE STUDY 1: ROBERT FLAHERTY   217
From social commentary to propaganda to poetic actuality   219
CASE STUDY 2: HUMPHREY JENNINGS   220
Propaganda as documentary myth   222
CASE STUDY 3: LENI REIFENSTAHL   222
From documentary bias to direct cinema and cinéma-vérité   224
CASE STUDY 4: FREDERICK WISEMAN   227
From radical documentary to television, diversity and popular forms 229
CASE STUDY 5: HOOP DREAMS (1994) AND WHEN WE WERE KINGS (1996)   231
Notes   234
Further reading   234
Further viewing   235
Resource centres   235

■ 8 Animation: forms and meanings 237

PAUL WELLS

Introduction   238
What is animation?   238
Early animation   239
The legacy of Disney   241
CASE STUDY 1: DECONSTRUCTING THE CARTOON – DUCK AMUCK (1953)   242
Orthodox animation   245
CASE STUDY 2: GIRLS NIGHT OUT (1986)   248
UPA and Zagreb Studios   250
Developmental animation   250
CASE STUDY 3: CREATURE COMFORTS (1990)   251
CASE STUDY 4: NEIGHBOURS (1952)   252
CASE STUDY 5: THE TANGO (1991) AND THE CRIMINAL (1992)   254
Experimental animation   255
CASE STUDY 6: A COLOUR BOX (1935)   258
CASE STUDY 7: DEADSY (1990)   258
CASE STUDY 8: COMPUTERS AND CONVERGENCE   259
Conclusion   261
Notes   261
Further reading   262
Further viewing   262
Resource centres   263

PART FOUR: REPRESENTATION OF GENDER AND SEXUALITY   265

■ **9 Women and film**   267
JILL NELMES

Introduction   268
No job for a woman – a history of women in film   268
Women working in documentary film in Britain   269
The feminist revolution   273
Feminist film theory and practice in Britain   274
Reassessing feminist film theory   282
Feminist film theory in the 1990s   283
Women in the mainstream film industry   286
CASE STUDY 1: RED FLANNEL   291
CASE STUDY 2: MAM (1988)   292
CASE STUDY 3: A QUESTION OF SILENCE (1982), DIRECTOR: MARLENE GORRIS   293
CASE STUDY 4: SALLY POTTER, FILM-MAKER   296
CASE STUDY 5: THE GOLD DIGGERS (1983)   297
CASE STUDY 6: ORLANDO (1993)   298
CASE STUDY 7: THE PIANO (1993)   299
Notes   303
Further reading   304
Further viewing   304
Resource centres   305

■ **10 Lesbian and gay cinema**   307
CHRIS JONES

Representation   308
Definitions and developments – homosexual and gay   309
Audiences   310
Lesbian and Gay Film Festivals   311
Gay sensibility   313
Lesbian and gay film study   315
Critical re-readings   315
Some films with gay themes   320
CASE STUDY 1: VICTIM (BASIL DEARDEN, UK 1961)   321
CASE STUDY 2: DESERT HEARTS (DONNA DEITCH, US1985)   324
CASE STUDY 3: THE LIVING END (GREGG ARAKI, US 1993)   327
CASE STUDY 4: LOOKING FOR LANGSTON (ISAAC JULIEN, US 1994)   330
CASE STUDY 5: GO FISH (ROSE TROCHE, US 1994)   332
Conclusion: a queer diversity   335
Further reading   341
Further viewing   341
Resource centres   344

PART FIVE: NATIONAL CINEMAS   345

■ **11 British Cinema**   347
LEZ COOKE

Part 1: Approaches and definitions   348
What do we mean by 'British Cinema'?   348

What is a 'British' film?   349
British Cinema as 'national cinema'?   350

Part 2: British film culture – a historical overview   351
From cottage industry to mass entertainment   351
Government legislation in the 1920s   352
Class and culture in 1930s British cinema   353
'Realism and tinsel' in wartime cinema   356
The postwar period   359
New films for new audiences: Hammer horror and the 'new wave'   361
Popular cinema: the *Carry On* and Bond films   363
British Cinema and Hollywood in the Sixties   366
The 1970s: mainstream decline and the rise of independent cinema   366
1980s 'renaissance'   367
'Heritage' cinema   368
Channel Four and the new multicultural British Cinema   369
The 1980s: postscript   371

Part 3: 1990s renaissance   371
From art house to mainstream   372
CASE STUDY 1: TRAINSPOTTING *(1996)*   373
CASE STUDY 2: THE FULL MONTY *(1997)*   375
A brief survey of other 1990s British films   377
Conclusion   378
Further reading   379
Further viewing   380
Resource centres   380

■ **12 An introduction to Indian cinema**   381
        ASHA KASBEKAR
Introduction   382
The narrative structure   382
CASE STUDY 1: DILWALE DULHANIYA LE JAYENGE   391
History of the popular Hindi film   396
CASE STUDY 2: MEHBOOB KHAN *(1904–64)*   402
CASE STUDY 3: RAJ KAPOOR *(1926–88)*   403
CASE STUDY 4: BIMAL ROY *(1902–66)*   403
CASE STUDY 5: GURU DUTT *(1925–64)*   403
Colour and the triumph of romance   405
CASE STUDY 6: SATYAJIT RAY *(1921–92)*   408
The distribution network   410
Satellite television   411
The influence of Hollywood   411
Consumption of popular Hindi films in Britain   412
Conclusion   413
Further reading   413
Recommended viewing   413
Further viewing   414
Resource centres   414

■ **13 The Soviet montage cinema of the 1920s**   417

MARK JOYCE

Introduction: why study the Soviet cinema?   418

Historical background   418

Pre-revolutionary Russian cinema   419

Soviet cinema and ideology: film as agent of change   420

Economics of the Soviet film industry   421

Form: montage   422

Other features of the Soviet montage cinema   425

The key Soviet montage film-makers of the 1920s   425

CASE STUDY 1: LEV KULESHOV, THE EXTRAORDINARY ADVENTURES OF MR WEST
IN THE LAND OF THE BOLSHEVIKS (1924)   426

CASE STUDY 2: SERGEI EISENSTEIN, STRIKE (1924); BATTLESHIP POTEMKIN (1925);
OCTOBER (1927); OLD AND NEW (1929)   428

CASE STUDY 3: VSEVOLOD PUDOVKIN, THE MOTHER (1926); THE END OF
ST PETERSBURG (1927)   437

CASE STUDY 4: ALEXANDER DOVZHENKO, ARSENAL (1929); EARTH (1930)   441

CASE STUDY 5: ESFIR SHUB, THE FALL OF THE ROMANOV DYNASTY (1927)   443

Audience response   443

Theoretical debates: montage versus realism   444

Postscript to the 1920s   445

Notes and references   446

Further reading   448

Further viewing   449

Resource centres   450

■ **14 New German Cinema**   451

JULIA KNIGHT

Introduction   452

The American legacy   452

The development of the film subsidy system   458

The artisanal mode of production   461

The quest for alternative images and counter-representations   463

CASE STUDY 1: YESTERDAY GIRL (1965–66)   463

CASE STUDY 2: THE AMERICAN FRIEND (1976–77)   474

CASE STUDY 3: GERMANY, PALE MOTHER (1979–80)   476

Sponsorship or censorship?   479

Conclusion   481

Notes   482

Further reading   483

Further viewing   483

Resource centres   483

Glossary of key terms   485

Bibliography   501

Index   513

Illustrations

The following were reproduced with kind permission. While every effort has been made to trace copyright holders and obtain permission, this has not been possible in all cases. Any omissions brought to our attention will be remedied in future editions.

Part 1 title page
    Le Voyage dans la lune, Star Film Studio, courtesy Kobal Collection   11
Part 2 title page
    Cinématographie Lumière, Lumière Brothers., courtesy Kobal Collection   89
Part 3 title page
    Daffy Duck from *Bugs Bunny*, Walt Disney Productions, courtesy Kobal Collection   209
Part 4 title page
    Looking for Langston, Isaac Julien, courtesy Sankofa Film and Video   265
Part 5 title page
    The Tin Drum, Franz Seitz GMBH Filmproduktion, courtesy British Film Institute   345

2.1	Nickelodeon in New York City, courtesy Kobal Collection	15
2.2	Paramount production facility, Paramount Pictures, courtesy Kobal Collection	20
2.3	Warner Bros. logo, Warner Bros., courtesy Kobal Collection	22
2.4	*Footlight Parade*, Warner Bros., courtesy Kobal Collection	23
2.5	Vitaphone sound system, courtesy Kobal Collection	24
2.6	*Jezebel*, Warner Bros., courtesy Kobal Collection	24
2.7	*Mildred Pierce*, Warner Bros., courtesy Kobal Collection	25
2.8	*The Robe* in Cinemascope, Twentieth-Century Fox, courtesy Kobal Collection	27
2.9	*My Beautiful Laundrette*, SAF/Channel Four, courtesy Kobal Collection	34
2.10	Steven Spielberg filming *Jaws*, Universal Pictures, courtesy Kobal Collection	35
2.11	UK poster for *The Crying Game*, Polygram Filmed Entertainment/ Pictorial Press	37
2.12	*Fellow Traveller*, Silver/Zon, courtesy Kobal Collection	40
2.13	Queue outside the Odeon, courtesy Kobal Collection	42
2.14	*No Down Payment*, Twentieth-Century Fox, courtesy Kobal Collection	43
3.1	*Terminator 2: Judgment Day*, Tri-Star Pictures, courtesy Kobal Collection	61

3.2	*King Kong*, RKO, courtesy Kobal Collection	63
3.3	*Le Voyage dans la lune*, Star Film Studio, courtesy Kobal Collection	67
3.4	*Tron*, Walt Disney Productions, courtesy Kobal Collection	74
3.5	*The Lawnmower Man*, First Independent/Allied Vision, courtesy Kobal Collection	75
3.6	*Mars Attacks!*, Warner Bros., courtesy Kobal Collection	77
3.7	*The Crow*, Entertainment Films, courtesy Kobal Collection	80
4.1	*RoboCop*, Orien Pictures, courtesy Kobal Collection	94
4.2	*The General*, Buster Keaton Productions and United Artists, courtesy Kobal Collection	96
4.3	*Shane*, Paramount Pictures, courtesy Kobal Collection	99
4.4	*Johnny Guitar*, Republic, courtesy Kobal Collection	100
4.5	*All that Heaven Allows*, Universal-International, courtesy Kobal Collection	102
4.6	*Strangers on a Train*, Warner Bros., courtesy Kobal Collection	103
4.7	*Mildred Pierce*, Warner Bros., courtesy Kobal Collection	104
4.8	*Mildred Pierce*, Warner Bros., courtesy Kobal Collection	105
4.9	*The Last Seduction*, ITC Entertainment Group, courtesy Kobal Collection	108
4.10	*Psycho*, Paramount Pictures, courtesy Kobal Collection	113
4.11	*Vertigo*, Paramount Pictures, courtesy Kobal Collection	118
4.12	*The Searchers*, Warner Bros., courtesy Kobal Collection	119
4.13	*The French Lieutenant's Woman*, United Artists, courtesy Kobal Collection	122
4.14–15	*Rashomon*, Daiei Films, courtesy Kobal Collection	123
4.16	*If …* Paramount Pictures, courtesy Kobal Collection	125
4.17	*If …* Paramount Pictures, courtesy Kobal Collection	126
5.1	*The Great Train Robbery*, Edison Company, courtesy British Film Institute	133
5.2	*Apocalypse Now*, Zoetrope Studios, courtesy British Film Institute	138
5.3	*Natural Born Killers*, Warner Bros./J.D. Productions/Ixtlan Productions/New Regency Pictures, courtesy British Film Institute	138
5.4–5	*Pulp Fiction*, A Band Apart/Jersey Films/Miramax Films, courtesy British Film Institute	151
5.6	*Pulp Fiction*, A Band Apart/Jersey Films/Miramax Films, courtesy British Film Institute	152
5.7	*Arrivée d'un train en gare à la Ciotat*, Lumière Brothers, courtesy British Film Institute	156
6.1	*Meet Me in St Louis*, Metro-Goldwyn-Mayer, courtesy Kobal Collection	165
6.2	*Cabaret*, Allied Artists/ABC, courtesy Kobal Collection	165
6.3	*Angels with Dirty Faces*, Warner Bros., courtesy Kobal Collection	168
6.4	*GoodFellas*, Warner Bros., courtesy Kobal Collection	168
6.5	*RoboCop*, Orion Pictures Corporation, courtesy Kobal Collection	173
6.6	*Stagecoach*, United Artists, courtesy Kobal Collection	173
6.7	*Braveheart*, B.H. Finance C.V./Twentieth-Century Fox/Icon Entertainment International/Paramount Pictures/The Ladd Company, courtesy Pictorial Press	173
6.8	*Independence Day*, Twentieth-Century Fox, courtesy Pictorial Press	173
6.9	*Sense and Sensibility*, Columbia, courtesy Pictorial Press	174

6.10	*Clueless*, Paramount Pictures, courtesy Pictorial Press	174
6.11–12	*Raising Arizona*, Twentieth-Century Fox, courtesy Kobal Collection	177
6.13	*On The Town*, MGM, courtesy British Film Institute	179
6.14	*New York, New York*, United Artists, courtesy British Film Institute	179
6.15	*New York, New York*, United Artists, courtesy Kobal Collection	179
6.16	Leonardo DiCaprio in *Titanic*, Twentieth-Century Fox, courtesy Kobal Collection	185
6.17	Brad Pitt, Zuma Press, courtesy Pictorial Press	185
6.18–19	*Raging Bull*, United Artists, courtesy Kobal Collection	187
6.20	*Cape Fear*, Tribeca Productions/Cappa Films/Universal Pictures/Amblin Entertainment, courtesy Pictorial Press	187
6.21	*Taxi Driver*, Columbia, courtesy Kobal Collection	187
6.22	*The Bodyguard*, Warner Bros., courtesy Kobal Collection	191
6.23	*New York, New York*, United Artists, courtesy Kobal Collection	193
6.24	*Written on the Wind*, Universal Studios, courtesy Kobal Collection	201
6.25	*New York, New York*, United Artists, courtesy British Film Institute	204
6.26	*New York, New York*, United Artists, courtesy British Film Institute	204
7.1	*Nanook of the North*, United Artists, courtesy Kobal Collection	217
7.2	*Nanook of the North*, United Artists, courtesy Kobal Collection	218
7.3	*A Diary for Timothy*, Crown Film Unit for the Ministry of Information, UK, courtesy British Film Institute	221
7.4–6	*Triumph des Willens*, Universurn Film Aktiengellschaft (UFA), courtesy British Film Institute	223
7.7	*Woodstock*, Warner Bros., courtesy Kobal Collection	226
7.8	*Woodstock*, Warner Bros., courtesy Kobal Collection	227
7.9	*High School*, Warner Bros., courtesy Kobal Collection	228
7.10	*When We Were Kings*, DAS Films Ltd./David Sonenberg Production/PolyGram Filmed Entertainment, courtesy Polygram	232
8.1	*Gertie the Dinosaur*, Winsor McCay, courtesy Kobal Collection	240
8.2	Daffy Duck in *Bugs Bunny*, Walt Disney Productions, courtesy Kobal Collection	243
8.3	*Girls Night Out*, Joanna Quinn (photographer), courtesy British Film Institute	248
8.4	*Creature Comforts*, Aardman Animation, courtesy British Film Institute	251
8.5	*Neighbours*, National Film Board of Canada, courtesy British Film Institute	253
8.6	*The Criminal*, Toccafondo (artist), courtesy of Paul Wells	255
9.1	*Blue Scar*, National Coal Board, courtesy British Film Industry	271
9.2	*To Be a Woman*, Outlook Films, courtesy British Film Industry	271
9.3	*The Seventh Veil*, Sidney Box/Ortus Productions, courtesy Kobal Collection	272
9.4	*Thriller*, Sally Potter, courtesy British Film Institute	279
9.5	*North by Northwest*, Metro-Goldwyn-Mayer, courtesy Kobal Collection	283
9.6	*Orlando*, Adventure Pictures (Orlando) Ltd, courtesy British Film Institute	287
9.7	*Dream On*, Amber Films, courtesy British Film Institute	288
9.8	*Bhaji on the Beach*, Christine Parry (photographer), courtesy British Film Institute	288
9.9	*The Unforgiven*, Warner Bros., courtesy Kobal Collection	290

9.10	*Thelma and Louise*, Metro-Goldwyn-Mayer, courtesy Kobal Collection	291
9.11	*Mam*, courtesy Red Flannel Films	293
9.12	*A Question of Silence*, Sigma Film Productions, courtesy of Kobal Collection	294
9.13	*The Tango Lesson*, Adventure Films/OKCK Films/PIE, courtesy Kobal Collection	296
9.14	*The Gold Diggers*, Sally Potter/BFI Production Board, courtesy Kobal Collection	297
9.15	*Orlando*, Adventure Pictures (Orlando) Ltd, courtesy Kobal Collection	298
9.16	*The Piano*, CIBY/2000/Jan Chapman Productions, courtesy British Film Institute	302
10.1	*Girls in Uniform*, Deutsches Film Gemeinschaft, courtesy British Film Institute	308
10.2	*Un chant d'amour*, Jean Genet estate, courtesy British Film Institute	310
10.3	*Before Stonewall*, Before Stonewall Inc., courtesy British Film Institute	312
10.4	*Parting Glances*, Contemporary Films Limited, courtesy Kobal Collection	312
10.5	*The Boys in the Band*, Cinema Centre Films, courtesy Kobal Collection	314
10.6	*Rebel without a Cause*, Warner Bros., courtesy Kobal Collection	316
10.7	*All That Heaven Allows*, Universal Studios, courtesy Kobal Collection	318
10.8	*The Wild Party*, Paramount Pictures, courtesy Kobal Collection	319
10.9	*Victim*, Rank, courtesy Kobal Collection	321
10.10	*Desert Hearts*, Mainline Pictures, courtesy Kobal Collection	325
10.11	*The Living End*, Mainline Pictures, courtesy Kobal Collection	328
10.12	*Looking for Langston*, Sunil Gupta (photographer), courtesy Sankofa Film and Video	330
10.13	*Go Fish*, Samuel Goldwyn/Islet Pictures, courtesy Kobal Collection	333
10.14	*Edward II*, Palace Pictures, courtesy Kobal Collection	336
10.15	*Khush*, Andre Cooke (photographer), courtesy British Film Institute	339
11.1	*The Scarlet Pimpernel*, CTE (Carlton) Limited, courtesy British Film Institute	354
11.2	*Sally in Our Alley*, Lumière Pictures Limited, courtesy British Film Institute	355
11.3	*In Which We Serve*, Two Cities, courtesy Kobal Collection	357
11.4	*The Wicked Lady*, Gainsborough, courtesy Kobal Collection	359
11.5	*The Curse of Frankenstein*, Hammer, courtesy Kobal Collection	361
11.6	*Saturday Night and Sunday Morning*, Woodfall/British Lion, courtesy Kobal Collection	363
11.7	*Carry On Doctor*, Adder Productions, courtesy Kobal Collection	364
11.8	*Dr No*, United Artists, courtesy Kobal Collection	365
11.9	*Chariots of Fire*, Enigma/Twentieth-Century Fox, courtesy British Film Institute	368
11.10	*My Beautiful Laundrette*, Channel Four International, courtesy British Film Institute	370
11.11	*Trainspotting*, Channel Four Films/Figment Films/PolyGram Filmed Entertainment/The Noel Gay Motion Picture Company, courtesy Polygram	374
11.12	*The Full Monty*, Twentieth-Century Fox, courtesy Kobal Collection	376
11.13	*Brassed Off*, Mirimax/Film Four, courtesy Kobal Collection	378

12.1 *Mohra*, courtesy Asha Kasbekar   386
12.2 *Phool*, courtesy Asha Kasbekar   387
12.3 *Mohra*, courtesy Asha Kasbekar   401
12.4 *Afsana Pyar Ka*, courtesy Asha Kasbekar   404

13.1 *The Extraordinary Adventures of Mr West in the Land of the Bolsheviks*,
Contemporary Films, courtesy British Film Institute   427
13.2 *Sergei Eisenstein*, Contemporary Films, courtesy British Film Institute   428
13.3 *Strike*, Contemporary Films, courtesy British Film Institute   429
13.4 *Strike* montage, Contemporary Films, courtesy British Film Institute   430
13.5 *Battleship Potemkin*, Contemporary Films, courtesy British Film
Institute   432
13.6–9 *Battleship Potemkin*, Contemporary Films, courtesy British Film
Institute   433
13.10 *October*, Contemporary Films, courtesy British Film Institute   434
13.11 *October*, Contemporary Films, courtesy British Film Institute   435
13.12 *Old and New*, or *The General Line*, Contemporary Films, courtesy
British Film Institute   435
13.13 *The End of St Petersburg*, Contemporary Films, courtesy British Film
Institute   438
13.14 *The New Babylon*, Contemporary Films, courtesy British Film Institute   440
13.15 *Earth*, Contemporary Films, courtesy British Film Institute   441

14.1 Wim Wenders, courtesy British Film Institute   453
14.2 Rainer Werner Fassbinder, courtesy British Film Institute   453
14.3 Werner Herzog, courtesy British Film Institute   454
14.4 Alexander Kluge, courtesy British Film Institute   457
14.5 Margarethe von Trotta, courtesy British Film Institute   460
14.6 *The Tin Drum*, United Artists/Franz Seitz GMBH Filmproduktion/
Bioskop, courtesy British Film Institute   461
14.7 *Yesterday Girl*, Kairos Film/Independent/Alexander Kluge, courtesy
British Film Institute   464
14.8 *Katzelmacher*, Antiteater-X-film, courtesy British Film Institute   466
14.9 *Shirin's Wedding*, Westdeutscher Rundfunk Cologne, courtesy British
Film Institute   467
14.10–11 *Deutschland im Herbst*, Futura Film, courtesy British Film Institute   469
14.12 *The Second Awakening of Christa Klages*, Bioskop, courtesy British
Film Institute   470
14.13 *The All-round Reduced Personality*, Basis Film Berlin/ZDF Maine,
courtesy British Film Institute   471
14.14 *Germany, Pale Mother*, Helm Sanders-Brahams/Literarisches
Colloquium Berlin/Westdeutscher Rundfunk Cologne, courtesy British
Film Institute   471
14.15 *Kings of the Road*, Wim Wenders Productions/Westdeutscher Rundfunk
Cologne, courtesy British Film Institute   473
14.16 *The American Friend*, Road Movies Berlin/Westdeutscher Rundfunk
Cologne/Wim Wenders Productions Munich, courtesy British Film
Institute   474
14.17 *Hitler – a Film from Germany*, TMS Film-Gesellschaft mbH, courtesy
British Film Institute   476
14.18 *The Marriage of Maria Braun*, Albatros/Trio/Westdeutscher Rundfunk
Cologne/FdA, courtesy British Film Institute   477

14.19   *Heimat*, Edgar Reitz Filmproduktion, courtesy British Film Institute   478
14.20   *The German Sisters*, Bioskop, courtesy British Film Institute   481

Contributors

Lez Cooke is a Principal Lecturer in Media Studies at Staffordshire University, where he teaches courses on British cinema, British television drama and alternative practices in film and broadcasting. He has written several book chapters on British cinema and is currently researching a a book on British television drama.

Chris Jones has taught Literature, Theatre and Film Studies at Brooklands College for a number of years. He has participated in gay-related theatre and video work. He wrote about Derek Jarman for his MA in film. He has recently taught film theory and creative writing at the University of Greenwich.

Mark Joyce is a lecturer in Film, Media and Communication Studies at West Kent College of Further Education, Tonbridge. He also lectures in Cultural Studies on the West Kent College/University of Greenwich BA degree programme in Media and Communication.

Asha Kasbekar graduated from the National School of Drama in New Delhi, India, before studying French Drama at the Sorbonne in Paris. She was a film and drama critic for the *Indian Express* newspaper. She has taught courses on Indian cinema at the School of Oriental and African Studies, University of London, and worked at the British Board of Film Classification as a film and video examiner.

Julia Knight is a senior lecturer in the Department of Media Arts at the University of Luton. She is the author of *Women and the New German Cinema* (1992), editor of *Diverse Practices: A Critical Reader on British Video Art* (1996), and has written for a number of film and video publications.

Searle Kochberg works as a senior lecturer in Film Studies and Cultural Studies at the University of Portsmouth, and as the co-ordinator of the mature students' Access Programme in Art, Design and Media at the same institution.

Jill Nelmes is Senior Lecturer in Film Studies at the University of East London and has taught a range of courses from Access to A Level and Higher Education. She has been an examiner for WJEC Media Studies and is on the subject panel for WJEC Film and Media Studies. She is interested in film scriptwriting and film production, and has two scripts in development.

Patrick Phillips is Chief Examiner for A level Film Studies. He teaches Film Studies at Middlesex University where he is responsible for the first year undergraduate programme. He is also Course Director for Film Studies within the University of Cambridge Board of Continuing Education. He has a particular interest in film studies education, looking at the relationship between the film experience of students and the academic study of the subject.

Allan Rowe has lectured in Film, Media and Sociology since the mid-1960s. He has taught Film A-Level since the original consortium in 1984, and is an assistant examiner in Film. At present he combines these activities with directing Quality Assurance at Epping Forest College.

Chris Webster is Head of Professional Design Studies at the Glamorgan Centre of Art and Design and is a lecturer in Animation. Initially trained as a graphic designer and illustrator, he has worked as a classical 2D animator for the last thirteen years on adverts, children's series and features. He continues to write on the subject and remains a practising professional animator.

Paul Wells is Chair in Cultural Studies at the University of Teeside. He is the author of *Understanding Animation* (Routledge 1998) and editor of *Art and Animation*. He is currently writing books on British animation and American cartoons and cultural history, and preparing a documentary series for the BBC on British film-makers.

Preface to the second edition

Since the early 1990s, interest in film studies as an academic discipline has increased greatly. The subject is now taught at GNVQ, at A level and on many degree courses, from modular to specialised media and film degrees. This rise in interest in the subject has brought about a surge in academic writing, often fascinating and important but much of it aimed at a post-introductory, if not at postgraduate level. The difficulty in finding material accessible at an introductory level, but which also gave an overview of the subject and was likely to engage the student, originally gave rise to the conception of this book. Indeed, since publication of the first edition in 1996, comments and sales have been testament to the need for such a text. Feedback from lecturers and students suggests that it has been used by the market intended and also as an introduction to specific areas for some second- and third-year degree modules. It is also seen as a useful reference book for teachers, particularly those who are new to teaching the subject. This second edition has been updated, expanded and improved upon, in response to comments and feedback from the first edition.

As an introductory text, it is felt that the book should be approachable and inviting in format, clearly laid out, with a good range of film stills to complement and advance the subject matter.

The book provides a background to film studies, introducing key areas, influential theories and debates without neglecting film history and development. The film industry and its working practices are examined, and the differences between Hollywood and other countries in their systems of production, distribution and exhibition are explored. No one method or theory is subscribed to and the book is not theory-led. Each chapter demonstrates the diversity of thinking in film studies and its richness as a field of study.

By referring to a wide range of films, particularly through the use of case studies, it is hoped that the application of theory to film texts will be made easier. The book has a contemporary feel, whilst not neglecting the history and development of cinema. Films discussed give an overview of the depth and breadth of cinema, from early silent cinema such as Buster Keaton's *The General*, to Eisenstein's *Battleship Potemkin* and world cinema such as the films of Satyajit Ray or Rainer Werner Fassbinder. There is a strong focus on recent cinema, with case studies of *Pulp Fiction*, *The Piano* and *The Full Monty*. It is hoped that by using popular films as study points, students will then transfer the skills learned to more 'difficult' films. The book is seen as a tool from which students will make the leap to more specialised areas of study and explore film more widely. In this light, a list of further reading and viewing is given at the end of each chapter and a detailed bibliography at the end of the book.

Jill Nelmes

Acknowledgements

I would like to thank the contributors who have given their time so freely and put so much hard work into the second edition. My thanks also to Rebecca Barden and Moira Taylor for being so encouraging during the birth of the new edition. I would also like to thank readers and academics for their constructive and helpful suggestions made in response to the first edition and which have been considered when planning the new one. Finally I would like to thank my daughter, my family, friends and colleagues who have been so supportive regarding the project.

Jill Nelmes

Chapter 1

Introduction

Jill Nelmes

We all enjoy watching films, whether in the cinema or on TV. Cinema attendance, after many years of decline, is increasing each year and a new generation of film-goers is appreciating the pleasures of the 'big screen', a pleasure which even a 30-inch TV set cannot provide. The study of film is also becoming increasingly popular and there are now many courses in film and media at the 16-plus and undergraduate level. Although film is often seen as part of media studies, it has particular qualities which separate it from the other media. How film is viewed, its history, conditions of production and the huge wealth of film available from not only Hollywood but also countries such as India, Senegal in West Africa and the Caribbean, surely requires that film should be seen as a discrete area of study. Yet film cannot be seen in isolation; films are shown on TV, satellite and video, and frequently referred to by the other media. Developments in computer technology and multimedia also, directly and indirectly, affect film. How images are put together, used and understood is of relevance to all the visual media. Issues such as technology, ownership, censorship and representation in the media are often the subject of intense debate, not only in colleges, but within society as a whole.

An Introduction to Film Studies does not subscribe to one particular method of studying or analysing film, but hopes to draw the readers attention to the diversity and range of opinion within the subject. Methods of study discussed include: a structuralist approach, psychoanalytic theory, feminism, cultural studies, lesbian and gay analysis and a literary/textual approach. These are all areas which have made their presence felt in the contemporary study of film. The book also works from the basis that contemporary film theory is in a constant state of flux, although certain theories may be given prominence. There has been criticism of the tendency of film studies to rely on what Bordwell and Carroll, in their book *Post-theory, Reconstructing Film Studies*, call the 'Theory' in which they criticise film studies for being so influenced by 1970s Anglo-American film theory, a combination of psychoanalysis, structuralism and semiotics, post-structuralist literary theory and varieties of Althusserian Marxism, leaving little room for the development of new ideas and ways of studying film. All these theories are, to some extent, discussed in this book because they have been so important to the historical development of film studies and indeed are still useful tools for the analysis and understanding of film. Film studies continues to thrive because of its heterogeneity, its ability to draw in contemporary thinking and to apply what is relevant to the analysis of film.

This book has been written with the intention of expressing the idea that film studies is a dynamic subject, and to encourage the reader to argue with, question and challenge its content and to go on to read and view further afield.

HOW TO USE THIS BOOK

The book covers a huge range, although it is by no means definitive and it is not meant to be read from cover to cover in one sitting. It is designed as a resource which the reader will be able to study at appropriate times, either as part of a course or for general interest. It is hoped that the reader will be interested in reading further, and extensive cross-referencing to other chapters suggests where to look for related topics and concepts.

Useful features

Features of the book which helped to make it an accessible and useful tool for the reader in the first edition have been revised and extended and include the following:

- Coverage of a wide range of concepts, theories and ideas about film studies.
- In-depth discussion of the film industry in Hollywood and Britain, with reference to other cinemas and their conditions of production.
- Reference to a wide range of films from different periods and different countries.
- Generous use of film stills as referents but also to give a sense of the pleasure of 'looking' at film.
- Self-contained chapters which can be seen as introductions to the areas discussed.
- Key terms highlighted in the text, with short definitions given in the margins the first time they are used.
- A glossary of key terms at the end of the book.
- Highlighted text which picks out particular areas of note in a chapter; this may be a particular point which is being identified.
- Case studies giving suggestions for the way a text may be approached. The second edition has a number of new case studies.
- Updated further reading sections at the ends of chapters to encourage the reader to look further afield. Other references in the text appear in the bibliography at the end of the book.
- Updated further viewing sections for each chapter, suggesting films which would further the reader's knowledge and understanding of the area under discussion. Where possible, video availability is given, although contemporary films may still be on general release at the time of publishing.

New features of the second edition:

- All the chapters have been revised and updated, some have changed focus and been substantially modified. Most chapters include new case studies.
- Cross-referencing has been added with the intention of unifying the book, making it easier for the reader to link common concepts, terms and connections between chapters, and sometimes within a chapter. For example, the chapter on New German Cinema is cross-referenced to Hollywood as a contrasting cinema.
- 'Think Points' are included in boxes with the aim of encouraging the reader to go beyond the chapter to develop independent thinking and to encourage engagement with the book.
- A new chapter on 'The Film Spectator' examines how we view film and includes a detailed case study of *Pulp Fiction*.
- Useful Internet sites have been added because of the mass of information now

available regarding film on the Internet. Much of the material available is general and non-academic, and in this section we try to steer the reader to particularly helpful sites.

■   Useful addresses are given as a resource for both lecturers and students.

An Introduction to Film Studies works on three levels: first, it provides a general background to the subject which is comprised of key issues and concepts, a discussion of particular forms and practices of film and a historical tracing of their development; second, to encourage questioning and engagement with debates and thinking in the area of film studies, and, finally, to appreciate film as a means of communication.

The book is divided into five sections, fourteen chapters in total, each section looking at a particular aspect of film.

PART ONE: INSTITUTIONS, AUDIENCES AND TECHNOLOGY

This section explores the relationship between cinema as a technology and as an industry, its existence as a business being dependent on gaining an audience to watch the films it produces. In Chapter 2 Searle Kochberg explains that the film industry is a complex organisation, an institution with set rules and methods of working which have evolved from the early days of cinema through the studio system to their present state. The focus is generally on US film which has so dominated film style and production in the twentieth century. The chapter details the rise of the studio system in the 1930s and 1940s, and explains why Hollywood was dominated by five companies, through a process of vertical integration, in which these film companies had control of production, marketing and exhibition. The control of the film industry by major studios was challenged at the end of the 1940s, resulting in many more independent companies producing films, an effect which has more or less continued to the present.

Contemporary distribution and exhibition in both the UK and the US are examined. Discussion of the British film industry points out that its films are usually low to medium budget, often funded by the terrestrial TV companies, particularly Channel Four. Case studies of mainstream and independent films in the US and UK are given to put in context the difference in size and budget of particular films.

The section on cinema audiences analyses why cinema attendance dropped so dramatically from a high point in the mid-1940s to a low point in the UK of one million per week in 1984. Since 1990 there has been something of a revival in the film industry and attendance had risen to 2.4 million per week in 1996.

Finally the chapter examines censorship in the US and the UK, considering the arguments for and against the system. A form of self-censorship exists in the US as an outcome of the NC-17 rating system. Films will find it difficult to get distributors if they gain a NC-17 rating, as no one under 17 will be admitted. In the UK, censorship is in the hands of the British Board of Film Classification, and a case study on the classification of *Platoon* (1986) demonstrates how a decision is made as to a film's suitability for a younger audience.

Chapter 3, written by Chris Webster, discusses the development of film as a technological medium, and addresses some of the issues technology confronts us with, as well as the relationship between art, technology and society. The first section outlines the development of film technology from the magic lantern of the seventeenth century to the special effects of Georges Méliès in the early 1900s. The representation of computers and technology in such films as *Metropolis*, *2001* and *Alien* is considered. This chapter also examines the development of computer-generated imagery in such films as *Jurassic Park* and *Toy Story*, using *Mars Attacks!* as a case study of the application of this technology to film. The impact of the Internet and Virtual Reality on film and, indeed, the entertainment industry as a whole is considered.

PART TWO: APPROACHES TO STUDYING FILM TEXTS

This section addresses methods of interpreting and analysing film, showing how a text is understood and interpreted by an audience; it is probably the most theoretically focused section of the book. The most influential theories in film studies are applied to a range of texts in a manner which is accessible for students new to the subject. Detailed case studies and suggestions of how to apply these theories to film are given.

Chapter 4, by Allan Rowe, can be seen as an introduction to how film is constructed, shaped and formed. The codes and conventions used in film-making have evolved over a period of time and are now accepted as 'real', as 'normal' to an audience. The development of these filmic conventions are explored using Buster Keaton's *The General* (1925) as an example of the early studio film, in contrast to *RoboCop* (1987), which demonstrates many of the conventions of a contemporary Hollywood action film. This chapter outlines key aspects of a film's construction; *mise en scène*, which comprises the look of the film, its setting, props, costume, character performance, movement and lighting; camera; editing; sound; and finally – and perhaps most importantly for Hollywood film – a detailed discussion of the role of narrative in film. This section discusses methods of narrative analysis, applying theory to a wide range of films. The contrast between the codes of realism in mainstream narrative cinema and alternatives to the mainstream is also discussed.

Chapter 5, 'The Film Spectator' written by Patrick Phillips, is a new chapter which has been included because of a growing interest in understanding how the audience make sense of films. This chapter discusses prominent and popular theories about the relationship between the audience and the cinema. Psychoanalytic theory has identified the 'look' or 'gaze' as a means by which the film-maker draws the audience into the film and places them in a particular position, i.e. controlling the 'look'. This view of film tends to see the spectator as passive, and thus easily manipulated by film. Cultural studies argues in response that the reader of a film text reacts in a far more complex way, suggesting that how we respond to a film will depend on many factors such as class, gender and age. A detailed case study of *Pulp Fiction* (1994) suggests how we might approach an analysis of a film, focusing on spectatorship. It notes how we recognise, align and show allegiance with particular characters in the film. The chapter concludes that there are many possible readings of a film and the viewer takes a far more active role than early spectator theory allowed for.

In Chapter 6, approaches to analysing genre, star and auteur are discussed, by Patrick Phillips, in relation to Hollywood cinema. This is explored through a case study of *New York, New York* (1977), a musical which pays homage to the studio system. Directed by Martin Scorsese it stars two very different actors, Robert De Niro and Liza Minnelli. This chapter suggests that genre, star and auteur are useful structures from which to study film, but they are by no means the only ones; genre for instance is very much defined by the narrative of a film. Different approaches to genre study are discussed, from narrative theory to analysis of binary opposites to Schatz's approach which identifies only two genres: the 'genre of order' and the 'genre of integration'. The star is a combination of the real person, performer of roles, a persona (how the combination of the real and the performer appears to the public) and image – a representation of particular qualities of the star. As in genre, there is a high degree of predictability when looking at the qualities a star brings to the screen. A star is more than an actor;

he/she represents a mythical figure embodying perfection, and is thus a powerful form of ideological reinforcement. An auteur director is seen as being able to exert his/her own creative and controlling influences when making a film. This section examines the auteur/director in Hollywood, as opposed to the art film auteur/director, and discusses the difficulties of working within the commercial requirements of an institution while producing creative work. Finally the chapter suggests that the structuralist approach taken is useful for analysing genre, stars and auteur but should not exclude other methods such as cultural studies which explores how we watch and use film in a very different way.

PART THREE: GENRE FORMS – REALISM AND ILLUSION

Part 3 examines two different and often neglected categories or genre of film: documentary and animation. The documentary form aspires to record 'reality' as opposed to fiction, yet is very much a construction of events. In Chapter 7 Paul Wells asks 'what is documentary?', focusing on the notions of 'truth' and 'authenticity'. A history of the non-fiction film is given which covers the work of post-Russian Revolution documentary film-maker Dziga Vertov, and of Robert Flaherty, whose use of the documentary as an ethnographic tool for studying other cultures was so influential. In the UK during the 1930s John Grierson, influenced by Soviet film-makers such as Vertov and Eisenstein, saw the documentary form as a political tool which was able to educate the people. The potential for propaganda in documentary is also explored. Case studies of Humphrey Jennings and Leni Riefenstahl discuss two approaches to the documentary form during the 1930s and 1940s.

The impact of new technology in the form of lightweight cameras has enabled film-makers to go anywhere. The cheapness of video has allowed marginalised groups such as women's groups and lesbian and gay film-makers to have a voice. Case studies of *Hoop Dreams* (1994) and *When We Were Kings* (1996), both recent successful films, show that there is still an interest in the form as a means of documentation. Finally the chapter argues that the search for documentary 'truth' still seems relevant and has value in recording and raising awareness of our cultural history.

In Chapter 8, Paul Wells suggests that animation should be recognised as a significant art form with its own codes and conventions. Often seen as merely being 'cartoons' it demonstrates a wide range of styles, from Disney to the social commentary of Nick Park. This chapter looks at the many schools of thought as to what animation is, outlining the development of animation from the days of the first moving images in the 1800s. The legacy of Disney is discussed along with his use of anthropomorphism, endowing creatures with human qualities, which gave a sense of 'realism' to his films. Three styles or types of animation are identified: 'orthodox animation' is the dominant language of animation; 'developmental animation' can be defined as an intermediary stage between orthodox and experimental animation and this is where most animation is sited; 'experimental animation' embraces many different styles and approaches often having much in common with art film and experimenting with new forms such as sand on glass. In recent years computer animation has enabled animators to work in different ways and to invent fresh approaches to their work. In conclusion, the chapter argues that it is the ability of animation to make anything possible which makes it such a significant and contemporary art form.

PART FOUR: REPRESENTATION OF GENDER AND SEXUALITY

The chapters in this section examine how two sectors of society are represented in film. In Chapter 9, 'Women and Film', Jill Nelmes analyses feminist film theory and films by women which could either be considered feminist or have content which could be termed 'feminist'. A historical background is given to women working in film, and the factors which enabled the development of feminist film and feminist film theory are outlined.

The work of two founders of feminist film theory, Claire Johnston and Laura Mulvey, is discussed in some detail. Johnston argues for a counter-cinema which will break the codes and conventions of mainstream cinema, whereas Mulvey's work has become more noted for her ideas regarding the use of psychoanalytic theory and the way the 'look' in film is directed at the male. She argues that the role of the woman in film is reduced to being the object of the 'look'. More recent feminist film theory argues that this is only one method of analysing film, and other influences such as cultural studies should be taken on board. Feminist film theory and film practice tended to converge in the 1970s and early 1980s but, as academia accepted the theorists, feminist film-making in its experimental form began to decline. More women film-makers wished to increase their accessibility to the audience, and looked for ways of working within main-stream film. A wide range of films are referred to and case studies are given of classic feminist films such as *A Question of Silence* (1982) and, more recently, the Oscar-winning *The Piano* (1993).

Chapter 10, written by Chris Jones, argues for a separate theory to account for lesbians and gays both in the way they are represented on screen and how they inter-pret film as an audience. Film theory generally assumes the viewer is heterosexual and film has tended to see homosexuality as a problem, a sickness. This chapter examines work by key theorists such as Vito Russo, Richard Dyer and Andrea Weiss. Russo's work outlines the lesbian and gay contribution to Hollywood cinema, suggesting they had been either invisible or marginalised. Richard Dyer explains how sexual ideology is transmitted by cultural artefacts such as film, but points out that representation of social groups is by no means fixed and can change. Andrea Weiss is a feminist, lesbian film-maker and writer who suggests that identification in film is a much more complex process than just being binary opposites of either male or female. Case studies are given of key films important to lesbian and gay cinema, such as *Victim* (1961) and *Go Fish* (1994).

The 1990s has seen an explosion of lesbian and gay films showing tremendous diversity. Termed the 'New Queer Cinema', such films break down the negative conno-tations of the term 'queer' and reappropriate the term in a positive sense.

PART FIVE: NATIONAL CINEMAS

In western society we tend to think of Hollywood as being the dominant form of cinema. Yet other national cinemas, past and present, have made an impact for many reasons, ranging from their productivity and popularity to their formal, aesthetic, political and social value. It would be neglectful to ignore other forms of film when their contribution has been so important. Cinema in such countries as Tunisia and China have produced an exciting range of film that presents interesting alternatives to the dominance of the Hollywood system and its conventions of film-making which so predominates in the western world. This part of the book focuses on four very different types of national cinema, with two more general studies (British cinema and Indian cinema), and two at particular moments in their history (Soviet cinema of the 1920s and New German Cinema).

British cinema has produced a diverse range of films, from the socialist-inspired documentary film movement of the 1930s to the international success of such films as *Four Weddings and a Funeral* (1994). In Chapter 11, Lez Cooke examines what we mean by 'British cinema' and whether it is in any sense a 'National Cinema' with its own cultural identity. One aspect highlighted is the continual threat to the survival of British cinema because of the dominance of Hollywood. Also outlined is the way in which film has been used to encourage the perpetuation of the class system, such as Korda's films of the 1930s which projected images of a Britain centred upon the upper classes and the aristocracy. Aspects of immediate postwar film are identified and outlined, while other key periods referred to include Hammer horror films, the British 'new wave', the *Carry On* films and the success of the Bond films which are all discussed in terms of representing a break with the 'old' British cinema.

The final section looks at British cinema in the 1980s and 1990s, from 'heritage cinema', to the influence of Channel Four on producing films that supported the representation of a multifaceted, multicultural Britain. In the latter part of the 1990s there has been something of a revival of the British film industry, and such films as *Trainspotting* (1995) (see case study) and *The Full Monty* (1997) (see case study) as well as being financial and critical successes suggest a culture which is represented as diverse and complex. The UK, the chapter argues, now has its own indigenous small-scale, low-budget cinema.

Indian cinema, often termed 'Bollywood', is even more prolific than Hollywood, producing more than 900 films a year. Film is a central part of Indian culture, and Chapter 12, written by Asha Kasbekar, explores its history and development while looking at forms of popular Indian film. This chapter concentrates on Hindi cinema, although there are many regional films made in a variety of languages. The form and narrative structure of Indian film is very different to Hollywood cinema, the plot tending to centre on family relationships and familiar story lines. Song, dance and spectacle are essential to the Hindi film, and extravagant visuals are expected. It is difficult to classify Indian films into a particular genre as they are always a combination of 'musical' and 'melodrama', mostly with a romantic plot. The latter section gives a history of popular Hindi film, which had established a successful studio system by the 1930s but was drastically changed by the onset of the Second World War when new independent producers entered the market. In the 1970s art cinema offered an alternative to the commercial films in their pursuit of western realism: perhaps the films of Satyajit Ray are the most famous of this style. Chapter 12 argues that although the influence of US culture is evident throughout the nation, the flexible narrative structure of Indian film will help it to survive future competition from the likes of satellite TV and Hollywood cinema.

Soviet cinema of the 1920s emerged out of the Russian Revolution in 1917 as a vehicle for propaganda, spreading the message of socialism. As a form of film-making, Mark Joyce argues in Chapter 13, Soviet montage cinema has had a lasting impact and theories developed out of this cinema are still influential today. Film was seen as crucial to the success of communism and the climate was right for experimentation in film to take place, and for montage cinema to flourish, based on the concept of the audience creating meaning from viewing two unrelated pieces of film side by side. Whilst Hollywood cinema would aim to cover up any graphic dissimilarities, 'montage' cinema would emphasise them.

Chapter 13 looks at key Soviet montage film-makers such as Kuleshov, Eisenstein, Pudovkin and Vertov, giving case studies and a discussion of their films. Vertov experimented with the documentary form, believing that the camera could capture the 'truth', and documented events around him. By the 1930s montage cinema was no longer supported by the Soviet authorities (Eisenstein was one of the few who continued to make films) and, combined with the coming of sound, the death knell was sounded for this experimental and innovative form of cinema.

New German Cinema really only existed for a brief period, from the 1960s to the early 1980s. In Chapter 14, Julia Knight explores the reasons for its emergence, often attributed to the brilliance of auteur directors such as Wim Wenders and Werner Herzog. This chapter argues that the social, economic and political conditions which existed in postwar Germany were also important contributory factors. New German Cinema has some common elements but can be seen as a body of work partly defined by its diversity. The chapter examines the dominance of Hollywood film in postwar Germany, ensuring any German cinema would remain small-scale and of poor quality because of lack of investment. Condemnation of the quality of West German cinema reached its peak in the early 1960s and this eventually resulted in the government setting up a film subsidy agency, producing twenty-five films within two years. The chapter argues that New German Cinema could not have emerged without the film subsidy agencies.

The style of films produced by the New German Cinema encouraged an auteur approach, where the film-maker had an all-round training rather than being a specialist. This meant that directors had a great degree of control over their films and the freedom in which to experiment. A vibrant women's cinema emerged at this time which was closely connected with the women's film movement. Film-makers like Margarethe von Trotta addressed such issues as terrorism and feminism in their films. The mid-1980s saw the demise of New German Cinema. This was partly because many of its directors had moved abroad and its leading figure, Fassbinder, was dead, but also because a right-wing government came into power and no longer supported a system of film subsidy.

FURTHER READING

Bordwell, D. and Carroll, N. (eds) *Post-theory, Reconstructing Film Studies* (University of Wisconsin Press, Wisconsin, 1996)

RESOURCE CENTRES

http://jimmy.qmced.ac.uk/
For producers and distributors in the UK, with links to all aspects of films and film industry: BFI, British Film Commission, Oscars, academic sites, stars. This is a website of Queen Margaret College, University of Edinburgh.

http://us.imdb.com/
This is a film and video reference source with hyperlinks within the database and links to thousands of external sites, covering the earliest cinema and latest releases: movies and events 1892–99, genres, and releases country by country (also try http://uk.imdb.com/ for the UK based Internet Movie Database).

http://www.moviefinder.com
This website provides film synopses, distributors, directors, producers, lists of casts and on-line reviews.

http://www.reel.com
A film video order company based in the US with discounts on films (*My Left Foot*, $4.99; *Titanic*, $9.99).

http://www.mediacube.de/links/Misc_Film.html
A website that contains miscellaneous information about cinema and films, with a reference guide to women in cinema, listings for the African Film Festival, Independent Film and Video Makers Resource Guide, and a link to the US National Film Registry.

http://www.cs.cmu.edu/Unofficial/Movies/NFR-Titles.html
A website of the US National Film Registry which, since 1988, has preserved twenty-five 'classic' films each year, including *Citizen Kane*, *Casablanca*, *Nanook of the North* and *The Searchers*.

Part one

Institutions, audiences and technology

Chapter 2

Cinema as institution

Searle Kochberg

■ **Introduction**   14
■ **The origins of the American film industry (1900–15)**   14
■ **The studio era of American film (1930–49)**   17
☐ Case study 1: Warner Bros.   21
■ **The contemporary film industry (1949 onwards)**   26
☐ Case study 2: a major US production, *Jaws* (1975)   34
☐ Case study 3: a medium-budget UK production, *The Crying
  Game* (1992)   37
☐ Case study 4: a low- to medium-budget UK production,
  Fellow Traveller (1989)   39
■ **Film audiences**   44
■ **Censorship and classification**   48
☐ Case study 5: US – The Hays Code   49
☐ Case study 6: UK censorship – interwar and Second World
  War   51
☐ Case study 7: UK contemporary – *Platoon* (1986)   52
■ **'Cinema as institution' – summary**   53
■ **Notes**   53
■ **Further reading**   57
■ **Further viewing**   57
■ **Resource centres**   58

■ Cinema as institution

INTRODUCTION

Films do not exist in a vacuum: they are conceived, produced, distributed and consumed within specific economic and social contexts.

The chapter that follows is a journey through the institutional framework of mainstream film from the beginning of the twentieth century to the present day. The American film industry has dominated all others during this time, and for this reason the section largely centres around it. I do not claim the itinerary to be definitive, but I have sought to cite some key issues and moments in the social and economic history of American and British film.

The origins and consolidation of the American industry are traced from 1895 to 1930 – a period which saw a fledgling industry harness new industrial practices and quickly grow into an important popular medium, organised into highly defined exhibition, production and distribution components.

The Hollywood studio era (1930 to 1948) is the next stop on the tour. Monopolistic practice and the finely tuned industrial organisation of the Hollywood 'factories' are discussed at some length. This section looks specifically at Warner Bros. as an example of a vertically integrated film company during the studio era.

There follows an exploration of the contemporary institutional framework of commercial film, starting with a review of the position of the 'majors' in the light of multimedia empires and mainstream independent US production. Mainstream UK film production is also reviewed. The production/distribution histories of *Jaws* (1975), *The Crying Game* (1992) and *Fellow Traveller* (1989) are taken as case studies.

The film-going habit is an important part of social history in the twentieth century: the changing nature of UK and US audiences since the Second World War is reviewed.

The chapter ends with a review of the systems of censorship and classification that have operated in the US and UK since the 1920s. Contemporary and historical case studies are looked at.

THE ORIGINS OF THE AMERICAN FILM INDUSTRY (1900–15)

The American film industry has been in existence for as long as there has been American film. This section looks at how the film industry organised itself into three main divisions in the early years of the twentieth century, divisions that exist to this day – **exhibition**, **distribution** and **production**.

Exhibition to 1907

By 1894, the exhibition of moving pictures had been established in New York City with the introduction of the box-like Kinetoscope. This allowed an individual customer to watch a fifty-foot strip of film through a slit at the top of the machine. In 1895, a projector called the Pantopticon was demonstrated, again in New York City, and for the first time more than one person could watch the same moving images simultaneously.

Once projectors were available, single-reel films started to be shown in vaudeville theatres as novelties. Exhibition outlets began to multiply and by the first years of the twentieth century small high-street stores and restaurants were being converted to small-scale cinemas or nickelodeons. As the name suggests, the cost of entry to these cinemas was 5 cents – an amount affordable to the (predominantly) working-class audi-

exhibition
Division of the film industry concentrating on the public screening of film.

distribution
Division concentrating on the marketing of film, connecting the producer with the exhibitor by leasing films from the former and renting them to the latter.

production
Division concentrating on the making of film.

ences of nickelodeons. By the end of 1905 there were an estimated 1,000 of these theatres in America, and by 1908 there were 6,000.

For an account of the invention of film, see Chapter 3, pp. 65–8.

Distribution to 1907

As the film industry expanded, exhibitors had a growing commercial need for an unbroken supply of films to show. To meet this need, the first film exchange was in operation by 1902 and acted as a go-between for the producers and exhibitors.[1] The exchanges purchased (later leased) films from producers, and distributed films to exhibitors by renting to them. By 1907 there were between 125 and 150 film exchanges covering the whole of the US.

Production to 1907

Until 1900 the average length of films was around 50 feet. Three major companies dominated production in the US: Edison, Biograph and Vitagraph. Although filming on location was very common at this stage, as early as 1893 the world's first '**kineto-graphic** theatre' or film studio was in operation. This was built by the Edison Company and called the 'Black Maria'.

kinetograph
Edison's first movie camera.

After 1900, films started to get longer, and by 1903, films of 300 to 600 feet were

• **Plate 2.1**
A nickelodeon (5¢ entry fee) in New York City in the first decade of the twentieth century. Converted high-street stores like this one were typical of the first cinemas.

fairly common. The Edison Company's *The Great Train Robbery* (1903) was over 1,000 feet long[2] and is an example of Early Cinema utilising increased running time and primitive continuity editing to tell, for then, a fairly ambitious story. By this time there were several major film producers in the US, including (as well as the companies mentioned above) Selig, Kalem, Essanay and Lubin. These companies ensured their dominant position in the industry by holding patents in camera and projection equipment.

The industrial organisation of film production until 1907 has been referred to as the 'cameraman' system of production.[3] As the name suggests, films were largely the creation of one individual, the cameraman, who would be responsible for planning, writing, filming and editing. Edwin Porter, working for the Edison Company, is a good example of such a craftsman.

Thus, by 1907, the American film industry was already organised into three main divisions: exhibition, distribution and production. The creation of these separate commercial divisions demonstrates pragmatic, commercial streamlining by a very young industry, which was designed to maximise profits in an expanding market.

The Motion Picture Patents Company and industry monopolies (1908–15)

patent pool
An association of companies, operating collectively in the marketplace by pooling the patents held by each individual company.

In 1908, the Edison and Biograph companies attempted to control the fledgling film industry through the key patents they held in camera and projection technology. They set up the Motion Picture Patents Company (MPPC), a **patent pool**, which issued licences for a fee to companies on a discretionary basis. Only licensed firms could legally utilise technology patented by or contracted to the MPPC without fear of litigation. The MPPC was soon collecting royalties from all sectors of the industry, including manufacturers of equipment, film producers and exhibitors. The MPPC's ultimate ambition was to monopolise the film industry in the US. Its goal was a situation in which films would be shot on patented cameras, distributed through its General Film Company and screened on its patented projectors.

Exhibition and audience during the MPPC era

An important contribution to the profits of the MPPC was from the licensing of projection equipment to exhibitors. In 1908 the most important exhibition outlet was the nickelodeon.

1910 marked the peak of the nickelodeon theatre, with an estimated 26 million people attending the 10,000 'nickels' in the continental US every week.[4] The meteoric rise of the nickel theatres was remarkable and reflected the general expansion of popular entertainment during the prosperous start to the twentieth century in the US. Enormous expansion in film exhibition occurred there, and inner-city locations were particularly important due to their concentrated populations. The growth of the nickelodeon in large American cities has been well documented and may in part be attributable to mass working-class immigration to the US at the time.[5]

The exhibition industry understood that its successful future lay in securing a wide audience base. It appears to have accomplished this even in its nickelodeon years, by successfully positioning 'nickels' in middle-class as well as working-class districts. Exhibitors realised, however, that even greater profit lay in larger theatres and more ambitious narratives. As early as 1909, large movie theatres were being constructed.[6] Film producers were also being encouraged by exhibitors to provide films that would appeal to middle- as well as to working-class audiences, including 'women's' stories and one-reel adaptations of literary classics.[7] This process continued to gather momentum in the final years of the MPPC era, when large luxurious theatres began to supplant the nickels in movie exhibition,[8] and audiences reached 49 million per week.[9] Feature-length films at an average length of four to six reels also became established.

Distribution during the MPPC era

Soon after its inception, the MPPC turned its attention to film distribution, and licensed 70 per cent of the film exchanges operating in the US. By 1910, the MPPC had set up its own distribution company – the General Film Company – which soon had nationwide cover through the purchase of forty-eight key exchanges in the US.[10] By 1911, the MPPC had constructed the first effective example of **vertical integration** in the film industry through a combination of takeovers and patent rights.

Changing conditions were soon to challenge the MPPC's supreme position in the industry. First, independent distributors, exhibitors and producers quickly and successfully organised themselves in response to the MPPC's attempted monopoly.[11] Then, a charge of anti-**trust** violation was filed against the MPPC by the Department of Justice in 1912.[12] The outcome of the case (announced in 1915) was that the MPPC was ordered to break up. Ironically, by this time, other vertically integrated companies were being organised within the industry (see next section).

Production during the MPPC era

The years 1908 to 1915 were not only marked by the rise and fall of the industrial giant – the Motion Picture Patents Company – but also by the rise of the multi-reel feature film and the relative demise of the single-reel film. Greater length and greater narrative complexity coincided with the application of scientific management principles to the industrial organisation of film production.

By 1908, the 'cameraman' system of production had already been discarded and replaced by the 'director system' (1907–9).[13] For the first time a director was responsible for overseeing a group of operative workers, including the cameraman. The director was central to the planning, filming and editing stages of film-making. Production was centralised in a studio/factory, permitting greater control of production, thus keeping costs down. Around 1909, this system was in turn discarded in favour of the 'director-unit' system.[14] Directors were now in charge of autonomous production units within companies, each with a separate group of workers. Companies were subdivided into various departments, for ever greater productivity and efficiency, informed no doubt by the then current 'scientific management' model of labour and workshop organisation popularised by F.W. Taylor.[15]

By the end of the MPPC era, the 'central producer' system[16] had been introduced, and was to dominate as a model in production management until the start of the studio era around 1930. This was a fully structured hierarchical system, with a strict 'scientific' division of labour. Production-line film-making was now the order of the day, all under the central control of a producer who used very detailed shooting scripts to plan budgets before giving the go-ahead to studio projects.

Summary

During the first twenty years of its life, the film industry increased in scale from a cottage-scale enterprise to an established, popular, mass medium. Its rapid and enormous growth was largely driven by the explosion in exhibition, which in turn triggered a streamlining in distribution methods and the industrialisation of production. The predominant position of exhibition within the industry was also to be a hallmark of the studio era of American film.

THE STUDIO ERA OF AMERICAN FILM (1930–49)

By 1930 the film industry in the US was dominated by five companies – all vertically

vertical integration
Where a company is organised so that it oversees a product from the planning/development stage, through production, through market distribution, through to the end-user – the retail consumer. In the case of the film industry, this translates to a company controlling production, marketing and exhibition of its films.

trust
A group of companies operating together to control the market for a commodity. This is illegal practice in the US.

oligopoly
Where a state of limited competition exists between a small group of producers or sellers.

integrated – known as the 'majors' or the 'Big Five": Warner Bros., Loew's-MGM, Fox, Paramount and Radio-Keith-Orpheum (RKO). Three smaller companies, the 'Little Three', were also part of the **oligopoly**: Columbia, Universal (both with production and distribution facilities) and United Artists (a distribution company for independent producers).

The origins of the studio-era oligopoly

Vertical integration made sense to the power-brokers of the film industry: companies with the financial resources to organise themselves in this way stood to dominate the market-place through their all-pervasive influence and their ability to block out competition.

Despite the alarm bells of the MPPC anti-trust case in 1915, film companies continued to seek out legal ways to construct vertically integrated companies through mergers and acquisitions.[17] In December 1916 an industry merger occurred which became the cornerstone of the future Hollywood studio era. This involved the Famous Players and Jesse L. Lasky production companies, and Paramount, a distribution company. By 1920 Famous Players-Lasky (as the new company was called) had established a pre-eminent position in the American film industry with the purchase of theatre chains throughout the US and Canada.[18]

The trend set by Famous Players-Lasky was soon copied elsewhere in the industry. In 1922 the distribution-exhibition giant, First National, became vertically integrated with the construction of a large production facility in Burbank, California.[19] By 1924 Loew's Incorporated, the major exhibition firm, had acquired both Metro Pictures (producer-distributor) and Goldwyn Pictures (producer-exhibitor). Henceforth, Loew's production subsidiary would be known as Metro-Goldwyn-Mayer (MGM).[20]

Exhibition during the studio era

Exhibition continued to be the most powerful and influential branch of the American film industry during the studio era. The reason for this was simple: it was where the money was made. Reflecting this, the majors channelled most of their investment into exhibition, which accounted for 90 per cent of the majors' total asset value during the years 1930 to 1949.[21]

first-run
Important movie theatres would show films immediately upon their theatrical release (or their 'first run'). Smaller, local theatres would show films on subsequent runs, hence the terms second-run, third-run, etc.

In spite of the fact that the majors owned only 15 per cent of the movie theatres in the US, they collected approximately 75 per cent of exhibition revenues there during the studio era.[22] This was possible because the 'Big Five' film companies owned 70 per cent of the **first-run** movie houses in the US during this period.[23] Their numbers were relatively small, but the first-run theatres accounted for most of the exhibition revenue because of their very large seating capacity (on average over 1,200 seats), prime locations (in key urban sites) and higher price of admission. The majors further strengthened their grip on exhibition by 'encouraging' the (30 per cent) independent first-run theatres to book their films, sight unseen, to the exclusion of competitors (see p.19). By bowing to the wishes of the majors, the independents safeguarded their access to the majors' popular films. All in all, it was the majors' control of cinemas during the years of vertical integration that ensured their profits.

The successful theatre chains

By the 1920s, American innovations in national wholesaling and chain-store retailing had been absorbed into cinema exhibition methods. The introduction of scientific management methods and economies of scale led to the building up of chains of theatres, lower per-unit costs, and faster, more efficient operations.

Exhibition and Balaban and Katz

By far the most financially successful and innovative of the exhibition companies in the lead-up to the studio era was Balaban and Katz,[24] with corporate headquarters in Chicago. Its success influenced the whole exhibition industry, especially at the top end of the market. Key innovations of Balaban and Katz included locating cinemas in outlying business and residential areas as well as downtown, building large, ornate, air-conditioned movie palaces (trips to which were 'events' in themselves for movie-goers), and accompanying screen presentations with quality vaudeville acts.[25]

The 1930s and 1940s saw a continuation of the scientific management practices inaugurated by innovators like Balaban and Katz. Changes were made in exhibition during the studio era, some a direct result of the fall in attendance brought about by the Great Depression which followed the Wall Street Crash of 1929. Vaudeville acts were eliminated in all but the grandest of movie houses and replaced by talkie shorts; new movie theatres were less elaborate; double bills were introduced; air conditioning was more universally adopted, and food and drink stands – in the form of popcorn (pre-Second World War onwards) and Coke/Pepsi (post-Second World War) – were introduced into foyers. These became major profit earners for exhibitors.[26]

The war years (1941–5) and the immediate postwar period were to mark the heyday of studio-era exhibition in the US: 1946 was the year of greatest profits for the Big Five.

Distribution during the studio era

The distribution of films in the US was effectively controlled by the Big Five during the studio era, even though the Little Three were also heavily engaged in the distribution business. The reason for this situation lay in the majors' complete domination of exhibition. To ensure access for their films to the nationwide cinema network controlled by the majors, the Little Three went along with the distribution system of the Big Five. Areas were zoned by the majors, and theatres designated first-run, second-run, etc. The average period between runs, or clearance, was thirty days or more.[27]

When booking films into their own theatres, each of the majors ensured that precedence was given to their own product, followed by films of the other majors. Any exhibition slots still available would be allocated to the Little Three.

Block-booking

In distributing films to independent theatres, the Big Five and Little Three utilised a system of advance block-booking[28] (films booked *en masse* and in advance). Under this system, independent exhibitors were often forced to book a full year's feature-film output of an individual film company, sight unseen, in order to secure likely box-office hits.[29]

It is worth noting that genre films and star vehicles of the studio era owed their popularity with distributors and exhibitors to the fact that they were useful marketing tools for distributors, and at the same time helped to provide box-office insurance for exhibitors.

For further discussion of genre, stars and marketing, see Chapter 6.

Production during the studio era

By the onset of the studio era, the major movie factories were each producing an average of fifty features per year to satisfy the voracious demands of the highly profitable exhibition end of the business. As in other areas of the film industry, production management was 'scientific': film studios were organised as assembly-line plants with strict divisions of labour and hierarchies of authority.

As early as 1931, Hollywood majors had begun to move away from the central-producer system which had dominated production since 1915. Columbia Pictures was the first company to announce the adoption of a producer-unit system in October 1931. Under the new organisational framework, the company appointed a head of production to oversee the running of the studio. Several associate producers were then appointed under the head, and each had the job of supervising the production of a group of films and of delivering the films on completion to the head of production.[30]

Those firms that adopted the new system (not all did)[31] were convinced that it was an advance in scientific management for several reasons. First, it was felt that the system saved money, since it allowed each associate producer to keep a closer control of individual budgets (overseeing far fewer films than a central producer). Second, the system was felt to foster 'better quality' films, and encourage specialisms in individual units, by investing in the creativity of the delegated producers.

Certain production units were associated with particular genres: Jerry Wald's unit at Warner Bros. specialised in noir melodrama, e.g. *Mildred Pierce* (1945); Arthur Freed's unit at MGM specialised in the integrated musical, e.g. *Meet Me in St. Louis* (1944).

Contracts and unions

It was standard studio practice during the 1930s and 1940s to employ personnel on long-term or permanent contracts. Workers' unions had firmly established themselves in American film production by the early years of the Roosevelt administration (in the mid-1930s).[32] Ironically, by defining and enforcing rigidly delineated areas of responsibility for specific jobs to protect their members' jobs, the unions were directly instrumental in reinforcing the hierarchical structure of film production practice.[33]

• **Plate 2.2** An aerial view of Paramount's production facility in Hollywood in the 1930s. This studio was one of the most modern talking-picture production plants in the world. It covered an area of twenty-six acres, had fourteen sound stages on the grounds, and employed 2,000 people.

Stars

Long before the 1930s, a whole subsidiary industry had grown up promoting the Hollywood 'dream factory', its films and its stars. This continued throughout the studio era, fuelled by the publicity machines of the film companies themselves.

Long-term contracts (normally seven years in duration) secured the ongoing services of stars for the film companies. This was the key to the financial security of corporations since the acting ability and personality of stars generated significant value for the films in which they appeared. Stars helped to differentiate films that were otherwise very standard in content and format. Their popularity reinforced consumer brand loyalty for the films of individual film companies, and provided the majors with the necessary 'carrot' with which to entice independent exhibitors into booking blocks of films sight unseen (or 'blind').

For further discussion of the star, see Chapter 6, pp. 181–95.

Summary

During the Hollywood studio era, a small group of manufacturers-cum-distributors-cum-retailers controlled the film market between them. Smaller US producers were forced to make do with subsequent-run cinemas in which to show their films or to arrange distribution deals with the Big Five and Little Three. Likewise, foreign films could not get a foothold in the US unless they too had arrangements with one of the eight US film companies comprising the oligopoly.

UK films and US distribution

Examples of UK production companies that had US distribution during the studio era were: London Films – distributing through UA, Imperator Films – distributing through RKO, and Rank Organisation – distributing through Universal.

It was not until after 1948 that the majors were forced to divest themselves of their cinema chains, as a result of the Supreme Court's decision in the Paramount anti-trust case (see next section).

☐ CASE STUDY 1: WARNER BROS.

From its origins as a small production company in the mid-1920s, Warner Bros. rose to become one of the five major vertically integrated film companies by the end of the decade. This was largely achieved through debt-financing – expansion financed through loans.[34] Key to Warners' exponential growth were the following financial deals: its take-over of Vitagraph Corporation (with distribution and production facilities) in 1925, its exclusive licensing of Western Electric sound equipment for 'talking pictures' in 1926, and its purchase of the Stanley Company cinema chain with its associated film company, First National in 1928.

Vitaphone

In 1926 Warner Bros. created a corporate subsidiary for its sound productions called Vitaphone Corporation. That year it premièred its Vitaphone 'shorts' and its first feature film with recorded musical accompaniment, *Don Juan*. The following year saw the release of WB's first feature-length part-talkie, *The Jazz Singer*.

The Great Depression seriously weakened Warners' financial base. The company could carry its enormous debt-load while big profits were being generated at the box-office. After 1930, however, box-office takings fell off so sharply that the company

• **Plate 2.3** The Warner Bros. logo.

• **Plate 2.3** The Warner Bros. logo.

began to lose money and had difficulty meeting its loan commitments. Warners was not to show a profit again until 1935.[35]

Warner Bros.' response to its financial crisis was to sell off assets,[36] introduce production units (to help control film budgets) and to make feature films as cheaply as possible.[37] Its series of studio-bound, fast paced, topical films in the early 1930s was the direct result of this corporate policy.

By 1935, the fortunes of the company had improved sufficiently for it to return to profit again. As profits increased, so did film budgets. Studio genres changed too, with the entrenchment of the melodrama, biopic, Merrie England and film noir genres in the late 1930s and early 1940s. As with the other majors, profits reached record levels for Warners during and immediately after the Second World War.

Warners as auteur (authorial voice):

The Warners' house style – cast, subject, treatment, technical standards – is discernable in the work of all its contract directors and over a wide variety of genres.

Warners' style during the studio era

As discussed, film production during the studio era was all about standardised assembly-line manufacturing practice. This is why there is such impressive consistency in the physical make-up of the classic Hollywood film of the period. Individual film companies needed to differentiate their product, however, if they were to develop brand loyalty with their customers.

Senior management control over Warners' house style is evident: staff workers were assigned projects by management, they did not choose them. Management retained ultimate authority on all matters concerning productions, and the corporation had direct control over the final cut. This practice was extensively exercised, much to the chagrin of directors and stars.

Throughout the studio era, Warners' films articulated a populist, liberal ethos. Several productions of the early 1930s were particularly hard-hitting social critiques. From 1933 onwards, however, Warners' films discarded their anti-government position and wholeheartedly supported the new Roosevelt (Democratic) administration and its **NRA programme**. The ultimate endorsement of the New Deal and Roosevelt must be *Footlight Parade* (1933), with its 'Shanghai Lil' dance routine incorporating images of the NRA eagle and Roosevelt, and its leading protagonist (played by James Cagney) apparently inspired by Roosevelt himself![38]

From the mid-1930s onwards, the radical streak in Warners' films may have been muted (due in part to a management eager for middle-class respectability), but the company's films still retained an incisive edge not apparent in the films of the other majors.

Warners (like most of the major film companies of the studio era) specialised in particular genres. Until the mid-1930s the company concentrated on low-budget contemporary urban genres such as the gangster cycle, the social conscience film and the fast-talking comedy/drama. The one costly genre that Warners specialised in during this period was the musical. Later, from the mid-1930s onwards, new genres began to dominate: the Merrie England cycle, the biopic, the melodrama and the film noir.

NRA (National Recovery Administration) programme
1930s government programme designed to rescue the US economy from the Great Depression (commonly known as the 'New Deal').

• **Plate 2.4** Still from *Footlight Parade* (1933): James Cagney's character at the helm in this NRA-inspired musical.

• **Plate 2.5** The Vitaphone sound system: a sound-on-disc system. An engineer monitors the wax disc during a recording in the late 1920s.

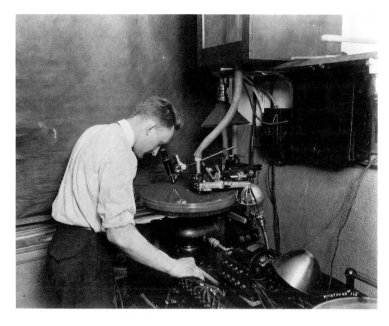

• **Plate 2.6** Production still from *Jezebel* (1938). Bette Davis and Henry Fonda are directed by William Wyler (seated on the camera crane).

As one might expect, Warners' roster of players during the studio era reflected to a large extent the studio's reputation for straightforwardness and toughness. It is worth noting that Warners' stars tended to be very genre specific – e.g. Bette Davis = melodrama, James Cagney = gangster film/musical, Humphrey Bogart = gangster film/film noir.

The factory-like regimentation of Warners' production methods meant that its studio style inevitably overwhelmed the individual creative talents of its contract directors. Pressure of work and division of labour meant that there was little active collaboration on projects between director and editor, or director and writer.[39] Directors were assigned projects and as soon as their task was done they were moved on to others, leaving editors to complete the post-production work. It is thus particularly problematic to assign individual authorship of films to Warners' contract directors such as Michael Curtiz, William Keighley, Mervyn Le Roy and Raoul Walsh.[40]

The cinematographic style of the company was very much in keeping with its tight budget policy. Studio cameramen such as Tony Gaudio (see e.g. *The Adventures of Robin Hood* (1938)), Sol Polito (see e.g. *Now Voyager* (1942)), and Ernest Haller (see e.g. *Mildred Pierce* (1945)) were exponents of a visual style based on low-key lighting, incorporating many night scenes. This aesthetic strategy suited Warners' genres and also helped to disguise cheap sets.

Art direction

Warners' art direction reflected a low-cost policy: location work was avoided, films were designed around a studio-bound look, and sets were regularly reused. The work of Anton Grot, a major art director at Warners during the studio era, typifies the studio's style. Grot not only designed sets, but also suggested camera angles and lighting for them. His sets conveyed a mood. They were not literal reproductions of life, but instead were impressionistic, using shadow, silhouette and angular perspective.[41] He is quoted as saying, 'I for one, do not like extremely realistic sets. I am for simplicity and beauty and you can achieve that only by creating an impression'.[42] The end result was art design that was both economic and atmospheric and in total sympathy with the studio's cinematography.

Costume design at Warners was very much in keeping with the contemporary stories of the films. The studio's principal designers, Orry-Kelly for instance, designed modern clothes for ordinary people, in keeping with Warners' up-to-date urban image.

Warners' films of the studio era, particularly in the early to mid-1930s, had a particular 'fast' editing style. Narratives were developed in a rapid succession of scenes, with extensive classic Hollywood montage sequences. The overall effect was one of dynamism and compression of time.

Finally, the background music of Warners' films was highly individual, and typified by the work of Max Steiner (e.g. *Now Voyager* (1942) and *Mildred Pierce* (1945)) and Erich

• **Plate 2.7** Still from *Mildred Pierce* (1945). This shot typifies the studio-bound cinematographic style and art direction of Warners during the studio era. The scene, photographed by Ernest Haller, is shot with low-key lighting; the art direction by Anton Grot conveys an impression of a quayside through its use of space, shadow, silhouette and perspective.

For a list of key Warner Bros. genre films, see the 'Further Viewing' section at the end of this chapter.

Wolfgang Korngold (e.g. *The Adventures of Robin Hood* (1938) and *King's Row* (1942)). From the mid-1930s to the end of the studio era, both composers created scores very much in the Middle-European tradition of romantic composition, using Wagner-like leit-motifs (recurring melodic phrases used to suggest characters or ideas) throughout.

Warners' style of the 1930s and 1940s can thus be identified as a composite one, the product of its creative personnel working under the control and direction of corporate management. The various signifying elements that made up this style were reinforced in film after film, year after year, producing what one now identifies as the studio-era Warner Bros. film.

As a useful summary exercise, consider the questions below in relation to the previous sections:

1   What are the three main divisions of the film industry?
2   What do you understand by 'scientific management'? How did scientific management inform on the industrial practice of film production before and during the studio era?
3   How did vertical integration of the majors assist oligopolistic practice in the studio era?
4   In what sense did Warners foster a corporate identity in its films?

THE CONTEMPORARY FILM INDUSTRY (1949 ONWARDS)

The late twentieth-century film industry is a very different affair from the system in operation during the studio era. This section looks at the contemporary institutional framework of film, first by examining the specifics within the film industry itself, and then by looking at the wider media context within which film exists today.

The 'Paramount' case

In the late 1940s an anti-trust suit was brought against the Big Five and the Little Three by the Justice Department of the United States (in the pipelines since the late 1930s).

Paramount and RKO were the first of the majors to agree with the US government to the terms of their **consent decrees** in 1949,[43] putting to rest the government's charge against them of monopolistic practice in exhibition. The terms agreed were the divorcement of their cinemas.

consent decree
A court order made with the consent of both parties – the defendant and the plaintiff – which puts to rest the law suit brought against the former by the latter.

1949 to the 1990s – a brief review

The majors were finally forced to divest themselves of their theatres at the end of the 1940s as a result of the 'Paramount' anti-trust suit filed against them by the US government. This divorcement of exhibition from production-distribution marked the end of the studio era.

The next few years saw a retrenchment of the majors. They no longer had a guaranteed market for their films and had to compete with independent producers for exhibition slots. Under the circumstances, they found their old studio infrastructure too expensive in the face of new market competition from the independents.

• **Plate 2.8** Early 1950s advertisement for the (then) new Twentieth-Century Fox widescreen Cinemascope system. The ad is intended to give consumers an idea of how the Cinemascope image (married with stereophonic sound) vastly improves the experience of cinema-going.

Meanwhile, for independents, things had never been better, with the majors only too willing to rent them studio space and to distribute their (better) films, and exhibitors eager to show them. The 1950s was to see an enormous explosion in independent production in the US. By 1957, 58 per cent of the films distributed by the erstwhile Big Five and Little Three were independent productions that they financed and/or distributed.[44]

UA and distribution

In the 1950s, United Artists led the industry in the distribution of independent films. With no studios to restructure and no long-term contract players, UA was able to respond very quickly to the post-1949 reality. In the year 1957 for instance, only Columbia Pictures distributed more films than UA.[45]

Another shock to the film industry around the early 1950s was the exponential growth of television, a product of TV's own popularity and a postwar focus on the home and consumer durables: between 1947 and 1950, the number of TV sets in the US rose from 14,000 to 4 million[46] (see section on audience, pp. 44–7). The film industry's response was twofold: differentiation from and collaboration with TV.

In the 1950s, various film presentation strategies were introduced to emphasise the difference between the film-going experience and TV viewing in a bid to stave off the harmful competition from film's rival. Widescreen, colour, 3D and stereophonic sound were all introduced in the period 1952 to 1954. However, at the end of the day it proved expedient for the industry to collaborate with 'the enemy'. Film companies began to sell (and later lease) their films to TV,[47] to make films for TV,[48] and to merge with TV companies.[49] By the late 1960s, the futures of the two media industries were inextricably linked. The situation by the mid-1980s was more complicated. The two industries had become integrated into multimedia conglomerates where they represented just two of the many associated interests of their parent corporations.

Cinema exhibition today

Throughout the studio era and before, the most powerful sector of the film industry was exhibition. In today's film economy, however, distribution is the dominant sector (see p. 29).

Theatre ownership in the US is still dominated by a small number of companies. For example, in 1987 twelve cinema circuits controlled 45 per cent of cinema exhibition in the US (and 29 per cent of the market was accounted for by the four leading circuits alone).[50]

And history does repeat itself. In spite of the consent decrees of the late 1940s and early 1950s, the majors are once again among those companies with substantial interests in cinema chains.[51] By the end of 1987 they had acquired interests in 14 per cent of US and Canadian theatre screens.[52] By 1989, four film companies (Universal, Columbia, Paramount and Warners) were subsidiaries of parent companies owning 3,185 screens in the US and Canada.[53]

Theatrical presentation is no longer dominated by large, select first-run movie theatres as in the studio era. Individual theatres are now usually small mini-theatres (average seating capacity 200–300 seats), and mainstream commercial films distributed by the majors generally open simultaneously at a large number of these 'screens'.[54] Several screens are commonly housed under one roof – in multiplex theatres – where economies of scale (several screens sharing overheads) allow for low per-unit costs. These cinemas are often purpose-built, located on major roads outside of town centres (where land is cheaper and more readily available), and associated with shopping-mall developments.

The multiplex theatre

One company to realise early on the potential of the purpose-built, multi-screen theatre was American Multi-Cinema (AMC) in the 1960s. Its success with the multi-screen formula was so great that by the 1980s AMC was one of the five largest cinema chains in the US. Based on the statements of AMC's senior management in 1983, its targeted audiences appeared to be the same as those of all exhibitors right back to the days of the nickelodeon theatres: 'we prefer to locate theatres in middle-class areas inhabited by college-educated families.... These groups are the backbone of the existing motion picture audience and of our future audience'.[55]

Another company notable for its development of the multi-screen concept is the Canadian company, Cineplex. It opened its eighteen-screen Cineplex in Toronto's Eaton

Centre in 1979, followed by a complex in the Beverly Centre, Los Angeles, in 1982. After its purchase of the Odeon chain in Canada in the mid-1980s, it began its US acquisitions in earnest, so that by 1988 it was the largest theatre-chain in North America.[56] Cineplex-Odeon's UK acquisitions began in May 1988 with the purchase of the ten-screen Maybox Theatre in Slough. Within a year its Gallery Cinema chain in the UK consisted of eleven multiplexes.[57]

From the mid-1980s, Cineplex-Odeon led the exhibition industry in its construction of several 'mini-picture palaces'[58] and the introduction of cafés and kiosks selling film-related materials.[59]

The company did find itself in a fragile financial position in 1989: its debt financing left it over-extended in a major recession (much like Warners in 1931). But by then the company's style and innovation had set the tone for mainstream exhibition practice for the 1990s.

Runs

It is worth noting that there are a variety of different types of cinema-run in operation today. A run can be **exclusive**, **multiple** or **saturation**. Combinations of runs are selected (largely at the discretion of distributors) on the basis of a film's likely performance. For instance, the exhibition of a word-of-mouth 'sleeper' – a small-budget film that does unexpectedly well at the box office – will usually begin with an exclusive run, until it has built up enough of a reputation to warrant a multiple run.

The UK scenario[60]

In Britain, some of the international majors have shareholding relationships with exhibition companies, others do not. Paramount, Universal and Warner Bros. are represented in UK exhibition: Columbia, Disney and Twentieth-Century Fox are not.

Despite there being around 200 exhibition companies in the UK, only six of them account for approximately 80 per cent of box-office revenues. They are: Odeon (Rank), Virgin, Warner Village (joint venture between WB International Theatres and (the Australian) Village Roadshow International Theatres), ABC, UCI (largely owned by Paramount and Universal), and National Amusements/Showcase. Odeon is the biggest of the exhibitors with approximately 400 'screens', with the other five major companies each having approximately 200 (as at 1998).

Independent cinema chains account for only 20 per cent of the box-office revenue in the UK. Under the label, 'Independent', are many different types of cinema organisation. Some independents are simply smaller chains showing mainstream fare. Others show a mixture of 'blockbuster', 'off-centre' (mainstream but not blockbuster) and 'art' films. Other cinemas specialise in the screening of minority interest/alternative films. In the public sector, the regional film theatres (RFTs), which are supported by the British Film Institute and regional arts councils, provide a circuit of exhibition for minority interest/alternative cinema. They also provide excellent education on film through newsletters, lectures, conferences and workshops. One exciting new venue is the publicly funded Lux Centre in London. Financed by the Arts Council and the National Lottery, the Lux is home to the London Film-makers Co-op and London Electronic Arts. Under one roof are housed a cinema, a gallery for media arts and production facilities (providing access to film-making equipment to individuals with little money).

Power and control are two hotly disputed areas in the film industry in the UK today. Some parties argue that despite the renaissance in cinema-going in the UK, structural domination by the majors in distribution, and their influence on exhibitors (exhibitors will not endanger the main source of their revenue), mean that UK films do not get a fair crack at the whip in UK cinemas.[61] Others dismiss the conspiracy theories and point out the obvious – that the Hollywood product has the advantage of high production

exclusive run
Where a film is only screened in one movie theatre.

multiple run
Where a film is shown simultaneously at a number of screens.

saturation run
Where a film is shown simultaneously at an enormous number of screens (usually a minimum of 1,000 screens in the US/Canadian market), accompanied by heavy media promotion.

For further discussion of contemporary British films, see Chapter 11.

costs, high marketing budgets and film stars, and that these are the films that the public wants to see and exhibitors want to show.

Whatever lies behind exhibition practice in the UK, most cinema-going is centred around multiplex theatres in the UK today. The turning point in UK exhibition is usually taken as November 1985 when the purpose-built multiplex, the Point, first opened its doors in Milton Keynes. However, it should be noted that the company, Screen 4, had been building four-screens in the North since the mid-1960s, and ones that were effectively purpose-built. Nevertheless, the success of the Point and other early multiplexes, like the Maybox in Slough, triggered a new investment in British exhibition and a resurgence in the cinema-going habit in the UK. A year prior to the opening of the Point, cinema attendance was down to 52 million admissions per year. By 1996, that figure had risen to 123.5 million admissions.[62] The multiplex has played a crucial role in this renaissance of cinema-going by offering the punter a choice of viewing in a modern, comfortable environment.

See section on 'Film Audiences', pp. 44–7, for more information on contemporary UK cinema-going.

Distribution today

The role of the majors today embraces film production, distribution and (since the mid-1980s) exhibition. In the area of exhibition, the majors' participation is very significant but not completely dominant. In the fields of production-finance and distribution, however, the majors rule supreme. Their names are all very familiar from the studio era: Paramount, Warner Bros., Columbia, Universal, Disney and Twentieth-Century Fox.

Since the late 1940s consent decrees, the powerbase in the industry has shifted from exhibition to production-finance and distribution, i.e. from the powerbase of the pre-1949 majors to the powerbase of the post-1949 majors![63] This shift reflects the fact that film revenue is no longer purely a function of cinema receipts. With the increasing importance of other distribution 'windows' (e.g. video, subscription TV and terrestrial TV) and merchandising spin-offs, access to a major's worldwide distribution/marketing network has become the determining factor in a film's financial success. Through their domination of marketing and promotion, the majors ensure that it is their films that the public wants to see and that cinema owners want to secure for their cinemas. Witness the reaction of the public and the exhibitors to the beat of the distributors' tom-tom with such blockbuster releases as *Batman* (summer 1989) and *Jurassic Park* (summer 1993).

For an interesting discussion on the importance of lesbian and gay film festivals in the area of distribution and exhibition, see Chapter 10, pp. 311.

Today, a major financier-distributor stands between the producer (if not directly producing the film itself) and the exhibitor. It will largely dictate the business terms which shape a film's finance and exploitation.

As noted by the ex-chairman of Cineplex-Odeon, Garth Drabinsky, in 1976:

If, but only if, a distributor … decides that the picture merits release and the kind of expenditures necessary to get it off the ground, the distributor will enter into a distribution agreement with the producer to govern their relationship.[64]

For the most part, the distributor dictates the terms of its deal with the exhibitor as well: the nature of the run, the length of the engagement, the advertising to be employed and the financial split of box-office receipts between the various parties. It has also been reported that it is common practice for distributors to exploit their upper hand with exhibitors and insist on blind-bidding and block-booking.[65]

Distribution windows

Up to the mid-1970s, apart from the theatrical release, the only distribution windows were network and syndicated TV. The new age of film distribution began in 1975 with the introduction of Time Inc.'s Home Box Office cable pay-TV (HBO) and Sony's

• **Plate 2.10** Steven Spielberg on location during the filming of Universal's *Jaws* (1975).

film rights to the book. Richard Zanuck and David Brown, independent producers working out of Universal Pictures, acquired the screen rights for approximately US$200,000.[77] Under the terms of the deal, Peter Benchley was to produce a screenplay for the film.

The director for the project was selected by the producers after the completion of the first draft of the screenplay. Steven Spielberg joined the package-unit production just as the producers and Benchley started work on the second draft.[78] As is typical in mainstream production, several drafts of the script were produced:

Benchley ultimately submitted three drafts of his screenplay but all were considered unsuitable for filming.... The final script was written by Spielberg and Carl Gottlieb.[79]

During pre-production, the budget was set at $4 million, with a two-month shooting schedule.[80] Universal Pictures was the financier-cum-distributor of the film. Meanwhile, during this period before filming began, the success of the hardback sales of *Jaws* (the book) was greatly increasing the value of the film 'property' all the time.[81]

Production and post-production

The production stage commenced in April 1974. There were many well-publicised difficulties on location, resulting in the extension of the Martha's Vineyard shoot (off Cape Cod) from two months to five and a half. Costs escalated accordingly, from an original budget of $4 million to $8 million.[82] Nevertheless Universal continued to support the project despite the financial pressures alluded to by Richard Zanuck:

something has driven the budget up a bit. There are pressures that bear on you.... You're out there someplace using somebody else's [Universal's] money. We sign our names to the budget and agree to bring it in at a certain price. When that price starts escalating ... pressures are applied.[83]

During location shooting on Martha's Vineyard, Universal didn't miss the opportunity to promote the film, and arranged free news junkets for the world's media:

Murray Weissman, chief of the motion picture press department at Universal, estimated [that] media representatives conducted more than 200 interviews with actors, the director, the producers and others while the film was on location, 'three times the normal for even a big movie'.[84]

In October 1974, filming shifted to Los Angeles for the last remaining scenes, including the final confrontation with the shark which had yet to be filmed. The final underwater footage was shot in 'the waters of the Pacific off Catalina [island], and in one or two studio tanks, where lighting could be carefully controlled'.[85]

Editing had commenced long before the completion of principal photography. The film's editor, Verna Fields, had assembled a rough-cut as the sequences were being shot. At the end of the production stage, only the rough-cut of the last third of the narrative was yet to be done. Spielberg worked closely with Fields to deliver the 'first answer print'.[86] In March 1975 the film was handed over by the producers to Universal Pictures for audience test-previews and distribution.

Universal retained the authority over the final cut of the film. But, in response to the excellent audience previews, only small changes were made by Spielberg and Shields.[87] The date set by Universal for the opening of *Jaws* was 20 June 1975.[88]

Distribution and exhibition

For the film's distribution and exhibition, Universal devised and co-ordinated a highly innovative plan. Universal and Bantam (the paperback's publishers) had designed a logo which would appear on the paperback and on all film advertising – an 'open-mouthed shark rising toward a lone female swimmer'.[89] Both publisher and distributor recognised the mutual benefits that a joint promotion strategy would bring. Such was the co-operation between the two parties that Zanuck and Brown 'embarked on a 6-city tour sponsored by Bantam books', to promote the publication of the paperback and also the up-and-coming release of the film.[90]

At the beginning of April 1975, Universal invited blind bids from US and Canadian exhibitors. Because of the enormous success of the paperback[91] and the film's excellent 'sneak' previews, Universal was able to command very stiff financial terms from exhibitors.

June 1975 marked the dawn of a new era in the promotion and distribution of major releases. For the first time the exploitation of a movie incorporated saturation booking technique with simultaneous nationwide media promotion on a massive scale. The concept behind this strategy was to create maximum exposure for the film as quickly as possible, so as to recoup production costs as quickly as possible:

Jaws has gotten a very massive release in about 500[92] theaters with a very intensive television campaign, probably the biggest, I would say, of all time.... It has become apparent to distributors today that they can get their money back faster and satisfy the demand to see a film by adopting a broader release pattern.[93]

Coinciding with the nationwide opening of *Jaws* was a media blitz which included approximately twenty-five 30-second adverts per night on prime-time network TV for the nights of 18, 19 and 20 June 1975.[94] Pre-opening promotion costs totalled $1.8 million, of which $700,000 went on this TV blitz campaign.[95]

The strategy paid off:

Jaws made 14 million dollars its first week in release.... Production costs were totally recouped within the first 2 weeks of release.... As of September 5, 1975, Universal declared *Jaws* the all-time box-office champion.[96]

Universal also exploited very profitable tie-ins/merchandising to help promote the film:

In eight weeks, over a half million *Jaws* T-shirts, 2 million plastic tumblers, and 2 hundred thousand soundtrack record albums were sold. *The Jaws Log*, a quickly produced paperback about the making of the film, sold over 1 million copies in the first month.[97]

By December 1977, the worldwide box-office gross for *Jaws* was over $250 million.[98]

Jaws was made before the era of domestic video and pay-TV, so it did not benefit from these lucrative distribution windows at the time. However, US network TV (ABC) did pay $25 million in the late 1970s for three screenings of it and *Jaws II*.[99]

☐ CASE STUDY 3: A MEDIUM-BUDGET UK PRODUCTION, *THE CRYING GAME* (1992)

This film has been chosen as a case study because it is a high-profile example of the TV co-production feature which has dominated UK production in the recent past. The project was conceived, written and directed by Neil Jordan.

Script development and pre-production

In 1982, Neil Jordan produced an outline and partial script for a project entitled *The Soldier's Wife*. The project was proposed to the then new terrestrial TV channel, Channel Four, but was turned down.

Nearly ten years later, in 1991, the project was set in motion again, to be directed by Jordan and produced by Stephen Woolley of Palace Productions. Despite many potential backers (including Miramax, ultimately the film's US distributor) being put off by what were perceived as 'difficult' themes – race, transgressive sexuality and Northern Ireland politics – a 'pack-of-cards' finance package was arranged through the summer and autumn of 1991. The participants included British Screen, Eurotrustees (a pan-European distribution alliance, one including Palace Pictures), Channel Four and Nippon Development and Finance (a Japanese distribution company). Financing was very tight – a modest £2.7 million (US$4.7 million) budget[100] – and hard won. To quote Stephen Woolley:

For an account of British Cinema in the 1990s, see Chapter 11.

• **Plate 2.11** UK poster for *The Crying Game* (1992), utilising a 'noir' visual vocabulary to promote the film.

It was only after literally begging on my knees to Channel Four and British Screen (which later became strong supporters of the film), and a handful of European distributors that we were able to finance the film at all, and then only because the entire cast and crew accepted substantial defer-ments.[101]

After script changes were made (at the behest of the backers), shooting commenced at the beginning of November 1991.

Production and post-production
Despite the fact that the financing of the picture was not fully completed until 10 November 1991, shooting of the picture commenced a week earlier, on location in Ireland.[102] As the film went into production, Palace Pictures – of which Palace Productions was a part – was in serious financial trouble. (The majority of its companies would be formally put into administration in May 1992.[103]) Despite Palace's problems, however, the production proceeded.

After less than a week's shooting in Ireland, the production shifted to London. Location work occurred in central London (in, for instance, Eaton Square and Fournier Street – Spitalfields). The rest of the film was shot at Shepperton Studios: shooting was completed just before Christmas 1991.

By the end of January 1992, a rough cut had been completed. Subsequently a new ending was shot at an extra cost of £45,000.[104] By April, 1992 the film was completed, and had acquired the title *The Crying Game*.

Initial UK distribution and exhibition
The film opened in the UK at the end of October 1992, having failed to secure a Cannes première, but having been seen at the Venice Film Festival that autumn.

Films with low budgets and no stars tend to have extended exclusive cinema runs upon release, to give the film the chance to build an audience through word of mouth. Not so here, unfortunately. Mayfair, the UK distributors, decided to book the film into cinemas across the country after only a few weeks' 'platform' exhibition in London.[105]

Anecdotal evidence suggests that the unfortunate coincidence of the film's release with an IRA bombing campaign on the British mainland, on top of the poor marketing, severely hampered the film's chances. For, despite generally favourable reviews, the film's initial box-office performance was weak (only around £680,000 gross by December 1992).[106]

US distribution and exhibition
In the spring of 1992, the partners in the film struck a US distribution deal with Miramax for $1.5 million. Miramax in the early 1990s was an independent distribution company (it is now owned by Disney) with a reputation for handling non-Hollywood product.

After screening the film at the Telluride, Toronto and New York Film Festivals, *The Crying Game* was released in the US at the end of November 1992. Miramax demon-strated its agility in non-blockbuster distribution with its careful marketing strategy. On its UK release, those marketing the film had requested that the press not reveal the film's 'secret' in their reviews. Miramax picked up on that idea as a promotional tool, and enlisted not only the media, but the audience *as well*, in a conspiracy of silence. The film was 'sold' to the public as an action thriller/film noir with a secret (the gay and IRA themes were played down). An inspired advertising slogan – 'The movie everyone is talking about, but no one is giving away its secrets' – certainly helped to fire the imagi-nation of the cinema-going public.[107] Meanwhile, Miramax also built a steady Oscar-nomination campaign for the film through late 1992 and early 1993.

The promotional campaign was supported by a carefully orchestrated theatrical release pattern. The film debuted on only six screens in the US at the end of November.[108] By early February 1993, Miramax had taken the film 'wide' – it was on at 239 screens[109] – and by 17 February, when the Oscar nominations were announced, the film was booked into 500 screens.[110] The film received six nominations (best film, best director, best screenplay, best actor, best supporting actor, best editing), and, on the weekend following the announcement of the nominations, grossed $5.2 million at the box office: a '400 per cent increase over the previous week'.[111] By the week preceding Academy Award night – 29 March – the number of screens had been increased to saturation level: 1,093 in total.[112]

In the event, the film won only one Academy Award, for best screenplay. Nevertheless, Miramax's effective handling of the film assured it continued box-office success. If US grosses for 1992 were a healthy $4.5 million,[113] grosses for 1993 were outstanding: at around $59.3 million.[114] By 1997, the total US gross figure was estimated at around $68 million.[115]

Miramax's handling of the film in the US proved to be a classic example of how to build an audience successfully for a relatively low-budget, non-US feature (see section on 'Film Audiences', pp. 44–7).

A footnote to UK distribution and exhibition

Although never outstanding, the UK box office did pick up again as a consequence of the film's US success. For the period December 1992 to December 1993, the UK gross was around £1.4 million.[116]

In summary, the UK distribution windows for *The Crying Game* were as follows:

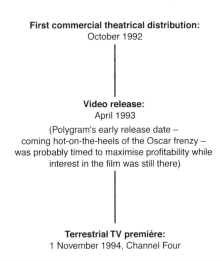

First commercial theatrical distribution:
October 1992

Video release:
April 1993

(Polygram's early release date –
coming hot-on-the-heels of the Oscar frenzy –
was probably timed to maximise profitability while
interest in the film was still there)

Terrestrial TV première:
1 November 1994, Channel Four

☐ CASE STUDY 4: A LOW- TO MEDIUM-BUDGET UK PRODUCTION, *FELLOW TRAVELLER* (1989)

This film was co-produced by the British Broadcasting Corporation (BBC), Home Box Office Showcase (HBO) in the US, and the British Film Institute (BFI).

Fellow Traveller, like *The Crying Game*, is an example of a UK TV co-production feature. The project was conceived and written by Michael Eaton whose interview with myself[117] forms the basis of this case study.

• **Plate 2.12** Still from
Fellow Traveller (1989).

Script development

The project began life in 1987 and was originally conceived by Eaton as a television play. He brought his idea to Colin MacCabe, then head of the production division at the BFI, who suggested that he write an outline and submit it to the BFI's production board to see if it would qualify for the (then) new scheme of monies for script development. On the basis of his 'pitch' document, Eaton received a modest sum to develop the script.[118]

Eaton prepared the first draft of the script on the basis of it being a low-budget (under £0.5 million), studio-shot telefilm. Its plot concerned an American writer who, blacklisted in the US, came to work in England during the early to mid-1950s. The script was rejected by the BBC and ITV companies, but was enthusiastically received when seen by HBO[119] in New York. As a result, Eaton met with HBO in early 1988. He was given a similar sum to that received from the BFI to develop a second draft of the script (modified to suit an enlarged budget, at HBO's request).[120] HBO indicated that if they liked what emerged from the second draft, they would co-finance the project.

Eaton arrived back in the UK to work on the TV-movie script, which was completed very quickly. The BBC then became interested in the project and agreed to co-finance with HBO, and like HBO before it, also made some suggestions regarding the script. Eaton's project was proving to be an ideal British/American co-production, with its narrative involving both countries' media histories – the McCarthy witch-hunts in Hollywood and the setting up of British commercial TV in the 1950s.

With both co-producers now coming from TV, it was looking less likely that the project would ever achieve a significant theatrical release, something Eaton was very keen on.

Pre-production

With the budget set at around £1.5 million, the next stage was assembling the production team and moving to pre-production. This began in earnest in autumn 1988. The BBC producer, Michael Wearing[121] was brought on-board to produce, with Philip Saville as director.

HBO was very enthusiastic about the production team selected for the film. During pre-production, its main area of activity was in the casting of the principal parts.[122]

Production

Production began in the new year, 1989. Most of the film was shot on location, except for the 'Robin Hood' scenes which were shot in a studio. The production schedule was five weeks in the UK and ten days in the US (Florida). Last minute funds contributed by the BFI enabled the film to be shot on 35mm.[123] This gave the film's *mise en scène* its very high visual clarity and definition.

Distribution/exhibition

The film received a theatrical première in New York City before HBO put it out on their cable channel. Although Time-Warner owned the rights to the film outside the US and the UK, the film was hardly exhibited theatrically outside Britain. It was, however, seen at international film festivals.

The film's distribution history in the UK is a little more extensive. Originally, the BBC had wanted to put the film on TV very quickly. However, the film's reception at its première at the Edinburgh Film Festival in August 1989, and at the London Film Festival a few months later, was so positive that it was decided to give the film a limited theatrical window in the UK. The film was shown at the Metro cinema in central London very successfully in early 1990.[124] It was also shown at the Cannon, Tottenham Court Road (London) and at regional BFI theatrical houses.

Eighteen months after first appearing at the Edinburgh Film Festival, *Fellow Traveller* was premièred on BBC2.

In summary, the UK distribution windows for *Fellow Traveller* were as follows:

Film festival première:
August 1989, Edinburgh Film Festival

First commercial theatrical exhibition:
January–March 1990, Metro cinema

Video release:
November 1990

Terrestrial TV première:
February 1991, Screen 2 (BBC)

For a case study of Red Flannel, a women's film and video production group, see Chapter 9.

Multimedia empires

For a discussion of the implications of Internet and computer digital technology, see Chapter 3.

Today, it is not adequate to consider the film industry in isolation, for it is only one part of a network of media, entertainment and communications industries controlled by vertically and laterally integrated multimedia conglomerates, 'each company controlling a vast empire of media and entertainment properties that amounts to a global distribution system.'[125] Examples of such organisations are Time-Warner (owner of Warner Communications), News Corporation (owner of Twentieth-Century Fox) and Sony Corporation of Japan (owner of Columbia Pictures).

At present, Time-Warner is the biggest media company in the world,[126] with interests in film and TV, publishing, cable and satellite systems, and the music industry.

Rupert Murdoch's News Corporation is the world's second-largest media conglomerate.[127] As an example of its **synergy strategy** – a strategy central to all multimedia conglomerates – we need only look at its UK BSkyB satellite service, which utilises press media[128] and film and TV production companies[129] owned by News Corporation to help promote it and provide programmes for it.

synergy strategy
Combined or related action by a group of individuals or corporations towards a common goal, the combined effect of which exceeds the sum of the individual efforts.

Sony Corporation of Japan purchased Columbia Pictures entertainment in 1989 for $5 billion. Underlying this purchase also was a synergy strategy.[130] Sony bought Columbia to boost sales of its home electronics hardware and to achieve synergy between its software and hardware enterprises.[131] Since it acquired Columbia, Sony has used the studio to showcase its electronic high-definition technology, such as high-definition TV and interactive multimedia video games.

The UK scenario

The global media conglomerates already have footholds in the UK as elsewhere (e.g. News Corporation and Time-Warner).[132] UK-based broadcasting organisations have been slow to join the global multimedia bandwagon. After a decade of government under-financing of the BBC, deregulation, and re-franchising of ITV companies, those British broadcasters which survived were hardly fighting fit at the end of the 1980s.

• **Plate 2.13** Queue outside the Odeon Leicester Square, London, in the late 1940s. The years immediately following the Second World War were to be the last ones where film held the position as number one mass medium of entertainment.

However, in 1991 the BBC launched its 24-hour satellite news service – World Service Television. WSTV was expanded in March 1993 with the setting up of a joint venture between the BBC and ABC TV (of the US) to form the world's biggest radio and TV news-gathering operation. WSTV is proving to be a popular alternative to CNN (Cable News Network), the US-based global satellite news service.[133]

UK producers do have a vested interest in a globally fit and healthy BBC. Some would argue that with it rests the ongoing sponsorship of UK media production.

For further discussion of new technology, see Chapter 3.

Summary

In a few years we could be looking at an integrated digital combination of TV, cable descrambler, personal computer, camcorder, and radio and phone set which plugs into a telephone outlet. [134] Products like these will revolutionise the communications business – of which film is a part.

The communications revolution is being orchestrated by only a handful of global players. Unless properly regulated, these few companies stand to enjoy an oligopolistic power not dreamed of in the far-off days of the MPPC and the studio era.

• **Plate 2.14** Still from *No Down Payment* (1957). The film industry in the 1950s would certainly have wished this fate on all domestic TV sets!

As a useful summary exercise, consider the questions below in relation to the previous section:

1 What was the long-term effect of the 'Paramount' case on the film industry?
2 How many distribution windows can you think of for a typical blockbuster film in today's viewing context?
3 To what extent do you think British films 'get a fair hearing' at the British box office?
4 If you were a part of a producer/director team in the UK, how would you go about setting in motion and developing a low- to medium-budget film project?

FILM AUDIENCES

Fundamental to the study of cinema as institution is a study of cinema audience. This section reviews the changes in cinema audience patterns/profiles from the end of the Second World War to the present day, and considers their likely causes.

The section ends with a review of how film companies attempt to build audiences for their films.

The 1940s: cinema-going as recreation

Before the 1950s, cinema-going was a very major recreational activity. According to one official report,[135] film-going was the number one recreational activity for most people in wartime America. The year 1946 marked the peak in cinema-going in the US, with an average weekly attendance of 95 million, a figure unsurpassed to this day.[136]

The late 1940s to the present

Studies of the composition of audiences in the 1940s identify certain key trends. Although men and women registered the same average monthly picture attendance,[137] a greater percentage of men constituted very high frequency cinema-goers.[138]

Age was the major determinant in the frequency of attendance. All surveys of the 1940s point to the fact that young people attended much more frequently than older persons.[139]

Statistics from the 1940s also indicate that expenditure on motion pictures increased with annual income and that those with higher levels of education (i.e. high school and/or college) were more frequent movie-goers than persons with only a grade school education.[140]

By the 1950s, cinema attendance was in rapid decline. Average weekly attendance figures had dropped in 1950 to 60 million (from their 95 million peak four years earlier), and by 1956 the number had slipped to 46.5 million.[141] What happened to bring about this sudden decline? Two reasons are most often cited: the first is the change in living patterns of Americans after the Second World War, and the second is the establishment of TV.

'Being at home' explains the drop in cinema attendance after the peak of the mid- to late 1940s. There was a radical change in social trends in the US after the war:

home ownership, suburbanization of metropolitan areas, traffic difficulties, large families, family-centred leisure time activities, and the do-it-yourself movement.[142]

These new trends put the focus firmly on domestic lifestyle, to the detriment of 'outside-the-home' film entertainment. An exception to this was the rise of the outdoor drive-in theatre in the early 1950s – itself a consequence of postwar suburbanisation. Now parents could choose to have a night out at the movies in the comfort of their own car, with the kids in the back of the vehicle. By 1954, there were 3,800 drive-ins in the US, whose box-office grosses accounted for 16 per cent of the total US box-office receipts.[143]

The early days of TV

The number of TV sets in the US grew from 250,000 in 1947 to 8 million by 1950 and to 42.2 million by 1956.[144] TV's rise was directly proportional to the demise of movie theatres, particularly those situated in the residential neighbourhoods. One can deduce that the audiences who previously frequented local theatres were now at home watching TV instead.[145]

The 1960s and 1970s saw an enormous growth in the leisure industry in the US. Yet, despite this, film-going continued to decline: by 1975, the average weekly attendance was down to 19.9 million.[146] A Gallup poll taken in 1977 underlined the dominance of home-based leisure pursuits as a 'favourite way to spend an evening'.[147] The survey also confirmed the long-standing trends of movie-going being more popular with younger persons,[148] those with higher incomes and those who were college educated.

The 1970s and 1980s saw the expansion of home-based, 'TV-related media' entertainment in the form of VCRs, subscription cable and satellite services, and video games, all of which weakened movie-going as a commercial leisure activity.[149]

The UK scenario

The history of cinema attendance in the UK since the Second World War mirrors US statistics to a large degree. As in the US, 1946 marked the peak in UK cinema-going. That year, the average weekly cinema attendance was 31.5 million.[150] and, as in the US, high-frequency cinema-going in the 1940s was predominantly the habit of the young.[151] However, unlike statistics in the US, working-class people went to the cinema significantly more often than others.[152]

Attendance figures fell dramatically in the 1950s: by 1956 weekly attendance was down to 21.1 million and by 1960 to 9.6 million.[153] As in the US, the precipitate drop correlated with the dramatic rise in the number of TV sets in circulation.[154] This phenomenon was symptomatic of a much larger social change of the 1950s: the growth of outlying residential areas[155] and the subsequent establishment of a home-based consumer culture. The decline in attendance among the frequent cinema-going age group (sixteen to twenty-four year olds) might also be attributable to the sudden appearance of a distinct youth culture in the 1950s, which led to new forms of recreation for teenagers.[156]

By the early 1970s, cinema-going was just one of many options in the expanding leisure industry. The long decline continued through the 1970s, so that by the mid-1980s, weekly attendance had plummeted to just over 1 million.[157] Other changes were apparent too: by the early 1980s the percentage of working-class people attending cinemas had declined significantly for the first time.[158]

Recent and future trends

Although the under-30s still account for the largest number of yearly admissions at movie theatres,[159] in recent years the percentage of the movie audience over the age of thirty has climbed significantly. For instance, between 1979 and 1987, the percentage of over-30s (in the US) in the total movie audience increased from 24 per cent to 38 per cent.[160] This trend is expected to continue. The figures will, of course, be affected by fluctuations in age distribution within the population.

There has long been evidence supporting the claim that increased education translates to increased frequency of cinema-going. If – and it is a big if – the number of college-educated individuals continues to rise, as it has in recent years, we can suppose that movie attendance may also go up.[161]

For discussion of contemporary British film, see Chapter 11.

Currently, film-going is enjoying a renaissance with the public, local multiplexes offering the 'supermarket' convenience of choice and car-parking facilities. But new films are also being delivered to their audience via pay TV and domestic VCRs. In the end, movie-going will continue as a social practice as long as the public and film industry show a willingness to support it.

The UK scenario

In recent years, multiplexes have also been at the centre of a renaissance in movie-going in the UK: attendance rose from a derisory 1 million per week in 1984 to 2.4 million per week by 1996.[162] Changes in audience profiles have also been noticed. Today, among sixteen to twenty-four year olds, demographic groups A, B and C1 are over-represented (in relation to their percentage in the general population), whereas C2 and D groups are under-represented. The shift towards better off, better educated young audiences is, in part at least, a consequence of the growth of purpose-built, out-of-town multiplexes which invariably need to be reached by car. This scenario will change in the near future, however, as a consequence of new planning guidelines laid down by the Government. In the next five to ten years, new developments of cinemas will be directed away from out-of-town sites, and back into city centres, in a policy of urban revitalisation.

Building an audience

Since the earliest days of the film industry, there have been attempts by makers, distributors and exhibitors to build audiences for their films. In today's film industry, building an audience is a sophisticated business: audience profiling, psychological testing and advertising (see previous section on the contemporary film industry) are all incorporated to help 'deliver' an audience for a film.

Audience profiling

Audience profile data – age, sex, income level, education, etc. – is influential in determining the kinds of films that get financed and the shape the projects take.

Audience data is sought by film 'backers' seeking evidence of potential audiences for films. For instance, in recent years the percentage of the total movie audience over the age of thirty has increased significantly. The effect of this statistic has been to spur Hollywood producers on to make more films that appeal to a wider range of audiences than just the teen-market. The summer 1993 releases reflect this policy – films like *The Firm*, *In the Line of Fire*, *Sleepless in Seattle*, *The Fugitive* and *Rising Sun*.

Psychological testing

Elaborate psychological test systems have been used in market research to help producers determine what audiences care to see or not to see in films. An early (and extreme) example of this was Sunn Classic Pictures who, in the late 1970s, identified a huge 'untapped audience for movies – working-class families which attended films only once or twice a year'.[163] By carrying out extensive market research on the narrative and formal elements that would appeal to this target audience, and by then submitting the data to computer analysis, the company was successful in creating a substantial audience for its low-budget nature movies, for example, *The Life and Times of Grizzly Adams*.[164]

Advertising

This topic has already been covered in the previous section on the contemporary film industry. However, it is important to restate that advertising is an essential tool in building audience interest for films. Consequently, advertising budgets tend to be very high: in recent years it has been noted that marketing an American mainstream film can 'devour' up to 25 per cent of a film's total revenue.[165]

TV promotion

Since *Jaws* (1975), concentrated national TV promotion (allied with saturation booking of theatres) has proven the most effective way of exploiting big-budget films: it is important that a lot of money is made in the first week of a film's theatrical release, before potentially bad reviews and word-of-mouth reduce the returns. *Jurassic Park* (1993) is a case in point: 'after taking $50 million in its first American weekend in June, [it] took half of that in weekend three'.[166]

Particularly in the case of the blockbuster, most of a film's advertising budget will be spent the week preceding and the week following its theatrical release. During this period, TV saturation advertising is predominant, though the printed media does play a key role in film advertising after this two-week period.

Summary

Film as communication is not unidirectional, with the producer presenting the consumer with a fixed diet of consumables. Quite the contrary. Increasingly, information technology allows market analysts to access accurate information about movie-goers – information which is used to determine production decisions. Whether these decisions can help to sustain the recent renaissance of film-going remains to be seen.

As a useful summary exercise, consider the questions below in relation to the previous section:

1 **What do you make of these statistics?**

	US weekly attendance (millions)	UK weekly attendance (millions)
1946	95	31.5
1956	46.5	21.1

2 **Who do you consider to be the typical frequent cinema-goer in the UK or US today? Are audience demographics reflected in the choice of films shown at neighbourhood multiplexes?**

3 **How do film companies try to build an audience for a blockbuster?**

CENSORSHIP AND CLASSIFICATION

Embarking upon a review of censorship, even when limiting the discussion to films, is a daunting task given the size of the topic. For this reason the content of this section is limited to a brief discussion of contemporary censorship in the US and the UK, followed by a look at specific historical examples of censorship in both countries.

Advocates versus critics of censorship

Those who argue in favour of censorship claim that it reflects and protects standards of morality generally held in society. Those who argue against it say that, rather than reflecting standards, it imposes them. There are strong arguments on both sides: advocates argue that depiction of graphic violence and sex on film shapes social behaviour, especially in young people, and that therefore its circulation needs to be controlled. Critics, on the other hand, argue that film censorship is only one example of where ideals and morals are imposed on the public by powerful groups within society.

For a discussion of censorship in German cinema in the 1970s, see Chapter 14, pp. 479–81.

The contemporary US scenario

Since 1952, film has been protected under the First Amendment to the Constitution of the US, along with other communication media such as newspapers and magazines. Under US law, individual states have the power to censor adult material, but only if it is deemed 'obscene'.[167] However, where children are concerned, state censors have extended legal powers to classify (or to rate) films as well.

The introduction of the 'ratings system' in 1968 is usually explained as an attempt by the film industry to offset the extended powers of state and municipal censors, granted that year by the Supreme Court which ruled that local authorities had the legal right to classify films for the protection of children.[168]

The ratings system is the film industry's 'voluntary' self-regulation system, and is administered by the Motion Picture Association of America (MPAA).[169] The ratings in current use are **G** (general audience), **PG** (parental guidance suggested), **PG-13**, **R** (persons under the age of seventeen must be accompanied by a parent or adult guardian), and **NC-17** (no one under seventeen admitted).

Key institution
The Motion Picture Association of America (MPAA) – administers the classification (ratings) system in the US.

Some observers argue that there is little censorship in the US, only classification. However, can one really argue that position with any confidence when film-makers are contractually obliged to deliver films to distributors that do not exceed an R rating, because exclusion of the pre-17 – frequent film-going – audience will mean that the films will do less well commercially? When this happens, as it does, censorship is in operation.

Other serious issues are raised by the current ratings system. First, what are the MPAA board's criteria for determining what should and should not be seen by children? Second, do major film companies, as the backers of the MPAA, receive preferential treatment, as has been suggested?[170]

Issues such as these need to be raised and discussed if we are to fully understand the motivation behind the promotion of certain moral positions and the suppression of others in films seen in the US.

The contemporary UK scenario

In matters of censorship and classification, the UK does share many similar strategies to the US: the only legally recognised censor bodies in the UK are local authorities; the nation's law cites 'obscenity' as a major reason for film censorship; and there exists a universally adopted system of film classification, administered by an industry-supported board – the British Board of Film Classification (BBFC) – which argues that the primary role of classification is the protection of children.

The BBFC operates a system of classification for film releases as well as video releases.[171] For the cinema, the ratings are: **U** (suitable for all), **PG** (parental guidance advised), **12** (restricted to persons twelve years and over), **15** (restricted to persons fifteen years and over), **18** (restricted to persons 18 years and over), and **R18** (restricted distribution only, through sex shops, specially licensed cinemas, etc.). For the video industry, an additional classification exists: **Uc** (particularly suitable for children). Video releases are classified separately from cinema releases. BBFC policy means that classification categories for videos are more rigidly imposed than for film releases, because videos are intended for home consumption, a 'sacrosanct ... protected place'.[172]

Unlike the US, however, films intended for adult consumption are subject to broad legal censorship as well as classification, and this job also falls to the BBFC.[173] Such is the widespread legality of censorship in the UK that a charge of obscenity, or any of the following, will likely result in cuts:

sexual violence ... emphasis on the process of violence and sadism ... glamorisation of weapons that are both particularly dangerous and not already well-known in Britain ... ill-treatment of animals or child actors that breaks the Cinematograph Act 1937 or the Protection of Children Act 1978 ... details of imitable, dangerous or criminal techniques ... blasphemous images or dialogue.

(From BBFC's *A Student's Guide to Film Classification and Censorship in Britain*)

The BBFC claims to be 'independent' of government and industry influences. But can this be fully justified, given its involvement with them? The organisation is funded entirely by the film industry, and

the appointment of the president and director have traditionally required the agreement of the local authorities, the industry trade associations, and the Home Secretary of the day.

(From BBFC's *Memorandum on the work of the BBFC*)

Given this, just whose interests does the BBFC represent?

There is no doubt that there is widespread support for the BBFC's role where the protection of children is concerned. However, its function in the censorship of films intended for adult consumption provokes a far less clear response. In the US, freedom of speech is guaranteed. No such position exists in the UK with the result that the BBFC can feel free to voice this statement on the population's behalf:

In the USA, freedom of speech takes precedence over all other considerations. This [is] not the case in this country where we argue that one freedom (e.g. to own a gun) may limit another freedom (e.g. to stay alive without fear of being shot) ... there is far more violence in the USA and American society is evidently prepared to accept more violence in its media. We do not feel there is any great pressure for us to follow suit.[174]

☐ **CASE STUDY 5: US – THE HAYS CODE**

For a period of approximately twenty years, from the early 1930s to the early 1950s, American commercial film was subject to rigid regulation from within the industry itself. The Production Code, or Hays Code, laid down specific ideological and moral principles to which all films shown commercially in the US had to subscribe.

Key institution
British Board of Film Classification (BBFC) – responsible for *both* classification and censorship of film shown in the UK.

Will Hays and the Production Code

The history of the Production Code dates back to 1922, and the appointment of Will Hays as president of the new, industry-sponsored, Motion Picture Producers and Distributors of America. He was an ideal front man for the organisation, having been a senior Republican politician – the ex-Postmaster General. Hays' brief was twofold: to improve the public image of Hollywood (following a series of very public Hollywood scandals around that time,[175] the film industry feared a backlash from state censors), and to protect Hollywood's interests in Washington and abroad, through his strong ties with the Republican party.

Key films exceeding the provisions of the code:
In their depiction of sex: *Red Dust* (1932), *She Done Him Wrong* (1932), and *Baby Face* (1933). In their depiction of violence: *The Public Enemy* (1931) and *Scarface* (1932).

Throughout the 1920s, Will Hays, as president of the MPPDA, saw to it that the influence of his organisation increased steadily within the industry. In the first few years of his appointment, Hays focused his energies on heading off state censorship boards,[176] under the banner of free speech. In 1924, the MPPDA introduced advice to film-makers on 'the suitability for screening of current novels and stage plays'.[177] In 1927, it produced a small document, called *The Don'ts and Be Carefuls*,[178] for producers. With the coming of 'talking pictures', a more formal code was announced (in 1930) – the 'Production Code'.

The code proved difficult to enforce until 1934, because producers, faced with falling box-office receipts brought about by the onset of the Depression, would not adhere to its principles.[179] Film producers saw sex and violence as 'box-office' insurance. The Hays office was not yet powerful enough to force the issue.

However, 1934 proved to be the decisive year. State censors, women's groups, education groups and religious groups were demanding action. The Roman Catholic church formed its Legion of Decency whose 'oath of obedience not to attend condemned films was recited by millions across the country during Sunday Mass'.[180] In this climate of threatened mass boycott of Hollywood films, the MPPDA could now rely on the complete support of the majors in implementing the Production Code.

Universal implementation of the code was finally assured with the arrival of the 'Production Code Administration' (PCA) that year, whereby the industry agreed that no film would be distributed or exhibited in the US that did not carry a PCA seal.

Thus, from 1934 until just beyond the end of the studio era, the code defined the ideological limits of the classic Hollywood film.

The content of the Production Code[181]

When depicting crime, producers were not allowed to include scenes on how to commit a crime, inspire the audience to imitate the crime, or make criminals seem heroic or justified. *The Public Enemy* (1931), for instance, with its glorification of the gangster, would in all likelihood not have been granted a PCA seal after 1934.

The code, in keeping with its project of pacifying the religious groups in the country, took a hard line on religion. No film could 'throw ridicule on any religious faith'. Ministers of religion could not be depicted as villains or comics and religious ceremonies had to be handled respectfully.

Under the terms of the code, representation of foreign countries and foreigners had to be respectful.[182] 'The history, institutions, prominent people and citizenry' of other nations had to be represented fairly.

Overt depiction of sex was banned of course. Other taboo subjects were sexual perversion, white slavery, miscegenation and sex hygiene! In the depiction of gender relations, films had to be sympathetic to marriage as an institution. 'Impure love' could not be represented as attractive, it could not be the subject of comedy, it could not be presented so as to 'arouse passion or morbid curiosity' in audiences, and it could not be portrayed as permissible. 'Compensating moral values' were required where the scenario depicted 'impure love': i.e. characters had to suffer in the scenario as a result of their behaviour.

Under the rules of the code, no adult nudity was permissible. Bedrooms had be treated with the utmost discretion, because of their association with 'sexual life or with sexual sin'. Vulgarities, obscenities and profanities[183] of any kind were all banned. Producers could not depict dances which suggested 'sexual actions'.

With so many restrictions, it is a wonder that Hollywood was able to dispense any 'pleasure' from its dream factories during the studio era!

Key Film
Compensating moral values:
Back Street (1941).

☐ CASE STUDY 6: UK CENSORSHIP – INTERWAR AND SECOND WORLD WAR

The British Board of Film Censors[184] was founded by the film industry in 1912 to neutralise the effect of local authority censorship (see above). From its inception, the BBFC operated a system of classification. It issued two categories: **U** (Universal) and **A** (Adult, denoting that the film was more suitable for an adult audience).[185] These categories were advisory until 1921, when the London County Council decided to adopt them. (An **H** category was introduced in 1933 for horror films.[186])

Although not an official censor, the BBFC protected ruling values and interests. Indeed, its personnel had established links with government. For instance, Lord Tyrell – the president of the BBFC from 1935 to 1947 – had been Head of the Political Intelligence Department and Permanent Under-Secretary of State at the Foreign Office before taking up his post at the BBFC.[187]

During the interwar years, most local authorities accepted a BBFC certificate as validation of a film's moral rectitude and therefore as fit for exhibition. Up until the end of the Second World War, the BBFC maintained a formal code of practice, like the MPPDA in the US. The BBFC was nothing if not conscientious in its crusade and, predictable censor fodder aside (i.e. sex and crime), made sure that any filmic material that was in any way 'sensitive' did not get passed. To quote Julian Petley:[188]

With its bans on the great Russian [Soviet film] classics, on ... newsreels critical of Nazi Germany and Fascist Italy, on 'references to controversial politics,' 'relations to capital and labour,'[189] 'subjects calculated or possibly intended to foment social unrest or discontent'... it is perhaps hardly surprising that in 1937 Lord Tyrrell could say to the exhibitors association: 'We may take pride in observing that there is not a single film showing in London today which deals with any of the burning questions of the day.'

Examples of films banned or severely cut by the BBFC in the UK in the 1920s and 1930s

Film	Reason for ban*/cut**
Battleship Potemkin (1925)*	pro-revolutionary propaganda
Mother (1926)*	pro-revolutionary propaganda
La Chienne (1931)*	an unrepentant prostitute was the central character
The Public Enemy (1931)*	subversive depiction of crime and gangsterism
Spanish Earth (1937)**	reference to controversial foreign politics – the Spanish Civil War

With the start of the Second World War, the state took a direct role in film censorship. The Ministry of Information (MoI) was set up to control the flow of public information, for the sake of national security: in other words, it became the official censor. (The BBFC's role during wartime was vastly reduced, as all films were first submitted to the MoI.) It was also responsible for presenting 'the national case to the public at home and abroad' and for 'the preparation and issue of national propaganda'.[190] Under the leadership of Jack Beddington (1940–6), the Films Division of the MoI conveyed the 'do-s and don't-s' to commercial film-makers, among others.

Around 1942, Jack Beddington initiated an Ideas Committee, included in which were eminent writers and directors of UK commercial film.[191] It operated as a forum for discussion, a kind of pro-active censorship group, where the wartime ideological (propaganda) strategy was formulated. A film that definitely was not a product of the Ideas Committee, and seems to have 'slipped through the net' during the Second World War, was *The Life and Death of Col. Blimp* (1943). Winston Churchill, no less, attempted to stop the production, because he felt it was 'propaganda detrimental to the morale of the army'.[192] Despite his attempts, the film was made and shown: the Ministry of Information deemed that it could not impose a ban on the film because it did not pose a threat to national security.[193]

☐ CASE STUDY 7: UK CONTEMPORARY – *PLATOON* (1986)

A review of the BBFC's handling of the classification of the 'Vietnam' film *Platoon* reflects a board which has abandoned a formal code of practice (eliminated after the Second World War), and which appears sensitive to social attitudes, with a willingness to reflect them (i.e. not merely to impose standards – as witnessed in the previous case studies).

After screening the film in January 1987, many BBFC examiners and members of the board felt it should carry an 18 certificate because of its graphic violence, but expressed regret that the fifteen to seventeen-year-old age group 'would be barred from a film that they were likely to find interesting'.[194] The UK distributor was then notified of the board's likely decision – that the film would receive an 18 classification – and appealed on the basis that the film was not a 'comic book war film' (like *Rambo: First Blood, Part 2* (1985)), but rather a serious discourse on the meaning of war (and no doubt on the basis that an 18 certificate would have seriously limited the audience for the film and its box office!).

After further screenings and discussions, the film was given a 15 certificate, with the stipulation that there be a test screening for fifteen to seventeen year olds, to ensure that they understood that the film was not glorifying violence and war. Their response supported the decision to grant the film a 15 certificate. A point worth raising, however, is whether a film that was not a big Hollywood picture would have been shown quite the same consideration by the BBFC.

Summary
There is no question that in the past, dominant groups in society were able to impose a strict code of values on films consumed by American and British film-goers. Today,

however, media penetration and accessibility (e.g. through satellite), and the democratisation of culture make a mockery of any attempt to fashion such a dogmatic policy. Nevertheless, the shaping of film texts to prescribed notions of what is 'suitable for chil-

---

As a useful summary exercise, consider the questions below in relation to the previous section:

1 **Does film censorship reflect or impose standards?**
2 **Why might classification/ratings systems be interpreted by some as censorship through the back door?**
3 **Taking the studio era blockbuster *Gone with the Wind* (1939) as an example, would you consider the film entirely in keeping with the spirit of the Production Code?**

---

dren' or what is 'obscene' still goes on. It must be left to society to debate the correctness and appropriateness of such a policy.

'CINEMA AS INSTITUTION' – SUMMARY

This chapter has centred on the institutional framework of mainstream film, and the historical relationship between text and context. Any change in production, exhibition or distribution practice, in communication technology (both hardware and software), in audience demographics, or in censorship will have repercussions for the films we see and how we see them.

Films and their socio-economic contexts are part of a much broader history, that of twentieth-century culture in general. The purpose of this (simplified) overview has been to go some way towards illuminating this point.

NOTES

1 T. Balio (ed.), 1976, p.14.
2 Ibid., pp. 7–9.
3 D. Bordwell, J. Staiger and K. Thompson, 1985, pp. 116–17.
4 T. Balio (ed.), 1976, p. 63.
5 See R. Allen and D. Gomery, 1985, pp. 202–5.
6 The 900-seat Princess Theatre (1909), see D. Gomery, 1992, p. 32.
7 T. Balio (ed.), 1976, pp. 73–4.
8 Ibid., pp. 76–7.
9 Ibid., p. 75.
10 T. Elsaesser (ed.), 1990, pp. 192–3.
11 Immediately after the formation of the General Film Company (GFC), independents began operating their own distribution company – The Motion Picture Distributing And Sales Company (May 1910). This was superseded by The Film Supply Company Of America, The Universal Film Manufacturing Company and Mutual Films in 1912. Later, the introduction of feature-length films further weakened the MPPC, when many of its own members began dissociating themselves from the GFC and distributed their features through alternative distribution organisations. See T. Elsaesser (ed.), 1990, pp. 194–6, 201.
12 Ibid., p. 198.
13 See D. Bordwell, J. Staiger and K. Thompson, 1985, pp. 113–20.
14 Ibid., pp. 121–7.
15 For instance, the Solax Company in 1912 was organised into the following departments: executive, production, direction, art, wardrobe, small properties, electrical,

mechanical, laboratory, sales, publicity, shipping, accounting. See ibid., p. 124.

16 Ibid., pp. 128–41.

17 See T. Elsaesser (ed.), 1990, p. 204, for an early case of vertical integration – Triangle Film Incorporated (1915).

18 D. Gomery, 1986, pp. 26–8.

19 T. Balio (ed.), 1976, p. 114. N.B. In 1928, First National was purchased by Warner Bros. Film Company.

20 D. Gomery, 1986, pp. 54–5.

21 Ibid., p. 14.

22 Ibid., pp. 12, 18.

23 The other 30 per cent of first-run theatres was owned by non-affiliated 'independent' exhibitors.

24 The company merged with Famous Players-Lasky in 1925 to form the New Corporation Paramount Publix. See D. Gomery, 1992, p. 43.

25 Ibid., pp. 40–56.

26 Ibid., pp. 77, 80–1.

27 D. Gomery, 1992, p. 67

28 An early form of block-booking called 'standing-orders' had existed during the days of the MPPC: see T. Elsaesser (ed.), 1990, p. 193.

29 D. Gomery, 1992, pp. 67–9.

30 D. Bordwell, J. Staiger and K. Thompson, 1985, p. 321.

31 N.B. This system was not universally adopted nor did companies refrain from changing production systems periodically. Taking 1941 as an example, it is interesting to note that the three most financially successful companies, in terms of box-office receipts, were all operating different production systems: United Artists had a system of director units and producer units; MGM operated a producer-unit system; Twentieth-Century Fox used a central-producer system. See ibid., pp. 320–9.

32 Through the National Recovery Act (NRA) and the Wagner Act: see D. Gomery, 1986, p. 10.

33 D. Bordwell, J. Staiger, and K. Thompson, 1985, pp. 311–3.

34 In Warner's case, this was arranged through the Wall Street investment merchant bank Goldman Sachs.

35 See WB's balance sheet for the studio era, in D. Gomery, 1986, p. 102.

36 WB theatres were sold off (or leases terminated) to help meet its debts; see D. Gomery, 1986, p. 110.

37 In 1932, the average production cost per feature was US$200,000 at WB, whereas at MGM it was $450,000. See R. Campbell, 'Warner Bros. in the 1930s', 1971, p. 2.

38 See M. Roth's essay, 'Some Warners musicals and the spirit of the New Deal', in R. Altman (ed.), 1981, pp. 41–56.

39 R. Campbell, 'Warner Bros. in the 1930s', p. 2.

40 For a discussion on the relationship of Raoul Walsh to Warners' studio style see E. Buscombe's essay, 'Walsh and Warner Bros.', in P. Hardy (ed.), 1974.

41 See drawings for Mildred Pierce sets in D. Deschner, 1975, p. 20.

42 Ibid., p. 22.

43 See T. Balio (ed.), 1976, p. 317.

44 See ibid., p. 353.

45 And 30 per cent of Columbia's releases were also produced by them: see ibid., p. 353.

46 See ibid., p. 315.

47 The first major film company to sell its film library to TV was RKO, in December 1955. See ibid., p. 322.

48 From the late 1940s onwards, film companies began producing programmes for TV, e.g. Warners' weekly series for ABC-TV, Warner Bros. Presents (1955). By the early 1960s, producing TV shows was standard film industry practice and a major source of its revenue. Shortly afterwards (from the mid-1960s onwards), TV networks began commissioning made-for-TV films from major studios and independent producers. Ibid., pp. 322–4.

49 E.g. In 1956, United Paramount Theatres (ex-exhibition arm of Paramount) merged with ABC-TV. See ibid., p. 324.

50 See G. Jowett and J. Linton, 1989, p. 43.

51 The majors started buying theatres again in the mid-1980s. The US government's view on this was that vertical integration was not such a threat to competition as in the studio era because of the diversified nature of the industry infrastructure – i.e. independent production, pay TV, video and the general increase in theatres outside the direct ownership of the majors. Ibid., p. 46.

52 Ibid., p. 46.

53 See Variety, 6 Dec. 1989, p. 3.

54 The pattern of exclusive first-run releases having been broken with The Godfather in 1972. See G. Jowett and J. Linton, 1989, p. 59.

55 J. Squire (ed.), 1986, pp. 329–30.

56 G. Jowett and J. Linton, 1989, p. 47.

57 Screen International, no. 750, 31 March 1990.

58 See D. Gomery, 1992, pp. 109–10, where comparisons are made between the centralised management style and innovation of Cineplex in the 1980s, and Balaban and Katz in the 1920s.

59 See Variety, 12 Dec. 1989, p. 3, and G. Jowett and J. Linton, 1989, p. 47.

60 Many thanks to John Wilkinson, of the UK-based Cinema Exhibitors' Association, whose interview with myself assisted in the compilation of the following information.

61 A useful précis of this argument was articulated in Wilf Stevenson's article 'Film jackpot solves nothing', Daily Telegraph, 15 May 1997.

62 Source: I. Wall et al., 1997.

63 See T. Balio (ed.), 1976, pp. 458–67.

64 G. Drabinsky, Motion Pictures and the Arts in Canada: The Business and the Law (McGraw-Hill Ryerson, Toronto, 1976). Quoted in G. Jowett and J. Linton, 1989, p. 56.

65 G. Jowett and J. Linton, 1989, pp. 43–4.

66 Reported in 'The Sunday Review', Independent On Sunday, 11 July 1993, p. 15.

67 D. Bordwell, J. Staiger and K. Thompson, 1985, pp. 330–7.

68 G. Jowett and J. Linton, 1989, p. 38.

69 US$600 million of the summer's $1.8 billion gross. The independent productions that were major box-office winners were, Terminator 2 (Carolco Productions), Robin Hood (Morgan Creek Productions), City Slickers (Castle Rock Productions), Backdraft (Imagine Productions), Point Break (Largo Productions) – reported in P. Biskind, 'Going For Broke', Sight and Sound, October 1991, p. 6.

70 In 1950 James Stewart's agent, MCA (Music Corp. of America), arranged for him to be paid 50 per cent of the net profits of the Universal film, Winchester '73, in lieu of his normal salary of $250,000. This arrangement would not have been possible under the terms of his MGM contract during the studio era. See N. Kent, 1991, p. 86.

71 See ibid., pp. 210–45.

72 A 1989 audience survey reported that the presence of stars was not an important factor in movie attendance

decisions, but only important as a means of publicising a film. See G. Jowett and J. Linton, 1989, p. 39.

73 A private company, partly financed by the Department of Trade and Industry, which endeavours to support the creation of low to medium budget features.

74 A public body funded by the Department of National Heritage. It puts money into films that enhance British culture.

75 In the form of writer/producer teams, writer/producer/ director teams, and unattached writers.

76 The EC Commission Initiative, Media II, loans money to producers, directors and writers for the development of film and TV fiction.

77 For details see D. Daly, 1980, pp. 106–9.

78 See interview with Zanuck and Brown, 'Dialogue on film', 1975, p. 40.

79 D. Daly, 1980, p. 107, note 4. However, changes were made to the script during production.

80 Ibid., p. 111.

81 The hardcover version of *Jaws* was on the *New York Times* Bestseller List for forty-five consecutive weeks. See D. Daly, 1980, p. 109.

82 Ibid., p. 111.

83 See 'Dialogue on film', p. 43.

84 D. Daly, 1980, p. 110, from comments reported in *LA Times*, 28 Sept. 1975, Section VII, p. 1.

85 See C. Gottlieb, 1975, p. 204.

86 I.e. the director's first cut.

87 C. Gottlieb, 1975, pp. 213–14.

88 D. Daly, 1980, p. 115.

89 See ibid., p. 113.

90 See ibid., p. 114.

91 By mid-March 1975 the paperback had sold 5 million copies. See ibid., p. 119.

92 Actually 464 theatres. By 15 August 1975, 954 theatres were playing *Jaws*. See D. Daly, 1980, pp. 124–5.

93 R. Zanuck's comments in 'Dialogue on film', 1975, pp. 51–2.

94 D. Daly, 1980, p. 122.

95 Ibid., pp. 122–3.

96 Ibid., pp. 124–5.

97 Ibid., pp. 137–8.

98 Reported in *Variety*, 10 December 1977, p. 5; quoted in D. Daly, 1980, p. 138.

99 Reported by D. Pringle, *TV Guide*, December 1979, pp. 39–40; quoted in G. Jowett and J. Linton, 1989, p. 125.

100 *Screen International*, no. 840, 17 January 1992.

101 S. Woolley, 'Last Palace Picture Show', *Guardian*, 30 October 1992.

102 A. Finney, 1997, pp. 25–8.

103 Ibid., p. 262.

104 J. Giles, 1997, pp. 36–37.

105 see A. Finney, 1997, pp. 272–3.

106 *Screen International*, no. 888, 18–25 December 1992.

107 See M. Fleming and L. Klady, 1993, p. 68.

108 Ibid., p. 68.

109 Ibid., p. 1.

110 Ibid., p. 69.

111 Ibid., p. 69.

112 Ibid., p. 1.

113 *Screen International*, no. 889, 8–14 January 1993.

114 *Screen International*, no. 940, 14–20 January 1994.

115 See J. Giles, 1997, p. 50.

116 *Screen International*, no. 940, 14–20 January 1994.

117 2 April 1993.

118 According to sources within the industry, BFI development money for projects of this type is currently in the region of £5,000+.

119 Via the BFI.

120 According to Eaton (interview 2 April 1993): '[The HBO development officer] told me, "in this next draft is there any chance you can make it more like a movie?". It was the opposite position I'd always been in in the past, which is like, "can you make this script cheaper". In the move from the first draft to the second draft, I put a lot more [of] America in there.' There was to be a big shift between drafts one and two, a shift from a TV studio drama to a TV film conceived entirely in terms of cinema.

121 Then head of drama at Pebble Mill, whose previous credits had included *The Boys from the Blackstuff*.

122 'They [HBO] have this incredible market research. It's done by another office than the development office. They know their market very, very well. They know which faces have recognition value within that [TV cable] market and they suddenly become extremely active at the time of casting' – Eaton interview, 2 April 1993.

123 With the quid pro quo that they would have theatrical distribution rights in the UK.

124 Between 5 January and 14 March 1990, the film was seen at the Metro (a small art-house cinema) by 16,357 people and grossed £60,455. This was a very good run for the cinema.

125 'Plenty of fish in pond Time-Warner wants to swim in', *Wall Street Journal*, 7 March 1989, p. B1, cited in T. Balio (ed.), 1990, p. 315.

126 Sales of $14 billion in 1992. See P. Koenig, 'Steve's world, and our own', The Sunday Review, *Independent On Sunday*, 21 February 1993, p. 2.

127 With sales of $12 billion in 1992. Ibid., p. 2

128 E.g. The *Sun*, and *News of the World*.

129 Twentieth-Century Fox and Fox TV in the US.

130 See 'Will SONY make it in Hollywood?', *Fortune*, 9 September 1991.

131 See ibid. Sony Corporation is convinced that its Betamax videotape format would have had greater success in the late 1970s if Sony had owned a studio and had thus secured for itself software for its hardware. (VHS succeeded as the standard format because it was promoted by European manufacturers – the first important domestic VCR market – and Hollywood studios adopted it as their standard format.)

132 Although its January 1993 bid to operate Britain's Channel 5 (with Thames TV) was rejected, it is a partner in Classic FM, and has a small stake in UK Cable TV (reported in P. Koenig, 1993, p. 4). One can safely assume that Time-Warner will continue in its attempt to infiltrate British media companies – ultimately to the detriment of companies trying to produce and deliver UK programming to UK consumers.

133 'The empire fights', *Sunday Telegraph Review*, 4 July 1993, p. 2.

134 See 'Wiring the world', *Newsweek*, 5 April 1993, pp. 28–35 (the above scenario no doubt underlies the News Corporation/British Telecom partnership announced on 1 September 1993).

135 Report by the US Department of Labor entitled *Family Spending and Saving in Wartime*, Bulletin no. 822; quoted in L. Handel, 1950, p. 104.

136　*Film Daily Year Book*, quoted in L. Handel, 1950, p. 96. By comparison, attendance figures for 1940 (pre-war) were 80 million a week, and around 85 million a week for 1945 (end of war). See B. Austin, 1989, p. 36.

137　Women: 3.75 times per month; men: 3.7 times per month – L. Handel, *Studies of the Motion Picture Audience*, New York, December 1941, cited in L. Handel, 1950, p. 100.

138　Defined as attending ten times a month or more: figures for men were 11.8 per cent, as opposed to only 7.5 per cent for women – source: A/A, cited in L. Handel, 1950, p. 100.

139　E.g. In a State-wide survey conducted in Iowa in 1942, 31 per cent of men and 24.9 per cent of women aged fifteen to twenty attended cinemas over five times a month, as opposed to only 11.4 per cent and 7.6 per cent respectively of those aged twenty-one to thirty-five – source: F. Whan and H. Summers, *The 1942 Iowa Radio Audience Survey*, Des Moines, 1942, cited in ibid., p. 103.

140　N.B. In actual numbers, persons with higher levels of education were a minority among cinema-goers in the 1940s – ibid., pp. 104–8.

141　*Film Daily Year Book*, quoted in I. Bernstein, 1957, p. 2.

142　I. Bernstein, 1957, p. 74.

143　Source: Department of Commerce's Census of Business for 1954, cited in ibid., p. 5.

144　Source: *Film Daily Year Book*, quoted in I. Bernstein, 1957, p. 73.

145　Ibid., p. 73.

146　The average weekly cinema attendance in the US for 1960 had been 40 million, and for 1970 had been 17.7 million: see B. Austin, 1989, p. 36.

147　Of those surveyed, 30 per cent cited watching TV as their favourite way to spend an evening, while only 6 per cent cited going to the movies – source: *The Gallup Opinion Index*, Report 146, pp. 14–15, September 1977; quoted in B. Austin, 1989, p. 40.

148　Defined in this survey as persons under the age of thirty.

149　Average weekly movie attendance for 1980 was 19.7 million: B. Austin, 1989, p. 36, 40–1.

150　D. Docherty, D. Morrison and M. Tracey, 1987, pp. 14–15.

151　In a 1948 Gallup poll, 79 per cent of people surveyed between the ages of eighteen and twenty, and 76 per cent of those between the ages of twenty-one and twenty-nine had been to the cinema within the previous three weeks: this declined to 57 per cent for those aged thirty to forty-nine – source: Gallup, cited in ibid., p. 17.

152　In a 1949 survey, 19 per cent of the working-class people surveyed (i.e. those persons with low levels of income and education) went to the cinema (at least) twice a week, as opposed to 13 per cent of middle-class people interviewed, and 8 per cent of upper-class people surveyed – source: Hulton Research, cited in ibid., p. 16.

153　D. Docherty, D. Morrison and M. Tracey, 1987, pp. 14–15.

154　'There was an increase in TV licences from 343k in 1950 to 10 million in 1960', ibid., p. 23.

155　Partly a product of 1950s prosperity and a move towards greater owner-occupation, and partly the result of the Town and Country Planning Act of 1947 which 'led to the clearing of slums, the growth of new towns … and, crucially, the resiting of large sections of the working class … around the edges of cities' (ibid., pp. 25–6).

156　Ibid., pp. 26–7.

157　Ibid., p. 29.

158　Dropping from half the total audience to one-third between 1977 and 1983 – ibid., pp. 30–1.

159　E.g. In the US in 1987, twelve to fifteen year olds accounted for 11 per cent of yearly admissions; sixteen to twenty year olds, 21 per cent ; twenty-one to twenty-four year olds, 15 per cent ; twenty-five to twenty-nine year olds, 15 per cent. Source: Motion Picture Association of America (MPAA), 1987; cited in G. Jowett and J. Linton, 1989, p. 90.

160　Source MPAA; cited in G. Jowett and J. Linton, 1989, p. 90.

161　'The US adult population with some college training increased from 15 per cent of the adult population in 1960 to 25 per cent in 1975, and by 1990 it is expected that over 1/3 of the adult population will have a year or more of college level work' – ibid., p. 134.

162　Source: I. Wall *et al.*, 1997.

163　See G. Jowett and J. Linton, 1989, p. 106.

164　'Every element of this heart-warming drama (*Grizzly Adams*), from the hair and eye colouring of the actors to the type of animals they frolic with, was pre-tested….Your family's every "ooh" and "ahh" was anticipated in tests taken by other families demographically identical to yours' – from P. Morrisroe, 'Making movies the computer way', *Parade*, Vol. 16, 3 February 1980; quoted in ibid., p. 106.

165　See ibid., p. 58.

166　Quoted from 'The Sunday Review', *Independent On Sunday*, 11 July 1993.

167　T. Balio (ed.), 1976, p. 438.

168　'The choice was not between a rating system and no rating system. It was between an industry rating system and fifty state classification boards (more if you add municipalities such as Dallas)' – quoted from S. Byron, 'Letter to Editor', *Film Comment*, Vol. 22, Issue 5, October 1986, p. 76.

169　Headquartered in L.A. The names and backgrounds of members of the board are kept secret. All that is known of the six board members who classify the films is that they are all parents and that one of them is nominated by the California PTA: see L. Sheinfeld, 1986, p. 11.

170　See L. Sheinfeld, 1986, p. 14.

171　As a result of the Video Recordings Act 1984, the BBFC now exercises for the first time a 'statutory function on behalf of central government' whereby it is the designated authority appointed by the Home Secretary to classify videos: see BBFC pamphlet, *Memorandum on the Work of the British Board of Film Classification*.

172　See BBFC pamphlet, *A Student's Guide to Film Classification and Censorship in Britain*.

173　Although statutory power to censor remains with the local authorities, the board's decisions are generally accepted.

174　Quoted from BBFC pamphlet, *A Student's Guide to Film Classification and Censorship in Britain*. N.B. Although the statement suggests otherwise, there is *no* decisive proof that films cause violence.

175　I.e. the Fatty Arbuckle scandal (rape and murder trial), the murder of William Desmond Taylor, and death (through drug addiction) of Wallace Reid: see C. Champlin, 1980, p. 42.

176　'Reformer-inspired censorship legislation' was on the rise at that time in more than half the States in the US: see T. Balio (ed.), 1976, p. 304.

177　Ibid., p. 308.

178　See C. Champlin, 1980, p. 42.

179 Despite the introduction of mandatory script submission by producers to the Hays office in 1931.

180 See C. Champlin, 1980, p.44.

181 Reprinted in full in L. Leff and J. Simmons, 1990, pp. 283–92.

182 As early as 1922, the Mexican government negotiated with the MPPDA over the representation of Mexicans in American films.

183 The dialogue, 'Frankly my dear, I don't give a damn', was allowed in *Gone with the Wind* (1939) only after a special appeal had been made by the producer to the Hays office.

184 As it was called until 1985.

185 N.B. In 1921, the classification A was modified to stipulate that children under sixteen had to be accompanied by a parent or guardian: see R. Falcon, 1994, Part 2, p. 4.

186 See J. Robertson, 1985, p. 58.

187 C. Barr (ed.), 1986, p. 44.

188 In his essay 'Cinema and State', in C. Barr (ed.), 1986.

189 E.g. A ban was imposed on the scenario, *Love on the Dole*, until the outbreak of the Second World War. In 1940, the project was given the go-ahead.

190 I. McLaine, *Ministry of Morale* (Allen & Unwin, London, 1979), quoted in A. Algate and J. Richards, 1986, p. 18.

191 Including (at various times): M. Balcon, M. Powell, S. Gilliat, L. Howard, C. Frend, A. Asquith.

192 From Prime Minister's Personal Minute M.357/2, 10 September 1942, reprinted in I. Christie (ed.), 1978, p. 107.

193 However, the film was cut at the request of the MoI before an export licence (for America) was granted it. See ibid., p. 110.

194 R. Falcon, 1994, p. 92.

FURTHER READING

Algate, A. and Richards, J. *Britain Can Take It* (Basil Blackwell, London, 1986)

Austin, B. *Immediate Seating: A Look at Movie Audiences* (Wadsworth Publishing Co, Belmont, CA, 1989)

Balio, T. (ed.) *The American Film Industry* (University of Wisconsin Press, Madison, 1976)

—— (ed.) *Hollywood in the Age of Television* (Unwin Hyman, Boston, 1990)

Barr, C. (ed.) *All Our Yesterdays* (BFI Publishing, London, 1986)

Bernstein, I. *Hollywood at the Crossroads* (Hollywood Film Council, L.A., 1957)

Bordwell, D., Staiger, J. and Thompson, K. *The Classical Hollywood Cinema* (Routledge & Kegan Paul, London, 1985)

British Board of Film Classification *A Student's Guide to Film Classification and Censorship in Britain*

Daly, D. *A Comparison of Exhibition and Distribution Patterns in Three Recent Feature Motion Pictures* (Arno Press, New York, 1980)

Docherty, D., Morrison, D. and Tracey, M. *The Last Picture Show?* (BFI Publishing, London, 1987)

Falcon, R. *Classified! A Teacher's Guide to Film and Video Censorship and Classification* (BFI Publishing, London, 1994)

Finney, A. *The Egos Have Landed*, (Mandarin, London, 1997)

Giles, J. *The Crying Game* (BFI Publishing, London, 1997)

Gomery, D. *The Hollywood Studio System* (Macmillan, London, 1986)

—— *Shared Pleasures* (BFI Publishing, London, 1992)

Handel, L. *Hollywood Looks at its Audience* (University of Illinois Press, Urbana, 1950)

Jowett, G. and Linton, J. *Movies As Mass Communication* (Sage Publications, Newbury Park, CA, 1989)

Kent, N. *Naked Hollywood* (BBC Books, London 1991)

Leff, L. and Simmons, J. *The Dame in the Kimono* (Grove Weidenfeld, New York, 1990)

Robertson, J. *The British Board of Film Censors: Film Censorship in Britain, 1896–1950* (Croom Helm, Kent, 1985)

Roddick, N. *A New Deal in Entertainment* (BFI Publishing, London, 1983)

FURTHER VIEWING

Key Warner Bros. (genre) films

gangster film

Little Caesar (1930)
The Public Enemy (1931)

Bullets or Ballots (1935)
Marked Woman (1937)
The Roaring 'Twenties (1939)

social conscience film

I Am a Fugitive from a Chain Gang (1932)
Wild Boys of the Road (1933)

fast-talking comedy/drama

Five-Star Final (1931)
Lady Killer (1933)
Hard to Handle (1933)

musical

42nd Street (1933)
Gold Diggers of 1933 (1933)
Dames (1934)

biopic

The Story of Louis Pasteur (1936)
The Life of Emile Zola (1937)
Juarez (1939)

Merrie England cycle

Captain Blood (1935)
The Adventures of Robin Hood (1938)
The Sea Hawk (1940)

melodrama

Jezebel (1938)
The Letter (1940)
Now Voyager (1942)
Mildred Pierce (1945)

film noir

The Maltese Falcon (1941)
The Big Sleep (1946)
Dark Passage (1947)

RESOURCE CENTRES

http://www.bfi.org.uk
The website for the British Film Institute.

British Film Institute Library
21 Stephen Street, London W1P 1PL
Tel: 0171 255 1444

http://europa.eu.int/eac
Website for the European Audio Visual Conference, in conjunction with the British Screen Advisory Council.
British Screen Advisory Council
19 Cavendish Square, London W1M 9AB
Tel: 0171 499 4177

http://win95.cns.ohiou.edu/movies10/links.html
A website of Ohio University with links to homepages of major movie studios (Twentieth-Century Fox, Paramount, Castle Rock, Sony, October, Orion, TNT, Roughcut, etc.) and links to Hollywood Hotline and Hollywood On-Line.

http://jimmy.qmced.ac.uk
For UK producers and distributors, with links to all aspects of films and the film industry: BFI, British Film Commission, Oscars, academic sites, stars. This is a website of Queen Margaret College, University of Edinburgh.

Chapter 3

Film and technology

Chris Webster

■ Introduction   60
■ Film and the technology of illusion   62
■ In the beginning   64
■ From toys to Tinseltown   66
■ Somewhere between then and now   69
■ Computer-generated imagery   73
□ Case study 1: *Mars Attacks!* (1996)   77
■ Other ways of seeing   79
■ World economics and new technologies   84
■ Final frame: conclusion   85
■ Further reading   86
■ Further viewing   87
■ Resource centres   87

■ Film and technology

INTRODUCTION

For many of us, the rate of change within our society is simply frightening. Central to that change and fear is technology. We seem to engage in endless debate about the evils and benefits of the modern world, about eroded values and new opportunities; some fear that technology is getting out of hand, that technology is becoming an end in itself – that the tail is beginning to wag the dog. This may point towards a deeper, more far-reaching anxiety, that our efforts will somehow be our undoing and that, ultimately, man-machines are destined to take over and wreak revenge on a feeble mankind, as in James Cameron's *Terminator*.

The impact that new technologies are having – and are increasingly going to have on our lives, on the values we hold dear, on the manner in which we deal with and communicate with each other – is going to be profound. It is through technology that we will increasingly inform ourselves about one another, and it will be technology that helps to formulate our views about ourselves and others. And with that will come, hopefully, understanding and empathy which will ultimately mean the eradication of the fear of the unknown and a chance to begin to celebrate our differences, rather than be threatened by them.

Not least to be affected by these changes will be the media. Indeed the media will be at the forefront of those changes, driving them along in search of a democratisation and decentralisation of the processes.

The pessimist's future

A pessimistic view of the development of new technologies may focus on the drive by market forces, observing that the capitalism of the media merely reflects the capitalism of the free market. The proponent of this view believes that cost effectiveness, distribution, targets, market reach, viewing figures and returns on investments will no longer be seen simply as the necessary considerations affecting production methodologies, but increasingly they will be the *sole reason* to engage in any form of creative activity. Quality issues and breadth of product provision will take a back seat. The result: the systematic dumbing-down of society through the global mass distribution of homogeneous, non-specific digital pap, a harmless sop for the disenfranchised and disinterested.

The optimist's future

An optimistic view of the advancements in new technologies may focus on the increase in choice. To see market democracy shaped and led by public opinion that echoes a worldwide political shift towards democracy as we have seen in recent years – the unification of Germany, the death of apartheid in South Africa, the dissolution of the Soviet bloc into its constituent member states, and a more united Europe. They may identify developments that will open new global markets and bring about new opportunities for employment, in part brought about by deregulation and the new union laws and employment regulations more fitting to the twenty-first century than to the nineteenth. They may envision a buyers' market being central to this process, whereby customers no longer have to tolerate heavily subsidised forms of marginalised art: the cost of opera would be the same as soap opera, or at the very least paid for by the consumers on an equal footing. They may feel that – as production costs tumble due to faster, cheaper computers and the development of new distribution methods through the **Internet**, coupled with a likely convergence of terrestrial television broadcasting and computer technology – the benefits will be passed directly on to them in

Internet
A system of interlinking computers in a world-wide network (WWW/World Wide Web). Since the Internet was privatised in April 1995 the rise in monthly traffic on the Net has been such that it represents a hundredfold increase in less than three years. See Gilder, 1998.

• **Plate 3.1** *Terminator 2: Judgment Day* (US 1991)

the form of a more interesting and diversified media, a decentralised media in which they have a say.

Whether pessimist or optimist, one thing is for sure: we need to manage the change and to ensure that it is to our benefit. Those who successfully manage change have been seen not only to survive but to thrive. Those who ignore change and refuse to respond in an appropriate manner will lose out: the technological steamroller will flatten them. Unfortunately there are many examples of these individuals throughout the history of cinema. George Méliès, Emile Raynaud and Pat Sullivan, while pioneers in their own right and successful to a point, all failed to take advantage of new technologies and either chose to ignore the public's desire for new and innovative attractions or were unable to respond in a positive manner.

We may well look back ruefully on the opportunity such technology offers us, to recognise finally that film and television are mediums by which we could enhance and enrich our lives, to use it to promote the finer qualities of what it means to be human, to rejoice in our endeavours, our progress towards the stars, to be a cornerstone of civilisations. Instead they have become mediums by which we sell stuff we do not want to people who cannot afford it, to instil petty jealousies, to promote greed and to encourage apathy, to sell ourselves and each other short.

The rate at which technological changes and developments continue to come about are so fast that this book, indeed any publication, is almost out of date by the times it reaches its readers. This begs the question: 'How new is a new technology?' In this chapter we will look at some of the more important developments in film technology and the associated issues relating to technology, how these have helped to shape cinema, and what effect this process has had on the way in which we 'read' film; we also examine the financial and political implications and how our expectations of cinema have altered as a result of technological developments and our own cinematic experiences.

FILM AND THE TECHNOLOGY OF ILLUSION

Technology and art come together in a unique way to create the sensation event we call cinema. So tightly are art and technology interwoven that technology is the very substance of film. Not merely in the practical processes of getting ideas on to screens, it is increasingly at the very heart of the *content* of the cinematic experience. Technology alters and shapes film and cinema, not just how it is made but *how* we see it and *what* we see. It has a fundamental impact on the storytelling process. Modern film-makers have just learned to add a bit more sparkle to the process. The cinematic experience is no more or less than our wildest dreams and fantasies played out in public, a way in which society identifies and communicates with itself and with others, a way of confronting its fears, hopes, aspirations and neuroses through an age-long tradition of storytelling and myth-making. Part of that confrontational communication is humanity's often uneasy relationship with new technologies.

Form and content

For the purpose of this discussion I have chosen to divide the cinematic form into two separate and distinct areas – 'physical film form' and 'film content'. Cinema is born out of the integration of the two. Cinema and other closely associated technological areas such as television, video and other, more peripheral methods of audio-visual storytelling such as computer games, Virtual Reality, simulations and multimedia, have always been a forum for public exposure of new technologies. This has often taken the form of startling new effects: multiple exposures (Méliès' *L'Homme à la tete de caoutchouc*), montage (Eisenstein's *Battleship Potemkin*), sound (*The Jazz Singer*), colour (*Flowers and Trees*), back projection (*King Kong*), computer animation (*Jurassic Park*). The list goes on. Though, almost as often, the scientific and technological discourse within cinema has stemmed from the storytelling aspects. The Jules Verne and H.G. Wells tradition of predicting future technological societies quickly found public favour and was to become a prime source of cinematic material. First exploited by Méliès in *Le Voyage dans la lune* (1902) (see Robinson, 1993), it is a tradition that continues to fascinate and thrill audiences to this day.

persistence of vision
The phenomenon of 'persistence of vision' is due to the momentary retention of an image on the eye's retina. This retention was found to be approximately one-tenth of a second by Chevalier d'Arcy in 1765 when he successfully carried out one of the first systematic scientific studies and presented his findings to the French Académie des Sciences.

Film, the practical techno-mechanical activity of recording, synthesis and projection and distribution of sound and images, was born out of the development of lens technology, photography and the experiments with phenomenon we know as **persistence of vision**. This dates back to d'Arcy in the sixteenth century and Kircher in the seventeenth century (Coe, 1981).

Film content has its roots firmly fixed in aural storytelling traditions and can be traced back thousands of years through the theatrical art forms – literature, shadow plays, theatre, opera and vaudeville. The development of a structured filmic language has its foundations in these traditions, though it has become a malleable and richly versatile cinematic syntax specific to film and its related forms.

There are some very good and compelling reasons why new technological developments have been continually embraced throughout the film industry's short history.

As with any production process, the use of technology opens up opportunities to create new products and improvements on existing ones. Practical developments have meant that processes can be speeded up, making films cheaper and quicker to produce. Early improvements in negative film stock enabled cameramen to film in situations of low lighting, while smaller, less heavy cameras and sound recording equipment gave added mobility to film crews. Advances such as sound and colour had a major impact on the film industry; careers were made and broken on these issues alone and, although improvements continue to be made, the impact on the content of films is not always as easy to see or hear. Perhaps in recent years the advent of computer-generated images and special-effects work has been the most prominent development. Film-makers are able to produce alarmingly realistic representations of people, animals and other organic forms. The progress in such technology is easy to identify when a comparative analysis is drawn between such films as *Jurassic Park* and *Jumanji* and those of the great pioneers of effects animation, Willis O'Brian (*King Kong*) or Ray Harryhausen (*Jason and the Argonauts*). While there can be no doubt about the genius of these two ground-breaking film-makers, their efforts still look crude by comparison with more recent work .

With the development of new technologies comes the sophistication of the viewers. As a child I found *King Kong* to be a truly terrifying experience, and to this day it remains a favourite of mine, though it is now possible to create similar animation and effects for a fraction of the cost using just an ordinary personal computer. Such simple

• **Plate 3.2** *King Kong*
(US 1933)

effects would no longer be acceptable to the public: our expectations have risen, and along with them the production values and costs. While it may be difficult for us to appreciate the level of excitement felt by early film buffs as they witnessed the Lumière brothers' film of a train arriving at a station, we are fortunate that we are presented with increasingly spectacular and believable images, including everything from the internal workings of the human body to the outermost reaches of the universe: dinosaurs walk among us, ghosts talk to us, starships transport us to the surface of alien planets, we can shake hands with President Kennedy, we witness men of metal walking through flames, columns of water that smile at us and Batman really lives in Gotham City. These and many more examples of high-tech wizardry are made to such a high degree of finish that they convince us that these things *exist*.

On the downside, it would seem that at times within the film industry, script content, original ideas and creativity are out and a disposable facile techno-gloss is in. However, the use of animation techniques, pyrotechnics and weird camera effects cannot be the solution to a poor concept and bad script. In the hands of an incompetent film-maker, these techniques become a crass representation of what Hollywood *thinks* the public wants. Used appropriately and as a support to a good idea, the use of new technologies for stunning effects can transform a film into an unforgettable event. At their best these technological advances are the very magic that makes cinema the most exciting of art forms. At their worst such effects become merely a cynical attempt to cover up creative weaknesses while pandering to the juvenile desire for bigger, louder and brighter bangs and flashes.

Using *Titanic* as a case study consider the following:

Do we view the ship as a prop/set, albeit an elaborate one, to support the storyline and acting, or does it transend that role and become a focus of attention, upstaging the actors?

How does the 'making of' documentaries and associated hype affect our understanding of the cinematic process?

How does an understanding of production processes affect the reading of the film?

IN THE BEGINNING

We now take for granted the level of technology that we see nightly on our TV sets. Almost every programme, no matter how modest, is preceded by the (now obligatory) flying logo, and usually contains aspects of computer-aided design of one sort or another. Cinema, and by this term I include the early magic lantern shows, has always been a marriage of entertainment and technology, of the aesthetic and the industrial.

Shadow puppets

See Chapter 8 for further referencing to early development in moving image technology.

The earliest known form of visual entertainment/experience using the elements of artificial light and objects in an attempt to create a synthetic 'other' reality that could, in some way, be described as 'cinema' was happening several thousand years ago in the form of shadow plays. Shadow puppet characters were constructed from thin pieces of stiffened leather, heavily decorated with intricate patterns of perforations that allowed light through. These were attached to rods of cane that enabled the puppet operator to work the jointed arms and legs. The performances were usually accompanied by orchestral music and narration, and dealt with the myths and legends surrounding the gods and demons of the societies. Throughout the late Middle Ages the popularity of such plays had spread through the Middle East and to Europe. Later, the use of optical devices was to bring about the change in approach to the projection, and ultimately the recording, of images.

Early opticals

In the early seventeenth century a number of individuals were carrying out experiments with the separate components that go to make up basic elements of photography – i.e. light source, subject and lens. In a document published in 1646 by the Jesuit Athanasius Kircher, various methods of projecting images by the use of lenses were discussed. These first experiments are considered to be the forerunners of **magic lantern** technology.

Probably the most famous of all lanternists was the Belgian Etienne Gaspard Robert. This remarkable man, commonly known as Robertson, took his very spectacular lantern show, *Phantasmagoria*, across Europe, thrilling audiences with a display of macabre sensationalism. This involved, among other things, the projection of skeletons, ghosts and devils on to screens and even on to columns of smoke situated in front of and alongside the audience. So alarming did audiences find this experience that men were known to draw their swords in alarm and anxious excitement. With the use of a variety of lenses, screens and movable lanterns Robertson was able to achieve a wide range of effects. The simple magic lantern show was soon improved upon with the introduction of dual lenses, triple lenses and devices to achieve **zooms**, **fades and mixes** and even very basic forms of animation and special effects. Quite a feat considering the date, 1798.

During the nineteenth century a variety of optical devices, little more than toys, began to appear. The first, the **Thaumatrope**, was a simple disc of card with images on both sides which was spun by using twisted cords attached to opposite edges. As the card revolved at high speed, both images were seen simultaneously creating the illusion of a single image. The popularity of this quaint optical trinket ensured that other devices quickly followed. The **Phenakistoscope**, the **Zoetrope** and the **Praxinoscope** all found favour with a public who sought novelty, though few of them could have been aware of the importance of these trivialities and the further developments they would lead to.

The Praxinoscope, invented by the Frenchman Emile Reynaud, was the forerunner of his famous Théatre Optique. Utilising the lantern technology of the day, coupled with a complex cranking mechanism and a series of transparent perforated picture bands, Raynaud was able to rotate whole sequences of animated images slowly in front of a lantern lens. This enabled him and his small team to create short screenings with accompanied music and sound effects of the most delightful nature, lasting up to twelve or fifteen minutes. Unlike other lantern shows, Reynaud's device was placed behind a translucent screen which was set into a proscenium arch reminiscent of theatres of the day. The first public showing, greeted with great public acclaim, was in Paris in October 1892. Though popular at the time, Reynaud found increasing competition from the photographic moving image which would ultimately bring about the demise of this charming, though short-lived, form of entertainment. The public, ever eager for new forms of 'realism', found what they wanted in photography and particularly cinematography. Increasingly the Théatre Optique began to look like something belonging to a bygone age, and in February 1900 the final show took place. So distraught was Raynaud that he destroyed his devices and consigned his picture bands to the waters of the Seine. It was the end of an era.

magic lantern
A projection system comprised of a light source and a lens, used to project an image. Usually oil-lamp fired, though many were later converted to electricity. Earliest known use was by Athanasius Kircher, recorded in a work published in 1646.

zoom
A technique whereby the image appears to advance towards or recedes away from the viewer.

fade and mixes
Where one image fades from view to be replaced by a separate image. When this is done with two images simultaneously the effect is known as a 'mix' or a 'dissolve'.

Thaumatrope
Attributed to the London physician Dr John Ayrton, this was first made in Paris in 1826. It consists of a disc of card on either side of which are printed two separate images, such as a bird and a cage. With the use of twisted threads attached to opposite edges of the disc, a spinning motion is achieved which enables both images to be viewed simultaneously due to the phenomenon of persistence of vision.

Phenakistoscope
Invented by the Belgian physicist, Joseph Plateau, in 1832, this is an optical device consisting of a disc with slots cut into its edge. When rotated, images on one side can be viewed with the aid of a mirror. The resulting stroboscopic images give the illusion of movement.

Zoetrope
The forerunner of the Praxinoscope, this consists of a drum with vertical slots cut into the top edge. As the drum is rotated, the images on the inner surfaces, when viewed through the slots, achieve the same illusion of movement as with the Phenakistoscope.

Praxinoscope
Invented by the Frenchman Emile Raynaud in 1878, the device was a more advanced and sophisticated version of the Zoetrope. Utilising mirrors and its own discrete light source, this was the forerunner of Raynaud's spectacular and charming, though ultimately short-lived, Théatre Optique.

For further discussion on early years of the Hollywood film industry see Chapter 2.

FROM TOYS TO TINSELTOWN

Partially as a result of the experiments first carried out around 1800 by Thomas Wedgwood and later by Nicéphore Niépce, Louise Daguerre and William Henry Fox Talbot, by 1840 it had become possible to make a permanent, fixed photographic image. However, photography was still in its infancy and sequences of photographic imagery remained impractical to create. It was Edward Muybridge who was to make the breakthrough. Using banks of individual cameras connected to each other, so that each spring-loaded shutter mechanism was fired in sequence at split-second intervals, Muybridge found it possible to record the action of a galloping horse. In the years that followed Muybridge made over 100,000 sequential photographs of all kinds of subjects, animals and people. To this day his work is used as an invaluable source of reference, by artists and animators alike, and remains a milestone in the history of photography and cinematography.

Cinematography

While Muybridge was conducting his work using many cameras in unison, which made for an unwieldy and static process, his French counterpart, Etienne Jules Marey, was struggling with the similar problem of recording animals in motion. He was experimenting with a device that would enable him to be mobile and record a number of sequenced images quickly and on a single photographic plate. The 'Photographic Gun' designed by Marey in 1882 was the result. It was both light and portable enough to be used much in the same way as a conventional gun, and was capable of capturing a series of twelve exposures in one second on a photographic disc that revolved through the gun's stock with the aid of a clockwork mechanism. Though Marey's Photographic Gun was a direct forerunner of the cinecamera, it was not until he built a more reliable apparatus, capable of much faster shutter speeds, that the necessary equipment for recording of motion photography became available. His later cameras with their improved mechanisms enabled him to achieve film speeds of 100 pictures per second, though to achieve this it was dependent upon a pliant, strong and very reliable film stock. By 1889 George Eastman, the founder of the Kodak company, had developed translucent celluloid roll film, the ideal material to be used in conjunction with Marey's more advanced equipment. Others were to succeed him with improved and more reliable cameras and projectors, and over the following few years a great many such devices appeared. It was only a matter of time before the industrial application of these new scientific discoveries and inventions would be fully developed and a market niche found and exploited.

Few did as much to popularise the new 'art form' and to help define that market as the French brothers August and Louis Lumière (though it is interesting to note that they themselves thought that the new cinematic novelty was merely a novelty and destined to be short-lived). Not only were they the first to achieve a satisfactory system for recording and projecting motion pictures, they were a major influence in developing the cinema as a mass form of entertainment. Long queues began to form at all of their shows, at which they presented a number of films, such as *Feeding the Baby*, *Workers Leaving the Lumière Factory* and *Delegates at the Photographic Congress*.

Only ninety-five years had transpired from Wedgwood's first tentative experiments with light-sensitive materials to the birth of what was to become an industry. Cinema had arrived.

Trick film

During these early years of cinema, the public demand for new films far outweighed supply, and this situation led to a major growth in film producers. One such producer was the wealthy shoemaker's son, George Méliès. Although his initial interest was in magic and illusion (he had sold his share in the family business and purchased a famous theatre of illusion, the Théatre Robert-Hudan, at which he gave regular performances), he was to become one of the greatest pioneers of cinema and in particular the film form of **trick film** and animation, perhaps because of his love of magic and illusions. As part of the night's entertainment Méliès began to show short films during his theatrical illusion programmes in an effort to compete with the increasing popularity of the cinématographes that were opening throughout Paris. It was only after he refused to pay the high prices demanded by the Lumière brothers and other producers of such films that Méliès decided to make his own short subjects. While shooting a sequence of a street scene in Paris Méliès' camera jammed. No one, not even Méliès himself, could have realised what a seminal moment this was to be in cinematic history. By the time he had rectified the problem and was able to continue filming, the pedestrians and traffic had moved on about their business to be replaced by other vehicles and individuals. When Méliès viewed the resulting footage he noticed that the mistake caused by the camera jam had created an illusion of carriages and people suddenly turning into different vehicles and people. This was something that closely resembled one of his own favourite magic tricks – the vanishing lady. His excitement at this 'mistake' was to give him the inspiration to carry out a series of experiments based on his already highly developed interest in illusion and magic. Méliès began to make films using his **substitution technique** and experimenting with **multiple exposures**, **mattes** and dissolves.

trick film
The generic term for the development of cinematic special effects using such techniques as mattes, multiple exposures, proto-animation and substitution techniques. Generally attributed to the pioneering French filmmaker George Méliès.

substitution technique
An early trick film technique used by George Méliès. It involved one object being filmed, the camera being stopped during filming and the object being replaced by a second object before filming recommenced. This was the basis of his famous vanishing lady effect, used in many of his films.

multiple exposures
A number of exposures being made on a single frame of film. This usually entails the film being rewound in the camera for subsequent passes and further exposures. Multiple exposures are normally made with the assistance of mattes.

mattes
Opaque images that mask out certain areas of the film negative. Subsequent passes through the camera allow the initial matted-out space to be exposed with another image.

• **Plate 3.3** *Le Voyage dans la lune/A Trip to the Moon* (George Méliès, France 1902).
Partly inspired by Jules Verne's science fiction work, *De la terre à la lune* (1865), and H.G. Wells' novel *The First Men in the Moon* (1902), the film was an immediate success, mixing traditional stagecraft with special effects.

Both an accomplished artist and film-maker, with a flair for solving the technical problems involved in creating his cinematic illusions, his work became ever more ambitious and popular. At the height of his career Méliès had a large studio employing many people turning out a large number of films each year, of which perhaps the most famous is *Le Voyage dans la lune*, probably the earliest science-fiction movie.

The amazing special effects developed by George Méliès became collectively known as trick film. This could be said to be the direct forerunner of **animation** and other **stop-motion** techniques as well as the more elaborate technical effects that we are familiar with today. His legacy lives on in such special effects and animation extravaganzas as *Star Wars*.

Animation

The English-born artist J.S. Blackton, while working at the Vitograph film company in New York, began to make films using the trick film techniques of Méliès. In 1906 he made a film utilising his skills as a 'Lightening Cartoonist', a term he used to bill himself in his **vaudeville** act. This short film, *Humorous Phases of Funny Faces* created on a blackboard using chalk, is the most likely candidate for the title of earliest drawn animation. Hot on the heels of Blackton was one of the most noted pioneers of early animation, Emile Cohl. Born in Paris in 1857, Cohl began his career as a cartoonist and political satirist. His work in the sequencing of drawings in strip cartoon form led to his interest in film. His first film, *Fantasmagorie,* made in 1908, while owing a lot to the work of Blackton, created even more interest in this new technique. Gaumont, for whom Cohl worked at the time, had him make a colossal amount of footage, turning out one film a month (Crafton, 1990). Even in their simplest form this is an astounding achievement. While Blackton and Cohl are accredited with being the first to create animation using sequential drawings and puppets, it was the work of the American cartoonist Winsor McCay that did the most to popularise the medium of animation. Whereas Cohl and Blackton thought it necessary to simplify their drawing styles in order to complete the necessary amount of drawings for animation, not so McCay. His animation displayed all the detail of his cartoon work, for which he was already famous. The film *Gertie the Dinosaur* was to ensure him of a place in the annals of animation and cinematic history (Maltin, 1987).

animation
The creation of artificial movement through a variety of techniques. Usually recorded one frame at a time, animation replicates naturalistic movement and creates the illusion of life in objects and images.

stop-motion
An animation technique whereby a 3D model is filmed a single frame at a time, the model being moved by the animator between exposures.

vaudeville
A type of variety entertainment popular in the early part of the twentieth century, chiefly in the US, consisting of short acts such as song and dance routines, acrobats and animal acts.

For further discussion of animation, see Chapter 8.

Using *Toy Story* as a case study consider the following:

What are there differences between the toys in Andy's room, the mutant toys belonging to Sid and the non-toy characters: Sid, Andy, Sid's dog Scud and Andy's mother?

Are some characters more suited to the CG environment than others?

How believable are Woody and Buzz as characters?

How does *Toy Story* compare with other traditional non-computer animated films? How does the use of camera moves differ? How does the use of environmental space (the sets) vary, and does it affect the action?

If we consider *Toy Story* to be a 'buddy movie' how does it compare with live-action films of the same type?

SOMEWHERE BETWEEN THEN AND NOW

Along with the development of cinema as a form of popular entertainment goes the development of new and ever more creative methods of making and showing film. This became very important for studios wishing to present the public with increasingly novel cinematic forms in an attempt to extend the market share and boost profits. It has been argued that it was not the animation talent or creative ideas that set Disney apart from his competitors but his pursuit and exploitation of new technologies, primarily the use of synchronised sound and later through the use of colour. This was not merely a matter of increased profitability for Disney but a matter at the heart of the organisation's very survival (see Gomery in Smoodin, 1994 pp. 72–3).

Sound and vision

The use of sound within the cinematic experience had been around a long time even before the invention of photography. The shadow puppet plays of Java utilised musicians in their performances. The audience would watch the flickering images on the screen surrounded by members of a **gamelan** orchestra creating a strange (by western terms) rhythmic accompaniment.

Emile Raynaud gave performances of his Théâtre Optique to the accompaniment of music and sound effects. The accompaniment of films by musicians took place in even the most modest of cinemas, although it was an expense that the exhibitors sought to do without. In addition to the problem of cost must have been the issue of sound quality, a hit-and-miss affair at best, being dependent upon the quality of the players. Sound effects could be provided through such devices as the Allfex sound-effects machine for cinemas. Wind, rain, steam trains and gunshots were all available at the turn of a handle, or so the adverts claimed. Since it was the cost of live musicians that was proving to be prohibitive to many exhibitors, any system that could mechanically replace them would drastically reduce costs and ensure commercial viability in an increasingly competitive marketplace.

The first practical device for recording sound, the **phonograph**, was created by the great inventor and industrialist Thomas Alva Edison in 1877. The **gramophone** was an improved system created by Alexander Graham Bell, Chicester Bell (A.G. Bell's cousin) and Charles Sumner Tainter in 1885. While adequate for home use, the device was unable to achieve sufficient volume for use in a sizeable auditorium, though it did provide a great advance in technology which resulted in the development of a number of devices more than capable of producing sufficient volume to fill a large hall.

The greatest problem film-makers faced was not just the recording of sound but the accurate synchronisation of sound and vision. Difficulties in achieving this, coupled with the expense of research and development, meant that studios were somewhat reluctant to get involved in the creation of sound-synch systems. Many thought they were doing just fine without sound, as the popularity of the cinema continued to grow at a steady rate. The first demonstration of synchronised sound and image was at the 1900 Paris Exposition. It was not entirely successful due to speed variations between the phonograph mechanism and the projector.

While a number of devices appeared (and disappeared) it was not until 1926 that a programme of musical shorts and a feature, *Don Juan,* successfully used synchronised music and sound effects using the **Vitaphone** system. However, the real turning point for the development of synchronised sound was the release of *The Jazz Singer* in 1927, starring Al Jolson.

While the Vitaphone system proved to be somewhat cumbersome, it was a more preferable arrangement than hiring costly musicians and it did fulfil its promise of making major

gamelan
An ensemble of musicians playing tuned percussion instruments – mostly gongs, drums, cymbals and metallophones (similar to a xylophone but with metal bars instead of wooden ones).

phonograph
A mechanical sound-recording device utilising a brass cylinder covered with metal foil. As the cylinder was rotated, vibrations of the sound being recorded would cause a metal stylus to score grooves in the foil. These same grooves would provide the information through which the original recording could be reproduced through ear tubes.

gramophone
A device similar to the phonograph. Initial models utilised wax-covered cardboard cylinders, though later ones used hard rubber discs pressed from a metal master disc. Models were fitted with a sound horn to enhance volume.

Vitaphone
A synchronised sound system based on the use of gramophone discs. This system could be fitted to any make of projector and was relatively easy to use, unlike earlier systems such as the cinematophone and the cinephone.

savings to the exhibitors. Suddenly everyone wanted talkies. There were casualties on the way, as not all of the stars of the silent screen made a happy progression into the talkies, though for some of them – a rather non-nondescript mouse for example – the new sound technologies elevated them to superstardom. In 1928 *Steamboat Willy*, the third of the Mickey Mouse shorts, was set to be yet another financial disappointment as had the first two Mickey films, *Gallopin' Gaucho* and *Plane Crazy*. However, the inclusion of a synchronised soundtrack turned one more mediocre animated short into a classic of cinematic entertainment, and created a milestone in the animated art form. More importantly for Disney at the time, it set the company firmly on the road to financial security. Though that road proved to be pitted and it was to be a rough ride, it ultimately led to the Disney corporation becoming one of the largest companies in the world. Sound changed the very nature of film. The broad, almost pantomimic action was replaced by a more naturalistic style. Subtle dialogue and sophisticated scripts added a depth and breadth to cinematic storytelling that was hitherto impossible.

The recording of optical sound – whereby sound waves appeared as a visual image on the same film strip as the image – was designed to ensure synchronisation. This was first demonstrated in 1923 by Lee de Forest and Theodore Case with their system, Phonofilm. Initial results were disappointing as the sound quality was poor. However, after a split with Forest, Case went on to develop a more successful version in 1927, Movietone. This led to the first sound newsreels, Movietone News, made by the Fox Film Corporation which had acquired the rights from Case.

Still the search for improvements continued, and by 1940 stereophonic sound was possible. Once again it was Disney who was at the forefront of the technological advance. The first major film production using stereo sound was Walt Disney's *Fantasia*, released in November 1940, demonstrating once again his belief in the utilisation of technology and its link with commercial success. Initially the use of stereophonic sound proved to be impractical, as new sound systems had to be installed and subsequently dismantled in the theatres where *Fantasia* was showing. It was not until after the Second World War that stereophonic sound was fully exploited in cinemas.

Not all sound is recorded during the filming process, indeed many of the most notable effects are achieved during post-production. Separate sound recordings for effects may be recorded within a **foley stage**, and for some sounds it is the only place where it is possible to achieve the desired effect.

The art of recording sound effects that are difficult or impossible to obtain during principal photography or are unavailable within a sound library are undertaken by foley artists. These sound artists are responsible for all types of effects that create illusions and mood. Anything and everything is done here, from the realistic (e.g. ambient sounds of a rain forest), to the fantastic (e.g. a fleet of spaceships attacking a giant Death Star), to the downright ridiculous (e.g. a T-Rex plucking his human victim off a toilet and breaking every bone in his body).

Dolby Sound, developed by Ray Dolby in 1965, continued to push the limits of quality sound. In addition to the stereophonic left and right channels, the Dolby Stereo system utilises a centre channel in order to create focus of sound, and a surround channel used to immerse the audience in ambient sound.

Progress continues to be made in the search for better sound quality, though this does come at a price. **THX**, instigated by George Lucas in response to audience reaction to his film *Star Wars*, is one such initiative. The THX system is not a way of recording sound but a designation of sound quality in cinemas, with the standards established by Lucasfilm Limited. THX standards are high and the costs to the exhibitor are substantial, with cinemas inspected regularly in order to achieve THX approval. Consequently THX cinemas are currently not the norm.

foley stage
Named after the sound editor Jack Foley, the foley stage is a sound recording room equipped with a screen and the necessary items for the creation of sound effects.

THX
A designation of sound reproduction quality in cinemas. The standards established necessitate the installation and maintenance of sound equipment to the specifications and guidelines laid down by Lucasfilm Limited.

Colour

The use of colour in film was initially a laborious, hand-done process. Added frame by frame to film by large teams of workers, colour proved to be a time-consuming and costly process, though some of the effects were stunning and proved very popular with the cinema-going public.

The principles of colour photography are based upon those described by James Clerk Maxwell in 1855. Maxwell demonstrated in a lecture at the Royal Institute in London that all the natural occurring colours could be created through the mix of red, green and blue light.

In an attempt to automate film colouring the Pathé company developed their own procedures. The Pathécolor stencil process introduced in 1905 addressed the mechanisation of tinting black and white prints. Stencils were cut and a series of coloured dyes were applied to the print, as many as six separate stencils for each frame. This method was still labour intensive, and in order to make the process economically viable it was necessary to produce 200 prints of a single film.

The British film-maker George Alber Smith developed the idea by which a practical colour film process, Kinemacolor, became possible. Smith used a camera which utilised two rotating colour filters that passed between lens and film. The results were first shown in 1908 and became a regular feature of programmes in London, Paris, Berlin and New York. Imitations of the Kinema color process soon followed, as did legal proceedings due to infringement of patent rights. However, so successful was the Kinemacolor process that it remained in continuous use until well into the First World War.

A number of companies entered the field with their own two-colour process, each possessing their own distinctive qualities. Among these was a process made by a company that was to set the highest standards for the next fifty years or so – **Technicolor**.

Technicolor went on to produce a three-colour process, though the cameras were extremely expensive to produce and were very cumbersome to operate, which presented film-makers with difficulties when shooting location footage.

The three-colour process developed in 1932 produced remarkable results, and Disney's *Flowers and Trees* became the first three-colour Technicolor film. Landing an exclusivity deal with Technicolor, Walt Disney once again managed to set himself apart from his competitors as he cornered the market in full-colour cartoons for the next two years, ensuring the Disney corporation's continued expanded share of the market.

Further improvements of colour film stock made by companies such as Agfa, the Eastman Kodak Company and Fuji have since made the three-strip Technicolor cameras obsolete. Today, manufacturers are making colour film stock that have become compatible with one another and it is doubtful that an audience would be able to detect differences between them.

Bigger, wider, curvier

Since the early days of magic lanterns, the desire for brighter, bigger images has been part and parcel of the cinematic experience. A number of devices were developed in an attempt to give audiences the feeling of immersion within the overall experience.

Even before the invention of movie photography, entrepreneurial exhibitors were looking for new ways to entertain a public seeking ever more novel forms of amusement. One such method was the **Panorama**. Created by the painter Robert Barker and first exhibited in 1788, the Panorama consisted of a huge cylindrical building fitted out with a 360° painting. These were very popular and a number of them began to appear throughout Europe, but were eventually succeeded by a more elaborate system, the **Diorama**. Like the Panorama, the Diorama consisted of a circular building though this

Technicolor
The first successful Technicolor process was introduced in 1922. This involved the use of a two-colour camera with a beam splitter which recorded red and green images of the scene. The three-colour Technicolor process developed in 1932 used three separate negatives. However this was replaced in 1932 by a prism beam splitter.

Panorama
Created by the painter Robert Barker, the Panorama was first exhibited in 1788. It consisted of a huge cylindrical building fitted out with a 360° painting.

Diorama
A circular building housing translucent paintings where, through the manipulation of shutters and screens, the transformation of the various scenes was effected.

used a series of translucent paintings. Through the manipulation of shutters and screens, the transformation of the various scenes was effected. This was invented by Louis Jacques Mandé Daguerre, the famous photographer and inventor of the daguerreotype photographic process.

Popular though these were, the public demand for ever more spectacular experiences led to the development of an 'animated' version of Barker's invention. The first attempt to create a moving version of the Panorama was made by Raoul Grimoin Sanson, a Frenchman who in 1897 presented to an eager public the **Cinéorama**. By the use of lantern technology, the creation of sophisticated scenes using dissolves, pans and even 'animated' effects was possible.

Although very popular with the public, the Cinéorama was deemed to be a serious fire risk, as the unventilated projection booth, housing ten 40-amp electric arc projectors and their operators, was located directly below the wooden structure which housed the audience. The Cinéorama was eventually closed down by the police.

Widescreen

The desire for bigger images continued into the cinema. While a variety of film formats was used for movie film, almost from the beginning **35mm film** became the standard format. As early as 1900 there were those who began to show an interest in wider formats, though this was short-lived. A revival of interest in widescreen cinema began in the 1920s, but due to the added cost of larger format cameras and expensive screen size conversions the widescreen format met with little general enthusiasm in the industry. This lack of interest may have been due, at least in part, to the costs exhibitors were already facing by the installation in their theatres of sound reproduction equipment, an expense that was very necessary if they were to remain competitive. It was not until the 1950s that once again interest began to grow in wide format film.

The Cinerama process opened in a Broadway theatre in New York. The system used three film strips recorded on separate synchronised cameras and required three synchronised projectors to throw the separate images on to a deeply curved screen. Alignment was vital, as was a special projection device to soften the edges of the individual film strips in order to achieve a satisfactory composite of the three images. The final composite image was so large – covering a visual field of 145° horizontally and 55° vertically – that, when seen from the optimum position, it virtually filled the viewer's field of vision. Once again competitors were quick to respond to the popularity of this new format in an attempt to hang on to their market share, and a proliferation of wide formats began to appear.

CinemaScope was one of the more successful competitors. The process, developed by Twentieth-Century Fox, lacked the visual impact of Cinerama but had the advantage that it could more easily be installed into existing theatres.

Paramount developed a system, Vista Vision, that used a horizontal configuration moving the film strip through the camera and projectors sideways. This method effectively doubled the size of the photographic image.

There were so many variants on the widescreen theme fighting for superiority in the market place that almost all the studios had their own version. The strange formats were only outdone by the outlandishness of their names – Techniscope, Technirama, the Todd-AO System, Cinemiracle, Wonderama. And yes, even Disney had their own system, Circarama. Specifically designed for use in Disneyland it utilised eleven interlocking cameras to project 360° images. A spectacular version of the Cinéorama.

So popular did the wide format become that after 1953 most films were shot to accommodate it and, as importantly, most theatres were equipped to show wide formats.

Cinéorama
A large circular structure with a tower in the centre, in which the audience stood. A number of lanterns situated below the audience projected images outwards on to huge curved screen.

35mm film
The measurement of film in millimetres (16mm, 35mm, 70mm) describes the length of the individual film negative frames which are exposed in order to capture an image: the larger the negative, the higher the resolution of the projected image. Larger format film such as 70mm, while superior in quality, is cumbersome to use and comparatively expensive to work with. There are also fewer cinemas able to screen formats other than the now-standard 35mm print.

3D or not 3D

Far from being a unique cinematic film experience, the use of 3D technology had been implemented in magic lantern shows as early as the 1890s. The first recorded demonstration of stereoscopy had taken place in 1856: two separate images (one green, one red) were shown in quick succession and through the persistence of vision achieved the illusion of a single deep image. Further advancements of the process in 1891 involved the superimposition of a pair of twin images through red and blue filters. The viewer was required to wear glasses with corresponding red and blue filters. For the next thirty years little more was made of these developments until once again in the 1920s interest in this 3D process began to reappear. However it was not until the 1940s that 3D films began to appear at regular intervals. As a result of this new interest, Paramount made *Bwana Devil* which opened in 1952 in Los Angles and was an immediate phenomenal success. This was followed in 1953 by Warner Bros.' *House of Wax* starring Vincent Price which was an even greater success. Hollywood's response was quick. Over sixty 3D films were made in 1953 though public interest was short-lived. By 1954 only around twenty 3D films were in production, and by the end of the year 3D was dead and buried.

The fad of 3D movies has long gone but the desire of audiences for new experiences has not. The development of new formats such as IMAX and OMNIMAX (see p. 82) are a testament to that. And while new developments in technology undoubtedly make for an increasingly spectacular cinematic experience, it is doubtful that such novelties will replace or be a substitute for the principal objective of cinema – storytelling.

COMPUTER-GENERATED IMAGERY

The way in which computer-generated imagery (CGI) and computer animation are used and appear within film can be seen to take on two very distinct and separate aspects. First, as a way of improving technical and design processes, and replacing some of the labour-intensive tasks previously carried out solely by human hands: this is usually the case with certain traditional animation techniques and processes. Second, as a way of making imagery within a computer environment. The nature of such images having their own integrity, being inseparable from the medium with which they were constructed.

The recent introduction of this second type of computerised image has enabled a broadening of the filmic language that has been with us since the early days of cinema. If the suspension of disbelief is the aim of cinema, to make the impossible plausible, then the introduction of new technologies has created a whole new version of reality – a pseudo-reality, a virtual reality.

Computers within cinema

From the early days of film, man's schizophrenic love–hate relationship with the Brave New World of technology has been part of the cinematic experience. In Fritz Lang's *Metropolis* (1926) we are witness to the human celebration of technology. Its beautiful possibilities and its potential for disaster and misery, like a roller-coaster ride, were at once thrilling and frightening. Were the audience seeing this film for the first time aware of this new electronic modernity extending beyond the images on the silver screen? Did they perceive that cinema was an example of this modernity and, by their very presence in the theatre, they were part of that 'technological future'? Perhaps this is overstating the effect cinema had on the public consciousness.

Computers began to appear in films in a small way. This was in part due to the large amounts of money involved in creating even the simplest of computer animation sequences. One of the earliest examples was *2001: A Space Odyssey* (1968). A

• **Plate 3.4** *Tron* (US 1982)
A complete computer environment.

wire frame
Three-dimensional
shapes, with neither
surface colour nor
texture, illustrated
through a pattern of
interconnecting lines.
Literally a framework of
'wires' on a two-dimen-
sional surface – the
computer screen.

sequence involving a space ship docking with an orbiting space station used a degree of computer animation for the control consoles on the flight deck. These were seen only in **wire frame** basic shapes representing the converging craft. At the time of release the sequence was state-of-the-art entertainment and was reputed to have cost a small fortune. By today's standards it looks simplistic bordering on the primitive, certainly not representative of the computer technology of the year 2001.

By the time *Alien* was released (1979), the computer entertainments industry was well under way and the public's understanding of computers had begun to be established. As with *2001*, *Alien* did little more than use computers for the creation of certain elements of set design, such as control panels, and while Mother, the spaceship's computer, had a degree of characterisation, it lacked the degree of sophistication of HAL in *2001*. It was not until 1982, with the release of *Tron*, that computer animation took a major leap forward, becoming a landmark in the way computers were used in a cinematic context. More than that, the film gave a deeper insight into the world of computers, its imagery and terminology. Not only did *Tron* use computers as a story-telling vehicle, but its entire world was one of technology, its very substance electronic and binary, set as it was *within* the computer.

Despite its lack of commercial success *Tron* initiated a development in the role of the computer-generated image. Not only used for the creation of control panels, the computer image in *Tron* had become a central characteristic of the film.

Ten years later, with the release of *The Lawnmower Man* in 1992, another step forward was made in the way computers were used as part and parcel of cinematic

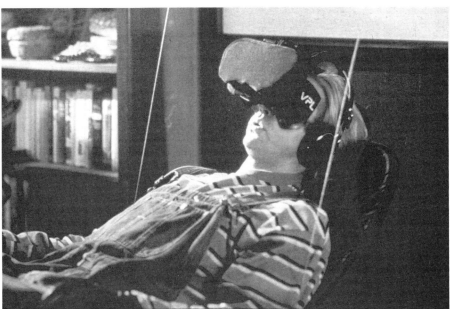

• **Plate 3.5** *The Lawnmower Man* (First Independent/Allied Vision, US 1992)

experience. *Lawnmower Man* relies heavily on our perception and understanding of computers, their language and environments. Not only do computers appear as computers, they are used to generate an entire environment within cyberspace, a place where people become computer-generated images. The film begins to question our perception of ourselves as beings occupying a given space within a three-dimensional world. The distinction between people and computer software, between the actual and the virtual, becomes unclear. In the film this notion is taken to its logical conclusion, such that the man experimenting with Virtual Reality no longer exists on a physical plane but is incorporated entirely into the computer system, existing only as information. The creation of artificial cyberspace landscapes as depicted in *Tron* and *Lawnmower Man* leaves us feeling that we know more about these places.

Computers were used to create another kind of reality in 1993 in the film *Jurassic Park*. Prehistoric animals that had roamed the earth millions of years ago were brought back to life with the aid of computer wizardry. On their own the computer graphics are very impressive, but used in conjunction with **go-motion** and combined with live-action footage the results become sensational.

One of the problems encountered by the special-effects artists on *Jurassic Park* involved the question of how to create a surface for the computer-generated dinosaurs that would give the impression of skin. Replicating man-made substances, such as plastic or chrome, is relatively easy with a computer and looks convincing to the viewer, but no one had ever attempted anything quite as complex as what was required for *Jurassic Park*. (Since the release of the sequel, *The Lost World*, these illusions have become commonplace.) The final result was achieved with several layers of textured mapping which produced the colouration and texture required to imitate the animals' reptilian skin. Working with live-action and model animation, an effect of hyper-realism is generated. The computer techniques behind the creation become transparent, merely part of the process. The audience are no longer watching computer graphics: they are viewing wildlife footage of extinct creatures. *Jurassic Park* must be the finest example to date of how computers can be used as an integral part of the on-screen entertainment, creating animation sequences that go far beyond the imitation of live-action. To all intents and purposes it *is* live-action.

The integration of computer animation with more traditional methods of animation has been one of the Disney studio's major concerns for a number of years. Computers were first used for animated sequences in the 1986 feature *The Great Mouse Detective*, and then more extensively in *The Rescuers*, *The Rescuers Down Under* and *Beauty and the Beast*. The use of computer-generated animation within an otherwise traditionally animated film took on a different aspect with *Aladdin* in which computers were used to generate not only backgrounds but also animated effects and character animation. With *The Lion King* the Disney studio took computer-generated imagery even further, creating huge herds of stampeding wildebeest and zebra, footage that would be almost impossible using solely traditional hand-drawn methods.

With the release of the blockbuster *Toy Story* in 1995, computer animation entered a new phase of development and with it took the development of cinema itself into another phase. For the first time the public was presented with a completely computer-animated feature film. Any doubts about the viability of such a process for the purpose of creating a feature must have quickly evaporated in the face of tremendous public and critical acclaim. *Toy Story* was one of the first films in which computer-generated images (CGI) were not simply needed to create a 'look' or even to provide objects that animated well. For the first time in a feature film, CGI were required to act and to possess believable characterisation (Lasseter and Daly, 1995). The director John Lasseter, who himself had trained at Disney as a traditional classical 2D animator, had for some time been creating short computer-animated subjects. His earliest, *The Adventures of Andre and Walley B.* was made by the computer graphics group of Lucasfilm in 1984. This group was later to become the now-famous computer animation company Pixar (Richard Auzenne, 1994).

While there can be no doubt that the use of CGI has had a major affect on cinema, its greatest use in film has not been restricted to animation. It encompasses a plethora of special effects that are present in almost every film, almost to the point of tedium. In fact we seem to be somehow short-changed if there is not at least one shot that can easily be recognised as CGI in origin.

go-motion

A refinement of stop-motion. Animated puppets are controlled with motorised rods. Their actions are determined by computer which permits a predetermined amount of motion during the film's exposure. The result is a slight blurring of the image, eliminating the somewhat stiff action associated with traditional model animation.

For further discussion of the marketing of Jurassic Park, *see Chapter 2.*

Generally speaking there are two classifications of special effects: those you see, and those you do not see. Almost every Hollywood film to hit the screen today, certainly those made since 1990, contain their fair share of flashes, bangs and crashes topped off with a liberal sprinkling of **Disney dust**. Unfortunately in some instances the effects are the only thing within the film that comes close to what one could call 'content'.

Disney dust
The term given to the glitter and sparkle that usually accompanies any form of magic or unearthly effect such as the glowing dust trail left by the flying Tinkerbell in Disney's *Peter Pan* (1953) and again in *Hook* (1991).

Using *Independence Day* as a case study consider the following:

Is it evident what techniques were used to create the effects?
Is it apparent which of the special effects were computer-generated and which were made using traditional methods?
How well do the special effects sit within the frame? Are they composited in an appropriate manner so as to make them believable?

☐ CASE STUDY 1: *MARS ATTACKS!* (1996)

The Tim Burton film *Mars Attacks!* is a prime example of the use of special effects. At one point or another it demonstrates the use of perhaps every kind of special effect used in Hollywood today. Burton was seeking to return to low-budget films, to create something that had the feel of the science fiction B-movies he had been so fond of as a child (Jones, 1996). Based upon a series of bubble-gum trading cards called *Mars Attacks!* first published by the bubblegum company Topps in 1962, the film is centred on the bug-eyed, big-brained aliens illustrated in the cards. The whole look of the film was intended to mimic the original trading cards and to be a nostalgic homage to 1950s science fiction. Taking itself only slightly seriously, *Mars Attacks!* sets out to be more of a B-movie than a B-movie, although with much higher production values than those afforded most of these films in the 1950s (Cotta Vaz, 1996).

Originally designed to be a combination of live-action and 3D-model stop-motion

• **Plate 3.6** *Mars Attacks!* (US 1996)

background plates
An optical process whereby foreground elements are placed over background artwork, CGI elements or models.

flocking routine software
In simple terms this is a computer program whereby the movement of a single designated computer element, for instance an animated bird, influences and determines the nature of movement of a selected group of elements. Animation of the primary element is followed by the subordinate objects. An elaborate form of this process was used to achieve the cavalry charge sequence in Disney's *Mulan* (1998).

match-move
Shots that have separate elements within them that need to be accurately matched, frame by frame. Usually involves live-action elements being coupled to animation or effects elements.

wire removal
The process of digitally removing any unwanted elements within a shot, such as a support for an animated object, puppet or prop. Used in the flying motorbike shot in *Terminator 2*.

blue screen
A process that involves the subject being filmed in front of a blue screen. Optical manipulation of this footage creates imagery of the actor against a black background. Additionally, the actor's silhouette is set against a clear background. Using these two elements as mattes it is possible to place the action into any scene required.

animation, *Mars Attacks!* is primarily computer-generated though, as with most films involving special effects, it is really an amalgamation of a number of techniques – CGI, pyrotechnics, in-camera effects, live-action and computer animation. In all the film is comprised of approximately 450 special-effects shots involving hundreds of flying saucers, scores of Martians, dozens of explosions and a handful of the most startling combinations of live-action and CG effects.

The Martians

A combination of processes was necessary to bring the Martians to the screen. In order to create them in the numbers needed for an invasion (at one point up to fifty Martians are in a single shot) it was necessary to create them using CGI techniques. New computer software was developed specifically to enable the animators to work on groups of characters instead of a single image. For some of the close-up shots, as in the autopsy of a Martian corpse and the sequence in which the remnants of the defeated Martian hordes are being mopped up, full-size urethane figures were used.

Saucers

As the massed ranks of the Martian saucers rose from within the surface of the red planet and began to head towards earth in preparation for their attack, earth lay blue and quiet unaware of the impending doom. To achieve this sequence involved creating a number of composite shots involving the use of large-scale models as **background plates** and the computer animation in the foreground. Most of the hundreds of separate saucers were manipulated using **flocking routine software**, thus avoiding the necessity of large numbers of objects being animated separately.

The footage of the interior of the alien mother ship centred around the use of a huge detailed model. Designed initially for use with 3D models in line with Burton's initial plans for the size of the model – eighteen feet across and eight feet high, featuring a central dome with columns. Such a large-scale model allowed the film-makers to achieve much more detail and realistic lighting effects. The switch from stop-motion animation to CGI also allowed the animators far more freedom when moving the Martians around the set. Working with such large scale sets enabled animators to film 3D puppets as if they were on location. This was done in order to first test the motion of the intended computer animation and provide the animators with a guide for the staging and timing of action. **Match-movers** would then link up the CGI work to the live-action model shot.

As the Martians finally succumb to the painful yodelling of Slim Whitman, a giant saucer, out of control, crash lands into a lake. The creation of this shot involved a twenty-five foot model saucer suspended by cables from a construction crane which swung at an angle before plunging it into a tank of water at the Universal Studios. **Wire removal** techniques were used to get rid of the supporting rigging.

Unspeakable experiments

This sequence, depicting the vivisection of an earth-woman (Sarah Jessica Parker) and the subsequent head transplant with her pet chihuahua, called for a combination of techniques. Separate **blue screen** shots were needed of the dog barking and the actress simulating the action of barking – as these two actions were to be married together in a composite frame, this necessitates a separate series of mattes being made for each of them. Accurate tracking of both actions was needed using 2D computer software. A separate CG wound element, complete with metal staples, was then created and superimposed over the join. It was then necessary to place a group of

CG Martians over the top of this composite shot, animating them turning to camera in close-up and slowly revealing their experimental handiwork. The reverse of this shot, Sarah Jessica Parker's head on the dog's body, required the creation of a CG dog, as the real thing was just too uncooperative during filming.

Earth destroyed

As the Martians set about destroying the earth, many famous landmarks fell victim to the death rays of the alien saucers, the Pentagon, the Taj Mahal, the Easter Island statues and Mount Rushmore among them. The destruction of the Houses of Parliament involved a large sixteen-foot tall, highly detailed model of Big Ben and the careful use of **pyrotechnics**. These explosions were designed to go off in sequence, starting with the blowing-out of the clock face and culminating in a hit at base level, causing the tower to drop vertically. Burton took the opportunity of shooting live-action footage of the actual razing of one of Las Vegas' more spectacular buildings, the Landmark Hotel, which was to become the Galaxy Hotel in the film. The live-action plates were incorporated into the final footage through film compositing, using elements comprised of additional lighting effects, background plates, foreground live-action and CGI animation.

pyrotechnics
The description given to effects involving the use of fire, fireworks and explosives.

The combination of these techniques, coupled with the sharp wit of the director, a humorous script and convincing performances from the actors and animators, makes *Mars Attacks!* a marvellous example of tongue-in-cheek escapist fantasy and humour.

Dead actors live again

With the untimely death of Brandon Lee in 1993, killed in a tragic shooting accident on the set of *The Crow*, the producers were faced with a terrible dilemma. They could scrap the film and start again, or they could try to finish the film without Lee. Fortunately a good deal of the principal photography was already in the can, but for the film to work it required additional footage of Lee. The answer was to approach an effects company which used digital photocompositing processes to create the necessary scenes. Using this technology they were able to take an image out of one frame, and place it and animate it within another piece of film. In at least two scenes, action shots were filmed using Lee's double for the required extra footage, Lee's face then was superimposed on the double's body using photo-imaging software. The new footage then had to be colour enhanced to match the rest of the scenes.

Such techniques have been used in other films to great effect. In *In the Line of Fire* (1993), Clint Eastwood plays the role of a secret service agent detailed to the bodyguard of the US President. Eastwood, playing a man of around fifty, experiences flashbacks to a time when he was much younger and assigned to guard President Kennedy and his wife, Jackie. We see Eastwood and the Kennedys on screen together, seemingly filmed alongside each other. Using computers and image photocompositing software, the two individual films were integrated on a single separate reel of film. This reel was then visually enhanced to ensure that both sets of footage 'sat well' together. Further treatment of the composite footage was then needed to give the appearance of the quality of newsreel footage of the day. More recently this same technique has been used to great effect in *Forrest Gump* (1994).

OTHER WAYS OF SEEING

As outlined at the beginning of this chapter, the continuing developments in film and

• **Plate 3.7** *The Crow*
(Brandon Lee, US 1994)

related media will mean that we are going to witness a change in the way we see and read film, and the way in which films are distributed will be a major factor in this process.

Distribution

Will we continue to gather together in large darkened rooms to view a flickering screen? I certainly hope so. But I doubt that this will continue to remain as it is at present. The forces impinging upon film may be too great to resist. Will we continue to use celluloid film stock? Why print off hundreds of copies of a film and then send them out to the furthest corners of the earth if you can centralise the process. Wouldn't it be better to have a central broadcast point which distributed films digitally along fibre-optical lines at a given time to cinemas around the country, which then simply replayed these? The situation would be better still if the films could be accessed at any time, taking into account the local variations in time over large continents (using satellite communications there is no reason why you couldn't even access films from another part of the world). And if distributors manage to overcome those difficulties, why be content with distributing films at a centralised point (cinemas)? After all, cinemas are costly institutions, often located in the centre of cities where real estate is at a premium. Faced with all the inherent transportation problems within cities, wouldn't the public prefer to view their movies in the comfort and safety of their own home? So why not distribute direct to the viewer's home? It sounds a little far-fetched perhaps, but then again television must have sounded improbable only seventy-five years ago.

In the next few years we are almost certain to see new forms of film distribution, and while these will probably not herald the end of cinemas they will certainly compete with them. It is the very fact that cinemas *are* these large darkened rooms where strangers gather together to laugh, weep and gasp in a communal worship of Hollywood that will ensure their continuing survival. There is nothing quite like that experience. Long may they live.

For further reference to film distribution in the US and the UK, see Chapter 2.

Television and the Internet

Foremost among new forms of distribution could well be the Internet. There continues to be a lot of discussion concerning the Internet and cable technology and the impact these will have on television, film and the media in general. Faced with problems on the Internet due to the lack of adequate bandwidth capable of dealing with the amount of data necessary for high resolution images, stereo sound and real time motion, distribution remains somewhat of a stumbling block. Though if **Moore's 'law'** is to be believed, the increase in processing power of computers is set to solve at least one of these problems and make this goal achievable in the not too distant future.

Moore's 'law'
'The capacity of processing power of computers doubles every 18 months': this 'law' is named after Gordon E. Moore, the co-founder of Intel, who first described it.

There are many people who see the benefits (not least of them financial) in the convergence of computer technology and television broadcasting. Issues of funding, ownership, distribution control, censorship and regulation will be at the forefront of the development of any such convergence. How, if this amalgamation of television and computer technology (and by inference the Internet) comes about, will it affect traditional film-making? The question to ask then becomes not how will it affect film but how will the big studios respond to it? Will we see a change in the way in which 'films' are funded, made and distributed? And how will this affect the content of the films? MTV films for an MTV generation?

No one knows how the convergence of the two technologies will be resolved, but with Bill Gates poised to embed RealVideo (a company heavily involved in bringing video on to the Net) into the Microsoft operations it would be safe to say that it is only a matter of time before such a convergence happens. As it stands at the moment (1998), the images on the Internet are small, jerky and of low quality, though there are some film-makers who have begun to make experimental forays into this new medium. Director Spike Lee has already made three short pieces exclusively for the Internet. All around five-minutes long, one features the actor John Turturro, another the students from a Brooklyn school and the third film features the dancer, Savion Glover (Reid, 1997).

As the cost of computer hardware and software tumbles and the processing power increases, we are almost certain to see the emergence of small groups of enthusiastic film-makers creating their own versions of cinema and distributing it to a wide audience through satellite TV, video and the Internet.

While the science of television has made great advances, the art of television has not (and in many regards it has gone into reverse). Discussions seem to be centred around quality of image and distribution and much less about content. Typical of this attitude was a dispute between SMPTE (Society of Motion Pictures and Television Engineers) and ASC (American Society of Cinematographers). At a joint meeting in October 1997 they gathered together to discuss issues related to the convergence of film and digital technologies and its impact on television. While it is safe to say that both associations are concerned with quality, even though the methods of distribution vary greatly (cinema and television), the concerns of both parties focused around the 'letterbox' format. The manner in which productions are shot does have some affect on the content of a film and can severely affect the composition of the shots and hence the reading and meaning of the film. This 'letterboxing' involves images being squeezed through a process known as 'panning and scanning' for television broadcast. However, research would seem to suggest that there is division between audiences, some still showing resistance to seeing films on television within the letterbox format (Bishop, 1997). This division makes the argument somewhat redundant in one way or the other. It would be better, surely, to concentrate on the advent of DTV (Digital Television) and the increase in low-cost television broadcasting, and their impact on quality issues. We may be faced with wall-to-wall soap operas and game shows, but with SMPTE and ASC and other similar organisations fighting the good fight we can rest assured that it will at least be high-quality letterbox soap opera.

IMAX and OMNIMAX

As with television, the film industry seems to be mesmerised by the development of new technologies such as digital sound, computer-aided video editing and an ever-increasing number of film and video formats, including the huge IMAX and OMNIMAX.

The IMAX and OMNIMAX cinemas offer quite a distinct experience from the cinema of the high street. The underlying principle behind both these systems is to utilise to the maximum the human field of vision. Images of such large proportion are projected on to a curved screen that extends beyond the range of peripheral vision – wraparound vision. This means that to view certain areas of the screen it is necessary to turn ones head so as to focus on the action. The effect of this is to seemingly envelop the viewer within the film imagery. Physically, the format of the IMAX negative is much larger than the 35mm or 70mm formats used for 'standard' cinematic releases. This larger format obviously necessitates not only special cameras and lenses when shooting the footage, but also a completely different projection system. In the case of OMNIMAX it entails the use of a huge curved screen that extends not only well beyond the lateral range of vision but beyond the vertical range as well. The nature of this large format medium lends itself well to film subjects involving large and impressive geographic shots such as the Grand Canyon, the Great Barrier Reef, the Taj Mahal and the Great Wall of China. It has also been used to great effect to film 'activity' shots such as shooting the rapids on the Colorado River, surfing in Hawaii, and aerial stunts such as wing walking. One film even depicts astronauts spacewalking in orbit above the earth.

IMAX has certain advantages over other types of cinema. It presents exhilarating footage beyond the scope of 'standard' cinema and as such has a huge novelty factor attached. This type of cinematography, while very spectacular, does have its draw-backs, however. It tends to depend on the 'spectacle' without the involvement of emotional or intellectual elements to be found in drama. Directors have found that the format creates problems when trying to sustain a subject involving character action, dialogue and relationships. The very size of the screen makes it difficult to use the same filmic language that is used to create cinematic storytelling. Edits between scenes need longer intervals for the viewer to register the image properly, so quick cutting is out. Close-ups can create strange images and bring with them problems of picture quality – due to the size of the screen there is low tolerance of grainy images.

Presently there are only a few such cinemas throughout the world. Because the IMAX experience is such a different one from the cinematic 'norm', the marketing potential has yet to be fully explored. There is no doubt in my mind that such techno-logical advancements should be undertaken to maximise the audience's cinematic experience and entertainment, and to widen the realm of film.

Virtual Reality

Robertson's *Phantasmagoria* created a sensation in the eighteenth century as did the Lumière brothers' Cinématographe shows in the nineteenth century. *King Kong* and the broadcast of Orson Welles' radio production of *War of the Worlds* did much the same in the twentieth century. The live broadcast of *War of the Worlds*, which was produced using a semi-journalistic style with on-the-scene reporters and complete with sound effects, had a particularly devastating impact on the public consciousness. So convincing was it that panic broke out among some members of the audience listening at home. Some people called the police for help and advice, others jumped in their cars and took to the hills in fear of their lives. There is even one account of a farmer blasting holes in a water tower with his shotgun as he mistook it for an alien war machine in the evening gloom. These major events did much more than to extend our understanding of cinematic language or new communication 'languages' – they raised our expectations of those forms of communication. In a very real way the responses they elicited were symptomatic of the rapidly changing pace of communication systems and our inability to adapt easily to them. Although still in its infancy, Virtual Reality is already with us and, as we face the twenty-first century, it may well take up the running in the expansion of the cinematic experience. It may even redefine the parameters of cinema, into a literally three-dimen-sional space. Direct parallels can be drawn between our response to Virtual Reality and the early days of cinema. The unsophisticated audiences of the nineteenth century were happy to witness what was, by our standards, mundane footage of everyday Parisian life or scenes from the seaside. Few of them could have imagined in their wildest dreams where the art form was to lead. The same is true of Virtual Reality: the truth is that we simply do not yet know the full extent of the impact Virtual Reality will have on society.

What is Virtual Reality?

Virtual Reality is a computer system whereby the operator, or perhaps it would be truer to say the 'experiencer', is in direct communication with the computer via a headset. Three-dimensional graphic images are viewed through a visor at the front of the helmet, while stereo sound is experienced via built-in headphones. As the user turns their head to the left or to the right the computer can trace the headset's spatial relationship to the computer via sensors in the helmet. It processes this information and returns modified images to the visor that give the impression that the wearer of the headset has turned their head within the computer-generated three-dimensional cyberworld. Other spatial information can be collected through the use of data gloves, which incorporate sensors that behave in a manner similar to those within the helmet. Pressure pads within the gloves, linked to the computer, enable the user to experience an illusion of picking up and moving virtual objects within this computer-generated world.

Presently the application of Virtual Reality has, by and large, been an industrial one. Architects and designers have used it to create 3D representations of their proposals before committing to the costly process of manufacture. The military has also used Virtual Reality as a training tool, simulating armoured vehicle control and fighter aircraft flight in combat situations.

The real potential for the entertainments industry, and particularly the film industry, has yet to be explored. Imagine a time when 'films' are made to be experienced not only in two dimensions, within the confines of a cinema, but on another level altogether. Wild fantasy? Maybe, but it was not that long ago that the Lumière brothers were amazing all and sundry with their footage of *Feeding the Baby*. We have come a long way since then. Recent developments within Virtual Reality technology have meant that it is possible to screen virtual worlds for a group audience. Although still in development, this could lead to another form of interactive cinema.

Our infatuation with the creation of 'other' realities and 'virtual' worlds seems a little odd coming at a time when mankind appears to be ill-equipped to deal with the actual realities of our physical world.

Using new technologies as a focal point consider the following:

Who are the the main users of the Internet for the disemination of information about film – studios, film-makers, journalists, enthusiasts?
How does the Internet encourage critical debate regarding individual films, film-makers and the industry in general?
Are there examples of films being written with the game industry in mind? If so, how do these films vary from non-game orientated films in terms of storyline, action, locations and characterisations?

WORLD ECONOMICS AND NEW TECHNOLOGIES

As with other forms of industry, the cost of film production is on the increase. As a measure to improve profits and maintain production values, studios and producers are ever on the lookout for new ways to cut costs. Within the traditional drawn animation studio system, exploitation of labour is nothing new, particularly where the unskilled tasks are concerned. Most notable of these is the use of 'paint and trace'. After the animation at the drawing stage is completed, the images are transferred on to clear sheets of celluloid, either by hand or Xerox. These are then individually painted by hand, a very expensive but necessary element of the production. When unemployment is high, it is easy to find people willing to train to carry out this semi-skilled task. During the 1980s a lot of this work moved away from the UK-based studios and went to Ireland and Spain where labour costs were low and there existed studio systems able to complete the work. By the late 1980s even this option was unacceptable to many producers and more work began to move out to the Far East. The Chinese in particular were not slow to take advantage of the West's desire for cheap paint and trace and, with the creation of their newly formed 'economic zone' work, began to pour into the area. As the work heading East began to increase, industry there became involved in other areas of production such as layout, animation and camera. The Pacific basin, the Philippines and, in particular, Manila, is now the heartland of this end of production. With a massive, easily renewable workforce, willing to work for extremely low wages and with no union representation, the lure of the East is far too much for profit-hungry producers to resist. The introduction of electronic paint systems is set to completely revolutionise animation production. Not only will wages be even lower than the work-hungry Filipinos are willing to tolerate but it will mean that production can be carried out in the country of origin. This will enable producers to keep a closer eye and a tighter rein on production schedules. As for other aspects of traditional animation production, we are likely to see a move towards the development of a computer lightbox that does away with the need for paper at all.

FINAL FRAME: CONCLUSION

The development of new technologies for both the manufacture and distribution of film, television and, increasingly, the new medias (multimedia, Virtual Reality, etc.) is not only inseparable from those processes but increasingly impacts upon the content of film and television and affects the way in which they are read. The use of technologies more familiar within multimedia, print and pop video not only informed the very nature of the image-making process in Peter Greenaway's *Prospero's Books* (1991), it impacted upon the way in which the film was 'read'. The multi-layered images incorporating the use of text and other typographical elements could indeed be read; they demanded of the viewer a double, simultaneous reading that went far beyond the standard use of subtitles, the text being woven into the screen image. Computer animation and CG imagery is increasingly becoming so central to the process of film-making that it is no longer restricted to a technical support role within live-action film-making, but is extending the realm of the cinematic experience.

When it [computer animation] is not calling attention to the limitations of photographic realism, it is recalling its own codes and conventions and, most significantly, developing new ones.

(Wells, 1998)

The success of film production companies has long been associated with the creation of new products linked to the adaptation of new technologies and production methodologies. A clear example is found in the Disney studio's utilisation of sound for the third Mickey Mouse short *Steamboat Willie* and the development of new camera processes and techniques – for example, the use of the multiplane camera in *The Old Mill*. This adaptation not only enabled Disney to survive in a very competitive marketplace during a period of general economic hardship – when many of their competitors were struggling and some were even forced to close their doors for good – it gave Disney the competitive edge. This enabled them to thrive and gave them the opportunity to develop the organisational framework needed to develop the business into one of the largest organisations in the world (see Gomery in Smoodin, 1994, pp. 71–5).

It is evident that there is a link between the popularity (and hence the financial success) of a film, and the technology within the film content, as distinct from production methodologies. While there are obvious exceptions to this – low-budget, low-technology films such as *The Full Monty* – the popularity of the science fiction genre has ensured that technology remains central to film content in films such as *Independence Day*, *Men in Black*, *Lost in Space* and *Godzilla*. Far from being limited to a single genre, the use of technology creates acting opportunities for 'real' Hollywood stars such as Tom Hanks in *Forrest Gump* where he comes face to face with dead US presidents, Robin Williams as the mad inventor in *Flubber*, and Jim Carrey in *The Mask*. Technology even manages to create stars of its own, such as tornadoes in *Twister*, boats in *Titanic* and insects in *Bugs*. Indeed it may well be that the new stars of Hollywood are the CG animators who bring these examples of digital magic to our screens.

Even the nature of the screens themselves may be an issue in the future, at least that is what some pundits would have us believe. There has been much discussion about interactivity and convergence of technologies, TV and computers, and the impact this will have on cinema. However there is not, as yet, any clear evidence of enough public interest in this. And, after all, it is the public interest that determines success or otherwise, shaping the future of the film industry and any media-related area. Given the harsh experience of Emile Raynaud and the public's response to his pioneering work I am sure he would endorse that sentiment.

FURTHER READING

Aronowitz, S., Martinson, B. and Menser, M. *Techno Science and Cyber Culture* (Routledge, London, 1996)

Bishop, H. 'Can Film and TV Ever Dance in Step?', *Clips* (No. 79, Nov. 1997)

Coe, B. *The History of Movie Photography* (Eastview Editions, Westfield, NJ, 1981) pp. 8–10

——*The History of Movie Photography* (Eastview Editions, Westfield, NJ, 1981)

Cotta Vaz, M. 'Martial Art', *Cinefex* (No. 68, 1996)

Cotta Vaz, M. and Rose Duignan, P. *Industrial Light and Magic: Into the Digital Realm* (Virgin, London, 1996)

Crafton, D. *Emile Cohl, Caricature and Film* (Princeton, NJ, 1990)

Gilder, G. 'Happy Birthday Wired', *Wired* (6 January 1998)

Hayward, P. and Wollen, T. *Future Visions: New Technologies of the Screen* (British Film Institute, London, 1993)

Jones, K.R. *Mars Attacks! The Art of the Movie* (Titan Books, London, 1996)

Lasseter, J. and Daly, S. *The Art and Making of the Animated Film* (Hyperion, NY, 1995) p. 18

Maltin, L. *Of Mice and Magic. A History of American Animated Cartoons* (Nal Penguin, NY, 1987)

Mealing, S. *The Art and Science of Computer Animation* (Intellect, Exeter 1992)

Millar, D. *Cinema Secrets: Special Effects* (Apple Press, London, 1990)

Monaco, J. *How to Read a Film* (Oxford University Press, 1977)

Reid, R.H. 'Real Revolution', *Wired* (5 October 1997)

Richard Auzenne, V. *The Visualization Quest. A History of Computer Animation*, (Associated University Presses, NJ, 1994) pp. 78–9

—— *The Visualisation Quest: A History of Computer Animation* (Fairleigh Dickinson University Press, London and Toronto, 1994)

Robinson, D. *George Méliès the Father of Film Fantasy* (British Film Institute, London, 1993)

Sklar, R. *Film: An International History of the Medium* (Thames & Hudson, London, 1993)

Smoodin, E. (ed.) *Disney Discourse; Producing the Magic Kingdom* (Routledge, London, 1994)

Sobchack, V. *The Persistence of History. Cinema, Television and the Modern Event* (Routledge, New York, 1996)

Wells, P. *Understanding Animation* (Routledge, London, 1998)

FURTHER VIEWING

The Last Machine (BBC)
Early Cinema Vols. 1 and 2 (British Film Institute)
The Making of Jurassic Park (CIC Video)

Europe. The Other Hollywood? (BBC)
Visions of Light (Academy Video)

RESOURCE CENTRES

Useful addresses

ASIFA – International Animated Film Association,
61 Railwayside, Barnes, London SW13 0PQ
BBC Multimedia, White City, 201 Wood Lane, London E3 3RW
British Council Film Department, 11 Portland Place, London
W1N 4EJ
British Film Commission, 70 Baker Street, London W1M 1DJ
BFI (British Film Institute), 21 Stephen Street, London W1P 1PL
Museum of the Moving Image, South Bank, Waterloo, London
SE1 8XT
National Museum of Photography, Film and Television, Prince's
View, Bradford, W. Yorkshire

Websites
www.422.com
4:2:2 Video Production Company

www.cgimag.com
CGI Magazine

www.computerarts.co.uk
Computer Arts Magazine

www.cyfle.demon.co.uk
CYFLE Training Agency

www.framestore.co.uk
Framestore Film and Video Graphics, Post-production and
Computer Animation

www.pixar.com
Pixar Computer Animation

www.sgrinwales.demon.co.uk
SGRIN Media Agency for Wales

www.skillset.org
Skillset National Training Organisation for Broadcast, Film, Video
and Multimedia

www.wired.com
WIRED Magazine

Chapter 4

Film form and narrative

Allan Rowe

■ **Introduction: the act of viewing**   92

■ Case study 1: *RoboCop* (1987)   92

■ Case study 2: beginning of Keaton's *The General* (1925)   95

■ **Cinematic codes**   98

■ **Narrative**   115

■ **Alternative narratives**   121

□ Case study 3: *If...* – an alternative text (1968)   124

■ **Notes**   127

■ **Further reading**   127

■ **Further viewing**   128

■ **Resource centres**   128

■ Film form and narrative

INTRODUCTION: THE ACT OF VIEWING

See Chapter 5 for a further discussion of the process of watching films.

The experience of watching films – particularly in the cinema – is an intense one. We sit in near-darkness, in rows of seats directed towards a screen. We are separated from one another by the lack of illumination and the armrest between the seats, and yet we are part of a shared experience. We view large images – allowing a closeness rarely afforded in everyday life, except in situations of extreme intimacy. Often we are given access to experiences which, if they were *real*, would be a major intrusion into the lives of the participants. The images are accompanied by a co-ordinated, concentrated and often loud soundtrack, further directing our attention if it threatens to wander, and encouraging us to respond in a prescribed way. It is small wonder that the viewers of the Lumière Brothers[1] took evasive action as that train first pulled into the station. Elvis Presley is alleged to have been concerned with the script of his first movie. He was required to hit a woman, and that was 'against his nature'. He could not be convinced that what occurred on screen did not actually have to take place. Yet we are ultimately aware of the fantasy nature of what we see – Edward G. Robinson went on to make many more films after the 'end of Little Rico' in *Little Caesar*[2] without provoking doubts or outcry among his fans. What occurs is a process of 'suspension of disbelief' whereby we seem to accept temporarily the reality of what appears in front of us, while having the capacity to switch off this belief at a moment's notice, if someone talks to us or the celluloid breaks.[3]

noise
In the film industry, it refers to any barrier to successful communication.

drama-documentary
Any format which attempts to re-create historical or typical events using performers, whether actors or not.

mainstream
Feature-length narrative films created for entertainment and profit. Mainstream is usually associated with 'Hollywood', regardless of where the film is made.

For a further discussion of the active–passive debate regarding audience see Chapter 5.

It is this capacity to switch on and off, rather than the poorer quality of the visual image, that accounts for the reduced potency of a horror film when watched at home with the remote control at hand. It is not the fidelity of image and sound that creates the illusion of reality for us. The early viewers of film accepted the shades of grey that appear in a black and white film. Viewing these films today, we find it hard to accept the illusion of films made in a period with different technical standards – the **noise** gets in the way. The mere recording of events in front of the camera – and the use, for instance, of everyday speech by non-actors in a **drama-documentary** – often appears strange to us. The 'illusory reality' of **mainstream** cinema is created for us by a number of devices, involving the use of camera, microphone and lighting. These devices are not fixed – a 'correct' way of recording the truth – but conventions developed over a hundred years of cinema. These are ingrained in us as viewers – and we can feel disturbed or cheated if these conventions are broken. If we are 'duped' by this, we are willingly duped. We participate in this process of suspension of disbelief as a price for the pleasures we get from film viewing – including that of 'surviving' being scared by a horror movie.

However, our role in this process is not merely a passive one. We work actively at making sense of the individual scenes, and particularly at predicting the story. To do so we retain an awareness of the conventions of film and are able to retain a critical distance from what we see. I would maintain that this is not a capacity possessed solely by 'film students', but rather is integral to the act of viewing.

☐ CASE STUDY 1: *ROBOCOP* (1987)

The process of making sense of a movie is first manifested at the beginning of a film when we are first drawn into its world. We will explore the film *RoboCop*[4] to see how this process works. This film operates in an area between genres, that of comic strip construction – a recently deceased policeman transformed into an indestructible robot –

and the environment of police precinct work in a form recognisable from TV police fictions and those of news programmes, an uncontrollable urban area and a political climate of privatisation. For the film to 'work' there is a need to absorb the impossible into the all-too-probable. The film's popular and critical acceptability suggests that this has worked.

After an initial aerial shot showing a modern, sky-scrapered city, with the film title (maybe suggesting that this could be any modern city), we are presented with a sixteen-picture grid dominated by images of urban violence, followed by a shot of a male and female facing directly to the camera. Before they start talking, a voiceover addresses the unseen TV audience, which in effect is us, the viewers of the film; 'This is Media – you give us three minutes, we give you the world'.

We are aware that this is a TV news item. Apart from TV lights and the studio backdrop, there is a direct address to the audience. In doing so the shot acknowledges the presence of a camera and, by implication, an audience. As a strategy, this has been denied to main-stream fictional cinema since the early days. Although what we see is not an identifiable TV station and we are aware that we are viewing a fictional film, the film-maker presumes our capacity to read the **conventions**. The first news item, a nuclear threat in the besieged white city-state of Pretoria, suggests a future, but not too-far-future, scenario; the second, a jokey news item on the Star Wars Initiative (a reference to a nuclear defence strategy popularly referred to after the George Lucas cycle of films and which would be familiar to audiences at the time) suggests a comic element within the news and hence the film, but also a world without clear moral values. A television commercial for artificial hearts follows. On first viewing we cannot place these as belonging to a story. However we 'trust' the narrative to make sense of them, as it does with the construction of the artificial policeman within the corrupt environment. Nothing in a mainstream narrative is there by accident.

The final item relates directly to the narrative of the film: the killing of three policemen, the taking over of policing by a private corporation and the introduction of two villains – the corporate boss Jones, in an insensitive interview, and the crime boss Boddicker, through a soft-focus shot from a newspaper. The TV introduction is not only an economical introduction to the narrative but authenticates the reality of the situation. It also places us at a distance from those in authority.

The next scene – set in the police precinct – is constructed with long moving shots using **Steadicam**, overlapping dialogue and a high level of verbal violence, all familiar as the style of TV police series such as *NYPD Blue*. However, the futurist nature of the scene is implied by the unremarked upon unisex locker room, a convention later repli-cated in *Starship Troopers*. There is a newcomer to the precinct, who is seen taking the place of a murdered policeman. We **read** this through his action in taking over a locker and replacing the name. He joins up with a partner, Lewis, who, in a stock scene, subverted by her gender, proves herself in a fight. The two ascend in the car to the 'real world', he driving the car, she blowing her bubblegum in his face.

The film cuts, without an **establishing shot**, to the inside of an ascending lift in the corporation building, suggesting a link organisationally if not physically between the two buildings. The locations show similarities, but also contrasts.

Uniforms are worn in both buildings (the dark-blue bullet-proofing of the police and the mid-grey of the 'suits'), the walls are predominantly single coloured (a grubby light green at the precinct and light grey at the corporation building); the clutter at the precinct contrasts with space at the corporation, a blackboard at the precinct with a high-tech bank of TV screens at the corporation.

The focus of this scene, used widely in the marketing of the film, is the presentation by Jones of a robot 'Future of Law Enforcement, ED, 209'. This robot is shot predomi-nantly from below, indeed from ground level, initially dominating the frame of the open doors leading from the boardroom, with corresponding **high angle** shots of the terrified

---

For further discussion of film genre see Chapter 6 pp. 166–81).

conventions
Conventions are estab-lished procedures within a particular form which are identifiable by both the producer and the reader. The implication of the idea of conventions is that a form does not naturally mean anything, but it is an agreement between producer and user.

Steadicam
A technical development from the late 1970s which permits the use of a camera held by hand which walks with the action, but with the steadiness of a camera moving on rails.

Starship Troopers (1997, dir. Paul Verhoeven) presents a world in the future where the military have taken control, nuclear weapons are commonplace and public executions take place on television.

reading a film
Although films are viewed and heard, the concept of 'reading' a film implies an active process of making sense of what we are experi-encing.

establishing shot
A shot using distant framing, allowing the viewer to see the spatial relations between char-acters and the set.

high angle
A shot from a camera held above characters or an object, looking down at them.

reality
The concept of the 'real' is problematic in cinema, and is part of the focus of this chapter. The concept is generally used in two different ways:

First, the extent to which a film attempts to mimic reality so that a fictional film can appear indistinguishable from documentary.

Second, the film can establish its own world and can, by consistently using the same conventions, establish the credibility of this world. In this later sense a science-fiction film such as *RoboCop* can be as realistic as a film set in a contemporary and recognisable world such as *Sleepless in Seattle*.

mediation
A key concept in film and media theory, it implies that there are always structures, whether human or technological, between an object and the viewer, involving inevitably a partial and selective view.

• **Plate 4.1** *RoboCop* (Paul Verhoeven, US 1987) ED 209, the future of law enforcement

executives. The robot's movements are heavy, metallic and jerky – and are accompanied by a high volume soundtrack. Its appearance with large bulky 'legs' and 'arms' suggests something subhuman – particularly when compared later with the human-based RoboCop. The crude mechanical 209 proceeds to destroy a junior executive in a demonstration of its power, failing to recognise that the executive has disarmed. This reflects the attitude of the corporation: 'It's life in the Big City.'

The first few minutes of the film have established its **reality** – part drawn from contemporary images, such as the boardroom, but with an invented technology such as the robot inserted in it. However, the construction of this reality is not just through a selection of the world outside, but rather through the judicial use of existing images and conventions that have already been **mediated** through film – or other related forms. We understand the film through our experiences and comparisons with other films or media products. These in turn assure the authenticity of the film to us, as an audience. We believe in the world of *RoboCop* because it has been validated by a spoof of recognisable TV news programmes. We can 'place' the film because we can identify both the images and the way they are presented from their similarity to images and representations with which we are already familiar.

The reading of film

RoboCop rests, therefore, on a number of cultural readings of the content by the viewer (e.g. the locker room), but also on a reading of film and its conventions. It appears relatively easy for us to read such a film because we have seen it all, or nearly all before. The film has been made fairly recently and, for people like ourselves, there is general agreement among members of the audience as to what it is about, what is happening, how we identify with characters and so on. The reading of early films, made a hundred years ago, appears on first sight to be easier, because they are less 'busy'. The language of the films of Lumière and Méliès[5] appears simpler – the visual equivalent of children's picture-books – and it is tempting to regard the early film-makers and their audiences with condescension. The conception of a 'Primitive Mode of Representation',[6] applied to the first two decades of film-making, encourages us to read these as the first faltering steps to the irresistible final product of the modern Hollywood movie.

Although the first extant movies are documentary records of either public or private events, such as the Lumières' home movie of feeding a baby or the reconstruction of events as in Edison's early boxing pictures for the Kinetoscope,[7] the normal format soon became fictional narrative. The earliest fiction films are the so-called 'tableau' films, including most of the work of Georges Méliès. These films are characterised by a succession of scenes recorded in long shot, square on to the action. Each scene begins with a cut to a black and is replaced by another scene in a different (later) time and place. Characters walk on and off either from the side of the frame, or alternatively through 'stage doors' in the frame, like the 'crew' walking into the space ship in Méliès' *Voyage to the Moon*. These films draw strongly on a theatrical tradition. They appear to be shot from the 'best seat in the stalls', and represent a series of scenes, albeit short ones, without the need to wait for the scene to be shifted.

Such films can still be enjoyed as 'spectacle' – the special effects, the hand-painted colour, the sets and costumes. These are connected by a narrative linking each shot to the whole, and usually each shot to the next one, by a pattern of cause and effect. However, the narrative is hard to follow for the contemporary viewer. This is in part due to the absence of **close-up** or identification with character. However, in a number of instances Méliès relies upon our knowledge of the narrative. *Ali Baba* (1905 Méliès from the BFI Early Cinema video) depends on the audience's pre-knowledge of the story. The individual tableaux appear to be operating as illustrations of the narrative rather than driving it.

The shift to a cinematic narrative and formal structure occurred fairly swiftly, so that by the mid-1910s most films are recognisable to a contemporary audience as fiction films. While there may be some dispute about who 'invented' the language of film – most accounts ascribing a major role to D.W. Griffith[8] – it is generally accepted that changes that had occurred by the end of that decade make the films of the late silent period resemble modern films more than the 'primitive' cinema.

See Chapter 3 pp. 62–9 for discussion on Lumière and Méliès, and Chapter 5, pp. 132–6, for a discussion of early cinema in relation to spectatorship.

close-up
Normally defined as a shot of the head from the neck up.

For further study
Consider the opening ten minutes of any commercial film of your choice (preferably one that is new to you):

How does the film introduce you to its main characters?
How does it establish the time and place of the world of the film?
In what ways is the film similar to other films that you have seen (try to draw specific comparisons)?
At the end of the sequence, what questions have been asked that you expect to be answered?

☐ CASE STUDY 2: BEGINNING OF KEATON'S *THE GENERAL* (1925)

Directed by Buster Keaton, this 1925 film is an example of the **Institutional Mode of Representation (IMR)** (Burch, 1973). Many of the conventions of mainstream cinema had already been established. Despite being a silent film it has a complex narrative structure, it tells a story set in a concrete historical setting, and lasts for nearly an hour

IMR
The Institutional Mode of Representation is a broad categorisation of systems of film form and

narrative characterising mainstream cinema from around 1915 onwards. It was perceived as replacing the Primitive Mode of Representation (a set of conventions used in early film between 1895 and 1905) as a gradual process in the first twenty years of cinema.

and a half. It is also strongly based on identification with character. We get to know the world of the film through the experience of a single player. In this sense the mainstream film is drawing on the conventions of the nineteenth-century novel which is focused on the psychological experience of one or two 'rounded' characters.

The credits prioritise Keaton as both star and co-director. The film starts with a title establishing place (Marietta, Ga) and time (1861), a device that continued into the sound era. The title does suggest that the spectator is able to 'read' this, the time being just prior to the American Civil War, and the 'Ga' signifying Georgia and the South. This message, however, is subsequently reinforced by dialogue, uniforms and indeed the whole narrative. A classic Hollywood film using the Institutional Mode of Representation aspires for *closure*: it is complete and understandable in its own right.

This title is followed by an establishing, long panning shot of a train, cutting to a medium shot to identify Johnny Gray (Keaton) as driver, and continuing to track forward to identify 'The General' – the name of the train. It then cuts ahead to the arrival of the train in the station.

There is then a reverse shot of the other side of the train. As Johnny descends he is admired by two children and checks with a colleague the time of the arrival of the train (implying the high status of the job and his proficiency).

This is followed by an inserted title – 'There were 2 loves in his life his engine and...' – and a cut to a close-up of a portrait of a young woman which he has in his cab.[9] This title suggests an external narrative commentary, the 'writer' is telling us what to think. This is a 'primitive' device that was destined to disappear from mainstream cinema, although it has re-appeared recently in the work of Martin Scorsese, such as in *The Age of Innocence* where Edith Wharton's words are read by a narrator as *a* commentary on the action. Classic Hollywood aspired to tell its stories through what we see and hear immediately. The narrator is absent and the story 'tells itself'.

After the title, Keaton walks off towards frame right. The following fade to black implies a different place or time and cuts to Annabelle (Marion Mack), identifiable as the woman in the portrait. She is looking away to frame right, the opposite direction from Johnny, and receives a look from an unseen admirer(?). The viewer can read that this is not Johnny, who should have appeared from the left of the frame as he walked off from

• **Plate 4.2** *The General* (Buster Keaton, US 1925) Johnny Grey (Keaton) and admirers

the right of the previous frame. This was one of the conventions of editing that had been adopted by early film-makers, and which by the 1920s seemed 'natural' to the audience.

Keaton is discovered walking from left to right followed by the two children (the same direction as he left the previous frame and the same direction as the train). Annabelle hides and deceives him by following the children (parallel to her deception of him with the admirer). She ends the joke and invites him in, with the children following. This creates a 'family', but not a real one and Johnny has to tell the children to leave. (This parallels her trick on him and suggests a similarity between them – they are a 'proper couple'.) He gives her a picture of himself standing in front of the train, a parallel of her portrait but significantly different: he is active and in control, the driver and The General.

There is a cut to an older man in a different room who, after looking off frame to the right, moves into the sitting room and a younger man enters from the door (right). The exchange that follows is 'in depth' and on a different plane to the 'lovers'. The first dialogue title appears, announcing the war and the wish to enlist. After the two men leave we get a subjective shot from Annabelle to Johnny, who is left alone and on the sofa (due to her absence they are no longer a couple). The shot places him on the edge and suggests imbalance and discomfort.

As Johnny leaves to try to enlist we are shown his awkwardness and inexperience; she kisses him and he tries to hide his embarrassment. He waves to an imaginary person over her shoulder and falls over.

There is no fade to black before the recruiting office scene, thus implying the speed of the action. This scene is largely in long shot. After his initial rejection, we pull away from Keaton and discover the reason for it. We know why he has been rejected, but he does not. The withholding of information from characters but revealing to the audience is a key device in Hollywood narrative and most particularly in comedy. Johnny, however, remains the centre of the narrative and we identify with him in his attempts to make sense of his rejection. For instance, he is placed next to a very much taller man in the queue and we realise before him that he would consider this the reason for his rejection. We also admire and identify with his attempts to trick his way in (there is a slightly strange cut where he appears on opposite sides of the frame in consecutive shots taken from the same angle thus breaking the 30° rule and thus confusing us as to where he actually is).

In the following scene there is a false 'eye-line' match from Johnny sitting on the side of the engine to Annabelle looking from the gate (we 'know' this is false from the journey Keaton takes to get to the house early in the film). His absence is stressed by the arrival of her father and brother who have enlisted and are where Johnny ought to be (both physically and in the narrative).

In the final scene Annabelle accuses Johnny of not trying to enlist and therefore of being a coward. We know (because we have seen it) that this is untrue. Our identification with the unjustly treated Johnny is therefore complete. In the final shot the train accidentally takes him away, establishing that he is not in control. The dilemma is set and we know, first, that he must regain control, second, that he must prove to be a hero and, third, that he must gain the love of Annabelle.

This sequence, although not cinematically complex, shows a strong sense of narrative and **identification**, and is **economically presented**. All elements are used to develop our knowledge of the narrative, including the use of *mise en scène* (the photographs), Keaton's body language, framing of shots and the continuity of editing. There even appears to be a **modernist** editing with a false cut. Although we cannot assume that the contemporary audience would read all that we have done into the sequence any more than would a modern audience, to make sense of the

See section on editing, pp. 110–13.

identification
The process of identification allows us to place ourselves in the position of particular characters, either throughout or at specific moments in a movie. The devices involved include subjectivity of viewpoint (we see the world through their eyes, a shared knowledge, we know what and only what they know), and a sharing in their moral world, largely through narrative construction.

economic presentation
All the components are designed to help us read the narrative. An examination of the first few minutes of almost any mainstream fictional film will reveal a considerable amount of information about characters, their social situation and their motivation.

modernist
Any device which undercuts the invisible telling of the story. A modernist device draws attention to itself and makes us aware of the construction of the narrative. It would be unclear in this instance whether the device is a consciously modernist one or a primitive one which unconsciously draws attention to itself.

sequence does presume, however, an understanding of film language. It is also a 'self-contained text' in that it is possible to understand the film without any previous knowledge of, for instance, the American Civil War. This contrasts to Méliès tableaux films like *Ali Baba* which do not make sense without a pre-knowledge of the narrative.

For further study
Consider an extract from any silent film to which you have access:

How do the performers convey their feelings without the use of words?
How are props used to tell us about the characters and the situations they are in?
How is the film edited to show changes of time and place?
If the film-maker had access to synchronised sound, how do you think the sequence would have been shot differently?

CINEMATIC CODES

With the addition of sound to film in 1927, the 'message' coming from film was relatively complete – strange experiments like 'sensorama' or the 'smellies' notwithstanding. In normal film viewing we experience simultaneously a number of codes: visual, sound and the codes controlling the linking of one sound or image to another. The division of the components we use in reading film are relatively arbitrary, but it will help in analysis to theoretically separate them.

Mise en scène

This term derived from the French, literally 'having been put into the scene', is used to describe those visual aspects that appear within a single shot. The term has been used differently by writers about film, some limiting it to those elements that are recorded by the camera – objects, movements, lighting, shadow, colour and so on – while others have included the art of recording itself, the focusing of shots and the movement of the camera. In the former sense *mise en scène* is limited to some kind of 'pro-filmic event'; those elements that are there before we start filming. In documentary films such events are perceived to have a 'real world' existence and hence appear not to be 'encoded', or at any rate only coded to the extent that the elements in the real world are. For instance, we may only expect certain categories of people with appropriate dress to be found in a hospital theatre. Not surprisingly, Early Cinema either used pre-existing events – the workers leaving a factory[10] – or alternatively it constructed events, such as the early boxing scenes used by Edison in his Kinetoscope showings. Subsequent developments involved the use of theatrical performance, vaudeville turns, even performances of plays, albeit silent and much condensed. This history, however, reinforced a 'common-sense' notion that filming was solely the recording of reality or theatrical performance.

The concept of *mise en scène* was developed by those theorists interested in issues of authorship, or the role of participants, and particularly directors in constructing the

See Chapter 2 for further details on production, distribution and exhibition in the Early Cinema, 1900–14.

See Chapter 6, pp. 195–205, for detailed discussion of authorship.

meaning of film.[11] During the classic period of the Hollywood studio, from 1920 to 1950, the director's control was limited to those processes that were recorded during shooting. The overall narrative was clearly established, and the script would be written before the director was even engaged.

Similarly the editing of the film, and the post-dubbing of the soundtrack, were taken out of the control of the director, sometimes involving a re-cut to meet the needs of the studio, or the responses of an audience at a preview. It was therefore the capacity to control what happened on the set, and the way this was recorded by the camera, which was the sign of filmic art as displayed by the director. The quality of a director's work could be read through his style, his control over the *mise en scène*.

We shall now look at specific elements of *mise en scène*:

Setting

In the context of studio shooting, the predominant form in the 1920s to 1940s, all elements in front of the camera were controlled and chosen, even if sometimes the director took over a set already existing on the back-lot (an inheritance, perhaps, from a more highly

• **Plate 4.3** *Shane* (George Stevens, US 1953)
A romantic view of the West

• **Plate 4.4** *Johnny Guitar* (Nicholas Ray, US 1954)
A darker view of the West

budgeted film). While settings are usually perceived as a signifier of authenticity, the place where the events are happening, they are nevertheless a constructed setting for action. This becomes clear if we examine the different 'look' of the West in films such as *Shane*, *My Darling Clementine*, *Johnny Guitar*, *A Fistful of Dollars* and *The Unforgiven*. Although each of these five films is recognisable as 'the West', they all emphasise different kinds of settings: the wilderness, the small town and the large ranch.

Most viewers have no concept of the nature of the historic West against which the images the films are to be judged, although films have been defined as more realistic at particular moments in time. The 'Spaghetti Westerns' of the 1960s, although shot in Spain, were seen as particularly authentic, settings and clothes being dirtier than the viewers were used to. The landscape and settings of a Western are probably better read against the conventions of the Western genre, than as a representation of the real West.

For a further discussion of genre see Chapter 6.

Jim Kitses in *Horizons West* describes the Western in terms of the opposing focus of wilderness and civilisation, 'the contrasting images of Garden and Desert'.[12] These oppositions permeate through the themes of the Western, the definition of characters and the status of particular settings and locations. The Starrett homestead in George

Stevens' *Shane* is presented as an isolated place, overlooked on one side by the mountains, from where Shane comes and where he goes to, with the town, a scene of danger and evil, on the other.

The setting can also function to place the performers. In *The Cabinet of Doctor Caligari* the characters are 'enclosed' in a two-dimensional set, with 'lighting' painted over the backdrop and the stage. The setting constantly suggests danger and paranoia which is revealed, at the end of the film, to be a relocation of the interior world inhabited by the 'crazy' narrator. This film was a precursor of Expressionism, a movement that can be seen in a number of influential German films from 1919 to 1931. Drawn from a contemporary movement in the visual arts, including the work of Munch and Nolde, its aim was to convey the crude force of human emotion in a total cinematic experience. It overtly rejected ideas of realism in the visual arts. While it never replaced the dominant realist aesthetic of mainstream cinema, leading protagonists of Expressionism, such as Murnau and Lang moved to Hollywood in the 1920s and 1930s. The influence of Expressionism can be seen in the horror films of the early 1930s, such as James Whale's *Dracula* and *Frankenstein*, and in film noir of the 1940s. In Frank Capra's *It's a Wonderful Life*, George Bailey (James Stewart), on the point of suicide, is taken by his guardian angel away from the world of middle America where he has grown up, with its model estate that he has helped to build, to a neon-lit 'modernist' rebuilt town which would have existed but for his help. Similarly, in *Blade Runner* Ridley Scott invents a futurist location that does not exist anywhere – a **dystopia** that we can recognise, possibly as much from other films as from extensions of a contemporary inner-city location, such as *The Fifth Element*, *The Fisher King* and *Terminator 2*.

Locations can not only be recognised and help us to place the characters within a film, but can also through the film itself create their own space and meaning. In Douglas Sirk's *All that Heaven Allows*, the principal action takes place in a family house, lived in by a family whose father has died before the film begins. While we learn little directly about this man, his presence lives on in the house, his trophies over the mantelpiece. The house with its oppressive lighting becomes almost the 'tomb' in which his widow Cary (Jane Wyman) is obliged to live out the rest of her life. The main room is divided up by screens. These divide Cary from her children, and particularly the son. Throughout the film he resists any attempt to change the house from the way it was when the father lived, and most particularly resents the presence of other men in the house. However, after he decides to leave, it is the house, and the implied memory of the father, that 'gets in the way' of a new relationship with his mother.

dystopia
A world of the future where everything has gone wrong.

Props

Films are also dependent on 'props' as a device for conveying meaning. In a familiar sense, props are definers of genre, such as the weapons in 'action' genres, or the arcane paraphernalia of the horror films – garlic and crosses. However, props can also become unique signifiers of meaning in a particular film. While all scenes are constructed around a number of props – to make the sequence 'look right' – our attention can be drawn to particular objects by the use of close-up and dialogue. This in itself suggests the significance of these objects – we know that such objects will be of importance in the narrative. In Hitchcock's *Strangers on a Train* a cigarette lighter changes hands from Guy, the 'innocent' tennis player with a wife he would rather be rid of, to Bruno, the plausible psychotic whom he meets on the train. The lighter is decorated with crossed tennis rackets, and the initials of Guy and his lover. The crossed rackets signify a number of 'crossings' within the movie: the 'crossed lovers', the offer of an exchange of murders by Bruno, the choices offered to Guy in the exchange, and so on. However, the lighter remains the significant 'icon' throughout the movie; it repre-

• **Plate 4.5** *All that Heaven Allows* (Douglas Sirk, US 1956)
The father still dominates the home even after his death

sents Bruno's threat to expose Guy if he does not keep his side of the bargain; its temporary loss delays Bruno's attempt to frame Guy; and its presence in the dying Bruno's hand at the end of the movie releases Guy from the hold that is upon him.

Props can also be used to 'anchor' characters into particular meanings.[13] In the complexities of possible ways in which an individual character may be read, an object may be used to clarify meaning. While Hannibal Lector in *Silence of the Lambs* may appear increasingly civilised, even charming, in relation to his fellow inmates and warders, the danger from his mouth, whether in terms of his speech or more obviously in his capacity to bite, is exemplified by the face-guard placed over him when he is being transported. The significance of this guard is that it denies the viewer full access to him in the way that we are permitted in the earlier exchanges through the reinforced glass. In *The Godfather* the entire film is suffused with props relating to family life. At the key moment when members of the Corleone family 'go to the mattresses' to prepare for the shoot out, the domestic world, exemplified by the cooking of a pasta sauce, is taken over by the men, exemplifying the contradiction of these family-centred and very traditional men who are prepared to murder to preserve family honour.

Costume

Costume is a variant of the prop but is, of course, tightly connected to character. Minor characters are often primarily identified on the basis of costume, which uses the codes of everyday life such as uniforms, or the cinematic codes such as the wearing of white and black to signify virtue and villainy in the early Westerns. Subtle changes in the costume of a single character can be used to signify changes of status, attitude and even the passing of time. In many 1930s gangster movies such as *The Roaring 'Twenties* and *Scarface*, the rise of the gangster, and his increasing separation both from his roots or from 'acceptable society', are exemplified by a change into clothes that are signifiers of affluence, if not taste. In *Mildred Pierce* we see the process in reverse. Our initial viewing of Mildred Pierce is as a smart, rich and powerful woman in a fur coat. In the first flashback we are introduced to the same character wearing an apron, in a clearly suburban domestic setting. We are presented with an 'after and

• **Plate 4.6** *Strangers on a Train* (Alfred Hitchcock, US 1951)
A significant icon

• **Plate 4.7** *Mildred Pierce* (Michael Curtiz, US 1945)
Joan Crawford translated from housewife (above) to businesswoman (opposite)

before', raising for us not only the dominant issue of the storyline at the moment – who killed Mildred's husband – but also the more complex issue of how this transformation has taken place.

Costume can also be used to signify mismatches. We bring to a costume a series of expectations, which are then subverted by the action. The 'false policeman' is regularly used as a plot device – either simply a robbery device, as in *The Wrong Arm of the Law*, or alternatively in films such as *The Godfather* where police act or speak in ways that we deem to be inappropriate.

A further example of mismatch is cross-dressing, usually a male in female clothing. Normally such devices are humorous, as in *Some Like it Hot* and *Tootsie*, where our expectations of appropriate behaviour and that of the male characters in the film, given the signifying props, are a mismatch with our knowledge of the gender of the character. In *The Crying Game* our knowledge is at least problematic, and the mismatch only appears retrospectively.

See case study of The Crying Game, *Chapter 2, pp. 37–9.*

In *Desperately Seeking Susan*, rather than using a uniform, Roberta, a suburban housewife with aspirations to a more exciting lifestyle, acquires a jacket belonging to

• **Plate 4.8** *Mildred Pierce* (Michael Curtiz, US 1945)

Susan, a woman with bohemian and underworld connections. This distinctive jacket, allegedly previously worn by Jimi Hendrix, allows Roberta to be 'misread' by other characters as 'being' Susan, but equally allows the viewer to place her in her aspirational world.

Performance and movement

Probably the richest source of *mise en scène* is the performance of actors. While there is more to consider in performance, it may help to consider the performer – whether human or animal – as an object for the camera's gaze. As with costume, there is a strong, coded element in the facial expressions and body positions held by performers. These codes, broadly referred to as 'body language', are of course part of everyday life. While there are cultural and temporal variations in body language, the body language of American film has become almost universally understood due to our familiarity with Hollywood. Indeed one of the consequences of the spread of film has been the global penetration of particular aspects of language such as the 'thumbs up' or the 'high five' signs.

For a brief discussion of Kuleshov's relation to actors in the Soviet cinema of the 1920s, see Chapter 13, p. 426.

The presentation of characters by actors using body language is a key element in the creation of a 'performance'. It is perhaps significant that the much-vaunted performances of recent years – Dustin Hoffman in *Rain Man*, Tom Hanks in *Forrest Gump* – have been characterised by bodily styles, conventionally associated with marginal figures in society. Again, body movements can be used to express both change of emotion and change of time. In *Citizen Kane*, the decline of Kane can be identified from the animated young man to the almost robotic, lumbering figure who smashes up his second wife's room when she threatens to leave him.

While early film was often dependent on the kind of exaggerated body movements that in the theatre were recognisable from the upper gallery, with the development of the close-up, meaning can often be expressed by the slightest movement, whether the wringing of hands in D.W. Griffith's *Intolerance* or the maintenance of facial expressions to be observed in almost any contemporary film. In an acting master-class, Michael Caine, that most minimalist of screen actors, ably demonstrates what can be conveyed by the flickering of the eye, the raising of the eyebrows or the turning of the lip.

See Chapter 6 for more detailed discussion of the star.

Finally, and briefly, the performer, and particularly the 'star', brings to the film a meaning derived merely from their presence. While some performers such as Jennifer Jason Leigh deliberately appear to present themselves differently in the films that they make, most operate with a high degree of consistency both in terms of appearance and type, a consistency which will usually be reinformed in terms of non-filmic appearances. As such, stars will bring in with them a level of expectation and an implied meaning from their previous films. This becomes obvious when performers attempt to take parts that move away from type, often with disastrous effect at the box office. It may be useful, therefore, to consider the (known) performer as part of the language of film, having a meaning that can be stretched and reused, but only to a limited extent.

'Putting into the scene'

Having assembled other components of our shots, the next procedure involves a process of recording these elements. However, such a distinction between content and form is an artificial one, in that we have already had to have recourse to concepts of close-up in order to describe individual constituents. Nevertheless, it is helpful to separate the processes, and hence those codes that characterise them from the codes of the objects themselves. While the latter are related to wider cultural artefacts and the meanings they have – like the meanings of ways of dressing – the former can be perceived either as strictly cinematic codes or, at any rate, as strongly related to the codes of other representational forms, painting, drawing and of course photography.

Lighting

Lighting of film is the first of the 'invisible' codes of cinema. While there are apparent sources of light within a shot, the lighting of a shot is off camera. Even with an outside location lighting is used to guarantee that the light level is adequate both to produce a sufficient level for recording and also to highlight particular aspects of the image. This activity is not separate from the shooting of the film, but is integral to it – and hence the term 'lighting cameraman', which is applied to the principal operator within the camera crew.

For further discussion on Bazin and realism, see p. 444–5.

Whereas Early Cinema relied on a relatively flat field of action, with the development of faster film stock it became possible and indeed desirable to establish a source of depth in the action. This, coupled with a small aperture lens, has enabled the camera to record over a number of fields of action. The French theorist André Bazin argued that such a form of shooting was both more 'realist' in the sense that the shots closely resemble the capacity of the eye to recognise objects across a wide depth (or at least to rapidly adjust focus to do so) and also more 'dramatic' in allowing the viewer the capacity to choose, within a given shot, where to direct attention.[14] In practice, deep focus shots and, in particular, a number of shots in *Citizen Kane* (such as the attempted suicide of Susanne Alexander, with a close-up of the sleeping draught and the distance shot of Kane breaking in through the door), allow little choice of attention. The planes of action are immediately joined as Kane rushes to the bed.

Lighting involves choices of level and direction of light. Classic Hollywood lighting involves a strong level of lighting on the main objects of a shot with fill lighting designed to eliminate shadows. The set is then backlit to enable those elements at the front of the set to be distanced from that which appears at the back, to give an illusion of diversion. However, lighting is also characterised by its absence.

Light and shade can be used to direct our attention to a particular part of the frame. This is most usually done by the movement of characters through a variously lit set. A more dramatic variant can be seen in Sergio Leone's *Once Upon a Time in the West*. In an early scene in the trading post a mysterious character, 'Harmonica' (Charles Bronson), is identified as present only through his characteristic theme music. He is dramatically exposed by 'Cheyenne' (Jason Robards) who propels an oil lamp on a horizontal wire across the room, producing a **low-key image** of Harmonica. This, the first meeting of these characters, who maintain an ambiguous relationship, is sudden, the characters revealed from out of the dark, and is followed by the flashing on and off of the light as a 'consequence' of the swinging of the oil lamp.

Sometimes, however, lighting can be used as a characteristic of the style of a whole film or over a number of scenes – rather than just a specific light to light a specific set-up. The classic realist film is usually characterised by a full lighting effect – high-key lighting – seemingly as a device to ensure that we see all the money that has been spent on constructing the effect. However, widespread use of shadows can be used to convey their own meaning. The use of reflective light scenes, and the often apparently dominant use of shadows, originated in German Expressionist cinema, but was incorporated into a Hollywood style of lighting in the 1940s and 1950s which later became known as **film noir**. This style was largely to be found in films within the detective/thriller genre, and was characterised by a world of threat and danger, but also one where characters' motivations were hidden from one another and, by implication, from the viewer. Lighting effects usually appear to be 'motivated', in that they come from sources such as table lamps that are in the shot. In an early scene of *Mildred Pierce*, the leading character Mildred 'frames' an old acquaintance Wally for a murder that she appears to have committed. The scene commences in a nightclub where the low level of lighting, together with Mildred's wide-brimmed hat, creates shots in which the face is half in shadow, with the eyes in particular in darkness. Later, returning to the beach house where the murder was committed, the interior is a kaleidoscope of lighting from the low table lights and the seeming dappled effect on the ceiling which is implicitly caused by reflections from the sea. It is within this scene that Wally is apparently trapped by the shadows that cut across him at every turn. The style of film noir is one of few formal characteristics that have come to be widely recognised, and indeed it survives into contemporary films such as John Dahl's *The Last Seduction*. This perhaps can be in part explained through its seeming difference from the visual effects of realist film, usually fully 'high-key' lighting, and its connection with a particular genre. The style of film noir is linked in an obvious way to themes of paranoia and alienation and other characteristics such as the *femme fatale*, a woman who is not what she immediately appears to be. In this instance the use of lighting enables the knowing viewer to be one step ahead of the protagonists within the film.

low-key image
Light from a single source producing light and shade.

film noir
A term developed by French film critics in the postwar period to describe a number of films produced in the 1940s. It has subsequently become a marketing device used to describe films with some of the lighting and narrative conventions of the period.

• **Plate 4.9** *The Last Seduction* (John Dahl, US 1994)
The style of film noir survives in contemporary films

Camera and camera movement

Having created the pro-filmic event and having lit it, the next set of choices surrounds the positioning of the camera. Early Cinema was largely characterised by a steadily held camera, at least as steady as hand-cranking permitted, and by the predominant use of the long shot incorporating all the action. Technological developments up to the Steadicam permitted greater flexibility and choice, both of movement and angle, as well as offering the option of different ratios with the variety of wide-scene formats operating since the 1950s. This 'progression' has not necessarily been continuous, particularly at the point of the introduction of sound when the cameras were initially installed within sound-proofed booths, thus restricting their movement. However, the techniques and 'language' of camera use had to be both developed by film-makers and 'learnt' by the audience.

Drawing primarily from the already existing art forms of photography and theatre, the camera was held static, with movement being derived from the actors in front of the camera. The camera was placed in the 'best seat in the stalls', square on to the action, with actors moving in and out of the shot as if from the 'wings'. The development of alternative camera positions and movements evolved in the first decade of the twentieth century. Probably the best introduction to this process and its effects can be gleaned from Noel Burch's film *Correction Please*, which combines early cinematic footage with a period narrative, progressively filmed using a range of methods. Within the capacities of focus the camera is able to move anywhere from the extreme close-up to the use of widescreen shots limited to pairs of eyes, as in the final shoot-out in *Once Upon a Time in the West*, to the extreme long shot of the field hospital in *Gone with the Wind*. The close-up has a particular place in the development of film, however, permitting us to 'know intimately' the faces of leading characters, and hence by implication to read their thoughts and feelings. This operates without needing to use either the knowing subtitle of the Early Cinema, or even the voice of the narrator to take us into the character.

It is also necessary to decide on the angle of the shot[15] and the relative height of the camera to the object being filmed – a low-angle shot looking up to the object or a high-angle shot looking down. Conventional accounts suggest that low-angle shots imply the power of the object – usually a human figure – and a high-angle shot its weakness. Such a rule can be seen to operate in many exchanges between characters – such as those between Kane and Suzanne Alexander in *Citizen Kane*, as she pieces together her jigsaw puzzle and he looks down on her. However, such rules cannot be applied to read off automatically the meaning of an individual shot. After the assault by the birds on the Brenner household in Hitchcock's *The Birds*, there is a tracking shot of the three members of the family taken from a very low angle. The suggestion is of their dominance; the birds have indeed disappeared, yet the anxious look on their faces and their isolation from one another suggest an alternative meaning. Our experience throughout the film suggests that danger comes from above – and indeed we are soon to discover that the birds have broken into the house and are waiting in an upstairs room.

While the camera is normally held level, it can also be tilted to one side. Such a shot is read as an indication of instability, either that of the characters or of the situation that the shot is recording. In an early scene in Nicholas Ray's *Rebel without a Cause* there is a series of shots on the staircase where James Dean's family is rowing. The shots are sharply tilted – an effect exaggerated by the Cinemascope screen.

While shots are classically in sharp focus, a soft focus can be used either to enhance the romantic effect of a scene or, alternatively, to expose the incapacity of a character to register the world around them.

Finally, the camera is able to move. The earliest moving shots were dependent on the movement of objects – cars or trains – so shots mimic the experience of viewing. Similarly, pans (horizontal movements) and tilts appear to reproduce eye movements and are motivated by the action that is occurring. Shots can also be developed to reproduce the movements of the characters within the set, originally using rails (hence the 'tracking shot'), or in a more liberated way using a hand-held or a Steadicam camera, walking the action. These shots give a strong sense of identity and place. For instance, in Scorsese's *GoodFellas*, Henry displays his power by entering a popular restaurant through a side door and impresses both his girlfriend and us with his capacity to walk through the back passageways and the kitchen, acknowledged only by the most important figures.

While such shots are perceived as naturalistic, and replicate the natural movements of the eye, the use of the crane moves beyond this to display a degree of control by the director of the world of the film. Such shots involve positions and movements that are inaccessible to us on a day-to-day basis. Crane shots can take us from the wide panorama of a scene to focus in on the object of our attention. In Hitchcock's *Marnie* a crane shot at a party takes us from Marnie's point of view on the landing above the expansive entrance hall of her husband's mansion to a close-up of her previous employer, Strutt, who has the potential to expose her earlier misdeeds. While this shot bears no relation to any possible human movement towards Strutt, it reflects the sense of powerlessness and inevitability felt by Marnie at that moment. The crane can also be used to dramatically reveal what has previously been hidden. In *Once Upon a Time in the West* there is a connection between Harmonica and the villain Frank, although this is not known by Frank. Only at the moment of death is this link established. In a flashback, Harmonica is revealed as a boy in close-up, with the camera craning back, first to reveal his elder brother standing on his shoulders, and then literally suspended by a noose from a ruined archway in the desert, waiting for the boy to weaken and plunge the brother to his death, and finally Frank laughing. A similar effect is produced in John Carpenter's *Halloween* where, following a lengthy Steadicam shot from behind a mask where the 'camera' searches through a house and discovers and kills two lovers, the mask is removed revealing a small boy. The camera cranes back and upwards stressing both the vulnerability of the child and the judgement of the local community.

While there has been a concentration in the preceding pages on some of the more obvious effects of the camera, the predominant style of Hollywood film-making is the use of a camera which is largely invisible, a predominance of shots being within the medium distance ('le shot American'), using very slight variations from the horizontal shot and involving limited camera movement, usually motivated by the action or the interest of the characters. Yet every shot is selected from a range of possibilities, even when it continues to appear to be the 'natural', the only, one.

Editing

See Chapter 13, p. 422–3, for discussion on Kuleshov and montage editing.

Having established the codes contributing to our understanding of the single shot, and hence *mise en scène*, we can now look at the combination of shots which construct a film flowing over time. While most of the characteristics of the film shot are related to codes developed in still photography, the joining of strips of films is specific to cinema, and as such has been seen as the component that is the essence of cinematic art. The Soviet film-maker Lev Kuleshov engaged in a number of 'experiments' linking shots and 'proving' that with adept editing it was possible to create alternative readings of the same facial expression – or to bring together shots occurring in completely different locations.[16] However, notions of the essential nature of film are certainly unfashionable and probably unhelpful in any attempt to read the meaning into sequences of film.

Historically, the first editing was between scenes, with individual extreme long shots recording a self-contained sequence at a particular time and place, followed by a cut to black. This device, drawing on the theatrical black-out, could easily be read by the early audiences, although for a contemporary audience a pre-existing knowledge of the storyline seems necessary in order to understand the narrative flow. In the first twenty years of cinema a 'vocabulary' of linking devices between scenes was established and largely attributed to D.W. Griffith. In particular, his method involved the distinction between 'slower' devices: the fade to and from black, and the dissolve between the image and the cut. While the fade implied a change of scene and the change of time, the cut was used within a scene or, in the case of cross-cut editing, signified that two events although separated by space were happening simultaneously.[17] This device was used particularly by Griffith to build up suspense in the rescue scene in *The Birth of a Nation*. Other devices such as the 'wipe', 'push off' and the 'turn over', while popular in the 1920s and revised as relatively simple techniques of the TV vision mixer, have largely been reduced to comic effects. The revival of linking devices by French New Wave directors such as Truffaut in *Tirez sur la pianiste* extended the use of the devices, in particular the use of the dissolve within a sequence to suggest the passing of time. The fade to black, which after time becomes almost an invisible device, was replaced by a dissolve to white, drawing attention to the uncertain status of the narrative in *Last Year in Marienbad*, and to other colours with specific emotional readings. However, the inventiveness of the New Wave directors, far from creating a universal language of the linking device, gave a number of alternative readings that had to be anchored through the *mise en scène*. The passing of time, for instance, would normally be doubly signified by use of *mise en scène*, the movement of characters, facial expressions, consumption of food and drink, or even the movement of the hands of the clock. New Wave directors felt free to ignore these conventions if the viewer was able to identify the passing of time through what was happening in the narrative.

While the linking devices described above have the function of signifying to the viewer the discontinuity of the action – the change of time and place – the major development in film editing has been to minimise the sense of disruption. Unlike studio TV, film is shot with considerable breaks, with changes of set, positioning and lighting. As a consequence film-makers are rarely able to record more than two to three minutes of usable stock in the course of a full working day. Those separate shots designed to be in the 'ideal' viewing place (for instance, a close-up on the speaker) have the potential to disrupt the viewers' attention. A system of conventions governing editing developed in the first two decades of cinema (although there were some changes following the introduction of sound) and these have become known as the 'rules of continuity editing'.[18] The intention of the rules is to produce a system to tell a story in such a way as to set out the action of the narrative and its position in space and time so that it is clear to the viewer while remaining unobtrusive. In particular, the storytelling should do nothing to draw attention to itself or to the apparatus of cinema (in the physical sense of equipment), but also should be such that strategies employed appear to be 'transparent' to the viewers, in the sense that they would not be aware of their existence.

For a further discussion of how the audience watches and understands film see Chapter 5.

These rules can be briefly summarised as follows. A scene will normally start with an 'establishing shot', a long shot which enables spectators to orientate themselves to the space of the scene and to the position of the performers and objects, as well as to reorientate them from the different space of the previous scene. All subsequent shots can therefore be 'read' within the space already established. Such a shot, a 'master shot', can of course be reintroduced in particular moments in the scene, whether to re-establish the space or to show significant movements of characters.

The 180° rule involves an imaginary line along the action of the scene, between actors involved in a conversation or the direction of a chase. The 'rule' dictates that this line should be clearly established and that consecutive shots should not be taken from opposite sides of the line. The consequence of this is the establishment of a common background space (either implicitly or explicitly) in static shots, and a clarity of direction of movement when, for instance, characters are running towards or away from one another. An extension of this is the principle of the 'eye-line match'. A shot of a scene looking at something off-screen is then followed by the object or person being looked at. Neither shot includes the viewer and the object together, but on the basis of the established space we presume their relationship.

The 30° rule proposes that a successive shot on the same area involves at least a 30° change of angle, or at any rate a substantial change of viewpoint. Although this involves a reorientation for the viewer, it does not involve the noticeable 'jump' of objects on the screen, which would produce a 'jump-cut'. Again, assuming the establishment of the narrative's space, the viewer is able to place the action.

Finally, the movement of actors and the reframing of the camera is so arranged and planned that the movement of the camera does not 'draw attention to itself'. This involves, for instance, the cut on action, so that the cut anticipates the movement to be made, such as a long shot of a character standing up or a cut to the person talking. The cut both takes the viewer where she/he as reader of the narrative wishes to be, and implies the control of the film-maker over the narrative. The cut appears to be 'motivated' by the need to tell the story.

This style of editing, including as it does decisions on the placement of camera and characters, is integral to the Hollywood classical realist text, a film that 'effaces all signs of the text's production and the achievement of an invisibility of process'. As such it is very hard to cite examples of the operation of the rules, or indeed to be aware of them when they are happening (although a full account does exist of a scene in the *Maltese Falcon*[19]).

*For a discussion of
Scorsese as auteur see
Chapter 6.*

However, we are made aware of these conventions when they are broken or in any way subverted. It is not unusual to commence a sequence with a close-up. In the post-sequence scene in Scorsese's *GoodFellas* we have an extreme close-up of the adolescent Henry before the reverse shot and pan reveals the gangsters across the road as the object of his gaze. Henry's voiceover stresses this boy's-eye view of the action ('They were able to stay up all night playing cards') rather than an objective narrative viewpoint. The initial close-up thus reinforces the subjective reading of the action before it is presented to us. The 180° was perhaps most forcibly broken in John Ford's *Stagecoach* as the Indians attacked the coach, seemingly riding from both directions. However, the strength of the narrative line and the clear visual distinction between the Indians and the cavalry present us with no problems in identifying narrative space. In *Who's That Knocking at My Door?*, the concluding dialogue between Harvey Keitel and Zina Bethune, the breaking of an 'impossible' relationship, again breaks the 180° rule as the camera plays on the invisible line.[20] The effort is disturbing, but only reflects the concern we have about where to 'place' ourselves emotionally in the sequence. The jump-cut was used widely by the French New Wave directors, notably Jean-Luc Godard in *A Bout de souffle*. The device used within conversations and during car journeys has the consequence of producing an ellipsis – the reduction of time spent on a sequence. Such a process is a necessary part of feature film narrative – films rarely operate in 'real time', equating the time of the action with what we see on the screen. However, the usual form of continuity editing hides this process by making the sequences within, say, a car journey appear continuous. It is not that Godard's use of the jump-cut makes the film's narrative incomprehensible, but rather it draws attention to the process of selection that has taken place.

While continuity editing dominates classic narrative, other strategies have been used – and were perhaps more formally developed in the silent era before the requirements of continuity in both sound and image restricted, at least temporarily, the expressiveness of successive images. The 'montage' sequence entailed a number of shots over a period of time to demonstrate a process of change. In *Citizen Kane*, the disintegration of Kane's first marriage is shown in a scene of breakfast, with the couple eating in silence hiding behind rival newspapers. A similar device is used in *The Godfather* where a sequence of killings occurs in different locations, while the baptism of Michael Corleone's child is taking place. In the sequence, the soundtrack of the church service is held over the images, not only contrasting the pious words of the protagonists with their actions, but also establishing the contemporaneity of the action.

*For a further discussion
of Eisenstein and* Strike
*see Chapter 13
pp. 428–32.*

An alternative form of editing is the so-called 'non-diegetic insert' which involves a symbolic shot not involved with the time and place of the narrative to comment on or express the action in some alternative way. Eisenstein in *Strike* uses the image of a bull in a slaughterhouse to represent the killing of strikers by the mounted soldiers. The primacy of realist narrative has made this kind of device less prevalent in 'Hollywood' cinema,[21] although such coded inserts proved useful as devices to circumscribe censorship in earlier eras. Hitchcock used the clichéd train entering the tunnel as an expression of the consummation of Roger Thornhill's marriage at the end of *North by Northwest*. In *Goodbye Columbus*, the 'seduction' of the daughter in the attic is similarly expressed by an abrupt cut to the carving of roast meat at the family lunch.

The cutting of film stock can also be expressive in itself. While the speed of cutting appears, particularly in dialogue sequences, to be determined by the pro-filmic event, the meaning of action sequences can be determined by editing. The length of a shot is in part determined by the amount of information within it. However, rapid or slow cutting can convey meaning in itself. Rapid cutting reflects the degree of excitement with a sequence, and cutting speeds can be accelerated to convey mood, so that the viewing of individual shots becomes almost subliminal. Perhaps most famously, the *Psycho*

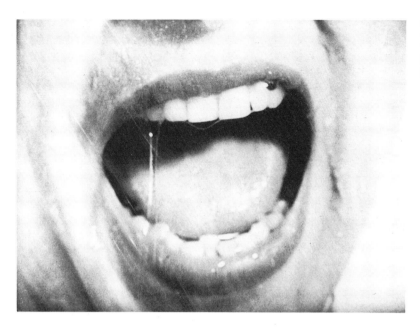

• **Plate 4.10** *Psycho*
(Alfred Hitchcock, US
1960)
Highly fragmented
images

shower scene exemplifies the use of rapid and highly fragmented images to present a climactic moment. The viewer, including the original American film censor, may often claim to see things that were not actually there.

For a discussion on sound and animation see Chapter 8.

Sound

The final element in constructing the 'image' of a film is the soundtrack. Sound as an integral part of a film only developed after 1927. While films were rarely seen in silence (they were sometimes accompanied by a speaker, a piano, organ or small orchestra), the nature of the sound was rarely in the control of the originators of the film and certainly not for all showings of the film. Unlike other innovations such as colour and widescreen, sound, once introduced, became a virtually universal format in a very short period of time. Ed Buscombe argues that the speed of this innovation arose from the need for a more realistic narrative.[22] Certainly, while Warner Bros. saw music as being the appealing part of sound, it was the talking element that attracted the first audiences. The role of the soundtrack was seen as one of reproducing the sounds that would normally be associated with the images, whether the unenunciated words in almost any 'silent movie' or the silent but ringing alarm in Porter's *Life of an American Fireman*. In this sense sound is perceived as diegetic, arising from objects in a scene either inside the frame, or logically related outside the frame – say, for instance, the sound of knocking on a door heard within a house.[23]

However, it would be unwise to assume that a soundtrack can merely be read off from the visual image. Soundtracks are equally 'sound images', constructed and selected in much the same way as the visual image is created. Components on the soundtrack may be simulated at the moment of shooting, but rarely except in a documentary is the soundtrack laid down at the same time. With the development of sound mixing the quality of the track is constructed over a period of time, whether the sound is diegetic or a music track laid over the top of it. A visual image tends to be simplified, Bazin's theory of deep focus notwithstanding – the eye tends to take in different aspects of the image sequentially, whether within or between shots. The ear, by contrast, is able to absorb a number of distinct sound sources simultaneously. Early sound films tended to display a relatively unilateral soundtrack – with dialogue, sound effects and music operating successively. Sound effects, in particular, were only included because they were integral to the narrative (in much the same way as visual effects). By the 1960s, Robert Altman, in particular, was developing soundtracks using the mixing devices available for music sound recording to produce dialogue where individuals interrupted or spoke over other actors (overlapping dialogue), but which also used locations such as the mess-hall in *M*A*S*H**, where conversations could be picked up apparently at random. The logical extension of this were sequences in *Pret-à-Porter*, when, using multi-camera and microphones, the sound and image appear to be collected almost randomly on the set.

Sound can be used to reinforce the continuity of the action. While the image is fragmented by the cuts from one shot to another which we 'know' can hide temporal ellipsis – a character not shown crossing a room for instance – an unbroken soundtrack signifies a continuity of time. This is perhaps best illustrated by an example that deceives the spectator. In an early scene in Scorsese's *Mean Streets*, Charlie (Harvey Keitel) climbs on the stage to perform with an exotic dancer. The soundtrack, playing the Rolling Stones' 'Tell me, (you're coming back)' appears to be running continuously, and yet Charlie appears in consecutive shots to be on the stage and then to be in the audience viewing the dancer, thus challenging the 'reality status' of one of the shots. Our understanding of the narrative certainly suggests on subsequent viewings that the first shot is Charlie's fantasy.

Sound also has a continuity role in establishing links across scenes. Orson Welles, drawing from his radio experience, used sound to bridge between sequences. In *Citizen Kane*, Welles uses Thatcher's 'Merry Christmas' as a bridge between Kane's boyhood greeting and adulthood. Such extravagant devices do not, however, disguise transitions in the way of continuity editing but, rather, celebrate it. More commonly, soundtracks marginally precede the visual image as a preparation for what we are about to see. Sound can also access experiences not immediately evident to the viewer. In *Psycho*, Marion Crane 'remembers', while driving along, the demands of her boss to deposit the money which she has purloined. More problematically she also 'hears' the discovery of the theft of the money and the reaction of her boss and the man she has robbed. The latter sound must at the moment of hearing be a projection of the sound which she could not in reality possibly hear, as she dies before the office is opened.

Sound can also be used to direct us into the past through the use of the voiceover as in *Mildred Pierce*, where Mildred takes us back on three occasions as part of her confession in the police station. Voiceovers, while providing a seemingly useful device to accelerate storytelling, to comment on the action and to admit us into the thoughts of the protagonists in the way of a novelist, are rarely used in feature films, and even then sparingly. A flashback sequence once introduced is normally allowed to return to a conventional mode in which the visual narrative is dominant. Martin Scorsese maintains a voiceover throughout *GoodFellas*, in keeping with its presentation as a 'true life' filmic representation of the life of a sub-Mafia wise guy. Yet the voiceover narrative appears often to be contradicted by the visual narrative, at the very least suggesting Henry's explanation and indeed control of the narrative is partial. At one stage he even loses control of the voiceover, which is taken over by his wife.

A predominant form of sound, and indeed the original function of soundtracks, is the use of non-diegetic music. Primarily music is used to inform the audience of appropriate emotional responses or, having established a response, to enhance it. The emotional pull of music and its high level of connotative meaning allow these processes to operate almost subliminally. While the impact of the *Psycho* shower scene can be attributed to the rapid cutting (described on pp. 112–3), it can equally be attributed to

Bernard Hornmann's 'shrieking strings', not least because they are a magnified reprise of Marion Crane's growing hysteria as she drives the car in the heavy rain. With the general denial of the use of voiceover to provide 'inner thoughts', and given the stress on the surface reality of the classic realist film, music appears to give us direct access to the emotions of the characters.

Music also plays the role of 'confirming' the emotional response of the spectator, seemingly leading us to a particular way of seeing a sequence, or at any rate editing a 'preferred reading' of the image. As such it can be seen as a way of anchoring meaning, eliminating ambiguities of response. In this sense music is often seen to be a final track. Indeed the adding of the sound to a pre-existing image and diegetic soundtrack, whether Miles Davis improvising to *Lift to the Scaffold* or a 'classical' orchestra playing a carefully choreographed score, is the more common method of construction. However, whether the final soundtrack or similar, music may be used at the editing state as a rhythmic device to inform the pace of the cutting. Sergio Leone describes the cast and crew of *Once Upon a Time in the West*, 'throughout the shooting schedules, listening to the recording [Morricone's score] acting with the music, following its rhythms and suffering its aggravating qualities, which grind the nerve'.[24]

Sound effects are normally perceived as part of the narrative realism, authenticating the images and informing the narrative attention. At the beginning of *Mildred Pierce* we hear gunshots while viewing the exterior of the beach house, only to cut to the conse-quential dying body of the victim. The denial of the image of the murderer, either at the moment of shooting or the subsequent reaction shot, is a key to the remaining narrative when the murderer is revealed. Increasingly, sound effects have come to be used to evoke mood. Peripheral sound can be used to establish the wider environment. Hospital or police precinct movies will normally feature telephone rings, not as a cue to the protagonist lifting the receiver and furthering the narrative, but to create other unseen and unrecorded narratives occurring at the same time, or simply to invoke the busyness of the location. David Lynch in *Eraserhead* extends this to a non-specific industrial background sound, permeating a number of interior domestic scenes and establishing without elaborate visual images the quality of the environment. The distinc-tion between non-diegetic music and sound effects can become blurred with the electronic production of both. At the beginning of *Nightmare on Elm Street* we are presented with a dream sequence involving a chase among the furnaces. What sounds to be modernist, horror film mood music also includes human sighs, muffled screams and the mechanical sounds relating to the working of furnaces, all integrated into a seamless music/soundtrack, and only loosely linked to the visual images.

Music may also be used to identify character (for example, themes associated with particular performers in *Once Upon a Time in the West* and *Dr Zhivago*), locations and time. In *GoodFellas*, Scorsese uses an elaborate soundtrack with some forty-two tracks, a mixture of American commercial ballads and rock music, Italian opera and traditional songs. The music is used to contrast the Italian-American from the American-Italian and to identify age distinctions between the protagonists. It is also used to delineate the time of the action in a movie which tells a story with a twenty-five year time span, but using only limited changes in the appearance of the characters.

NARRATIVE

Throughout our consideration of the components and coding that make up film, there has been explicit the idea of a narrative – the idea that films have a primary function of telling a story. The images are organised and are made sense of around this function.

*See Chapter 12
pp. 382–8 for a discus-
sion on narrative in
Indian Cinema.*

This is particularly true of the feature film, which is developed, given a 'treatment' in terms of its plot line, and this is perceived as being what a film is 'about'.

It may be useful to start with distinctions between parts of the narrative process that are sometimes confused. There is a distinction between the story that is represented, and the representation of it that is perceived by the spectator. The story, referred to by the Russian literary theorist, Shklosky, as the 'fabula', is the basic succession of events arranged in a chronological order. A film summary, appearing alongside a review in a magazine such as *Sight and Sound* comprises the fabula. However while this is in itself a form of narrative, it is not the narrative of the film itself. In many instances the summary as it appears bears little relationship to our experiences in trying to make sense of a film, particularly one like *Trainspotting* with a fractured style of storytelling. However it would be wrong to see the fabula as some kind of raw material available to the film-maker before a film is made. As spectators, we attempt to reconstruct the fabula from the film as we view it. In some instances, for example Luis Buñuel's and Salvador Dali's *Un chien andalou*, our wish to place a film into a simple cause-and-effect chain can get in the way of our understanding.

The second term that is used to describe narration is the plot, or syuzhet. The syuzhet works on the story by giving the events a logic. In particular the events are linked in a causal way, for instance being derived from character traits and their relationship with events that have occurred. In Ang Lee's *The Ice Storm*, a synopsis of the film ends with 'Ben (Kevin Kline) bursts into tears'. The syuzhet of the film has been devoted to an examination of two affluent families and their fragile personalities, confronted with a particular set of events: a wife-swapping party, teenage sexual experimentation, and the death of the son in the storm. We are led to make sense of the bursting into tears from the relation of these components. Equally the syuzhet constructs the fabula in a particular temporal order and with specific spatial reference. This construction is not merely the filling-in of the details of time and space from the fabula, but establishes the relationship between the events. *The Ice Storm*, for instance, starts with its ending (the morning after the storm), and then tells us what happened up to that moment, but eschews any of the conventional signifiers of the flashback, such as the dissolve. This technique reinforces a sense of inevitability in the actions and reactions presented – we know how it is all going to end. Again while the two families are presented as neighbours, the houses are significantly apart, separated by a woodland path, enabling actions such as adultery in the two houses to be distinctive and unknown to the other. Like the fabula, the syuzhet, is in itself media-free. However the syuzhet may in many circumstances direct the film-maker towards particular effects.

Finally we need to consider those aspects of narrative that are film specific. These are the elements that we have already considered in this chapter: the use of editing (and in particular continuity editing), the use of *mise en scène* in its widest sense and the use of sound. The spectator who is both plot literate (i.e. who understands the conventions of plotting derived from the nineteenth-century novel) and film literate (i.e. has an understanding of the codes of cinema) will try to make sense of a narrative film. As spectators, we attempt to absorb a succession of on-screen events as a continuum, as activities occurring in particular settings, and as unified by the organisation of time and causation. In so doing we try to fit our experiences into formulae or templates that we already understand, in order to recreate for ourselves the individual fabula of the film. The closer we are able to fit the individual film into our existing templates, the easier it is for us to 'understand'.

*For further discussion on
film audience and spec-
tatorship see Chapters 5
and 9.*

The cinema has often drawn its plots and, to some extent, its storytelling strategies from literature, most notably the novel. Work on film narrative has therefore often drawn from work on other media, notably literary criticism, expressing an interest in the similarities and differences in the ways stories are told in different media.

At the simplest level, narrative analysis is concerned with the extent to which those things that we see make sense. It is assumed that those elements that we see cohere in some way, that they are part of a whole. While all elements of an image will not be of equal importance, there is a supposition that if a film draws attention to something it will have a consequence in the development of the story. One of the pleasures of a film such as *The Usual Suspects* is the attempt by the spectator to determine what are the important components or 'clues' from among the 'red herrings'. By contrast, in *North by Northwest*, Roger Thornhill lights a cigarette for Eve Kendall using a personalised matchbook bearing the initials 'ROT'. The significance of this artefact is marked by a conversation ('what does the "O" stand for?' – 'nothing') signifying a man with nothing at the centre. Yet, at the level of the story, the matchbook re-emerges at the end when Thornhill uses the matches to alert Eve of his presence in the villain VanDamm's house. In general terms all that is of significance in the narrative has a subsequent conse- quence. Narrative develops on the basis of a chain of cause-and-effect. An event happens and is shown to have (likely) consequences. As experienced film-goers, we learn to expect and anticipate this chain, or any rate to recognise the causal links when they are made. At the simplest level these links are consecutive, the effect from one cause becoming the cause of the next link, as for instance the succession of trials facing Indiana Jones in the search for the Holy Grail in *Raiders of the Lost Ark*. However, the example from *North by Northwest* illustrates that causal links can operate over a longer period, with other plot devices intervening.

Narrative involves the viewer in making sense of what is seen, asking questions of what we see and anticipating the answers. In particular, narrative invites us to ask both what is going to happen next and when and how will it all end. Narrative operates on the tension between our anticipation of likely outcomes drawn from genre conventions and the capacity to surprise or frustrate our expectations. Some sixty minutes into *Dirty Harry* we appear to have the final link of the cause–effect chain as Inspector Callaghan arrests the serial killer Scorpio after a chase across a football field. Yet the force entailed in the arrest becomes, in turn, the cause of Scorpio's release, and the beginning of a new cause-and- effect chain leading to an apprehension from which Scorpio can never be released.

While film narrative can be viewed as a number of cause-and-effect links, it may also be perceived in terms of larger structures incorporating the entire film. Todorov sees the start of narrative as a point of stable equilibrium, where everything is satisfied, calm and normal. This stability is disrupted by some kind of force which creates a state of dise- quilibrium. It is only possible to re-create equilibrium through action directed against the disruption. However, the consequence of this reaction is to change the world of the narrative and/or the characters so that the final state of equilibrium is not the same as the initial state. Although this analysis is a simplified one, it is a useful starting-point – delineating the differences between individual films or genres.

For a discussion of Todorov, narrative and genre, see Chapter 6.

The initial equilibrium state of the film is often very brief, little more than an establishing shot or, at most, an establishing sequence. Our expectation of narrative disruption, together with our capacity to 'read' the equilibrium state rapidly, has led to shorter and shorter equilibrium sequences. The beginning of *Jaws* involves a brief scene of teenagers on a beach enjoying a night-time party before two of their number engage in a swim dramatically interrupted by the shark attack. Horror films, in particular, have become increasingly characterised by immediate disruption, as for instance in the dream sequence at the beginning of *Nightmare on Elm Street* referred to on p.115. Even when they return to a temporary equilibrium (the girl wakes up), this is an unstable state capable of easy disrup- tion. *Vertigo* commences with a particularly disruptive act, a chase across the rooftops, culminating in Scottie's loss of nerve and consequent retirement from the police force. If there is a stable equilibrium state, it is implicit and occurs before the movie begins.

See the case study on Jaws, Chapter 2, pp. 34–7.

Initial equilibrium states are also particularly unstable in melodrama. It is clear from the beginning of the flashback sequence in *Mildred Pierce*, in effect the beginning of the

• **Plate 4.11** *Vertigo*
(Alfred Hitchcock, US
1958)
A disruptive act

10344-12

narrative, that this is not a harmonious family setting, despite the iconography of the mother baking cakes and wearing an apron. The nature of Mildred's relationship with Vida suggests that trouble is in store, quite apart from the somewhat incongruous image of Joan Crawford as a petit bourgeois housewife. As a consequence the apparent cause of the disruption – Bert's decision to leave the family – is in no way an unexpected disruption to a stable state.

Equally in the 'romance' genre, the initial equilibrium is signified by an absence or a 'lack' (of a partner) by one, Richard Gere in *Pretty Woman*, or two, Billy Crystal and Meg Ryan in *When Harry Met Sally*. The initial equilibrium is perceived as integrally unstable, to be resolved within the movie, and the 'disruption' involves the first meeting of the characters, usually disharmoniously, in which the misunderstandings of motive are the beginning of the resolution.

Disruptions similarly are variable, although they tend to be genre specific. Action genres are often disrupted by an external threat or raid, for instance the raid of the Indians in *The Searchers*, or the arrival of the vengeful Max Cady in *Cape Fear*. The leading characters may be forced to disrupt their normal lifestyle due to a chance experience – for example, Jack Lemmon and Tony Curtis try to pass as female musicians after viewing the St Valentine's Day massacre in *Some Like it Hot*. Within the genres the disruption may be equally important to the characters and their drive towards some particular goal. Travis Bickle in *Taxi Driver* is not so much driven into disequilibrium by external events (his meetings with Betsy, the appearance of Iris and Sport in his cab) as by his determined drive to transform the world.

The actions to restore equilibrium, of course, become the narrative drive of the movie. Such re-equilibrating processes are resisted, whether by the protagonists or by chance events. The pleasure associated with conventional narrative is, at least in part, related to our recognition of the strategies employed to delay the pleasure. Opposition to equilibrium can be attributed to the 'villain', a function within the narrative, and the stronger the 'villain', the greater the pleasure in the triumph of the 'hero'. This will often involve a number of moments where there appears to be a temporary equilibrium – involving the seeming defeat of the hero (the 'cliff-hanger') or, more rarely, of the villain. Since the 1970s the horror film has developed the temporary equilibrium state of the defeat of the villain at the end of the movie, only for him to reappear in subsequent movies (for example, the Hammer *Dracula* series, *Halloween* and *Friday the 13th*). The struggle to resolve, while usually explicit in the revenge movie, in other genres may be present and obvious to the viewer, but not to the protagonists. In romantic comedy (*Bringing Up Baby*, *What's Up Doc*, *When Harry Met Sally*) the resistance to an early resolution comes from the characters themselves who are unaware of the mutual attraction (of opposites) that is 'obvious' to the viewer.

The final resolution again differs between films. There is a drive towards the 'happy ending' – we assume that Hugh Grant and Andie MacDowell will end *Four Weddings and a Funeral* in domesticity rather than death. Films often end with an 'establishing' long shot which is similar to the one with which they began – even where this involves other characters with no place in the new equilibrium 'riding off into the sunset' (*Shane*, *The Searchers*). Occasionally such an ending appears ironic, the conflicts within the movie are seen as ultimately unresolvable in the way that conventional narrative

• **Plate 4.12** *The Searchers* (John Ford, US 1956)
No place in the new equilibrium

demands. At the end of *All that Heaven Allows* a relationship between Rock Hudson and Jane Wyman, separated by age and class and resisted by family and community, is allowed to develop, but at the cost of a fractured leg. However, the film ends with a kitsch shot of a baby deer playing in the snow, suggesting that the resolution is no more than the false harmony of a traditional Christmas card. The 'happy ending' of *Taxi Driver* similarly strains belief. The European art movie and American 'independent' cinema, while ending with a resolution, is more often associated with character development and a recognition by protagonists of the inevitability of an unsatisfactory state of affairs.

A more elaborate analysis of narrative structure has been associated with the work of Vladimir Propp. Drawing on an analysis of Russian folk-tales, he concluded that regardless of individual differences in terms of plot, characters and setting, such narratives would share common structural features. There were the functions of particular characters: 'the villain', 'the donor', 'the helper', 'the princess', 'her father', 'the dispatcher', 'the hero' and 'the false hero'. There were also thirty-one narrative units descriptive of particular action, for instance: 'a member of a family leaves home', 'a prohibition or rule is imposed on the hero', 'this prohibition is broken', etc. The characters were seen as stable elements from story to story, despite individual variations of appearance or idiosyncrasies of personality. The narrative units were sufficient to describe all of the stories, although not all units appear in all of the stories, but when they do appear they are in the prescribed order. While it might appear that such narrative structures are specific to a given genre or culture, the model has proved adaptable to Hollywood movies, such as *Sunset Boulevard*, *Kiss Me Deadly* and *North by Northwest*. They inevitably had to be 'translated' from the original. For instance, in Peter Wollen's article on *North by Northwest*, Eve Kendall, a double agent, becomes a princess. However, the accounts do have a degree of credibility, and at the very least have the function of making the analysis of a narrative 'strange'. The very force of narrative often makes it difficult for even the trained viewer to stand back and observe what is really going on.

See Chapter 6 for a discussion of Propp in relation to narrative and genre.

The Proppean analysis does, however, depend on the existence of a single narrative operating in a linear way. The examples chosen to illustrate the analysis are characterised by a strong central storyline – although one of them, *Sunset Boulevard*, does have a framing device. Even mainstream movies have tended to develop a system of subplots, often with a 'romantic' subject subservient to the action plot. While this is recognised within Propp – the resolution involves a wedding as a consequence of the success the hero has had in the action plot – the main plot and the subplot often exist in a state of tension. Police movies have increasingly stressed a tension between the demands of the job, the successful solution of a crime and the satisfaction of the hero's romantic and domestic needs. The very principle of a linear narrative is being increasingly challenged – and not merely outside the mainstream. Robert Altman's *Short Cuts* combines a number of short stories, but with many of the characters appearing in more than one story, who have, in Proppean terms, alternative character functions. Quentin Tarantino's *Pulp Fiction* extends this technique, using three stories with overlapping characters, but also inserts the final resolution – Bruce Willis with girlfriend riding off on his motorbike, the final moment in the time of the narrative – around two-thirds of the way through the film. *Pulp Fiction* does not conform to mainstream narrative structure, and it is only comprehensible because we as viewers hold on to an understanding of narrative and formal conventions through our experience of the mainstream.

Todorov and Propp's work stresses the simplicity of film narratives which are media-specific. In particular, the classic realist text appears to narrate itself. Despite the example of *GoodFellas* (see p. 114), the film does not usually appear to have a narrator, an 'I' who tells the story. Novels can either have a 'teller', a character or observer within the text, or an author, who by implication has privileged access to some of the characters. Similarly, in much television news or documentary coverage there is either a voiceover or a presenter who operates as the authoritative voice. In the absence of a presenter, the narrative itself is seen as the embodiment of the truth of what is happening, no matter how far-fetched.

For further study

Consider any mainstream Hollywood film with which you are familiar:

What is the initial state of equilibrium, how is it disrupted and how is it resolved?

Try to identify how individual characters fit into Propp's typology of 'hero', 'villain', 'princess' etc.

List the oppositions that exist within the film.

To what extent can the film be considered 'realist'?

ALTERNATIVE NARRATIVES

The concentration in this chapter has been on mainstream cinema. However, there has always been a tradition in European cinema for the production of films that challenge or at least subvert the conventions of the mainstream. Peter Wollen has distinguished a tradition of counter-cinema exemplified in the work of Jean-Luc Godard, which is contrasted with mainstream in a succession of oppositions as follows.

See Chapter 9, p. 274, for a discussion on feminism and its relation to the avant-garde and counter-cinema. See Chapter 14 for a discussion of New German Cinema and its attempt to challenge Hollywood cinema. For reference to experimental animation see Chapter 8.

Narrative transitivity versus narrative intransitivity

In mainstream cinema there is a flow of action with a clear developmental pattern and a cause-and-effect chain. In counter-cinema the narrative is subject to a series of breaks where the narrative's hold on the spectator is broken. This can be in the form of inserted titles, which were eliminated from mainstream cinema with the coming of sound, or the presence of scenes that either break with the narrative drive or style of the film. In *Natural Born Killers* we are presented with the story through a multiplicity of devices or forms; cartoon, situation comedy (including canned laughter), dance and sequences constructed in a documentary format. The culmination of this is a film in which the veracity of anything we see is challenged.

Identification versus estrangement

In mainstream cinema we are drawn into the film through the leading protagonists, sharing their experiences and learning to see the situations within the film from their point of view. In counter-cinema we are not expected to be in thrall, and indeed are distanced from the leading characters. This may be because they are presented as less than attractive as people, or because the performers are seen to step out of character, to address us directly and to reflect on the film and the characters they are playing. Karel Reisz's *The French Lieutenant's Woman* uses the device of a film within a film to allow the *actors,* played by Jeremy Irons and Meryl Streep, to reflect on the circumstances of their characters within the costume drama which is the main narrative.

• *Plate 4.13* The French
Lieutenant's Woman
(Karel Reisz, UK 1981)
Actors playing actors:
Jeremy Irons and Meryl
Streep as actors
discussing the plight of
their characters

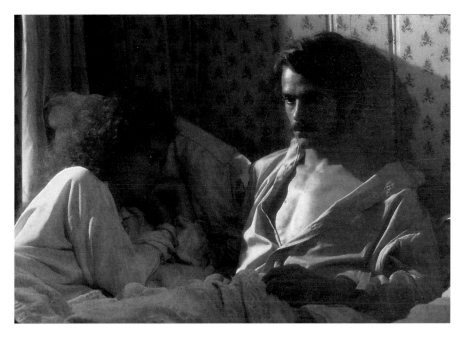

Transparency versus foregrounding

In mainstream cinema the film-maker hides the work of film production (see *RoboCop*, p.92–4). In counter-cinema the film-maker may draw attention to the processes involved by, for instance, talking to the camera operator and allow the conversation to remain on the soundtrack. In Ingmar Bergman's *Persona*, the film starts by showing film stock running through the projector. Bergman then cuts to the numerical countdown that appears in the leader tape on all films, but which is never shown to the audience.

Simple versus multiple diegesis

In mainstream cinema there is a single coherent storyline with a drive towards uniformity; the soundtrack is compatible with the visual images, and all disruptions, such as flashbacks or scene changes, are absorbed into a single linear narrative. In counter-cinema different narratives can not only appear within the same film, but indeed can be contradictory. In Kurosawa's *Rashomon*, the same event, a rape and a killing, is told and shown from the point of view of four characters, without in the end privileging any of the four contradictory accounts over the others.

Closure versus aperture

In the mainstream, cinema narratives are designed as self-contained worlds, both understandable in themselves but also resolving all the issues raised within the film. In counter-cinema, the film will make reference to a world outside itself, for instance by referring to other films or experiences, which the spectator may or may not be able to bring to the viewing. Consequently, the experience of the individual spectator cannot be determined by the author of the film. In many of Godard's films, characters will read extracts from books without placing them for the spectator. The sense we make of these extracts, for example whether we are meant to

• **Plates 4.14 and 4.15**
Rashomon (Akira
Kurosawa, Japan 1950)
Alternative realities: the
same scene within
Rashomon replayed with
different accounts

approve of them, will depend on our cultural background and whether we can contextualise them. In this sense counter-cinema films may be more 'open' to interpretation than the mainstream text.

Finally, Wollen sees the role of mainstream films as being to produce pleasurable fictions. Hollywood films are created to be consumed and enjoyed, and the contradictions of everyday life magically resolved in the happy ending. Counter-cinema, by contrast, is designed to give an 'unpleasurable' reality, presenting a non-narrative, non-escapist world, whose contradictions have to be resolved in real life. While Wolllen's presentation of oppositional tendencies was highly apposite in the 1970s when it was written and when there was a distinctive counter-cinema shown in an art house circuit and a relatively monolithic mainstream cinema from the remnants of the studio system, it is less clear whether the distinction can be drawn today. Many of the illustrative examples above were quoted for their accessibility, and could not be regarded as a pure form of counter-cinema. One of the hit films of 1998, *Sliding Doors*, has a fractured narrative with two alternative fabula dependent on a chance event – whether the leading (female) character catches a tube train or not. The alternative narrative is foregrounded by a reverse action sequence before she is allowed to get into the second account. The film then cuts between the two narratives, sometimes privileging one rather than the other. It denies the viewer an insight to a preferred reality. Due to the fairly rapid scene changes and the absence of editing devices such as fades or cuts to black to inform us of changes in storyline, the film depends on both a familiarity with *mise en scène*, specifically different haircuts, and the constant dredging of our memory as to where we last left the other story, in order for us to make sense of what we see.

□ CASE STUDY 3: *IF...* – AN ALTERNATIVE TEXT (1968)

In 1968, Lindsay Anderson, after working in the subsidised theatre, as a film critic and producing both documentaries and 'social realist' fiction films, made *If...*. It was financed by a major studio, Paramount, who at that stage were interested in investing in British filmmakers. Although based on an existing book, *Crusaders* by David Sherwin, it is nevertheless a highly personal film using for its locations and backdrop Anderson's own public school background. Furthermore, the film draws upon Anderson's interest in Brechtian theatre, and is an attempt to explore the 'alienation effect' in a cinematic setting. The film, however, was targeted at a commercial audience, and rested upon the understandings of a mainstream audience. Far from producing a detached, analytical spectator, the film produced in its contemporary audiences an involved and committed response.

See Chapter 11 for more details on British films of the 1960s.

There are two immediately strange devices, disturbing for a viewer inbued in realist text. The film is divided into sections, each with a heading rather like the chapter heading of a book. Since the coming of sound such disruption is rarely to be seen except as a comic effect. More speciously, however, the film stock changes from colour to black and white at frequent intervals within the film. Normally these changes are between scenes, but they sometimes occur within sequences. Such shifts provoke a need in the viewer to explain, possibly to discover, the 'code'. Anderson's explanation at the time was simply that of budgetary constraints, not enough money to film in colour throughout. Whatever the status of that explanation, the consequence is to foreground the process of film production throughout the film.

I would like to briefly consider the sequence 'Ritual and romance' that occurs about halfway through the film. The sequence in plot terms involves the transgression of school rules – not to attend the house rugby match, to escape out of bounds, to steal a motorbike and to meet a young woman in a transport café.

• **Plate 4.16** *If...*
(Lindsay Anderson, UK
1968)
A mixture of filmic
styles

The sequence involves an approximate balance of colour and black and white shots, but also a mixture of filmic styles. Although narrative cinema has involved a range of stylistic practices, a Frank Tashlin/Jerry Lewis comedy, Spaghetti Westerns, British drama-documentary, there is normally a characteristic unity of style within a film. However, even within this sequence we get a black and white documentary realist sequence in the school chapel, predominantly long shot; an accurate slow-motion sequence with a boy performing on parallel bars from the admiring gaze of his lover; a colour sequence of a performance on a motorbike by three characters to popular music; a long shot 'candid camera' sequence; as well as sequences filmed with conventional narrative strategies involving continuity editing and eye-line matches. There are also variable uses of sound, a variety of microphone positions sometimes giving 'tight' sound designed to clearly pick up dialogue, but elsewhere a distant and echoey sound as if from a documentary. Music is fragmented and inter-cut with silence. Sound is overlaid from one scene to another in such a way as to draw attention to itself – yet at the same time the narrative appears to be constructed along a conventional cause-and-effect chain. The rebels are instructed to attend the game; cut to the game, and they are not there; cut to the town where they are seen drifting; cut to motorcycle shop where they steal a bike; cut to the open road where they escape; and cut to the transport café. The transport café scene commences with narrative continuity. The rebels continue to behave in the boorish and chauvinist way we have learnt to expect from the narrative so far. The female waitress responds by slapping the face of Travis as a response to his advances. He turns to the jukebox on which he plays (or maybe does not) the African mass which he has on his record-player back at school. In the following sequence the waitress appears to make her own animal advances and after a jump-cut they appear naked play/fighting/loving on the café floor. They then appear fully clothed and, unfazed by their experience, resume drinking the still warm cup of tea.

This scene problematises the 'reality status' of what we see. Do we accept the truth of what appears in front of us, despite both the improbability and the continuity breaks, or do we read the sexual encounter as 'only a fantasy'? However, if we attempt to read this as a fantasy then the status of the rest of the scene is thrown into question. Given that there is no consequence from the theft of the bike is this also a fantasy, despite its realistic depiction? If this scene is a fantasy how do we read the subsequent scenes where the young woman appears within the school setting? While the sequence subverts the process of the classic realist narrative, it is none the less only comprehensible on the basis of our knowledge of this process.

• **Plate 4.17** *If...*
(Lindsay Anderson, UK 1968)
Do we believe what we see?

For further study
Consider any film outside the mainstream:

How do Wollen's categories of counter-cinema apply to the film?
To what extent does the film frustrate you in your wish to draw pleasure from it?
Do you regard the film as realistic or unrealistic? How would you justify your opinion?
What do you think was the intention behind making the film in the way it was (and not in the classic realist way)?

NOTES

1 Auguste and Louis Lumière are credited with developing a lightweight movie camera and a system of projecting moving images on the screen. They gave their first public projection of single-shot films on 28 December 1895.

2 Warner Bros. 1929.

3 For a full account of the process of viewing film and its parallels with the process of dreaming, see the chapter on 'Cinema as image and sound' in John Ellis, *Visible Fictions: Cinema, Television, Video* (Routledge, London, 1982).

4 Directed by Paul Verhoeven, available as a Virgin video.

5 Georges Méliès, a pioneer of film, developed short narrative films as an entertainment within magic shows.

6 See Noel Burch, *Theory of Film Practice* (Secker & Warburg, London, 1973); also the film *Correction Please* and the accompanying booklet, published by the Arts Council of Great Britain, which reconstructs the development of film language in the first decade of the century.

7 Thomas Edison developed a peepshow system of viewing moving pictures which predated the Lumière system of projection.

8 Griffith directed about 400 single reel (eleven-minute) films between 1908 and 1913 and subsequently developed the full-length feature film with *The Birth of a Nation* (1915).

9 This title would seem to suggest an external narrative commentary – a 'primitive' device that was destined to disappear, though see *GoodFellas* on p. 114. In the IMR the narrator is absent – the story 'tells itself'.

10 One of the original Lumière shorts.

11 There are a number of examples of work relating to *mise en scène*, particularly by those critics involved in *Movie* magazine. One accessible example is Victor Perkins, 'The Cinema of Nicholas Ray' in I.F. Cameron (ed.), *Movie Reader* (November Books, London, 1972).

12 Jim Kitses, *Horizons West* (Thames & Hudson, London, 1969).

13 The concept of anchorage was developed by Roland Barthes and has been particularly used to show the way that captions are used in magazines to limit the choice of meanings of a particular photographic image.

14 See André Bazin, *What is Cinema?*, Vol. 1: *Ontology and Language* (Editions du Cerf, Paris, 1958). There are also many summaries of Bazin on realism, for instance, Andrew Tudor, *Theories of Film* (Secker & Warburg for the BFI, London, 1974).

15 For a straightforward account of the 'grammar' of film shots see John Izod's *Reading the Screen: An Introduction to Film Studies*, (Longman Harlow; York Press, Beirut, 1984).

16 Lev Kuleshov (1899–1970) attempted to prove that the meanings of shots could be changed by altering the juxtaposition of shots. This involved a close-up of an actor playing a prisoner, which was then linked to two different shots: a bowl of soup and the open door of freedom. The audience were said to be convinced that the actor's expression was different even though the same shot was used.

17 For an account of cross-cut editing and parallel editing in the Early Cinema see D. Bordwell, J. Staiger and K. Thompson, *The Classical Hollywood Cinema* (Routledge & Kegan Paul, London, 1985).

18 A full account can be found in Karl Reisz and Gavin Millar's *The Technique of Film Editing* (Focal Press, London, 1953), but also can be traced in any beginner's guide to film editing.

19 In K. Bordwell and K. Thompson, *Film Art* (Knopf, New York, 1990).

20 *Who's That Knocking at My Door?*, directed by Martin Scorsese, was released under a number of titles between 1965 and 1970. The reference here is to the 1969 version.

21 Quotation marks around Hollywood are often used to indicate the commercial American cinema which is not necessarily produced in a particular geographical location.

22 E. Buscombe, 'Sound and Colour', *Jump Cut* (no. 17, 1977).

23 Diegesis refers to the world of the narrative. In this sense anything that is not 'happening' within the story, whether an image or a sound used as a commentary of what is going on, is 'non-diegetic'. See below for the use of non-diegetic music.

24 Cited in Christopher Frayling, *Spaghetti Westerns* (I.B. Tauris, London, 1998).

FURTHER READING

Three introductory texts of increasing level of difficulty

Turner, G. *Film as Social Practice* (Routledge, London, 1988)

Andrew, D. *Concepts in Film Theory* (Oxford University Press, Oxford, 1984)

Lapsley, R. and Westlake, M. *Film Theory: An Introduction* (Manchester University Press, Manchester, 1988)

General works

Bazin, A. *What is Cinema?* Vol 1, *Ontology and Language* (Editions du Cerf, Paris, 1958)

Bordwell, D., Staiger, J. and Thompson, K. *The Classical Hollywood Cinema* (Routledge & Kegan Paul, London, 1985)
An encyclopaedic and scholastic look at the development of film and narrative in Hollywood. Its wide set of references to films of the first fifty years of cinema is daunting but stimulating.

Bordwell, K. and Thompson, K. *Film Art* (Knopf, New York, 1990)
Probably the most comprehensive text, with a wide range of examples.

Burch, N. *Theory of Film Practice* (Secker & Warburg, London, 1973)

Cameron, I.F. (ed.) 'The Cinema of Nicholas Ray', in *Movie Reader* (November Books, London, 1972)

Cook, D. *History of Narrative Film* (Norton, New York, 1991). Fluctuates from detailed analysis of particular 'significant' films to lists of films outside Hollywood mainstream.

Ellis, J. *Visible Fictions*: *Cinema, Television and Video* (Routledge & Kegan Paul, London, 1982)
A provocative account of film and TV which requires a full read rather than dipping in.

Izod, J. *Reading the Screen: An Introduction to Film Studies* (Longman, Harlow; York Press, Beirut, 1984)

Kitses, J. *Horizons West* (Thames & Hudson, London, 1969)

Tudor, A. *Theories of Film* (Secker & Warburg for the British Film Institute, London, 1974)

In a sense almost any viewing would be applicable to work on this chapter. Nevertheless, the 'non-obtrusiveness' of much mainstream cinema creates difficulties in observing the processes whereby meaning is created. This suggests that initial work on form and narrative is perhaps most productive with work characterised by 'excess'.

At the risk of appearing to be an unreconstructed auteurist, this might suggest the work of the following directors as a possible way in: Altman, Argento, Bertolucci, Bresson, Coen brothers, Fuller, Hitchcock, Jamusch, Lynch, Minnelli, Murnau, Ophuls, Powell and Pressburger, Ray, Scorsese, Sirk, Sternberg, Tarantino, Vidor and Welles.

A more austere approach would extend this list to include perhaps more self-consciously 'modernist' directors: Anderson, Buñuel, Eisenstein, Godard, Oshima, Potter, Resnais and Straub.

http://www.filmeducation.org
Useful for investigating topics discussed in this chapter

Chapter 5

The film spectator

Patrick Phillips

■ Introduction: spectators, audiences, screenings   130

■ What we can learn from Early Cinema   132

■ Some characteristics of the spectator of film and cultural theory   136

☐ More on the spectator as 'subject'   143

☐ More on communication models and response   147

☐ Case study 1: *Pulp Fiction*   148

☐ Some notes on spectatorship and regulation   157

■ Notes   159

■ Further reading   160

☐ The film spectator

INTRODUCTION: SPECTATORS, AUDIENCES, SCREENINGS

See Chapter 6.

The most obvious reasons for studying film are concerned with issues of meaning and response. In a textual study we attempt to establish what are the film's meanings, and consider how these meanings are communicated, for instance through generic conventions or star images. In a response study, we ask how and why we react as we do, both emotionally and intellectually. We may extend this to consider reasons for the uniformity or diversity of reactions among a group of people.

Film studies has distinguished between the response of social groups, collectives of people called *audiences*, and the response of the individual, called the spectator. Most of this chapter will concentrate on ways of thinking about the individual as spectator. However, the importance of audience studies will also be recognised.

Film theory, in assigning great importance to spectatorship since the late 1960s, has tended towards three working assumptions:

1   spectatorship is something that happens in traditional cinema auditoria
2   the audience ceases to exist for the individual spectator for the duration of the film
3   spectator study concentrates on the consumption of films that are 'popular' and are geared towards providing typical forms of cinematic pleasure: spectacle, emotion, plot, resolution, within conventional narrative and generic forms

Let us consider each of the above.

Spectatorship is something that happens in traditional cinema auditoria

See Chapter 4, p. 92, for further discussion of how we watch a film.

You or I are referred to as spectators when we position ourselves in front of a screen and engage in watching a film. As a spectator, you or I are assumed to be alone in the presence of the film – even if we are surrounded by other people.

This immediately begs a number of questions:

What kind of screen? A screen in a cinema receiving a projected image? A television screen transforming electronic signals from an external transmission source or from a video recorder?

What kind of space? A large auditorium more or less completely dark? A screen outdoors? A small screen in a living room with the lights on?

How many and which people are also present? A full cinema auditorium of strangers? A group of friends out together socially? A family at home in front of their television set?

What kind of film? An emotive melodrama in Hollywood tear-jerking style? A reflective and intellectually demanding film, maybe with subtitles?

For an extended discussion of the differences between watching a film in a cinema and watching television, see John Ellis' *Visible Fictions* (Routledge, London, 1992).

The cinema experience is much more completely separated from the rest of our lives than is the act of watching television. We enter a public space having paid an admission charge. We are predisposed to a certain level of investment of ourselves in the film screening – if only because we have paid for it. The fact that we have paid also indicates that we have certain expectations which will further increase our willingness to concentrate. The cinema is, in a peculiar way, both more public and more private than our own homes. As a public place we are offered the chance to enjoy a different set of comforts and facilities from those at home. While the lights are up and the advertisements or trailers are playing, we are aware of the people around us. The popcorn being crunched and the drinks being slurped do not annoy us particularly. When the lights go down and the film credits appear we are suddenly alone with the images on the screen and the sounds coming from the speakers. Now the crunchers and the slurpers run the risk of seriously annoying us – we suddenly realise we want to be alone. (Unless, of course, you are with a special friend and the reason for paying to go into a comfortable darkened space has been motivated by reasons other than wanting to watch a movie!)

The technology of cinema exhibition holds us much more powerfully than does television. The size (and shape) of the screen, the quality of the images, the clarity of the sound all invite much more attention – indeed they demand it. We are held in our comfortable seats; all around us is near-darkness, except for exit signs. We have no control over the film. If we go to the toilet we cannot put the film on pause. Not only that, but we can only engage in the briefest of whispers about what has happened in our absence.

See Chapter 3 for further discussion of film and technology.

If you are in any doubt about the differences between cinema and television film consumption, consider the very significant up-turn in cinema visits at a time when VCRs and multi-channel satellite/cable TV dominate domestic entertainment. The cinema 'experience' is acknowledged as special and different – and is considered to be worth taking seriously as a topic of study.

The audience ceases to exist for the individual spectator for the duration of the film

We have already commented on the dark of the auditorium and about how distracting it can be to become aware of people around us during a film screening. However, the relationship between the spectator and the audience is more complex than this. First, we enter the auditorium as a member of the audience, our expectations possibly enhanced by the chat around us. Second, many people go to the cinema accompanied by one or more other people and their physical proximity is something that cannot easily be put out of our mind. Third, even if alone, we are conscious of shared reactions during a screening; sometimes this takes an audible form – laughter, groans, screams – any of which can be infectious, altering the individual spectator's response.

On a broader front we can say that we exist as audiences for a movie well away from the cinema. We are constructed as members of a 'potential' audience in at least two ways. We become exposed to the promotional and marketing hype designed to create expectations. We are also drawn into conversation about issues relating to a movie which may be circulating within our culture, resulting particularly from the profile the film enjoys in other media. In moving from 'potential' to 'actual' audience member, we have an individual and a collective sense of what we are doing – we are self-aware. After the screening we may well engage in yet another expression of audience membership as we discuss our reactions in a variety of contexts – on the bus, in the pub – maybe for days afterwards.

Nevertheless, for better or for worse, theories of spectatorship have tended to isolate the self that exists more or less alone with the film for the duration of its screening. We will have more to say about this later.

Spectator study concentrates on the consumption of films that are 'popular' and are geared towards providing typical forms of cinematic pleasure

Most work on spectatorship has focused on the act of engaging with popular main-

Discuss the 'film event' with a group of friends. Consider:

1 What is said about the specific experience of watching a film in a movie auditorium

and

2 How much the experience is enhanced by the ways we engage with the film through the media, with friends, etc. before and after the screening.

stream films. This is partly because so much of the emphasis of film theory was concerned with making sense of Hollywood cinema at the time when spectatorship became an important concept.

Much of film theory evolved from the political left and was characterised by a double-take on popular culture generally. On the one hand, popular culture was seen as having huge potential for harm by feeding people forms of entertainment which did not encourage new ways of seeing and thinking about the world – and thus of changing it. On the other hand, popular culture was seen as the people's culture, and was thus something deserving respect rather than something simply to be rubbished. There have been very interesting shifts within film studies from a model of a 'passive' spectator dangerously controlled by the overwhelming mechanisms and physical presence of the popular film screening. The emphasis is now much more on an 'active' spectator who makes meaning and 'negotiates' within the film in the very act of consuming it. This key debate around the 'active' and 'passive' spectator and the extent to which different kinds of film are likely to produce the one rather than the other will be explored further below.

WHAT WE CAN LEARN FROM EARLY CINEMA

For further discussion of the development of the codes and conventions of Early Cinema, see Chapter 4, pp. 95–8.

Very often the best way of trying to understand something with which we are so familiar that we take it for granted, is to look at how things used to be and speculate on how things might have developed differently. One of the best ways of understanding the relationship between mainstream commercial film and spectatorship is to study how the two evolved together in the period referred to as 'Early Cinema' from around 1895 to 1917.

Film historians tend to agree that by about 1917 nearly all of the fundamental features of what we now consider as mainstream film 'language' were in place. Film had in just twenty years evolved ways of managing time and space, particularly through editing, and of managing the distance between object and audience, particularly through camera movement, which made the experience of cinema very different from the theatre. Though it must also be said that films still very much showed their relationship to popular forms of theatre such as melodrama and vaudeville, especially in storylines and character types.

The evolution of film form

In very early films the camera is static before action and character. This can be accounted for purely by reference to the technical limitations of the equipment. However, there is also an assumption being made about spectator viewing position –

the camera 'eye' assumes the position of a member of the audience sitting in the middle of the stalls of a proscenium arch theatre. The theatre spectator cannot move closer to a key character or observe a key event in more detail. Early films seem particularly clumsy to our eyes in that they often include shots full of people and a variety of action without any guidance as to which action or indeed which character is particularly significant for the development of the plot.

Not only do the earliest films not offer us close-ups but they do not offer in any systematic way the kind of point-of-view shots which we are so familiar with and which we have become so dependent upon to draw us into the action and emotion of an event.

It is useful to list some of the ways in which the spectator began to be drawn in to a particular relationship with the screen through control exercised by camera movement, *mise en scène* and editing:

- camera movement towards and away from an object – usually the camera fixed to a train or car – in order to give the spectator a greater sense of physical involvement
- camera position nearer or further from an object – long, medium and close shots motivated by a concern to 'direct' the spectator's attention and increase engagement with the emotions of characters
- *mise en scène* organised to enhance the meaning and emphasise the significance of particular actors or objects – through positioning, set design, lighting
- the frame of the *mise en scène* exploited to create interest and desire in what cannot be seen beyond the edges of the shot
- editing used as the means by which shots can be organised and, thereby, the means by which the spectators seeing is 'managed', for example:
  - parallel editing so that two events can be followed simultaneously, encouraging the spectator to make and respond to assumed dramatic and thematic connections

For a vivid account of the evolution of film form, see Noel Burch's *Correction Please – or How We Got Into Movies* (1979). This film mixes short films from the period 1895–1903 with Burch's own amusing film which builds up a sequence from the static camera to the close-up and shot-reverse shot. However, some caution is required. Burch is clearly reflecting a specific view of the development of the cinema apparatus and the spectator which is increasingly under challenge. *See pp. 136–7.*

• **Plate 5.1** *The Great Train Robbery* (1903) This still from Porter's *The Great Train Robbery* illustrates the static camera of early silent cinema. For a spectator used to the 'standard' film language established twelve to fourteen years after this film was made, films such as this provide major problems. For example, the static camera does not create the expected involvement or draw attention to significant objects in the frame which might help create narrative clarity.

□ editing used as montage – to encourage a particular interpretation of one shot
by the influence exercised on the spectator's mind by the shots on either side
of it

□ editing used particularly to move the spectator between different points of
view within the *mise en scène*

The 'look' and the 'gaze'
developed as central
concepts in relation to
the control of the spec-
tator. Cinematic looking
has also been associated
with theories of desire
and pleasure, theories
often founded in psycho-
analysis. *(See below,
especially pp. 142–5).*

A way of pulling much of the above together is by reference to the concept of the '*look*'.

The evolution of spectatorship

Early cinema needed to find ways of controlling the look of the spectator, essentially in
order to try to:

■ ensure that the meanings intended by the film's makers were those taken by the
members of the audience

■ replicate for realism of effect the ways in which we engage in the act of looking
outside the cinema

■ provide greater pleasure in the act of looking

*See Chapter 4 for more
on spectatorship in rela-
tion to film form and
narrative.*

It is possible to talk about developments in the use of the camera, *mise en scène* and
editing as ways of controlling the look.

The camera offers a particular 'eye' on the world of the film. This 'eye' may be the
camera as the impersonal storytelling device or it may be the 'eye' of a character within
the film as represented by the camera. These are literally 'points-of-view'. Even when
the camera is not aligned with the viewing position of a particular character but is
'objectively' pointing at a *mise en scène*, the spectator look could be directed by the
looks and glances exchanged by the on-screen characters in order to draw attention to
a significant object or a development in a relationship. Editing allows the spectator to
adopt different viewing positions; to share in an exchange of looks, most commonly in a
shot-reverse-shot dialogue sequence.

One spectator 'effect' of the development of film form is particularly important. It is
the way in which the spectator is drawn into the world of the film, caught inside and
between characters. This is achieved through editing and point-of-view, and results in
the interpellation of the spectator inside the psychic and physical life of the fiction. This
'effect' is at the heart of so many debates around spectatorship and manipulation in
popular cinema.

*For more on interpella-
tion (*not *interpolation),
see section on 'Key
concepts' below.*

Two of the most famous
films featuring
voyeurism are
Hitchcock's *Rear Window*
(1954) and Powell's
Peeping Tom (1960).

Of all the ideological aspects of spectatorship, none have received as much attention as those around notions of *voyeurism* – the look of the peeping Tom, able to see
without being seen. Early cinema very frequently represents the female dissected by the
close-up into a fetishised object of the male look. It is certainly interesting in relation to
ongoing debates around Laura Mulvey's famous 'male camera' proposition, that the
evolution of this out of crude peepshow technology should be so evident from the
beginning of popular cinema.

Laura Mulvey's *Visual
Pleasure and Narrative
Cinema* (1975) and her
*Afterthoughts on Visual
Pleasure and Narrative
Cinema* (1981) are
discussed in Chapter 9.

Practical solutions, common sense or ideology?

It is fascinating to study these developing strategies in Early Cinema. The development
does not appear to have been systematic. Some are used, then discarded, then used
again. By trial and error, film-makers found a set of procedures that worked – aesthetically,
emotionally and intellectually and, most of all, commercially. There are different ways for
accounting for how mainstream commercial film form developed the way it did by 1917.

It can be interpreted as entirely 'natural':

- a common-sense set of solutions to problems of representing how the spectator engages with the real world through the act of looking
- a set of practical solutions to the problem of making the film more intelligible to an audience

Alternatively, it can be interpreted as ideological:

- a reflection of the ways of seeing of western culture and particularly of the male within western culture
- a recognition of the medium, if only for commercial reasons, as a powerful manipulative medium, capable of controlling representation and response

In fact these two positions are not opposed: what appears 'natural' and 'common sense' is rooted in a set of **hegemonic** choices and constructions. The very naturalness of these choices makes them largely invisible and, therefore, more effective as forms of control.

A study of Early Cinema forces us to ask questions, the most fundamental of which is this: could film have been different from what it is and still have developed a mass audience? It can be argued by those particularly opposed to mainstream commercial cinema that the period of Early Cinema can be seen as a kind of Garden of Eden. It is possible to think what other ways film form – and, therefore, spectatorship – could have developed. For example, a model for a radical alternative form of cinema might be conceived as one which does not guide us every step of the way through close-up, shot-reverse-shot, and so on. In a static camera long shot, for example, we are given freedom to choose for ourselves what we wish to focus upon. In not being interpellated, we are free to engage more objectively and thoughtfully with what we see and hear. There is not the space here to explore these arguments. However, it is necessary to recognise that much of the interest in Early Cinema is motivated precisely by a need to find other forms of spectatorship than that established by the kind of cinema which Hollywood (and not just Hollywood) had evolved by 1917.

Early Cinema audiences

In the introduction to this chapter, the inter-relationship of spectator and audience studies was pointed out. With regard to Early Cinema, just as interesting as the study of the development of film form as it relates to spectatorship is the development of film exhibition as it relates to audiences.

Film gradually emerged from 1895 as a fairground attraction to the nickelodeons of the early 1900s. Audiences were overwhelmingly working and lower-working class. The medium had a very low cultural status. The commercial concern was to raise the social image of movies and this had to involve both making them more sophisticated artefacts and placing them within more 'theatrical' auditoria.

An anarchy in film response had to be contained if film-going were to be more appealing to the middle classes. This anarchy derived partly from the fact that the films were silent. This gave them a wonderful 'universality' on the one hand, but also offered them as particular to different audiences – for example, to the vast diversity of immigrant groups arriving on the east coast of the US. More specifically this anarchy derived from the lack of a controlled viewing position prior to the development of a standardised film form as described in the outline on pp. 95–6 and from the inter-active (i.e. talkative) behaviour of audiences. Neither the film's textual operations nor cinema's organisation

Some elaboration of her very influential work can also be found in the section, 'More on the spectator as subject', pages 143–7.

For further discussion of ideology, see Chapter 9, Chapter 10 and Chapter 11.

hegemony
An important concept in this chapter. A set of ideas, attitudes or practices becomes so dominant that we forget they are rooted in choice and the exercise of power. They appear to be 'common sense' because they are so ingrained, any alternative seems 'odd' or potentially threatening by comparison. Hegemony is the ideological made invisible.

In relation to the development of cinema, it can be seen how Hollywood developed hegemonic status and power. The Hollywood form of genre-based narrative realist film is considered a 'common sense' use of the medium. Other forms of cinema, by comparison, are more or less 'odd'. In looking at the early history of cinema we can begin to understand how and why Hollywood assumed this position.

There are now several very good histories of Early Cinema. See the Further Reading on p. 160.

of the viewing event was able to isolate and control the spectator. The peculiar nature of the film experience as both isolated (in spectatorship) and collective (in audience membership) was itself evolving – or rather, being constructed.

The fact that film audiences were socialised into a particular cinema practice (e.g. sitting in quiet) at the same time that film form had been evolved to manage the act of spectatorship (e.g. control over the look) is highly significant. The standardisation of both film form and of cinema exhibition from very early in the history of cinema has encouraged film theorists to develop ideas based on:

- a normative spectator unified as the 'subject' addressed by the film
- regarding the viewing situation as a constant (rather than as variable according to who is the spectator, when and where they are and what they are watching).

The strengths and shortcomings of this approach are considered in the next two sections.

Consider the questions raised in this and the previous section. Do you think that the emergence of what we now recognise as the dominant mainstream kind of cinema, together with normative forms of exhibition and audience behaviour were:

1   the 'natural'

and

2   the 'best solution' in developing the medium?

SOME CHARACTERISTICS OF THE SPECTATOR OF FILM AND CULTURAL THEORY

A negative view of the spectator

At almost any point in film history one can find essentially negative assumptions about the behaviour of the movie-goer as spectator. Even contemporary debates about media 'effects' are based on a view that the spectator is extremely vulnerable to the manipulative qualities of the film text and the cinema experience. What is particularly interesting is the approach of critics from the political left during a period extending from the 1930s to the 1980s. One might expect support for the 'people's culture' and a positive attempt to interpret how mainstream commercial cinema was used by audiences. In practice the approach over a fifty-year period was both critical and pessimistic.

The Frankfurt School, made up of left-wing intellectuals who escaped Nazi Germany in the 1930s, presented Hollywood-style films as a kind of twentieth-century 'opium of the people', a form of mass culture which entertained and seduced people into an undemanding acceptance of the values, attitudes and fantasies presented to them. Film theory, developed out of a mix of structuralist and psychoanalytical theories in the early 1970s, also portrayed the spectator as someone made passive, dominated by and thus vulnerable to the powerful representational mechanisms of the movie. Popular cinema could only reinforce in people a conventional way of making sense of their world – rather than inspiring them with new and different ways of thinking about their own lives and the lives of others.

See the section 'Some notes on spectatorship and regulation' in this chapter p, 157–9.

For more on structuralist and psychoanalytic theories, see Chapter 9.

Key concepts in 'classic' film theory

The power of cinema as a system of communication, holding the spectator in place, was referred to as the *cinema apparatus*. The very term 'apparatus' conjures up ideas of being tied into place, controlled. The term describes the technical process and the effects produced in the act of projecting images on to large screens in darkened auditoria.

One of the key effects is to **interpellate** the spectator. We have already used this word but it is sufficiently important to deserve some elaboration here. The word was brought into film studies from the writings of the French philosopher Louis Althusser, himself influenced by the psychoanalytical theories of Jacques Lacan. Althusser argued that we are all 'subjects' of ideology through the ways in which we are interpellated or positioned into society by its structures and systems. The spectator is similarly interpellated into the film, is similarly the 'subject' of its largely invisible or taken-for-granted operations. Arguably, interpellation is both one of the basic pleasures of the movie experience and one of the most obvious ways in which popular narrative realist cinema can be said to have ideological effects. Associated with interpellation is **suture**. This French word literally means 'to stitch' and is another way in which the process by which the spectator, drawn into the world of the film, has been described.

From the above it can be seen that it was thought appropriate to talk about the spectator as a function of the cinema apparatus, as its 'subject'. The subject is a way of talking about the hypothetical spectator. The subject within established film theory became the dummy figure who ideally demonstrated the effects of the cinema apparatus, being:

For a brief exposition of these complex theories, see the section 'More on the spectator as subject', pp. 143–7.

- interpellated into the film in very specific ways
- more or less, the passive 'subject' of overwhelming physical and psychic forces

Underpinning these key concepts was a deterministic model of cinema built out of linguistic, psychoanalytical and political-cultural theories. Each reinforced the other in explaining how the spectator is positioned/absorbed/controlled. Even in more modified versions in the late 1970s and early 1980s, when acknowledgement was given to the spectator as having some manoeuvrability, some choice, that choice was seen as circumscribed and, therefore, limited by the cinema apparatus and by film form.

Thus, the spectator of film theory was:

- the 'subject' of an 'apparatus' which imposed the 'look' of the camera, a 'look' which was implicitly or explicitly ideological in its preferences,
- within an overall physical and psychic experience, including 'interpellation' which prompted regressive behaviour
- and thus suppressed critical faculties which might otherwise offer a defence against the ideological messages and representations of the film.

Responding to the spectator of film theory

Each of the above propositions can be challenged:

- Does the spectator automatically or necessarily become aligned with the camera's view?
  If not, then even if we accept the idea that the camera's view reflects ideological choices, the spectator need not endorse those choices uncritically.

■ Does the spectator really lose himself or herself in the cinema experience, becoming so 'stitched' (sutured) into the formal systems of the film, that he or she becomes entirely absorbed?

If not, then we can talk about a more complex process involving self-awareness; the spectator as simultaneously 'inside' and 'outside' the experience.

■ Does the spectator surrender a sense of self so completely that his or her own particular class/gender/sexual/ethnic/cultural identity counts for nothing?

If not, then we can talk about more complex ways in which the spectator handles the messages and representations of the film.

What do you think of the ideas put forward in this section? When you watch a film do you surrender to its effects or remain critically alert? Does it depend on the kind of film? Does it depend on your own state of mind at the time? Does it depend on who you are with?

Is it possible to surrender to the film *and* remain critically alert?

See also 'More on the spectator as subject', p. 143, and the model presented in the section 'More on communication models and response', p. 147.

Film studies as a discipline has tried to move away from the very heavy determinism based on theories of the subject and the apparatus. Cultural studies has provided useful alternative approaches to the question of how we respond to media messages. In particular, the terms 'preferred', oppositional' and 'negotiated' proved valuable.

A *'preferred' reading* of a media text is one in which the spectator takes the intended meaning, finding it relatively easy to align with the messages and attitudes of those who created the text. An *'oppositional' reading* is one which involves the rejection of the ideas and points of view contained in the text. Most often a 'preferred' response will be associated with pleasure, if only the pleasure of reassurance that comes from the comfortable and familiar. Most often an oppositional response will be associated with

• Plate 5.2 *Apocalypse Now*

• Plate 5.3 *Natural Born Killers*

Both Coppola's *Apocalypse Now* (1979) and Stone's *Natural Born Killers* (1995) are satires. However, 'preferred' readings of the two films cannot be guaranteed. For example, *Apocalypse Now*, rather than being viewed as an anti-war movie, could be seen as offering pleasure in the spectacle of war; *Natural Born Killers*, rather than being viewed as an indictment of contemporary media culture and values, could be seen as celebrating the values of the central characters. Meaning and response cannot be separated.

displeasure, or perhaps better, unpleasure. More crudely, there may be the temptation to associate a 'preferred' reading with the 'passive' spectator and an 'oppositional' reading with an active spectator. Maybe in practice, the most common form of response is one which involves 'negotiation'.

A *'negotiated' reading* is one which involves a certain give and take between our own views and experiences and those presented in the film text. It is a mature and complex response which is dependent on our familiarity with and experience in handling the medium – or to put this slightly differently it is to do with our 'competence' as spectators (see also section two of the *Pulp Fiction* case study, p. 154). We may well be aware that in a real world we would find a certain representation unacceptable, a certain moral attitude repulsive – but we can 'place' this within the context of a fictional experience. We are aware of being 'inside' and 'outside' the world of the film. In fact, one might argue that only psychotic spectators, incapable of distinguishing between fiction and reality, find it difficult to negotiate a position between themselves and the constructed fiction-as-reality with which they are presented.

For further discussion on the relationship between film and cultural studies, see Chapter 10, pp. 283–6.

....

If we take Spike Lee's *Do the Right Thing* (1989) or *Jungle Fever* (1990), we can identify strong differences in audience response which can be described in relation to 'preferred', 'oppositional' and 'negotiated' readings. Lee's films are also challenging in terms of analysing our alignment and allegiance with film characters (see 'Spectatorship and character' in the *Pulp Fiction* case study, p.148.

Lee's films are clear in the positions they adopt. Some films, especially ones which use irony, are much more diffi-cult to define in terms of their 'preferred' reading. Coppola's *Apocalypse Now* (1979) should be seen as an anti-war movie. Does this mean that those who enjoy its spectacular battle sequences and who consider the film to be cele-brating war are giving an *aberrant reading* – one which is simply 'wrong'?

A more recent film which demonstrates the difficulty of describing responses in terms of 'preferred', 'oppositional', 'negotiated' or 'aberrant' is the American independent film *In the Company of Men* (Labute, 1996). The difficulty is rooted in distinguishing between the film's *intention* and its *effect*. This in turn highlights a problem with this approach in general. These descriptive terms are applied on the assumption that the film has a set of meanings separate from the spectator. An alternative view is that the film has no meaning without the spectator. His or her response cannot be measured against a 'right' or 'wrong' interpretation but only in terms of their experience of the film – the affective, phys-ical and cognitive pleasures that are taken from the experience by a particular individual (see the section 'Spectatorship, audience and pleasure', p.141).

....

The most extreme reaction against the model of cinema, as described in structuralist film theory, presented the view that there are in fact as many 'readings' of a film as there are spectators. Each of us comes to a film with our own personal 'formation' – the result of all our life experiences. These will predispose us to certain interpretations of char-acter, certain attitudes towards moral and political issues and certain emotional responses to events.

So, the challenge to the deterministic theory of spectatorship contained in 'subject' and 'apparatus' theory is the proposition that audiences display independence and diversity of response. In fact it is more complex than this. It can be argued that if we put aside the inevitable differences from one person to the next which results from partic-ular details of their personalities, audiences respond remarkably uniformly to a film. It is necessary to ask why this might be.

One answer may be found in the idea that we all carry out essentially the same 'work' using the same skills and strategies. We are all familiar with the structures and formulae of popular cultural forms – the plots, settings and character types of different genres. We recognise these conventions and transform them through our imaginations, 'suspending our disbelief'.

I choose to enter a cinema. That choice will be in response to information (publicity, marketing, word-of-mouth, etc.) and in response to my particular needs, most often the result of information about the kind of film on offer and the expectations aroused by that information. If I choose to buy into the latest James Bond experience, it is in the context of the hype surrounding it, the particular expectations it offers. My particular knowledge and predisposition will be shared by others who make the same choice. If the information I have informs me that there is a choice between one film which is intellectually demanding, one which is politically provocative and a third which is throw-away spectacular fun, I will decide which one best matches my needs. It is likely that the choices of others will reflect the same need. In choosing the James Bond movie, I am not expecting to have intellectual needs met nor am I going to take too seriously the politics of the film. In other words, I will be able to make a 'preferred/negotiated' reading – rather than an 'oppositional' one, even though I may, in a more serious frame of mind, have to acknowledge that the sexism, militarism and violence portrayed is not something I would endorse in life.

To put this slightly differently, in responding to an impulsive need for escapist fun, it may be argued that I am freely choosing to become the spectator of film theory. In other words I *want* to become the 'subject' of the apparatus, I want to be interpellated into the action, I want to be aligned with the look of the camera. Rather than denying the model of spectatorship offered by film theory, one may want to accept its accuracy in describing the film experience, but within the contexts of choice and pleasure.

There is also a second possible answer to the question of why it is that at any particular screening, a large majority of the individuals appear to show remarkably similar behaviour as spectators. This involves looking at their shared social and cultural 'formation' as an audience. In choosing the same film, the same film experience as many others and in responding to it in the same way as most of the other people who made the same choice, I am not participating in a 'plural' audience.

So at one level it is simply enough to talk in terms of this uniformity of response as being the result of self-selection – in sharing a taste in a certain kind of movie there is a good chance of a fairly uniform response to the pleasures it offers. We will work *with* (rather than against) the film. However, this still begs a larger question. Why did I, together with my fellow spectators, make the choice that we did? Why did we choose a spectacular fun movie and why could we be so comfortable watching its formulaic representations of gender, ethnicity and so on? Or, to go back to the previous paragraph, how could we 'allow' ourselves the pleasures of the film?

For a summary in diagrammatic form of the ideas covered in this section see the section 'More on communication models and response' (p. 147).

To explain this we could fall back on traditional models of media manipulation. We are persuaded by advertising and promotional hype to buy a ticket. We are then further manipulated once we 'surrender' as spectators to the medium. A more profound explanation would be that most of us are 'subjects' of the same ideological messages which circulate within our western corporate capitalist culture. We are, in the abstract, capable of 'oppositional' readings but are most likely to conform to the 'common sense' attitudes and understandings which constitute the political, social and cultural hegemony. We are not so much manipulated into a response as immersed in a mind-set through the wider culture in which we live and act. We find ourselves negotiating within a narrow range, rather than across the kind of broad spectrum of possible responses which a genuinely pluralist culture might be expected to encourage. In other words, the fairly small variation in response within an audience is a reflection of the relatively small range of perspectives actively circulating in the wider society. There is, in the abstract, a large spectrum of responses; in practice very few.

Maybe you disagree that audiences respond in broadly the same way to a film. Is there evidence of much greater diversity of response to popular films – for example, *The English Patient*, *The Full Monty*, *Titanic*?

Spectatorship, audience and pleasure

Another way of trying to bring together theories of spectatorship is in relation to pleasure. Pleasure is what motivates us to enter the cinema. The kinds of pleasures we seek may be described (and judged!) by different criteria – aesthetic, moral, social, intellectual, emotional, erotic, etc. In a typical situation our motives may be mixed, the pleasures we are seeking diverse.

The following attempts to present in diagrammatic form different pleasures which have their origin in the cinema institution. Some of these are spectator pleasures, some broader based audience and social pleasures. The diagram incorporates much of what has already been outlined in the chapter so far.

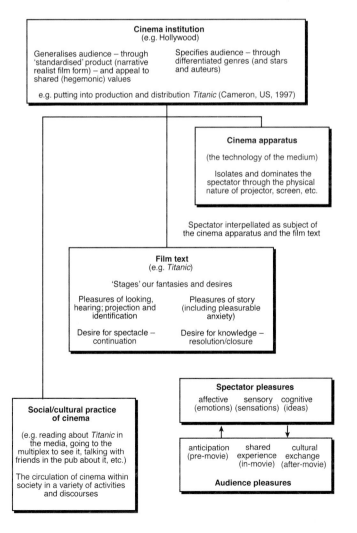

Cinema as an institution produces both film texts and the 'cinema experience' as constituted by the 'apparatus' (see section on 'Key concepts', pp. 137–40). In addition, however, the cinema institution is the dynamo which sustains a cinema culture in wider society.

Narrative realist film is the dominant form in cinema. When we buy into the experience of such a film we are buying into the promise of two kinds of pleasure. One is very general – the promise offered by a form of cinema that we can handle comfortably because we are able to understand its familiar form. The other is rather more specific – the promise offered by the specific genre, star or auteur billing. This helps us to decide whether we will join an audience for the film.

The psychoanalytical theories on which apparatus–subject theory is based would indicate that the pleasure cannot be in fulfilment of desire, only in the 'staging' of it. So the film experience can be seen as a pleasurable 'tease' in which we have dangled before us forms of fulfilment which we cannot actually reach out and take. In psychoanalysis this is the unfulfillable object that we will pursue through the repeated search – the next trip to the movies. *See the section, 'More on the spectator as subject', pp. 143–7, for further discussion of these ideas.*

The way the cinema apparatus and the film text interpellate the spectator has already been discussed. For the spectator it is seductively pleasurable to surrender to this position (leaving to one side debates about how vulnerable we may be to ideological effects). The pleasures provided by the film text can be described in many different ways – one is to talk of how the film 'stages' our desires and fantasies. In the cinema auditorium, sitting in front of the screen and its images, we are in a state which seems simultaneously to involve passive surrender and active engagement. We surrender to what we cannot control (the unfolding of the narrative, the subject positions we are given); and engage with what delights us (visual images, sound, character identification). We have a desire for the film to continue so we can continue to enjoy these pleasures. Simultaneously we have a desire for the film to end and thus 'close' the uncertainty and anxiety which the narrative induces in us. We desire different kinds of knowledge (for example, relating to plot and character) and different kinds of experience (for example, relating to the stimulation offered by sight and sound).

Overall we can identify different kinds of spectator pleasure: emotional as in our empathy with character and situation; physical as in the stimulation our senses are provided with; cognitive as in the complexities of plot and theme. Forms of desire may run through all of these.

Our experience of very personal and maybe quite idiosyncratic pleasures as spectators in the movie auditorium may be reinforced or modified by our formation as members of an audience. Certainly it is valuable to take into account the broader kinds of pleasures we enjoy by participating in cinema culture and social practice is valuable. It helps to 'locate' the spectator and avoid an approach which discusses the spectator as an abstraction. For example, the spectator exists prior to the screening as someone already formed as a 'potential' member of an audience with expectations and prejudices. The spectator leaves the screening to 'negotiate' their response with friends and reviewers.

How would you reconstruct the diagram on page 141 to account for the pleasures of viewing a film on video at home with a couple of friends or with family?

While acknowledging the importance of this larger framework within which pleasure can be explored, there remains a particular attraction in focusing on desires set in motion in the act of spectatorship. We are forced to recognise the importance of unconscious as well as conscious aspects of the film experience. It is possible to talk in terms of a spectator 'actively' working to find some material in the film experience to satisfy their desire. The rejection of a film because it fails to find common ground with the spectator's desires is likely to lead to an 'oppositional' position every bit as strong as an oppositional response to the film's more visible, conscious material.

In practice we need to recognise that the power of the cinema apparatus and the film text lies in the way it envelops both our conscious *and* our unconscious selves. A model of spectatorship needs to account for the pleasures available to us at both levels.

Maybe the fundamental reason for the fear of cinema expressed by different kinds of social and cultural analysis for almost the entire length of film's history has not been because of concern over the conscious self made passive, as described above. Maybe the real fear has been over film's capacity to make the unconscious self active! Censorship is never related to film passivity – it is always concerned with the potential of film to *activate* the spectator's imagination.

For more on pleasure see the case study on p. 148 where different responses to Pulp Fiction *are discussed.*

> **Rather than writing a response to a film which is an interpretation of its content and an analysis of its formal features and style, try putting together a response based purely on desire and pleasure. This may include a critical analysis of any un-desire and un-pleasure.**

MORE ON THE SPECTATOR AS 'SUBJECT'

What was the basis for a model of the spectator in 1970s film theory as passive and vulnerable? Three powerful sets of theories were brought together, around language, the mind and ideology. They focused upon the power of the text in controlling the spectator and determining response.

The control of language and spectatorship

A theory of language derived from the work of Ferdinand de Saussure presents the individual as locked into language structures which limit our thinking to the forms – the words, the grammatical rules – already available. We cannot think outside the terms language provides us; indeed language does our thinking for us, *it speaks us*.

If we consider popular cinema as a language which works according to its particular rules and conventions (be they on the large scale of narrative and genre or on the small scale of the continuity edit), then we can argue that the spectator is locked into the film text, placed within the operations of film form. In the supposedly passive activity of watching a film, the spectator is interpellated (see p.137) into the film on its terms, manipulated into forms of identification by the system of looks at work within the film and by the irresistible drives contained in the narrative.

Psychoanalytical theory and desire in spectatorship

A psychoanalytical theory developed by Jacques Lacan encouraged a comparison to be made between the act of spectatorship and a specific period in the development of the young child. The theory says that a child is born with a sense of incompleteness, a 'lack'. There is thus a desire from birth to fully 'be', with life spent trying to overcome or fill the lack, something which we can never accomplish. To compensate for the failure to re-establish a sense of personal completeness or unity, the child will console itself with imaginary solutions, especially idealised images of itself as 'complete'. The child's first illusion of wholeness is the mirror and the sense that 'that must be me'. More profound is the mirror provided by the mother who 'reflects' a particular identity back on to the child. The mirror image is a kind of mirage, a narcissistic self-idealisation, a **misrecognition** because the imagined 'real' is always, in fact, unattainable.

Film theory compared the act of spectatorship to this 'mirror phase' in order to explain both the pleasure and the ideological effect of surrendering to the film image. The pleasure is that of experiencing, at least temporarily, 'wholeness', however imaginary. The ideological significance is that the spectator accepts images (and, by implication, the ideas they bear) which are a misrecognition, not truly representative of his or her identity or ideological needs.

It is interesting to note the relationship between theories of language and theories of the mind. After the 'mirror stage', also referred to as the 'imaginary', Lacan talked about the child entering into language or the 'symbolic'. Because language pre-exists the child, he or she can only enter it on its terms. Identity appears to be offered by the way language orders and names things. Different discourses – such as discourses of gender – seem to offer the possibility of greater self-recognition, greater wholeness. In fact what increases is the risk of misrecognition. The child must submit to the rules of language and in so doing his or her subjectivity is actually formed by language which 'speaks' the permissible roles and identities available to the child. The 'symbolic' appears to offer liberation but in fact offers constriction.

Lacan further argued that everything that will not fit into the terms of language is consigned to the unconscious. More will be said about this later.

On finding the 'symbolic' world of language just as incapable of answering a sense of 'lack', the child, according to Lacan, will look to some other person for an unconditional love which will answer this need to achieve wholeness. A projection takes place, most obviously again on to the mother. But the mother or some other person can never provide fully what is being desired. This becomes the launchpad for a lifelong unfulfillable search for the 'lost object', never ending desire.

Film theory adapted this description to account for the *desire* which takes us to the cinema and the desire which is awakened in the act of spectatorship. No film can ever satisfy the spectator's profound desire for some kind of sense of completion. What film does is to produce the fantasy which nourishes desire. The fantasy sets out and screens the desire. This is enough to provide intense *pleasure* for the duration of the film, but is so insufficient that the desire to return for more, for other screenings of desire, will be very strong.

Ideology and spectatorship

The ideological effects of cinema if conceived in terms of either of the above – a controlling language system or as some sort of materialisation of mental processes – is clear. The film locks spectators into structures and plays out for them experiences which are irresistible. The language of mainstream cinema is 'invisible' in that it is the language the spectator has been born in to. The endless exploitation of desire with partially satisfying texts of pleasure allows the continuing exploitation, teasing of the spectator – both for commercial gain and, more profoundly, for ideological manipulation. The forms the spectator's desire takes are those offered by the dominant culture – particular representations of sexuality, lifestyle, consumerism, individualism.

The above 'effects' can be placed within Antonio Gramsci's reworking of traditional Marxist theory. Gramsci helped to explain through the concept of hegemony how, in a sophisticated twentieth-century society, the dominant groups retain power not through physical force but through perpetuating particular attitudes and values which appear so

misrecognition
This idea can be related to the Marxist concept of 'false consciousness'. As the victims of a dominant ideology we can only understand ourselves and our relationship to the world on its terms. We are, therefore, likely to be persuaded to act against our own interests and in the interests of those whose ideology we are contained by. Marx talked about how people can be persuaded to service the capitalist system both as workers and consumers and believe it is in their interest rather than of the owners of capital to do so. To put it differently, we are *interpellated* into *'subject'* positions by the structures which give us identity and purpose.

obvious that they are more likely to be described as 'common sense' than as ideology. The taken-for-granted values at the heart of a culture become dominant by what appear to be purely natural processes rather than through any imposed system of authority. Popular cinema could be seen as playing a part in 'naturalising' particular ways of seeing and understanding the world – not just in particular on-screen representations but in the form of film (narrative realism) and the psychology of the communication process.

Two examples of theories deriving from 1970s film theory

Of the theories which emerged from the theoretical study of film and spectatorship, two produced by English academics were given particular attention.

Colin MacCabe in an article entitled 'Realism and the Cinema'[1] extended the analogy of language to film by considering the different discourses at work within a particular film. One might think that an interplay of different viewpoints within a film would give the spectator freedom to choose. One spectator may side with character A and hope for one resolution of the plot while another spectator may side with character B and hope for a very different resolution. MacCabe argued that although there are various 'voices' within a film (or novel), they are organised into a hierarchy and there is one voice/point of view or 'discourse' which dominates, controlling our overall response. MacCabe argued that a typical narrative realist film is controlled by the invisible and taken-for-granted presence of the film's impersonal storyteller. This storyteller, rather as a 'god-like' third person controlling presence in a novel, manages all the more visible and dramatically contrasting voices in the text. Discourses operate in a hierarchy – some are more valued, more emphasised than others. In a film, MacCabe argued, the dominant discourse is contained in the visual, the organisation of looks – what was described as 'dominant specularity'.

MacCabe develops his ideas by reference to Pakula's Klute *(1971). Like the films referred to on p.134,* Klute *deals with voyeurism. Interestingly, it couples voyeurism with eaves-dropping in ways which raise further issues about the particular 'pleasure' cinema provides in allowing us to invade private experience, private space.*

Laura Mulvey in 'Visual Pleasure and Narrative Cinema'[2] focused particularly on the subject position offered to the spectator. In as much as she identified the dominant discourse (in MacCabe's approach) as the camera itself and that the camera's way of seeing the world, in the points of view offered, was masculine rather than feminine, she was able to propose the idea that the subject position offered to the spectator is male. The subject – the one who does the looking is male. The 'object' of the look is woman.

This raised very significant issues. First, it brought gender into the ideological account of the cinema apparatus and subject. Second, it raised the extremely challenging question – if the spectator is offered a male 'subject' position, what is the female spectator doing if not allowing herself to become 'male' for the duration of the film? One answer is that she engages in a masochistic over-identification with the women characters on screen; another that she reflects the images back onto herself in an act of narcissism.

See Chapter 9 for further discussion of Mulvey's ideas.

Certainly both MacCabe and Mulvey quickly modified their own ideas. The strengths and weaknesses of their basic propositions have not only been debated widely but in the process of being debated have been moved on. The reason for giving so much space to these ideas is partly because they have been so influential and partly because they illustrate the consequences of establishing such a central part of film studies in a particular theoretical approach to cinema.

Modifications to 1970s film theory

Spectatorship theory was presented above as having three sets of roots: in language, in psychoanalysis and in Marxism. In the early 1980s there was a move away from notions of the text as the overwhelming determinant of meaning. What is now referred to as **post-structuralism** acknowledged that the spectator is a more active agent in a dynamic model of meaning–response.

Deriving from the work of the French philosophers and cultural theorists Jacques Derrida, Roland Barthes and Michel Foucault, ideas of language emerged which countered, to some extent, those of Saussure, especially in claiming that there are any fixed and final meanings in language. These moved from the idea that language does our thinking for us, emphasising instead language either as a game or as a competing struggle between alternative discourses. At the very least this introduces a more active subject; one who negotiates with the given language. Meaning is much more obviously dependent on the reader (spectator).

Modifications in the adaptation of Lacan's work began to suggest that the spectator is not so much constructed and held in place by the apparatus and the film text. The structuralist description of the spectator as fixed in place by an (imaginary) unified self-image projected on to the screen was replaced. Instead the spectator was now considered capable (as in what was said about language in the previous paragraph) to 'play' or 'struggle' with different positions. He or she could occupy different and contradictory positions – male/female, hero/villain, protagonist/victim – and thus was able to exercise conflicting fantasies within the self.

Film theory from the 1970s emphasised the relationship between spectator and screen images as voyeuristic. However, the balancing opposite in Freudian theory has become important as well: the exhibitionist. The screen performer in the act of exhibiting themselves 'draws' the look, wishing to be the object of the spectator's look rather than its 'victim'.

More broadly, a Marxist-style ideological analysis had to adjust to incorporate the idea of a more active spectator. If the spectator was now to be seen as an active producer of meaning as much as a passive subject produced by the cinema apparatus/film text, then a simple deterministic model had to be modified. More attention would have to be given to the spectator as an individual whose response is based on a vast range of variables.

However, the notion that there are as many 'readings of a film as there are spectators' bares as little relationship to experience as the opposite notion that spectators are simply steam-rollered by all powerful mechanisms.

The reasons for a remarkable uniformity in response despite the potential for diversity can be explained in relation to hegemony. This is explored in the sections on plurality of meaning and 'More on communication models and response' (opposite).

Different theories, different films

What has been written here may give the impression that films are fairly uniform and that what changes are the theories designed to help us account for them. Of course there are different kinds of film, and films themselves evolve in response to theoretical perspectives. Although there is no space here to elaborate, it is worth looking at the differences between a conventional mainstream Hollywood film and a low-budget independent film. *Waiting to Exhale* (Whitaker, 1995) and *Just Another Girl on the IRT* (Harris, 1991) each focuses on the lives of black women and is specifically targeting black female audiences. *Waiting to Exhale*, with a star cast, offers pleasures for male and female spectators respectively within a standard ideological and psychic framework. For example, women spectators are invited to (a) identify with hegemonic values and aspirations, and to (b) engage in the kind

Extending these ideas further, the voyeuristic is associated in Freud's work with the sadistic and exhibitionism with the masochistic. If we take a film such as Harlin's *The Long Kiss Goodnight* (1996), we find a central female performance (by Geena Davis) which could be considered at least as much a masochistic exhibition as an act of sadistic objectification by the cinema apparatus for the spectator-voyeur. One of the best films for focusing this debate is Charles Vidor's *Gilda* (1944) in which Rita Hayworth fends off sadistic male treatment by acts of exhibitionism, including the famous 'Put the blame on Mame, boys' routine.

of over-identification and narcissism which are, at least according to film theory, the inevitable results of their spectator positioning. *Just Another Girl on the IRT* offers something different. First, there is a much more critical take on hegemonic values and the film works out, rather than simply accepts, its attitude towards them. Second, there is a different kind of central performance, much more exhibitionist, much more resistant to the normal look of the spectator.

Without doubt, the only way to test out film theories is through the careful study of films representing different kinds of practice. To paraphrase the title of a book listed in the bibliography to Chapter 6, film theory must go to the movies.

MORE ON COMMUNICATION MODELS AND RESPONSE

Models of communication

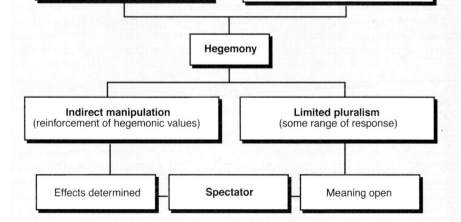

Manipulative model	**Pluralist model**
Based on the view that media 'effects' are the consequence of forms of stimulus carefully calculated to hit their target. Response is highly determined.	Not the opposite of a 'manipulative model' – but proposes that 'effects' are more varied and less predictable. Media sophisticated audiences are well capable of resisting the 'preferred' response.
The passive spectator (vulnerable)	The active spectator (competent)
Media pessimists	Media liberals
Pro-censorship/regulation	Anti-censorship/regulation
but	**but**
The idea of response determined entirely by the text is considered too simple, especially when represented in terms of stimulus→response theories. Determination is achieved by more subtle means in a media-sophisticated society.	The large majority of spectators making up an audience have very similar 'formations' as a consequence of the political-social-cultural environment in which preferences are formed and choices made.

Hegemony

Indirect manipulation
(reinforcement of hegemonic values)

Limited pluralism
(some range of response)

Effects determined   **Spectator**   Meaning open

This diagram attempts to show the key function of hegemony in reconciling two quite different approaches to media (including cinema) messages. On the one hand hegemony is seen as an additional and very powerful form of manipulation, producing more sophisticated forms of persuasion by appealing to shared values and aspirations in the audience rather than trying to push cruder, more visible and obvious kinds of messages. On the other hand hegemony can be seen as limiting the range of responses that seem, at least in theory, to be possible if we adopt a 'pluralist' position.

This model goes some way towards explaining what has been called 'openness of meaning yet determinacy of effect'.[3] This is a highly convenient compromise for theorists who had originally proposed the very deterministic set of theories around structuralism and subject-apparatus theory. Accepting that the spectator had to be reconceived as less of a cabbage-like creature, this allows for something much more positive. At the same time it seemed a denial of the truth to accept the notion that 'there are as many responses as there are spectators'. Hegemony embraces both text and spectator, media producer and media consumer in a communications model which requires a lighter, more subtle feel for the complex ways in which we 'negotiate' meaning.

☐ CASE STUDY 1: *PULP FICTION* (1994)

Pulp Fiction is a useful film to use in exploring spectatorship and audience. On the one hand, it is a very self-aware film which plays with some of the basic conventions of narrative realist film. On the other hand, sequence by sequence, it employs standard aspects of mainstream film form – such as in the section discussed here.

In this section we will focus on a well-known episode from Quentin Tarantino's *Pulp Fiction*. In the first part Vincent (John Travolta) picks up Mia (Uma Thurman) on the instructions of his gangster boss, Mia's husband, and takes her out to a diner. In the second part he has to cope with her overdosing, resorting to some rather shocking emergency treatment!

In exploring the first part of the episode, the study of spectatorship will be extended by looking in detail at an aspect ignored by much film theory – character and character identification. In exploring the second part, we will try to test out different theoretical approaches outlined above in the previous section.

Spectatorship and character

By thirty minutes into *Pulp Fiction* we have established that Vincent is a ruthless hit man but also a rather ordinary guy, appealing, even slightly vulnerable, in whom the audience can take an interest. (He is also John Travolta.) Immediately before his arrival at Mia's house he has taken drugs. We have no significant knowledge of Mia, although our expectations based on the gangster genre (the schema we rely upon to 'navigate' through fictional films) may lead us to expect a typical 'moll' or 'femme fatale'. So, in different ways, we are already working as spectators, either in placing and coming to terms with a character we have some knowledge of or in anticipating one we have yet to get to know.

See p. 162 for an explanation of schemas.

There are (at least) three aspects to the work the spectator carries out with a screen character. In the first instance we must *recognise* the character. By this I mean that we must be able to translate the fictional 'construct' – which, at one level, we know is the product of screenwriter, actor, director and others, into a credible person. This is something we do automatically most of the time, unless the film is deliberately making it difficult in order to force us to adopt a more detached position (see *Suture* (Samuel Goldwyn, 1993), a film which even in its title shows an awareness of spectatorship issues). At another level, our ability to recognise a character will depend in part on our knowledge and experience of the world. At yet another level it will depend on our

I am indebted to Murray Smith's excellent book, *Engaging Characters – Fiction, Emotion and the Cinema* (Oxford University Press, 1995) for much of what follows here.

knowledge and experience of the textual conventions (and mental 'schemas') at work generally in fictional film. When we are aware of the creation of a character by a well-known actor/star, there is a different kind of recognition which may have a number of consequences. Familiarity with the star persona-image may provide us with additional insights and expectations. It may lead to 'over'-recognition in which it is difficult to move beyond the star presence in order to engage with the character as a self-contained entity in the fictional world of the film.

See Chapter 6 on genre, star and auteur.

Second, we become *aligned* with a particular character. We see and feel parts of the story through this fictional person. Classical film theory would say that this alignment is involuntary – we are placed by the complex and powerful technical and textual mechanisms described above (in the section on the spectator and cultural theory). If we have more access to the point-of-view and subjectivity of a character, we may become dependent on them for our 'take' on the film as a whole and, in the process, form a particularly close bond, an 'identification' with them. However, care must be taken not to assume that in aligning or being aligned with a particular character, we identify with them – in the sense of endorsing their behaviour and attitudes. It is perfectly possible for a film to create structures of alignment which place the spectator in the point-of-view/subjective consciousness of a homicidal maniac or a robot.

Third, we show *allegiance*. In so doing we make evaluations about the 'appeal' of the character to us. This may well be a moral/ideological allegiance, but if, for example, a spectator expresses a strong allegiance with Micky and Malory in Stone's *Natural Born Killers*, this involves a positive evaluation of their wild anti-social, anarchic moral positions. As with alignment, classical film theory would tell us that allegiance is constructed by forces outside our control, that we are manipulated into allegiance, sometimes with characters whose views are ideologically counter to our needs and circumstances in the real world. Such manipulated allegiances could be described as inducing what Marxist theory calls 'false consciousness'. The application of concepts such as false consciousness to film studies fails, however, to come to terms with the spectator as 'imaginative worker'. This spectator is someone who can try out different identities in aligning with different characters within a fiction film and someone who is quite capable of exercising their personal judgement when forming allegiances.

See the section 'More on the spectator as subject', pages pp.143–7, for a discussion of false consciousness and the related concept of misrecognition.

Take any film of your choice and consider your relationship to two contrasting characters in terms of *recognition*, *alignment* and *allegiance*. Does your study show movement and change in your response across the length of the film? Does it show that we have a capacity to align with and even show allegiance to:

1 a variety of different sorts of characters
and
2 characters whom we would not feel drawn to in our actual lives?

Pulp Fiction is full of surprises, including those which derive from playing with character alignment and allegiance. The most shocking to the spectator is the death of Vincent in the episode where Butch (Bruce Willis) is the central focus. It is a shock partly because, in narrative terms, it is so casual and unannounced but primarily because it fails to respect the allegiance we have formed with the Vincent character previously – especially in the episode I now wish to turn to.

Vincent and Mia: 1

Vincent approaches the house of his employer Marsellus Wallace. The spectator follows him from behind, first in long and then in medium shot. As he takes a message from the door, there is a cut to close-up and we hear what we assume (from our familiarity with film conventions) is the voice of the person who has written the note, Mia. The voice invites Vincent to enter. There is a cut to the interior as Vincent feels his way gingerly – he is on unknown territory; he is high on heroin. The spectator is then presented with a shot of Mia from behind as she sits in front of four televisions relaying close-circuit surveillance pictures of Vincent. During the rest of the two-minute sequence, until Mia's fingers pick up the stylus, Dusty Springfield's version of 'Preacher Man' provides an accompaniment to what we see. There is next a big close-up of Mia's lips at a microphone. Her call 'Vincent' startles him. All his movements seem to require additional thought. The spectator processes a range of information contained in the *mise en scène*, soundtrack, dialogue and performances. The information is controlled by the film's maker. To this extent the spectator is in a dependent situation. However, it is precisely because of this limited access to information that the spectator becomes active

In terms of recognition, alignment and allegiance, the sequence is interesting. In the twenty-two shots before the couple leave the house, we do not see Mia's full face. The spectator's curiosity is increased, partly for this general reason, partly for the specific reason that she has been in control throughout. She is in a position of power because (1) she is the boss's wife, (2) she controls camera and sound technology, and (3) Vincent's condition is not likely to produce assertiveness! Our alignment is increasingly with Mia, all the key point-of-view shots are hers, including ones where she prepares and then snorts cocaine. Our allegiance, however, is with Vincent. He is the object of the camera's look – which becomes the object of the female look. Our recognition is based on what we know of him from the first thirty minutes of the film. If an allegiance has formed, it is based partly on the attributes of the Vincent character as already established and partly on the attributes of the Travolta star persona. We quite literally do not recognise Mia yet (although it is almost certain we will have an image already in our minds from publicity material in circulation outside the space of the cinema auditorium) and must move towards forming an allegiance based only on her behaviour, voice (and lips!).

A moral evaluation of the two characters will, for experienced film spectators, depend less on judging them against a set of moral criteria from the real world than from those that are operative within the world of Tarantino's film. The recognition given by someone with no awareness of Travolta and with little ability or willingness to engage imaginatively within the terms of the film's genre and form may well be very different. In other words, we can anticipate the spectrum of 'preferred', 'negotiated' and 'oppositional' responses. Another way of discussing this topic is in terms of the competence of the individual spectator, which refers to the skills possessed by the spectator, most obviously their 'cine-literateness'. One could imagine a spectator who is either too inexperienced in contemporary popular cinema or too unsophisticated to pick up Tarantino's tone and his attitude towards his characters.

There is a cut from the Wallace residence to a red Chevrolet. The camera pulls out and pans left to establish that Vincent and Mia have arrived in the diner car park. We see Mia's full face for the first time. One minute seventeen seconds of screen time is used to establish the world of Jack Rabbit Slim's diner and get the two characters to their seats. In looking at the sequence from Mia's 'What do you think?' to when she goes to 'powder' her nose, we are presented with a very familiar shot-reverse-shot dialogue sequence. As is typical of such a sequence, there are a large number of edits – seventy-five in five minutes thirty seconds of screen time, with the average shot length 4.4 seconds. In such a sequence it is appropriate to apply the concepts of interpellation and suture (see p. 137). The spectator is very much drawn into ('stitched' into) the space between the two characters. However, there is no obvious sense in which this involves spectator passivity. In terms of working with the visual and verbal information we are provided with, very considerable 'active' processing is taking place. This is partly a consequence of the specific nature of this shot-reverse-shot dialogue: each character is objectifying the person opposite them. It is intended that the spectator becomes fascinated by the complex of forces put into play: Mia's power over Vincent; Vincent's odd mix of coolness and vulnerability; the separate knowledge we have of the state of mind of each of them. This becomes particularly

• **Plate 5.4** Uma Thurman in medium close-up

• **Plate 5.5** Travolta and Thurman in two-shot

The diner scene from *Pulp Fiction* between Mia (Uma Thurman) and Vincent (John Travolta) is made up in large part of a classic shot-reverse-shot rhythm which 'sutures' (stitches) the spectator into the space between the characters producing intense involvement. Plate 5.4 is a typical example of the spectator 'sutured' into the sequence. However, Tarantino can surprise us as in the side-on two-shot (Plate 5.5). Suddenly the spectator is on the outside in much more of an observer role.

• **Plate 5.6** Travolta and Thurman re-enter the apartment

Vincent returns Mia to her home. The spectator has been drawn into alignment with these two characters. As a consequence of our involvement, further anticipation and tension is created. After their very flirtatious night out, will Vincent risk taking things further with the boss's wife? Our privileged information on Mia's condition leads us to consider a different scenario. We care because we have been drawn into the situation by the calculated use of film techniques in the previous scenes. An unusual feature of *Pulp Fiction* is that our caring, our allegiance, is sometimes set up only to be wiped out by some turn in the plotting or structure of the film.

apparent during the 'comfortable silence' when the spectator is shifted from point-of-view shots to side-on 'observer' views of each character separately. The sequence, and its continuation after Mia returns from the Ladies, requires the spectator to be both caught up within the exchange of looks and yet remain observant, responsive to the character information being revealed.

The spectator is very often both '*privileged*' in possessing information which an on-screen character lacks and '*restricted*' in that key information is withheld. Both are ways in which our interest is created and maintained. We may feel we have limited access to information at various points in this episode but in one important way we are in a position of superior knowledge: we know that *both* characters are high on drugs. Relative to Vincent, the spectator is 'privileged' on three separate occasions: before, during and after the trip to the diner we see Mia taking cocaine. Not only does this inform our understanding of and alignment with the Mia character, it also significantly shifts the spectator's expectations on what dramatic results are likely to follow. Having returned from Jack Rabbit Slim's, Vincent is observed in a bathroom of the Wallace home telling himself not to become sexually involved with Mia, but to go home. This is a darkly comic situation, intensified by the Vincent character/Travolta performance and made dramatically ironic by the knowledge given to the spectator that Mia is in the sitting room with very different preoccupations.

There is then a sudden shift in tone after Vincent's bathroom monologue:

So you're gonna go out there, drink your drink, say 'Goodnight, I've had a lovely evening,' go home and jack off. And that's all you're gonna do...[3]

We do not expect a close-up of Mia's face, suddenly deathly white, sick coming from her mouth, blood from her nose.

Vincent and Mia: 2

After Mia has overdosed, there is a two minute ten second sequence involving Vincent driving towards the house of Lance, trying all the while to communicate the desperateness of his situation on his mobile phone (while the *Three Stooges* play on Lance's TV). There then follows just under two minutes of frantic activity, much of it in a hand-held shot. (Tarantino's script offers the following description: 'everything in this scene is frantic, like a documentary in an emergency ward, with the big difference here being nobody knows what the fuck they're doing'.) There is then a quieter but hardly calmer one minute twenty-five seconds preparing for and giving the adrenaline shot to the heart which causes Mia's instant recovery.

The entire six minutes ten seconds before we see Mia, ghostly white, being driven home by Vincent is simultaneously suspenseful, shocking and comic. In the act of spectatorship there are undoubtedly some responses which are involuntary, just as there are in our responses to shocks and surprises outside the cinema. In this sequence, the most obvious illustration of this involuntary response is when Vincent, after a long pause, takes aim and plunges the syringe into Mia's heart. The shock of an entire audience is audible! However, for most of an action sequence, spectator involvement is far from involuntary. We need to *care* what happens – and this is directly related to the allegiances we have formed with the two central characters, specifically here as a result of our 'participation' in the previous long sequence in the diner.

In considering some of the alternative ways of responding to the 'overdose sequence', it is first necessary to list some of the alternative ways of responding to the episode as a whole:

A   primarily at the level of character and the emotions generated by their circumstances – a very 'affective' response
B   primarily at the level of genre/form in which characters and situations are understood in relation to familiarity with the 'schemas' of different kinds of cinema – a 'cine-literate' if usually quite automatic response
C   primarily at the level of the film as 'construct' in which there is a strong awareness of the film's makers – a very 'cognitive' response

These can be mapped against pleasure (1) and unpleasure (2). In the abstract the alternatives can be presented in diagrammatic form (see over).

One way of interpreting these divergent responses is by reference to 'preferred', 'oppositional' and 'negotiated' readings.

Perhaps the most notorious example of the mixing of tones is in the accidental shooting of Marvin by Vincent as he sits in the back seat of a car.

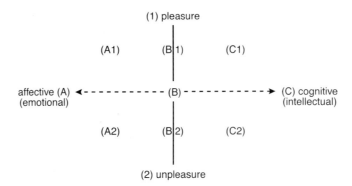

In relation to the particular sequence, different responses may include the following:

A1 Intense concern for Mia (that she recovers) and for Vincent (that he does not suffer the consequences of Mia's death)
B1 Amusement at the mix of black comedy and farce
C1 Delight in the way Tarantino mixes melodramatic intensity (1) with the comedy and farce (2)
A2 Distaste for Mia and Vincent, their behaviour and the values they represent
B2 Disorientation at the mix of black comedy and farce in a situation involving a drug overdose and possibly outrage as a consequence
C2 Irritation at the 'smart' way Tarantino mixes melodramatic intensity (1) with the comedy and farce (2)

Of course, these can be mixed: A1 could operate alongside B2 and C2, for example. And, of course, these are not the only responses.

Try out this model on a film of your choice. What is the range of responses? Which of these are more likely and why?

The tone of *Pulp Fiction* needs to be carefully measured. It is most appropriately approached as a black comedy – arguably, the 'preferred' response. So, for example, Mia is hardly treated with respect or care after her overdose. She is unceremoniously dropped on the grass outside Lance's house while Vincent begs for help for his *own* survival. 'That was fucking trippy' is the summary offered by Jody, Lance's girlfriend at the end of the 'emergency', and, in relieving the tension of the situation, is meant to speak on behalf of the spectator. By contrast, one could well imagine a spectator who finds the world of the characters, the attitude towards drugs in particular, so disturbing as to 'oppose' the film. Some fairly hard 'negotiating' would be required by the spectator who is simultaneously delighted and shocked by the characters and events and the manner in which they are depicted. We could also imagine a different kind of spectator, one who is committed to crime, violence and drugs. In seeing the film as endorsing criminal lifestyles would they be closer to a 'preferred' reading?

See the special section 'Some notes on spectatorship and regulation', pp. 157–9.

A complementary way of trying to explain different responses is again in relation to the concept of spectator 'competence'. In some respects 'competence' and evaluative judgement are clearly separable from one another. For example, I may be perfectly capable of appreciating artistically, cinematically what Tarantino is doing – and despise it morally, ideologically!

In other respects, however, it is more difficult to disentangle competence from evaluative judgement. For example, the inexperienced spectator may not be able to engage with fictional characters in the kind of playful, imaginative way a film such as *Pulp Fiction* clearly requires. The film invites us to take pleasure in all of A1, B1 and C1 as identified above. It is only possible to do so if the spectator is simultaneously 'inside' and 'outside' the fiction, able to empathise with character, imagine the situation and yet to recognise its fictional nature. The active spectator, like the active reader of literature, is able to use fiction to expand their experience, to become capable of new insights, more mature judgements – beyond the limitations of their actual experience in the 'real' world.

In a variety of formulations this remains the key debate running through the whole of this chapter: *Is the spectator 'passive' or 'active'; 'worked upon' or 'working'? The provisional answer offered here is that the films do have 'effects' (otherwise we would not be bothered to go and see them). These effects are the product of powerful communication processes. These effects will be handled by different spectators differently – on the basis of their 'formation' and their 'competence'. Most spectators, constituted as an audience, behave more or less the same way because, other than in personal detail, their formations and their competences are very similar within a given society. This is even more so if, as is probable, the spectators making up a given audience are largely self-selecting, having made their decision to enter the cinema on the basis of information available to them about the likely nature of the film experience on offer.*

None of this, however, deals directly with the central function of spectatorship: *imagining*. The 'passive' spectator is seen as one who somehow surrenders completely to the film experience in a form of imagining which can only be compared to some sort of infantile regression. The 'active' spectator is seen as one who is able, in the simple term used several times already, to be simultaneously inside and outside the world of the film. A somewhat different way of expressing this is by considering two different kinds of imagining:

In *The Thread of Life*, Richard Wollheim makes a fundamental distinction, corresponding to a big divide between two modes of imagination': 'central' imagining and 'a-central' imagining. A rough guide to the distinction can be found in linguistic clues. While central imagining is often expressed in the form 'I imagine...', a-central imagining is expressed in the form 'I imagine that...'.[5]

There are certain times when a spectator experiences 'central' imagining, particularly when a film recreates a physical sensation like falling or walking in a daze. The move towards ever more spectacular forms of visual and aural cinema – such as with the IMAX technology – we are being offered are forms of cinema providing more opportunities for central imagining.

See Chapter 3, pp. 82–3, for more on IMAX technology.

I imagine sitting on the rollercoaster ... I imagine the sensation of paragliding over mountains ...'. What is being created is the effect recorded as early as 1896 of spectators imagining a train coming towards them in Lumière's *Arrivée d'un train en gare à la Ciotat*, and made fun of as early as 1901 in Paul's *The Countryman and the Cinematograph*.

Most of the time the spectator operates in the 'I imagine that...' mode. *I imagine that it must be pretty scary to have a gangster's wife overdosing in front of you when you are responsible for her! I imagine that having to plunge a syringe into a woman's heart in order to bring her out of a coma must be, well, quite stressful and I can't imagine that I could ever do such a thing!*

By contrast, the 'subject' of classical film theory is conceived as being at one with the camera/projector and thus involved in central imagining. In practice it seems wisest to approach spectatorship as a complex mixture of central and a-central imagining.

See the special section 'More on the spectator as subject', pp. 143–7.

Vincent and Mia: 3

Consider two incidents in the 'Vincent Vega and Marcelus Wallace's wife' episode which draw particular attention to the film as a textual construct rather than something striving to disguise its construction, and which enable the 'suspension of disbelief'.

The first is a brief moment when Vincent and Mia are still in the car having just arrived outside Jack Rabbit Slim's.

Vincent:　　Come on, Mia, let's go get a steak.
Mia:　　　　You can get a steak here, daddy–. Don't be a...
Mia draws a square with her hands. Dotted lines appear on the screen forming a square. The lines disperse.
Vincent:　　After you, kitty-cat.[6]

This is the most blatant admission to the spectator of the film as textual construct. It is a characteristic particularly common in 'postmodern' art (see next chapter). The spectator is invited to take pleasure in a certain complicity with the film-maker – this is a 'game' made possible because of the coming together of the 'playful' imaginations of both.

The second incident is when Mia demands that Vincent join her to dance the twist. The spectator is confronted with a fine distinction between John Travolta's role and his star identity as the dancing star of *Saturday Night Fever* (1977). The relationship between textual and extra-textual information is clearly being exploited here in order to acknowledge the star 'myth'. A model of spectatorship which presents the inter-action between spectator and film text as closed off from wider contexts of audience and culture seems particularly inadequate in explaining what happens at moments such as these. Again, this can be described as a characteristic moment of postmodern cinema, this time involving a 'play' between the role of a character within the fiction and the persona image of a star who exists outside that fiction. Tarantino mobilises a knowledge and a set of associations held by the spectator, not to enhance the fiction but to intensify a sense of the spectator and director creating meaning together.

Maybe we can talk of two tendencies in contemporary cinema. One is the ever more costly attempts to produce the spectacular realist illusion, especially in action movies –

Again, for more on the potential disruptive effect of stars in realist films, see Chapter 6.

● **Plate 5.7** Lumière's *Arrivée d'un train en gare à la Ciotat* (1895). Movement towards the camera thrilled and terrified the first cinema audiences. There are a number of examples of the sadistic delight taken in 'running down' the audience: for example, in R.W. Paul's *The Motorist* (*circa* 1902), a car 'hits' the spectator head-on.

moving towards the kind of IMAX experience discussed above. The other is towards an ever more 'playful' kind of cinema – like that exemplified by *Pulp Fiction*. Maybe we need different conceptions of spectatorship for each: 'I imagine…' for the first, 'I imagine that…' for the second. However, the point holds from the end of the previous section above: for the majority of films it seems wisest to approach spectatorship as a complex mixture of central and a-central imagining.

Mixing it in spectatorship studies

There has not been space here to illustrate adequately any of the theoretical approaches to spectatorship described. Certainly you are invited to explore them further by engaging in a more detailed analysis of the episode from *Pulp Fiction* which has been the subject of this section.

Within such a study, there are valuable insights to be gained by adopting a mixed approach.

- The strong emphasis on the way the spectator is 'determined', deriving from the *'subject' theory* of 1970s film studies, may be less fashionable today but it still offers valuable insights, for example in the study of unconscious processes in spectatorship.
- The emphasis for much of this chapter has been on *response theory* with its emphasis on the detailed study of the relationship between the 'working' spectator and the aspects of the film text such as character.
- The political formation of both film text and spectator is emphasised in a *cultural studies* approach which opens up for study the social practice of cinema and thus places spectatorship much more within audience study.

See Chapter 9, pp. 283–6, for discussion of feminism and cultural studies.

Whichever approach is adopted, it is clear that spectatorship study must be closely linked to the study of film form. Also, there is undoubtedly the need to support spectatorship/audience study with solid empirical information – which, in keeping with too much writing on the subject, this chapter singularly lacks!

SOME NOTES ON SPECTATORSHIP AND REGULATION

Assumptions and biases

Debates around film regulation and censorship should be informed by *studies* of spectatorship. Instead they are nearly always informed by *assumptions* about spectatorship which are grounded neither in empirical nor theoretical studies.

In the UK there has existed for almost the entire history of cinema a paternalistic approach based on a set of assumptions about the power of the cinema 'apparatus' and the vulnerability of an audience to the manipulative potential of the film medium. The spectator has been regarded as in need of protection from the 'effects' of the cinema experience. This is particularly stridently stated during times of so-called 'moral panics'. When a different view about 'effects' has prevailed, more closely reflecting a cultural studies/response theory model of spectatorship, this has been the result of a more libertarian cultural climate in general, such as developed throughout the 1960s and 1970s.

For more on censorship see Chapter 2, pp. 48–53.

Often the debate on film 'effects' appears characterised by no more than those in one corner of the room shouting 'Oh, yes it does!' and those in the opposite corner shouting 'Oh, no it doesn't!'

I wish to refer briefly to four arguments and offer a summary overview.

Film and spectator disinhibition

This is a more sophisticated version of the simple stimulus→response idea that underlies much crude discussion of the spectator. Disinhibition refers to the gradual wearing-down of the moral/ideological 'rules' that the spectator adheres to as a member of a particular society. So, for example, the 'effect' of a sexual crime represented on film may appear negligible, but watching such events repeatedly within film fiction will, according to the argument, wear down the 'natural' inhibition the spectator has grown up with and which protects him/her from any tendency within themselves to carry out such an action.

Film and 'what if'

This can be related to ideas of central imagining and a-central imagining.

By contrast, there is the view that through fiction of all kinds, including film, we 'try out' experiences, some of which are not possible, some of which are not permissible. In so doing, we extend our experience – as we do when we watch television news. 'What if ... such a thing happened outside my front door?' It is argued that no matter how often we watch, for example, acts of gross violence in film, we will remain just as capable of being shocked and appalled by an act of violence witnessed in reality.

Film and catharsis

An extension of the 'trying out' argument is that film is unique as an art form because of the circumstances of reception in a darkened but public place. Within this space we can 'let go' the 'darker side' of our nature in a controlled, safe and ultimately therapeutic experience. The analogy is made with ancient Greek theatre and the notion that through the ritualistic blood-letting of theatre and religious forms, any craving to do these things in reality is safely channelled.

Liberal theories of spectatorship and the 10 per cent

Even if we are relaxed about the ideas put forward here, one question will not go away: What about the 10 per cent who are incapable of the imaginative processing required? (It may not be 10 per cent – this is the problem; without empirical data, numbers and percentages are thrown around quite wildly. Some spectators may indeed be incapable of distinguishing between fiction and reality. Some spectators may seek out certain films not in order to 'safely channel' some dangerous craving but in order to stimulate it. Should all spectators be controlled by legislation in order to protect society from a relatively small minority?

Political and social positions

The following attempts to superimpose political and social attitudes to censorship on to spectatorship theories. The model is crude and invites elaboration. The vertical axis represents the difference between a paternalistic government/state (such as in the UK) and a libertarian one (such as in Sweden, the Netherlands). Against each is attached a view on the spectator. The horizontal axis represents two ways in which a government/state can operate: one is a free market which puts as few restrictions on business as possible, promoting capitalist enterprise; the other is interventionist, believing that in order to protect certain social or moral values enterprise should be controlled.

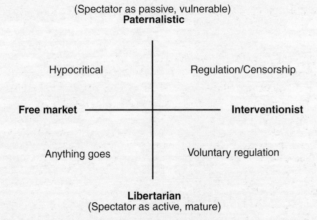

(Spectator as passive, vulnerable)
Paternalistic

Hypocritical   Regulation/Censorship

Free market ——————————— **Interventionist**

Anything goes   Voluntary regulation

Libertarian
(Spectator as active, mature)

Of the four quadrants, the one which may appear to make least sense is the left upper. It may seem difficult to imagine a state system which both promotes a free-market system while having strong paternalistic tendencies – perhaps caricatured as 'You can sell anything you like at whatever price you can get to anyone prepared to buy it … but oh, how can you sell this to these people – what effects it will have on them!' It may be reasonable to associate the last Conservative government in Britain with this contradictory position.

As a further footnote here, it is interesting that the long-held fear of cinema 'effects' from the dominant power groups in society should be shared by both the political right (e.g. conservative) and the political left (e.g. socialist) for similar and different reasons. Crudely speaking, the policing function of the state has been concerned by the potential of cinema for undermining core social values. The left has feared the opposite: that cinema lulls people into a state of passivity which prevents them from challenging the system in which they live. However, both are based on the shared assumption that the apparatus and the film text are somehow irresistible and overwhelming.

The demand is repeatedly for more empirical studies of how spectators actually behave. There is the ongoing need to refine descriptions of the spectator of theory so that he or she resembles as closely as possible the spectator sitting in a seat in the darkened auditorium of the cinema.

 **NOTES**

1   C. MacCabe, 'Realism and the Cinema: Notes on some Brechtian Theses', *Screen*, Vol. 15, No. 2, Summer 1974.

2   L. Mulvey, 'Visual Pleasure and Narrative Cinema', *Screen* (Vol. 16, No. 3, 1975).

3   R. Lapsley and M. Westlake, *Film Theory: An Introduction* (Manchester University Press, Manchester, 1988), p. 66.

4   Q. Tarantino, *Pulp Fiction – the screenplay* (Faber & Faber, London, 1994), p. 69.

5   M. Smith, *Engaging Characters* (Oxford University Press, Oxford, 1995), p. 76.

6   Q. Tarantino, *Pulp Fiction – the screenplay* (Faber & Faber, London, 1994), pp. 51–2.

 **FURTHER READING**

Accessible overviews of spectatorship and audience issues

('Accessible' is relative here – even basic writing on spectatorship quickly becomes quite demanding.)

Ellis, J. *Visible Fictions*, revised edn, (Routledge, London, 1992)

Hayward, S. *Key Concepts in Cinema Studies* (Routledge, London, 1996)

Lapsley, R. and Westlake, M. *Film Theory: An Introduction* (Manchester University Press, Manchester, 1988)

Mayne, J. *Cinema and Spectatorship* (Routledge, London, 1993)

O'Sullivan, T. *et al.* (eds) *Key Concepts in Communication and Cultural Studies* (Routledge, London, 1994)

Stacey, J. *Star Gazing: Hollywood Cinema and Female Spectatorship* (Routledge, London, 1993)

Turner, G. *Film as Social Practice*, 2nd edn, (Routledge, London, 1993)

More specific studies in spectatorship-related theory

The following list puts particular emphasis on spectatorship discussed from feminist and psychoanalytical perspectives:

Erens, P. (ed.) *Issues in Feminist Film Criticism* (Indiana University Press, Bloomington, 1990)

hooks, bell *The Oppositional Gaze: Black Female Spectators in Black American Cinema: Aesthetics and Spectatorship* (ed. Manthia Diawara, Routledge/AFI, London)

Kaplan, E. Ann (ed.) *Psychoanalysis and Cinema* (American Film Institute/Routledge, London, 1990)

Mulvey, L. *Visual and Other Pleasures* (Macmillan, London, 1982)

A different approach to spectatorship is one which gives no particularly privileged place to psychoanalysis. The following work, which has had a strong influence on the approach to *Pulp Fiction* offered in this chapter, focuses more on cognitive and social explanations for our response to films:

Smith, M. *Engaging Characters* (Oxford University Press, Oxford, 1995)

On Early Cinema and the development of spectatorship

The first two volumes of the University of California *History of the American Cinema* are particularly useful:

Musser, Charles, *The Emergence of Cinema: The American Screen to 1907* (University of California, Berkeley, 1994)

Bowser, Eileen, *The Transformation of Cinema 1907–1915* (University of California, Berkeley, 1994)

With the exception of Robinson's book, the following are quite advanced:

Bordwell, D. *On the History of Film Style* (Harvard University Press, Cambridge, Mass. 1997)

Burch, N. *Life to Those Shadows* (University of California, Berkeley, 1990)

Hansen, M. *Babel and Babylon – Spectatorship in American Silent Film* (Harvard University Press, Cambridge, Mass. 1991)

Robinson, D. *From Peep Show to Palace – the Birth of American Film* (Columbia, New York, 1996)

Censorship/Regulation

Three different approaches are represented here. The first looks at 'effects' and 'moral panic' debates; the second takes a cultural approach arguing that response to violent material relates to the particular 'formation' of that society. The third is an interesting response study looking at audience reactions to recent violent films. The fourth considers a range of examples of censorship around the world and the various motives for this censorship.

Barker, M. and Petley, J. (eds) *Ill Effects – the Media Violence Debate* (Routledge, London, 1997)

Duclos, D. *The Werewolf Complex: America's Fascination with Violence* (Oxford University Press, New York, 1998)

Hill, A. *Shocking Entertainment* (Libbey Books, Luton, 1997)

Petrie, R. (ed.) *Film and Censorship – The Index Reader* (Cassell, London, 1997)

Pulp Fiction

Tarantino, Q. *Pulp Fiction – the screenplay* (Faber and Faber, London, 1994)

Woods, P. *King Pulp – The Wild World of Quentin Tarantino* (Plexus, London, 1998)

There is, of course, much, much more on the Internet.

Chapter 6

Genre, star and auteur – critical approaches to Hollywood cinema

Patrick Phillips

■ **Introduction**   162
□ Case study part 1: genre, star and auteur critical
    approaches to *New York, New York*   164
■ **Genre**   166
□ Case study part 2: *New York, New York* as problematic
    musical   178
■ **Stars**   181
□ Case study part 3: *New York, New York* as clash of the
    stars   193
■ **Auteurs**   195
□ Case study part 4: Scorsese and *New York, New York*   202
■ **Beyond a structuralist critical approach to**
    Hollywood cinema   204
■ **Notes**   207
■ **Further viewing**   207

■ Genre, star and auteur – critical approaches to Hollywood cinema

INTRODUCTION

Introductory overview

It is possible to apply the principles of genre, star and auteur to other popular cinemas such as Hindi cinema (*see Chapter 12*).

In this chapter we will consider the significance of genre, star and auteur studies in trying to make sense of popular films made within the institution called Hollywood cinema. Beyond a very basic set of questions – what is genre study? what is star study? what is auteur study? – we will consider what they have in common as critical approaches. This will be done by focusing upon them as communication or 'meaning' structures. Such analysis may appear very cold and formal, but it enables us to see clearly how genre, star and auteur function to contain meaning within the film text. It also allows a very interesting extension to the study of spectatorship undertaken in Chapter 5. If we can see that genre, star and auteur structures work as systems of 'potential' meaning, then we can consider how they become 'actual' in the response of the spectator to them.

See Chapter 5 on spectatorship.

One way to explain how spectators make meaning is by reference to schemas, a concept used in studies of the human thinking process. When we are confronted by a new experience, we look for familiar patterns which allow us to orientate ourselves and make sense of what is in front of us. The structures within the film text provided by genre, star and auteur function as schemas for the human mind to work within the act of spectatorship.

Thus, in what follows, genre, star and auteur will be considered separately as discrete, well established critical approaches, and collectively as structures which work to put in place meanings within the film text, and as schemas which spectators can use as the basis for their imaginative work in making meaning.

For clarification of the difference between the Hollywood studio system and the 'new' Hollywood, see Chapter 2 on 'Cinema as Institution'.

The focus will be on a single film – *New York, New York* (1977).

There are several reasons for choosing this film: it exemplifies characteristics of genre, star and auteur which can easily be transferred to other Hollywood films; it is interesting because it is clearly a film of the 'new' Hollywood but pays homage to the product of the studio system; it is provocative for the purposes of this chapter because it demonstrates that the concepts of genre, star and auteur are dynamic, not static, and that critical approaches based on these concepts can be critical and questioning, not just descriptive. In relation to spectatorship, the film certainly makes demands, demands which it will be shown are met by the application of the schemas we bring with us, based on genre, star and auteur structures.

postmodern
This includes a complex set of ideas. It is defined below in the section entitled 'Playing with Genre', p. 175–8.

And just maybe you will be encouraged to seek out this film which is a key work in appreciating Martin Scorsese as an auteur; a fascinating text in trying to understand the relationship between 'classic' genre and '**postmodern**' cinema; and a rich example of stars slugging it out using very different performance styles. It is a flawed work – but flawed works are often the most interesting!

It is often said that when an agent or producer puts together a 'package' to present to a Hollywood studio for finance and distribution, it should have three saleable 'elements' – such as two stars and a well-known director, or a star, a director and a property such as the rights to a best-selling novel. If the studio likes the 'package', a 'deal' is done.

Ways of approaching Hollywood film: institution, form, audience

New York, New York is a film produced in Hollywood in 1977 by United Artists. It contains 'bankable' elements around which a characteristic Hollywood deal could be struck by producers Irwin Winkler and Robert Chartoff: a director (Martin Scorsese) and two stars (Robert De Niro and Liza Minnelli). Previous remarkable collaborations between Scorsese and De Niro, most recently *Taxi Driver* of the previous year, further guaranteed the financial viability of the project. What was less certain was the box-office potential of a film dressed up as a classic studio system musical. However, the confidence of the backers was clear; they agreed to a budget of $9 million. In return they got a film 153-minutes long costing $11 million. Any film of this length will have exhibition problems; in fact the film was first released in a version of (only) 136 minutes and got longer on re-release. The director had enough power to insist that what he considered a crucial scene – one which cost $350,000 to shoot – be included despite a general perception that the narrative needed to be tighter rather than more expansive. *New York, New York* was a commercial failure, although it has been passionately defended by some critics and audiences.

A study of *New York, New York* could elaborate on some of the stark details outlined in the previous paragraph. The film could be seen in relation to the *institution* which produced it, in this case, the Hollywood industry as it was operating in the second half of the 1970s. *New York, New York* is very much the product of the 'New' Hollywood of independent producers, powerful directors and autonomous stars drawn together in one-off projects. The study could focus on the financing of the project, the power-broking involved during the different stages of production. A study of the marketing, distribution and exhibition of the film would, perhaps, consider the particular challenges presented to the industry in handling a musical – and one of such length. Of particular concern might be the perennial conflict between financial restraint and artistic licence, a conflict which would reach a high point five years later with Cimino's *Heaven's Gate*, which brought United Artists to financial ruin. Another area of study could focus on production under the new Hollywood system, making comparisons with production under the studio system – a comparison with particular significance in this case where a deliberate attempt was made to recreate what appears, at least on the surface, to be such a typical studio-system product in a very different production context.

A different approach to *New York, New York* would be one which focuses not on institutional issues but on *film form*: the organisation of narrative, the use of *mise en scène*, editing, cinematography and sound. For example, the narrative of this fictional musical melodrama/**biopic** is conventionally linear, one event follows the preceding one in a chronological way, conveying in the process a cause→effect→cause→effect pattern. Much more unusual, by comparison, is the film's use of very long sequences, themselves partly the result of an unusual improvisational, documentary-style approach. In editing, the rejection of the master shot – that is, one which provides an overview of the setting and the location of the characters within it – in favour of a rhythm of tracking shots creates, along with the use of colour, a distinctive visual style. The anti-naturalistic look which results is the most obvious challenge in a study of the film's form. Scorsese has said:

> In the city streets I'd seen in MGM and Warner Brothers musicals, New York kerbs were always shown as very high and very clean. When I was a child, I realised this wasn't right, but it was part of a whole mythical city, as well as the feeling of the old three-strip Technicolor with lipstick that was too bright and make-up even on the men.[1]

One pleasure of *New York, New York* is in the contrast between this studied artificiality of the film's look and the edgy improvisational acting of its stars, especially Robert De Niro.

A third approach would be to focus on *audiences* for *New York, New York*. This could be done by looking at reviews and critical writing on the film in the period immediately after its release. It could also involve a study of audience response, although doing so over twenty years after the release of a film is fraught with difficulties. A historical

See Chapter 2, pp. 26–43, for a discussion of the US and UK film industries after 1949. Also see Steve Neale and Murray Smith (eds), *Contemporary Hollywood Cinema* (Routledge, London, 1998).

See Steven Bach's *Final Cut: Dreams and Disaster in the Making of Heaven's Gate* (Faber & Faber, London, 1986).

See Chapter 4 'Film form and narrative'.

biopic
A film which dramatises the biography of a real or imaginary person. It is usually characterised by a linear narrative. Examples of musical bio-pics range from *The Glenn Miller Story* (Mann, 1954) to *The Doors* (Stone, 1991).

approach, looking at the cultural status and significance of *New York, New York*, might tell us a lot, not only about the film but also about attitudes, preoccupations and tastes – and how these might have changed over time.

In choosing to focus on genre, star and auteur studies, it is impossible to isolate them from a study of institution, form and audience. On the other hand, however, the interaction between them is so complex that it is sometimes necessary and useful to artificially limit the scope of a study. The emphasis will be on *meaning* – as contained within genre, star and auteur elements – and *response* – as demonstrated in what spectators do with these genre, star and auteur elements.

☐ CASE STUDY PART 1: GENRE, STAR AND AUTEUR – CRITICAL APPROACHES TO *NEW YORK, NEW YORK*

Consider these three statements:

- *New York, New York* is a musical melodrama. It has a generic identity.
- *New York, New York* is dominated by two stars who impose their distinctive identities on the film.
- *New York, New York* is directed by an auteur, someone who imposes his distinct artistic identity on to the film.

The need to create an identity for a film is obviously crucial from the industry's position in having to sell a commodity. Audiences also need these identities in order to be able to identify what they are being offered, what expectations or 'promises' a particular film appears to contain, and in order to communicate with others about the film. Reviewers and media presenters whose work involves talking about films need to be able to latch on to easily understood identities. (It is significant how often a film with an unclear or ambiguous identity struggles at the box office – for example, Scorsese's (1982) *King of Comedy*.)

Genre, star and auteur are, like narrative and realism, important **discourse systems** working within and on behalf of the larger discourse system we call 'film studies' or 'cinematics'. A discourse is a mode of speech which has evolved to express the shared human activities of a community of people. So, for example, there is the distinctive discourse of the medical and legal professions, and there is the discourse of different academic disciplines. Film studies has, like other academic disciplines, developed its own language – its own discourse system – to make possible the identification and 'mapping' of that area of human activity and experience with which it is concerned.

These discourses enable discussion and debate to occur. For example, in naming things we categorise them: 'a musical', 'a De Niro film', 'a Scorsese film', 'a De Niro–Scorsese collaboration'. Disagreements over categorisations open up critical debate and encourage more detailed analysis. The very names we give things forces critical reflection and doubt – Can we be content with these names and identities? Are they sufficient to represent the film?

In the case of *New York, New York* a major difficulty arises over its *generic identity*. Is it a musical? Could it be better described as a melodrama involving musicians? If it is a musical, can it best be assigned to the sub-genre of musical biopic? Is it a celebration of or a critical reflection on the classic MGM musical, especially with its refusal of a happy ending? (The dismissal by Jimmy Doyle – De Niro – of the lavish 'happy-endings' film-within-the-film as 'sappy endings' will be touched upon in the next section.) These interesting questions arise because of a

See Further Viewing on p. 207 for examples of the MGM musical.

focus on genre. Whether we can agree in some definitive way on what exactly is the generic identity of *New York, New York* is less important than the encouragement that a critical approach through genre study gives to a wide ranging consideration of the film's complexities and ambiguities.

If we turn to the star identity of *New York, New York*, the presence of Liza Minnelli brings a number of elements associated with her star image. What precisely are we to make of the fact that the film is consciously re-creating the look of her father's (Vincente Minnelli's) MGM musicals and melodramas, or that her on-screen vulnerability may be informed by knowledge of her mother, Judy Garland?

Are either of these important in the final third of the movie which seems designed primarily as a vehicle for Liza Minnelli to 'do her thing' – belt out musical numbers in her distinctive performance style? Is the increasing sassiness of her character/performance – established in her Sally Bowles role in *Cabaret* (1972) – primarily there for itself or to provoke the De Niro character and thereby fire the melodrama of the film? In trying to arrive at some critical understanding of Minnelli's contribution to *New York, New York*, we can start from any of the above questions. Again, the fundamental point here is that the critical approach – here, star study – allows us to enter into a potentially rich and wide-ranging analysis of the film.

An understanding of *New York, New York* is very much enhanced by an appreciation of the auteur identity Martin Scorsese brings to the film. Without an awareness of the thematic and stylistic preoccupations of this director in his films either side of *New York, New York*, it may appear a far less rich and interesting work. Reference has already been made to his conscious 'homage' to the classic Hollywood musical on the one hand, but his rejection of its easy optimism on the other. The excess and abundance of the classic Hollywood musical is here overlaid by an introverted and dark melodrama of the male-in-crisis. The tension of the film is added to by his deliberate use of improvisational

Vincente Minnelli was a theatre designer brought from Broadway to Hollywood in the early 1940s. He specialised in directing musicals and melodramas. His second, after the remarkable black musical, *Cabin in the Sky*, was *Meet Me in St Louis* in 1944. He married Judy Garland, the star of that film. Judy Garland was one of the greatest of Hollywood talents. At a young age she was prescribed drugs to which she became addicted for the rest of her life. She became increasingly unreliable and developed a persona which included a mixture of vulnerability and strength. To a remarkable degree, her daughter seems to have repeated her mother's life.

Later in this chapter, the idea is put forward that it is common for contemporary film-makers to make reference to the history (and myths) of Hollywood cinema in order to produce additional levels

• **Plates 6.1 and 6.2** Mother, father and daughter. Plate 6.1 Vincent Minnelli directs Judy Garland on the set of *Meet Me in St Louis* (US 1944); Plate 6.2 Liza Minnelli in *Cabaret* (US 1972).

of meaning, additional resonance. It may be argued that Vincente Minnelli and Judy Garland have a shadow presence in *New York, New York*.

Discussion of *New York, New York* continues below in Part 2 of the case study, p.178.

For a list of Scorsese's feature films (his filmography), see Part 4 of the case study (p. 204).

realist performance techniques on the one hand, and very artificial *mise en scène* on the other. Now, it may be possible to discern each of the above characteristics of the film without any knowledge of Scorsese's other work, but again the point to be made is that the critical approach – here auteur study – opens up these conflicts and emphasises them in a particularly direct way, forcing our critical attention to be paid to them.

As each of the three preceding paragraphs has emphasised, it is the surprising difficulty that we encounter in working with questions of categorisation and identity that push us on to ask further and more interesting questions. This is even more the case when we acknowledge that genre-star-auteur work in combination and that our analysis must involve seeing the film as a complex whole. The combination

musical/melodrama – De Niro/Minnelli star vehicle – Scorsese auteur film

produces a film distinctive from one in which any of these elements are changed. In analysis, knowledge of the identity of each will inform an understanding of the other three.

Take some examples of Hollywood cinema, past or present and consider the following:

1 **How easily identifiable are genre, star, auteur in the 'image' of the film created by those responsible for promotion and marketing?**
2 **How far does 'talk' around these films, be it television reviewing or book publishing or conversation among movie-goers, depend on reference to genre, star, auteur?**

GENRE

What is genre?

This question needs to be answered by reference to a field of study broader than that of films and cinema. Genre is a fundamental means by which we communicate, especially in storytelling. Genres allow us to take the actual world in which we live and transform it into something much more controllable, much more rule-bound, in which imaginary solutions can be offered for real problems. A 'genre world' is one in which there are a limited and predictable range of features; where characters and events are more predictable and where our expectations are more likely to be fulfilled. Genres function in the way that any language system does – offering a vocabulary and a set of rules which allow us to 'shape' reality, thus making it appear more coherent and contained, less random and disordered. Transforming the experience of living into a set of predictable conventions and patterns provides us with some basic pleasures, the most important of which are based on the security they provide, compared to the relative shapelessness of real-life experience.

Extending this broad definition of genres as 'language systems', they can be seen to perform two essential communicative functions:

as structures used by those making meaning, both film-makers and spectators
as discourses for those who wish to talk about their response to the film: audiences, reviewers, critics, film students (see previous section above)

A structure is a combination of elements, this combination is governed either explicitly or implicitly by 'rules' which can be identified as a result of study. The elements available for inclusion within a particular structure are limited by these 'rules' which usually appear as based on convention or common sense. If these 'rules' are not adhered to, communication will become problematic.

The following diagram represents the basic elements of a communication structure, whether that communication is verbal, visual or musical. The horizontal axis is the syntagmatic (the rules which govern how words can be combined in sentences, visual images in a composition, notes in a piece of music, etc.). The vertical axis is the paradigmatic (the choice of words, images, musical notes, etc., which can be selected for a 'slot' (x) within the structure).

Selection
(limited) choice from
range of options

X   X   X   X

rule of combination
Construction

In applying this to film genre, we have the opportunity to appreciate how a genre works like other communication systems, based on acts of *construction* and *selection*. The fact that these are usually so automatic and taken-for-granted is an indication of how central they are to popular cinema.

Genre: selecting

The most common starting point in the study of genre is **iconography** – characteristic props, costumes and settings. In the terminology of semiotics these are 'signs', visual signifiers which can often allow us to identify instantly the genre of a film. The *visual signifiers* of a Western, such as *Stagecoach* (1939), are clearly different from those of a techno-action thriller such as *Terminator* (1984). We cannot arm John Wayne in *Stagecoach* with the weaponry carried by Arnold Schwarzenegger, while it would look odd to have the latter dependent on a horse to move around in the world of the *Terminator* movies. The distinctive visual signifiers of some genres, most notably film noir, are less to be found in objects than in a characteristic *mise en scène* of shadows and diagonals.

The paradigmatic options available to a film-makers working in two traditional Hollywood genres can be compared as follows:

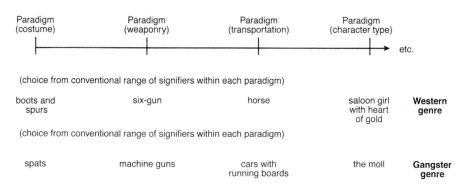

Paradigm (costume)	Paradigm (weaponry)	Paradigm (transportation)	Paradigm (character type)		
					etc.

(choice from conventional range of signifiers within each paradigm)

boots and spurs	six-gun	horse	saloon girl with heart of gold	**Western genre**

(choice from conventional range of signifiers within each paradigm)

spats	machine guns	cars with running boards	the moll	**Gangster genre**

If these words appear alien, consider this simple verbal sentence structure: *The dog bit the postman in my garden.* The syntagmatic rule tells us that we must put the words in a certain order and cannot write: *Bit the dog in my garden the postman.* The paradigmatic tells us what alternatives we can put in each 'slot'. So we might substitute cat for dog, milkman for postman and clawed for bit: *The cat clawed the milkman in my garden.* This is a reasonable alternative, but there comes a point where our playing around with paradigms comes up against common sense, as in: *The lion shot the movie star in my garden.* In other words, there are 'norms' which limit paradigmatic alternatives unless we wish to deliberately create some surreal image. Here is an example which keeps the same paradigms as in the first sentence but plays with their placement within the syntagm: *The postman bit the dog in my garden.* Playing with rules is something we will look at in the section 'Playing with genre' p. 175.

In all forms of communication, such as in the above, we select and construct. We do so in relation to rules and conventions.

See Chapter 4, pp. 99–103, for a discussion of mise en scène *and setting, and pp. 103–5 for a discussion of costume and* mise en scène.

However, iconography does not provide a sufficient basis for defining genre. Consider the way the traditional signifiers of the gangster genre are used to 'dress' the musical *Bugsy Malone* (1976) or how in *Westworld* (1974) the iconography of the Western is appropriated for a science-fiction movie.

When cross-overs do occur, they are sometimes integrated into the plot and themes of the film. This can be seen, for example, at the beginning of *The Shootist* (1976) when a number of signifiers such as a tram are deliberately introduced to indicate that the traditional world of the West has passed – and with it the hero of that world. When 'common sense' choices are not made the surprise can sometimes be disturbing, sometimes comic. The introduction of a motor car, and even more disconcertingly, a camel at the beginning of Peckinpah's Western *Guns in the Afternoon* (1962) illustrates the shock effect of going outside the conventional paradigms. The strategy of mixing genre elements has become increasingly common since the mid-1980s. It is illustrated in a simple and brash way by the arrival in the American West by the central characters of *Back to the Future 3* (1991) and in a more complicated, subtle way by elements from the horror movie in *The Quick and the Dead* (1995).

Again, see the section 'Playing with genre' (p. 175).

In addition to visual signifiers, genre paradigms include *musical signifiers* and *verbal signifiers*, particular kinds of speech which have become conventionalised in dramatising certain character types and situations. Some genres cannot be identified instantly by their visual signifiers. A film in a contemporary setting could be a crime thriller or a comedy. However, it is usually the case that in combination with musical signifiers (e.g. characteristic soundtrack) and verbal signifiers (e.g. characteristic dialogue), it is possible to quickly establish the kind of genre world we are entering.

An important underlying point here is that we have learnt how to decode these signifiers through growing up in a culture where they are part of everyday media communication. Film-makers and audiences share a common language or, rather, sets of languages which allow effective communication to take place.

• **Plates 6.3 and 6.4** Paradigms of dress as illustrated here in *Angels with Dirty Faces* (Michael Curtiz, US 1938) and *GoodFellas* (Martin Scorsese, US 1990), may help identify a genre – but not always. We often need to look beyond iconography.

Genre: constructing

Within Hollywood cinema, genre depends on narrative. Can we say that different genres have different rules of combination, that different kinds of construction show themselves in distinctive kinds of narrative? The work of theorists such as Propp and Todorov[2] has focused on the similarity in narrative across different genres. Genres which are clearly different from one another in terms of visual, verbal and musical signifiers operate according to the same overall narrative structures.

See the section on Narrative in Chapter 4, page 115–21.

Star Wars has proved to be a useful illustrations of how Propp's 'Morphology of the Folktale' can be applied to popular film. All the features which give *Star Wars* its generic identity as science fiction derive from the selection of signifiers (as discussed in the previous section). It could be 're-costumed' as a Western or as a thriller quite effortlessly.

See Graeme Turner's Proppian analysis of *Star Wars* in *Film as Social Practice* (Routledge, London, 1993).

Todorov's basic narrative theory with its concepts of equilibrium–disequilibrium–restoration of equilibrium is so general that it can incorporate any narrative in mainstream Hollywood from a musical such as *Singin' in the Rain* (1953) to a blockbuster action movie such as *Jurassic Park* (1994).

There remain, however, interesting differences between genres in terms of:

A practical guide to writing screenplays for Hollywood also demonstrates how much the film story is based on generic conventions and common myths – Christopher Vogler, *The Writer's Journey: Mythical Structure for Storytellers and Screenwriters* (Boxtree, London, 1996).

the nature of the disequilibrium
the methods used to try to restore/renew it
the degree of 'closure' and associated security in the new equilibrium at the end

This takes us beyond narrative structure as such, to consider the motives and methods which lie beneath the surface features. In so doing we move away from an abstract framework to the particular thematic preoccupations and ideological emphases of different genres. *Singin' in the Rain* explores ideas of individual authenticity and 'true' romance; *Jurassic Park* responsibility in the application of science and technology. *Singin' in the Rain* works through its thematic preoccupations using the methods of the musical genre, leading towards a set of utopian solutions and possibilities. In the process, a range of ideological issues around sexuality, gender, capitalist enterprise and work ethics are explored with a characteristic lightness which is based on a comfortably complacent set of assumptions easily intelligible to the film's audience. *Jurassic Park* works through its thematic preoccupations using the methods of the action movie, leading to a containment of the central problem of the film and thus a new, if rather provisional, equilibrium (space has to be left for a sequel!). In the process the ideological issues focus on 'natural' and scientific law with particular emphases on the individual and the group and professional competence. The negative values which create the disequilibrium and then exacerbate it, and the positive values which are applied in restoring order are, as with *Singin' in the Rain*, sufficiently familiar to be comfortably endorsed by the film's audience.

Another way of looking at the structuring principles of genre films is through the application of a **binary analysis**. This approach derives from cultural anthropology and particularly the work of Claude Lévi-Strauss. His work focuses on how storytelling is used as a means of coping with the fundamental contradictions and unresolvable difficulties of a society. Storytelling produces imaginative solutions which 'manage' or 'negotiate' across these divides. Each culture produces its **myths**.

myth
A key term within media and cultural studies: a myth is something which is not true but which is repeated so frequently that it becomes part of the 'reality' of the people who share it. In some instances it can become part of a culture's 'common sense' (see p. 167). Myth is a means by which the ideology of a culture takes form.

It is possible to identify the binary structure of a Hollywood genre and, in the process, not just list the typical thematic issues with which it deals but locate the 'ideological work' of that genre, the particular myths it constructs and perpetuates. We can see how this fits with the definition of genre offered above – 'genres allow us to take the actual world in which we live and transform it into something much more controllable, much more rule-bound, in which imaginary solutions can be offered for real problems'. Consider the typical binary structures at work in the Western and the musical respectively.

The Western		The musical	
Open space	Containment	Scarcity	Abundance
Wilderness	Cultivation	Exhaustion	Energy
Individualism	Institution	Manipulation	Transparency
Natural law	Institutional law	Fragmentation	Community

I am indebted to Kitses' work on the Western and Dyer's on the musical (see Bibliography, p. 503).

The focus on thematic structure is most interesting when we begin to look at the spaces between the binary oppositions. The 'leaps' from one side to the other carried out within the narratives of Hollywood genre films are possible because genre conventions make them permissible.

This 'leap' is often achieved through the extraordinary personal qualities of the star. For more on this see section on 'Stars and ideology' p.189.

Such 'leaps' offer imaginative solutions to the real contradictions that face us in everyday life as we work with different kinds of value systems and different sets of aspirations. The pleasure (and 'escapism') of popular film is located in the mix which involves exploring important and personal issues of value and identity in the spectator, and then resolving these issues more effectively and more ideally than is possible in life. (Not least because in life we cannot rely on a Hollywood plot with its convenient turns of event to help us out!)

In summary, what is being suggested here is that there are two principles in the construction of a genre film. One is the basic shape and trajectory of the movie and which is more or less the same for all popular mainstream films; the other is more varied and is based on the recurrent themes and solutions we identify within different genres. The combination of different ideological themes and solutions within the standard narrative (disruption of equilibrium→overcoming the resulting crises→restoration of equilibrium) makes possible complex films and interesting critical analysis.

Take a film with which you are familiar. Consider:

1   **the thematic issues and problems at the heart of the film in binary terms**
2   **the way these problems are worked through by the end of the film**
3   **how far there is a dependence on the extraordinary qualities of a central character in this working through**
4   **the extent to which the issues and problems have actually been resolved – as opposed to simply displaced or skirted over.**

How many genres?

Polonius' list raises an important point about how we identify and name genres. He uses much broader categories than is common in film studies. (See the work of F. McConnell, note 3, p. 207.)

Based on Todorov's formulation of popular narrative we may be tempted to answer that there is only one genre dressed in many different types of clothes. At the other extreme, if we enter the labyrinth of signifiers and their classification according to their particular combination we may end up endorsing the words of Polonius in Shakespeare's *Hamlet*:

The best actors in the world, either for tragedy, comedy, history, pastoral, pastoral-comical, historical-pastoral, tragical-historical, tragical-comical-historical-pastoral...

By contrast, there has been a number of attempts to classify the range of stories that exist within western culture into very few archetypes. These archetypes are 'core' stories which contain the basic experiences, values and beliefs of the culture. The way a culture makes sense of itself, involves, as already discussed, mythologising. The most common myths relate to national identity and the key events which at different points in a culture's history have formed or consolidated that identity. British cinema, for example, is often studied in relation to national myths of 'Britishness' and how the qualities contained in this concept are particularly clearly represented at defining historical moments – such as the Second World War. In the US the mythologising of nineteenth-century history (particularly by Hollywood) produced the 'Wild West', a place and a state of mind which may not be very accurate historically but which contains many of the fundamental values and beliefs of the nation.

See Chapter 11 for a discussion of British cinema.

In a particularly imaginative study, Frank McConnell offers just four character types and four genres which correspond to the four-stage historical cycle of a culture:[3]

> The King establishes the state – EPIC
> The Knight consolidates the state – ADVENTURE ROMANCE
> The Pawn is trapped in the institutionalised state of laws – MELODRAMA
> The Fool points out the craziness of the institutionalised state – SATIRE

Beyond this McConnell posits a fifth stage in the cycle – apocalypse – a breakdown into anarchy and decadence which requires the establishment of a new order – and a new cycle.

One of the things that McConnell's work helps us to recognise is the significant concentration of Hollywood genres within what he calls melodrama. In some genres, like film noir, the 'pawn' becomes increasingly trapped while in others, most exceptionally the musical, the pawn finds release into a utopian world. McConnell's work encourages us to pay particular attention to the 'borders' between his different categories. The Western, for example, deals with a fascinating paradox: the 'knight' who rides the open spaces extending and consolidating the advance of so-called 'civilisation' is, in the process, creating the world of 'law' and his own demise. This is, for example, very consciously the subject of John Ford's *The Man Who Shot Liberty Valance* and, more subtly, Clint Eastwood's *The Outlaw Josey Wales* (see the Western binary structure in the previous section). McConnell's work may also force us to make a distinction between different kinds of comedy: one which is ultimately conservative because it remains within melodrama, laughing with the 'pawn' and his or her necessary compromises – like the parenting comedies of the late 1980s to mid-1990s such as *Look Who's Talking* and *Parenthood*; and one which is potentially much more radical – like the war comedies *Dr. Strangelove* and *Mars Attacks!*. Finally, and in anticipation of the section 'Playing with genre' (p. 175), I suggest that McConnell forces us to consider what 'apocalypse' might look like in relation to a contemporary 'postmodern' cinema.

Whether or not one finds McConnell's work specifically useful, it is worth pursuing the more general idea that a large number of superficially different Hollywood genres actually represents a relatively small number of basic mythical/ideological themes. Furthermore, these themes are contained within narrative structures which are remarkably similar. In turning to the work of Thomas Schatz we find another critic looking for approaches to genre classification which emphasise similarity and overlap.

For a discussion of genre and the postmodern, again see 'Playing with genre' p. 175.

Schatz, in his definitive study, *Hollywood Genres* (1981), adopts a thematic and ideological approach which identifies only two genres: the 'genre of order' and the 'genre of integration'.[4]

Genres of order	Genres of integration
(for example, Western, gangster, science fiction)	(for example, musicals, comedies, melodramas)
Hero	**Hero**
Individual (male dominant)	Couple or collective – e.g. family (female dominant)
Setting	**Setting**
Contested space (ideologically unstable)	Civilised space (ideologically stable)
Conflict	**Conflict**
Externalised (expressed through violent action)	Internalised (expressed through emotion)
Resolution	**Resolution**
Elimination (death)	Embrace (love)
Thematics	**Thematics**
The hero takes upon (him)self the problems, contradictions inherent in his society and acts as redeemer	The couple or family are integrated into the wider community, their personal antagonisms resolved
Macho code of behaviour	Maternal – familial code
Isolated self-reliance (either through his departure or death, the hero does not assimilate the values/lifestyle of the community he saves – but maintains his individuality)	Community co-operation

One strength of Schatz's approach is that it allows films which are superficially different in their iconography and other aspects of their signifying systems to be studied in terms of their common underlying thematic structuring principles (see above). *Braveheart* and *Independence Day* both concern heroic individualism in which male characters engage in 'externalised' conflict in 'contested' space – in one case thirteenth-century Scotland, in the other the US/world of the near future. The hero figures take upon themselves the problems of their societies to act as redeemers, employing male codes of conduct. At the end, they remain apart from the peoples they have fought on behalf of. *Sense and Sensibility* and *Clueless* both concern groups in a 'civilised' space – in one case early nineteenth-century England, in the other Beverley Hills of the 1990s. The female group is integrated into the wider community and the issues of the films are resolved through reference to community and family.

Again reminding ourselves that critical analysis is a creative act and that no one theory or model should be applied slavishly, it is clear that Schatz's categories are broadly helpful but sometimes break down in detail. Interrogating just a little further the films referred to in the previous paragraph, we might ask whether *Independence Day* is as much about 'isolated self-reliance' as is *Braveheart*; whether 'the integration into the wider community' with 'personal antagonisms resolved' is really comparable in *Sense and Sensibility* and *Clueless* (*Sense and Sensibility* and *Clueless* are in their very different ways, based on Jane Austen novels). To take another pair of examples, both Tom Hanks movies, we would want to place *Forrest Gump* and *Philadelphia* in the 'genre of integration'. Both deal with an individual male central character but one who

• **Plate 6.6** *Stagecoach* (Ford, 1939)

• **Plate 6.5** *Robocop*
(Verhoeven, 1987)

Is it possible to see four genre films, which at face value appear completely different from one another, as having important things in common? (See the discussion of 'Genres of order' on p. 172).

• **Plate 6.7** *Braveheart*
(Mel Gibson, 1995)

• **Plate 6.8**
Independence Day (Roland Emmerich, 1996)

• **Plate 6.9** *Sense and Sensibility* (Ang Lee, 1995)
Have these films more in common than appears at first sight?

• **Plate 6.10** *Clueless* (Amy Heckerling, 1995)

works through 'internalised' conflict to resolve problems through love. By contrast, a different kind of 'cross-over' is represented by the *Alien* series, firmly placed in the 'genre of order' though the heroic individual is female.

What the critical application of Schatz's classification is forcing us to do is to think more carefully about genre. His classification is a basic binary opposition and in such a system the spaces between are nearly always of greatest interest as we have already seen. Perhaps one of the reasons for the continuing fascination with film noir, such as *Mildred Pierce*, is because they work a space between 'order' and 'integration', between crime and melodrama.

Perhaps the interest in *Thelma and Louise* lies primarily in the way it negotiates between the two kinds of genre Schatz identifies.

For further discussion of film noir and Mildred Pierce, *see Chapter 4, p. 108.*

How useful do you find Schatz's classification in relation to the output of contemporary Hollywood?

A genre-based critical approach

The characteristic qualities of a film genre can be studied in isolation. It is possible to list the characteristic choices of signifiers ('Genre: selecting') and the characteristic combination of elements ('Genre: constructing'). On the other hand, there is the opportunity to go beyond the single-genre approach and to play off features of one genre against another (see previous section).

The first approach has clarity but is, arguably, circular. The critic starts off with a check list of conventional features already in place and then demonstrates their applicability by measuring a film or group of films against them. At worst, this reduces genre study to a 'ticking off' of features based on an 'essentialist' methodology. Like the formal function of genre itself, this critical approach runs the risk of producing a containment and closure of the world it represents rather than an opening up of that world to a more curious gaze. If a genre is seen as free-standing, appearing to make reference only to its own internal 'systems', there is little incentive to think beyond this fictional construct to the real world it somehow represents and to ideological issues at the heart of the film.

The second approach is potentially messy and confusing. The 'check list' is still used – but only as the launchpad for a much more open, exploratory approach. If genre study is to be of real value it is in encouraging a marauding approach across the *whole* of Hollywood – from Western to techno action-thriller and from road movie to teen comedy. In their different ways McConnell and Schatz offer models of flexible rather than pedantic approaches to genre classification, an approach which promotes creative and productive comparisons to be made across formal generic boundaries. In fact a 'marauding' approach to genre is best exemplified today from within Hollywood, from screenwriters and film-makers, as will be discussed in the next section.

A third approach to genre study involves a very different emphasis – away from film texts and their 'meaning structures' – and towards spectators and their 'work'. In Chapter 5 on spectatorship, as well as at the start of this chapter, the concept of schemas has been touched upon. Clearly, genre helps spectators to become orientated, to navigate their way through the world of the film by reference to familiar features. Of particular interest is the pleasure that a genre film offers through offering an experience which is almost entirely predictable while weaving just enough variation and suspense to make it different from the previous encounters which the spectator has had with films of the same genre. The imaginative work of the spectator involves a complicity with the genre, engaging with it through an acceptance of the ways in which it works. If a genre works, it does so because the spectator allows it to. How and why are among the most fascinating questions in film studies.

> **Trace the changing popularity of a genre such as the Western or the musical over time and try to offer an explanation.**

It can be said that we inherit language insofar as we are born into it and learn to make sense of our world through the terms language offers. This language we inherit is not 'innocent'; rather, it bears all the marks of the history through which it has developed. We inherit language and we also inhabit language. We live inside language, so much so that some linguists and philosophers argue that language does our thinking for us: we are only able to process our world to the extent that our language allows us to. To extend further the analogy between language and genre offered earlier, it can be said that both film-maker and spectator inherit genre with all the additions and ideological colourings of its history. And just as we inhabit verbal language, film-maker and spectator inhabit genre.

For a discussion of gender and language, see Chapter 9, p. 277.

The more appreciation of the inheritance, the more understanding of the habitation, the richer and more productive will be the creative process of 'making meaning'. Film-makers such as Scorsese, Lynch, the Coen brothers and Tarantino work through their generic 'inheritance' and 'habitation' to produce creative and exciting work. Those working in genre studies have the potential to be equally bold, to demonstrate that in grouping films and making connections across films they are themselves involved in important and exciting work.

Playing with genre

Awareness today of genre among film-makers and audiences alike is such that it has become a defining characteristic of what is often referred to as 'postmodern

Hollywood'. John Belton in his excellent *American Cinema/American Culture* identifies three characteristics of **postmodern** cinema:[5]

First, it is based on pastiche of traditional generic material.
Second, much of the imitation is of images from the past, offered as a nostalgic substitute for any real exploration of either the past or the present.
Third, this referencing the past reflects another problem the film-maker faces today: not being able to say anything which has not already been said.

The postmodern film-maker struggles to make meaning from what appear as a vast and meaningless assembly of detail – visual, verbal and musical signifiers – in contemporary culture. As Belton comments, 'in transmitting the reality of their social and cultural context, they reproduce only its incoherence'. This can produce work which is superficially exciting, both thematically and stylistically, but which begs questions about any substantial meaning. The work of the Coen Brothers is often cited to illustrate postmodern Hollywood – *Barton Fink* (1991) providing a particularly good example. Stone's *Natural Born Killers* (1994) is also often referred to as postmodern. In this latter case, however, it is truer to say that it is a film *about* postmodernism.

Bricolage is a term used to describe the playful mixing of elements from different artistic styles and periods. This tendency can be found in the way some Hollywood films from the mid-1980s onwards have included self-conscious references, especially generic references, from the vast storehouse of images and memories of film accumulated through the repeated viewing of films from the past. The access to this 'storehouse' through television, and particularly through video, has created a genre-literate culture of considerable sophistication. Jim Collins describes the contemporary Hollywood film text as a narrative which operates simultaneously on two levels:[6]

in reference to character adventure
in reference to a text's adventure in the array of contemporary cultural production

The 'text's adventure' can be described as in large part the free use of generic signifiers, disconnected from their conventional paradigmatic use in stable narratives (see 'Genre: selecting' p. 167). *Raising Arizona*, the 1986 film by the Coen Brothers, provides a vivid illustration of this playfulness. Its overall hybrid generic identity – comic melodrama, social satire, thriller – is intensified by its appropriation of signifiers from an even broader range of genres. The 'Mad Max' biker figure and the escaped convicts come from other generic worlds; their presence manages to be both comic and disturbing. Adapting the simple diagram from page 167, the generic hybrid, *Raising Arizona*, can be represented as follows:

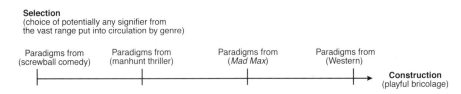

Selection
(choice of potentially any signifier from
the vast range put into circulation by genre)

Paradigms from (screwball comedy)	Paradigms from (manhunt thriller)	Paradigms from (*Mad Max*)	Paradigms from (Western)	

Construction
(playful bricolage)

The heightened awareness of genre is also producing a more subtle 'postmodern' experience. This can be seen in the relationship of both film-makers and spectators to films which are not extravagant 'hybrids' but apparently straightforward genre films. Coppola's *Bram Stoker's Dracula* (1992) uses the signifiers and structures of a particular

• **Plates 6.11 and 6.12**
Raising Arizona (Coen Bros, US 1986) This baby has genre problems!

genre in a conventional way – even if elaborated upon by some blockbuster special effects and an understated AIDS theme. In *Cape Fear* (1991), Scorsese offers a psychological thriller which contains a range of features typical of the genre. Dahl's *The Last Seduction* (1994) has characters and a narrative which conform to a standard film noir check list. However, in all these films there is a '*knowingness*', a self-consciousness on the part of film-maker in deploying generic features and on the part of spectators in interpreting them.

In fact a closer examination of any of these three films reveals 'excess' of one kind or another – in performance, visual style or plotting – suggesting that 'knowingness' and postmodern 'playfulness' go together. Critics of postmodernism discuss how artistic work becomes less concerned with representing an external reality and more preoccupied with **intertextuality**, texts 'talking' to other texts.

See final section p. 204–6.

It is interesting to speculate, as Jim Collins has done,[7] on the extent to which there is a new genre divide in Hollywood today – between the 'eclectic' or 'hybrid' film on the one hand, smart and 'knowing', and a more traditional kind of film keen to endorse 'authentic' values and a solid, traditional sense of reality, as opposed to a playful set of representations.

It is worth considering again *Pulp Fiction* (discussed in Chapter 5). The popularity and critical success of the film is based on its 'playfulness'. One can, however, understand a reaction against such a representation of reality.

Certainly the very strong box-office and critical reception given to more traditional genre films, from Costner's *Dances with Wolves* (1990) through Eastwood's *The Unforgiven* (1992) to Minghella's *The English Patient* (1997), suggests, at the very least, a nostalgia for the Hollywood conventions to which they conform.

> Are some genres less touched by postmodern 'playfulness' than others? If so, which and why? In answering these questions you will need to reflect on the relationship between film and the broader culture.

☐ CASE STUDY PART 2: *NEW YORK, NEW YORK* AS PROBLEMATIC MUSICAL

Three moments from the film illustrate the demands *New York, New York* makes on its audience:

1   Jimmy Doyle observes a sailor dancing with a girl late at night. The couple is alone and there is no music. This manages to be both a ***hommage*** to MGM's *On the Town* (1949) and a re-enactment of the kind of masculine crisis and alienation associated with the period immediately following the end of the Second World War. This period produced both film noir, with its dark studies of male entrapment, and the celebratory MGM musicals produced by Arthur Freed.

2   Jimmy Doyle decides to marry Francine Evans (Minnelli) – in the middle of a snowy night (of studio-set artificiality). He drives her to the registry office without having proposed or even explained his actions. The scene that follows has elements of both comedy and romance, but it is uncomfortable, at times embarrassing to watch. Neither the comedy nor the romance promises any meaningful 'integration'.

3   Jimmy and Francine have divorced. Francine is now a movie star. Jimmy goes to see her latest film, *Happy Endings*, which contains Busby Berkeley-style choreography and exuberant display (highlighting in its extravagance the starkness of the musical called *New York, New York* which contains it). Afterwards, Jimmy lightly dismisses the sequence as 'sappy endings' – in so doing dismissing the film's own *hommage* to the classical musical. This is followed by the closure of the narrative in which no reconciliation between Jimmy and Francine occurs – no happy ending.

Andrew Sarris wrote of *New York, New York* in *The Village Voice*: 'What is it like? people ask me…it is mixed moods and delirious dialectics – two crucial ingredients for box office poison.'

How might a genre-based critical approach (a) explain the difficulties the film has caused, and (b) take us towards a better understanding and appreciation of the film's qualities?

Normally the superficial generic identity of a film will trigger in the minds of audiences certain schemas, and these will be used as mental frameworks for making meaning. The first difficulty to be acknowledged with regard to *New York, New York* is that we are uncertain about what we are being presented with, constantly unsettled by having to adapt the schemas we would normally expect to apply effortlessly in making sense of a Hollywood genre film.

Does breaking the film down into its constituent sub-genres help? For example, we can say that the film contains elements of four different kinds of musicals: the artificial sets and the particularly extravagant 'Happy Endings' sequence place this within the MGM musical of Vincente Minnelli and Stanley Donen/Gene Kelly from the late 1940s and early 1950s; De Niro's role conforms to the big-band era which preceded the MGM musical; Liza Minnelli's role conforms to the individualistic star celebration exemplified

---

hommage
The French word for an act of paying homage, sincere respect.

On the Town is a musical about three sailors who have twenty-four hours shore leave to enjoy New York. It includes the song 'New York, New York'.

The 'Happy Endings' sequence repeats a convention of MGM musicals from the late 1940s and 1950s – a film within a film. See, for example, the climactic sequences of *Singin' in the Rain* or *Band Wagon*.

Cabaret (Fosse, 1972) and *New York, New York* are worth comparing not just for their casting of Liza Minnelli. There is, for example, a similar refusal of the standard happy ending of the musical.

Interestingly, Scorsese, in his excellent video history *The Century of Cinema* (1995) identifies the three key Hollywood genres as those most indigenous to the US: the Western, the gangster movie and the musical.

• **Plate 6.13** *On The Town* (MGM, US 1949)
• **Plates 6.14 and 6.15** *New York, New York* (Martin Scorsese, US 1977)
(Plate 6.13) The three sailors at the centre of MGM's 1949 musical *On the Town*, enjoy their twenty-four hours shore leave. *New York, New York* picks up images and sounds from this film but with a sense of melancholy for things lost rather than exuberance at life's possibilities. (Plate 6.14) Francine Evans (Minnelli) and Jimmy Doyle (De Niro) at their midnight wedding in *New York, New York* – a scene which is uncomfortable, even in its comedy. (Plate 6.15) Happy (sappy?) endings – the musical climax to the film – both a *hommage* to the great MGM musicals and a self-conscious commentary on their romanticism.

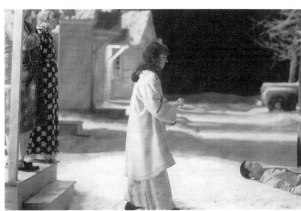

in the late 1960s and early 1970s by various Barbra Streisand vehicles; in narrative the film most resembles the musical biography of the 1940s.

Reference to the visual and musical signifiers is not enough. From them alone we find ourselves unable to place this film unambiguously in the musical genre. These do not capture either the comedy or the darkness of the film. We might, instead, be encouraged to describe the film as a melodrama with music. Scorsese himself has emphasised the melodrama:

It could have been a film about a director and a writer, or an artist and a composer. It's about two people in love with each other who are both creative. That was the idea: to see if the marriage would work.[8]

Does an attempt to place the film within McConnell's melodrama category or within Schatz's 'genre of integration' take us farther? Certainly the struggle of Jimmy Doyle in institutional structures, especially marriage, dramatises the tension between the free-spirit of the 'knight' and the entrapment of the 'pawn'. The Schatz model is useful in amplifying the tension we sense at the heart of the film. It provides us with a framework within which we can see Jimmy Doyle caught between 'macho code' and 'contested space' on the one hand and 'familial code' and 'stable space' on the other. The closure of the film leaves antagonisms unresolved, the central male character in a state which Schatz describes as 'isolated self-reliance'.

We can also begin to see more clearly how different thematic/ideological issues are embodied in the film. These may be further opened up by the application of a binary analysis.

Richard Dyer identifies the distinct 'product' of the classic MGM-style musical as feeling – abundance, energy, community.[9] These qualities provide imaginary solutions to a real world of scarcity, exhaustion, manipulation and fragmentation. *New York, New York* singularly lacks this 'feel-good factor' and does not offer a 'utopian solution' to the problems of living in a real social world. The sets, for example, manage simultaneously to conjure up the colour and style of the classic musical, and at the same time to convey something eerie, often barren. Their obvious artificiality is used to convey distance, disconnectedness, alienation.

The film refuses us the normal 'leap' across binary opposites. As a consequence we are refused the normal pleasures that we expect from popular cinema, pleasures that

New York, New York	*The Hollywood musical*
Alone	Community
Authoritarian	Accommodating
Assertive individuality	Harmonious ensemble
Comedy of embarrassment	Comedy of delight
Anger	Charm
Respected	Celebrated
Self-sufficiency	Family
Energy turned inwards	Energy externalised
Introspective performance	Extrovert performance
Success as meaningless	Success as abundance
Jimmy Doyle (as problematic)	Francine Evans (as unproblematic)

derive from the imaginary overcoming of some of the inherent contradictions and limita-tions of real life. *New York, New York* may not quite be the world of *Taxi Driver*, but it certainly suggests a world darker and more troubled than anything we would associate with the musical or the romantic melodrama. Indeed, the more one confronts the main conflicts within the film (what Sarris called the 'delirious dialectics), the more we are able to appreciate how far removed the whole structure is from one which might be associated with a 'genre of integration'.

A sensitivity to Hollywood genre will also allow us to see how this film depends for some of its power and effect on its intertextuality, its 'play' with the heritage of Hollywood film. As a text *New York, New York* can be said to 'inherit' and 'inhabit' genre. Sometimes the effect is celebratory, sometimes ironic and sometimes both at the same time – as in the three examples quoted at the start of this section.

I would argue that the application of a genre-based critical approach is useful here both in explaining the difficulties of the film and in helping us to think through them.

Discussion of New York, New York *continues below in Part 3 of the case study. p. 193.*

STARS

What is a star?

First of all, a star is a *real person*. It may be thought that this obvious fact is hardly worth stating. Surely in star study we are interested in the transformation of the ordi-nary, the presence in our lives of the extraordinary. While this is true, our interest in these figures is intensified by the sense of their ordinariness. Throughout the twentieth century the cult of the star has depended on a simultaneous sense of the star's excep-tional qualities and the fact that at some level of everyday living they have experiences just like we do and can be communicated with as friends we know. The appeal of the star is, in part, because he or she exists and could, by some quirk of fate, enter our lives. Certainly when a star dies, the loss we feel is for a real person.

Second, a star is a public performer of *roles*. The primary encounter we have with a film star is in the roles they play. We come to know them through their roles – which bring us close to their physical bodies, to characteristic features of their voice, look, gesture. Through their roles we begin to associate them with particular attitudes and ideological positions.

Third, and arising from what has just been said, the star is a *persona*. This involves a merging of the real person and the roles they play, particularly in cases where the star takes on the same type of role repeatedly. This is a figure constructed maybe by fans, maybe by publicists, maybe by the media, maybe by all three working in combination. The persona may indeed represent significant elements of the real person, but not necessarily.

Fourth, a star is an *image*. He or she becomes a sign – a cultural 'signifier' of a particular concentration of qualities, most often relating to gender and sexuality. He may represent a particular male image; she a particular female image. Both are likely to be objects of desire. They 'em-*body*' a set of values which are fashionable and which capture the *zeitgeist* – the spirit of the time. The image is the most unstable of the four components of the star listed here. It can shift over time and it can mean different things to different groups in society at the same moment.

See Richard Dyer's *Stars* (BFI, London, 1998). The basis for much of what follows here is found in C. Gledhill (ed.), *Stardom* (Routledge, London, 1991), Chapters 13–16.

See Chapter 12, p. 388–9, for a discus-sion of stars in Indian cinema.

Consider Marilyn Monroe as a star. She can be known to us through biographical study as Norma Jean Baker, a *real person*. In *role*, she is known to us as a 'dumb' blonde, a comedienne and singer. Her *persona* merges the real person with these roles. We imagine we know the real person as the person on screen. Her *image* lies beyond the first three. It is an image signifying stardom itself – something quite 'other' and outside our experi-ence. However, the image is not stable within culture; it becomes contested. The Monroe image of the 1950s is very different from the Monroe image of the 1990s, demonstrating how a star image can change over time. Equally the Monroe image may mean different things to different groups in society at the same moment. For example, the image of Monroe is appropriated by feminism in a different way to the way it is appropriated by the advertising industry.

> **Consider two stars of your choice. Apply the concepts – person, role, persona, image – to each of them. Does the approach work more easily for one than the other? If so, why?**

The star is accessed through films which often function specifically as 'vehicles' (see 'The star as structure, p. 184). In addition there is the promotional material produced by the industry (including the agency acting on behalf of the star) and media commentary (including review and feature writing) which, in a circular way, simultaneously speak on behalf of the star's public and to that public.

The real person, the roles and the persona are most often the objects of *biographical study*. The image takes us into broader areas of *cultural study*. The inter-relationship of real person–role–persona–image may be approached through *institutional study* or *audience/fan study*, depending on where the emphasis is placed in exploring how the star has been 'constructed'.

A different way of talking about stars is in terms of their functions.[10]

For more on stars and their function within the film industry, see Chapter 2, pp. 21 and 33.

A star can be said to offer '*insurance value*' to the film industry by guaranteeing the success of a film production project. Whether in the studio-system period when they were under lengthy contracts, or under the new Hollywood where they become 'elements' in a 'package', stars have been major attractions for film audiences. (Of course, a miscalculation – such as the choice of a wholly inappropriate star for a genre film – will undermine the 'insurance value'. In contemporary Hollywood, the star may come so expensively that the gamble on the insurance premium has to be carefully considered!)

A star can also be said to offer a '*production value*'. He or she will bring something unique to the film which can be exploited in achieving the overall meaning and effect of the film. This production value is based on the star's persona and image as discussed above. A very simple but effective way of getting a measure of the production value a particular star brings to a film project is by substituting that star for another in a specific film role. This 'commutation test' can be both revealing and fun.

For more on the commutation test, see 'The star as structure' p. 184, which includes a 'swapping' of Leonardo DiCaprio with Brad Pitt.

A star can also be said to offer a '*trademark value*' which contains elements of the previous two values. What is specifically referred to here is a set of characteristics which can be mobilised for publicity and marketing purposes. However, the trademark is more than just a sign of quality – as in a 'guarantee'; it is also a condensed meaning – a communication of what the film will be about and how it will feel.

In 1991 Richard Dyer offered an analysis of Julia Roberts which employed the concepts used above.[11] With the benefit of hindsight, it is particularly interesting that he talked about 1991 as 'the year of Julia Roberts', raising an interesting question around the idea of the '*star moment*' – the extraordinary meeting of the particular meanings signified by the persona/image of the star and the attitudes, values/ideologies foregrounded in society at that particular historical moment.

The 'real' person called Julia Roberts was described as likeable, attractive and talented. But this only begged the question of why *this* particular likeable, attractive, talented young woman? One explanation is simply that Roberts was lucky enough to be the particular individual, chosen from among many young women of virtually identical attributes, to be hyped by the marketing machinery of Hollywood. But hype itself cannot guarantee stardom. The history of Hollywood is littered with examples of aspiring actors who did not reach stardom, despite having huge amounts of money invested in them. A different explanation is in relation to what Dyer called charisma: the fact that some people naturally 'glow'. 'We often talk about people whom the camera loves. Perhaps it is not so much that the camera loves some people than that some people love the camera.'

What this suggests is that some people but not others are capable of becoming icons. These are people whose extraordinary energy draws the camera to them, rather than those whom the camera constructs. In looking at ways in which Roberts 'drew the camera to her' in films between 1989 and 1991 we also see ways in which she functions in sequences which have no purpose other than display, trying on different images – particularly in *Pretty Woman* and *Sleeping with the Enemy*.

Star 'image', however, must be more than just visual image. The persona (the mix of real person and character role) must also engage interest, produce meaning. In modern stars like Roberts this often is focused on the idea of 'authenticity', encouraging a linkage between the real person and the character role in the mind of the spectator. The stories told about Julia Roberts in the media, about her relationships with the male leads in her films, convey the idea that she is just being herself. The characters she played at this time demonstrate a powerful mixture of strength and vulnerability, suggesting a very direct embodiment of these roles by Roberts-the-real person. The spectator is presented by the paradox of stardom: the star seems knowable, accessible, ordinary and yet, at the same time, extraordinary and only attainable in the everyday world of the spectator in forms of desire and fantasy.

Dyer concluded by claiming that the particular 'moment' of Julia Roberts was the result of a coming together of the qualities she possessed and meanings she signified with a historical moment which they perfectly represented. Dyer suggested that Roberts embraces feminism in as much as it was no longer credible to a female audience for her to be a 'bimbo' or a housewife. At the same time she was not so far suppressing the bimbo or the housewife that she failed to appeal to the male spectator. She was no pushover, no victim in the parts she played at this time, and yet 'there are some of the disturbing implications of female desirability – she's vulnerable, that's to say eminently hurtable'. Dyer concluded his analysis as follows:

Julia Roberts is so sexy and yet so very much her own woman that she's the very embodiment of the so-called post-feminist woman. She's prepared to allow herself to be sold as a sex object and yet at the same time she gives the impression that she's in charge of her image.… Playing with your image, shopping is the only thing worth doing; these are very 80s images – but Julia Roberts is just soft and old fashioned enough to reconcile them with what we flatter ourselves are the more caring attitudes of today. And she does light up the screen.

More is said about Julia Roberts in the section 'Stars and ideology', on p. 189.

The kind of critical synthesis contained in this last quote needs to be broken down into its different components. In order to do this the next three sections will consider the following approaches:

the star as a 'structure' within the text of the film;
the star as performer;
the star as bearer of ideological meaning.

Take a star who is particularly popular at the moment and try to explain why this is their 'moment'?

The star as structure

In any particular film, the star's presence is likely to be made up of recurring features which lead to a high degree of predictability and associated audience expectations. (Indeed this is the basis of what was described in the previous section as 'insurance' and 'trademark' values). As in a generic structure (see above), a star can be said to be made up of a definable set of paradigms. These generate both the repetition and variation from one film to the next. They include visual signifiers (appearance, gesture, movement) and aural signifiers (voice), as well as specific performance signifiers – the star 'doing his or her thing', be it shooting things up, dancing, singing or whatever.

In fact, the relationship between star and genre is an intimate one. The star persona often evolves in relation to the requirements of a particular genre, with individual genre films providing 'vehicles' for the star to 'do their thing'. In the marriage something distinct is often produced – like Clint Eastwood's work as 'the Man with No Name' in Leone Westerns of the 1960s and as Dirty Harry in the detective films of the 1970s. The relationship between genre and star is two-way. The star may depend on the opportunities the genre conventions provide (like Wayne and the Western). The conventions of the genre may become more clearly defined as a result of the dominant presence of a particular star (like the Western and Wayne). Genre and star paradigms can sometimes be observed to develop simultaneously, as with the rise of the gangster movie: Edward G. Robinson's defining role in *Little Caesar* in January 1931 and James Cagney's in *Public Enemy* three months later.

To demonstrate how a structuralist approach can be extended from genre into star study and how the two interrelate, consider the following diagram (adapted from the one which appeared in the section 'Genre: selecting, p. 167'). Here one of the paradigms of a genre – a principal character type – is amplified by reference to a particular star and the paradigms which constitute his star identity.

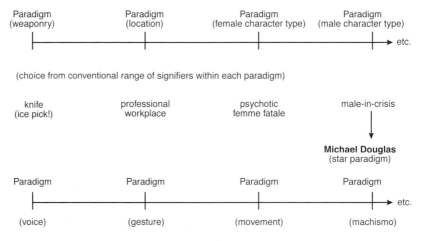

Psychological thriller (*Fatal Attraction, Basic Instinct, Disclosure*)

| Paradigm (weaponry) | Paradigm (location) | Paradigm (female character type) | Paradigm (male character type) | etc. |

(choice from conventional range of signifiers within each paradigm)

| knife (ice pick!) | professional workplace | psychotic femme fatale | male-in-crisis |

Michael Douglas (star paradigm)

| Paradigm | Paradigm | Paradigm | Paradigm | etc. |
| (voice) | (gesture) | (movement) | (machismo) |

In this example, the star persona of Michael Douglas is reinforced as he plays more roles which conform to a particular paradigm of the 1980s and 1990s psychological thriller/melodrama. In turn the genre allows Michael Douglas to do his 'star thing'. In addition to the vehicle, the star is accessed through the exposure his image receives in supplementary media forms. For example, the Douglas persona is amplified by stories of the 'real' Michael Douglas, most notably of his attending a clinic to overcome 'sex addiction'.

There is some value in seeing a star as a structure, especially in order to isolate, for the purposes of study, the star as a signifying system from the star as a person. However, whereas earlier in this chapter a genre 'meaning structure' was identified as having two axes – selection and construction – this is not directly appropriate to a star. The choice for film-makers lies in which star, with their 'bundle of paradigms' already fixed in place, will best *signify* a specific character in their movie. Alternatively, the choice for the star is in which role best accommodates the 'bundle of paradigms' which is his or her star identity. If stars are constructed ahead of the film, then we cannot talk about their construction as an active part of the film-making process. What we can do, however, is look at ways in which other forms of construction, particularly genre and narrative, exploit the star as a predetermined meaning structure.

In this respect casting is a key function within Hollywood cinema. From a structuralist perspective what the casting team must do is find the most appropriate combination of paradigms for the role. This is almost literally a process of 'slotting' different features in and out of an imagined 'role structure' to identify the best fit. (Although, of course, there will be other major considerations such as the relative box-office pulling power of the individuals being considered.) For the purpose of illustration, let us imagine that in casting the romantic male lead for James Cameron's *Titanic* (1997), a choice was to be made between Leonardo DiCaprio and, say, Brad Pitt.

This commutation test reminds us how determining is the choice of star. Different stars bring different meaning structures to a film. *Titanic* would be a different film with Brad Pitt in the lead role.

There are many stories about Hollywood casting. Perhaps the most famous surrounds the casting of Scarlett in *Gone with the Wind*. One of the most vivid illustrations of how casting could alter the meaning of a film and our response to it is to consider what so nearly happened with the role of Rick in *Casablanca* – played not by Humphrey Bogart but by Ronald Reagan.

A commutation test is 'used to assess if a particular unit in a syntagm carries meaning, and if so, what meaning. The test involves changing the unit for another in the same paradigm'.[12]

• **Plate 6.16** Leonardo DiCaprio   • **Plate 6.17** Brad Pitt

Interchangeable? Or does each star bring a different set of meanings to a film? Imagine DiCaprio in *Seven* or Pitt in *Titanic*.

Star One: Leonardo di Caprio

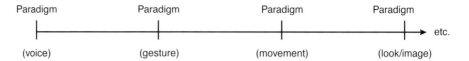

Paradigm   Paradigm   Paradigm   Paradigm

(voice)   (gesture)   (movement)   (look/image)

Star Two: Brad Pitt

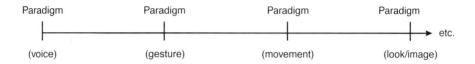

Paradigm   Paradigm   Paradigm   Paradigm

(voice)   (gesture)   (movement)   (look/image)

> Try to identify the key paradigms of two stars of your choice.
> Having done this, try to relate these paradigms to the films in which they appear. Is there a good fit with roles?
> Is there a relationship between the star paradigms and the ideal requirements of a particular genre?

Actors and stars

A different way of looking at the idea of stars as 'fixed' is by comparing them with actors. This allows us the opportunity to make a rather sensitive but very important distinction. It is particularly pertinent in the context of modern Hollywood where one can be forgiven for thinking that there are as many stars aspiring to actor status as there are actors aspiring to star status.

Let us consider two different ways of creating a role in performance: impersonation and personification.[13]

For a brief discussion of Kuleshov's relationship with actors in Soviet Cinema of the 1920s, see Chapter 13, p. 426.

Impersonation involves the actor creating a role from the range of skills and imagination they possess. Successful impersonation involves disappearing into the role and leaving the real self behind. The actor as impersonator is evaluated in relation to the range of roles they can successfully take on and the degree to which they are perceived as psychologically realistic. It is most often associated with serious acting in the theatre.

Personification involves the actor stepping into a role by virtue of their physical appearance and behaviour patterns conforming to the 'type' of that role. The actor as personifier is evaluated in terms of what they are – rather that what they can do. It is most often associated with cruder forms of melodramatic theatre – and with popular cinema. Hollywood star performing has traditionally been dependent on a very high degree of personification. Wayne *is* the Western hero; Bogart *is* the noir private eye: Monroe *is* the (not so) dumb blonde: Stallone *is* Rocky. Sometimes it is difficult to describe a role at all: Garbo or Dietrich or Madonna primarily personify their own personas!

Since the late 1940s, interestingly coinciding with the breakdown of the studio system, Hollywood performance has been strongly marked by the development of the American Method. People like Marlon Brando and Rod Steiger – famously together in *On the Waterfront* (1954) – put into effect the concepts of Lee Strasberg and in so doing

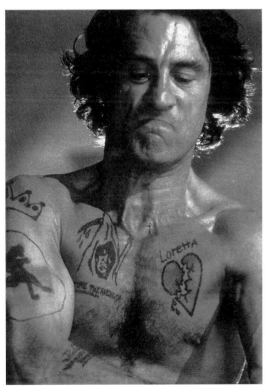

• **Plate 6.18** and **Plate 6.19** *Raging Bull* (Scorsese, US 1980); **Plate 6.20** *Cape Fear* (Scorsese, US 1980); **Plate 6.21** *Taxi Driver* (Scorsese, US 1976)

The method actor: De Niro in *Raging Bull*, *Cape Fear* and *Taxi Driver*. In *Raging Bull* De Niro put on over 60 pounds in moving from the young Jake La Motta (top left) to the middle-aged boxing has-been (top right).

reshaped Hollywood performance and introduced the phenomenon of the star-as-actor which has extended into contemporary cinema, exemplified by people as diverse as Meryl Streep and Al Pacino. The star personifier appeared to become the actor impersonator.

See Chapter 3, page 105–6, for discussion of performance and movement in film.

In order to appreciate the significance of this, we need to refer back briefly to the previous discussion. There, the 'meaning system' of the star was presented as more or less fixed and stable. Using the 'Method' the star appeared to become something very different: a genuinely fluid combination of paradigms, selected by the performer in relation to the requirements of the role; and these, in turn, combined in fresh and imaginative ways.

However, unlike the classic methods for character construction and impersonation advocated by Stanislavski, which encourages the actor to work from the imagination, the process advocated by Strasberg demands that actors work from within their own person, their own conflicts and personal experiences.

Maybe the opposition between the work of Stanislavski (1863–1938) at the Moscow Art Theatre and Strasberg (1901–82) at the New York Artist's Studio is overstated. Arguably, the twentieth century's two most influential theories and practices of acting are on a continuum as explained here – rather than in stark opposition to one another.

It can lead to the painful self-exposure of Brando in *Last Tango in Paris* (1972) and the self-mutilation of De Niro in *Raging Bull* (1980). The method is in fact a more intense, psychologically-based form of personification. As described above, personification involves the star physically embodying the role. The method adds to this the requirement that a star psychologically and physically 'becomes' the role.

One way of exploring definitions of 'star' and 'actor' performance is to consider Oscar winners. This is the list working back from 1997 to 1991:

Jack Nicholson *As Good as it Gets*	Helen Hunt *As Good as it Gets*
Geoffrey Rush *Shine*	Frances McDormand *Fargo*
Nicholas Cage *Leaving Las Vegas*	Susan Sarandon *Dead Man Walking*
Tom Hanks *Forrest Gump*	Jessica Lange *Blue Sky*
Tom Hanks *Philadelphia*	Holly Hunter *The Piano*
Al Pacino *Scent of a Woman*	Emma Thompson *Howards End*
Antony Hopkins *Silence of the Lambs*	Jodie Foster *Silence of the Lambs*

What this list indicates is a mix of Hollywood stars, non-Hollywood actors and some who could be defined as actor-stars. To accommodate such a range, the following diagram may be of value:

Performance types

Personification ←——————— ——————→ **Impersonation**

(embodying role)   (creating role)

Method

Paradigms fixed using   Paradigms selected and
signifiers of star idenity   constructed using signifiers
                                                               from actor's repertoire

One further issue arising from consideration of star performance concerns the illusion of realism which is believed to be such a fundamental feature of Hollywood narrative 'realist' film. Nothing so obviously or so frequently challenges the 'believability' of a Hollywood film than the presence of a star. However much the conventions of Hollywood narrative realist cinema are intent upon making invisible the constructed nature of its product through, for example, naturalistic *mise en scène* and continuity editing, the star presence has the potential to undo this. The spectator is only too aware of, say, Schwarzenegger-in-performance. Why then, does the illusion 'gap' opened up by star in performance rarely provide a problem for the spectator?

One answer is not very different from that we might use in relation to how we cope with predictable generic elements. Spectators are skilled in '**suspending disbelief**' and working with the conventions on screen. The star is simply another set of conventional features, a 'schema' which the spectator can work with. A somewhat more complex answer is based on ideas we have used here around concepts of signification and persona. The relationship between the star (signifier) and role (signified) appears 'natural' because the characteristics of the star persona are suited to those required by the role. When the star brings to the role a very powerful image which has a strong presence in the wider culture, their signification is too great. In other words, the meanings they bring to the role are excessive, and so the spectator risks being distracted from the realist illusion of the narrative. The most obvious examples of this are films which use a star from a wider area of popular culture, Elvis Presley or Madonna, for example. Some films are self-referential, deliberately drawing attention to the star's presence. This is most common in comedies, such as Schwarzenegger in *Twins* (1990) or 'light' action movies such as the same star's *Last Action Hero* where the star plays with his own image.

Stars and ideology

Stars have been described as 'meaning systems' or 'meaning structures'. Since meanings are always ideological, star study allows the analysis of their ideological significance, both in specific films in which stars appear and in general culture in which star images circulate.

Earlier in this chapter, genres were described as performing 'mythical' work. They contain imaginary solutions to real-life problems. In their repetition from one film to another, these mythical solutions take on a kind of 'truth', even though they only really work within storytelling. As was illustrated by reference to the work of McConnell and Schatz, these mythical forms require archetypal, mythical heroes and heroines who embody the values and qualities required. Stars are the 'magic' figures of popular cinema, the 'shamans' who are capable of bringing about illusory solutions to real-life difficulties. The major differences in how they do this are found in characteristics of the genre or genres in which they work. More minor but more varied differences are to be found in the particular components of their star images.

At a straightforward level we can list the meanings a particular star brings to a role – as we previously did in looking at Julia Roberts. At a more complex level we can list these qualities and identify the oppositions/contradictions between them. For example, with Julia Roberts these were identified as:

Sex object	In charge of own image
Vulnerable	No pushover
Playing with image	Authenticity
Consumerism	Caring attitudes
Bimbo ⟷	Housewife

By embodying these different values and qualities, Julia Roberts as star brought them into

suspending disbelief
This refers to the ability a person has when engaging with a constructed object – film, play, novel – to repress their knowledge that the object is in fact just a 'construct', and respond to it as though it is real. (*See Chapter 5 on spectatorship*.)

This playing with the star image might be seen as a further quality of Hollywood 'postmodern' cinema (see above). A catchphrase associated with postmodernism is 'the signifier without the signified' – in other words, the sign (image, sound) has no 'thing' in the real world which it represents. Images of stars from the past such as Bogart and Monroe have become simply signs – available for decorative, playful effect.

Stars in the present have more opportunity to exploit the interplay of role-persona-image. At its most extreme, the distinction between the star (signifier) and the role (signified) disappears. Schwarzenegger plays Schwarzenegger.

play as part of the dramatic structure of her films during the late 1980s and early 1990s. In representing opposites, the star not only dramatises these values and qualities but appears to navigate a course between them. She becomes a fantasy role model (primarily for a female audience) and a fantasy figure of desire (primarily for a male audience). Either way, the star is offering a fascinating synthesis of things an audience finds very difficult, if not impossible, to bring together in real life. The Julia Roberts 'star structure' offers a set of mythical solutions to ideological contradictions – fantasies which are all the more powerful because they seem to indicate ways of reconciling values and forms of behaviour which, in society outside the walls of the cinema, seem unachievable.

Consider a different example: the classic hero from Schatz's 'genre of order' ('How many genres?', p. 172)

Disequilibrium around:	**Hero characteristics applied to the task**	Restoration of equilibrium around:
Institution	**Self-reliance**	Institution
Restriction	**Existential freedom**	Restriction
Rule-based discipline	**Rebellion**	Rule-based discipline
Law	**'Natural' law**	Law
Conformity	**Authenticity**	Conformity
Weariness	**Energy**	Weariness
Physical limitation	**Physical expression**	Physical limitation

Be it Bruce Willis or Pierce Brosnan, Harrison Ford or Mel Gibson, the star embodies and communicates fantastic qualities – fantastic in two senses: extraordinary and make-believe. The capacities the star-as-hero brings to action-genre films are truly 'mythical'. The fact that these capacities are employed to put the world back into the kind of 'order' which is the very *opposite* of what the star-as-hero represents is a central irony of popular cinema.

When they operate as signifiers within narrative and genre, providing an audience with the pleasures of recognition and expectations fulfilled, the meanings of a star appear controlled and predictable. However, the star-as-signifier operates not just within the textual space of a genre-based narrative realist film. He or she also exists in broader culture and in this existence can have more diverse meanings. The relative instability of the star image circulating in culture allows us to describe it as **polysemic**. The '**uses and gratifications**' offered by the star image to diverse groups of people allows us to study the star in relation to the values, fantasies, desires and myths they signify for specific groups and communities within the culture. A study of the different meanings a star signifies can open up an investigation of ideological faultlines within the culture. For example, a whole critical industry has grown up around the image of Madonna. Through her persona-image, she has been seen as both highlighting contradictions, especially in relation to gender and sexuality, and negotiating these contradictions. The attraction to the gay community of the star image of Judy Garland (and, to some extent, her daughter, Liza Minnelli) is an example of how the ideological meanings of a star, experienced as forms of fantasy, can be perceived as valuable – and so as a source of pleasure – to a particular section of society.

Of course, meanings circulating outside the world of the film text will find their way back in to it. The film can become destabilised in a way similar to that referred to in the brief discussion of stars and realism (above). Madonna, for example, is scarcely, if at all, 'confined' by the textual system in which she is placed. For an audience of today, the

polysemic
Having many meanings – a polysemic text is likely to be less stable, more hotly contested by different sections of an audience.

'uses and gratifications'
A specific approach to the study of audiences. It considers how individuals and groups may consume a film or some other media product to satisfy their particular needs.

same could be said of Marilyn Monroe. The very fact of her 'confinement' in generic roles contributes to the way we read her wider cultural image, her *sign*-ificance. She has come to signify, in an archetypal way, the objectification and exploitation of a talented woman by an industrial complex.

A more general ideological meaning is contained in all Hollywood stars – the central ideological value of US society: individualism.

The fact that the star is a '*maximised type*', that is as perfect an embodiment of a set of characteristics as can be imagined, allows the culture to perpetuate its myths, be they of masculine heroism, female beauty or of self-actualisation through lifestyle. Inasmuch as western consumer capitalism is built on the cult of the person, the development of a unique individualised identity through image, the ideological reinforcement provided by the star image is very powerful.

Take, for example, the 'maximised types' personified by Kevin Costner and Whitney Houston in *The Bodyguard* (1992). Both star personae are displayed 'doing their star thing' as action hero and singer respectively. Narrative exists primarily as a platform for the spectacle of the two stars as bodies, as performers, as extraordinary individuals. Neither star creates character so much as embodies 'type' traits which appear unique because mediated through their specific star personas/images. The star is recognisable yet unique, caught in a melodramatic narrative but capable of expressing extraordinary individuality, enclosed in a recognisably naturalistic world and yet able to exist as an autonomous self able to gain control of the world they inhabit.

See Chapter 3 of Richard Dyer's *Heavenly Bodies* (BFI, London, 1987).

Consider a star of your choice in terms of the following:

1 **their polysemic meaning**
2 **their impact in reflecting – or even defining – aspects of their culture**
3 **their function as maximised types**

• **Plate 6.22** *The Bodyguard* (Warner Bros., US 1992) *The Bodyguard* as star vehicle for 'maximised' types, Whitney Houston and Kevin Costner

A star-based critical approach

One approach to star study is to subordinate the star to the requirements of the film text, asking what is specific about the contribution of the star. This may put a focus on representation and the particular qualities the star contributes as a 'signifier' of meaning. A more particular question might be in relation to the requirements of the film as a generic text. This will raise issues about the star as 'type' within the operations of a conventional story form.

The work of stars within a genre and the movement of a star across several genres are each very interesting points of focus for the film student. Star study can be advanced through a study of genre. James Stewart's star persona in Capra melodramas, Mann Westerns and Hitchcock thrillers exemplifies the possibilities of a star study informed by genre (*and* by auteur studies – see p. 195–201). In turn, genre study can be advanced through a focus on stars. One could look, for example, at the shifting dynamic of the Western through a comparative and chronological study of the John Wayne and Clint Eastwood star images.

A second approach to star study is to focus directly on the star in themselves. This may focus on their valuation within the cinema institution, shifting attention to what are primarily financial and marketing areas.

Another interesting example of a star 'in transition' is offered by John Travolta. See the case study on *Pulp Fiction* in Chapter 5.

However, their value will depend on the relationship of their persona-image to the wider culture at that particular cultural 'moment'. The commutation test (mentioned on p. 185) can lead to a more precise description of what is indeed in one persona-image over another. A variation on the commutation test is to look at a star in transition from one persona-image to another. A spectacular example is offered by Jane Fonda whose career has represented major transitions. These include, rather crudely, a range from Hollywood starlet to bimbo to left-wing political activist to successful businesswoman. A study may consider whether there is a 'core' identity which remains across these transitions. (In Fonda's case, the 'core' identity will include paradigms of voice, gesture, mannerism and gesture. The latter can be related specifically to her 'method' performances. Beyond these features we can consider more evaluative qualities such as sincerity, competence, independence, and so on.)[14]

A third approach to star study is in relation to audiences – and, in a broader context, the culture from which the audience comes. We begin not with the film text but with the meanings the audience brings to the film text. These meanings reflect meanings circulating within the culture and which are symptomatic of that culture. We can start with a very simple question of popularity and extend this into questions of ideology. What, for example, is the significance of Whoopi Goldberg's mixed popularity (and meaning) to sections of the black community in the US? What is the significance of Jodie Foster's popularity (and meaning) to the lesbian community?

See Chapter 9, for further discussion of gender, sexuality and audience.

Communicating in critical, academic terms about stars has proved very difficult. There is pressure to avoid sounding like a gushy fanzine and instead to bring real critical rigour to the 'object' of study. But there is also the counter-pressure to represent adequately the felt presence of the star as a figure of desire and fantasy within popular culture. An exemplary approach is offered by Richard Dyer, whose work has been referred to directly or indirectly throughout this section.

Returning to the introduction to this chapter, we can say that stars as structures offer schemas with which an audience can work in order to engage more fully with the film. Stars are a central focus for our study of meaning and response.

☐ CASE STUDY PART 3: *NEW YORK, NEW YORK* AS CLASH OF THE STARS

Three more moments from the film:

1   VE Day, the beginning of the film. Jimmy Doyle, loud, brash in manner and dress, moves through the crowd. He decides to chat up a young woman in military uniform, Francine Evans. His approach is aggressive and obstinate though with just enough self-irony for him to avoid appearing merely boorish. She is witty and resourceful, a mix of sophistication and street sense. The scene between them is the film's opening sparring match and lasts twelve minutes. It establishes that the drama will revolve around two people, different in so many ways from each other, but most interestingly, different in the way they 'act'.

2   Jimmy is waiting for the pregnant Francine to emerge from the recording studio. He is in a new car. She is astonished to discover this extravagance. Jimmy, as so often, appears shockingly self-centred but also defensive, vulnerable. When Francine asks him if he will spend more time supporting her in her pregnancy, he takes his saxophone and leaves the car, asking if he should break it against the wall. The imagery is clear: he feels he is being threatened with castration by the woman. The intensity of Jimmy's character is wrapped up so much in his masculinity. The 'feminine' seems all the more provocative in Francine's reason-ableness, her understated distress. (But to balance this, comedy immediately follows when Francine rather than Jimmy lets rip at a couple impatient for their parking space.)

3   Francine as movie and cabaret star sings 'New York, New York' to her adoring fans. She has been separated from Jimmy for some time. He is in the audience. Compared with his introspective performances on the saxophone, her singing is big and extrovert. Jimmy as spectator is almost impassive although he claps with appreciation at the end along with the rest of the audience. He is on the outside looking in on a world he does not seem able to possess, a world he maybe does not want. He remains wrapped in his self-sufficiency and introspection while Francine is fully 'integrated' into a social world.

In another scene shortly afterwards, Francine is in a Harlem jazz club where Jimmy has established himself. As she approaches the stage, intending to join him in a duet, he physically drives her back with his saxophone playing.

• **Plate 6.23** *New York, New York* (Martin Scorsese, US 1977) De Niro and Minnelli engage in combat: their first encounter – VE Day, 1945

We can rephrase the question we asked regarding a genre-based critical approach to the film in part 2 of this case study (p. 178): How might a *star*-based critical approach (a) explain the difficulties the film has caused, and (b) take us towards a better understanding and appreciation of the film's qualities?

Robert De Niro and Liza Minnelli have a determining effect on the meaning of the film because of the specific qualities they bring with them – of appearance, voice, manner, etc. Jimmy Doyle and Francine Evans would be somewhat different in a re-make starring Kevin Costner and Whitney Houston or, say, John Travolta and Madonna! Beyond this, they bring with them specific meaning associations from their roles in other films/performances and from the personas that developed out of this. Their images in circulation in the mid-1970s would arouse expectations and inform the viewing situation – De Niro's intensity and avoidance of publicity; Minnelli's mix of strength and vulnerability, her 'Garland image'.

The two stars perform within the terms of melodrama. *New York, New York*, in focusing so exclusively on a relationship by reference to psychology and emotion, illustrates Hollywood's typical avoidance of other determining factors – social, cultural, political. However, the film is unusual in demonstrating so vividly two contrasting star performances. First, how the application of the 'method' performance to a melodramatic scenario can produce characterisation of depth: De Niro's Jimmy Doyle has real complexity. Second, how this performance is countered by a much more old-fashioned and increasingly powerful form of star performance from Minnelli in which she 'personifies' a character close to herself. She brings the charisma of her image to bear throughout the film, and not only in her on-screen performances. The explosion of energy after the divorce when she achieves stardom is contained from the beginning in the 'promise' of Liza Minnelli as superstar.

Thus a principal source of interest in the three scenes outlined above, and throughout the film, lies in the interplay between a star (Minnelli) whose personification in the role of Francine Evans is constructed from a traditional Hollywood base in star persona/image and De Niro's method entry into role.

Scorsese has said: 'we were just doing it – rewriting, improvising, improvising, improvising until finally twenty weeks of movie had gone by and we had something like a movie'.[15]

It is uncommon in Hollywood commercial cinema for narrative and character development to be so dependent on the way character evolves through improvisation. In favouring the 'method' approach to performance, the film suited De Niro. By contrast, Minnelli seems much of the time at a disadvantage. Her character seems dominated for much of the film. It has been argued that the film privileges the male point of view, even in the latter part of the film when the Minnelli character appears strong, since her performance is seen through and judged from a male perspective.[16]

Much of the film seems like an interrogation. This extends from the dialogue within the film to one between the film and its audience. We seem to be asked questions by the mix of genre and star elements – what has been described previously as the 'meaning structures' of the film. Certainly the formal contrasts between the two stars intensify this sense of interrogation. We are more aware than usual of these star presences threatening to undermine the illusion of 'reality' we expect from Hollywood entertainment. They question, probe each other in long scenes which produce a **surplus of meaning**. This 'surplus' derives from their different roles; from their different star personas/images, which they bring with them to the film; and from their very different performances.

Narrative, genre and star collectively provide a highly conventionalised form of communication which makes available to an audience two forms of fantasy pleasure. One is the artificial security created by the formal organisation of the film; we know the

---

As discussed earlier, we also have to consider how images change over time. How might we approach these two stars today – what are their images *now*? In terms of meaning and response, we only ever consume films in the present.

For this film De Niro prepared himself in classic 'method' fashion, spending eight months learning how to play the saxophone. He had spent two weeks, twelve hours a day, driving the streets of New York in preparation for *Taxi Driver* the previous year, and as he would spend twelve months in training for his boxing role in *Raging Bull* two years later.

surplus of meaning
Meaning in excess of what is required to fulfil the functional requirements of the narrative; a 'surplus' will include ambiguity, complexity rather than clarity and simplicity.

real world is far less comprehensible and manageable than that constructed by narrative and genre (see the introductory overview to this chapter). The second is the intense personal potential embodied in the star – either for simply existing or more specifically for the resolution of crises. We know the real world cannot be imposed upon or acted upon so directly, so effectively by ordinary individuals.

David Thomson in his entry on Robert De Niro in his *Biographical Dictionary of Film* David Thomson writes the following:

'*New York, New York* is so painful a film because De Niro's drive prefers private, sinister ecstasies to the wholesome bliss of the 1940s Musical. He makes the musical noir. In the long opening sequence he "wins" Liza Minnelli not out of sentiment, but because she is the available target that his fierce boredom selects. His Jimmy Doyle overpowers people or ignores them; he cannot deal with them. Thus the abrupt humour, the compulsive routines just like sax solos (he never makes it to sex) – and that steel-trap grin. Communication systems, but not the natural gestures of feeling. How astute it was in *Taxi Driver* to have him talk to himself.'[17]

If *New York, New York* appears to be a relatively 'difficult' film, it is partly because these two forms of pleasure are in limited supply. The narrative and genre elements provide little security, while the 'intense potential' of the stars seems cloaked in unresolved conflict and loneliness. *New York, New York* is a film which asks us to seek pleasure precisely in its unsettling play of different formal features. Star study can make a significant contribution to the understanding of the issues and processes involved.

AUTEURS

What is an auteur?

An auteur, at least in film study, is nearly always a director. This does not mean all directors are considered to be auteurs. An auteur director is one who brings to a film signs of their own individuality – perhaps in the way the narrative is constructed, the way certain themes are explored or in the visual style. Beyond this, there is an understanding that the auteur is able to function as the main creative force and controlling presence. Within certain kinds of cinema – most obviously independent and **art-house** – an auteur approach appears entirely justified. In relation to Hollywood cinema, an auteur critical approach is of more debatable value.

Since the late 1950s, following the work of critics in France, it has been considered both possible and necessary to distinguish the auteur in Hollywood cinema from what they called the *metteur en scène*, the director who 'merely' brings competence to the specialist role of directing within a production over which they have no overall artistic control. Of course, it is difficult in practice to decide precisely when a *metteur en scène* becomes an auteur.

Early Hollywood auteur theory was based on the idea that some directors, those whose work consistently demonstrated a set of identifiable characteristics, had been able to rise above the 'restraints' of formulaic genre film-making. The underlying 'politics' of the *politique des auteurs*, the name given in France in the 1950s to promote Hollywood directors as 'authors' of their work, included the admirable desire to have Hollywood cinema respected as a significant art form. One way of doing this was to identify artists for this art form. Certainly auteur theory has made two fundamental contributions to film studies:

art-house

This is a crude shorthand way of referring to films in which artistic ambition and intellectual challenge are more important than the simple motive to provide entertainment. 'Great' art-house directors such as Bergman and Godard are unquestionably considered to be auteurs.

For a discussion of the auteur in German cinema, see Chapter 14.

For detailed discussion of mise en scène, *see Chapter 4, pp. 98–108.*

- In the most general sense it encouraged the serious study of popular Hollywood cinema
- More specifically, it did so by demanding a close analysis of *mise en scène* – as the principal site where the auteur identity could be 'excavated'

While genre and star can be seen as 'meaning systems' rooted in the whole Hollywood industrial process, auteur study takes us in a different direction, emphasising individual creativity and control. Previous sections of this chapter have emphasised how genre and star are phenomena of importance to audiences; a genre or star can signify myths and desires which circulate at the heart of popular culture. By contrast, the presence of an auteur is neither so easily 'felt' nor, as a consequence, so direct a focus for response. If genre and star studies can be said, in broad terms, to have been developed out of the lived experience of Hollywood cinema, auteur study is a construct of criticism. For these reasons its centrality within film studies has long been a cause of dispute. This is compounded not only by problems of definition touched upon above, but by fundamental questions surrounding the very idea of 'authoring' a film in a complex and collaborative production process which involves many creative people.

In pursuing the idea of the individual creative figure, conceived as romantically fighting against the odds to impose their unique mark on the text, it can be argued that much more was lost than gained:

- Directors whose work did not reveal the marks of some essential underlying personal force were relegated to the status of *metteurs en scène* – and their work relegated with them.
- The evaluation of a film was carried out in terms of whether or not it possessed an auteurist identity – leading to some absurd conclusions (a bad film by an auteur was 'better' than a great film by a non-auteur).
- In regarding the Hollywood studio system as that which the creative individual struggled against, auteur theory diminished the strengths and achievements of the industrial production process, what Thomas Schatz has called the 'genius of the system'.[18]
- Rather than broadening the study of film into wider political and cultural debates, auteur theory led inwards towards pedantic and trivial debates about who was and who was not an auteur, and what precisely were the features that constituted the auteur 'signature'.

The auteur 'sign' and the industry

The director in modern Hollywood can function much like a star in offering an insurance value to the industry – the guarantee of financial success – and a trademark value to the audience – the guarantee of quality. Increasingly films are bought and sold on the basis of the director's name which takes on the function of a 'sign'. This sign will carry much information of significance concerning the popular and critical 'credit' of the director, based on their previous work and the kind of promise offered by a new film bearing their name.

The auteur sign, by contrast, signifies a set of stylistic and thematic features to be found in the film itself, and is thus much more specific. An auteur possesses a sign(ature).

This 'signature' may or may not be connected with the personal characteristics and biographical details of the auteur. Early auteur theory tended towards this approach, which is common in other areas of study such as literature and art appreciation. By the late 1960s, however, there was a shift away from the auteur-as-person towards the approach we have already seen in this chapter in relation to genre and star study.[19] The auteur-as-structure still requires individual names – a 'Hawks structure', for example. However, there is no particular interest in discovering the essential characteristics of the man called Howard Hawks. The intention is to understand better and appreciate a film or group of films. We become aware of an additional meaning system at work within the film text, an additional schema we can work with to produce meaning, in our role as spectators.

This is not to say that biographical information about the auteur is irrelevant. It may be useful in helping to confirm observations made about the distinctive 'presence' communicated by the auteur structure. The sign(ature) is a set of formal elements, a set of paradigms working in combination. For an example, see the list of paradigms we can identify for the 'Scorsese structure' in part 4 of the *New York, New York* case study (pp. 202–4). The choice remains for the student as to whether to engage in character analysis of Scorsese-the-man based on the signature identifiable in the films.

A critical approach based on paradigm, structure and signature is helpful in trying to reconcile the concept of the auteur with that of film production as a co-operative enterprise involving the contributions of an assortment of creative personnel. In specific scenes the work of one or more of these may be particularly foregrounded – the actor, the set designer, the scriptwriter, the editor, the music composer – but the controlling, creative authority and deployment of these contributions is that of the auteur director. The contributions of others are expressions of specific aspects of the auteur's overall imaginative vision and to that extent they become inscribed with the auteur's identity. For example, disputes as to whether Saul Bass's scenario or Bernard Hermann's music constituted the crucial creative contributions to the shower scene in *Psycho* become irrelevant if we accept that these elements exist only as 'potential' until mobilised and made coherent within a meaning structure with a unitary identity – in this case something called 'Hitchcock'.

What this suggests is in fact something of a compromise between early auteur individualism and a purely structuralist conception. The auteur structure called 'Hitchcock' leaves room not only for the individual called Alfred Hitchcock to be seen as a 'catalyst' but as the final determining creative force. In addition, this does not preclude the possibility of a 'combination' structure, in which a text is 'authored' by different codes working together in an identifiable, recurring form, for example: the Hitchcock–James Stewart–psychological thriller structure or the John Ford–John Wayne–Western structure.

Certainly the identification of a single 'author' has been embraced by all those who must classify and catalogue films. The listings produced both by other media and by academia embrace the single name – perhaps for convenience as much as anything. However, this simple justification sidesteps the contested reading of this name: as originating genius, as catalyst, as structure. And, convenient or not, it is difficult to accept uncritically a discourse which so powerfully diverts attention away from the collaborative and complex creative relationships between a large number of people which are at the heart of Hollywood cinema.

Another issue concerns the kind of institutional context which best suits auteur creativity. Was the auteur better off in the security of a studio system or now in the wheeler-dealing of the 'new' Hollywood? (see Chapter 2); in the formal conventions of narrative and genre or in the 'free play' of postmodernist 'play' referred to above?

Within the 'new' Hollywood, it would appear at first sight that directors are much more free to develop their own personal projects. The director, often also acting as producer or writer, can be one of the key 'elements' in a 'deal'. However, the pressures of the box office remain. Francis Ford Coppola acknowledges this:

As an extension of the point made about 'art-house' cinema (p. 195), it is clear that auteur study takes us into the contentious area of 'low' and 'high' art. One of the more obvious ways of giving films a 'high' art status is to name and catalogue them by reference to the 'artist' responsible for creating them.

The problem is I have a double life and I work for the commercial film industry, which basically wants to take old formulas and make them with new actors. It's like Boeing – they have to make planes that will fly. They can't make one that flies on its side, even though that might be a good idea.… People are particular about films, they don't want to be put into an incredibly unusual situation. It's like the little kid who says 'Tell me the story of the Three Bears again'.[20]

At the same time, in pursuing debates about the pressures imposed on the auteur in the 'new' Hollywood by the deal system of one-off film production, it is necessary to take on board the opposite pressure to the one referred to by Coppola: the increasing expectation in audiences of *textual* '*excess*' in production values and stylistic flourishes. A young director wishing to be noticed must leave his 'calling card' on screen. All directors in the 'new' Hollywood must aspire to the status of auteur, while prioritising audience requirements (box office) over their own individuality. Maybe this is the way it has always been, but the current Hollywood system exposes the conflict particularly starkly (Altman's *The Player* captures these issues with sharp, ironic humour).

Coppola is also an interesting point of focus in relation to debating the benefits or otherwise of working within a studio system. His attempt to make films with an auteur signature across a range of genres and to enable others to do the same under the 'new' Hollywood institutional system led him to create, in 1969, a 'studio' (Zoetrope) which would offer the kind of security and continuity creative personnel had not been offered since the end of the studio system.

Under whatever production system and regardless of the film form in vogue, the auteur needs to enjoy a significant level of control and independence in the various stages of production if the auteur structure is to assert itself on the screen. To refer back to an earlier point, his '*catalyst*' *function* must be secured. This is equally true of those working on mainstream commercial projects – directors like Steven Spielberg, Oliver Stone, Clint Eastwood and Spike Lee – as it is for those working in the lower-budget 'independent' sector – directors such as John Sayles, Jim Jarmusch, Gus Van Sant and Hal Hartley. In this regard the *de facto* producer role of the director is fundamental. In the studio system directors such as Howard Hawks and John Ford enjoyed either actual or *de facto* producer power. However, it is difficult to precisely define the amount of control a director needs to enjoy before he can be considered sufficiently enabled to impose his sign(ature) on a film. Using right to the final cut as a benchmark of an auteur's controlling presence within the film is to go too far. Clearly *The Magnificent Ambersons* would have been the better for Welles retaining control through to final cut, but the film in the form in which it survives is still very visibly marked by the Welles' auteur presence. Is Sluitzer's Hollywood remake of his own Dutch-language film *The Vanishing* (with an entirely different ending) an example of loss of auteur control? The case of *Blade Runner – the Director's Cut* raises the interesting idea that it is possible to become the auteur of a film ten years after its original release through being granted additional power. At what point precisely did Ridley Scott make the transition from *metteur en scène* to auteur?

> It is worth comparing Coppola's *One From the Heart* with *New York, New York* – both are auteurist attempts to do something new while exploiting the conventions of the 1950s studio musical and melodrama – and both were box office failures.

Compare an auteur with a *metteur en scène* in terms of:

1 **the critical reputation of the films they made**
2 **their positions within popular and academic film discourse**

This example of the foregrounding of Ridley Scott in the re-release of *Blade Runner* also indicates the extent to which the industry is keen to promote directors to the auteur ranks for marketing reasons. 'A film by ——' or 'A —— film' is a typical feature of film promotion today even when the director clearly has not enjoyed the producer power described above (for example, *Fatal Attraction* – an Adrian Lynne film?). Thus for marketing purposes all directors seem to have assumed or had thrust upon them auteur status. Is this to undermine fatally the auteur concept, or does it highlight how absurd it has been all along to try to make meaningful distinctions between those who 'direct' and those who 'create'?

The tension between auteurist innovation and commercial requirements continues in writing on the work of directors in the 'new' Hollywood. In other words the romantic view of the 'heroic' embattled creative artist is perpetuated. Consider, for example, the following. Dudley Andrews writes that:

to 'begin' a project is not to originate a work, but rather to deflect a flow, to branch off in a direction. This limited sense of novelty retains the power of individual effort and critique while recognizing the greater power of the social system within which anything that makes a difference must begin…. Why not apply [this view] in some degree, to a Ridley Scott, whose attempt to branch out from the road picture in *Thelma and Louise* seems more heroic for its collapse in the film's final chase sequences.[21]

Andrews here sees Ridley Scott as, at best, 'deflecting a flow' of larger processes. So his attempt to do something different with *Thelma and Louise* is seen as 'heroic' precisely because it is certain to be compromised by these larger processes – such as institutional caution, narrative and generic conventions, social and ideological conservatism – all of which can be reduced to issues of 'box office' – what will sell.

A more positive interpretation of the relationship between creativity and institution involves seeing the conventions of commercial genre cinema as facilitating expression. A system of rules provides both security and the opportunity for inventing variation. The auteur, it could be argued, enjoys both a safe anchorage within an artistically self-enclosed world and the incentive to push against the edges of this world to discover new possibilities. More questionable is whether compromise in terms of artistic control is balanced by much greater financial security.

Pulp Fiction is an obvious example – see the case study in Chapter 5.

Other kinds of auteur

Within a commercial cinema such as Hollywood, we must ask whether, in fact, the director is always the most suitable candidate for auteur status.

For example, it is possible to consider the studio as having auteur status, in relation to a particular 'house style', most obviously Warner Bros. and MGM in the 1930s. Certainly a strong case can be made for the producer as auteur, with recurring characteristics observable across a range of films. This might be particularly appropriate in looking at groups of films from the studio system produced by men with characteristic personal visions – such as Thalberg, Zanuck or Selznick. It is particularly appropriate in relation to producers co-ordinating their own distinctive production units, such as Val Lewton at RKO (gothic horror/film noir) or Arthur Freed at MGM (the musical). In the period since the collapse of the studio system, it is still possible to identify producers with a determining presence, such as Cubby Broccoli who co-ordinated the James Bond series for thirty years, maintaining its distinct identity. In contemporary Hollywood, arguably, Spielberg is as much an auteur in his role as producer as he is in films which he personally directs.

And what of the star as auteur? The vehicle can be so controlled by the star that he

See Chapter 2, pp. 17–21, for a discussion of the Hollywood studio era.

becomes the producer-star determining the stylistic as well as the thematic content of the film. Is Schwarzenegger or Stallone an auteur? A claim can be made for Kevin Costner as auteur not only in his role as director-star in *Dances with Wolves* (including a 'Director's Cut') but in his role as producer-star in *The Bodyguard* and *Waterworld*. In relation to what was said about the star above – as having a determining effect on the film because of the distinctive 'meaning system' he or she brings to the film – it seems quite reasonable to talk of the star 'signature'.

The most radical claim is for the spectator as auteur. Meaning is only created in the act of reading – an encoded message (text) remains only as potential meaning until it is decoded by a reader (or spectator). Further, different readers come to a text with their own specific social, cultural and psychological formation as individuals. The logical deduction from this is that the text is 'authored' by the reader rather than by the text's originator. Roland Barthes, for example, talked of the 'death of the author' and the 'birth of the reader'.

If there are more questions than answers here, this is because traditional auteur theory stands on insecure ground in relation to the whole issue of origination – where the film comes from. Its undoubted value is in putting in place another meaning structure, another creative dimension (whether deriving from auteur-director, auteur-producer or even auteur-studio) to intersect with those of genre and star already discussed, thus enabling a closer interrogation of the film text.

An auteur-based critical approach

Like a star, an auteur director can be regarded as a 'persona', similarly made up of a combination of a real person and the films which he or she is identified through (see section 'What is a star?' p. 181). The principal difference, of course, is that the auteur director does not appear in films (with notable exceptions, ranging from Hitchcock's on-screen 'signature', to Scorsese's and Tarantino's occasional cameo roles in their own films, to Spike Lee's and Woody Allen's central roles). So, whereas the star-in-role is visible, the auteur-in-role must be 'excavated' through critical analysis.

Whether the focus is on Hitchcock or Scorsese or Woody Allen, an emphasis on the biographical, and especially the more speculative forms of the biographical, is commonplace. What can this film tell us about the real person behind its creation? This is a legitimate activity. However, the emphasis throughout this chapter has been on what we can learn about the film itself as a complex 'meaning system'.

As with genre study, there is a peculiar circularity in the way we go about auteur analysis. In order to 'excavate' the auteur characteristics of any particular film, we need to already have the auteur structure to hand – just as when we identify the generic characteristics of a film, we need to already have available the generic structure, against which the film under scrutiny will be 'checked'. The Scorsese auteur structure is assembled deductively from the films Martin Scorsese has directed. The structure is then applied to the text under scrutiny.

To take another example, a 'Douglas Sirk' film will be read in response to knowledge about the 'Douglas Sirk' auteur structure, and if that knowledge is absent, the auteur structure will not be read at all – it will be a meaning 'potential' left untouched by the reader.

Sirk was thought of in the 1950s as a director of traditional melodramatic 'weepies' set in a bourgeois world. Only with the work of auteur critics such as Andrew Sarris in the 1960s was a different view of Sirk's work put forward: that he was in fact offering a scathing critique of the world depicted in his films. Sarris argued that in visual style and in his 'narrative attitude' Sirk was a remarkable auteur – delivering films to Universal as per contract which appeared to be standard genre product but which were charac-

For more about this, see Chapter 5 on spectatorship.

Arguably, the auteur can also be related to other star characteristics identified above (in the section entitled 'star-based critical approach'). The auteur as artist is a 'maximised type', while the promotion of the auteur as creative individual furthers the ideology of individualism at the heart of western culture.

The extent to which this auteur structure is also the result of inductively applying biographical information about Martin Scorsese the person is more debatable and will be touched on in Part 4 of the case study p. 202).

• **Plate 6.24** *Written on the Wind* (Douglas Sirk, US 1956) Rock Hudson and Dorothy Malone: American soap or auteur masterpiece?

terised by an individual way of seeing and telling. One of Sirk's celebrated films, such as *Written on the Wind*, may well appear of little or no special interest unless the spectator is aware of the Douglas Sirk auteur structure. The claims made for it as a 'subversive' text rather than as a regular 1950s melodrama and star vehicle require validation through reference to the determining additional meaning structure – 'Sirk' – operative within the text. In other words, the film becomes a more significant and interesting text if mediated through the process of auteur criticism.

Some of the surplus of meaning contained in *Written on the Wind* (1956) can be confirmed by reference to its stars, much more by reference to the 'Sirk' auteur structure – and the same can be said of *New York, New York* when an additional level of 'coding', the 'Scorsese' auteur structure, is examined.

Even if the spectator is ignorant of the auteur structure, the simple power of *naming* remains significant. The classification which the auteur name allows means that texts can be differentiated from one another, most particularly in terms of the status which can be conferred upon them. The act of spectatorship will be influenced by the power of the name. This returns us to the auteur as 'guarantee' and 'trademark'. It also returns us to the observation that in contemporary Hollywood nearly all films have placed upon them the name of an auteur, whether or not any auteur structure has been established behind that name. The name exists purely as a name-tag on a commodity – indeed the name-tag is itself a commodity: 'Spielberg'.

Auteur study attempts to establish a recognisable set of thematic and stylistic features (a signified) for the auteur name (the signifier). Increasingly, this is done by the auteur who quite consciously puts in place the components of an identity which his name can then be said to signify. Thus we can trace a transition since the late 1950s, when critics constructed an auteur meaning structure out of a body of films put in place more or less intuitively by a director in active collaboration with other creative individuals within enabling institutional structures. Today the director often strives, self-consciously, to construct a recognisable auteur identity to confirm the commercial and critical existence of the name she or he bears.

The real challenge in auteur criticism is in examining the work of directors whose work is so varied that we are tempted to artificially limit the range and scope of the work for purposes of critical 'neatness'. It is much easier, for example, to develop a 'check list' of Woody Allen characteristics for application to any particular film bearing his name than it is in approaching the work of, say, Oliver Stone.

Overall, we can say that, unlike genre or star structures, an auteur structure does not offer itself so obviously as a schema for the audience to work with. However, additional layers of meaning and response can emerge if we are prepared to study a body of films which have a shared auteur origin.

> **Why do you think the auteur is at the centre of so much film studies work? Why, to quote Richard Dyer, should auteur theory have become film studies 'greatest hit'?**[22]

☐ CASE STUDY PART 4: SCORSESE AND *NEW YORK, NEW YORK*

The Scorsese auteur structure can, at least in part, be deduced from films which lie chronologically on either side of *New York, New York* in which Martin Scorsese enjoyed the kind of producer-director control discussed above. Thus *Who's That Knocking at My Door?*, *Mean Streets*, *Raging Bull* and *King of Comedy* offer themselves as texts to be searched for the kind of recurring features which will allow us to construct an auteur structure. *Boxcar Bertha* and *Alice Doesn't Live Here Anymore*, films over which Scorsese did not exercise such personal control, are excluded from consideration. (But should they be? Perhaps they are in some respects the most interesting; projects where the director had to 'negotiate' a relationship, an identity with the material.)

We discover the following principal thematic preoccupations in two or more of Scorsese's 'auteur' films:

- a strong focus on masculinity: on male friendship, on male sexuality and on the ways in which these are threatened or experienced as areas of personal crisis
- more specifically, the male attitude to women as 'other', as unknowable, definable as 'whores' or 'virgins', as the source of the threat to masculinity, as the cause of male paranoia, and consequently as objects of abuse within relationships where the male seeks to assert dominance
- explicitly or implicitly the male character is placed within a framework of guilt, sin, retribution, redemption;
- the male existing within a closed world, either a community (New York Italian) or a mental state of alienation and reality distortion
- this reality distortion is sometimes linked to wider forms of reality distortion within American culture (*Taxi Driver* and *King of Comedy*)
- generally the resolution of internal conflict by means of external violence
- as an extension to this, the dominance of the physical over the verbal – male characters are characteristically inarticulate but physically expressive
- a representation of blacks which reflects either the overt or implicit racism of the protagonists

We also note the following features of form and style recurring in two or more of the above named films:

- documentary-style realism in 'method' performances and locations
- the expressive use of mobile camera, lighting, editing and sound which works against the documentary realism, placing it within a stylised artificiality
- thus, point-of-view is a complex interaction of the spectator's observations of an 'objective' world and the character's 'subjective' perception of that world
- the primary role assigned to soundtrack in the creation of meaning
- the adoption (and subsequent problematising) of generic forms and, in particular, the ambiguity and perplexity of the films' closures

These paradigms, these features observable within the films can be amplified by reference to biographical information concerning Martin Scorsese. So, for example, his close identification with Little Italy in New York City, with its distinctive social formation, may be cited. More specifically, his Catholic background provides useful corroborating evidence, and some (overly neat?) personal statements such as that in which he says that as a boy he wished to be either a priest or a gangster. His immersion from a very early age in film culture helps to explain something of the rich repertoire of styles and images he is able to bring to the screen. His interest in the films of Powell and Pressburger, as well as the more obvious homage to the MGM classic musical, may, for example, advance our appreciation of *New York, New York*.

Keeping Scorsese-the-person at arm's length by working with Scorsese-the-structure in order to make meaning out of *New York, New York* may appear absurdly purist. Biographical information such as that outlined in the previous paragraph clearly contributes to the composite auteur structure which we are applying to the film. However, the question must be considered: what kinds of biographical detail are useful? For example, during the filming of *New York, New York* Scorsese was having a relationship with Minnelli while his nine months pregnant wife, co-screenwriter Julie Cameron, stalked the set. There were also strong rumours of on-set cocaine use. When considering the improvisational approach used throughout the film, is it necessary to probe the madness in this method?

In placing *New York, New York* within an auteur structure called 'Scorsese' it is possible to identify more sharply both stylistic and thematic elements and in so doing move towards a more complex understanding and appreciation of the film.

One of the themes which is amplified by application of the auteur structure is the male struggling to find expression and identity within a heterosexual relationship. For example, Jimmy Doyle's saxophone as phallus is most dramatically referred to in the scene with Francine just before the birth of their baby when he accuses her of provoking him to smash it. (Also referred to above.)

One of the stylistic features which is amplified by the application of the auteur structure is the placing of method performance against the artificiality and visual excess of its studio-bound locations. At the same time, the film does not demonstrate some of the key elements of other Scorsese films, such as the placing of the central character within a Catholic theological context of guilt and redemption (the rejection of 'Happy Endings' actually makes this a less 'redemptive' film than those apparently much bleaker films made on either side of it). The fact that there is not a perfect 'match' between auteur structure and film is perfectly reasonable. The structure offers us a schema. It is enough if we can 'map' some of the features of the film on to this schema. The auteur structure should not wrap the film being studied in a strait jacket.

This superficial sketch of auteurist features of *New York, New York* nevertheless allows some evaluation of the use of auteur study as a critical approach to Hollywood cinema. Most obviously, elements of theme and style become foregrounded, confirming what might otherwise remain a spectator's tentative interpretation of the film's meaning. Perhaps new significance can be read into detail, and a richer appreciation becomes possible of aspects of the film's form.

While remaining philosophically and methodologically suspect, an auteur approach offers an additional layer of coherence to the text and helps us to come to terms with some of the text's important 'surplus' meaning. The more auteur structures/identities that enter into general circulation and become visible, the more expectations are raised and fulfilment sought by audiences always on the lookout for patterns of repetition and variation as part of the pleasure of cinema.

See case study part 3, pp. 193–5.

• **Plates 6.25** and **6.26** *New York, New York* (Martin Scorsese, US 1977)
Male introspection and violence are both conveyed through the sax playing of Jimmy Doyle (De Niro). Can we identify these as auteur preoccupations during this period of Scorsese's career?

The following Scorsese filmography includes only his feature films. It is organised chronologically in two groups, films with and without De Niro:

Scorsese feature films with De Niro:
Mean Streets (1973)
Taxi Driver (1976)
New York, New York (1977)
Raging Bull (1980)
King of Comedy (1982)
GoodFellas (1990)
Cape Fear (1991)
Casino (1995)

Other Scorsese feature films:
Who's That Knocking at My Door? (1969)
Boxcar Bertha (1972)
Alice Doesn't Live Here Anymore (1974)
After Hours (1985)
The Color of Money (1986)
The Last Temptation of Christ (1988)
The Age of Innocence (1993)
Kundun (1997)

It is much easier to devise an auteur structure around the first group than the second. *Who's That Knocking at My Door?* can clearly be placed in the first group. As a test of the auteur critical approach, take, for example, *The Last Temptation of Christ* and consider how it becomes a more interesting film, a film with more meaning, more to respond to, if placed with the Scorsese auteur structure.

Consider these two quotations from an article by Amy Taubin on Scorsese's *Kundun* (1997), a film about Tibet and the Dalai Lama, which at first sight seems very difficult to connect with other Scorsese films: (1) 'Tibet may be worlds apart from the mean streets of Manhattan, but Kundun is unmistakably a Scorsese picture. Like *Taxi Driver* (1976), it cleaves to a first-person point-of-view; like *The Age of Innocence* (1993), it's a fetishistic examination of a highly ritu- alised culture; *like The Last Temptation of Christ* (1988), it narrates the spiritual struggles of a holy man.'; (2) 'The third act maps the Dalai Lama's journey into exile, which is also an interior spiritual journey. Like the climactic set pieces in *Taxi Driver* and *GoodFellas* (1990), this is the projection of what might be called an altered state of consciousness. Travis Bickle's explosion of homicidal rage and Henry Hill's cocaine-induced psychosis are the perversions of the Dalai Lama's spiritual transcendence.'[23]

The reader must decide whether this kind of comment, based on an auteur approach, is of value in helping us to get more out of the film under discussion.

BEYOND A STRUCTURALIST CRITICAL APPROACH TO HOLLYWOOD CINEMA

A structuralist approach to film study can be very useful. It allows a *common approach* to be adopted not only to a large number of apparently very different films but also to different critical discourses within the subject – such as genre, star and auteur. It also allows for sufficient *containment of all the surface variables* that make every film different from every other film for a study of a film text or a group of film texts to become manageable.

However, these advantages – a 'common approach' and 'containment' – can also be regarded as disadvantages, *overdetermining* how a film is read and critically 'processed'. Also, comment has been made throughout this chapter on the increasing *difficulty or desirability of containment*, of limiting for the purpose of study all the mean- ings in play.

In relation to genre, star and auteur, the chapter has emphasised the loosening of traditional categories in contemporary popular cinema:

The range of paradigmatic features 'permissible' within a genre film has been freed up considerably, with films showing an increasing tendency to 'borrow' paradigms from the whole of Hollywood cinema.

In relation to star study, the shift from 'star' to 'actor' has made it much more difficult to fix in place a set of recurring characteristics, in relation to either roles or persona.

With the industry's incorporation of many directors into the ranks of auteurism, if only for marketing purposes, and with the free movement by auteurs between 'personal' and 'commercial' projects (Scorsese provides a good example of this), it is as difficult as it has always been to agree what might actually constitute an auteur in Hollywood cinema.

intertextuality
This refers to the ways in which a (film) text refers to other films, either explicitly or implicitly, and thereby triggers ideas and associations which might enrich our response.

All those elements which cannot be contained and which, with reference to *New York, New York*, have been described as 'surplus meaning' or 'excess' or even 'delirium', are the very things we might most want to explore. Particularly intense forms of pleasure and meaning are precisely in those aspects of the film which escape structural containment. The film illustrates not only the rich complexities of **intertextuality**, of the 'dialogue' which is going on between this film and a whole Hollywood history, rich in association, but also how much internal 'dialogue' is going on within and between the different paradigmatic elements, genre, star and auteur, which the simple musical bio-pic narrative (just about) holds together. The imposed logic of structuralism needs to be balanced by a sensitivity to these forms of 'dialogue'.

To continue the analogy made throughout with language, a finite set of rules and a limited vocabulary can generate an infinite number of meanings. It is very useful to learn the vocabulary and the structures, but the purpose of doing so is to participate in the real world of communication. In the real world of interaction between film industry–film text–film audience, a limited vocabulary in the form of paradigms, structured in ways which are sufficiently conventionalised to be called 'rules', are capable of producing an infinite number of meanings. Pleasure is to be found both in the artificial containment of the real world in structured forms and in the 'play' which these structured forms allow.[24]

Within culture, cultism is a particularly interesting phenomenon – and one which has the potential to extend the study of film genre, star and auteur. We can take the horror genre, for example, in order to explore the relationship between a 'formal meaning system' and its fans and what they do with it. Fans may define and bestow cult status on stars and auteurs who cannot be seen to have been constructed by the industry or by reviewers and critics.

For this reason the formal study of genre, star and auteur must be balanced by a very different approach to film studies, which emphasises reception and the actual uses to which a film text is put by specific groups of people differentiated by gender, class, race or age at the particular historical moment of viewing. A film is a text with complex internal structures put into circulation as a commodity by an industry. But it is also an experience, a cultural event in which the commodity form of the film can be appropriated by an audience as part of their own cultural production. (For example, the meaning of Schumacher's vigilante thriller *Falling Down* for lower middle-class white US urban audiences; the appropriation of Lisa Minnelli's mother, Judy Garland, by gay audiences.) This is where the exploration of genre and star in particular must move along the continuum from textual to *cultural studies*, from structuralism to *ethnography*, from theories to the way people actually watch and use films within their lives.[25]

Take a genre and star auteur from another area of popular culture such as music or sport. Consider:

1 **How far the critical approaches described in this chapter are transferable**
2 **Whether fresh insights into the study of cinema, especially contemporary cinema, can come from such a comparative approach across different areas of popular culture**

NOTES

1 D. Thompson and I. Christie (eds), *Scorsese on Scorsese* (Faber & Faber, London, 1989), p. 69.

2 See J. Fiske, *Television Culture* (Routledge, London, 1987), Chapter 8.

3 See F. McConnell, *Storytelling and Mythmaking* (Oxford University Press, New York, 1979).

4 See T. Schatz, *Hollywood Genres: Formulas, Filmmaking and the Studio System* (McGraw Hill, New York, 1981), pp. 29–36.

5 See J. Belton, *American Cinema/American Culture* (McGraw Hill, New York, 1994), pp. 305–10.

6 J. Collins, 'Genericity in the Nineties', in J. Collins *et al.* (eds), *Film Theory Goes to the Movies* (AFI/Routledge, New York, 1993), p. 254.

7 Ibid., pp. 257–62.

8 D. Thompson and I. Christie (eds), *Scorsese on Scorsese* (Faber & Faber, London, 1989), p. 72.

9 R. Dyer, 'Entertainment and Utopia', in R. Altman (ed.), *Genre – The Musical* (Routledge, London, 1981).

10 See P. Cook (ed.), *The Cinema Book* (BFI, London, 1986), pp. 50–2.

11 This is taken from Richard Dyer's piece on Julia Roberts broadcast on BBC's *The Late Show* in March 1991.

12 T. O'Sullivan *et al.*, *Key Concepts in Communication* (Routledge, London, 1983) p. 44.

13 See B. King, 'Articulating Stardom', in C. Gledhill (ed.), *Stardom – Industry of Desire* (Routledge, London, 1991).

14 See R. Dyer, *Stars* (BFI, London, 1979), pages 72–98.

15 Thompson and Christie (eds), op. cit., p. 72.

16 See the articles by R. Lippe and L. Cooke, in *Movie*, vol. 31–2, Winter 1986.

17 D. Thomson, *A Biographical Dictionary of Film*, (Andre Deutsch, London, 1994).

18 See T. Schatz, *The Genius of the System: Hollywood Filmmaking in the Studio System* (Pantheon, New York, 1988), an excellent study of the studio system.

19 P. Wollen, *Signs and Meaning in the Cinema* (Secker & Warburg, London, 1972).

20 See The *Guardian*, 21 January 1993.

21 See D. Andrews, 'The Unauthorised Auteur Today', Collins *et al.* (eds), op. cit., pp. 82–3.

22 R. Dyer 'Introduction to Film Studies' in J. Hill & P. Church Gibson (eds), *The Oxford Guide to Film Studies* (Oxford University Press, Oxford, 1998), p. 5.

23 A. Taubin, 'The Road Not Taken', *Sight and Sound*, Vol. 8, Issue 2, February 1998, pp. 6–8.

24 See, for example, Fiske op. cit., Chapter 12.

25 See J. Basinger, *A Woman's View – How Hollywood Spoke to Women, 1930–1960* (Chatto & Windus, London, 1994), for a very entertaining example of how genre and star study can be refocused on how audiences actually 'use' films.

FURTHER VIEWING

For an excellent introduction to Hollywood cinema and to the personality of Martin Scorsese:

A Century of Cinema: A Personal Journey Through American Movies (Scorsese, BFI Videos 1995)

If you wish to engage in a detailed study of the musical genre, you are recommended to view some of the following films:

The musical

The biopic
The Glenn Miller Story (Mann, 1954)
A Star is Born (Cukor, 1954) – also for Judy Garland
Evita (Parker, 1996)

The star vehicle
Funny Girl (Wyler, 1968)
Cabaret (Fosse, 1972) – also for Liza Minnelli

The MGM product
(all of the following were produced by Arthur Freed)
Meet Me in St Louis (Minnelli, 1944) – also for Judy Garland and Vincent Minnelli
On the Town (Donen/Kelly, 1949)
An American in Paris (Minnelli, 1951)
Singin' in the Rain (Donen/Kelly, 1952)
Band Wagon (Minnelli, 1953)

It is interesting to compare the MGM musicals listed above with the Warner Bros. product of the 1930s such as:
42nd Street (Bacon, 1933)
Gold Diggers of 1933 (Le Roy, 1933)

Rick Altman in his *The American Film Musical* (Indiana University Press, Bloomington, Ind., 1987) identifies three categories of Hollywood musical. All but three of the films listed above come from one of those categories, 'The Show Musical'. The exceptions are *An American in Paris* (a 'Fairy Tale' musical) and *Meet Me in St Louis* and *On the Town* (Folk Musicals)

De Niro and Scorsese

If you wish to engage in a detailed study of the principal star and auteur featured in this chapter, see the filmography on p. 205.

As mentioned in a marginal note, it is also useful to compare Scorsese's *New York, New York* with Coppola's *One From the Heart* (1982).

To compare De Niro in Scorsese films with his work for other directors, a useful range might include:

The Godfather, Part II (Coppola, 1974)
The Last Tycoon (Kazan, 1976)
The Deer Hunter (Cimino, 1978)
True Confessions (Grosbard, 1981)
Once Upon a Time in America (Leone, 1984)
Angel Heart (Parker, 1986)
The Untouchables (De Palma, 1987)
Midnight Run (Brest, 1989)
A Bronx Tale (De Niro, 1993)
Jackie Brown (Tarantino, 1998)

The study of genre, star and auteur invites list-making. Over eighty films are referred to in this chapter. You may find it useful to use some of them as the basis for constructing your own lists. These may be based on conventional generic or star or auteur identities: a list of Westerns, for example; a chronological list of films by star or auteur.

However, it is through the construction of more imaginative lists which go across these obvious categories that critical discussion is opened up. These may be along the lines of Schatz's 'Genres of order' and 'Genres of integration' (see p. 171–4) or Collins' 'authenticity' and 'eclecticism' (see p. 177). They may be film lists reflecting combinations of stars and genre or stars and auteur. The vital thing to remember is that interpretation and critical analysis are creative acts. We are free to construct different shapes and patterns out of the vast range of films available to us at cinemas, on video and on television. We should see this as an opportunity for making new and interesting meaning.

Part three

Genre forms – realism and illusion

The documentary form: personal and social 'realities'

Paul Wells

■ **Introduction**   212
■ **What is documentary?**   213
■ **Some developments in non-fiction film**   215
■ **From travelogue to authored documentary**   216
□ Case study 1: Robert Flaherty   217
■ **From social commentary to propaganda to poetic
  actuality**   219
□ Case study 2: Humphrey Jennings   220
■ **Propaganda as documentary myth**   222
□ Case study 3: Leni Reifenstahl   222
■ **From documentary bias to direct cinema and
  *cinéma-vérité***   224
□ Case study 4: Frederick Wiseman   227
■ **From radical documentary to television, diversity
  and popular forms**   229
□ Case study 5: *Hoop Dreams* (1994) and *When We Were
  Kings* (1996)   231
■ **Notes**   234
■ **Further reading**   234
■ **Further viewing**   235
■ **Resource centres**   235

■ The documentary form: personal and social 'realities'

INTRODUCTION

See Chapter 6, for
further discussion of film
genre.

Recent years have seen a re-emergence of the documentary form from its cultural 'ghetto'; a shedding of its traditional connotations of 'dryness', 'fact' and 'everyday-ness', and a movement towards a proper recognition of its role as a model of cinematic and televisual practice which can entertain, provoke, persuade and affect audiences emotionally. Peter Moore, Channel Four's senior commissioning editor for documentaries, suggests that '[d]ocumentary is in a permanent state of crisis and so documentary makers, who are highly critical people, turn their critical faculties on the discipline itself. They are so inventive they keep the genre alive'.[1] Tracing the survival and redefinition of the genre is part of the project in the following chapter.

It is often the case that documentary is believed to be the recording of 'actuality' – raw footage of real events as they happen, real people as they speak, real life as it occurs, spontaneous and unmediated. While this is often the case in producing the material *for* a documentary, it rarely constitutes a documentary in itself, because such material has to be ordered, reshaped and placed in sequential form. Even in the shooting of the material, choices have to be made in regard to shot selection, point of view, lighting, and so on, which anticipate a certain presentation of the material in the final film.

For further discussion of
film form and film
construction, see
Chapter 4.

Andrew Britton extends this point by suggesting:

> In the first place, truly great documentaries are analytical, in the sense that they present the corner of reality with which they deal not as a truth there to be observed, but as a social and historical reality which can only be understood in the context of the forces and actions that produced it. Secondly, they are engaged, in a sense that they lay no claim to objectivity, but actively present a case through their structure and organisation of point of view.[2]

It is important to stress then that, just like any 'fiction' film, the documentary is *constructed* and may be seen not as a recording of 'reality', but as another kind of representation of 'reality'. The **documentary** form is rarely innocent and is defined in a number of ways, ranging from 'Travelogue' to 'Radical Essay', and these forms must be studied with regard to their specific address and purpose.

documentary
A non-fiction text using 'actuality' footage, which may include the live recording of events and relevant research material (i.e. interviews, statistics, etc.). This kind of text is usually informed by a particular point of view, and seeks to address a particular social issue which is related to and potentially affects the audience.

See Chapter 5 for further
discussion of audience
and spectatorship.

Most people see many documentaries on television and have become very familiar with their dominant codes and conventions, so much so that they have ceased to interrogate and question these texts. Audiences regularly watch documentaries characterised by the use of voiceover, a roster of experts, witnesses and opinionated members of the public, an apparently 'real' set of locations, footage of live events and 'found' archive material. All of these recognisable conventions have a particular history and place in the development and expansion of the documentary as a *cinematic* form. This is an important point to stress because in many ways the documentary form has been neglected and marginalised as a film art because it has been absorbed by the more journalistic tendencies of television. Further it has essentially become cheap prime-time television, finding a large popular audience. The *Discovery Channel*, dedicated to broadcasting documentaries and available only through satellite and cable, for example, now broadcasts to over forty countries and has worldwide audiences of over 100 million.[3] There is evidence to suggest, however, that with such a proliferation of 'news-style' documentaries there has been a movement back to a more 'cinematic' approach by individual film-makers which recalls the very traditions and styles discussed here. While it is clear that there are more broadcast contexts for documentary, film-makers working in a more cinematic style still seek the widest possible distribution of their films in cinemas, colleges and universities and film societies. Further, the increasing number of festivals showing documentaries have enhanced their profile, often providing the context for critical acclaim that both activates wider distribution on the major exhibition circuits and often ensures prime-time broadcast on terrestrial channels predicated on a public service ethos.

WHAT IS DOCUMENTARY?

John Grierson first coined the term documentary in a review of Robert Flaherty's film *Moana* (1925), indicating the ability of the medium to literally produce a visual 'document' of a particular event. Grierson, though fiercely committed to the educational and democratic capabilities of the documentary, clearly recognised that film itself was a relative form and, in typically combative style, suggests that '[c]inema is neither an art nor an entertainment; it is a form of publication, and may publish in a hundred different ways for a hundred different audiences'.[4]

For further reference to Grierson and documentary film, see Chapter 9, pp. 269–70 and Chapter 11, pp. 356–7.

The documentary form is one method of cinematic 'publication' which in Grierson's terms is defined by 'the creative treatment of actuality'.[5] Supporting Britton's earlier point, Grierson acknowledges that the filming of 'actuality' in itself does not constitute what might be seen as the 'truth'. He recognises that 'actuality' footage must be subjected to a creative process to *reveal* its truth. This apparent manipulation of material is both a recording of 'reality' and a statement *about* 'reality'. As screenwriter and director, Bela Balazs notes: '[t]his presentation of reality by means of motion pictures differs essentially from all other modes of presentation in that the reality being presented is not yet completed; it is itself still in the making while the presentation is being prepared. The creative artist does not need to dip into his memory and recall what has happened – he is present at the happening itself and participates in it'.[6] It remains necessary, therefore, to examine the nature and extent of the intervention and manipulation of the film-maker, and the subsequent generic aspects that are being explored, and possibly redefined.

See Chapter 5 for discussion of realist film and the spectator.

A useful starting point is Richard Barsam's list of categories which constitute and seek to define what he generically terms 'the non-fiction film'.[7] This list effectively demonstrates the different types of film which have been perceived as documentary, and clearly share some of its possible codes and conventions. The categories include

- factual film
- ethnographic film
- films of exploration
- propaganda film
- *cinéma-vérité*
- direct cinema
- documentary

Barsam essentially locates the documentary itself outside the other categories because he suggests that the role of the film-maker is much more specific in determining the interpretation of the material in these types of film. In other words, he views the documentary as a medium which, despite its use of 'actuality' footage, is still what we may term an 'authored' form, and this arguably provides a useful distinction by

**reactive observation-
alism**
Documentary film-
making in which the
material recorded is
filmed as spontaneously
as possible subject to
the immediacy of obser-
vation by the camera
operator/director.

**proactive observation-
alism**
Documentary film-
making in which specific
choices are made about
what material is to be
recorded in relation to
the previous observation
of the camera
operator/director.

illustrative mode
Approach to documen-
tary which attempts to
directly illustrate what
the commentary/
voiceover is saying.

associative mode
Approach to documen-
tary which attempts to
use footage in such a
way as to provide the
maximum degree of
symbolic or metaphorical
meaning on top of the
literal information available in the image.

overheard exchange
The recording of seem-
ingly spontaneous
dialogue between two or
more participants
engaged in conversa-
tion/observation.

testimony
The recording of
solicited observation,
opinion or information by
witnesses, experts or
other relevant partici-
pants in relation to the
documentary subject.
The primary purpose of
the interview.

exposition
The use of voiceover or
direct-to-camera
address by a figure who
is essentially directing
the viewer in the recep-
tion of information and
argument.

which the other categories may be evaluated in regard to their common characteristics
and divergent methods.

Barsam's categories attempt to distinguish different uses of 'actuality' footage. We
may view this footage as raw footage, which though subject to processes of selection
as it is photographed may be viewed as an unmediated recording of an incident, an
interview, an event etc. *as it happened*. This footage then becomes subject to specific
compilation and organisation which defines its context. In its turn that footage can then
become:

the Newsreel (record of current events), the Travelogue (description of a place, often for the
purposes of promotion or advertising), the Educational or Training film (to teach an audience how to
do or understand something), and the Process film (to describe how an object or procedure is
constructed).[8]

These films, having determined their context, that is, their purpose and perspective,
are then constructed in a specific way. John Corner suggests that we may address
these films and their claim to be defined as documentary by looking at three key areas
which inform all non-fiction films.[9] These are:

1   technological factors;
2   sociological dimensions;
3   aesthetic concerns.

Clearly, technological developments have been absolutely intrinsic to the changing
styles and approaches that characterise the non-fiction film. Advanced technology
enables advanced technique. Light, hand-held cameras capable of recording sound
and using sensitive film stocks or digital video discs, able to record footage for a
considerable length of time, will obviously produce a different kind of film to that
produced by a static, heavy camera unable to record sound or photograph material for
more than a few minutes.

The sociological dimension of these films is important because the documentary
medium is a specifically social form. In attempting to record certain aspects of 'reality'
in a particular time and space, the documentary implicitly and explicitly locates itself in
the historical moment and focuses on the personal and cultural codes and conventions
of that time.

It is in the aesthetic concerns of documentary that there is considerable debate,
because it is largely in creating an aesthetic approach that documentaries and other
non-fiction films begin to challenge, distort and subvert notions of documentary 'truth'
and 'authenticity'. The aesthetics of a piece ultimately determine its proper context.
Useful here are Corner's four modes of visual language and three modes of verbal
language in the documentary form.[10] Corner suggests that **reactive observationalism**
operates as the most apparently unmediated recording of actuality footage, while
proactive observationalism includes a higher degree of choice in what is actually
recorded. The **illustrative mode** looks to directly echo what is being eschewed in
commentary, while the **associative mode** involves the highest degree of manipulation
in the sense that the footage is used in the service of overtly symbolic and metaphoric
purposes. Verbal evidence in the documentary may be in the mode of **overheard
exchange** between filmed participants; **testimony**, mainly through the voices of inter-
viewees; and finally **exposition**, through voiceover or direct-to-camera address. These
approaches in relation to visual and verbal language help to determine the kind and
extent of construction and self-reflexivity in the documentary – a key tension in the
evolution of the non-fiction film.

A key aspect of this discussion concerns the role of the documentary film-maker. For further study, when you are watching a documentary, consider the following points:

1 **How does the documentary film-maker use *mise en scène*, editing, sound, cinematography and narrative devices to create a point of view/argument?**
2 **The documentary film-maker in dealing with 'actuality' and real social issues may encounter certain problems in the making of a text. What might these problems be and how can the documentarist resolve them?**

In a number of the case studies in this chapter, the political and ethical stance of the film-maker is crucial to the way we understand and perhaps support or oppose the implied or explicit argument of the documentary. When watching future documentaries consider and evaluate the behaviour, attitude or position of the film-makers. Do you believe that they are correct in the ways that they pursue 'documentary truth'?

See Chapter 4 for further discussion of film language.

SOME DEVELOPMENTS IN NON-FICTION FILM

The history of the non-fiction film has its origins in the development of the earliest motion pictures. Following on from still photography, and motion studies like those photographed by Edward Muybridge, and yet further extending a trend in the arts to record 'reality, in the most accurate way',[11] 'actualities' or 'documentaries' filmed by the Lumière Brothers in 1895 constitute some of the first non-fiction films. These films included *Workers Leaving the Lumière Factory* and *Arrivée d'un train en gare à la Ciotat*, and are merely examples of everyday events recorded with a static camera. Audiences were astonished by the images because they were seeing moving pictures of 'reality' for the first time. Similar short films were recorded by Edison in America and soon the phenomenon spread worldwide with examples emerging from Spain, India and China.

   Perhaps the first major examples to characterise the documentary form were the films emerging after the Russian Revolution of 1917, and particularly the work of Dziga Vertov, who edited a newsreel series called *Kino-Pravda* (literally 'Film-Truth'), and developed an approach to film called *Kinoki* ('cinema-eye'), informed by twelve major theoretical points. In the space available here, I only intend to stress three of the points, but they are representative of the highly politicised and, indeed, highly aestheticised view Vertov had of the cinematic medium as a documentary tool:

See Chapter 13, pp. 442–3, for further discussion of Vertov's work.

The Cameraman uses many specific devices to 'attack' reality with his camera and to put facts together in a new structure; these devices help him to strive for a better world with more perceptive people.

He continues:

Knowing that 'in life nothing is accidental', the cameraman is expected to grasp the dialectical relationships between disparate events occurring in reality; his duty is to unveil the intrinsic conflict of life's antagonistic forces and lay bare the 'cause and effect' of life's phenomenon.

And concludes:

All this is necessary if kinoks [documentarists] want to show on the screen 'Life-as-it-is' in its essence, including the 'life' of the film itself – the process of cinematic creation from shooting and laboratory, through editing, up to the final product, i.e. the film being projected to the audience in a movie auditorium.[12]

Vertov's use of the film medium is a highly creative one, stressing simultaneously the importance of the art of film-making and the politicised 'reality' it records. It is this tension between revealing the 'form' of the recording (that is, the unusual use of the camera, complex editing, etc.) and the 'content' it shows, which confuses the notion of the films as documentaries, especially in regard to his later and most renowned work, *The Man with the Movie Camera* (1929). *Cinéma-vérité* director Richard Leacock says that Vertov's newsreels were persuasive, even if they were superficial in their recording of famine or disaster, but adds:

[Vertov]…went on to film *The Man with the Movie Camera*, which was accused of being formalistic, and to me it was. It was tricks, games, and I don't see that it really has any connection with his expressed desire to show life as it is.[13]

For further discussion of realism and Soviet cinema, see Chapter 13, pp. 444–5.

It is Vertov's aesthetic sense which in Leacock's mind ultimately distances him from the true spirit of the documentary enterprise in showing 'reality' as it is, without the addition of foregrounded 'formalist' principles of film-making practice. A similar kind of formalism occurs in what became known as the *City Symphony* documentaries which include *Rien que les heures* (1926), directed by Alberto Cavalcanti, and Walter Ruttman's *Berlin, Symphony of a Great City* (1927), both of which were characterised by avant-garde and surrealist techniques. The films were essentially impressions of each city, using footage of real locations to reveal the disparity between rich and poor. Despite their formalist pretensions, the films succeed in making social comment, and are influential in their achievement in using images of everyday people, objects and locations for symbolic and political effect. Arguably, Vertov, Cavalcanti and Ruttman are working primarily in an *associative* mode which would later be challenged by Leacock's preferred mode of *reactive observationalism*, which he believes is closer to authentic documentary.

FROM TRAVELOGUE TO AUTHORED DOCUMENTARY

In America, the non-fiction film had primarily been defined and sustained by the travelogue (a term coined by Burton Holmes), which was footage shot in foreign lands and shown at lectures and slide-shows to introduce audiences to different cultures and exotic locations. In 1904, at the St Louis Exposition, George C. Hale's *Tours and Scenes of the World* was particularly successful, but did not reach the mythic proportions of the footage from President Teddy Roosevelt's African safaris or Robert Scott's expedition to the South Pole. These kinds of travelogues appealed to the American public because they demonstrated the American spirit of enterprise and adventure, supporting the view that the American consciousness was informed by a pioneering spirit and an enduring sense of 'the frontier'. This outlook underpins the Romantic tradition of film-making which begins with travelogue footage of real cowboys and Indians and comes to its apotheosis in the films of Robert Flaherty. Special mention must be made though of Merian C. Cooper and Ernest Schoedsack who shot *Grass* (1925), a film about Iranian nomadic tribes searching for fresh pastureland, and *Chang* (1927), which followed a Thai family's experiences in the jungle, and included scenes of predatory animals attempting to abduct women and children, which had a profound influence on Cooper and Schoedsack's most famous feature film, *King Kong* (1933).

It is Robert Flaherty, though, who most embodies the development of the documentary form as an ethnographic (the scientific study of other races from a position 'within' the community) and anthropological tool.

☐ CASE STUDY 1: ROBERT FLAHERTY

His films were travelogues to places that never were.

(Richard Barsam)[14]

Flaherty's films are not just moving pictures. They are experiences, similar in a geographic sense to visiting Paris or Rome or seeing the dawn rise over the Sinai desert. Flaherty is a country, which having once seen never forgets.

(Arthur Calder-Marshall)[15]

Sponsored by the fur company Revillon Freres, Robert Flaherty made *Nanook of the North* (1922), a study of the Inuit Eskimos of northern Canada, which is acknowledged as one of the most influential films within the genre. It perhaps provides us with all the clues we require to define both the documentary and its acceptable limits. As is indicated above by Barsam and Calder-Marshall, Flaherty's films are 'authored' films with a specific intent; an intent that we might characterise as not merely to record the lives of the Eskimos, but to recall and restage a former, more primitive, more 'real' era of Eskimo life. This nostalgic intent only serves to mythologise Eskimo life and to some extent remove it from its 'realist' context, thus once again calling into question some of the inherent principles that we may assume are crucial in determining documentary 'truth'.

For further discussion of authorship and film, see Chapter 6.

• **Plate 7.1** *Nanook of the North* (Robert J. Flaherty, Canada 1922) Filmed August 1920–August 1921 in the area around the Hudson Strait, Canada, and along the shore of the Hopewell Sound, Quebec

Though Flaherty was an advocate of the use of lenses that could view the subject from a long distance so as not to affect unduly the behaviour of the Eskimos, and deployed cinematography (using long uninterrupted takes) instead of complex editing, it is Flaherty's intervention in the material that is most problematic when evaluating *Nanook* as a key documentary. Flaherty was not content merely to record events; he wanted to 'dramatise' actuality by filming aspects of Eskimo culture which he knew of from his earlier travels into the Hudson Bay area between 1910 and 1916. For example, he wanted to film Eskimos hunting and harpooning seals in the traditional way, instead of filming them using guns, which was their regular practice. Similarly, he rebuilt igloos to accommodate camera equipment, and organised parts of the Eskimo lifestyle to suit the technical requirements of shooting footage under these conditions. In *Moana*, Flaherty staged a ritual tattooing ceremony among the Samoan Islanders, recalling a practice that had not been carried out for many years, while in *Man of Aran* (1935) shark-hunts were also staged which did not characterise the contemporary existence of the Aran Islanders.

John Grierson argues that Flaherty becomes intimate with the subject matter before he records it and thus '[h]e lives with his people till the story is told "out of himself" ' and this enables him to 'make the primary distinction between a method which describes only the surface value of a subject, and a method which more explosively reveals the reality of it'.[16] This seems to legitimise Flaherty's approach because *Nanook*, *Moana* and *Man of Aran* all succeed in revealing the practices of more 'primitive' cultures –

• **Plate 7.2** *Nanook of the North* (Robert J. Flaherty, Canada 1922)

cultures which in Flaherty's view embody a certain kind of simple and romanticised utopianism.

Clearly, then, Flaherty essentially uses 'actuality' to illustrate dominant themes and interests that he is eager to explore. In some ways Flaherty ignores the real social and political dimensions informing his subjects' lives, and indeed does not engage with the darker side of the human sensibility in order to prioritise larger, more mythic and universal topics. There is almost a nostalgic yearning in Flaherty's work to return to a simpler, more physical, pre-industrial world, where humankind could pit itself against the natural world, slowly but surely harnessing its forces to positive ends. Families and communities are seen as stoic and noble in their endeavours, surviving often against terrible odds. Flaherty obviously 'manipulates' his material and sums up one of the apparent ironies in creating documentary 'truth' by suggesting '[s]ometimes you have to lie. One often has to distort a thing to catch its true spirit'.[17]

FROM SOCIAL COMMENTARY TO PROPAGANDA TO POETIC ACTUALITY

If Flaherty established a tradition of documentary which emerged out of the travelogue and aspired to celebrate humankind, then it was John Grierson in Britain who defined the documentary in more politicised terms. Grierson theorised the documentary, produced a number of films (all influenced by his political stance) and created a distribution network for them. His outlook suited a period in which the mass media (film, radio and the press) and advertising industries were having considerable impact, while the idea of mass political democracy was emerging in a way that necessitated the education of ordinary people in its principles.

For further discussion of Grierson and documentary film, see Chapter 9, pp. 269–70, and Chapter 11, pp. 356–8.

Enamoured by the view that documentary could serve the processes of democracy in educating the people, Grierson pursued his aims which characteristic zeal. He was influenced by the ideas of Walter Lippmann (who believed that the complexity of modern life prohibited ordinary individuals from participating in a society to a proper extent) and the works of Sergei Eisenstein (whose 1925 film *Battleship Potemkin* Grierson admired as a 'glorified newsreel' and consequently organised a showing of it in England). Grierson wanted the documentary to be more sociologically aware and less formally aesthetic than the work of Vertov. Grierson's documentary film unit was initially sponsored by the Empire Marketing Board, under the leadership of Sir Stephen Tallents, who sought to reach Commonwealth nations both in a commercial and ideological sense. (Tallents sought to promote Britain as much as its trade.) The unit came under the auspices of the General Post Office (GPO) in 1933 and finally became the Crown Film Unit in 1940, predominantly working with the Ministry of Information on wartime propaganda.

See Chapter 13, pp. 423–5 and 427–36, for discussion of Eisenstein and his contribution to Soviet montage cinema.

The films produced by Grierson fall into Dennis De Nitto's definition of the social commentary film, which he divides into three distinct sub-groups: The documentary of *Social Description* has its primary purpose to present to an audience social conditions, particularly how an environment and institutions affect the lives of people. Any criticism of these conditions is oblique, implied rather than stated. In a documentary of *Social Criticism*, the director is less objective, and his intention is to make audiences conscious that something is wrong in their society and should be remedied. When a director is angry about a situation and wishes to induce outrage in his audience and even provoke them into action, he creates a documentary of *Social Protest*.[18]

Most of Grierson's output falls into the first category, beginning with *Drifters* (1929),

propaganda
The systematic
construction of a text in
which the ideological
principles of a political
stance are promoted,
endorsed and made
attractive to the viewer
in order to influence the
viewer's beliefs and
preferences. Such a text
may often include critical
and exploitative ideas
and imagery about oppo-
sitional stances. 'Point of
view' in these texts is
wholly informed by polit-
ical bias and a specificity
of intention to persuade
the viewer of the
intrinsic 'rightness' of
the authorial position.

the only film actually directed by Grierson, and concerned with herring fishermen in the North Sea. Other significant films followed: *Granton Trawler* (1934), directed by Edgar Anstey, also about fishing; *Song of Ceylon* (1934), directed by Basil Wright, which featured the first attempt to counterpoint sound to visual images rather than use music or dialogue; *Housing Problems* (1935), co-directed by Anstey and Arthur Elton, which deployed a journalistic newsreel style in interviewing ordinary people living in slum housing conditions; *Nightmail* (1936), directed by Basil Wright and Harry Watt, which features music by Benjamin Britten and poetry by W.H. Auden in its highly lyricised view of the night-time mail train on its journey from London to Glasgow; and *North Sea* (1938), produced by Alberto Cavalcanti, and directed by Harry Watt, which tells the story of ship-to-shore radio, using dramatised reconstructions.

During the Second World War, the Ministry of Information appointed Jack Beddington as the film liaison officer to work with Grierson's newly christened 'Crown' film unit to produce works of documentary information and **propaganda**. These films addressed domestic and strategic issues and were characterised by a desire to educate the public and invoke a consensus among the people in the conduct of the war at a personal and social level. Films like *Squadron 992* (1939), *Dover Front Line* (1940) and *Target for Tonight* (1941) established Harry Watt as one of the most important film-makers of the period, but it is the work of Humphrey Jennings which represents some of the finest and most influential aspects of British documentary film-making.

□ CASE STUDY 2: HUMPHREY JENNINGS

Having read English at Cambridge University, and become interested in theatre and costume design, Humphrey Jennings immersed himself in the arts and joined the GPO film unit in 1934. He designed sets for Cavalcanti's *Pett and Pott* (1934) and directed *Post Haste and Locomotives* in his first year. By 1936, he was part of the organising committee for the International Surrealist Exhibition in London, and working on ideas concerning an 'anthropology of our own people' which would be the catalyst for the Mass Observation Movement, principally taken up and established by journalist and anthropologist Tom Harrison. Mass Observation sought to observe and record detailed aspects of human behaviour, including the 'Shouts and Gestures of Motorists', 'Bathroom Behaviour', 'Distribution, Diffusion and Significance of the Dirty Joke' and 'Female Taboos about Eating'.[19] Clearly, this reflects some of the aspirations of Jennings' work as a documentarist, particularly in his film following the journey of the picture postcard, *Penny Journey* (1938) and his record of working-class communities' leisure pastimes, *Spare Time* (1939).

When war broke out, Jennings made two films, *The First Days* (1939) and *Spring Offensive* (1939), but his first major achievement was in collaboration with Harry Watt. Entitled *London Can Take It*, the film dealt with how the British people survived the Blitz, demonstrating their indefatigable spirit and endurance. The film was especially made to appeal to markets in the Empire and in the US. *Heart of Britain* (1940) followed, but it was *Words for Battle* (1941) that established Jennings as a distinctive film-maker not afraid to develop aspects of the form that he was working within. In a letter to Cicely Jennings in March 1941, he defends the technique he employed to heighten the emotional impact of Britain's purpose in fighting the war:

*See Chapter 13,
pp. 420–1, for discus-
sion of propaganda and
Soviet cinema of the
1920s.*

I have been accused of 'going religious' for putting the Hallelujah Chorus at the end of 'This is England' [*Words for Battle*]. This of course from Rotha and other of Grierson's little boys who are still talking as loudly as possible about 'pure documentary' and 'realism' and other such systems of self-advertisement.[20]

Jennings simultaneously demonstrates a sceptical view of documentary and signals a more poetic and emotive approach to emotional realism. *Words for Battle* is composed of seven sequences, each with a commentary by Laurence Olivier, each demonstrating a juxtaposition of images with a specific piece of poetry or public oratory – these include William Blake's 'Jerusalem', Rudyard Kipling's 'The Beginnings', Winston Churchill's speech made on 4 June 1940 and Abraham Lincoln's Gettysburg Address. Jennings effectively poeticised 'actuality', simultaneously rehistoricising public monuments and buildings and elevating the human worth of ordinary people as they stoically endured the hardships of war. This redefined the documentary as a genre which not merely recorded events and locations but appropriated them as illustration for the poetic muse.

Listen to Britain (1941) and *Fires Were Started* (1942) continue this approach which attempts to lyricise and celebrate ordinary working practices that had been ignored until their importance was heightened and their value was acknowledged during the war. It was suggested by certain distributors and critics based at Wardour Street in London that *Fires Were Started* should be cut further. This drew a response from Jennings which is revealing about his position on documentary: 'Well, of course one expects that from spineless well-known modern novelists and poets who have somehow got into the propaganda business – who have no technical knowledge and no sense of solidarity or moral courage.'[21]

Significantly, Jennings rejects the idea that his films are propaganda, and indeed that they fit easily into any Griersonian category of documentary achievement. Moreover, he aligns himself with the power of film itself to *evoke* and *provoke* consensus through moral and emotional empathy. *A Diary for Timothy* (1946) completes Jennings' war cycle, and is perhaps his finest achievement in this mode of documentary film-making, for it anticipates the baby Timothy's growing up in postwar Britain. With a script by E.M. Forster, read by Michael Redgrave, the film has an elegiac and ambiguous feel because Jennings' normal emotional optimism has become emotional uncertainty. Documentary 'actuality' has been imbued with the inconsistency of 'feeling' rather than the consistency of 'fact'.

• **Plate 7.3** *A Diary for Timothy* (Humphrey Jennings, UK 1945) With a commentary written by E.M. Forster spoken by Michael Redgrave, and 'produced with the help of the people all over Great Britain, among them Dame Myra Hess', it represented the condition and mood of Britain in the final stages of the war

For further study, either from your knowledge of documentaries that you have already seen, or from current documentaries you see on television or at the cinema, try and apply De Nitto's three categories of documentary: *Social Description*, *Social Criticism* and *Social Protest*, suggesting why you have reached your conclusion. Consider *who* says *what* to *whom*, *when*, *how* and *why*, and with *what* effect.

PROPAGANDA AS DOCUMENTARY MYTH

A European tradition of documentary film-making would necessitate a chapter in its own right, but figures like Joris Ivens (Holland) and Henri Storck (Belgium) contribute a great deal to the understanding of pre-war Europe in their films. Ironically, one of the greatest European documentary film-directors, Leni Riefenstahl, emerges from a more sinister context, in that she was responsible for Nazi propaganda film, and created what has become acknowledged as one of the greatest films, documentary or otherwise, of all time. In 1935, Riefenstahl made *Triumph of the Will*, a record of the 1934 Nuremberg Party rally, and with this one film initiated an enduring debate. Should such a film, which so effectively glorifies the Nazi ideal, become divorced from its propagandistic context to be celebrated as 'art' and championed as one of the finest examples of documentary? Only by addressing the approach of Leni Riefenstahl can one posit an answer.

☐ CASE STUDY 3: LENI RIEFENSTAHL

Leni Riefenstahl began her career as an actress, most commonly in Arnold Fanck's 'mountain' movies, which featured aspirant climbers scaling alpine ranges in search of spiritual truth and mythic grandeur; Riefenstahl herself directed and starred in a 'mountain' movie entitled *The Blue Light*. This served to confirm her as an emergent talent which had already been acknowledged by Hitler himself. The themes of the 'mountain' movie – the search for purity and higher knowledge, the pursuit of personal excellence in the face of the elemental and the primitive, notions of self-discipline and spiritual purpose – chimed readily with the politicised High Romanticism of National Socialism, later distorted into the criminal agendas of Nazi policy. This inherently 'fascist' genre clearly informs Riefenstahl's later work.

Riefenstahl made *Triumph of the Will* after she completed *Victory of Faith* (1933) celebrating Hitler's first National Socialist Party Congress, and *Day of Freedom: Our Army* (1934), a tribute to the discipline and regimented efficiency of German soldiers. *Triumph of the Will* essentially combines these two themes and develops them into the notion of documentary propaganda as myth. Seemingly fully supported by Hitler and Goebbels, and given full co-operation and funding by government agencies, Riefenstahl deployed some 120 crew members and over thirty cameras in the shooting and construction of the film. The rally itself was staged to accommodate the film and essentially operated as a highly artificial, planned piece of theatre. This directly refutes Riefenstahl's claim that *Triumph of the Will* is *cinéma-vérité*, because as Susan Sontag indicates, '[i]n *Triumph of the Will*, the document (the image) is no longer simply the record of reality; 'reality' has been constructed to serve the image'.[22]

This construction of documentary 'myth' corresponds to the fascist aesthetics Sontag outlines in her evaluation of Riefenstahl, where she indicates that the 'ritual' of

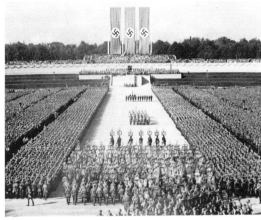

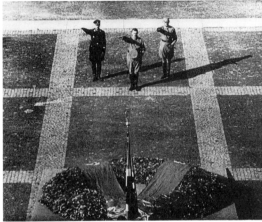

• **Plates 7.4, 7.5 and 7.6** *Triumph des Willens* (*Triumph of the Will*)
(Leni Riefenstahl, Germany 1935)
Filmed 4–10 September 1934 in Nuremberg at the Nazi Party
Congress. Winner of the National Film Prize of Germany, 1935, and
the Venice Biennale Gold Medal, 1936

the Nuremberg Rally is characterised by 'domination' and 'enslavement' and this is
reflected symbolically in:

the massing of groups of people; the turning of people into things; the multiplication of things and
the grouping of people/things around an all-powerful, hypnotic leader figure or force. The fascist
dramaturgy centres on the orgiastic transaction between mighty forces and their puppets. Its choreography alternates between ceaseless motion and a congealed, static, 'virile' posing. Fascist art
glorifies surrender, it exalts mindlessness: it glamorises death.[23]

Sontag usefully shows how a film like *Triumph of the Will* constructs its 'actuality'
around consciously conceived choreographic principles which recognise and deliberately deploy symbolic relationships. Documentary 'actuality' acts as a set of metaphors
which are informed by rich mythical and political associations. An examination of the
opening sequence of the film supports this view because it begins with the emergence
of a plane from parting clouds, which casts its shadow over Nuremberg as it flies over
excited crowds staring up towards it in anticipation. Needless to say, this is Hitler's
aircraft, which serves the symbolic function of defining Hitler's Godhead as he
descends from the heavens, literally overshadowing his people as he arrives to
dispense his glory and wisdom. Hitler is constantly looked up to in the film and individualised and elevated above the dehumanised masses of both people and soldiers.

In making the film in this fashion, Riefenstahl uses film form in a sophisticated way to construct power relations and define Hitler's mystical identity in the light of faceless, highly regimented groups of undifferentiated 'ordinary' people. Hitler becomes an icon which is apparently authenticated and naturalised by the 'realism' inherent in the documentary form. It is only by understanding that 'actuality' may be extensively manipulated that we can understand the relativity of documentary practice and question the whole notion of documentary 'truth'. The combination of Riefenstahl's compositional skill and the specific choreography of the proceedings succeed in making a great film 'fiction'. 'Actuality' is not actual; the filmic record of the event is highly mediated; the material is edited not to reveal the 'truth' but a set of symbolic relationships with a specific political purpose; the rally in becoming an illusion of 'reality' becomes 'documentary myth'.

Representation is a key issue in film-making practice. It has stimulated some highly contentious debates in relation to mainstream cinema. Documentary has a social mission, and is perceived as a democratic medium. For further study, consider issues of representation in the documentary form. Does the representation of people and events in documentary differ significantly from those, for example, in an action-adventure film, an animation, the news? If so, in what ways, and to what effect? Consider also, groups traditionally marginalised in films: how does documentary treat gender, race, age, class, social difference, etc.?

FROM DOCUMENTARY BIAS TO DIRECT CINEMA AND CINÉMA-VÉRITÉ

Riefenstahl's work may be understood as both highly aestheticised and (to use Corner's terms) determinedly 'associative'. Another kind of approach to political documentary informed the work of the Workers' Film and Photo League of America (1930–5). Overtly left wing in its outlook, it championed the ordinary working people of America, and sought to educate, inform and politicise blue-collar groups in securing better pay and conditions. Griersonian in spirit, the League recorded key historical moments of the Depression, which included protest marches about unemployment and pictures of families in bread-lines. The League's work was later overshadowed by the emergence of 'Nykino', who were also dedicated to socialist principles and a commitment to support union activity in working environments. Dutch documentarist Joris Ivens, while working in America was influential upon the group's political film output, particularly in Nykino's newsreel, The World Today, which was essentially a left-wing version of the popular mainstream newsreel, The March of Time[24] (satirised in Orson Welles' Citizen Kane, 1941). Though not a left-wing sympathiser, Pare Lorentz, another key figure in American non-fiction film-making, made two important films in the style of Nykino, employing a number of the group's key personnel. These films were entitled The Plow that Broke the Plains (1936) and The River (1937), and were both sponsored by the government and attempted to sustain 'the American Dream' in spite of less than ideal social realities. In principle, Lorentz tried to create films that provided ideological justification for potentially unpopular or difficult to understand programmes of reform which necessitated a high financial commitment by the government.

The River was a thirty-minute documentary made on 16mm film, designed to be shown in farmhouses, schoolrooms and any suitable venue, in order to educate the people of the Mississippi Valley about the disastrous effects of flooding and 150 years of exploitation of the land's resources. The documentary centres on the experience of one poverty-stricken family and clearly attempts to create sympathy for the people on emotional terms, suggesting that they are 'ill-clad, ill-housed, ill-fed' and 'a share of the crop their only security'. It is suggested that the people lack 'a frontier'; they have no new continent to build, they have to be instrumental in saving their land – 'the greatest river valley in the world'. Roosevelt's 'New Deal' administration had already established the Tennessee Valley Authority and the Farm Security Administration in 1933, and successfully justified state intervention in that area. The film attempts to prove that state intervention in this instance had rehabilitated the land, so that it might gain the support of Midwestern audiences in financing further state reform in the Mississippi Valley.

Significantly, the family that the film focuses on is white, when it is more likely that a black family would be working in the area, and thus be more representative. It is possible that 'the argument' of the film may have been strengthened by showing a black family, and engaging 'race' sympathy. Any film's 'argument' is targeted to specific audiences, however, and it is clear that Lorentz was using his film to engage white power élites, legislators and voters in order to secure change. In short, the film was not for black audiences, though, of course, many black families were affected by the situation. Here, it is important to note that 'actuality' is once again subjected to politicised choices and adjustments. The film attempts to relate a 'national' issue through a regional policy; thus it makes specific decisions about which audiences it can *initially* speak to, even if its intentions are ultimately more democratic and universal. Documentary film is here used as a specific tool in the process of communication between government and its people. In the American tradition of documentary, it is this very premise that over thirty years later American film-makers were to reverse. New leftist film-makers wanted to directly intervene in the process of communication between the government and its people by revealing how government created institutions which oppressed and misrepresented its people in the name of democracy.

Robert Drew headed the television production section of Time Inc. and worked with key **direct cinema** directors, Richard Leacock, Donn Pennebaker and Albert and David Maysles, initially within the context of ABC TV. The company was at first responsive to Drew's fresh approach to news and current affairs coverage, but scheduled the programmes unfavourably, still prioritising a more mediated style of 'talking head' analysis. Ironically, the most influential film by Drew and his associates was made before joining ABC TV. Called *Primary* (1960), it followed Hubert Humphrey and John F. Kennedy on the Democratic Party campaign trail at the Wisconsin primary election, and attempted to view the proceedings through the candidates' eyes. Using shoulder-mounted camera work, the film echoes the candidates' experience and proves very revealing in its concentration on the 'liveness' of the event. This approach greatly influenced the 'fly-on-the-wall' documentaries by many British TV documentary directors, particularly in the *Space Between the Words* and *Decisions* series made by Roger Graef,[25] and in the ultimately more interventionist style of Paul Watson in *The Family*. Direct cinema seemed to record 'actuality' in a way that achieved historical authenticity and accuracy. Documentary could provide 'documents' which appeared to offer veracity, and did not apparently operate in the more self-conscious style of *cinéma-vérité*.

On leaving Drew Associates, Pennebaker pursued his interest in the popular culture of the period, making *Don't Look Back* (1966), a film of Bob Dylan's tour of England in 1965, and *Monterey Pop*, featuring performances by The Who, Simon and Garfunkel, and Jimi Hendrix. Pennebaker, like his colleague Leacock, seemed to have an affinity with music as a barometer of popular attitudes and communal energy. Pennebaker

See Chapters 12 and 14, for further reference to the use of film as a means of communicating a 'national' message.

direct cinema
American documentarists of the 1960s and 1970s believed that the advent of light, portable, technically sophisticated camera equipment enabled a breakthrough in the ways that documentary film-making could reveal personal and social 'truth'. The fact that the documentarist could literally film anywhere under any conditions meant that a greater intimacy could be achieved with the subject, heightening the sense that 'reality' was being directly observed, and that the viewer was party to the seemingly unmediated immediacy of the experience. Less controlled, unscripted, apparently spontaneous, the look and feel of 'direct cinema' arguably demonstrated a less deliberately authored approach.

viewed his films in a less political light than his direct cinema colleagues. He says: 'They're not documentaries. They weren't intended to be documentaries, but they're records of some moment.' He continues:

My definition of a documentary film is a film that decides that you don't know enough about some- thing, whatever it is, psychology or the tip of South America. Some guy goes there and says 'Holy shit, I know about this and nobody else does, so I am going to make a film about it'.[27]

Pennebaker views documentary as the use of film for exploratory, investigative and analytical purposes. He sees his own films as films of 'record', free from these agendas. Once more, the definition of the documentary seems to be intrinsically bound up with the intention of the film-maker and the nature and emphasis of the 'intervention' in the finally produced film. Films like Pennebaker's 'records' of popular culture became the staple of non-fiction film-making and continued to test traditional views of the docu- mentary form and make controversial statements about the era.

This is significantly illustrated by comparing Mike Wadleigh's *Woodstock* (1970) (with the sing-along 'bouncing ball' sequences directed by a young Martin Scorsese) and *Gimme Shelter* (1970), made by the Maysles brothers. If *Woodstock*, a record of the most famous rock festival of all time, was a celebration of the spiritual value of peace, love, community and the use of mind-expanding drugs, then *Gimme Shelter*, a record of the Rolling Stones' American tour, featuring a murder which takes place at the band's Altamont concert, policed by Hell's Angels, suggests the era is over.

The Maysles made many documentaries about popular cultural figures, for example, The Beatles in *What's Happening! The Beatles in the USA* (1964), Marlon Brando in *Meet Marlon Brando* (1965), Mohammed Ali and Larry Holmes in *Mohammed and Larry* (1980) and visionary artist Christo, who wraps geographical landmarks like islands, valleys and bridges in silk, in *Christo's Valley Curtain* (1974), *Running Fence* (1976) and *Islands* (1986). One of their most important films, though, is *Salesman* (1969), which follows four members of the Mid-American Bible Company in their attempts to sell bibles. The Bible, of course, is more than 'a book', more than 'a commodity', so what the film ultimately becomes about is a tension between commercial and spiritual values. In order to buy or sell a bible it is necessary to address what you have 'faith' in, and

• **Plate 7.7** *Woodstock*
(Mike Wadleigh, US
1970)

• **Plate 7.8** *Woodstock*
(Mike Wadleigh, US
1970)

Paul Brennan, 'the Badger', whom the film mainly focuses on, clearly exhibits an inner crisis in doing his job. As well as prioritising the direct cinema approach, the Maysles also looked for different methods of recording or deploying 'the interview', for example contextualising the footage of the murder in *Gimme Shelter* by asking Mick Jagger and Keith Richard to observe and comment upon the incident and its inclusion in the film. This raised issues about the nature of documentary, in that the film seemingly distances itself from the stabbing of a black man by a white youth, and does not prioritise raw 'actuality' as enough to substantiate a viewpoint. The relativity of documentary is once again called into question – a relativity never denied by one of its greatest American exponents, Frederick Wiseman.

☐ CASE STUDY 4: FREDERICK WISEMAN

> I think the objective/subjective stuff is a lot of bullshit. I don't see how a film can be anything but subjective.[28]

Ex-lawyer, Frederick Wiseman, though committed to the filming of 'actuality', recognised the role of the film-maker as intrinsic to the purpose and ultimate creation of documentary. Rather than trying to make a film with a certain ideological position, however, Wiseman wished to make socially conscious films, which essentially established his own position about the people and events he was encountering. At the same time, he attempted to work in a style that enabled his audiences to do the same. Wiseman resisted the kind of documentary approach that prioritised figures or events in popular culture. He was more concerned with a particular kind of film-making which involved the viewer in the everyday day life of familiar American institutions. Wiseman said:

What I am aiming at is a series on American institutions, using the word 'institutions' to cover a series of activities that take place in a limited geographical area with a more or less consistent group of people being involved. I want to use film technology to have a look at places like high schools, hospitals, prisons and police, which seem to be very fresh material for film.[29]

Wiseman wished to address these institutions because they operate as part of the intrinsic structure of a democratic society yet seem so integrated in that society that their activities remain unexamined and uninterrogated. By not concentrating on an individual story with an imposed 'narrative', Wiseman created a 'mosaic' of events, interactions and working processes, revealing patterns of behaviour, which ultimately reflected the morality of the institution, and the social values of the society that established and defined the role of that institution. In order for an audience to recognise and interpret the material it was viewing, it was important that they were not 'passive' viewers but actively engaged in perceiving the world they, like Wiseman, were encountering. Consequently, Wiseman did not use voiceover or music to guide the viewer's understanding of the film. Although Wiseman clearly wished the audience to make up its own mind, he also wanted the audience to make the imaginative leap in understanding that any institution is a model of society, and its activities serve as symbols and metaphors for some bigger themes about power and authority.

Wiseman has made many films. Some of the most important include *Titicut Follies* (1967), *High School* (1968), *Basic Training* (1971), *Model* (1980) and *Central Park* (1989). *Titicut Follies*, Wiseman's first film, perhaps remains his most controversial, as it is about the Bridgewater State Hospital for the criminally insane in Massachusetts. Effectively banned for over twenty-five years because of continuing legal action, the film created considerable controversy in its revelation of the conditions and treatment the

• **Plate 7.9** *High School* (Frederick Wiseman, US 1968)

inmates had to endure. The film, named after the annual revue staged by the staff and patients, shows the inhumane attitudes and actions of authorities and the lack of proper care for seriously disturbed patients. It is the first example of one of Wiseman's key themes, which is the attempt by any one individual to preserve their humanity while in apparent conflict with institutional rules and regulations which have a dehumanising effect.

High School, concerning the NorthEast High School in Philadelphia, illustrates the theme in another form by showing how pupils are forced to conform unquestioningly to the rigid principles of the school. Blind obedience and a lack of personal identity are seen as practical and valuable in the school's understanding of a proper induction to the institutional frameworks operating in society as a whole. The film concludes with a sequence of Dr Haller, the school's principal, reading a letter from ex-student Bob Walter, who requests that his GI insurance money be given to the school if he is killed in Vietnam. In the letter, he says 'I am only a body doing a job', and this in many ways serves as Wiseman's position about the school, and indeed, the army which the boy is to serve in, a context Wiseman took up in his film *Basic Training*. Once more illustrating the effects of the processes of dehumanisation, Wiseman shows the initiation of recruits at the Fort Knox training centre in Kentucky. Key questions are raised about the humiliation of certain soldiers (the film was later an influence on Stanley Kubrick's *Full Metal Jacket*) and the regimentation achieved through manipulative strategies which focused on the fears of individuals and the perceptions they had of their own masculinity.

Ultimately a **liberal humanist**, Wiseman raises questions about the assumptions of, and the conduct within, 'institutional' life. The irony inherent in Wiseman's approach is that it is simultaneously an intimate portrait of an institution, showing its 'real' interactions and effects, yet his style remains remote. At one and the same time Wiseman is completely present in making the film, but absent in its final completion. This achievement in itself creates documentary in a spirit which refuses to take sides, blame particular people or offer solutions to problems, but still operates with a forceful commitment. These documentaries are informed 'comments' but not overt 'opinions'.

liberal humanist
A political perspective in which the emphasis is placed upon an openness of democratic discourse and a multiplicity of perspectives which directly relate to the actual experiences of people and the fundamental principles relating to what it is to be 'human'.

FROM RADICAL DOCUMENTARY TO TELEVISION, DIVERSITY AND POPULAR FORMS

The direct cinema school in America was significantly opposed by film-maker Emile de Antonio,[30] who felt the ambition of such film-making – an unmediated, apparently unbiased version of 'reality' – was naïve and unachievable. De Antonio imbued his films with Marxist politics and fierce intellectual criticism of American institutional hypocrisy. This meant that he was monitored by J. Edgar Hoover, the FBI and the CIA throughout his career. His films are largely compiled from found footage taken from a number of sources, particularly a lot of film taken but not used in network news coverage. He deliberately made films which created an alternative view of American culture as it had been mediated through television and government agencies. These films included *Point of Order* (1963), which showed the demise of Senator McCarthy at the Senate army hearings of 1954; *Rush to Judgement* (1967), which was the first major documentary to challenge the findings of the Warren Commission in regard to the assassination of John F. Kennedy in 1963; *In the Year of the Pig* (1969), an uncompromising view of American conduct in the Vietnam War; and *Milhouse: A Whitehouse Comedy* (1972), a satirical portrait of Richard Nixon. De Antonio feels that his work is a necessary antithesis to bland and highly censored news reporting on the main television networks, which in his

See Chapter 4, pp. 121–6, for discussion of alternative narratives and counter-cinema.

view have sanitised current affairs and documentary. De Antonio, for example, believed that ABC constructed a sensationalised view of the Vietnam War, which misrepresented the Vietnamese people, did not show illegal American activity, and privileged media personnel as key figures. He also condemned the commercial context of American news programming as inevitably trivialising the horrors of war and leading to the desensitisation of audiences. De Antonio fundamentally believed that television as a medium was misused, banal and ideologically ineffective.

In many senses, this very realisation has influenced and provoked documentarists, eager to revalidate the documentary form. This has led some documentarists to use the television medium for more radical narratives, or to work in ways which make their approach to documentary film more distinctive and experimental. Alongside this more highly politicised use of documentary has been the development of more populist forms hybridising documentary with soap opera, dramatic fiction and news reconstruction. Further, with the advent of affordable camcorder technology in the high street, amateur footage has been used in *Video Diaries* and for entertainment purposes, like those modelled on variations of *Candid Camera*. It was television that essentially absorbed the documentary form in the 1970s and 1980s. Diversification has meant that filmmakers from previously marginalised groups have grasped the opportunity to privilege specific voices with particular concerns. This has been crucial to the maintenance of the documentary as a necessary social vehicle upholding democratic principles. Important feminist non-fiction films have emerged that directly challenged the predominantly male concerns and outlook of the documentary form.[31] These include Kate Millett's *Three Lives* (1971), Donna Deitch's *Woman to Woman* (1975), Connie Field's *The Life and Times of Rosie the Riveter* (1980)[32] and Michelle Citron's *Daughter Rite* (1978). These films sought to both reclaim 'film language' and express the historical, social and personal concerns of women. Similarly, lesbian and gay film-makers have found a voice in documentary, for example, in *Before Stonewall: The Making of a Gay and Lesbian Community* (1984) by Greta Schiller, John Scagliotti and Robert Rosenberg, and, most movingly, in Robert Epstein's *The Times of Harvey Milk* (1984), about the murder of Harvey Milk, the gay and lesbian rights campaigner and official in San Francisco.

Further, black film-makers have used documentary to reclaim history and identity, perhaps most notably in Henry Hampton's *Eyes on the Prize* (1989), and within the British context, John Akomfrah's *Handsworth Songs* (1986).[33] Oppressed or underrepresented groups have been enabled to tell their 'truth', demonstrate their 'fact' and illustrate their 'actuality', and in this the ironic flexibility of the documentary form has served them well.

Increasingly, the documentary has become a hybrid of forms, often erring towards the cinematic vocabularies of narrative 'fiction' to apparently present 'fact' in a critical (yet sometimes populist) mode which Bill Nichols sees in the light of the **reflexive or performative**.[34] In the 1990s more documentaries are being made comparatively cheaply with new digital technologies, filling ever expanding television schedules, and speaking to a seemingly insatiable interest by audiences worldwide to engage with another aspect of themselves and the world they live in.

Arguably, the grand project of the new Information Age in enhancing communication and providing more time by which humankind can communicate more effectively has not been successful. Documentary has therefore become an increasingly valuable form in attempting to critically evaluate the supposed progress of society, and the real implications of cultural history. Important works like Claude Lanzmann's *Shoah* (1986), a nine-hour epic of interviews with survivors of the holocaust; Errol Morris' *The Thin Blue Line* (1988), a study of a roadside murder case in which Randall Adams, the man imprisoned for the crime, was proved innocent; and Michael Moore's *Roger and Me* (1990), a

See Chapter 9 for further discussion of feminism and documentary film.

See Chapter 10 for further discussion of gay and lesbian documentary film.

reflexive/performative documentary
Documentary which is much more subjective and self-reflexive in its construction, foregrounding the arbitrariness and relativity of 'objectivity', 'reality' and 'truth'.

For further discussion of the impact of new technology, see Chapter 3.

concerned citizen's perspective on economic and social betrayal by General Motors, were all internationally successful, an indication of the documentary form's continuing power in the contemporary era. Distinctive **iconoclasts** like Nick Broomfield, Molly Dineen, Clive Gordon, Robert Gardner and Trinh T. Minh-ha are stretching the boundaries of the form, continually and sometimes controversially engaging with issues not addressed in other cinematic or journalistic contexts. Perhaps most significant, though, is the interface between documentary and populist forms – in the recent era, most notably, sport.

iconoclasts
Documentarists committed to challenging the received construction and meanings of images, partially through the critique of those images, and mainly through the reconfiguration of imagery in a subjective style.

☐ CASE STUDY 5: *HOOP DREAMS* (1994) AND *WHEN WE WERE KINGS* (1996)

Aaron Baker and Todd Boyd have identified sport as one of the master narratives of twentieth-century culture.[35] They suggest that the conduct of sporting activity globally has historically provided a crucial touchstone for a range of highly mediated political discourses, concerning gender, race and identity. The institutional structures, commerce and competitive action at the heart of sport, aligned with its representational agendas and dramatic uncertainties, are attractive to film-makers in general, in that they are imbued with persuasive narrational incident and an intrinsic emphasis upon the psychological, emotional and physical limits of the human condition. Sporting feature films, though there are successful examples – *Rocky* (1976), *Raging Bull* (1980), *Field of Dreams* (1989), *Tin Cup* (1995) – are largely characterised by a sense of fictiveness in the sporting performances of actors or the execution of staged matches, which inevitably undermines their effectiveness. Television broadcasts, though 'fictions' in themselves, have educated audiences to expect an authentic 'liveness' and an almost mythologised, electronic model of theatre which further renders sporting film fictions redundant.

Documentary successfully reconciles the recording of sporting activity with the enhanced sense of context and implication afforded by narrativised actuality, related to but outside the sport itself. Leni Riefenstahl's *Olympia* (1938) and Kon Ichikawa's *Tokyo Olympiad* (1965) are perhaps the finest examples of documentaries concerning the world's greatest sporting event. Ken Burns' epic series, *Baseball* (1994) is 'about race … about class … about wealth … about labor and its tensions. [It] is a metaphor for the country'.[36] Barbara Kopple's *Fallen Champ* (1993) is a compelling address of the demise of heavyweight boxing champion Mike Tyson. Powerful examples of the sporting documentary genre which have reached wider audiences and gained critical acclaim in recent years are *Hoop Dreams* (1994) and *When We Were Kings* (1996).

Steve James', Frederick Marx's and Peter Gilbert's *Hoop Dreams*, the story of two black Chicago teenagers, Arthur Agee and William Gates, in their aspirant struggle to become professional NBA basketball players, has been recognised by Arthur and Cutler as a film which works like fictionalised sports movies, almost to its cost as a social commentary, but which, nevertheless, delineates a 'largely unexamined system of inequalities and exploitative practices'.[37] Of greater concern to Arthur and Cutler, however, is the impact of the film-making process upon the boys and the fact that the film-makers do not foreground their own practices in making the text. Further, they note the media 'noise' suggesting that it was unjust that the film had not won an Oscar. Clearly, Arthur and Cutler speak to some of the concerns outlined in this chapter about the construction and status of the documentary form, perhaps fearing that in the critical eagerness to acclaim the film in the name of political correctness, endorsing the need for films which exposed the continuing inequalities for black people in America, that insufficient attention was given to the way in which the documentary was merely

endorsing the mythic narrative of the rise to sporting celebrity and not properly criti-cising it in the way that socially constructive documentaries should.

Leon Gast's and Taylor Hackford's Oscar-winning *When We Were Kings* is an account of the 1974 World Heavyweight Boxing Championship bout between Mohammed Ali and George Foreman staged in Zaïre, which has since been popularly known as the 'Rumble in the Jungle'. The fight itself has taken on legendary status in the popular memory for the way in which Ali overcame seemingly insurmountable odds to defeat Foreman through guile, strategy and an overtly politicised will-to-win. *When We Were Kings* tells the story of the encounter but places emphasis on Ali as a man clearly aware of, and articulate about, his own role as a political subject, and is careful to offer a critical, if sometimes romantic, commentary by figures including film-maker Spike Lee; journalist George Plimpton; novelist and essayist Norman Mailer; and artist Malik Bowens.

The film has a key thematic which stresses the importance of Africa in the modern Afro-American psychology, especially in relation to an increasingly dehistoricised youth culture, using Ali as a site of black discourses from slavery to separatism. Ali is played out as prophet, wit, athlete, political activist and popular hero, defined within President Mobutu's ruthless ambition for the former Belgian Congo; the economic machinations of professional sport, illustrated through the dealings of promoter, Don King; and the tropes of Afro-American entertainment epitomised by soul singer James Brown and blues guitarist B.B. King. Gast and Hackford use Ali as a mediator of the primal integrity of African identity, culture and tradition; the overtly political implications of sporting confrontation; and the stated resistance to white supremacist ideologies at the centre of global structures and spectacle. Above all, Ali's personality works to make this accessible and amusing, partially through the (unfair) textual construction of Foreman as complacent, integrationist and 'Negritude', and the extra-textual contemporary sympathy concerning Ali as a sufferer from Parkinson's disease. Nostalgic longing for the heightened moments of black cultural presence and achievement in the wake of civil rights activism mixes with a model of narrative which entertains and enthuses, a basic reminder to its intended audience that it should not lose sight of its formative history, perhaps, in itself, one of the primary motivations of the documentary enterprise.

Literally thousands of documentaries have been made throughout the world. This chapter can only touch on a few of them. The documentary is a constantly evolving form, crucial to the understanding of ourselves and others. At all times it has tried to find the 'truth' inherent in all contexts and situations. It is this fundamental purpose that defines the documentary form as intrinsic to democratic and humanist cultures.

1 For further study, consider the implications of 'hybridisation' in documentary. For example, what aspects of 'soap opera' and 'documentary' combine in a 'docu-soap' and to what effect?

2 Further, what issues arise out of 'drama-documentary' and 'reconstruction'. Is dramatised documentary a useful and/or legitimate way of 'telling the truth'?

3 With video cameras and other new recording technologies becoming available to more people, consider the implications and consequences for documentary practice.

NOTES

1 Quoted in J. Willis, 'What's Up, Docs?', The *Guardian*, 6 October 1997, p. 9.
2 A. Britton, 'The Invisible Eye', *Sight and Sound*, February 1992, p. 29.
3 Willis, op. cit., p. 9.
4 F. Hardy (ed.), *Grierson on Documentary* (Faber & Faber, London, 1979) p. 85.
5 J. Grierson 'The Documentary Producer', *Cinema Quarterly* Vol. 2, No. 1, p. 8.
6 B. Balazs, 'Filming Death', from K. Macdonald and M. Cousins (eds), *Imagining Reality: The Faber Book of Documentary* (Faber & Faber, London and Boston, 1996) p. 31.
7 R. Barsam, *The Non-Fiction Film* (Indiana University Press, Bloomington and Indianapolis, 1992) Preface, p. 1.
8 D. De Nitto, *Film: Form and Feeling* (Harper & Row, New York, 1985) p. 325.
9 J. Corner (ed.), *Documentary and the Mass Media* (Edward Arnold, London, 1986) pp. xiii–xx.
10 J. Corner *The Art of Record: A Critical Introduction to Documentary* (Manchester University Press, Manchester and New York, 1996) pp. 27–30.
11 See Barsam, op. cit., pp. 13–17.
12 V. Petric, 'Dziga Vertov as Theorist', *Cinema Journal*, Vol. 1, Autumn 1978, pp. 41–2.
13 Interview with Richard Leacock, cited in G. Roy Levin, *Documentary Explorations* (Doubleday, New York, 1971) p. 202.
14 Barsam, op. cit., p. 53.
15 A. Calder-Marshall, *The Innocent Eye: The Life of Robert J. Flaherty* (Harcourt Brace & World, New York, 1966) p. 229.
16 Cited in Hardy (ed.), op. cit., p. 148.
17 Cited in Calder-Marshall, op. cit., p. 97.
18 De Nitto, op. cit., p. 330.
19 M.L. Jennings, *Humphrey Jennings: Film-maker, Painter, Poet* (BFI, London, 1982) p. 17.
20 Ibid., p. 27.
21 Ibid., p. 35.
22 S. Sontag, 'Fascinating Fascism', from B. Nichols (ed.), *Movies and Methods* (University of California Press, Los Angeles, 1976) p. 34.
23 Ibid., p. 40.
24 For information on the American newsreel series, *The March of Time*, see Barsam, op. cit., pp. 163–5.
25 For information on Graef's work, see A. Rosenthal, *The Documentary Conscience* (University of California Press, Los Angeles, 1980) pp. 171–82.
26 For information about Jean Rouch, see Barsam, op. cit., p. 301, and Roy Levin, op. cit., pp. 131–47.
27 Cited in Roy Levin, op. cit., 1971, pp. 234–5.
28 Cited in Roy Levin, op. cit., 1971, p. 321.
29 A. Rosenthal, *The New Documentary in Action* (University of California Press, Los Angeles, 1972) p. 69.
30 For information about Emile De Antonio, see Rosenthal, op. cit., pp. 205–27.
31 See H. Keysaar, 'The Toil of Thought: On Several Non-Fiction Films By Women', from C. Warren (ed.), *Beyond Document: Essays on Non-Fiction Film* (Wesleyan University Press, Hanover and London, 1996) pp. 101–37.
32 For a useful essay on this film, see Corner, op. cit., pp. 125–39.
33 See Corner, op. cit., 1996, pp. 171–81.
34 See 'Performing Documentary' in B. Nichols, *Blurred Boundaries* (Indiana University Press, Bloomington and Indianapolis, 1994) pp. 92–107. Some aspects of Nichols' work here have been applied to the field of animation in P. Wells, 'A Consideration of Animation and the Documentary Aesthetic' from P. Wells (ed.) *Art and Animation* (Academy Group/John Wiley, London, 1997) pp. 40–6.
35 A. Baker and T. Boyd (eds), *Out of Bounds: Sports, Media and the Politics of Identity* (Indiana University Press, Bloomington and Indianapolis, 1997) Preface, p. xi.
36 Quoted in Baker and Boyd (eds), ibid., p. 193.
37 P. Arthur and J. Cutler, 'On the Rebound: *Hoop Dreams* and its Discontents' from K. Macdonald and M. Cousins (eds), op. cit., p. 305.

FURTHER READING

Barnouw, E. *Documentary: A History of Non-Fiction Film* (Oxford University Press, Oxford, 1974)

Barsam, R. *The Non-Fiction Film* (Indiana University Press, Bloomington and Indianapolis, 1992)

Corner, J. (ed.) *Documentary and the Mass Media* (Edward Arnold, London, 1986)

—— *The Art of Record: A Critical Introduction to Documentary* (Manchester University Press, Manchester and New York, 1996)

Guynn, W. *A Cinema of Non-Fiction* (Associated Universities Press, Rutherford, 1990)

Hardy, F. (ed.) *Grierson on Documentary* (Faber & Faber, London, 1979)

Macdonald, K. and Cousins, M. (eds) *Imagining Reality: The Faber Book of Documentary* (Faber & Faber, London and Boston, 1996)

Nichols, B. *Representing Reality* (Indiana University Press, Bloomington and Indianapolis, 1990)

—— *Blurred Boundaries* (Indiana University Press, Bloomington and Indianapolis, 1994)

Renov, M. (ed.) *Theorising Documentary* (Routledge, London and New York, 1993)

Rosenthal, A. *The New Documentary in Action* (University of California Press, Los Angeles, 1972)

—— *The Documentary Conscience* (University of California Press, Los Angeles, 1980)

—— (ed.) *New Challenges for Documentary* (University of California Press, Los Angeles, 1988)

Roy Levin, G. *Documentary Explorations* (Doubleday, New York, 1971)

Sussex, E. *The Rise and Fall of the British Documentary* (University of California Press, Los Angeles, 1976)

Warren, C. (ed.) *Beyond Document: Essays on Non-Fiction Film* (Wesleyan University Press, Hanover, 1996)

Winston, B. *Claiming the Real* (BFI, London, 1995)

FURTHER VIEWING

Olympia (Leni Riefenstahl, 1936)
The Spanish Earth (Joris Ivens, 1937)
The Power and the Land (Joris Ivens, 1940)
Night and Fog (Alain Resnais, 1955)
Chronicle of a Summer (Jean Rouch, 1961)
The Sorrow and the Pity (Marcel Ophuls, 1970)
Woodstock (Mike Wadleigh, 1970)
Naked Spaces: Living is Round (Trinh T. Minh-ha, 1985)

Forest of Bliss (Robert Gardner, 1985)
Shoah (Claude Lanzmann, 1985)
The Times of Harvey Milk (Robert Epstein, 1985)
The Thin Blue Line (Errol Morris, 1988)
The Ark (Molly Dineen, 1992)
The Unforgiving (Clive Gordon, 1994)
Heidi Fleiss: Hollywood Madam (Nick Broomfield, 1995)

RESOURCE CENTRES

The websites cited here provide a range of both academic and informational materials about the documentary genre, and engage with historical and contemporary models of documentary practice from a range of global contexts.

http://www.city.yamagata.jp/yidff/ff/box/en
http://humpc61.murdoch.edu.au/criteriuum/docu/links.htm
http://www2.dox.dk/dox

Chapter 8

Animation: forms and meanings

Paul Wells

■ **Introduction** 238
■ **What is animation?** 238
■ **Early animation** 239
■ **The legacy of Disney** 241
□ Case study 1: deconstructing the cartoon –
  Duck Amuck (1953) 242
■ **Orthodox animation** 245
□ Case study 2: *Girls Night Out* (1986) 248
■ **UPA and Zagreb Studios** 250
■ **Developmental animation** 250
□ Case study 3: *Creature Comforts* (1990) 251
□ Case study 4: *Neighbours* (1952) 252
□ Case study 5: *The Tango* (1991) and *The Criminal* (1992) 254
■ **Experimental animation** 255
□ Case study 6: *A Colour Box* (1935) 258
□ Case study 7: *Deadsy* (1990) 258
□ Case study 8: computers and convergence 259
■ **Conclusion** 261
■ **Notes** 261
■ **Further reading** 262
■ **Further viewing** 262
■ **Resource centres** 263

■ Animation: forms and meanings

INTRODUCTION

For discussion of film genre, see Chapter 6, pp. 166–81; for further discussion of main-stream codes and conventions, see Chapter 4.

The animated film has been intrinsically bound up with the development of the moving image and the emergence of 'cinema' itself. This has done much to hide the unique and distinctive qualities of animation as a film language in its own right. Regularly dismissed as children's entertainment or a television schedule filler, animation has often gone unrecognised as a significant film art with its own codes and conventions. The continuing success of the Disney Studios, the rise of Japanese *manga anime*, and the affecting individual achievements of contemporary animators as diverse as Nick Park, Frederick Back, Gianluigi Toccafondo, Erica Russell, Solveig von Kleist and John Lasseter, however, has necessitated the re-evaluation of the importance of the animated film.

WHAT IS ANIMATION?

A working definition of animation is that it is a film made frame by frame, providing an illusion of movement which has not been directly recorded in the conventional sense. Norman McClaren, one of the medium's acknowledged masters suggests that '[a]nimation is not the art of drawings that move, but rather the art of movements that are drawn', noting 'what happens between each frame is more important than what happens on each frame'.[1] McClaren is suggesting that the true essence of animation is the manipulation of movements between frames. Animators of the Zagreb School in the former Yugoslavia, however, seek to enhance this definition by stressing the creative and philosophic aspects of the craft: 'To animate [is to] give life and soul to a design, not through the copying but through the transformation of reality.'[2] The Zagreb School wished to emphasise that in literally 'giving life' to the inanimate something was revealed about the figure or object in the process which could not be privileged or effectively achieved in live-action. British-based animators John Halas and Joy

See Chapter 9, p. 269, for further reference to Joy Batchelor.

Batchelor confirm this point by suggesting that: '[i]f it is the live-action film's job to present physical reality, animated film is concerned with metaphysical reality – not how things look but what they mean.'[3] Animation essentially offers an alternative vocabulary to the film-maker by which differing perspectives and levels of address are possible.

Czech surrealist animator Jan Svankmajer[4] perceives the vocabulary in animated film as liberating, original and potentially contentious:

Animation enables me to give magical powers to things. In my films, I move many objects, real objects. Suddenly, everyday contact which people are used to acquires a new dimension and in this way casts doubt over reality. In other words I use animation as a means of subversion.[5]

Svankmajer's view stresses how animation can redefine the everyday, subvert our notions of reality and challenge the orthodox understanding of our existence. Roger Cardinal goes as far as to suggest that '[t]he whole ideal of the animated film is to suppress the categories of normal perception; indeed its logic might even be to suppress all differential categories, and annihilate the very conditions of rationality'.[6] Animation can defy the laws of gravity, contest our perceived view of space and time, and endow lifeless things with dynamic vibrant properties. In short, animation can change the world and create magical effects – a point well understood by pioneer film-makers like Georges Méliès, and early animators J. Stuart Blackton, Emile Cohl, Winsor McCay and Ladislaw Starawicz.

EARLY ANIMATION

The development of the animated form is specifically related to the early experiments in the creation of the moving image. As early as 70 BC there is evidence of a mechanism that projected hand-drawn moving images on to a screen, described by Lucretius in *De Rerum Natura*. In the sixteenth century, 'flipbooks' emerged in Europe, often containing erotic drawings which, when riffled, showed the performance of sexual acts. (So much for those 'stickman' drawings of footballers and jugglers I drew in the margins of my textbooks!)

In 1825, Peter Mark Roget developed what was later to be called the *persistence of vision* theory, determining why human beings could perceive movement. Basically, the human eye perceived an essentially *static* image but because of its ability to create an 'afterimage', it operated as a link to the next static image that the eye perceived. This in effect created a continuity of perception in which the material world appeared to move, and this very much echoes the frame-by-frame construction of the film. This phenomenon is crucial in watching moving pictures in general, of course, but of particular significance for the kind of animated cinema achieved frame by frame. With developments like the **Phenakistoscope** in 1831; the **Kinematoscope** in 1861 and the **Praxinoscope** in 1877, there was the eventual emergence of the cinematic apparatus. Intrinsic to these diversionary 'toys' was the idea of the moving image as something magical – a colourful, playful, seemingly miraculous practice.

Also in place by the 1890s was the comic strip form in the American print media industries. This is important because the comic strip was to provide some of the initial vocabulary for the cartoon film: characters continuing from episode to episode; speech 'bubbles'; visual jokes; sequential narrative; and so on. By 1893, the *New York World* and *New York Journal* were using colour printing in their strips, and these may be seen as prototypes of later animated forms.

At the centre of the development of 'trick effects' in the emergent cinema was Georges Méliès. His discovery of the 'dissolve' (that is, when one image cross-fades into another) led him to pioneer a whole number of other cinematic effects that have become intrinsic to the possibilities available to animators. These included stop-motion photography, split-screen techniques, fast and slow motion, and the manipulation of live action within painted backdrops and scenery. Méliès was also a 'lightning cartoonist', caricaturing contemporary personalities, speeding up their 'construction' on screen by undercranking the camera.

By 1900, J. Stuart Blackton made *The Enchanted Drawing*. He appeared as a 'lightning cartoonist', drawing a man smoking a cigar and drinking some wine. By the use of stop-motion, one drawing at a time is revealed and the man's face is made to take on various expressions. Various similar films had preceded this including *The Vanishing Lady* (1898) and *A Visit to the Spiritualist* (1899). These films can be classified as **proto-animation** as they employ techniques which are used by later animators but are not strictly or wholly made frame by frame. Blackton achieved full animation of this sort in *Humorous Phases of Funny Faces* (1906). Though using full animation in key sequences, the film was essentially a series of tricks. Primitive notions of narrative animation followed in the early work of famous comic-strip artist Winsor McCay, who under Blackton's supervision at the Vitagraph Brooklyn Studio made an animated version of his most celebrated strip, *Little Nemo in Slumberland*, in 1911. Blackton clearly recognised that the animated film could be a viable aesthetic and economic vehicle outside the context of orthodox live-action cinema. His film, *The Haunted Hotel* (1907) included impressive supernatural sequences, and convinced audiences and financiers alike that the animated film had an unlimited potential.

In France, caricaturist Emile Cohl's *Fantasmagorie* (1908) created animation as

See Chapter 3, pp. 62–8, for further discussion of early developments in moving images.

Early developments in the moving image
The **Phenakistoscope** was made up of two rotating discs which appeared to make an image move. The **Kinematoscope** was more sophisticated and employed a series of sequential photographs mounted on a wheel and rotated. The **Praxinoscope**, pioneered by Emile Reynaud, was a strip of images mounted in a revolving drum and reflected in mirrors; a model later revised and renamed *Théâtre Optique*, that may claim to be the first proper mechanism to project seemingly animated images on to a screen.

proto-animation
Early live-action cinema demonstrated certain techniques which preceded their conscious use as a method in creating animation. This is largely with regard to stop-motion, mixed media and the use of dissolves to create the illusion of metamorphosis in early 'trick' films.

incoherent cinema
Influenced by the 'Incoherents' artists working between 1883 and 1891, a movement principally led by Cohl, this kind of animation was often surreal, anarchistic, and playful, relating seemingly unrelated forms and events in an often irrational and spontaneous fashion. Lines tumble into shapes and figures in temporary scenarios before evolving into other images.

personality/character animation
Many cartoons and more sophisticated adult animated films, for example, Japanese *anime*, are still dominated by 'character' or 'personality' animation, which prioritises exaggerated and sometimes caricatured expressions of human traits in order to direct attention to the detail of gesture and the range of human emotion and experience. This kind of animation is related to identifiable aspects of the real world and does not readily correspond with more abstract uses of the animated medium.

anthropomorphism
The tendency in animation to endow creatures with human attributes, abilities and qualities. This can redefine or merely draw attention to characteristics which are taken for granted in live-action representations of human beings.

incoherent cinema, less predicated on the comic strip, and more related to abstract art. In Russia, Ladislaw Starawicz was making extraordinary three-dimensional puppet films. *The Cameraman's Revenge* (1911) features insects in a melodramatic love triangle and self-consciously shows the power of cinema itself to show human life.

It is Winsor McCay, however, who must be properly acknowledged for his influence on Disney and American cartoonal tradition. McCay's *The Story of a Mosquito* (1912) is a mock horror story of a mosquito graphically feeding on a man until it is so bloated with blood that it explodes! This film anticipates his development of **personality or character animation** through the creation of *Gertie the Dinosaur* (1914). The playful dinosaur, Gertie, gleefully hurls a mammoth into a lake in the film and clearly displays an attitude. McCay included this film as part of his touring revue show and appeared to be directly talking to and acting upon his character. This **anthropomorphism** is key within animation in general, but most significantly in the films of Walt Disney that were to follow.

While Disney is acknowledged as the main figure in moving animation towards an industrial process, this neglects the work of John R. Bray, who pioneered the cel animation process using translucent cels in 1913 and made a film called *The Artist's Dream*. The Bray Studios then released a series of cartoons with a continuing character, *Colonel Heeza Liar*, and demonstrated the viability of animation as a commercial industry capable of mass production. Cartoons emerged in the market place in the US at the same time that more experimental abstract animation was beginning to emerge out of European avant-garde cinema practices, particularly through film-makers like Oskar Fischinger[7] and Walter Ruttmann. The work of individual artists like these sought to explore the aesthetic boundaries of the film-making art, while rapid advances in film-making technologies in America encouraged the emergence of a variety of organisations making films. These included the Fleischer Brothers, who made the *Out of the Inkwell* series, and later the *Betty Boop*, *Popeye* and *Superman* cartoons. Initially working at the Bray Studios, the Fleischers established an efficient, streamlined anima-

• **Plate 8.1** *Gertie the Dinosaur* (Winsor McCay, US 1914)

tion process, and were one of the first studios to experiment with sound. It is Walt Disney, however, who remains synonymous with animation, through his radical technical and aesthetic innovations between 1928 and 1942, perhaps the 'golden era' of cartoon animation.

Animated films regularly endow animals with human characteristics, giving them distinct personalities and identities. For further study, when you are watching an animated film consider the animal characters with regard to how they represent human issues, most specifically the representation of gender, race, class and physical capability. Some questions you might give thought to are:

1 **How far does the *received knowledge* about animal characteristics inform the construction of humanised characters?**
2 **Is Jerry a girl in the *Tom and Jerry* cartoons?**
3 **How should we view 'cross-dressing' (a regular occurrence in cartoons – for example, Bugs Bunny's 'Brunhilde' in *What's Opera, Doc?*)?**
4 **How should we interpret 'cross-species coupling'?**
5 **How is the 'body' constructed in animated films, and to what purpose and effect?**
6 **In what ways do animated films address issues of race – is the dominant use of 'caricature' in animation a problem in this respect?**

THE LEGACY OF DISNEY

Walt Disney Productions was founded in 1923. Disney himself was a draughtsman on his first 'Laugh-O-Grams' – fairytales such as *Puss in Boots* and *Cinderella* – but soon realised that his greatest flair was as an entrepreneur and artistic director. His film *Alice in Cartoonland*, a mix of animation and live action, was successful enough to secure distribution and finance to further develop his ideas. Fundamentally, Disney wanted to move towards the establishment of an industrial process and a studio ethos and iden- tity which was competitive with and comparable to the established Hollywood studios. In 1927, Disney began working on his 'Oswald the Rabbit' series of cartoons, and during this process he developed 'the pencil test' i.e. photographing a pencil drawn sequence to check its quality of movement and authenticity before proceeding to draw it on cels, to paint it and so on. In 1928, Disney premièred *Steamboat Willie*, featuring Mickey Mouse, which was the first synchronised sound cartoon. Following continuing experiments in the use of sound effects and music in differing relationships to the visual images, the cartoon began to standardise itself as a form which moved beyond the illustration of different kinds of music into one which accommodated narrative and a series of related jokes. Disney introduced Technicolor, the three-strip colour system, into his Silly Symphony *Flowers and Trees* in 1932, which later won an Oscar. All Disney's animators undertook programmes of training in the skills and techniques of fine art, in the constant drive towards ever greater notions of **realism** in his cartoons. Even though Disney was dealing with a form that arguably was more suited to abstract, non-realist expression, he insisted on verisimilitude in his characters, contexts and narratives. He wanted animated figures to move like real figures and to be informed by plausible motivation. Former Disney art director, and veteran of the 'golden era', Zack Schwartz suggests that even though the figures moved in an anatomically correct way,

See Chapter 2 for discussion of the Hollywood studio system.

realism
Live-action cinema has inspired numerous debates about what may be recognised as 'realism'. This is really a consideration of what may be recognised as the most accurate repre- sentation of what is 'real' in recording the concrete and tangible world. Clearly, the animated form in itself most readily accommodates 'the fantastic', but Disney preferred to create a hyper-realism which located his characters in plausibly 'real' worlds which also included fantasy elements in the narrative.

See Chapter 7, pp. 212–14, for discussion of realism and documentary film.

they still required an element of caricature which ironically appeared to make them 'more real' on screen, and that what Disney really wanted was a state of *conviction* in the characters that reconciled the realistic with the caricaturial.[8] This level of 'reality' was further enhanced by the development of the multi-plane camera. Traditionally, in the two-dimensional image, the illusion of perspective had to be created by the artist. The multi-plane camera achieves the illusion of perspective in the animated film by having the relevant image painted on a series of moveable panes of glass placed directly behind each other. Elements of the image can be painted in the foreground; other elements in the mid-spaces; other elements in the receding background. In this way the camera can move *through* the elements seemingly keeping them in perspective. This directly aped live-action shooting and was successfully demonstrated in another Oscar-winning Silly Symphony, *The Old Mill* (1937), with its most advanced aesthetic use in the first full-length, Technicolor, sound-synchronised animated cartoon feature, *Snow White and the Seven Dwarfs* (1937).

Animation had reached a position of maturity, acknowledged in this form as 'art'. *Pinocchio* (1940), *Fantasia* (1940) and *Bambi* (1941) only consolidated this prestige, moving the animated film into the contemporary era, effectively reconciling fine art, a sense of Classicism and a model of traditional American folk culture, drawn, ironically, from many European influences. The rise of Disney and the populist utopian ideology which appealed to the American mass audience has resulted in the neglect of other kinds of animation, and perhaps even more significantly the popular cartoon, as exemplified by the work of Tex Avery, Robert McKimson, Bob Clampett and Chuck Jones at the famous 'Termite Terrace' lot at Warner Bros. Studios. An analysis of Chuck Jones' classic cartoon *Duck Amuck* (1953) may usefully offer, however, some points which both valorise the art of the cartoon short, and provide a vocabulary by which it may be studied.

See Chapter 5 for discussion of how we as spectators are drawn into the world of the film.

☐ CASE STUDY 1: DECONSTRUCTING THE CARTOON – *DUCK AMUCK* (1953)

Duck Amuck, directed by Chuck Jones, is the perfect example of a cartoon which is wholly self-conscious and reveals all the aspects of its own construction. Consequently, it is possible to recognise the cartoon as a mode of **deconstruction**. As Richard Thompson points out:

> It is at once a laff riot and an essay by demonstration on the nature and conditions of the animated film (from the inside) and the mechanics of film in general. (Even a quick checklist of film grammar is tossed in via the 'Gimme a close-up' gag.)[9]

deconstruction
All media 'texts' are constructed. To understand all the components within each construction it is necessary to deconstruct the text and analyse all its elements. For example, the cartoon is made up of a number of specific aspects which define it as a unique cinematic practice, i.e. its frame-by-frame construction; its modes of representation and so on.

Daffy begins the cartoon in anticipation that he is in a musketeer picture and swashbuckles with due aplomb until he realises that he is not accompanied by suitable scenery. He immediately recognises that he has been deserted by the context that both he and we as the audience are accustomed to. He drops the character he is playing and becomes Daffy, the betrayed actor who immediately addresses the camera, acknowledging both the animator and the audience. Perceiving himself as an actor he localises himself within the film-making process, and signals its mechanisms, all of which are about to be revealed to us.

Trouper that he is, Daffy carries on, adapting to the new farmyard scenery with a spirited version of 'Old Macdonald Had a Farm', before adjusting once again to the arctic layout that has replaced the farmyard. The cartoon constantly draws attention to the relationship between foreground and background, and principally to the relationship

• **Plate 8.2** Daffy Duck
from *Bugs Bunny* (Walt
Disney, US 1953)

between the character and the motivating aspects of the environmental context. Daffy's actions are determined by the understanding of the space he inhabits. These tensions inform the basic narrative process of most cartoons: all Daffy wants is for the animator to make up his mind!

Each environment is illustrated by the visual shorthand of dominant cultural images, for example, the Arctic is signified by an igloo, Hawaii by Daffy's grass skirt and banjo! The white space, however, becomes the empty context of the cartoon. Daffy is then erased by an animated pencil rubber and essentially only remains as a voice. However, as Chuck Jones has pointed out, 'what I want to say is that Daffy can live and struggle on in an empty screen, without setting and without sound, just as well as with a lot of arbitrary props. He remains Daffy Duck'.[10] This draws attention to the predetermined understanding of Daffy as a character, and to the notion that a whole character can be understood by any one of its parts. Cartoon vocabulary readily employs the **synecdoche**, the part that represents the whole, as a piece of narrative shorthand. Daffy can be understood through his **iconic** elements, both visually and aurally. No visual elements of Daffy need be seen for an audience to know him through his lisping voice, characterised by Mel Blanc. We need only see his manic eyes or particularly upturned beak to distinguish him from Donald Duck and other cartoon characters, who all have similar unique and distinguishing elements in their design.

Upon the point when Daffy asks 'Where am I?', even in his absence the audience know of his presence. When he is repainted by the anonymous brush as a singing cowboy we anticipate, of course, that Daffy will sing, although the genre probably prohibits him singing 'I'm Just Wild about Harry', which remains one of his favourites! Initially, Daffy finds there is no sound and holds up a small sign requesting 'sound please', thus drawing the audience's attention to the explicit vocabulary of sound necessitated by the cartoon form, and one immediately familiar to the anticipated viewer. When Daffy attempts to play the guitar, it sounds first like a machine gun, then a horn, then a donkey, thus simultaneously showing the necessity of sound and image synchronisation for narrative orthodoxy, and the creation of comedy through the incongruous mismatching of sound and image. This is developed after Daffy breaks the guitar in frustration – a standard element of the cartoon is the process of destruction – and attempts to complain to the animator about his treatment, especially as he

synecdoche
The idea that a 'part' of a person, an object, a machine, etc. can be used to represent the 'whole', and work as an emotive or suggestive shorthand for the viewer, who invests the 'part' with symbolic associations.

iconic
The iconic is defined by the dominant signs that signify a particular person or object – Chaplin, for example, would be defined by a bowler hat, a moustache, a cane and some old boots; Hitler would be defined by a short parted hairstyle and a small 'postage stamp' moustache.

For further discussion of iconography, see Chapter 4 and Chapter 6.

considers himself 'A Star'. He is given the voice of a chicken and a cockatoo, and just when he is at his most hysterical in his attempt to speak, he is allowed his own voice, but at increased volume. Daffy is visibly humiliated and his attitude once again reveals to an audience his helplessness in the face of the power of the animator. The animator is at liberty to manipulate the image completely, and create impossible and dynamic relations which need not have any connection with orthodox and anticipated relations.

This manipulation of Daffy's image and identity also tells an audience about his essential character traits – egotism, ambition, frustration, anger and wilfulness – which are constantly challenged in most of the narratives through the resistance offered by the world around him. In *Duck Amuck* he is also defeated by the animated context he exists within. He pleads with the animator for orthodoxy and is greeted with a child's pencil drawing for a background, slapdash painting for the scenery and an absurd reconstruction of his own body in wild colours and a flag tied to his newly drawn tail indicating that he is a 'screwball'. Despite protestations that he has fulfilled his contract, Daffy continues to be treated with contempt. Just when he seems to have been granted the legitimacy of 'a sea picture' – an obvious reference to both Donald Duck and Popeye – Daffy is subjected to the standard cartoon gag of recognising that he is temporarily defying gravity by standing in mid-air only to drop into the sea the moment he realises. Seconds later he is on an island, but the image is merely a small frame within the normal frame, this time drawing the audience's attention to the compositional elements of the cartoon and, indeed, of film language itself. We can hardly hear Daffy as he calls for a close-up, and receives one at rapid speed, only showing us his eyes.

Once again calling upon the audience's recognition of the frame as a potentially three-dimensional space, Daffy then tries to cope with the sheer weight of the black background scenery which falls upon him like a heavy awning. He eventually tears up the 'screen' in sheer frustration and demands that the cartoon start, even though it has already been going several minutes. A screen card with 'The End' comes up accompanied by the Merrie Melodies theme. Daffy then attempts to take control of the film by returning to the key notion of himself as an entertainer performing a vaudevillian soft-shoe shuffle. He is trying to reclaim the idea of the cartoon as a medium for entertainment rather than deconstruction. His song and dance routine is interrupted, however, by the slippage of the frame as it appears to divide the screen in half and expose the frames of celluloid the film is supposedly composed of. The two frames, of course, reveal two Daffys, who immediately start to fight and disappear in a blur of drawn lines – the fight merely becomes a signifier of cartoon movement, a symbol of kineticism unique in embodying character and signifying form.

Narrative life improves for Daffy as 'the picture' casts him as a pilot. This is merely a device, however, to demonstrate a series of conventional cartoon gags, including an off-screen air crash, the appearance of the ubiquitous anvil as a substitute for Daffy's parachute, and an explosion as Daffy tests some shells with a mallet – by this time, however, he is a gibbering heap, devoid of dignity or control, the two qualities Daffy most aspires to. As he tries to assert himself one last time, Daffy demands to know: 'Who is responsible for this? I demand that you show yourself!' The frame as we understand it is then completely broken as the scene changes and the camera pulls back to reveal the drawing board and 'the animator' – Bugs Bunny, Daffy's arch-rival. As Thompson remarks: '*Duck Amuck* can be seen as Daffy's bad trip; his self-destruction fantasies and delusions, with their rapid, unpredictable, disconcerting changes of scene and orientation, are the final extension of ego-on-the-line dreams.'[11] This is an important point in a number of respects. It locates Daffy as a character firmly in a relationship between form and meaning. Each narrative establishes and develops the vocabulary which defines the underpinning imperatives of both character and the form the character inhabits. This leads to the cartoon animation embodying a number of **ideological**

ideological
Although a complex issue, ideology may be seen as the dominant set of ideas and values which inform any one society or culture, but which are imbued in its social behaviour and representative texts at a level that is not necessarily obvious or conscious. An ideological stance is normally politicised and historically determined. In the first instance, cartoons seem especially 'innocent' in this respect, but they are characterised by implicit and sometimes explicit statements about gender, race, nationality, identity etc., which are the fabric of ideological positions, and require interrogation and inspection.

positions. Disney's films, for example, often play out an orthodox narrative form to rein-force an ideological status quo. In other words, Disney's films support and illustrate what Robert Sklar calls 'the spirit of social purpose, the re-enforcing of old values'.[12] This idealised world is often challenged by the anarchic worlds of Tex Avery[13] and Chuck Jones, and, indeed, other kinds of animation which send complex and often subversive messages.

For further discussion of ideology, see Chapter, pp. 144–6.

The animated film reached maturity in the 'golden era' of the American cartoon, and in doing so had established Disney as synonymous with animation. This has led to animation being understood in a limited way. Disney perfected a certain language for the cartoon and the full-length feature which took its model from live-action film-making. This overshadowed other kinds of innovation and styles of animation which have extended the possibilities of the form and enabled other kinds of film to be made. Disney's art remains the dominant language of animation and we can term this **orthodox animation**. This kind of work must be compared though to two other areas of the form which we may classify as **developmental animation** and **experimental animation**. These areas reflect certain styles and approaches and characterise the particular objectives and intentions of some leading animators.

Animation is often perceived as an innocent medium. Many animated films do have overt political messages, however, and other, perhaps more seem-ingly innocuous animations are also underpinned by ideology. For further study:

1 **Consider how the 'Arab'/'Muslim' characters are represented in Disney's full-length feature *Aladdin*, taking into account that the film was made during the period of the Gulf War, and provoked protest from Muslim groups. How far can 'Jafar' be seen as a thinly veiled caricature of Saddam Hussein? Is Aladdin an all-American hero? How far does the film promote American culture and nationalism, and demote and 'villainise' the Arab/Muslim world?**
2 **Many animated films address environmental issues. For further study, look at full-length features like *Ferngully*, or children's series like *The Animals of Farthing Wood*, or short films like *Handle with Care*, and suggest how they offer an alternative point of view to the way that the world is currently governed. Does this offer an example of competing ideological positions?**

ORTHODOX ANIMATION

Cel animation remains the most convenient technique for the mass production of cartoons. These kinds of films are usually storyboarded first, after the fashion of a comic strip, and corresponding to a pre-recorded soundtrack. 'Key drawings' are then produced indicating the 'extreme' first and last positions of a key movement which are then 'in-betweened' to create the process of the move. After 'pencil-testing' (now often done on computers), the images are drawn on separate sheets of celluloid, painted and photographed frame by frame against the appropriate background. The music, dialogue and effects can then be synchronised with the images. This process enables a large number of animators to be involved and facilitates an industrial process.

Aside from the Disney Studios producing Silly Symphonies, Harman and Ising created the first of the Looney Tunes in 1930, entitled *Sinkin' in the Bathtub*. In the same year, the Fleischer Brothers introduced Betty Boop in a Talkartoon called *Dizzy Dishes*, and two years later translated Popeye from comic strip to cartoon. Harman and Ising moved to MGM and created the Happy Harmonies, while Warner Bros. created the Merrie Melodies. Walter Lantz, later creator of Woody Woodpecker, was appointed as head of Universal Studios animation team, and coincidentally, like Disney, chose to create an Oswald the Rabbit series. All these figures were evolving the language of the medium, which in turn became its orthodoxy. This orthodoxy was characterised by a number of dominant elements which I will now discuss.

Configuration
Most cartoons featured 'figures', that is, identifiable people or animals who corresponded to what audiences would understand as an orthodox human being or creature, despite whatever colourful or eccentric design concept was related to it. Thus Donald was recognisable as a duck whether he wore a sailor's suit or khaki togs and a pith helmet!

Specific continuity
Whether a cartoon was based on a specific and well-known fairy tale or story, or on 'riffing' (a sequence of gags developed around a specific situation), it had a logical continuity even within a madcap scenario. This was achieved by prioritising character and context. For example, Goofy was perpetually trying to succeed at a task and consistently failing. He is thus contextualised in the continuing attempts to complete the task, and creating slapstick comedy through his failure, but simultaneously he creates sympathy for, and understanding of, the fundamental aspects of his character.

Narrative form

For further discussion of film form and narrative, see Chapter 4; for reference to sound, see pp. 113–5.

As an extension of the previous point, it is necessary to stress the importance of narrative form. Most early cartoons echoed or illustrated the musical forms which provided their soundtracks. The soundtrack suggested a possible proto-narrative before particular visual scenarios or sight gags were developed. Most often, these were based on character conflict and chase sequences, where common environments became increasingly destabilised as they were subjected to (accidentally) destructive forces. However notional, the idea of 'a story' was essentially held in place by following the principle of establishing a situation, problematising it, creating 'the comic' and finding resolution, mainly through the principal character whom the audience has been encouraged to support and sympathise with.

Evolution of content
The orthodox cartoon rarely draws the audience's attention to its construction (though *Duck Amuck* (1953) – analysed above – and a number of Warner Bros. cartoons are an obvious exception to this). Rarely also does it tell the audience of its interest in the use of colour and the material of its making. Instead it prioritises its content, concentrating specifically on constructing character, determining comic moments and evolving the self-contained narrative.

Unity of style

The formal properties of the animated cartoon tend to remain consistent. Cel-animated or hand-drawn cartoons remain in a fixed two-dimensional style throughout their duration and do not mix with three-dimensional modes as later more experimental animation does. Visual conventions echo those of live-action cinema in the deployment of establishing shots, medium shots and close-ups, but camera movement, when it is employed, tends to be limited to lateral left-to-right pans across the backgrounds or up-and-down tilts examining a character or environment. However, one consequence of camera movement across a drawing can be the illusion of a change of perspective or angle to facilitate an unusual context for the character. This often happens, for example, when Wile E. Coyote chases Roadrunner and finds himself in an impossible predicament. An apparently safe rock formation suddenly presents itself at an impossible angle and becomes a dangerous landscape that defeats him once more. Story conventions like these inform most cartoons which mainly operate on the basis of a repeated formula and, most obviously, the chase. The chase informs the pace of these narratives, privileging speed and frenetic action and creating conventions such as visible movement lines around moving limbs and the blur of fast-moving bodies.

Sound in the animated film is entirely constructed. Sound conventions like 'the crash', 'the bo-ing' or the ascending and descending scale are also instrumental in determining a specific kind of film language in the cartoon. Although dissolves and fade in/fade out often provide the mechanism for scene changes, there is also the emergence of one of the most important terms in an animator's vocabulary: **metamorphosis**. The animator can thus tell the story by evolving the image rather than cutting from one image to another. While using all these conventions, colour, scenic design and character formation remain consistent.

Absence of the artist

Some later animation signals its codes and conventions and thus reveals the presence of the individual artist in creating the work. Conventional cartoons prioritise their characters and style and at no point privilege the artist or signal the process of their creation.

Dynamics of dialogue

Even though the fundamental appeal of the cartoon lies in its commitment to action, character is often defined by key aspects of dialogue. This was a particular feature of the characters created at Warner Bros. Studio for the Looney Tunes and Merrie Melodies cartoons. Bugs Bunny's laconic sense of superiority is established by his carrot-munching proposition, 'What's up, doc?', or by his call to arms when his current adversary temporarily gains the upper hand when he confirms, 'You realise, this means war!' Specifically based on the verbal dexterity of Groucho Marx, Bugs also qualifies any minor error in his plans by claiming 'I should have taken the right turn at Albuquerque!' Equally, Daffy is characterised by his persistent babble, arrested only when he has experienced complete humiliation and when he lispily claims 'You're despicable!' Elmer Fudd always insists upon quiet as he is hunting 'wabbits', while Yosemite Sam overstates his position when he says 'I'm seagoing Sam, the blood-thirstiest, shoot-em firstiest, doggone worstiest buccaneer that's ever sailed the Spanish Main!' All these verbal dynamics served to support the visual jokes and create a specific kind of 'noise' that is characteristic of these films. Philip Brophy suggests that the Disney soundtrack moves towards the *Symphonic* while the Warners soundtrack embodies the *Cacophonic*. The Symphonic is informed by classical aspirations towards the poetic, balletic and operatic; the Cacophonic is more urban, industrialised, beat-based and explosive in its vocabulary.[14]

metamorphosis
The ability for a figure, object, shape or form to relinquish its seemingly fixed properties and mutate into an alternative model. This transformation is literally enacted within the animated film, and acts as a model by which the process of change becomes part of the narrative of the film. A form starts as one thing and ends up as something different.

See Chapter 2, pp. 21–6, for a case study of Warner Bros.

A further example of orthodox animation which moves beyond the cartoon tradition and uses the animated form as a critique of live-action representation is Joanna Quinn's 1986 short, entitled *Girls Night Out*.

☐ CASE STUDY 2: *GIRLS NIGHT OUT* (1986)

See Chapter 9 for detailed discussion of film language and gender.

Joanna Quinn's *Girls Night Out* tells the story of Beryl, an ordinary Welsh housewife, who goes out for a 'quiet drink with the girls' and ends up enjoying a striptease routine by a male stripper. Quinn is careful to prioritise character and encourage our empathy with Beryl by stressing the mundaneness of her existence. The soundtrack is a constant babble of conversation as the film opens, simultaneously defining factory life and sexual titillation by focusing upon the image of a passing conveyor belt line of cakes as they are being individually topped with bouncing cherries. By the subtle implication of breasts, and the chorus of chatter, the factory and indeed the narrative form of the animation is gendered feminine. This is important as the film is attempting to reclaim the language of film which is predominantly gendered as masculine.

The sheer vitality of the film is expressed by endowing objects and figures with an excess of drawn movement – telephones shake and jump when they ring, drinks rattle fervently on a tray matching Beryl's bouncing bosom, figures literally blur into shapes which embody the visual dynamics of excitement and laughter. This energy drives the narrative and underpins the sexual agenda of the film. Beryl, for example, fantasises that the macho man of her dreams 'will take her away from all this' and make love with her on a desert island. These fantasies which are projected in the thought bubbles of the comic strip, become a whirling blur of lines and shapes as Beryl kisses her dream

• **Plate 8.3** *Girls Night Out* (Joanna Quinn, UK 1986)

man, exhibiting not merely sexual frenzy but uninhibited joy. This is juxtaposed with the static images of domestic boredom as Beryl's couch-potato husband and the family cat sit drowsily and unmoving in front of the television. Quinn skilfully keeps the scene static while giving it a visual interest by changing the look of the image through the use of the flickering light of the television set. Beryl's husband ignores her when she tells him she is going out and, clearly, the audience's sympathy and encouragement lie with Beryl.

She speeds off in a car that leaps across a street map representing the town where she lives. This juxtaposition of images is a good example of narrative and visual **condensation**. Quinn also deploys metamorphosis to provide this kind of condensation in the evolving passage of one scene into another. As Beryl speeds along, the pub sign of 'The Bull' swings in anticipation, and provides punctuation in the construction of her journey. When she arrives at the pub, Beryl buys her drinks and the image, in concentrating on the 'wobble' of her body, stresses her size, especially when she settles her large bottom on a creaking bar-stool. In a similar way to Daffy in *Duck Amuck*, the audience is invited to inspect and interrogate Beryl's body, in the spirit of acceptance, a point Quinn develops in a later film about Beryl entitled *Body Beautiful* (1989). Beryl is an ordinary working-class woman with a pedestrian existence who is looking for some excitement in an otherwise dull and oppressive life. The film is suggesting that the audience see life from Beryl's point of view by sharing Beryl's point of view. This is made explicit when the male stripper is made the obvious subject of the female gaze, a reversal of the dominant orthodoxy of women being the subject of the male gaze that characterises mainstream film.[15]

Beryl's body is set against the stereotypical ideal of the macho body as it is expressed through the stripper. Clad in a black vest and leopard skin G-string, the moustachioed, muscle-bound stripper reveals his hirsute chest and rotates his hips as the image concentrates on his bulging codpiece, toying with the idea of the exposure of his penis. The soundtrack consists of screams of delirium and encouragement – 'Get 'em off!' roars Beryl, as she sprouts horns of bedevilment and mischief. The girls enjoy both their excitement and their embarrassment as the stripper operates with increasing confidence and physical bravura. The film endows him with status over the women – he possesses an impossible physical dexterity as he bends over and wobbles his buttocks or moves across the stage balanced on one finger! His shadow looms over an initially terrified Beryl, who offers him a drink – the drink in essence being offered to the camera, and the mechanism by which Beryl's actions are disguised as she tugs at the stripper's G-string. Once more, in a frenzy of 'reaction' lines drawn around the stripper's face and body, the film stresses its agenda as a woman's film. The audience has identified with the heroine and enjoys how she undermines the sexual posturing of the stripper (which by extension is a metaphor for arrogant, oppressive masculinity) by tearing off his G-string, exposing a small penis.

The stripper is humiliated and the women, chiefly Beryl, feel empowered by the moment. She gleefully swings the G-string around after the fashion of the stripper himself, and clearly enjoys her moment of triumph and difference. Temporarily Beryl, in the symbolic act of challenging male dominance as it is coded through the stripper's sexual confidence and sense of superiority, undermines patriarchal norms. What Beryl achieves in the narrative, Joanna Quinn achieves in her manipulation of film form – a subversion enabled by the reclaiming of a cinematic language in the animated film, a language *not* wholly colonised by men, and often deployed by an increasing number of female animators creating a feminine aesthetic in the medium.[16]

condensation
The compression of a set of narrative or aesthetic agendas within a minimal structural framework. Essentially, achieving the maximum amount of suggested information and implication from the minimum amount of imagery used.

See Chapter 5 and Chapter 9 for further discussion of audience and gender positioning. Also see case study on The Piano, pp. 299–303, a film which also reverses the 'look' and so empowers its heroine.

UPA AND ZAGREB STUDIOS

Before addressing the concepts of developmental animation and experimental animation, it is important to note two studios who largely developed key aspects of orthodox
animation. As a consequence of the strike at Disney Studios in 1941, Canadian
animator Stephen Busustow left the company and established United Productions of
America (UPA). He, along with other talented animators John Hubley, Pete Burness,
Bob Cannon and Bill Hurtz, wanted to pursue a more individual style that the Disney
'look' could not accommodate. This led to work that was less specifically 'realist' in its
approach, and, as Ralph Stephenson has suggested, 'the cynicism, the sophistication,
the depth of adult attitudes are not ruled out'.[17]

Ironically, this 'sophistication' was achieved through non-naturalist, fairly unsophisticated technical means. These included minimal backgrounds, 'stick' characters and
non-continuous 'jerky' movements. The **squash and stretch** conception of movement
in conventional cartoon characters, based on a design where the body is thought of as
a set of circles, was replaced by the representation of a body as a few sharp lines;
backgrounds, which in Disney animation were positively voluptuous in their colour and
detail, were defined by a surrealist minimalism, where stairs led nowhere and lights
hung from non-existent ceilings. This kind of development expanded the vocabulary of
the animated film and served to define its potential in one particular style.

Most surreal, both in its design and its soundtrack, was Bob Cannon's *Gerald
McBoing Boing* (1951), in which a little boy speaks only through incongruous sounds.
More popular was the *Mr Magoo* series, featuring a short-sighted old man, voiced by
Jim Bacchus and based on W.C. Fields, who had endless encounters based on
mistaking the people and objects he saw for someone or something else. UPA established a new style and liberated many artists, despite economic limitations and the
initial resistance to a new aesthetic principle, an agenda which was fuelled by economic
as well as aesthetic necessity, an agenda shared by the Zagreb Studios in the former
Yugoslavia.

Influenced by UPA's *Gerald McBoing Boing* and *The Four Poster* (1952), designed by
John and Faith Hubley, the Zagreb animation industry developed around the two key
figures of Dusan Vukotic and Nikola Kostelac. Initially making advertising films, the two
progressed to making cartoons deploying **reduced animation**, which is described by
Ronald Holloway:

Some films took an unbelievable eight cels to make, without losing any of the expressive movement a large number of cels usually required. Drawings were reduced to the barest minimum, and
in many cases the visual effect was stronger than with twice the number of drawings.[18]

Liberated from the limitations of orthodox animation, these films increased the intensity
of suggestion located in the images and moved towards a more avant-garde sensibility
without neglecting key aspects of the vocabulary outlined above.

DEVELOPMENTAL ANIMATION

Developmental animation may be described as the intermediary stage between
orthodox and experimental animation, and it is in this category that the majority of
animation is located.

It may be defined as the kind of animation which deploys but extends the principles
of orthodox animation using other materials, that is, models, puppets, clay/plasticine,
objects and cut-outs, and so on. These films are made frame by frame but extend the

squash and stretch
Many cartoon characters
are constructed in a way
that resembles a set of
malleable and attached
circles that may be elon-
gated or compressed to
achieve an effect of
dynamic movement.
When animators 'squash
and stretch' these circles
they effectively create
the physical space of the
character and a partic-
ular design structure
within the overall pattern
of the film. Interestingly,
early Disney shorts had
characters based on
'ropes' rather than
circles and this signifi-
cantly changes the look
of the films.

reduced animation
Animation may be liter-
ally the movement of
one line which, in oper-
ating through time and
space, may take on
characteristics which an
audience may perceive
as expressive and
symbolic. This form of
minimalism constitutes
reduced animation,
which takes as its
premise 'less is more'.
Literally an eye move-
ment or the shift of a
body posture becomes
enough to connote a
particular feeling or
meaning. This enables
the films to work in a
mode which has an
intensity of suggestion.

vocabulary into the three-dimensional and visually innovative sphere. Each method-ology clearly creates its own agenda for analysis as the possibilities determined by the use of other materials becomes as large as the number of films made. In illustrating some of the types of animation in this category, I will suggest ways in which orthodox animation has been redefined and reformulated.

☐ CASE STUDY 3: *CREATURE COMFORTS* (1990)

Nick Park's Oscar-winning *Creature Comforts* essentially develops the anthropomorphic tendencies of the Disney cartoon into three dimensions by using plasticine models of zoo animals. They are voiced by real people talking about their own living conditions and those of animals in a zoo. This ambiguity is played out in the responses of each character as they are being interviewed by an unseen microphone-wielding film-maker, not unlike Park himself. The film emerges as a hybrid of the cartoon and a mock docu-mentary.

The humour of the film derives from the tension between the very ordinariness of the varied verbal responses on the soundtrack and the visual jokes, first, created by the design of the character, and second, by the activities which take place in the back-ground or alongside the main character speaking. These include a hippo doing 'number twos' while another is interviewed, a highly coloured bird having its beak 'twanged' as if it were a paper cone on an elastic band around someone's face, and a beach ball, which comes from off-screen, bouncing on a surprised tortoise's head! These visual jokes are directly drawn from Park's enjoyment of *It'll Be Alright on the Night*, which is a programme composed of 'out-takes' from other programmes, featuring mistakes and unexpected situations. Park found particular amusement in those 'out-takes' where a reporter is talking about a serious subject, only to be unknowingly undermined by an animal copulating or defecating in the background!

The soundtrack is characterised by different age groups speaking in different dialects, and these voices are skilfully matched to the appropriate animal. An old lady's

• **Plate 8.4** *Creature Comforts* (Nick Park, UK 1990)

voice, for example, is matched to a koala bear as it perches precariously on a euca-lyptus tree. The koala is endowed with large glasses to foreground its large eyes and its difficulty in seeing. This reinforces the vulnerability and 'cuteness' of the creature and the old lady it represents, especially when she says that she feels very secure just at the moment when the branch creaks before breaking!

While prioritising a more static image system than orthodox animation to focus on small details, especially in its jokes, *Creature Comforts* does localise its interest in char-acters and an evolving 'content' (making points about meat-eating, housing conditions and the benefits of double glazing along the way!). It also possesses a unity of style, but it is a style that enables Park to use a wider filmic vocabulary such as camera move-ments, effects of lighting and complex sets that exist in real space. He uses a conventional soundtrack for the zoo/jungle 'atmos' and sound effects to accompany jokes, but instead of deploying the 'dynamics of dialogue' he prefers the 'dynamics of monologue', carefully editing juxtapositional voices together.

It is clear, then, that Park uses the conventions of orthodox animation, but adjusts them to his own specifications. The result of this is to bring an intrinsic 'Englishness' to the piece in its irony and gentle reserve. Though informed by the influence of *The Beano*, the work of Terry Gilliam, and the whimsical humour of Laurel and Hardy and the British comedy film tradition of the 1930s and 1940s,[19] Park dilutes the craziness and surreality of 'cartoon' forms, preferring an unpretentious style that highlights the eccentricities of the everyday, and a nostalgic belief in the uncommon and unaddressed aspects of the ordinary.

☐ CASE STUDY 4: *NEIGHBOURS* (1952)

Norman McClaren is probably the most experimental film-maker in the animated field. He has explored a number of different styles, including direct animation (drawing directly on to celluloid), paper and object animation (stop-motion frame-by-frame constructions of movement with objects and cut-outs, etc.), evolution works (the gradual evolution of a pastel or chalk drawing) and multiple printing works (where movements are recorded as they evolve through the multiple printing of each stage of the movement). McClaren, then, is strictly an experimental film-maker, and many of his works would be rightly included in the final category I have defined on p. 255. *Neighbours*, however, sits neatly in the developmental animation category in its use of **pixillation** in the redefinition of the orthodox form.

As Cecile Starr has noted: 'His films are enriched with an abundance of childish playfulness, artistic subtlety, psychological insight and human concern.'[20] In *Neighbours* these qualities are played out, revealing McClaren's insight into how the language of the cartoon could readily be applied to a form that manipulated live action, the consequence of which would be to create a commentary on the representation of violence in cartoons and the presence of violent impulses in human nature. McClaren combines 'the childish playfulness' of the cartoon with a specific contemplation of aspects of the human condition, bringing to that agenda an artistic sensibility that reworks the codes and conventions of orthodox animation.

Employing pixillation, *Neighbours* works as an affecting parable. Two neighbours, seated in deckchairs, smoking their pipes, reading newspapers with the headlines 'War certain if no peace' and 'Peace certain if no war', become involved in a territorial dispute over the ownership of a wild flower. This dispute escalates rapidly, horrible violence takes place and the pair eventually end up killing each other. The method by which this

pixillation
The frame-by-frame recording of deliberately staged live action move-ment to create the illusion of movement impossible to achieve by naturalistic means i.e. figures spinning in mid-air or skating across grass. This can also be achieved by particular ways of editing material.

• **Plate 8.5** *Neighbours*
(Norman McClaren, UK
1952)

simple yet telling narrative takes place reveals as much about orthodox strategies of animation as it does about the inevitability of human conflict and, indeed, confirms that conflict is the key underpinning theme of the orthodox animated narrative.

McClaren alludes to the two-dimensional cartoon by employing this in his scenery. He creates the illusion of two neighbouring houses in the middle of a real field by erecting two hand-painted cartoon-like house fronts. He then concentrates on establishing **symmetry** in his frame before disrupting it with the chaos: first, of ecstatic responses by the men to the fragrance of the flower and, second, of their conflict. The wild exaggeration of their movements successfully parodies the dynamics of movement in the orthodox cartoon. Similarly, the electronic soundtrack echoes the role of sound effects in such films, creating mood, accompanying actions and replacing words. The effect of using these conventions but reinventing the means to create them is to draw attention to them.

This in turn signals that to reinterpret the conventions is to reinterpret the meanings inherent within them. To create cartoon conventions *showing* violence is to ignore that the conventions are *about* violence too. It is this very point that McClaren clearly understands, taking the exaggeration of cartoon violence to its logical extreme and showing the audience primitive barbarism. Two men die, two families die, and by implication two nations die, thus illustrating the futility and tragedy of war. If the close reworking of the cartoon in another kind of animated form has not done enough to signify the presence of the artist, then the final multilingual sequence of titles saying 'Love thy neighbour', certainly does, in the sense that the moral and didactic purpose of the film has been revealed.

symmetry
Direct balance of imagery in the composition of the frame using parallel or mirrored forms.

☐ CASE STUDY 5: *THE TANGO* (1991) AND *THE CRIMINAL* (1992)

The films of Gianluigi Toccafondo explore the space between the developmental mode of animation and the experimental codes that are discussed later in this chapter. Toccafondo and his collaborator Simona Mulazinni address what Toccafondo himself describes as the 'ambiguous area between painting and film'.[21] Incorporating the distortions and false perspectives of German Expressionism, the sometime hallucinatory quality of the **post-Impressionists**, the chiaroscuro shadow and light effects of 1940s film noir, and the dynamic themes and conventions of **Fauvist** art, Toccafondo's work uses the very materiality of paint to reveal the expressive yet imprecise nature of movement as it defines personal identity, and the roles and functions associated with that identity. Further, his approach redefines the body as a malleable entity; almost as an experiment in extending the corporeality of the body until it either becomes something completely different or reveals the symbolic aspects of figurative representation.

Perhaps Toccafondo's chief influence is his father, a potter by trade. The young Toccafondo was less impressed with the finished artefacts his father produced, preferring the intermediary stages in which the pot was shaped, where the form itself was dilated and transformed. This sense of something 'coming-into-being', a process with its own aesthetic vocabulary, is directly related to the animated form, and is readily enacted in Toccafondo's films.[22] Toccafondo especially enjoys the practice of charting the movement from a recognisably figurative approach with identifiable characters which then metamorphose into something different which is often surreal and provocative.

Like Erica Russell, Monique Renault and Norman McClaren,[23] Toccafondo also exploits animation's special relationship to dance. In *The Tango*, stills of Fred Astaire and Ginger Rogers are manipulated in a way that collapses the initial orthodoxy of their tango into a series of mutations and distortions of their moving form until it becomes unrecognisable as anything but abstract shapes and forms. The Busby Berkeleyesque choreography, with its specific sense of pattern and execution, is replaced by a blurring of scratched lines and elongated painted forms, until finally transforming into animals like lions, camels and pigs, who themselves are subject to reconfiguration with extended insect-like legs and flowing movement. Ultimately, the film becomes about the transition in the human form from elegance to animality, from control to chaos, from certainty to question, and speaks fundamentally to the conditions whereby animation uniquely reveals this state.

The Tango was initially based on tests in which the silent film comedian Buster Keaton was subjected to a range of physical redefinitions, taking up the premise of the very physicality of his comic performance and exaggerating it to its logical, yet perversely funny extreme. In a more serious context, Toccafondo plays out the issue of physical identity in *The Criminal*. Based on Lombroso's theories of a criminal typology that may be identified in the characteristics of offenders, the film takes up the escape of one such criminal and his pursuit by the police. The film draws explicitly on film noir for its look, but as importantly for its editorial style and camera movement. Unlike other kinds of animation which conceive 'moving painting' as the imperceptible metamorphosis from one image to another, Toccafondo actually uses his painterly approach to play out tensions between stillness and imprecise movement, blurring the image, constantly changing its pace and perspective in the style of a live-action noir, but purely through animation and not editorial construction. The criminal moves into an underworld and conducts a shooting. Figures remain in the dark. The sense of entrapment and claustrophobia is palpable as the criminal cannot be identified in his constant

post-Impressionism
After the Impressionist movement had determined pictorialness in a spirit of the felt experience of a context or place, the post-Impressionists re-imposed a more defined sense of structure which was still subject to a sense of dream-like softness and distortion.

See Chapter 4, pp. 108, for further discussion of film noir.

Fauvism
Fauvism literally means 'wild-beastism', and describes the vivid colours and distorted forms in the paintings of artists like Henri Matisse and André Derain, which emerged as part of the first modern art movement at the turn of the century.

See Chapter 4, pp. 95–8, for discussion of Buster Keaton's The General (1925).

For further discussion of cameras and camera movement, see Chapter 4, pp. 108–10.

• **Plate 8.6** *The Criminal* (Toccafondo, UK 1952)

movement. The final image catches the face of the criminal in a photographic snap only to reveal a blurred physiognomy which refuses stasis and identification – a final image then which comments on the condition of animation, painting and physical movement. Toccafondo exposes the processes towards 'fixedness' as the true machinations by which meaning may be understood, recognising ultimately that formal structures and categorial certainties are probably misrepresentative.

EXPERIMENTAL ANIMATION

Experimental animation embraces a number of styles and approaches to the animated film which inevitably cross over into areas which we may also term avant-garde or art

For further discussion of avant-garde film, see Chapter 4, pp. 121–6 and Chapter 9, p. 278.

films, and may only partially display aspects of animation in the form I have previously discussed. Of course, there has been experimentation in all areas of animation, but I am prioritising animation which has either been constituted in new forms (computer, photocopy, sand on glass, direct on to celluloid, pinscreen, etc.) or resists traditional forms. William Moritz has argued that this form of non-objective and non-linear animation is actually the purest conception of animation as its language is significantly different from its live action counterpart, and most explicitly reveals the distinctive range and extent of the animated vocabulary.[24] Following my definition of orthodox animation, I would suggest that there is another set of dominant strands to experimental animation which I will define as the signposts for analysis in this type of film.

Abstraction

This kind of animation tends to resist configuration in the ways audiences most often see it, that is, as an expression of character through the depiction of a human being or creature. Experimental animation either redefines 'the body' or resists using it as an illustrative image. Abstract films are more concerned with rhythm and movement in their own right as opposed to the rhythm and movement of a particular character. To this end, various shapes and forms are often used rather than figures.

For discussion of conventional film language and its development, see Chapter 4.

Specific non-continuity

While initially seeming a contradiction in terms, the idea of specific non-continuity merely signals the rejection of logical and linear continuity and the prioritisation of illogical, irrational and sometimes multiple continuities. These continuities are specific in the sense that they are the vocabulary unique to the particular animation in question. Experimental animation defines its own *form* and *conditions* and uses these as its distinctive language.

Interpretive form

The basis of experimental animation is aesthetic and non-narrative, though sometimes, as I will illustrate, aesthetics are deployed to reconstruct a different conception of narrative. Predominantly, though, experimental animation resists telling stories and moves towards the vocabulary used by painters and sculptors. Moving away from the depiction of conventional forms and the assumed 'objectivity' of the exterior world, animation, in enabling shapes and objects to move, liberates artists to concentrate on the vocabulary they are using *in itself* instead of giving it specific function or meaning. As Leopold Survage wrote:

I will animate my painting. I will give it movement. I will introduce rhythm into the concrete action of my abstract painting, born of my interior life; my instrument will be the cinematographic film, this true symbol of accumulated movement. It will execute 'the scores' of my visions, corresponding to my state of mind in its successive phases…. I am creating a new visual art in time, that of coloured rhythm and of rhythmic colour.[25]

This kind of subjective work has therefore necessitated a different response from audiences. Instead of being located in understanding narrative the audience is asked to bring its own interpretation to the work.

Evolution of materiality

The experimental film concentrates on its very materiality, that is, the forms in which it is being made, and the colour, shape and texture which is being used in the creation of the piece. These colours, shapes and textures evoke certain moods and ideas, but once again, film-makers of this type are suggesting that these aspects should give pleasure in their own right without having to be attached to a specific meaning or framework. Experimental animation thus privileges the literal evolution of materiality instead of content, showing us, for example, how a small hand-painted dot evolves into a set of circles, where the audience recognises the physical nature of the paint itself, the colour of the dot and its background, and the shapes that emerge out of the initial design. This sense of 'materiality' goes hand in hand with the emergent technologies which have liberated more innovative approaches to animation.

Multiple styles

If orthodox animation is characterised by a unity of style, experimental animation often combines and mixes different modes of animation. This operates in two specific ways: first, to facilitate the multiplicity of personal visions an artist may wish to incorporate in a film, and, second, to challenge and rework orthodox codes and conventions and create new effects.

Presence of the artist

These films are largely personal, subjective, original responses, which are the work of artists seeking to use the animated form in an innovative way. Sometimes these 'visions' are impenetrable and resist easy interpretation, being merely the absolutely individual expression of the artist. This in itself draws attention to the relationship between the artist and the work, and the relationship of the audience to the artist as it is being mediated through the work. The abstract nature of the films insists upon the recognition of their individuality. Sometimes, however, individual innovation is localised in more accessible ways that have a relationship with dominant forms, however tenuous the link. It may be, for example, that the experimental animation will try to create something aspiring to the condition of the dream-state, which, of course, has its own abstract logic, but conforms to a common understanding of 'the dream'. Dreams may be the vehicles for personal visions but they possess a universalised dimension.

Dynamics of musicality

The experimental animation has a strong relationship to music, and, indeed, it may be suggested that if music could be visualised it would look like colours and shapes moving through time with differing rhythms, movements and speeds. Many experimental films seek to create this state, and, as I have already suggested, some film-makers perceive that there is a psychological and emotional relationship with sound and colour which may be expressed through the free form that animation is.

Sound is important in any animated film, but has particular resonance in the experimental film as it is often resisting dialogue, the clichéd sound effects of the cartoon or the easy emotiveness of certain kinds of music. Silence, avant-garde scores, unusual sounds and redefined notions of 'language' are used to create different kinds of statement. It may be said that if orthodox animation is about 'prose' then experimental animation is more 'poetic' and suggestive in its intention.

☐ CASE STUDY 6: *A COLOUR BOX* (1935)

Len Lye's *A Colour Box* is a completely abstract film in that it is created with lines and shapes stencilled directly on to celluloid, changing colour and form throughout its five-minute duration. It has dominant lines throughout, with various circles, triangles and grids interrupting and temporarily joining the image, until it reveals its sponsors, the GPO film unit, by including various rates for the parcel post, that is, 3lbs for 6d., 6lbs for 9d., and so on.

The dazzling, dynamic images are set to a contemporary jazz-calypso score, which has the effect of bringing further energy and spontaneity to the piece. Lye believed that this kind of work should be seen as *composing motion* as it reveals the 'body energy' which connects the music and the images.[26]

☐ CASE STUDY 7: *DEADSY* (1990)

David Anderson's *Deadsy* is an example of the combination of xerography and puppet animation. Xerography, in this particular instance, involves the filming of a live perfor-mance by an actor, followed by the transfer of still images of his performance on to videographic paper. These images are photocopied and enlarged, and then rendered and drawn on before being refilmed on a rostrum. The effect is to distort and degrade the image to give a haunting and hallucinatory quality to 'the character' known as Deadsy, a symbol of apocalyptic despair aligned with shifting sexual identity.

Deadsy is located as one of the 'Deadtime Stories for Big Folk', thus signalling its relationship to the vocabulary of the dream-state and, most particularly, the nightmares experienced by adults. The film creates the dream-state of deep sleep and reveals profound anxieties about the fear of death and the instability of gender and sexuality in its central character, Deadsy, who oscillates between being represented by a skeletal model and a distorted human figure. The film continually blurs lines in regard to its representation of life and death, masculinity and femininity and the physicality of sex and violence. Particularly effective in reinforcing this uncertainty and ambiguity is the use of writer Russell Hoban's monologue for Deadsy, which echoes the corrupted nature of the images by creating a post-apocalyptic language which slurs and mixes words together, for example:

When Deadsy wuz ul he like din do nuffing big He din do nuffing only ul ooky-pooky Deadsy Byebyes like he do a cockrutch or a fly He din do nuffig big. He werkin his way up tho after wyl He kilia mowss o yes my my.

This kind of language *suggests* meaning; it does not formally fix meaning in the way that English-speaking peoples might readily understand it. It alludes to the escalation of violent behaviour in the development of humankind and the inevitability of the apoca-lypse. Deadsy as a character becomes aligned with the personality of a rock star motivated by inner voices and instinctive drives, and aroused by the spectacle of destruction. This sense of arousal either inspires or informs the shifting gender posi-tions Deadsy represents. Anderson shows the phallic relationship between male genitals ('sexothingys') and missiles, illustrating the masculine imperative to violence. Deadsy has a desire to change sex, however, to justify these actions. Deadsy assumes that if he becomes feminised, that is, 'Mizz Youniverss', then 'ewabody will luv me'. These gender shifts become symptomatic of the complex relationship between sexuality and violence and the socially unacceptable thoughts and feelings each individual may experience and repress. Anderson is suggesting that this kind of complexity under-pins the fundamental anxiety that humankind will inevitably destroy itself.

The film is clearly trying to break into the viewers' preconceived ideas both about animation as a form and gender, death and global politics as a set of issues. Anderson is attempting to re-engage an audience with an abstraction of visual and verbal languages which reflect an antirational stance. Deadsy is a notional configuration but is characterised by differing representations as a form (that is, as a photographed image and a model) and in regard to gender and expression. Dialogue is abandoned in favour of voiceover monologue, but only to privilege a corrupted language that is difficult to understand. Styles are mixed, narrative and continuity are blurred and ambiguous, sometimes resisting interpretation, and even the artist, while clearly present, is elusive. This is an attempt to create the post-apocalypse dream-state in the only form that could properly facilitate it.

☐ CASE STUDY 8: COMPUTERS AND CONVERGENCE

Animation can create the conditions to express new visions by creating a vocabulary which is both unlimitedly expressive and always potentially progressive because it need not refer to or comply with the codes and conventions that have preceded it. Orthodoxy, developmental and experimental animation are constantly changing.[27] Computer technology, for example, is enabling a new generation of animators to work with a different tool in order to both use traditional methods and invent fresh approaches to the animated form. Science, art and the moving image are conjoining to create a new digital cinema, enabling both a redetermination of the animated film and the enhancement of special effects in mainstream movies.

See Chapter 3 for discussion of computer-generated imagery and computer animation.

From the early experimental uses of computer animation at NASA and the Massachusetts Institute of Technology, the film exercises of James Whitney senior and junior, the work of Stan Vanderbeek (*Poemfields*, 1967–9), Lillian Schwartz (*Pictures from a Gallery*, 1976) and Peter Foldes (*Hunger*, 1973), and the output at the PIXAR company, there is already a tradition of animation in computing that is continually devel-oping a vocabulary that is extending the limits of the form. Ironically, it is ex-Disney animator, John Lasseter, who has created some of the best computer-animated shorts – *Luxo Jnr* (1986), *Tin Toy* (1990) and *Knick Knack* (1991) – by emulating the character animation of Disney and the gag structures of Warner Bros. and MGM cartoons. This has culminated in the first full-length fully computer-generated feature, *Toy Story* (1995), which ironically does not impress through its animation, simply because when the viewer is used to its principally live-action conventions they inevitably concentrate on the story of Woody and Buzz Lightyear rather than the 'effect'. The film does, however, demonstrate what computer-generated images uniquely offer. The toys are the perfect vehicle for the three-dimensional sense of smoothness and plasticity achievable using the computer; further, the playroom space is fully exploited for the sense of dynamic movement through three-dimensional space also afforded by the computer. Interestingly, the least persuasive factor is the human characters. This had led to a heightened interest in the movement back towards realism.[28] It is now standard practice in conventional live-action films like *Terminator 2: Judgement Day* (1991), *Jurassic Park* (1993), *Twister* (1997), *Jumanji* (1997) and *Starship Troopers* (1998) to employ computer-generated imagery which is indistinguishable from its live-action context (see Chapter 3). Though 'animated' in the sense that traditional techniques of three-dimensional stop-motion animation and two-dimensional drawn animation are used in the process towards creating the computer image, the sense that this is 'animation' as a form in its own right is negated. Essentially, the animated form is made explicit if computer generated when operating as part of the orthodoxy of Disney vehicles like *Aladdin* and *The Lion King*; or as part of distinctive developmental advertising campaigns and short sub-cartoonal films; or in the work of experimental artists. Yoichiro Kawaguchi in Japan has sought to be more abstract and experimental in his computer-generated films – *Eggy* (1990), *Festival* (1991) and *Mutation* (1992) – by emulating organic forms and developing random systems which create different shapes, forms and colour combinations. British animator James Lathan has also created software to execute designs in a similar spirit.

It may be useful then in this age of convergence when animation again is often subsumed by the dominance of mainstream live-action film, to consider that at the very beginnings of the cartoonal form in the films of the young Walt Disney and the Fleischer Brothers there was a concern to blend live action and animation in a way that revealed the distinctive aspects of both forms. The *Alice in Wonderland* and *Out of the Inkwell* series served to demonstrate the profound flexibility of the animated form set against the fixity of the real world. In 1940, Porky Pig featured in *You Oughta Be in Pictures* playing out his role as a movie star renegotiating his contract with live-action producer, Leon Schlesinger. Years later, *Who Framed Roger Rabbit?* (1985) constituted a state-of-the-art amalgam of live-action characters and contexts with seemingly three-dimensional cartoon characters out a range of studios from the 'golden era' – Disney, Warner Bros., MGM and Fleischer stars mixed for the first time. This integration further articulated the tension between the representational conventions of live-action realism and the freedoms of the cartoonal form.

In 1997, *Space Jam*, featuring basketball superstar Michael Jordan and the cartoon stars from the Warner Bros. Studio, Bugs Bunny, Daffy Duck and Porky Pig, continued this tradition, but enhanced it further with the use of computer-generated imagery. Cartoon characters work in a live-action space; live-action characters work in a cartoon space; and all the characters interact in a computer graphic space which is constructed as a three-dimensional virtual environment that the figures move through. Jordan's play is recorded in a green screen environment mapped with reference points that the computer can correspond to in post-production in order to map in the cartoon characters and the live-action context. The 'cybercam' creates three-dimensional images of live-action figures which may be translated into three-dimensional cartoon form and further manipulated. Cartoon characters are created in three dimensions and all is seamlessly mixed in the computer-generated environment, playing out and extending the widest dynamic of choreographed movement corresponding both to the aesthetics of physical sporting activity and the historically determined codes and conventions of animated film.

For further study, apply the definitions of *orthodox animation*, *developmental animation* and *experimental animation* to three films of your choice. How far are the categories outlined in these definitions useful in interrogating and interpreting the films?

CONCLUSION

Even without new technological apparatus animators are finding unique ways to express their individual vision. It is the intrinsic nature of animation itself which enables this to happen and animators to continually amaze, shock and amuse with their films. There is greater recognition that animation combines all the art forms from music to dance to painting to sculpture, and that it rightfully claims to be one of the most significant, and increasingly prominent, art forms of the twentieth century.

Having read this chapter, for further study consider the ways in which animation specifically *differs* from live-action film-making. Try to describe the distinctive characteristics of the vocabulary of animation, and the ways it might enable animators to achieve different kinds of meaning and expression as a film-maker. Develop an argument which stresses the value and importance of animation as an art form, against a view of animation as a 'second cousin' to mainstream live-action cinema.

NOTES

1 Quoted in C. Solomon, 'Animation: Notes on a Definition' in *The Art of the Animated Image* (AFI, Los Angeles, 1987) p. 11.

2 Quoted in R. Holloway, *Z is for Zagreb* (Tantivy Press, Cranberry, NJ, 1972) p. 9.

3 Quoted in T. Hoffer, *Animation: A Reference Guide* (Greenwood Press, Westport, CT, 1981) p. 3.

4 For a full discussion of Svankmajer's work, see P. Hames (ed.), *Dark Alchemy: The Films of Jan Svankmajer* (Flicks Books, Trowbridge, 1995).

5 Quoted in *The Magic Art of Jan Svankmajer*, BBC documentary, broadcast June 1992.

6 R. Cardinal, 'Thinking Through Things: The Presence of Objects in the Early Films of Jan Svankmajer', from P. Hames (ed.). op. cit., p. 89.

7 For a brief discussion of Fischinger's work, see P. Wells, *Around the World in Animation* (BFI/MOMI, London, 1997).

8 See the interview with Zack Schwartz in P. Wells (ed.), *Art and Animation* (Academy Group/John Wiley, London, 1997) pp. 4–9.

9 R. Thompson, 'Pronoun Trouble', in D. Peary and G. Peary (eds), *The American Animated Cartoon* (Dutton, New York, 1980) p. 221.

10 Cited ibid., p. 233.

11 Ibid., p. 233.

12 R. Sklar, 'The Making of Cultural Myths – Walt Disney,' in Peary and Peary (eds), op. cit., 1980, p. 61.

13 Tex Avery, vehemently anti-Disney in his style, essentially extended the vocabulary of the animated cartoon by exposing and extending its conventions, in a similar way to those described in my analysis of *Duck Amuck*. Using alienation devices (methods by which viewers are made to remember they are watching a cartoon), he broke the frame of the cartoon, showing the audience characters running past the edge of the celluloid, crossing from the end of Technicolor into black and white, acknowledging an audience by directly talking to them, and so on. He changed the pace of the cartoon, making it frenetic and surreal, and he prioritised the zaniest of gags which foregrounded adult concerns like irrational fear, status, power and most particularly overt sex and sexuality. For a full analysis of Avery's work, see J. Adamson, *Tex Avery: King of Cartoons* (De Capo, New York, 1975).

14 P. Brophy, 'The Symphonic Experience', in A. Cholodenko (ed.), *Illusion Of Life* (Southwood Press, Sydney, 1991) pp. 73–112.

15 For a full discussion of this issue see L. Mulvey, 'Visual Pleasure and Narrative Cinema' in *Popular Television and Film* (Oxford University Press/BFI, Oxford and London, 1981) p. 206, and the section on this film in P. Wells, *Understanding Animation* (Routledge, London and New York, 1998).

16 See J. Pilling (ed.), *Women and Animation: A Compendium* (BFI, London, 1992).

17 R. Stephenson, *Animation in the Cinema* (Zwemmer Ltd, London, 1969) p. 48.

18 Holloway, op. cit., 1972, p. 12.

19 See interview with Nick Park in P. Wells (ed.), op. cit., 1997, pp. 66–72.

20 C. Starr, 'The Art of Animation', in Starr, *Discovering the Movies* (Van Nostrand Reinhold Co., New York, 1972) p. 111.

21 See J. Pilling 'Everything Flows' in P. Wells (ed.), op. cit. 1997, pp 14–21.

22 The idea of a form 'coming-into-being' echoes Russian director Sergei Eisenstein's conception of *plasmaticness* that he identifies in the early cartoons of Walt Disney. See J. Leyda (ed.), *Eisenstein on Disney* (Methuen, London and New York, 1988).

23 For a discussion of Erica Russell's postmodern dance aesthetics in animation, see 'Dance Animation and the Post-Modern', in P. Wells (ed.) op. cit., 1997, pp. 35–40; for an analysis of Monique Renault's film *Pas à Deux*, see P. Wells, *Understanding Animation* (Routledge, London and New York, 1998); for information on McClaren and his use of dance in *Pas De Deux*, see 'Norman McClaren: Exhibition and Films' catalogue, Canada House Gallery, 26 October–25 November 1975, produced by the Scottish Arts Council; and A. Rosenthal, *The New Documentary in Action* (University of California Press, Los Angeles, 1971) pp. 267–81.

24 See 'Some Observations on Non-Objective and Non-Linear Animation' in J. Canemaker (ed.) *Storytelling in Animation: The Art of the Animated Image*, Vol. 2 (AFI, Los Angeles, 1988).

25 Quoted in R. Russett and C. Starr, *Experimental Animation* (Da Capo, New York, 1976) p. 96.

26 From D. Curtis, 'Len Lye' exhibition catalogue, Watershed, 24 October–29 November 1987 (Arts Council, London) p. 5.

27 Obviously, in a chapter of this length, no justice can be done to the many kinds of work in the animation field, nor the gifted animators who make it. While one could mention Svankmajer, Norstein, the Quay Brothers, Pitt, de Vere, Neubauer, Driessen and Rbycynski as important names, this already neglects many others, and it is hoped that the chapter raises a general awareness of the field in order that students will seek out new work and cultivate tastes and preferences.

28 An overview of special effects and aspects of computer animation is also given by Paul Wells in *An Introduction to Special Effects* (BFI/MOMI, London, 1994) with an accompanying video.

FURTHER READING

Adams, T.R. *Tom and Jerry* (Crescent Books, New York, 1991)

Adamson, J. *Tex Avery: King of Cartoons* (Da Capo, New York, 1975)

Beck, J. and Friedwald, W. *Looney Tunes and Merrie Melodies* (Henry Holt & Co., New York, 1989)

Brion, P. *Tom and Jerry* (Crown Publishers, New York, 1990)

Cabarga, L. *The Fleischer Story* (Da Capo, New York, 1988)

Canemaker, J. (ed.) *Storytelling in Animation* (AFI, Los Angeles, 1989)

Cholodenko, A. (ed.) *The Illusion of Life* (Power Publishers, Sydney, 1991)

Hollis, R. and Sibley, B. *The Disney Studio Story* (Crown Publishers, New York, 1988)

Klein, N. *7 Minutes* (Verso, London, 1993)

Maltin, L. *Of Mice and Magic* (NAL, New York, 1987)

Peary, D. and Peary, G. (eds) *The American Animated Cartoon* (Dutton, New York, 1980)

Pilling, J. (ed.) *Women and Animation: A Compendium* (BFI, London, 1992)

—— (ed.) *A Reader in Animation Studies* (John Libbey, London, 1997)

Russett, R. and Starr, C. *Experimental Animation* (Da Capo, New York, 1976)

Solomon, C. (ed.), *The Art of the Animated Image* (AFI, Los Angeles, 1987)

Wells, P. (ed.) *Art and Animation* (Academy Group/John Wiley, London, 1997)

—— *Understanding Animation* (Routledge, London and New York, 1998)

FURTHER VIEWING

Here are some key models of animated film which repay viewing and analysis:

Three Little Pigs (Walt Disney, 1933)

Popeye the Sailor Meets Sinbad the Sailor (Dave Fleischer, 1936)

Bad Luck Blackie (Tex Avery, 1943)

Springer and the S.S. (Jiri Trnka, 1946)

Red Hot Riding Hood (Tex Avery, 1949)

What's Opera, Doc? (Chuck Jones, 1957)

Ersatz (Susan Vukotic, 1961)

The Nose (Alexander Alexieff, 1963)

The Hat (John and Faith Hubley, 1964)

The Hand (Jiri Trnka, 1965)

Pas De Deux (Norman McClaren, 1967)

Great (Bob Godfrey, 1974)

The Street (Caroline Leaf, 1974)

Asparagus (Suzan Pitt, 1978)
Tale of Tales (Yuri Norstein, 1979)
Elbowing (Paul Driessen, 1981)
Tango (Zbigniew Rybczynski, 1981)
Dimensions of Dialogue (Jan Svankmajer, 1982)
Binky and Boo (Derek Hayes and Phil Austen, 1989)

Body Beautiful (Joanna Quinn, 1990)
Fatty Issues (Candy Guard, 1990)
Knick Knack (John Lasseter, 1991)
The Stain (Christine Roche and Marjut Rimmenen, 1991)
Triangle (Erica Russell, 1994)

RESOURCE CENTRES

Information compiled by Jayne Pilling and Paul Wells

http://www.aardman.com/
Aardman Animations

http://www.annecy-animation-festival.tm.fr/
Annecy Festival

http://www.chapman.edu/animation/
Animation Journal

http://www.awn.com/heaven_and_hell/
Animation Heaven and Hell
This site has nicely designed pages on model and stop-frame animation, including Svankmajer and George Pal.

http://www.awn.com/
Animation World Network
The database section is pretty minimal, and often incorrect; the best thing is the magazine's breadth of articles, mainly written by animators, critics or festival programmers. The What's New section in AWN is convenient for updates. The Animation Village has several listings and links to animators, organisations, festivals, etc. in the international animation world. Artists like Caroline Leaf and Alison Snowden/David Fine have their own home pages on AWN. The same has Nicole Salomon's AAA in Annecy, Folioscope, ASIFA Hollywood and ASIFA San Francisco, as well as The Society for Animation Studies, Motion Picture Screen Cartoonists Union Local 839 and The Writers Guild of America. There are also links to other similar home pages not hosted by AWN, such as ASIFA International.

http://www.swcp.com/animate/
ASIFA Central

http://www.yrd.com/asifa/
ASIFA East

http://www.awn.com/asifa_hollywood/
ASIFA Hollywood

http://Samson.hivolda.no:8000/asifa
ASIFA International

http://www.awn.com/asifa-sf/
ASIFA San Francisco
ASIFA East and ASIFA San Francisco produce quite informative articles, and information on current (US-based) projects, both commercial and independent, and opinion pieces.

http://www.nfb.ca/E/1/1/
National Film Board of Canada
The National Film Board of Canada has a really impressive site. You can go through their whole catalogue of films with descriptions, many of the most important film-makers have their own biography and the history of NFBC is extensively described. The main problem with the NFBC home page is that the entry page is too big, it takes minutes to download; skip it and go directly to the index.

http://www.awn.com/safo99/
Ottawa Festival

http://www.medios.fi/animafest/
Zagreb Festival

Part four

Representation of gender and sexuality

Chapter 9

Women and film

Jill Nelmes

■ Introduction   268
■ No job for a woman – a history of women in film   268
■ Women working in documentary film in Britain   269
■ The feminist revolution   273
■ Feminist film theory and practice in Britain   274
■ Reassessing feminist film theory   282
■ Feminist film theory in the 1990s   283
■ Women in the mainstream film industry   286
□ Case study 1: Red Flannel   291
□ Case study 2: *Mam* (1988)   292
□ Case study 3: *A Question of Silence* (1982), director:
   Marlene Gorris   293
□ Case study 4: Sally Potter, film-maker   296
□ Case study 5: *The Gold Diggers* (1983)   297
□ Case study 6: *Orlando* (1993)   298
□ Case study 7: *The Piano* (1993)   299
■ Notes   303
■ Further reading   304
■ Further viewing   304
■ Resource centres   305

■ Women and film

INTRODUCTION

This chapter looks at the role of women in film-making and film theory, with particular reference to the relationship between feminist film practice and feminist film theory from the late 1960s to the present day.

The emphasis is on giving a background to British women film-makers and film theorists, although frequent reference will be made to women film-makers and film theorists in other countries such as the US and the Netherlands – it would be difficult to ignore the contributions made by film-makers such as Jane Campion and Marlene Gorris, and the more recent contributions made to film theory by Teresa De Lauretis and Tania Modleski.

First, a broad background history traces women's place in film-making and focuses on the difficulties women had gaining positions of authority and control in the industry.

Second, the rise of **feminism**, the development of feminist film theory and the parallel rise of feminist film-making is discussed; in the 1970s feminist film theory and practice seemed to converge, but by the 1980s the links had become more tenuous. Many film-makers felt that they were being marginalised and needed to gain a wider audience; the concept of pleasure in watching a film which had been seen as fundamental to mainstream, conventional cinema had been denied in aspects of feminist film theory and practice. A number of women wanted their voice to be heard and felt that aspects of feminist film were in danger of alienating their potential audience.

Third, by the 1990s an increasing number of women in Britain and America had made mainstream films, yet the film and video workshops which had done so much to encourage women in film were in decline, mainly because of lack of funding; so although there has been a rise in the number of women directing bigger budget movies, such as Gurinda Chadha and Sally Potter in the UK and Penny Marshall and Nora Zephon in the US, conditions in the small budget, independent sector seem to be worsening.

Finally, a selection of case studies of differing aspects of women in film is given.

NO JOB FOR A WOMAN – A HISTORY OF WOMEN IN FILM

The first years

From the beginnings of the film industry in the late nineteenth century women were generally excluded from the film-making process, although it was traditional for women to work in non-technical areas such as continuity and make-up, or as a production assistant. Recent research, though, seems to suggest that woman's role has not been as silent as once thought and some women did, both directly and indirectly, exert their influence as directors, producers, editors and scriptwriters.

The only recorded early women film-makers were in France and America – there were apparently none in Britain. Two well-known Hollywood movie actresses, Mary Pickford and Lillian Gish, both directed films but did not want this known for fear of harming their image as stars.

France can claim to have raised the first woman director, Alice Guy Blaché, who gained access to equipment because she worked for Gaumont, a company that manufactured cameras. Her career began in 1896 with a one-minute short called *The Good Fairy in the Cabbage Patch*, which Blaché believed was the first narrative film ever made. After eleven years of working in the industry in France, she left for America and

feminism
This is based on the belief that we live in a society where women are still unequal to men; that women have lower status than men and have less power, particularly economic power. Feminists argue that the media reinforces the *status quo* by representing a narrow range of images of women; for instance, woman as carer, as passive object, as an object of desire. Many feminists now argue that the range of representations for both male and female is limited and slow to change. In recent years feminism has become fragmented and it is difficult to argue that feminism is a complete area of study; but gender and power relations in society can be seen as central to feminist thinking. For an interesting discussion on this area, see Liesbet van Zoonen 1994.

the greater opportunities it would give her. There she wrote, directed and produced many films including *In the Year 2000*, a film in which women ruled the world. Blaché found working conditions in the United States much easier than in France, where a working woman was frowned on. Her daughter, Simone Blaché, explained in an interview that: 'Mother was really cherished in the US. She used to say that people treated her so wonderfully because she was a woman, because she was a woman in film. The situation in France was quite the reverse' (Smith 1975: 6).

In the early 1900s there was an enormous expansion of the American film industry, which was making large profits because of the vast audiences attracted to the new medium. Although the new industry was cut-throat and competitive, it was also much more receptive and open to change than the European film industry and there was significantly less discrimination against women. It has been estimated that there were at least twenty-six women directors in America before 1930, but there were probably many more who directed and acted or were screenwriters and not credited with these roles. Lois Weber was the first female American film-maker and probably the most famous, often writing, producing and starring in her films, many of which dealt with social issues such as abortion and divorce. Weber directed over seventy-five films.

For discussion of the origins of the American film industry, see Chapter 2.

By the end of the 1920s silent movies were on their way out and talkies had arrived which, indirectly, brought about the demise of many women in film. Only the bigger studios could survive because of the expensive equipment needed in the change over to sound, and it was generally the many small, independent companies (who employed the majority of women) that had to close down, and so with them went many jobs for women in the industry.

Only one woman director, Dorothy Arzner, really survived the transition to talkies. She went on to make many famous movies such as *Christopher Strong* (1933) with Katharine Hepburn and *Dance Girl Dance* (1940). At one time Arzner was ranked among the 'top ten' directors in Hollywood.

Somewhat ironically, the changes in America drove directors like Elinor Glynn and Jacqueline Logan to the UK and Europe, which already had an extremely poor record of women working in film.

The UK did not seem to have given much encouragement to its indigenous women film-makers; the earliest woman known to have directed British films was Dinah Shurey, though very little is known about her other than that she made two films, *Carry On* (1927) and *Last Port* (1929).

Until the Second World War, hardly any women could be termed film-makers in the UK, but some had key roles in the film-making process: Alma Reville, married to Alfred Hitchcock, assisted him in many films, such as *The 39 Steps* (1935) and *The Lady Vanishes* (1938). She also helped to write other scripts, such as *Suspicion* (1941) and *Shadow of a Doubt* (1943). Mary Field worked in documentary from 1928 and became executive producer of children's entertainment for J. Arthur Rank from 1944 to 1950. Joy Batchelor worked mainly in animation from 1935 and co-directed the first British feature-length cartoon, *Animal Farm* (1954), continuing to make animation films until the 1970s.

For further reference to animation films and Joy Batchelor, see Chapter 8, p. 238.

WOMEN WORKING IN DOCUMENTARY FILM IN BRITAIN

The British Documentary Film Movement, of which John Grierson was the founder, had a huge influence on British film and has continued to exert its influence to the present day. Grierson's sister, Ruby, worked alongside him on a number of films and was involved in making films herself, such as *Housing Problems* (1940). Many film-makers involved in the early documentary movement went on to make propaganda films during

For further discussion of Grierson and the documentary film, see Chapter 7.

the war. This was one area of film where a few women could be found working as directors and assistant directors. Some women were taken on in roles usually only open to men because of the increased demand for documentary propaganda film in wartime Britain and the shortage of available manpower.

Kay Mander is one woman film-maker who initially worked in continuity and was then able to work as a director, partly because of the increased opportunities the war gave to women. Her career as a film-maker is varied, having worked in both documentary and feature films, originally directing films for the Shell Film Unit and then working for the Department of Health, winning a British Film Academy award in 1949. Mander explained that she lost her desire to direct and eventually went back into continuity when she was told by a renowned feature film producer that, 'women couldn't control film crews', and the job was given to a man.[1]

Reflecting on the lack of women film directors and technicians, Mander felt that there were so few because the way of life was very different then; women had different expectations, many of the women involved in film had husbands or brothers or fathers whom they assisted, and for a woman to work in film 'you had to be desperate to do it, in those days you had to have some sort of special drive'.[2]

Other women film-makers such as Yvonne Fletcher and Budge Cooper directed documentaries for Paul Rotha. Mary Marsh directed educational films and Marjorie Deans started Touchstone Films in this period.

Jill Craigie continued the tradition of women making documentaries about social conditions, writing and directing a number of films such as *The Way We Live* (1946–7), *Blue Scar* (1950) and *To Be a Woman* (1951), a documentary short about women's employment, which promoted women as part of the labour force, arguing that they had a right to equal pay and should not be treated as cheap labour.

Very few women in the UK have directed fiction film, but two women who made a number of films in the 1940s and 1950s, Muriel Box and Wendy Toye, gained an international reputation. The lesser-known Wendy Toye made such films as *Raising a Riot* (1957) and *We Joined the Navy*, with Dirk Bogarde and Kenneth More.

Muriel Box – an outstanding career in film

Muriel Box is regarded as one of the outstanding British film-makers of the 1940s and 1950s, and possibly the most successful woman director to date. Her career in film began as a script girl but really took off in a husband-and-wife partnership with Sydney Box when they worked on films together from 1939 to 1964. The *British Film Guide* (1979) says of Box:

One of only two women directors regularly employed in British features ... sister-in-law of our only British producer Betty Box.... Her own films are for the most part 'women's pictures'.... They are part of the magazine fiction of the screen and no less competently organised than most magazine fiction.

(Cited in Heck-Rabi 1984: 10)

Critical opinion of Box's work was not, as the above quote suggests, high. *Movie Magazine* placed her in the bottom group of directorial talent, yet her films can be seen as part of the strong tradition of melodrama passed down from the Victorian and Edwardian theatre.

The Box team made profitable, popular, mass entertainment films and Muriel Box was a highly respected film-maker and scriptwriter who wrote and directed more than thirty films. Probably her most famous film, which she scripted, is a melodrama, *The*

• **Plate 9.1** *Blue Scar* (Jill Craigie, 1950) Miners being attended to by the women.

• **Plate 9.2** *To Be a Woman* (Jill Craigie, 1951) An early documentary short arguing that women should be an essential part of the labour force.

Seventh Veil (1945), which received international acclaim and was a great box-office success.

By the 1960s the number of women directors could be counted on one hand – Muriel Box made her last film in 1964, *Rattle of a Simple Man*. Mai Zetterling, the Swedish actress married to a British film-maker, made a few documentaries, such as *Polite Invasion* (1960) and *Visions of Eight* (1973) and Joan Littlewood directed *Sparrows Can't Sing* (1963). There seemed to be little reason for women to be hopeful of an expanding role within the British film industry which unfortunately was in a state of decline. By the end of the 1960s the American money which had helped to support the British film industry in the boom decade had been pulled out. The film industry could not provide for the men and few women already working in it, let alone produce conditions which were conducive to the acceptance of more women film-makers:

For further discussion of Hollywood investment in British film in the 1960s, see Chapters 2 and 11.

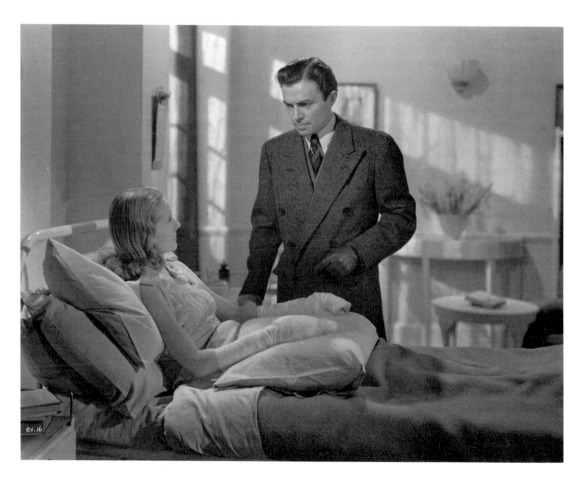

• **Plate 9.3** *The Seventh Veil* (Muriel Box, 1945)
A hugely successful melodrama.

The British film industry has, since the end of the First World War, staggered from crisis to crisis (with occasional very brief periods of health) because the British market is not large enough to support a film industry built on the classic *laissez-faire* model.

(Auty and Roddick 1985: 5)

Very few women film-makers existed in the UK before 1970 and even fewer could be termed commercially successful, Muriel Box being the outstanding exception. Yet the strong tradition of documentary film in this country did give women like Kay Mander, Jill Craigie and Yvonne Fletcher the opportunity to acquire film-making skills. It was virtually unheard of for women to work in technical areas like sound or camera, although women art directors and film editors were not so unusual – Ann V. Coates worked as an editor on Box's film *The Truth About Women* (1958) and David Lean's *Lawrence of Arabia* (1962). In general, though, it was rare for a woman to have a key role in film-making and, it could be argued, the rise of feminism in the 1960s was to be the great catalyst for change for women in film. This will be discussed in the next section.

THE FEMINIST REVOLUTION

The women's movement did not suddenly arrive; since the days of the suffragettes an increasing number of women had seen the need for equality with men. A new political and social climate was evolving in the 1960s and early 1970s which questioned the established order, encouraged radical reform and produced conditions that were conducive to the rise of the feminist movement. Although this radical dissatisfaction with contemporary society began in the US, its message soon spread to the UK and in both countries there was a questioning of woman's role in society. Betty Friedan's book, *The Feminine Mystique*, was published in 1963 and touched a chord in many discontented women. The time was ripe for the spread of the feminist movement,[3] as Friedan explained:

the absolute necessity for a civil rights movement for women had reached such a point of subterranean explosive urgency by 1966 that it took only a few of us to get together to ignite the spark – and it spread like a nuclear chain reaction.

(Cited in Banner 1984: 247)

Representation and stereotyping of women in the media

Feminists generally believe that the media is a contributory factor in perpetuating a narrow range of **stereotyped** images of women. How women are **represented** in the media may encourage particular expectations of women which are extremely limiting; for instance, that women are always based in the home, that they are inferior to men, that they like men who are violent, are just a few of the myths which are arguably perpetuated by the media. As Molly Haskell points out:

From a woman's point of view the ten years from, say, 1962 or 1963 to 1973 have been the most disheartening in screen history. In the roles and prominence accorded to women, the decade began unpromisingly, grew steadily worse, and at present shows no sign of improving. Directors, who in 1962 were guilty only of covert misogyny (Stanley Kubrick's *Lolita*) or kindly indifference (Sam Peckinpah's *The High Country*) became overt in 1972 with the violent abuse and brutalisation of *A Clockwork Orange* and *Straw Dogs*.

(Haskell 1973: 323)

For discussion of feminism and the New German Cinema, see Chapter 14, pp. 468–71.

stereotyping
A quick and easy way of labelling or categorising the world around us and making it understandable. Stereotypes are learned but are by no means fixed, yet are often resistant to change. They tend to restrict our understanding of the world and perpetuate beliefs that are often untrue or narrow. For instance, the concept that only thin women are attractive is a stereotype promoted by much of the media in the late twentieth century (though there are some exceptions like comediennes Dawn French and Roseanne); yet in other eras the opposite has been true. Stereotyping is not always negative, but tends to be very much concerned with preserving and perpetuating power relations in society. It is in the interests of those in power to continue to stereotype those with lower status in a negative light, thus preserving the status quo.

representation
The media *re*-presents information to its audience, who are encouraged by the mainstream media to see its output as a 'window on the world', as reflecting reality. Yet the process of representing information is highly complex and highly selective. Many feminists argue that the way notions of gender are represented by the media perpetuates and reinforces the values of patriarchal society; for instance, men tend to

take on strong, active roles, while women are shown as passive and relying on their attractiveness. There are exceptions to such narrow stereotyping, the 'strong' woman shown by Ripley in the *Alien* trilogy and the two heroines in *Thelma and Louise* could be seen as positive, although rather more cynically they could be seen merely as 'role reversal' films and thus as having purely novelty value.

Representations often make use of stereotypes because they are a shorthand, quick and easy way of using information. It could be argued that the media production process encourages the use of stereotypes because of the pressure of time and budget. Many feminists point out that because so few women hold key positions in the media hierarchies representations of women are bound to be from a male perspective.

For more discussion of representation, stereotyping and sexuality, see Chapter 10.

patriarchal society
A society in which it is men who have power and control. Women are generally disadvantaged and have lower status.

alternative cinema
Provides an alternative to the codes and conventions of mainstream, narrative cinema, often both thematically and visually.

avant-garde cinema
Essentially non-narrative in structure and often intellectual in content, working in opposition to mainstream cinema. Avant-garde film is often

Film, particularly in the early feminist period, was seen as one area of the media that would become a battleground for the women's movement. Film would be used as an ideological tool, which would counteract the stereotyped images of women presented by the male-dominated media and raise women's awareness of their inferior position in **patriarchal society**, where women generally take a subservient role. For instance, in film, women, as the historical section indicates, have usually taken supportive roles rather than key, decision-making ones.

> **Do mainstream films still represent women in a narrow range of predictable and stereotyped ways?**

FEMINIST FILM THEORY AND PRACTICE IN BRITAIN

The influence of alternative, independent and avant-garde film

Alongside the expansion of feminism and the women's movement **alternative** and **avant-garde cinema** was flourishing. **Independent cinema** could, at its simplest, be divided into two forms: documentary and avant-garde. British film has a strong documentary tradition, which was to some extent socialist-influenced, and feminist film initially saw documentary as a way of presenting the 'truth' about the lives of women. During the 1960s American avant-garde film-makers produced many innovative and controversial films, some of the most well known being 'gay' and 'camp' films that challenged traditional stereotypes of gender roles such as Andy Warhol's *Lonesome Cowboys* (1968) and Kenneth Anger's *Scorpio Rising* (1965). Also in Europe, avant-garde film had been taken up by a number of film-makers, Jean-Luc Godard and François Truffaut being its most famous exponents. Although gender roles in European films tended to be stereotypical, some feminist film-makers saw the potential of avant-garde film as a means of breaking away from the constraints of traditional cinema.

The expansion of independent film-making in Britain encouraged the formation of a number of workshops, which aimed to make film-making available to all and to destroy the élitism often found in the industry. Many workshops made films that were outside the sphere of mainstream film and television, often being concerned with areas that were considered radical in politics or content. Cinema Action was one of the earliest workshops. Formed in 1968, it toured the country screening films aimed at a working-class audience. Amber Films, based in Newcastle, began in 1969 and The Other Cinema opened in London as a distribution agency (an essential outlet for the distribution of independent films). Perhaps the best known of the workshops is the London Filmmakers Co-op which, alongside Amber films, is still in existence today.

The late 1960s and early 1970s was a period of great academic and cultural vitality. The government supported the arts and there was a commitment to film-making; in 1968 the Regional Arts Associations began funding individual films and in 1972 the Arts Council did likewise.

The first women's film group

The combination of the expansion of the women's movement and the rise of independent film-making brought about the conditions in which feminist film could thrive. In 1972 the first women's film group in Britain was formed, the London Women's Film Group, which aimed to spread ideas about women's liberation and enable women to learn film-making skills otherwise unavailable to them.

The London Women's Film Group, apart from making films by women, also campaigned for equal opportunities for women in the industry, and was instrumental in initiating the examination of the role of women within the ACTT (Association of Cinematographers, Television and Allied Technicians). Without acceptance by the union it was, and still is, virtually impossible to work in the industry. In the 1970s there were no more women working in high-grade jobs in the film and television industry than there had been in the 1950s. Demystification of the learning of technical skills was considered vital, but it was also necessary to make women familiar with all the stages in the film-making process so that they had a large pool of knowledge, which they would never have been able to obtain in mainstream film. Many film groups worked co-operatively, giving all members an equal say in the production process and rejecting the strict hierarchy of roles used in mainstream film production.

The feminist film movement was intentionally political, aiming to give all women, but especially working-class women, a chance to work in film. The films were often shown to trade unions, in factories and housing estates, and it was hoped they would help to raise women's consciousness about their place in society. Many of the early feminist films fitted into the black-and-white documentary realist tradition, the dominant mode of alternative, political film-making in the UK. Linda Dove, of the London Women's Film Group, explained in an interview:

We tended to reject commercial films wholesale as the ideological products of capitalist, sexist, racist society.... Originally our aim was to change the context in which a film is seen – we wanted to break down the audience passivity by always going out with films and discussing them when they were shown.

(Dove 1976: 59)

Film as a 'window on the world'

Left-wing documentary films had been seen as presenting the 'truth' and a form of reality, but the viewpoint that the visual media presented a 'window on the world' came under question in the early 1970s. The media, it could be argued, are manipulated by the ruling patriarchal ideology and what is seen as natural, as clear-cut and obvious, is in fact a concept produced by our society. The ambivalence about the meaning of film suggests its interpretation by the audience may be different to that intended by the film-maker. For instance, *Women of the Rhondda* (1972) has a naturalistic style with no voiceover and the images are intended to speak for themselves, but the message is somewhat ambiguous for a non-feminist audience because there are so many possible readings (this multitude of possible readings has been termed a polysemic text). This awareness resulted in a number of radical documentary film-makers becoming more didactic in their approach: for instance, *The Amazing Equal Pay Show* (LWFG, 1972) experimented with film conventions, developing links with avant-garde cinema, as does *The Night Cleaners* (Berwick Street Collective, 1972) which was concerned with better pay for office cleaners but used unconventional editing techniques.

Many feminist film-makers in the 1970s appropriated ideas from avant-garde art cinema and applied them to discuss questions that were of concern to the women's movement, such as representation. The avant-garde had always been male-dominated

self-conscious and frequently makes use of devices such as cuts to the camera crew, talking to the camera and scratching on film.

independent cinema
May be divided into two areas. First, independent mainstream cinema, such as HandMade Films, which aims to compete with the big studios, although without any large financial backing finds it difficult to survive. Palace Films was one such casualty; the success of *The Crying Game* came too late to save its demise. Second, the term is used to describe film-making outside the mainstream sector, for instance, film workshops, avant-garde film, feminist film. The boundaries between these two areas are not always clear and may overlap.

For further discussion of avant-garde and counter-cinema, see Chapter 4.

and narrow in its representations of women (see, for instance, Jean-Luc Godard's films such as *Breathless* (1960), *A Married Woman* (1964) and *Weekend* (1968)). But the avant-garde's political/anarchist basis gave an alternative form to the traditional use of realism in both fiction and documentary film. This influence was most profound in film-makers like Laura Mulvey and Sally Potter, whose films are discussed on pages 296–9.

Early feminist film theory

A key year for the women's film movement and the development of a feminist film theory and practice was 1972. In August, a women's event was held for the first time, in conjunction with the Edinburgh Film Festival, and proved to be very successful. In early 1973, Claire Johnston organised a season of women's cinema at the National Film Theatre in London.

The ideological sense of purpose and political debate behind feminist film-making ensured the development of a film theory. Feminist film theory was, in the early period, especially concerned with representation and sexuality and its relation to the domi-nance of the male power structure within a patriarchal society. A number of women, often from an academic background, encouraged this development, but it was perhaps Laura Mulvey and Claire Johnston who were the progenitors of feminist film theory. Both wrote seminal articles which were to have a huge impact on the study of film and the media and will be discussed in this chapter.

Developing a counter-cinema

Claire Johnston's 'Women's Cinema as Counter-cinema' (1973) is one of the earliest articles on feminist film theory and practice. Johnston shows how women have been stereotyped in film since the days of the silent cinema, and argues for a cinema that challenges such narrow conventions but which will also be entertaining. In mainstream cinema woman is seen as an extension of a male vision and Johnston criticises the narrow role she is given in film: 'It is probably true to say that despite the enormous emphasis placed on woman as spectacle in the cinema, woman as woman is largely absent' (Johnston 1973: 214).

The work of two female Hollywood directors, Dorothy Arzner and Ida Lupino, is considered by Johnston, who suggests that their films partially subvert the patriarchal viewpoint. An understanding of how these films work could be important for feminist film practice in breaking through and challenging the ruling ideology.

Johnston argues for a woman's cinema that will work both within and outside main-stream cinema, and that will work collectively in groups with no hierarchical structure but also more conventionally, using film as a political tool and an entertainment.

The importance of developing a film practice that questions and challenges main-stream dominant cinema and its patriarchal basis is stressed by Johnston. She terms it a counter-cinema movement which will have links with avant-garde and left-wing film.

Pleasure, looking and gender

Psychoanalytic theory, particularly the theories of Freud and Lacan, has been instru-mental in the development of a feminist film theory, although **structuralist** and **Marxist theories**[4] have also been influential to a lesser extent. Laura Mulvey's article 'Visual Pleasure and Narrative Cinema' (first published in 1975) emphasises the importance of the patriarchical viewpoint in the cinema; that the pleasure gained from looking (called scopophilia) is a male pleasure and that 'the look' in cinema is directed at the male, this is often referred to as the 'male gaze'. Scopophilia can be directed in two areas: first, voyeurism, that is scopophilic pleasure linked to sexual attraction, and, second, scopophilic pleasure which is linked to narcissistic identification. Mulvey argues that this identification is always with the male, who is the pivot of the film, its hero, while the female is often seen as a threat. Film reflects society, argues Mulvey, and therefore society influences our understanding of film. This viewpoint is linked with psycho-analytical theory to demonstrate the influence of patriarchal society on film. Patriarchy and phallocentrism are intrinsically linked; the phallus is a symbol of power, of having (note how guns are used in film: guns = phallus = power). The woman has no phallus, she is castrated, which relates back to Freudian theory that the woman is lacking and therefore inferior because she has no phallus.

Freud's theories on scopophilia centre around voyeurism and the desire to see the erotic and the forbidden, yet this desire is male-centred. The cinema provides a perfect venue for illicit voyeuristic viewing because the audience is in a dark enclosed womb-like world. Mulvey argues that the power cinema holds is so strong it can act as a temporary form of brainwashing (an argument which is still very much alive today!).

The woman in Freudian theory represents desire, but also the castration complex, and so there is a tension, an ambivalence towards the female form, and her 'look' can be threatening. As the male is the controller, taking the active role, the female is reduced to the icon, the erotic, but at the same time is a threat because of her difference.

Mulvey argues that woman has two roles in film: erotic object for the characters in the story and erotic object for the spectator. More recent feminist theory, though, seems to suggest the representation of women is far more complex, and later theory, including Mulvey's, looks at films where women do have a key role as subject rather than object. Melodrama is one such area (see Mulvey 1981).

Mulvey refers to Hitchcock because of the complicit understanding in his films that the audience gains a voyeuristic pleasure from watching a film, from looking: 'In *Vertigo* (1958) in particular, but also in *Marnie* (1964) and *Rear Window* (1954), the "look" is central to the plot oscillating between voyeurism and fetishistic fascination' (Mulvey 1975: 813).

The denial of pleasure

Mulvey points out that devices used in the traditional Hollywood narrative film have trapped film-makers into using certain codes and conventions that place the female in a subordinate, passive position, making her role as erotic object extremely limiting. Mulvey criticises the narrowness of this role and argues that to change woman's position in film a revolutionary look at cinema needs to be taken and the denial of cinematic pleasure be given a priority. The exclusion of woman as object, as provider of voyeuristic pleasure will then free her from the narrow limits she has been allocated in cinema. This may seem an extreme reaction to mainstream narrative cinema, but in the early 1970s feminists felt the only way to change female representation was to take extreme measures; a new radical cinema was needed, an alternative to the 'magic' of narrative cinema.

A new language

The importance of the creation of a female subject and the development of a new language is central to early feminist film theory, which argued that spoken, written and visual languages all placed women in a subordinate position and reflected a patriarchal ideology. A film theory and practice that had its own codes and conventions would replace the dominance of patriarchal cinema. Christine Gledhill echoes this desire in her article, 'Some Recent Developments in Feminist Criticism' (1985):

A feminist filmmaker then, finds the root of patriarchy in the very tools she wishes to employ to

Marxist theory
Argues that those who have the means of production have control in a capitalist society. The dominant class have control of the means of production and have an interest in perpetuating the dominant ideology. More recently exponents of Althusserian Marxism, particularly post-1968, have argued that main-stream narrative cinema reinforces the capitalist system and that a revo-lutionary cinema is needed to challenge the dominant ideology.

speak about women. So what is required of her is the development of a counter-cinema that will deconstruct the language and techniques of classic cinema.

(Gledhill 1985: 841)

Classic cinema was based on ideas which had been passed on from the old literary/realist tradition and many feminists felt that the realist tradition perpetuated a way of seeing, of understanding the world, that belonged to dominant patriarchal society and that feminists should break with this tradition.

Avant-garde feminist film

Film-makers like Mulvey and Sally Potter were interested in a film theory and practice which worked together and would produce a new feminist language. Avant-garde film was the ideal vehicle for these ideas because it broke the normal rules and conventions of mainstream cinema; its political/anarchist basis gave an alternative form to the traditional use of realism in both fiction and documentary film. Mulvey's article 'Film, Feminism and the Avant-Garde' (1979) explores this relationship, suggesting that both forms of film can be mutually beneficial, working towards similar goals. Mulvey's films, for instance, actively avoid any sense of being constructed for the male spectator, confronting the lack of representation of women in film; they are a mixture of avant-garde, melodrama and psychoanalytic theory. Mulvey has put her theories into practice, providing an alternative cinema in which:

pleasure and involvement are not the result of identification, narrative tension or eroticised femininity, but arise from surprising and excessive use of the camera, unfamiliar framing of scenes and the human body, the demands made on the spectator to put together disparate elements.

(Mulvey 1989: 125)

(For further analysis of avant-garde, feminist film see case study 4 on Sally Potter's films, p. 296.)

Make a list of the ways you could make a film which would break as many of the conventions of patriarchal cinema as you can think of.

The need for an audience

Avant-garde was limiting as a form in achieving feminist aims of reaching a mass audience precisely because of its upturning of the codes and conventions of mainstream cinema. Many avant-garde films were termed 'difficult' and only attracted a small audience which tended to be those familiar with 'art film'. Even though avant-garde-influenced film-makers, like Mulvey, did much to aid the understanding of their films by producing hand-outs and giving lectures, some feminists felt that avant-garde film was élitist and would be of no interest to a mass audience of women. Mulvey's and Johnston's theories, they suggested, would be more useful for the development of a feminist film theory than as a guide on how to make feminist films. Kaplan (1983), for example, points out that it makes more sense to use familiar and recognisable cinematic conventions to explain that the 'realism' of mainstream cinema is a fabrication.

Questioning representation

The need for a strong feminist film practice which provided an alternative view other than the gender stereotype was voiced by feminists. There had been a shift in attitude by the end of the 1970s when it was acknowledged that representation was a complex area and there need not necessarily be a direct link between media representations of women and their changing place in society. If the media does not represent a 'window on the world' it would therefore be naïve to assume that changes in representation in the media would automatically result in changes in society. Mulvey comments on the dangers of an overemphasis on representation and suggests that to bring about change by working within the conventions of patriarchal production could be counter-productive.

A period of optimism and defiance

Johnston's article 'The subject of feminist film theory/practice' was published in a spirit of optimism when the women's movement was still strong and the 'Feminism and Cinema Event' had been successfully held at the Edinburgh Film Festival in 1979. Johnston points out that feminists had achieved much in a short time span, and 'We are now at a stage when it is becoming possible to theorise a conception of ideological struggle within feminist film theory and practice more concretely' (Johnston 1980: 28).

• **Plate 9.4** *Thriller* (Sally Potter, 1979)
Explores the lack of female voice in society.

Feminist film theory and practice in the early period up to 1980 had been a joint ideological struggle; film theory analysed the patriarchal conventions that mainstream film worked within and film practice was physically able to break these rules. Yet there was only a limited audience for feminist film in this period, even though there was an increasing interest in academic circles in feminist film theory. In the strongly male-dominated world of film-making women were not seen as artists or film-makers, and feminist art was seen as a possible challenge to patriarchal society.[5] As Johnston explains, the female within patriarchy is seen as the 'other' and feminist art challenges these narrow conceptions of gender:

Feminist art, on the other hand, which asserts a woman's discourse about her position and ... the subjective relationships which constitute her as a female subject in history, is far more problematic and far less easily assimilated into the conception of woman as irrevocable 'other' by which patriarchy is maintained.

(Johnston 1980: 34)

By the end of the 1970s a feminist film theory and practice had been established, giving many women a new-found confidence and a belief that society could change. In the previous decade a number of influential articles on feminist film theory and practice had been written. A body of work had been formed by feminist writers and academics, Mulvey and Johnston being the founder writers who were to influence a generation of film and media critics. Janet Bergstrom, in 'Rereading the Work of Claire Johnston', explains how Johnston laid the groundwork for 'a recognition of the importance of an understanding of feminist criticism and theory, feminist filmmaking' (Bergstrom 1988: 83).

Films were being made by women and about women. More women's film groups had been formed. Sheffield Film Co-op, for instance, was formed in 1975 by a group of socialist feminist film-makers who made documentary and drama-documentary films about women in the local community, such as *A Woman Like You* (1976) and *Jobs for the Girls* (1979). Films such as Clayton and Curling's *Song of the Shirt* (1979) and Sally Potter's *Thriller* (1979) were received with interest and some acclaim.

Making feminist film accessible

Feminist film practice generally saw itself as separate from mainstream film. Yet in the next decade this was to become an area of debate. Strategies for gaining a larger audience for feminist ideas would be hotly argued. Lack of money and very tight budgets did not appear to have caused real frustration and the main concern was to develop a feminist film practice. Sally Potter, for instance, felt that although it was desirable to gain a larger audience, her ideological position excluded her from becoming involved in the mechanisms of the mainstream film industry: a feminist film would have little marketability and be a huge risk for a distributor. Potter argues that pleasure can be revolutionary:

I think that working for a wide audience is not a matter of compromise at all…and that pleasure need not be an ideological acceptance of a patriarchal society….There is pleasure in analysis, in unravelling, in thinking, in criticising the old stories. That was the premise from which *Thriller* worked.

(Cook 1981: 27)

While Sally Potter was developing fictional film and seeking a wider audience, a significant strand of feminist film, more Marxist-influenced than avant-garde/structuralist, was developing a documentary style aimed at working-class women with the intention of making feminist film more accessible. These documentary film-makers felt that there should not be just one authorial voice, a sole director, and a number of films were made co-operatively. Clayton and Curling's *Song of the Shirt* (1979) was one such project. This was initially instigated and researched by a feminist history group and then brought to the film-makers for completion.

At the beginning of the 1970s the focus was on representation in film and the media, but by the end of the decade attention was being diverted to the concept of 'pleasure' and whether this should be denied in film. Some feminists expressed the concern that by denying the pleasures of mainstream cinema feminist film-makers might alienate their audience. Yet feminists generally agreed that feminist film theory and practice had an important role to play in raising conciousness as to the marginalisation of women in a patriarchal society.

Many feminists still called for a counter-cinema and a deconstructive cinema in the early 1980s. Ann Kaplan and Annette Kuhn argued there is a need to break down the dominant forms of cinema, and the audience should become active rather than passive, gaining pleasure from learning rather than the narrative. Feminist counter-cinema can be broadly divided into three types of film: first, those films that look at the absence of a female voice in film and women's marginalisation in a phallocentric language and image system; Mulvey's films are an example here. Second, films that have points in common in their use of Lacanian psychoanalytic theory, and demonstrate that women have been used as an empty vessel, an extension of the male voice; Sally Potter's *Thriller*, for instance. Finally, films which are concerned with writing women into history and examining the problems of depicting women's role in society. Clayton and Curling's *Song of the Shirt* comes into this category.

Both Kuhn and Kaplan and film-makers like Sue Clayton were aware of the problems of using a cinema which rejects the mainstream, that is anti-conventional, and may therefore alienate its audience. Kaplan suggested that a way forward would be to work within and manipulate the conventions of mainstream cinema.

Moving towards mainstream narrative cinema

A number of feminists feared certain areas of feminist film practice had become so entrenched in promulgating a theoretical viewpoint that a barrier had been created between film and audience, and if these films were to appeal to a mass audience traditional narrative structures and conventions may have to be used.

In fact, by the early 1980s some films by women were working within mainstream film conventions. Alongside experimental films like *The Gold Diggers* (1983) and *An Epic Poem* (1982), more traditional narrative and documentary forms were being investigated by feminists such as Dutch film-maker Marlene Gorris, who made the excellent, but somewhat controversial at its time of release, *Question of Silence* (1982) (see case study 3, p. 293), and Lizzy Borden who made *Born in Flames* (1983), a mix of documentary and science fiction. Both films were received with interest and seemed to indicate a new way forward for feminist narrative film.

By the mid-1980s the documentary was being used to considerable effect by women's film groups, such as the now defunct Red Flannel, giving a voice to women's issues (see case study 1, p. 291). Formed in 1984, it benefited from the advent of Channel Four (in 1982) which gave financial assistance to a number of film groups and provided a wider audience through the mass medium of television. The feminist Sheffield Film Co-op continued to make films with strong representations of working-class women like *Red Skirts on Clydeside* (1983) which is a documentary concerned with reclaiming key points in women's history, in this case the 1915 Rent Strike in Glasgow.

REASSESSING FEMINIST FILM THEORY

Feminist film theory was going through a similar period of reassessment which also seemed to suggest feminist ideas could be expounded using mainstream cinema. In 1981 Mulvey published a 1980s response to her 1970s article 'Visual Pleasure and Narrative Cinema', which was so fundamental to the development of feminist film theory, entitled 'Afterthoughts on Visual Pleasure and Narrative Cinema' (1981). In the article Mulvey develops two lines of thought: first, examining whether the female spectator can gain a deep pleasure from a male-orientated text, and second, how the text and the spectator are affected by the centrality of a female character in the narrative. 'Afterthoughts' does seem to mark a shift in attitude, a move away from representation to studying the female response, to asking how women watch films and questioning the role of melodrama, which has traditionally been viewed as the woman's genre.

Feminist film theory has been especially influenced by psychoanalytic theory and particularly Freud and Lacan. Mulvey acknowledges her debt to Lacan who, she explains, has 'broadened and advanced ways of conceptualising sexual difference, emphasising the fictional, constructed nature of masculinity and femininity' (Mulvey 1989: 165).

Not all feminists supported a feminist film theory based on psychoanalytic theory. Terry Lovell in *Pictures of Reality* (1983) criticised Lacanian theory because of its emphasis on the individual rather than the collective, and argued that gaining pleasure from the text is rather more complex than a simple attribution to sexual desire.

In the latter part of the 1980s Freud's work had been re-examined by many feminists because of its phallocentric basis. Tania Modleski, for instance, in her book *The Women Who Knew Too Much* (1988), asks for a less male-centred version of spectatorship and calls for the development of a feminist psychoanalytic theory which is challenging and inventive. Penley, in the introduction to *Feminism and Film Theory* (1988), states that much feminist film criticism questions the patriarchal roots of current psychoanalytic theories, especially those of Freud and Lacan.

Modleski applies her ideas to an analysis of Hitchcock's films, which have been of great interest to feminists because of his extreme use of voyeurism and the 'look'. Reassessing earlier theory, Modleski points out that Mulvey's article 'Visual Pleasure and Narrative Cinema' (1975) does not allow for the complex nature of representation and raises questions about the stereotypical, passive female object and the active male. Modleski states: 'What I want to argue is neither that Hitchcock is utterly misogynistic nor that he is largely sympathetic to women and their plight in patriarchy, but that his work is characterised by a thoroughgoing ambivalence about femininity' (Modleski 1988: 3).

Many of Hitchcock's films are seen from the point of view of a female protagonist: *Blackmail* (1929), *Rebecca* (1940), *Notorious* (1946), for instance, or when the hero or heroine is in a vulnerable or passive, female position as in *Rear Window* (1954).

Modleski re-examines aspects of Mulvey's work , especially the suggestion that the patriarchal order has banished a strong female presence. In *North by Northwest* (1959), Cary Grant's role is that of hero and sex object, the desirable male; in *Marnie* (1964), Sean Connery plays a similar role, which also serves to heighten the irony that Marnie, the heroine and his wife, is frigid. In Hitchcock's films both male and female can become objects of the 'look'.

The strong and powerful female can exist within mainstream film, yet Hitchcock is patently not a feminist film-maker and his films seem to express Freud's assertion that the male contempt for femininity is an expression of the repression of their bisexuality – woman is a threat who must be destroyed: 'the male object is greatly threatened by bisexuality, though he is at the same time fascinated by it; and it is the woman who pays for this ambivalence, often with her life itself' (Modleski 1988: 10).

• **Plate 9.5** *North by Northwest* (Alfred Hitchcock, 1959) Cary Grant – irresistible to women.

Towards the end of the 1980s there was a certain ambivalence regarding the role of feminist film theory and practice; the close ties which had united and argued for a counter-cinema were now divorcing, theorists and practitioners felt to work within mainstream cinema was possible, if not essential, to gain a wider audience. Teresa De Lauretis in her article, 'Guerrilla in the Midst – Women's Cinema in the 1980s' (1990), suggests there are two distinct areas in which women film-makers could be most effective: the alternative 'guerrilla' cinema which is locally based, and mainstream film aiming at a nationwide or worldwide audience.

FEMINIST FILM THEORY IN THE 1990s

In the late 1990s feminist film theory appears to be thriving; many books have now been published on the subject, and it is an established area of study on higher education courses. Much current research though seems to provide more questions than answers;

indeed there is a fundamental understanding of the complexity of reading media texts and how they are interpreted by an audience. Feminist film studies could, in one sense, be seen as being in danger of fragmenting and becoming disunified. Yet it is the subject's heterogeneity, its ability to incorporate a range of theories from psycho-analysis to postmodernism, which should continue to ensure its useful contribution to a deeper understanding of film studies and women's place in society. Black feminist film theory and lesbian feminist film theory, for instance, have both suggested new ways of understanding how women from different social and ethnic groups interpret cultural messages.

In the last decade there has been a departure from Freud- and Lacanian-based psychoanalytic theory towards an appropriation of concepts from cultural studies; the emphasis has transferred from reading media texts, a move from studying the encoding process which asks how messages are produced, to a study of the decoding process, which asks how messages are received and understood by an audience. The historical tendency to favour psychoanalytic theory has proven to be problematic when applied to feminist film theory because of its dependence on the Oedipal trajectory, in which woman is seen as not only 'lacking' but also needing to be brought under control through the male gaze. If woman's role in film is to always be reduced to the 'other' by psychoanalytic theory, then it could be argued there is little place or room to open up patriarchal narratives to account for the female spectator, other than through identifica-tion with the male.

Yet some feminist film theorists such as Jackie Byars have reworked psychoanalytic theory to give a feminist perspective. Her analysis of melodrama suggests the woman can exist as a spectator in a positive way, she explains that in *All That Heaven Allows* the gaze is strongly female.[6] Jackey Stacey's analysis of *Desperately Seeking Susan* points out the film is not about sexual difference but the difference between two women, a view which cannot be read in terms of Lacan or Freud.[7] It would seem psychoanalytic theory needs to develop a new framework which will view the woman as a positive force rather than suffering from a state of lack. Susanna Walters asks: 'could it be that feminist textual analysis had replicated traditional ways of seeing by privi-leging the discrete moment of image production outside of its social and experiential context?' (Walters 1995: 99).

For further discussion of ideology and spectator-ship, see Chapter 5.

The reworking of psychoanalytic theory may provide a new model from which feminists could work. Mulvey's theories, based on Freud and Lacan, have had consid-erable impact in enhancing our understanding of the role of the spectator in film and how media texts place the viewer in a particular position. Application of these methods of analysis proves useful when analysing a film such as *The Piano*, which gives the female the power of the look and to some extent reverses conventional filming practices (see case study 7, p. 299). Cultural studies theorists argue that film studies tends to isolate the viewer from the text and is itself more concerned with studying how cultural systems produce meaning, how ideology is replicated through cultural institutions, texts and practices. Ideology can be seen as the means in which we interpret and make sense of our lives, the viewpoint from which we see the world. Ideology, in a capitalist society, needs constant re-establishing and this is carried out by, what Gramsci has termed, hegemony. This is the means by which a dominant social group maintains control of a subordinate group, a form of unconscious control, in which we take on certain beliefs, practices and attitudes as being natural or normal and carry those opinions with us, for instance the belief that in a patriarchal society it is entirely normal for woman to be the homemaker and have a low-paid, menial job. Hegemony therefore is constantly shifting, it is constantly negotiated and never fixed; from a feminist standpoint this means there is the potential for change in patriarchal society.

If cultural texts such as film are apparatus for transmitting cultural values, they are also sites for a struggle over meaning. The term given to describe the constant shifting of and multiple possibilities of meaning a text may have is polysemy, i.e. a text has no one fixed meaning. This then gives feminist film and cultural critics the opportunity to analyse audience response to texts as 'open' rather than 'closed' and the study of how gender differences work in the reception of texts becomes productive. Stuart Hall, in his early work, suggested that there are three ways in which a text may be received: (a) a dominant reading, as meant by its producer; (b) a negotiated reading, when the text is generally accepted but challenged in some areas; (c) an oppositional reading, when the viewer challenges the reading of the text.[8] In fact, more recent research argues for the possibility of a much more complex relationship between the reader and the text than had previously been thought.

The audience can be accredited with entering into a viewing situation with a range of skills and competences and a background of cultural knowledge. The audience is there-fore active rather than being a merely passive receiver of the message. This understanding has implications for feminist film theory, which breaks open the parame-ters of patriarchal definitions of feminine subjectivity. Christine Gledhill uses the term 'negotiation' of text, explaining that we negotiate with cultural texts at every level; from institutions, where feminists can put pressure on to negotiating the active meanings of texts, to the active process of reception.[9] Gledhill does though point out the need to be aware of the dangers of overemphasising the process of reception which could result in a move away from feminist political resistance.

Ethnographic research has proven to be of particular use to more recent studies of how women receive media texts. Janice Radway, in her research on romance fiction, found that the women she interviewed preferred a strong, independent heroine.[10] This tended to contradict previous feminist textual-based research which sees the romance novel as presenting women as passive and vulnerable. Jacqueline Bobo conducted group interviews to analyse the reception and interpretation of *The Color Purple*, the results of which she found surprising. The film contained many stereotypical images of black people and their culture and was filmed by a white male director, Steven Spielberg, yet the black women interviewed saw the film as positive, they 'not only liked the film, but have formed a strong attachment to it. The film is significant to their lives' (Bobo 1988: 101). Bobo believes those interviewed were able to filter out negative aspects of the film and highlight areas they could relate to.

Black feminist theory has found it problematic in applying what could be termed white, bourgeois film theory to an ethnic group which is so noticeably absent in film. bell hooks explains: 'many feminist film critics continue to structure their discourse as though it speaks about "women" when in fact it only speaks about white women' (hooks 1992: 123). Because black women are generally excluded from film, or given an extremely limited number of representations, a film like *The Color Purple* is of particular significance to the many black women who read the film favourably.

Lesbian and gay studies is now also beginning to be taken seriously as a method of cultural analysis. Lesbian writers question whether a theory of lesbian desire and its relationship to media texts and representation is needed; a separate theory from previous feminist film thinking which has been concerned with the relationship of the heterosexual woman to film and tends to place lesbian desire as radically other. (See Chapter 10, 'Lesbian and gay cinema' for a more detailed discussion.)

The variety and wealth of modes of research available to feminist film theorists are eclectic; psychoanalytic, semiotic-based textual analysis, social history, empirical and ethnographic study are just a sample of the tools available. Some feminists have been resistant to embracing cultural studies in its totality, arguing it is too concerned with examining the class structure. But there has been a shift away from solely concentrating on ideology and hegemony to studying identity and subjectivity, which can partly, at least, be attributed to the impact of feminism.

Feminist film theory seems now to be moving towards an understanding of the difference, the complexity of the audience response, depending on ethnic identity, nationality, class and sexuality. Yet feminist film theory needs to integrate rather than discard the range of analytical processes which have been made available and contribute to our understanding of how gender and, in particular, women communicate, are communicated to and interpret media texts, especially film.

> **How useful a contribution has feminist film studies made to the study of film?**

WOMEN IN THE MAINSTREAM FILM INDUSTRY

Although the number of women working in key roles in the film industry was still very small, by the late 1980s an increasing number of women were entering these areas after receiving training in a film school or gaining experience in the growing number of film workshops. The National Film School, for instance, increased its intake of female students from one out of twenty-five when it first opened in 1971 to around 30 per cent by the mid-1980s. In an interview, camerawoman Belinda Parsons explains how important a thorough preparation and training was in a male-dominated workforce: 'As a woman one was going to have a lot of other problems and I didn't need confidence problems on the technical side; so from that point of view film school was brilliant' (Fitzgerald 1989: 193).

By the 1990s more women were working in previously male-dominated areas like directing, camera, sound and lighting.[11] Diane Tammes, Sue Gibson and Belinda Parsons are all respected camerawomen; Diana Ruston and Moya Burns work in sound. Surprisingly, they have come across little sexism and feel that with more and more women coming into the industry men have no choice but to accept them. Moya Burns comments in an article entitled 'Women in Focus':

The industry has changed a lot in the last ten years, there are not so many hard-boiled areas, like big-budget features. The features that get made today are financed differently, a lot of the money seems to be coming from bodies like Channel Four. They have a different emphasis on the type of film they want to make, and this filters right down to the type of crew they want to employ.

(Burns 1992: 4)

> 1 Why are so few big-budget or Hollywood films made by women?
> 2 Study the credits in at least five or six films of different type and budget. What does this tell you about the roles women have in film production?

In the field of directing women film-makers are now beginning to break into mainstream film, often from the independent and workshop sector. Lezli-Ann Barrett made the 'arty' feminist film short, *An Epic Poem*, in 1982 and went on to make the political but more conventional *Business as Usual*, starring Glenda Jackson, in 1987; Zelda Baron had a minor success with *Shag* (1988) and then worked in the US; Beeban Kidron directed *Vroom* and then made the highly acclaimed TV series *Oranges Are Not the Only Fruit*. In 1992 she worked in the US on *Used People*, starring Shirley Maclaine, and completed *Great Moments in Aviation History* with John Hurt and Vanessa Redgrave in 1993. Kidron recently completed filming *Swept From the Sea* (1997), adapted from a Conrad story; it has already been released in the US and may well establish an international career in directing for her. Sally Potter moved from the avant-garde *The Gold Diggers* (1982) to *Orlando* (1993), a film based on a Virginia Woolf novel. Although the film is art-based in form, it is coherent enough in style to have gained a wide audience and much praise and attention from film critics in the UK and US (see case study 6, p. 298). Her latest film, *The Tango Lesson* (1997), has had a more mixed reception but is a brave, if not entirely successful, attempt at writing, directing and starring in her own film. One of the most striking films to come out of the workshop sector is Amber Films' *Dream On* (1992), focusing on a group of women who live on a Tyneside estate. Gurinder Chada's most recent film takes a wry and witty look at life for Asian women in Britain today; *Bhaji on the Beach* (1994) is a rich and colourful film that deserves to be seen by a wide audience. Chada is now working on a script for Disney titled *Mistress of Spices*.

The advent of Channel Four in 1982 proved beneficial for women and film. Apart from funding a number of film and video workshops the company also employed women in key positions who in turn encouraged a programme of work by women (Caroline Spry, for instance, is a commissioning editor for Channel Four). In 1990

• **Plate 9.6** *Orlando* (Sally Potter, 1993)
An elegant gender-bender.

• **Plate 9.7** *Dream On* (Amber
Films, 1992)
A supportive community of
women.

• **Plate 9.8** *Bhaji on the Beach* (Gurinder Chada, 1994)
Received a BAFTA nomination for best film.

Channel Four screened a series of films by women from all over the world. Entitled 'Women Call the Shots', it was a response to the wealth of cinema made by women that is rarely seen by a large audience. More recently, though, Channel Four has dramatically cut back on its workshop funding,[12] including financial support for Red Flannel and many other innovative workshops which provided a vehicle for women to gain work and experience in film and video without being part of the mainstream industry. The whole of the workshop sector is having to cope and remain solvent in the 1990s post-Thatcher recession and with growing competition from other independent film and TV companies.

Fragmentation of the feminist movement

Many women in film seem to have distanced themselves from the feminist movement, and, although retaining sympathy for its ideals, question what feminism and feminist film really means. The term post-feminism has frequently been referred to, suggesting that we are past feminism. Feminism seems to have become fragmented, yet Jane Pilcher argues that many women, especially those under thirty, are aware of the term in its widest sense: 'However, they also described feminism as being concerned with a wider range of issues, including, for example the sexual objectification of women or the politics of appearance. Others described feminism as being a wide ranging "philosophy of life" ' (Pilcher 1993: 4).

Pilcher also came across the 'I'm not a feminist, but...' syndrome in her research, women who were sympathetic to feminism but did not want to be associated with extremism. This is a dilemma that confronts women who work in film. As film-maker Sally Potter points out, in an interview with David Ehrenstein, to acknowledge being a feminist is problematic:

So if I said, 'Yes I'm a feminist', it would slot in with their definition, which was a cliché of a protesting radical – everything they fear. You've got to be clever. You've got to speak freshly with nice juicy words that intoxicate – not trigger jargon words that turn people off.

(Ehrenstein 1993: 17)

Perhaps a new term, 'feminist realism', should be applied to women working in film, who have to be sensitive to the demands of the mainstream film industry if they are to get backing for their films, especially in such a competitive industry when production funding for both men and women is so difficult to obtain.

A number of support agencies for women film-makers have been established which aim to provide the female equivalent of the 'Old Boys' Network'; 'Women in Film and TV' helps women in the mainstream sector and in the independent and workshop sector, groups like 'Real Women' hold regular seminars and screenings, while 'Networking' provides information and support for all women interested in film and video.

So much of the future for women in film seems to be dependent on funding; in the independent sector on government support for the arts, and in the mainstream sector on confidence and continued investment in the industry. Possibly, in a British film industry that is so reliant on television, there may be more openings for women film-makers there (Beeban Kidron, for instance, gained experience working in television drama and documentary before moving on to TV-funded films).

Whether changing attitudes towards women working in the film industry will produce more positive representations of women in film is open to question. Feminism has perhaps changed the way we look at film, and there is a greater awareness of how gender is represented in the media, yet many films, particularly genre films, still display woman as erotic object or passive and incapable (see Clint Eastwood's 1992 film *The*

For more discussion of government support for film-making and how British films are funded, see Chapter 11.

Unforgiven). *Thelma and Louise* (1992) was hailed as a feminist film (directed by Ridley Scott, but scripted by a woman, Callie Khouri), although a more cynical analysis reveals that the women are filmed quite conventionally, as objects of 'the look'.[13] As more women work in mainstream film, though, it does seem likely that there will be a widening out of representations of women both visually and thematically. Films like Sally Potter's *Orlando* (1993) and Jane Campion's *The Piano* (1993), for instance, have both had successful releases yet are concerned with subject matter that would not normally be considered mainstream. They are also both exquisitely photographed and sensual films which offer an alternative world-view to the Hollywood norm.

To what extent is *Thelma and Louise* merely a role reversal film? Are there points where a woman may have filmed it differently?

• **Plate 9.9** *The Unforgiven* (Clint Eastwood, 1992)

• **Plate 9.10** *Thelma and Louise* (Ridley Scott, 1992)

☐ CASE STUDY 1: RED FLANNEL

Red Flannel was a women's film and video production group based in South Wales. It was formed in 1984, partly as a result of working together on film projects during the miners' strike of 1984–5. It was originally envisaged that the group would provide a workshop where women could acquire training in film and video, but it would also provide media education, produce films and videos and be a facility for hiring equipment. Red Flannel was provisionally franchised by the ACTT (the union for the film and TV industry) in 1985 and was fully franchised in 1987, when it also gained Channel Four funding. In 1997 Red Flannel folded, unable to survive in such a competitive climate. The group has always been particularly concerned with portraying the lives of women in South Wales. Members defined themselves as being socialist, feminist and Welsh. The political slant to their work ensured that issues were examined from a women's perspective, drawing attention to areas which are often ignored by the mainstream media.

In an interview with Red Flannel, it was pointed out that working for a feminist film and video group enabled its members to gain invaluable experience and training: 'We could make mistakes and not have to defend ourselves from the male onslaught. These sorts of organisations are very important because women tend not to have much confidence in our industry.'[14]

The group emphasised how male-dominated the industry still is. From Hollywood downwards there is a lack of representation of women's ideas and issues. Even though the situation has improved over the last ten years there is much room for progress.

For discussion of Channel Four's role in the British film and TV industry, see Chapter 11.

The loss of funding from Channel Four in 1992 affected their ability to exist as a workshop. Channel Four funding had enabled Red Flannel to operate with an enormous amount of freedom; they provided an everyday running budget (to include wages), a generous budget to produce one documentary a year and money for community work, which Channel Four encouraged. Since the funding cuts the group had kept busy, making a number of programmes over the last two years, but were still under enormous financial pressure and running from commission to commission. Each commission provides a film budget and production fee of between 7 and 10 per cent of the budget (the production fee includes the running costs and wages). To remain solvent Red Flannel needed to complete at least four productions a year, and these were generally made on a much lower budget than previously; most of their films were local commissions costing around £1,000 a minute (about half the London budget). In 1993–4 Red Flannel put in twenty film proposals to television companies (HTV, BBC and Channel Four), approximately half of which were focused on women's issues. The response was positive; the BBC was interested in five of the proposals, HTV and Channel Four in one each. However, an interest in a proposal still does not mean a production is guaranteed and this caused a degree of uncertainty. Red Flannel were competing at a time when the government is committed to deregulating the television industry. Indeed, they are one of the few women's film and video groups to have survived into the late 1990s.

As a feminist and socialist group, Red Flannel had tried to work co-operatively whenever possible. This has been most successful in documentary programmes where everyone can be involved in the research side, rather than an individually conceived, expressionistic piece like *Otherwise Engaged* (1991) where an author is needed. *Mam* (1988) was devised by the group and worked well as a collective film: 'There were very long discussions about what should go in, right up to the editing stage, but in production we had a specific role.'[15] The next film, *If We Were Asked* (1989), was a less successful collaboration and after that, partly because of pressure of time, collective working became a less realistic option. Projects tended to become the overall responsibility of two people, with others giving comments at 'report-backs' on a film's progress.

For further case studies of American and British film production, see Chapter 2.

☐ CASE STUDY 2: *MAM* (1988)

Mam is a documentary film which uses a mix of archive footage and interviews to give a historical account of the role of the Welsh mother in the working-class mining communities of South Wales. The film explores how the 'mam' is a concept originally imposed by early Victorian patriarchy, when the morals of Welsh women were put under question by a report from three Anglican commissioners who investigated the state of education in Wales. Among other points made, the report stated that Welsh women were lacking in morals and domestic skills. It resulted in the 'Blue Book' which said women should be based in the home and serve their husbands and children. Many women had worked in the heavy industries such as coal and iron, which then became exclusively male preserves, emphasising the divide between male and female that was to continue well into this century.

The film focuses on a community in a state of change. By the early 1980s the pits had nearly all closed and the 1984 miners' strike was a catalyst for a number of women who became actively involved in protecting the future of the community and providing a positive role for women within it.

Women in the Valleys often work for pin money, are frequently isolated and lacking in confidence. Training is suggested as a way forward, as a means of empowerment.

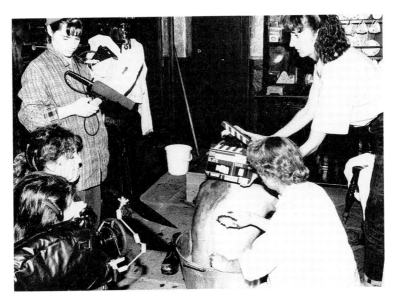

• **Plate 9.11** *Mam* (Red
Flannel, 1988)
Women working on the
production.

Shirley Powell, for instance, explains how she is part of a workers' clothing co-operative
that was formed when the company she worked for 'went bust'.

In a series of short 'talking heads' interviews women discuss why the male/female
divide has been so strong in the Valleys, and why the 'mam' has endured. It is argued
that mothers tend to reinforce these stereotypes. One woman suggests that it is the
'mam' herself who is to blame and sons should do more in the home; another points
out that the Valleys' man is twenty to thirty years behind the average male in his attitude
to women.

The film has a fairly conventional structure, although there is no single linking voiceover. This style developed from the influence of the British Documentary Movement on
independent film, ranging from early films like Humphrey Jennings' *Listen to Britain*
(1942) to the later *Women of the Rhondda* (1972) made by the London Women's Film
Group (a film well worth looking at in conjunction with *Mam* because of the similarity of
style and content). The style is often referred to as 'the storytelling technique' when the
visuals and interviews explain the narrative – there is no omniscient narrator to explain
how the film should be read. This method can produce ambiguity, but often leads to a
livelier, more creative work.

□ CASE STUDY 3: *A QUESTION OF SILENCE* (1982), DIRECTOR: MARLENE GORRIS

Marlene Gorris' career as a film-maker seemed to break off abruptly in the mid-1980s
after receiving much acclaim for *A Question of Silence* and *Broken Mirrors* (1983). More
recently though Gorris has directed two films which have revived her career; *Antonia's
Line* (1995) which received an Academy Award for best foreign language film and *Mrs
Dalloway* (1997), an adaptation of the Virginia Woolf novel.

A Question of Silence is an unusual and still topical film that gained some notoriety

• **Plate 9.12** *A Question of Silence* (Marleen Gorris, 1985)
One of the first feminist films to utilise some of the conventions of narrative film.

when it first came out because many men found its central subject matter offensive. The plot, at its simplest, tells the story of three women who are charged with murdering the male manager of a boutique. The story has an investigative structure that gradually reveals information about the murder, as the female psychiatrist assigned to the case attempts to find out why the murder took place.

The narrative is in certain aspects fairly conventional; it is the discourse of the film that is most disturbing to the audience, the acceptance of a 'logically' motiveless murder. Yet showing this film to male and female students in the 1990s generally elicits a response of interest tinged with amusement. This perhaps suggests a shift in attitude over the last decade: the film is not seen as threatening and there is an awareness of its black humour and playfulness, the poking fun at the ridiculousness of patriarchy. Masculine constructions in society such as the court system, for instance, are satirised in the film.

A Question of Silence challenges male authority, rendering it absurd and pointless, and examines women's lack of power and voice in a patriarchal society. It has been argued that the film supports a feminist separatist existence, a world apart from men; indeed, the film has no positive male characters. Even the psychiatrist's husband, originally presented as a liberal thinking 'new man', gradually reveals his underlying authoritarian, patriarchical values.

Jeanette Murphy argues that the murder is generally seen as a metaphor, a symbol of woman's oppression, but could also be seen as a literal device to show women's anger and frustration with patriarchy: 'How else to expose the insidious and deeply hidden forces of male dominance? How else to express the depth and degree of women's anger?' (Murphy 1986: 105).

The form of the film is often elliptical and only partly fits into the mainstream, although the investigative plot makes the form more acceptable and great pleasure is gained from the gradual revelation of events (Barthes named this the 'enigma' code).

Alternative cinema can use this form to attract an audience who may have antipathy towards anything other than mainstream cinema.

The film begins about half way through the timescale of events and is interspersed by flashbacks which reveal more and more about the events building up to the murder, which is then only partly shown to the audience. The murder is confusing and disturbing because there is no obvious motivation – a logical reason for murder is part of the expectation of the conventional narrative structure. Gorris makes fun of narrative expectations, often with a strong sense of irony; for instance, the murder weapons are everyday objects familiar to women, coat-hangers and shopping trolleys. The bizarreness of the plot creates a sense of the surreal, of wicked black humour which is particularly pointed against men and is continued after the murder when the three women show no sign of remorse: Christine goes to the funfair, Ann has a feast of fine food and Andrea prostitutes herself.

All three women are presented as being very ordinary, having little power or control over their lives, and their frustration is made clear: Ann, a barmaid, has to put up with sexist insults; Christine is a mother and housewife whose husband treats her like a servant; and Andrea, the most confident and assertive of the women, is an indispensable secretary, but patronised by her male bosses.

Janine Van Der Bos, the psychiatrist, initially represents authority and middle-class, patriarchal values. We see events through her eyes, and so how her role changes from inquisitor to supporter. As Janine begins to understand the women so she questions her role in society and her marriage, becoming distanced from her husband. The distance between them is heightened when he rapes her in their bedroom, a scene which is intercut with images of the women standing over the murdered boutique manager. Janine now identifies with the women.

Heterosexual sex is not presented as pleasurable for a woman – Janine's relationship is on her husband's terms, and Andrea coldly and unemotionally sells her body. Although the relationship between the women is not directly presented as sexual, there seems to be a mutual understanding that is almost telepathic. This is most evident when Andrea outlines Janine's body with her hands, in an emotional and potentially sexual scene which emphasises their closeness. There is certainly a hint that a lesbian relationship may be more satisfactory than a heterosexual one.

The final court scene begins with a wide shot of the court emphasising the all-male exclusiveness of those in power. At the same time a voiceover of the prosecutor represents the pompous and convoluted language of patriarchy that is designed to intimidate. Many feminists, particularly in the early 1980s, believed that a new language should be devised that would be sympathetic to women (at its simplest, words like history would become herstory). Throughout the film, language is problematic; Christine refuses to talk, the murder is carried out through a play of silent looks, as in the court scene when Janine communicates with the women by a series of looks, a more effective means of communication than language. Laughter is seen as an alternative to patriarchal language, as being able to subvert patriarchal authority, and is used to confuse the judge and undermine the court scene. The ripple of laughter that spreads across the women and finally to Janine effectively disrupts the seriousness of the court, making the legal process look ridiculous.

Janine's insistence that the accused are sane is received with disbelief because this does not make the crime understandable and rational. If the women were insane then the crime would be explainable. Janine's judgement is questioned by the prosecutor, who tries to ridicule and patronise her. After Janine walks out of court in solidarity with the others, her husband waits for her impatiently by the car, but we know that she will not go back to him, and there is even a repetition of the music motif from the murder scene which suggests he may be the next victim.

☐ CASE STUDY 4: SALLY POTTER, FILM-MAKER

Sally Potter is probably best known for three films: the film short *Thriller* (1979), the feature-length *The Gold Diggers* (1983) and the much acclaimed *Orlando* (1993). Her most recent film *The Tango Lesson* (1997) though has received a rather more muted reception. Potter worked in dance and performance for many years and in the 1980s worked in television. Her work has been termed avant-garde, yet *Orlando*, although having many of the qualities of an 'art' production, has a strong narrative drive.

Potter's earlier films could be termed feminist, but in more recent years she has found the term problematic and in an interview with Penny Florence explains, 'I can't use the word anymore because it's become debased' (Florence 1993: 279).

Whether Potter will be able to continue to make films with a strong personal vision, as Peter Greenaway and the late Derek Jarman have done, will depend very much on funding, but Potter is optimistic that there has been a change in attitude towards women film-makers, that they are now seen as just directors. *Thriller* (1979) is a feminist reading of Puccini's opera *La Bohème* (1895). Linking together feminist, Marxist and psychoanalytic theory, the film is a critique of the constraints of patriarchy, the lack of female voice and woman as object and victim. The film was funded by the Arts Council, and although avant-garde in style received much interest from quite a wide audience, though it was by no means a mainstream success. Ann Kaplan explains why the film aroused such interest: 'It is, first, an imaginative intervention in the dominance of a certain kind of classical narrative (the sentimental romance and the detective story) making a critique of such narratives into a alternative art form' (Kaplan 1983: 161).

• **Plate 9.13** *The Tango Lesson* (Sally Potter, 1997)
Sally Potter's latest film has wonderful cinematography but lacks the wit and sparkle of *Orlando* (1993).

☐ CASE STUDY 5: *THE GOLD DIGGERS* (1983)

The Gold Diggers is a full-length film made with a grant from the British Film Institute (BFI). The film explores the relationship between women and power, money and patriarchy: developing and continuing themes from *Thriller*. The film has two main characters, both women: the early nineteenth-century heroine (Julie Christie) and the modern heroine (Colette Lafone). Potter purposefully and ideologically chose an all-women crew to work on the film, including women musicians.

On its release in 1983 the film was poorly received, partly because of its complex yet plotless narrative which seemed to exemplify some of the problems of art and avant-garde cinema in the early 1980s – a lack of awareness of audience.

Potter has discussed the problems of the film, explaining the difficulties of working collaboratively with others (which was the case with *The Gold Diggers*). She said that the film 'came out of a practice in the theatre of going with the moment, incorporating ideas, and not being completely text-bound' (Ehrenstein 1993: 3).

Imagery in the film is visually arresting, often verging on the surreal, but the script is stilted, elliptical and difficult to follow, being almost a series of vignettes. A shorter, tighter script might have been more effective in retaining an audience.

The modern heroine in the film plays the part of investigator and observer of events, an observer of patriarchy, which is seen as disempowering women. Patriarchy is threatening, bureaucratic, intimidating and ultimately ridiculous (compare with *A Question of Silence*). In the scene when Colette is working at a VDU in an office with other women, the only male is the manager who imperiously surveys the scene. Colette asks him to explain what the information is on the screen, to which he patronisingly replies, 'Just do your job'.

The Gold Diggers was filmed in black and white, and is a bleak film suggesting that woman is either revered or reviled by man. *Orlando*, in contrast, is full of colour and optimism.

• **Plate 9.14** *The Gold Diggers* (Sally Potter, 1993)
A search for identity.

☐ CASE STUDY 6 : *ORLANDO* (1993)

Potter's film is an adaptation of a Virginia Woolf novel and is made by her own company, Adventure Pictures, formed with *Orlando*'s producer Christopher Sheppard. The film budget was £2 million, making it a medium-size British film, though the quality of the production gives it the look of a much more expensive film. In contrast to *The Gold Diggers*, in which the crew was all-female, a mixed crew worked on *Orlando*.

After the experience of *The Gold Diggers*, Potter took great care to ensure that the script was just right, doing endless rewrites until she was happy with it. The developmental process took years rather than months but ensured a clear narrative that drives the film powerfully forward.

The film is concerned with two central ideas: the concept of immortality and the changing of gender. Orlando travels 400 years, from the Elizabethan age (Queen Elizabeth is played by Quentin Crisp, introducing the theme of playing with gender) to the present day, changing sex in 1700. The *mise en scène* is sumptuous and exotic, richly coloured and textured, enhanced by the camera work; the scene when Orlando moves into the Victorian age, for instance, is full of movement and dynamism, the gorgeous costumes swirl forward into the future.

Aspects of feminism, gender, imperialism and politics are part of the narrative discourse – areas that are often anathema to a film's success. Yet *Orlando* has been received with much acclaim: David Ehrenstein in *Film Quarterly* compares the film to Orson Welles' *The Magnificent Ambersons*: 'Like no other film of the moment, it demonstates that art and pleasure are not mutually exclusive categories of experience' (Ehrenstein 1993: 2).

Potter is more concerned with gender than feminism, although the vulnerability of women is a key theme: when Orlando becomes female she loses her home, her financial power. She then only has her body, her femaleness to bargain with, which she refuses to share in marriage with the archduke, who sternly reminds her she has no property and will suffer the ignomy of remaining a spinster.

The film has a strong sense of playfulness, from the knowing looks that Orlando gives to the audience, to the confusion of sexual identity. When Orlando becomes

• **Plate 9.15** *Orlando*
(Sally Potter, 1993)

female in a beautifully filmed metamorphosis, she boldly states to the camera, 'same person, just a different sex'. Potter explains:

I don't think the book so much explores sexual identity as dissolves them, and it's that kind of melting and shifting where nothing is ever what it seems for male or female that I think is the strength of the book and which I wanted to reproduce in the film.

(Florence 1993: 283)

Potter put much thought into the development of Orlando's character. This led her to consider what it means to be 'male' and the dangers and difficulties of being masculine. At times gender differences are de-emphasised, for instance, the clothing worn by the young Orlando is not much less constricting than that worn by the female. However, when Orlando returns to England as a woman, her dress is used as a powerful symbol of her womanhood and the constraints and limitations that imposes. As a woman in the seventeenth century, Orlando must curb her sense of adventure and her inquiring mind. Orlando is offered the final insult when told that she may as well be dead as be a woman and has to endure the threat of house and wealth being taken away from her.

Orlando rebelliously enters the Victorian age, a heroine of melodrama ready to be rescued by a handsome, romantic hero who becomes her lover, and fathers her daughter. Although Orlando has lost her home and refuses to follow her lover, she retains her independence and moves forward in time to successfully negotiate life in modern Britain.

The film finishes on a positive note. There is hope for the future in the form of a child and we are told 'ever since she let go of the past she found her life was beginning'. Orlando is at peace.

Orlando, in style, has moved away from the avant-garde towards the mainstream without being conventionalised by narrative form. Potter's film is a stimulating and rich attack on the senses and has a discourse that, although concerned with gender, seems to suggest a blending of the sexes rather than a separation, which many of the earlier feminist films, like *A Question of Silence* (1982), *The Gold Diggers* (1983) and Lezli-Ann Barrett's *An Epic Poem* (1982), seemed to encourage.

☐ CASE STUDY 7: *THE PIANO* (1993)

Jane Campion is one of the few women directors who could justifiably be called an auteur director. Her early films, in particular, *An Angel at my Table* (1987) and *Sweetie* (1989) brought Campion's unusual and darkly humorous films to the attention of an art house audience. It was *The Piano* (1993) though, a complex, poetic film, which received international recognition, gaining a number of Oscar nominations and receiving the award for Best Script (Jane Campion), Best Actress (Holly Hunter) and Best Supporting Actor (Anna Paquin).

At times melodrama, at times art film in its expressionistic style, *The Piano* portrays the experiences of Ada, an elective-mute woman who emigrates to New Zealand from Scotland with her daughter Flora. Ada's father has arranged her marriage to Stewart, a man she has never met. Ada brings her beloved piano to New Zealand which causes conflict with her new husband. This tension results in an employee of Stewart, Baines, showing sympathy for Ada's predicament; Ada falls in love with him and they eventually have a passionate affair.

The conventions of melodrama are shown in the portrayal of the central relationships; Ada is wilful and stubborn, yet is desired by two men who try to control and contain her. The element of hysteria typical of melodrama is evident at the film's climax when Stewart severs Ada's finger, in a symbolic gesture that suggests castration. Music in melodrama is an important signifier in expressing emotion; in *The Piano* it is used as a motif for Ada's feelings and emotions that she cannot express verbally. Yet Ada's lack of voice makes it difficult to identify with her as a truly romantic heroine. The film also takes on many of the conventions of an art film in its heavy use of symbolism, its expressionistic style and a narrative which sees the piano as an extension of Ada, which in turn becomes a fetishised object of desire.

On one level the film recounts the tale of a woman at the mercy of a patriarchal society in which she has little power: Ada is forced into an arranged marriage by her father, treated as a commodity by Stewart, and is initially seen as little more than a prostitute by Baines; but it is Baines who is able to transfer the relationship from one of power to one of compassion and tenderness.

Many aspects of the film though represent the female as strong-willed and powerful. Ada is determined and obstinate, even though she loses a finger because of her insistence on continuing to see Baines. Flora is a replica of her mother, feisty and determined. The other female characters, despite having a two-dimensional, pantomime dame quality, are strong and vigorous. The interior scenes also infuse the film with a positive quality around the home, which is always a safe haven, whether as protection from the weather, the Maoris, or sensual and sexual pleasure.

Gender roles in *The Piano* are strongly defined through clothing. Ada is shown in tight-fitting tops and waist-clinching dresses, not only emphasising how tiny and delicate she is but also her sexuality. The whiteness of Ada's skin is contrasted by the dark clothing she wears; her voluminous Victorian clothing is shown to be impractical and absurd in the New Zealand climate, yet Ada often looks comfortable in her dress as opposed to Stewart, whose too-tight clothing makes him seem absurd and stiff (Campion purposefully made his clothes too tight to enhance this point.) Baines, in contrast, is at home in this environment and his dress is loose and casual which also reflects a shifting of his European values. The Maoris, although often seeming like comic caricatures, are shown dressed in a mix of male and female clothing suggesting an ambivalence regarding their gender roles.

Ada's underwear becomes an object of fascination for the audience and fetishisation for Baines. We frequently see Ada in petticoats and underwear, whilst playing with Flora but especially so in her relationship with Baines; in one scene Baines smells the top she has just taken off, in another sequence he becomes fascinated by a tiny hole in her stocking which reveals a glimpse of skin.

Campion undercuts conventional audience expectations of gender in the development of their relationship: it is Baines' first removal of clothing which is so startling for both the audience and Ada, until then it is Ada who has been placed in a vulnerable, feminine position. In this sequence there is a reversal of cinematic conventions, it is Ada who removes the curtain (coded red for danger) which reveals Baines unclothed, but he also represents a threat, the game has moved on from being sensual to directly sexual. Ada is confronted by Baines' naked body and, as we see this sequence from her point of view, we cut to a reaction shot which is at first startled but she does not look away, in fact her eye-line suggests a downward look. In this case the gaze, the look, is not male but female.

Much of *The Piano* is seen from Ada's point of view, emphasising our identification with her. Indeed Ada's lack of voice can be seen as a symbol of her withdrawal from patriarchal society. We hear Ada's voiceover at the beginning and end of the film, but all other communication is through the visuals and music. Although we frequently see shots of Ada's face, which is generally expressionless, almost blank, it is difficult to identify with her as one would in a conventional narrative.

The act of looking, the gaze, takes on a complex relationship between the audience, the spectator and the different characters in the film. A key sequence which exemplifies this is when the relationship between Ada and Baines changes to one of mutual attraction; firstly Flora spies on the couple and this changes her relationship with her mother, an element of jealousy is brought in but the scene also moves Flora into a new sphere, she is a voyeur made aware of her mother's sexuality. In a later scene Stewart spies on Ada and Baines making love, and stays there watching, clearly aroused by what he sees, in an instance of what is called the scopophilic drive. Yet the audience does not stay with Stewart, the film cuts to an interior medium-shot and the sequence is imbued with a golden hue, sensual rather than explicit or fetishising the female body, as is so usual in patriarchal cinema. There is no sense of the couple being aware of an audience, or Ada's body being the subject of the 'male gaze'. Neither looks at the camera, yet the camera contrasts Baines' muscular, squat masculine body with Ada's tiny feminine one. The sequence concludes with a shot of Stewart surveying the couple from underneath the floor boards, when a button from Ada's dress falls through a hole on to his face. Stewart is in the position of passive voyeur, but the scene also drives home his ineffectualness, his impotence, with a deep sense of irony.

A later sequence again reverses the traditional function of the look as instrument of the male gaze; when Ada is in bed with Stewart she explores his body by touching and stroking his back down to his buttocks, strangely sensual rather than sexual. It is unusual in film for the male body to be explored and eroticised in this way. Stewart is bathed in a warm light and has a passive position enforced upon him by Ada, when he attempts to be active Ada rejects him.

Patriarchal cinema generally fetishes sex by emphasising voyeurism and fragmenting the female body or associating it with related objects or clothing such as underwear. Campion plays with this convention by showing Baines fetishise Ada's clothing but extends this to include the piano; so although the piano functions as Ada's voice the fetishisation takes on a surreal, almost absurd quality. In a perceptive article on the use of clothing in *The Piano*, Stella Bruzzi comments that the film is a 'complex feminist displacement of the conventionalised objectification of the woman's form dominated by scopophilia and fetishism' (Bruzzi 1995: 257).

By the final stage of the film Ada's life has affected us deeply; the gradual building up of empathy with Ada has been subtly woven into the film, so that when the final confrontation between her and Stewart occurs we are almost as traumatised as Ada by what happens. Stewart's retribution is terrible and could be seen as a symbol of phallic dismemberment or clitoridectomy. Stewart's aim is to control Ada's sexuality and spiritedness. In this sequence we continually have reaction shots of Ada and are placed to suffer with her. She seems to visibly shrink before us as she falls to the ground fully punished for her transgression. Stewart has now taken on the role of evil persecutor and in the narrative of melodrama she has to leave or be destroyed. The axe can be seen as a symbol of phallic destruction associated with the Europeans; in the Bluebeard shadow play the axe is used to kill his wives and, in an acting out of the play in an earlier sequence, foreshadows Stewart attacking Ada; Stewart is identified with the axe, seen carrying it, chopping wood and trees which directly associate him with patriarchal and colonial destruction.

The landscape not only acts as a metaphor for Ada's state of mind but is also used to inform us about the people in the film and their characters. The boggy undergrowth which Ada finds it so difficult to move in suggests her inability to escape, she is trapped. This motif is constantly reinforced by the cinematography, where the forest is the limits of Ada's horizons; she lives in a dense, almost knotted forest paralleling the

• **Plate 9.16** *The Piano* (Jane Campion, 1993) Mother and daughter are isolated in an alien environment.

wild woods of folk tale which are suffused with erotic symbolic significance. Stewart's immediate world is surrounded by grey, petrified, half-dead tree trunks. He is referred to as 'old dry balls' by the Maoris and the contrast in landscape between him and Baines emphasises Stewart's impotence and inability to give love. Baines' hut is lush and verdant, part of the forest with which he is at ease.

Ada seems to represent western femininity in contrast with the Maori women who are coarse and loud, making lewd suggestions to Baines. Yet Ada, by her association with Baines, is different: she is able to blend in to the woods wearing garments which seem to take on the same hues of blue and green which predominate throughout the film. It could be argued that Campion uses stock stereotypes of the Maoris as noble natives, natural and easily able to express their sexuality, so giving a rather superficial look at the Maoris who are seen in terms of civilised versus uncivilised.[16]

Perhaps one of the most interesting aspects of *The Piano* is the mother/daughter relationship, a theme which is often explored through melodrama; in the film Ada and Flora seem to have a symbiotic relationship which is only broken by the intrusion of Stewart and Baines. Flora is literally Ada's voice, acting as a mediator between Ada and the rest of the world. The two are often shown in tight, claustrophobic shots, and there is a sense of almost Oedipal jealousy; for instance Flora is in her mother's bed whenever Stewart visits. When Flora eventually aligns with Stewart to stem Ada's affair with Baines, she precipitates his retribution on Ada; Flora chooses the path to Stewart rather than take the piano key, inscribed with words of love from Ada, to Baines. Flora has been introduced to the dangerous forces of sexuality and the film is to some extent a rites of passage for her. When these dark forces are unleashed Ada, in effect, uses her daughter as a go-between and their relationship is changed.

In the final stages of the film, the piano has become a tie with the past and in a symbolic gesture, when Ada is on the boat with Baines and Flora, she insists the piano is thrown overboard. Ada is pulled in too and we think the film will end on this tragic note, but she releases herself and in her voiceover tells us 'my will has chosen life'. Yet the life she has chosen, to live with Baines in Nelson as a piano teacher, does not seem convincing or a particularly satisfactory ending, at least not for a melodramatic heroine – she is now contained by Baines.

The Piano works on a visual, poetic level which is at times dark and disturbing, yet its central discourse is an exploration of sexuality, and especially female sexuality. Patriarchal filmic conventions are reversed in portraying a heroine who often has control of the look, the woman is subject rather than object and, at times, it is the male who is the object of the female gaze. But *The Piano* is much more than a reversal of patriarchal mainstream film conventions, it is one of the few films directed by a woman to achieve critical and financial success and yet still retain its art-house character.

NOTES

1 From an interview by the author with Kay Mander, film-maker, July 1990.

2 Ibid.

3 Suggested further reading: on the early feminist movement, K. Millett, *Sexual Politics* (Virago, London, 1977), and G. Greer, *The Female Eunuch* (Flamingo, London, 1971); and, more recently, M. Maynard, 'Current trends in feminist theory', *Social Studies Review* (Vol. 2, No. 3, 1987) p. 23.

4 Structuralism and Marxism have been, and still are, important concepts in the application of film theory and to some extent have affected film practice, particularly in the independent and workshop sector. For a good general background to these viewpoints read Chapters 1 and 2 of Robert Lapsley and Michael Westlake, *Film Theory: An Introduction* (Manchester University Press, Manchester, 1988).

5 For further discussion of woman's lack of place in art see Griselda Pollock and Roszika Parker, *Old Mistresses* (Routledge & Kegan Paul, London, 1981). Rosemary Betterton, *Looking On* (Pandore, London, 1987), is a useful and interesting collection of essays about images of women in art and the media.

6 See Jackie Byars, *All That Heaven Allows* (University of North Carolina Press, Chapel Hill, 1991), for discussion of melodrama and the female spectator.

7 See Jackie Stacey, *Desperately Seeking Difference* (Routledge, London and New York, 1992), for an interesting analysis of *Desperately Seeking Susan*.

8 If you are interested in reading more about Stuart Hall's important input into cultural studies theory, a good starting point is 'Encoding/Decoding', in *Culture, Media, Language* (Hutchinson, London, 1980).

9 For further discussion of how we negotiate with cultural texts, see C. Gledhill's 'Pleasurable Negotiations', in D. Pribram (ed.), *Female Spectators* (Verso, London and New York, 1988)

10 Janice Radway has thrown new light on to how women interpret fiction. Her theories can be usefully applied to other texts. For further detail see her *Reading the Romance* (Verso, London, 1987).

11 For further information on women working in the media read A.R. Muir's article 'The status of women working in film and television', in L. Gammon (ed.), *The Female Gaze* (The Women's Press, London, 1988). Also of interest is J.

Arthur's 'Technology and gender', in *Screen* (Vol. 30, nos 1 and 2, Winter/Spring 1989 pp. 40–59).

12 For a discussion of Channel Four's involvement with the workshop sector, see Lovell's article in *Screen* (Vol. 30, No. 1, 1990), pp. 102–8.

13 For Donald and Scanlon's article on whether *Thelma and Louise* is a feminist film, see their article 'Hollywood Feminism? Get Real!!', in *Trouble and Strife* (Vol. 25, Winter 1992) pp. 11–16.

14 Interview with Red Flannel, December 1993.

15 Ibid.

16 For further discussion on the relationship between the colonials and the Maoris portrayed in *The Piano*, see Linda Dyson's article in *Screen* (Vol. 36, No. 3, 1995) pp. 269–76.

FURTHER READING

Berger, J. *Ways of Seeing* (Penguin, London, 1972)

Betterton, R. *Looking On: Images of Femininity in the Visual Arts and the Media* (Pandora, London, 1987)

Brundsen, C. (ed.) *Films for Women* (British Film Institute, London, 1986)

Cook, P. and Dodd, P. (eds) *Women and Film: A 'Sight and Sound' Reader* (Scarlet Press, London, 1993)

Francke, L. *Script Girls* (British Film Institute, London, 1994)

Haskell, M. *From Reverence to Rape* (New English Library, London, 1973)

Kaplan, E.A. *Women and Film: Both Sides of the Camera* (Methuen, London, 1983)

Modleski, T. *The Women Who Knew Too Much* (Methuen, London, 1988)

Mulvey, L. *Visual and Other Pleasures* (Macmillan, London, 1989)

Penley, C. *Feminism and Film Theory* (Routledge/British Film Institute, London, 1988)

Pilling, J. (ed.) *Women and Animation: A Compendium* (British Film Institute, London, 1992)

Pollock, G. *Vision and Difference* (Routledge, London, 1988)

Pribram, E. (ed.) *Female Spectators* (Verso, London, 1988)

Tasker, Y. *Working Girls* (Routledge, London, 1998)

Thornham, S. *Passionate Detachments* (Arnold, London, 1997)

Women: A Cultural Review (Vol. 2, No. 1, Spring 1991) – the whole issue is devoted to women and the media.

Zoonen, L. van *Feminist Media Studies* (Sage, London, 1994)

A composite information pack on *Thelma and Louise* and *The Piano* is available from the BFI, 21 Stephen Street, London W1P 2LN.

Periodicals are extremely useful to refer to for further reading; they tend to be more topical and up-to-date. Look out for articles on women and film in the following: *Feminist Review*, *Women: A Cultural Review*, *Camera Obscura* and *Sight and Sound*.

FURTHER VIEWING

This chapter has focused mainly on women in independent film in the UK and is therefore a selective view, having only touched on cinema by women in other countries such as the US and the Netherlands. Worldwide, women's cinema is rich and varied – countries as small and culturally diverse as New Zealand and Tunisia have contributed to this upsurge. As more women enter the film industry and take on key roles, the number of mainstream films by women will hopefully increase. Films to look out for in this category which would provide interesting discussion regarding representations of men and women are: *Wayne's World*, Penelope Spheeris (US 1991); *The Piano*, Jane Campion (Australia/France 1993).

Other chapters in this book refer to films by women; see Chapters 8 and 10. Unfortunately, many films by women are difficult to obtain. The BFI and Cinenova (a film and video distributor which promotes films by women) hold a number of titles for rental. The latter's comprehensive catalogue is well worth looking through. The following films can all be hired through Cinenova at 113 Roman Road, London E2 0HN (Tel. 0181 981 6828): *To Be a Woman*, Jill Craigie (UK 1953); *Women of the Rhondda*, Esther Ronay (UK 1972); *A Comedy in Six Unnatural Acts*, Jan Oxenburg (US 1975); *An Epic Poem*, Lezli-Ann Barrett (UK 1982); *Born in Flames*, Lizzie Borden (US 1983);

Mam, Red Flannel (UK 1988); *Otherwise Engaged*, Red Flannel (UK 1991).

The following films are all available for rental from the BFI and provide stimulating viewing: *A Question of Silence*, Marlene Gorris (Holland 1982) (see case study 3, p. 293); *Orlando*, Sally Potter (UK 1993) (see case study 6, p. 298); *Wayward Girls And Wicked Women*, Vols 1, 2 and 3 (1992) (various women animators, often witty, poignant and hard-hitting); *Sweetie*, Jane Campion (Australia 1989) (better than *The Piano*, it's anarchic, funny and strange!); *Dream On*, Amber Films (UK 1992) (focuses on women on a north-east estate; realistic, hard-hitting, with some lighter moments); *Bhaji on the Beach*, Gurinder Chada (UK 1994) (an Asian women's group go to Blackpool! A sharp script takes on race, culture, gender and family in contemporary Britain).

Sally Potter's *The Tango Lesson* (1997) is well worth watching as part of a body of her films, and is now available on video. *Female Perversions* (1997), directed by Susan Streitfeld, contains many interesting ideas but fails to engage. It remains worth watching because it is so unusual for an avant-garde style film to have fairly high production values and be made by a woman! *Mrs Dalloway* (1997), directed by Marlene Gorris, would be interesting to compare with *Orlando*, as examples of adaptations of Virginia Woolf novels.

RESOURCE CENTRES

http://www.feminist.org
A website with information on film, arts and literature of particular interest to women.

http://www.mediacube.de/links/Misc_Film.html
A website that contains miscellaneous information about cinema and films, with a women cinema reference guide, listings for the African Film Festival, Independent Film and Video Makers Resource Guide, and a link to the US National Film Registry.

Chapter 10

Lesbian and gay cinema

Chris Jones

■ **Representation**   308
■ **Definitions and developments – homosexual and gay**   309
■ **Audiences**   310
■ **Lesbian and Gay Film Festivals**   311
■ **Gay sensibility**   313
■ **Lesbian and gay film study**   315
■ **Critical re-readings**   315
■ **Some films with gay themes**   320
☐ Case study 1: *Victim* (Basil Dearden, UK 1961)   321
☐ Case study 2: *Desert Hearts* (Donna Deitch, US 1985)   324
☐ Case study 3: *The Living End* (Gregg Araki, US 1993)   327
☐ Case study 4: *Looking for Langston* (Isaac Julien, UK 1994)   330
☐ Case study 5: *Go Fish* (Rose Troche, US 1994)   332
■ **Conclusion: a queer diversity**   335
■ **Further reading**   341
■ **Further viewing**   341
■ **Resource centres**   344

■ Lesbian and gay cinema

heterosexual
A word used to name and describe a person whose main sexual feelings are for people of the opposite sex.

gender
A name for the social and cultural construction of a person's sex and sexuality. Gender, sex and sexuality can overlap but are by no means an exact match. It is this 'mismatch' which has generated a fascinating body of film production and criticism.

REPRESENTATION

Representation is a social process which occurs in the interactions between a reader or viewer, and a text. It produces signs which reflect underlying sets of ideas and attitudes. In her essay 'Visual Pleasure and Narrative Cinema', Laura Mulvey (1995) suggested ways in which a viewer of classic Hollywood films is addressed as male by being encouraged to adopt the viewpoint, the 'look', of the male protagonist. Although she later adjusted these ideas to cater for such female-orientated Hollywood genres as the melodrama, Mulvey's argument is based on the traditional psychoanalytic notion of male/female definitions and oppositions. Nowhere does she take into account the extent to which her argument is geared towards a **heterosexual** look. Nevertheless, her ideas about the positioning of the film spectator and film-maker within the **gender** system have been very influential. They have led to much constructive critical investiga-

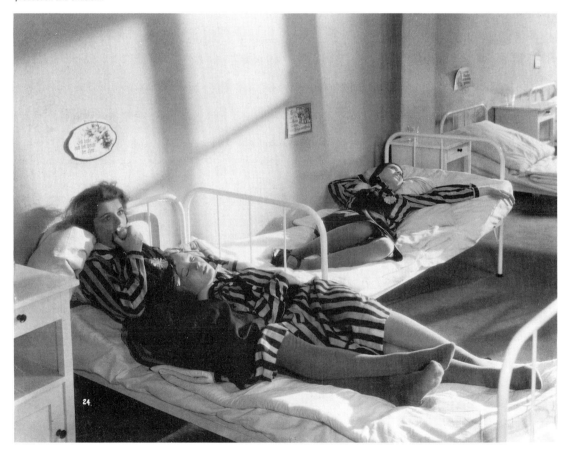

• **Plate 10.1** *Girls in Uniform* (Leontine Sagan, Germany 1931)
Based on the play by lesbian poet Christa Winsloe, the film portrays the friendship and support given to the main character, Manuela, in her love for her teacher.

tion into how different kinds of film-makers and viewers affect meaning-making processes according to their race and **sexuality**, as well as gender. Such investigation has also started to take into account a variety of viewing formats based on video and the TV screen.

An integral part of the process of reading a film is the use of stereotyping, the depiction of a character according to their perceived membership of a certain social group, such as Asians, mothers-in-law, businessmen, lesbians. This is a form of shorthand; a few visual or sound cues give the audience a view of a certain type of person which is widely accepted. The nature of this view is generally shaped by the dominant groups in a society.

In film, representation is organised through the signs of *mise en scène*, editing, sound and narrative patterns. The final part of this chapter will deal with the representation of gay people in a selection of films.

DEFINITIONS AND DEVELOPMENTS – HOMOSEXUAL AND GAY

Men and women who relate sexually to members of their own **sex** have always existed, but the modern term 'homosexuality' was invented in 1869 by a Swiss doctor. It was not commonly used in the English language until the 1890s, the decade that saw the birth of cinema. The term **homosexual** was partly inherited from nineteenth-century ideas of disease. Previously, same-sex relations had been predominantly characterised by notions of sin inherited from the medieval period. These commonly-held associations continued into this century as German film-makers produced a number of works campaigning for more enlightened attitudes in sexual and social matters. *Different from the Others* (*Anders als die Andern*, 1919) was a success on first release. Even though the main character, a homosexual musician, finally poisons himself, the dour storyline is countered by sections of the film in which Dr Magnus Hirschfield puts forward an affirmative view of homosexuality. Hirschfield was a sexual researcher and social reformer whose world-renowned Institute was later destroyed by the Nazis. Within a year of its release the film was subject to censorship and now exists only in fragments, although these have since been assembled and shown. *Girls in Uniform* (*Mädchen in Uniform*, Leontine Sagan, 1931) can still be seen today as a major portrayal of anti-authoritarianism, with the love for each other of its two female protagonists triumphing over the oppressive regime of their boarding school.

During the Second World War, with its movements of population and large numbers of servicemen and -women being thrown closely together in same-sex barracks, many people became aware of homosexuality on a personal and social level. This resulted in two parallel and contradictory developments in North America and Europe during the 1950s; increasing growth of communities of homosexuals and lesbians in big cities, and systematic attempts by those in authority to prevent such developments.

These communities began to demand and develop wider networks of meeting-places and entertainment, including film. Early examples of films made with such audiences in mind are the physique films of Dick Fontaine, who worked in San Francisco from the late 1940s. Such film activity mainly took place within the art-film world, and involved small-budget production and viewing in clubs and homes. Jean Genet's *Un chant d'amour* (1950), with its sexually charged images of handsome male prisoners, became a cult film, as did Kenneth Anger's *Fireworks* (1947), a young man's sexual fantasy involving sailors. From the 1960s the **homoerotic** films of Andy Warhol and George Kuchar began to find wider audiences. It was during this period that the word **gay** began to be used to both denote and describe a male homosexual person.

---

sexuality
A name for the sexual feelings and behaviour of a person. When applied to groups of people (e.g. heterosexuals) ideas of social attitude and organisation are implied.

For further discussion of representation and feminism, see Chapter 9.

See Chapter 11 for discussion of representation in British film.

For detailed discussion of spectatorship, see Chapter 5.

sex
A word used to denote and describe a person's physical type according to their genital make-up. In academic discourse, this is primarily a scientific term.

homosexual
A word used to name and describe a person whose main sexual feelings are for people of the same sex. Mainly, but not exclusively, used in reference to males.

homoerotic
A description of a text – prose, poem, film, painting, photograph, etc. – conveying an enjoyable sense of same-sex attraction.

gay
A description of strong, positive sexual love and attraction between members of the same sex, used by extension to describe cultural products, such as film and video, concerned with similar themes. Mainly referring to males, it can also be used for any person.

In 1969, for the first time in modern history, homosexuals in a small New York bar called the Stonewall Inn fought back against a police raid. A major riot ensued and the New York Gay Liberation Front was immediately formed, soon to be followed by similar organisations across the world. Members of the new movement adopted the word 'gay' for its positive connotations of happiness, and because they wanted to use a term to describe themselves that had not been chosen by outsiders. For them, the term represented a way of demonstrating pride in their identity, the power of political organisation, and a distinct culture. The term was initially conceived as describing both men and women, but women soon began to feel marginalised within the movement, and the term **lesbian** came back in general use during the 1970s to signal the distinctness and strength of women.

It is the very different emotional connotations of these varying terms which led critic Vito Russo to say: 'There never have been lesbians or gay men in Hollywood films. Only homosexuals' (Russo 1987: 245).

AUDIENCES

Gay men, like men in general, have on average more spending power than women, despite Equal Opportunities legislation in many countries. With gay liberation came a greatly expanded network of related commercial goods and services; nightclubs, shops, clothing, books and magazines, the majority of which were aimed at men. The same conditions apply in the developing structures of film and cinema aimed at lesbians and gays. Men constituted the main organised audience for this type of production. Even those films with non-commercial financial backing, such as the work of Derek Jarman and Isaac Julien, tended to attract funds partly because of the perceived existence of this established gay male audience.

Lesbian film and video developed in parallel with the emerging women's movement, almost always with less finance than its male equivalent, and found a base in film clubs

lesbian
A word used to name and describe a woman whose main sexual feelings are for other women. Coined as a medical term in the late nineteenth century, the word has been invested post-Stonewall with new ideas of openness and liberation. It can also be used to describe cultural products, such as film and video, dealing with lesbian themes.

See Chapter 2, pp. 44–7, for further discussion of film audiences.

and workshops. The American film and video artist Su Friedrich actively prefers this type of outlet as a way of reaching lesbian audiences with films such as *Damned If You Don't* (US 1987). As a result of this production and viewing background, and the modest financial levels this involves, many lesbian films are less than feature length. *Home Movie* (US 1972) by Jan Oxenberg is a modest but highly effective twelve-minute film, which edits home-movie footage from the director's own childhood with scenes of her adult life as a lesbian to make the viewer amusingly aware of the conventions of family life. Her *Comedy in Six Unnatural Acts* (US 1975; 26 minutes) presents six short, staged scenes dealing with the foibles of lesbian life, and debunking a few myths about **butch/femme** role-playing.

LESBIAN AND GAY FILM FESTIVALS

After 1945, film festivals became recognised across Europe and America as serving several useful functions. They act as a marketplace for film distributors to view and possibly buy new product and allow producers, scriptwriters and others to gather and discuss new projects. Critics attending festivals alert wider audiences to new and interesting work. Audiences can view and enjoy a wide range of films they would not normally see in the cinema.

Since the 1970s, a worldwide circuit of Lesbian and Gay Film Festivals has grown up. San Francisco was the first to start operating, followed by London, Paris, New York, Toronto, Berlin and others. These events, often accompanied by lively lectures and discussions, serve all the purposes already mentioned for lesbian and gay producers, directors, critics and audiences. Their development has gone hand-in-hand with the flowering of gay political consciousness; Rosa Von Praunheim's early gay liberationist film *It is Not the Homosexual Who is Perverse, But the Situation in Which He Finds Himself* (W. Germany 1970) was typical of the kind of work that found a viewing base in such festivals. In particular, these festivals have helped to bring small-scale film and video work and feature films from developing countries to the attention of wider lesbian and gay audiences. An example of the latter is the work of Lino Brocka from the Philippines, whose treatment of homosexual themes contains messages of tolerance and democracy not always acceptable to established authorities in his own country. Recent festivals have included work from Israel, Taiwan, Mexico, India and Japan.

Another form of film-making given wider distribution through the festival circuit is feature-length documentary. *The Times of Harvey Milk* (Robert Epstein, US 1985) chronicles the rise to power, and tragic assassination, of the San Francisco city supervisor who was one of the America's first openly gay elected politicians. *Before Stonewall: The Making of a Gay and Lesbian Community* (Greta Schiller and Robert Rosenberg, US 1985) vividly recalls gay and lesbian lives in the years during and following the Second World War. All these films wove together interviews, contemporary newsreel film and photographs. Through fostering cultural and historical consciousness, such films as these aided the growing self-awareness of lesbian and gay communities in the US and elsewhere.

As the AIDS crisis arose in the 1980s, this newly developed network of audiences and exhibition venues was particularly receptive to the wide variety of film and video work created around this topic, such as Rosa Von Praunheim's *A Virus Knows No Morals* (W. Germany 1986). Short videos such as John Greyson's *The ADS Epidemic* (Canada 1986) boosted morale by warning in a jokey way against ADS (Acquired Dread of Sex) while reminding people about safe sex. Bill Sherwood's outstanding independent film *Parting Glances* (US 1986) presents a mature, low-key portrait of a group of New Yorkers in the late 1980s. A central character of the group is Nick, who has AIDS. The character is portrayed with gentle humour and his condition is accepted and

butch
Description of behaviour-patterns – such as aggression, sexual dominance – traditionally associated with masculinity.

femme
Description of behaviour-patterns – such as gentleness, sexual passivity, concern with dress and appearance – traditionally associated with femininity.

For further discussion of film distribution and exhibition, see Chapter 2.

See Chapter 7 for further reference to lesbian and gay documentary film.

• **Plate 10.3** *Before Stonewall* (Greta Schiller and Robert Rosenberg, US 1985)
A full-length film documentary about the gay and lesbian movement in the US from the 1920s to the 1960s. This film vividly evokes lesbian and gay life in the US before gay liberation and forms part of a growing body of work on lesbian and gay history.

• **Plate 10.4** *Parting Glances* (Bill Sherwood, US 1986)
The two lovers live through their ups and downs with credible warmth and humour.

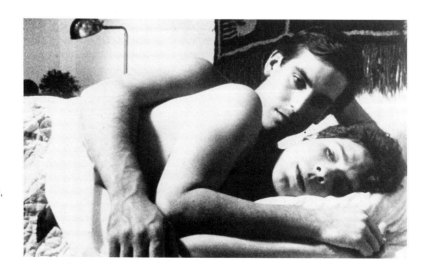

supported by those around him. *Common Threads: Stories from the Quilt* (Robert Epstein and Jeffrey Freedman, US 1989) is a full-length documentary chronicling the stories of a group of people who have lost loved ones to AIDS and contributed panels to the memorial quilt. We see moving interviews with, among others, the parents of a haemophiliac boy, the lesbian spouse of a gay man by whom she has had a child, the widow of a drug addict struggling to bring up her children, and Vito Russo talking of the death of his lover. The final scene, with acres of quilt laid out in the grounds adjoining the White House in Washington, is an inspiring tribute to human solidarity in a crisis.

GAY SENSIBILITY

In a book published by the British Film Institute to coincide with the first ever Lesbian and Gay Film Festival at the National Film Theatre, London, in 1977, the critic Jack Babuscio wrote:

I define gay sensibility as a creative energy reflecting a consciousness that is different from the mainstream; a heightened awareness of certain human complications of feeling that spring from the fact of social oppression; in short, a perception of the world which is coloured, shaped, directed and defined by the fact of one's gayness.

(Babuscio 1977: 40)

In a key essay, 'Rejecting Straight Ideals: Gays in Film', to be found in the book *Jump Cut* (Steven 1985 – see Further reading), Richard Dyer challenged Babuscio's emphasis on oppression as a mainspring for gay sensibility. He says this sensibility must be understood as 'something that has been and is produced and praised in history and culture' (ibid., p. 287). For Dyer, oppression 'merely provides the conditions in relation to which oppressed people create their own subculture and attendant sensibility' and is not the defining factor as Babuscio perceives it.

In his essay, Dyer makes a convincing and clear argument based on the idea of what he calls 'the sexual **ideology** of our culture', that is the idea that society and culture, through structures such as the family and artefacts such as film, impose a particular view of what it considers correct sexual behaviour (ibid., p. 294). This view includes a dominance of the heterosexual viewpoint and antipathy towards the homosexual one. Homosexuality, according to Dyer, is predominantly seen from a heterosexual viewpoint in most mainstream films. As examples he cites the image of homosexuality as a sickness and a problem in *Victim* (Basil Dearden, UK 1961) and an endless succession of gay and lesbian characters as vampires, psychos and criminals (which still continues). However, as Dyer points out, ideology is contradictory and ambiguous, full of what he calls 'gaps and fissures' through which film-makers and audiences can make new, alternative meanings (ibid., p. 294). This process sometimes involves an attitude of conscious, ironic distancing on the part of a spectator known as **camp**, traditionally associated with gay audiences. Critic Susan Sontag describes camp as 'one way of seeing the world as an aesthetic phenomenon ... not in terms of beauty, but in terms of degree of artifice, of stylisation' (Sontag 1982: 106). The concept is useful when considering how lesbian and gay audiences often view mainstream representations.

Critical awareness and discussion of gay sensibility and established sexual ideology, a concept that was later labelled 'heterosexism', started to be shared by increasing numbers of people: audiences, critics and film-makers. Film production in this area continued to take place mainly within the structures of alternative or art cinema, although Hollywood made occasional attempts to exploit what was seen as an increasingly open gay audience, and a greater interest in gay themes by non-gays. Examples

ideology
A set of ideas and attitudes held so much in common by most members of a society that they are seen as part of the natural order.

For further discussion of the relationship between film, ideology and society, see Chapter 9 and Chapter 11.

camp
A critical attitude which involves looking at texts less as reflections of reality than as constructed sets of words, images and sounds at a distance from reality. The attitude often involves irony or detachment when considering this distance. See 'Notes on Camp' (1982) by Susan Sontag.

• **Plate 10.5** *The Boys in the Band* (William Friedkin, US 1970)
This pre-liberation film contains an array of stereotypes, sometimes hilarious, often controversial.

of such products are *The Boys in the Band* (William Friedkin, 1970), which exploited the sensationalistic stereotypes of emotional trauma, and *Making Love* (Arthur Hiller, 1982), an over-sweet romantic treatment of male love. *Cruising* (William Friedkin, 1980) equates homosexuality with pathological violence. These, and many other mainstream films such as Jonathan Demme's *Philadelphia* (1993) could profitably be examined using Dyer's notion of sexual ideology.

As a concept useful in the study of film, gay sensibility can be defined as a developed awareness of sexual variation. This does not automatically mean that a film-maker or viewer has to be gay or lesbian to be able to present or appreciate themes and issues connected with gay people, but such awareness can open up rich creative possibilities. David Cronenberg's films, such as *Dead Ringers* (Canada 1988), make viewers uncomfortably aware of the fragile limits of conventional masculinity. While one can debate what exactly constitutes a 'lesbian film' or a 'gay film', gay sensibility can enrich film production and appreciation for gays and non-gays.

LESBIAN AND GAY FILM STUDY

The following elements can be identified as constituting lesbian and gay film study:

1 Re-readings of films by lesbian and gay audiences and critics, often producing meanings and messages that were not consciously intended by their original makers.
2 Film and video work dealing sensitively and/or positively with lesbian and gay themes, characters and issues, often but not exclusively made by and/or for gay people.

These elements are centrally concerned with the issue of representation. At times these two elements can overlap, as will be shown, for example, in the reading of *Victim* (see case study 1, p. 321).

CRITICAL RE-READINGS

The possible meanings of a film, as with all signifying practices, reside in the interaction between the viewer and the text. Much work has been done in recent years on how subgroups within the wider popular audience arrive at their own particular meanings when watching a mainstream film. Lesbian and gay critics have been at the forefront of such 're-readings'. Here are some examples (references are to the books included in the Further reading list).

Vito Russo

Russo's work as a film critic and journalist included articles for *The Advocate* in the US and *Gay News* in the UK during the 1970s and 1980s. Parker Tyler's book *Screening the Sexes: Homosexuality in the Movies* opened up the field of study and analysis of lesbian and gay cinema in 1972, but Russo's *The Celluloid Closet: Homosexuality in the Movies* is now regarded as a major landmark. First published in 1981 and revised in 1987, the book has continued to influence later critical work in this area.

Russo combines a historical view of lesbian and gay people's contribution to Hollywood cinema with an awareness of representation and audience. Although it deals mainly with Hollywood product, in contrast to Tyler's work, Russo's book is packed with examples and ideas which have formed the basis of further research by new generations of critics and academics. He traces the images of lesbians and gay men in Hollywood film from relatively open portrayals in the silent and early sound eras. He outlines the development of what he calls 'the sissy image' as a coded portrayal of gay men after the introduction of the Production Code and goes on to outline how 'as an outlet for unspeakable ideas, then, the sissy often became a monster or an outlaw' (Russo 1987: 42). One example of new insights Russo has to offer is his interpretation of the monster in the horror films of gay director James Whale. He sees *Frankenstein* and *The Bride of Frankenstein* as images of unnameable experiences and feelings outside normal society.

Using cogently argued examples, Russo outlines gay invisibility in the Hollywood films of the 1950s, followed by marginality and violence in the 1960s and 1970s: 'in twenty-two of twenty-eight films dealing with gay subjects from 1962 to 1978, major gay characters on screen ended in suicide or death' (Russo 1987: 52). At the same time, he makes out a powerful argument about how gay men derived particular subcultural messages from *Rebel without a Cause* when empathising with the relationship

• **Plate 10.6** *Rebel without a Cause* (Nicholas Ray, US 1955)
The star images of Dean and Mineo were strong precursors of later gay images.

between Jim (James Dean) and Plato (Sal Mineo). Among the few positive examples he cites from this period are some British films. *The Family Way* (Roy Boulting, 1966) and *The Leather Boys* (Sidney Furie, 1964), are seen as illuminating portrayals of the way in which fear of homosexuality limits the feelings between men. He praises *The L-shaped Room* (Bryan Forbes, 1962) for its sensitive portrayal of an elderly lesbian music-hall artiste, and sees the character Geoff in Tony Richardson's *A Taste of Honey* (1961) as relatively sympathetic.

The emergence of neurotic, shadowy gay characters is discussed using *The Boys in the Band* and *The Killing of Sister George* (Robert Aldrich, US 1968). Russo's final argument, in the revised 1987 edition, is that worthwhile gay and lesbian cinema can only be developed and encouraged outside the traditional Hollywood power structures, and he outlines a range of examples of such positive work.

Richard Dyer

Richard Dyer has been lecturing and writing about lesbian and gay film for about twenty years, and currently teaches at the University of Warwick. His book, *Now You See It: Studies in Lesbian and Gay Film* (1990), is a comprehensive academic survey of the German films outlined earlier, as well as the work of Jean Genet and Kenneth Anger. It contains a particularly useful introduction to lesbian film and video-making of the postwar period.

Dyer is the author of many illuminating essays. His work on sexual ideology has already been mentioned, but he is perhaps best known for his work on stars. In *Heavenly Bodies: Film Stars and Society* (1987) Dyer investigates the cultural associations between Judy Garland's star image and gay male audiences from the 1950s onwards. He shows members of this audience strongly allying themselves with Garland's much-vaunted ability to fight back against oppression and with the status of outsider which her behaviour and personality often conferred on her.

As part of his study of the film noir *Gilda* (Charles Vidor, US 1946), Dyer teases out the film's homoerotic subtext, the sexually-charged dockside meeting between the Glen Ford character and the casino-owner which leads to the two men working closely together and pledging the firm friendship with 'no women' that is subsequently destroyed by the appearance of the *femme fatale*, played by Rita Hayworth. He relates this subtext to film noir traditions and the dominant postwar view of sexual relations. His essay, 'Homosexuality in Film Noir' (in Dyer 1993a) coherently shows how gay characters in this classic Hollywood genre were negatively portrayed in both appearance and behaviour. This is an important topic to investigate because, as Dyer points out, 'some of the first widely available images of homosexuality in our time were those provided by the American film noir' (Dyer 1993a: 52).

Dyer's later studies of star image include a seminal essay on Rock Hudson in relation to public perceptions of sexuality, both before and after Hudson's homosexuality became public knowledge (Dyer 1993b). Dyer cogently argues how knowledge of Hudson's sexuality greatly enriches a viewer's appreciation of the gender-play in the 1960s sex comedies in which he starred. He shows how such knowledge gives extra depth to Hudson's star performances in the famous sequence of 1950s melodramas directed by Douglas Sirk, such as *All That Heaven Allows* (US 1955).

Andrea Weiss

The work of Andrea Weiss, like that of other writers on lesbian film such as Mandy Merck, B. Ruby Rich and Judith Mayne, was nurtured within the feminist movement. Weiss works primarily as a film-maker. She was chief researcher on the documentary feature *Before Stonewall*, and has produced an equally well-researched book on lesbians in film, *Vampires and Violets* (1993).

In her book, Weiss clearly tackles the critical problems associated with identification and representation for lesbians. She states that 'identification involves both conscious and unconscious processes and cannot be reduced to a psychoanalytic model that sees sexual desire only in terms of the binary opposition of heterosexual masculinity and femininity; instead it involves varying degrees of subjectivity and distance depending upon race, class and sexual differences' (Weiss 1993: 40). This judgement reflects the questioning of Laura Mulvey's ideas on cinematic 'looking' referred to earlier, a critical practice which has grown steadily since the 1980s. Weiss gives her readers a fascinating set of studies to show how lesbian audiences of classic Hollywood cinema have used their own interpretations to empower themselves, and how lesbian film-makers have been able to make their own images. These studies range across Dorothy Arzner's *The Wild Party* (US 1929), star performances by Greta

For further discussion of Mulvey's theories of gender and spectatorship, see Chapter 6 and Chapter 9.

• **Plate 10.7** *All That Heaven Allows* (Douglas Sirk, US 1955)
Rock Hudson becomes a wish-fulfilment figure for both Jane Wyman and the audience.

Dorothy Arzner
The work of the only woman to pursue a career solely as a director in classic Hollywood is currently undergoing reassessment by critics of lesbian film. Here are some key films:
The Wild Party (1929)
Christopher Strong (1933)
The Bride Wore Red (1937)
Dance, Girl, Dance (1940)

Garbo and Marlene Dietrich in the 1940s, lesbian vampire films, and 1970s radical lesbian films by Barbara Hammer. She offers fascinating, oppositional interpretations of the way in which lesbian audiences gained positive messages from the otherwise bleak and tragic lesbian characters and relationships in *The Killing of Sister George* (Robert Aldrich, US 1968) and *The Children's Hour* (William Wyler, US 1961).

Weiss clearly outlines the ongoing critical debate about the difficulties of representing autonomous female sexuality in a system of representation which continues to be focused on the male heterosexual look. A major part of this debate for lesbian film centres on the problems of producing scenes of woman-centred intimacy and lovemaking that remain satisfying for lesbian audiences while not falling into the traditional function of being a turn-on for heterosexual men.

Bearing in mind ideas of dominant heterosexual ideology, Weiss points out how Dolly, the lesbian character played by Cher in *Silkwood* (Mike Nichols, US 1983), is marginalised, made to look childlike, and seen predominantly through the eyes of the heterosexual characters – what she deftly calls the 'happen to be gay' approach to the depiction of lesbians and gays in film (Weiss 1993: 63). That is, the character is gay or

"IT'S THE SIGN OF THE HARD-BOILED MAIDENS' ~ NIFTY, WHAT?"

• **Plate 10.8** *The Wild Party* (Dorothy Arzner, US 1929)
The energetic college girls have such a fun time together that being paired off with the males at the end comes almost as an anti-climax.

lesbian but is presented within a completely heterosexual framework and outlook and is therefore found to be lacking. In a similar fusion of ideology and representation, she shows how the central lesbian relationship between Celie and Shug in Alice Walker's novel *The Color Purple*, is downgraded and put under male control in Steven Spielberg's film version (US 1985).

In her section on the lesbian aspect of art film, Weiss uses some key films to show how their directors have dealt in various productive ways with the male heterosexist narrative and viewing strategies of this kind of film tradition. In this context she gives clear readings of films such as Chantal Akerman's *Je, Tu, Il, Elle* (Belgium 1974) and *Joanna D'Arc of Mongolia* by Ulrike Ottinger (W. Germany 1988). She points out how Marlene Gorris' *A Question of Silence* (Netherlands 1983) sees lesbian relationships as part of a continuum of relations between women, which are privileged over those with men.

See the case study on A Question of Silence on pp. 293–5.

Weiss finishes her book with a look at the viewing strategies of recent film-making by and for lesbians. She has positive praise for the focus on racial and sexual diversity among women, as well as the fluid viewpoints used, in Lizzie Borden's *Born in Flames* (US 1983). On the other hand, she analyses a well-known lesbian film of the 1980s,

Sheila McLaughlin's *She Must Be Seeing Things* (US 1987) and sees it as being so caught up in conventional viewing strategies that it denies any positive pleasure or viewpoints for lesbian viewers. Finally, she rightly cautions against a simplistic view of lesbian film as progressing from hidden signs to liberated images, pointing out that 'the cinema has been and continues to be a contested terrain in which people and groups with often opposing interests have staked their claims' (Weiss 1993: 163).

> **In the light of Weiss' comments on viewing strategies, analyse the love-making scenes from *Desert Hearts*, *Go Fish* and another film of your choice.**

SOME FILMS WITH GAY THEMES

Stereotypes and characters

Richard Dyer, in his book *The Matter of Images* (1993a), has pointed out the dangers inherent in thinking rigidly in terms of stereotypes when dealing with representation: 'a **stereotype** can be complex, varied, intense and contradictory, an image of otherness in which it is still possible to find oneself' (ibid., p. 74). Stereotypes, he points out, are not always or necessarily negative, although some, such as the black mammy of Hollywood, are very limiting. The process of stereotyping involves power: the power of dominant groups to mould the accepted social view of themselves and of those groups that they perceive as marginal. This view can change and develop as certain social groups, such as gays and lesbians, grow in self-awareness, expression and power, so that dominant groups have to modify their available images. As an example, Dyer cites the 'sad young man' stereotype common in popular film and literature of the 1940s and 1950s, an image of the passive, unhappy, sexually troubled outsider which grew into the ambiguously attractive and strong image of the social rebel as embodied in James Dean and Montgomery Clift.

stereotype
A set of commonly-expected behaviour patterns and character-istics based on role (e.g. mother) or personal features such as race, age or sexuality. In society and cultural products, the depiction of a stereotype becomes a form of communicative shorthand, and often reflects the attitudes of dominant social groups.

For further discussion of stereotyping, representa-tion and gender, see Chapter 9.

> **Think about the films discussed in the following case studies. Do they contain any stereotypes that could be interpreted in several ways?**

Key European films
These films by major European directors are important as gay texts and as such will reward further study using the insights of gay history, psychoanalysis and auteur theory.
Beauty and the Beast (*La Belle et la Bête*) (Jean Cocteau, France 1946)
Theorum (*Teorema*) (Pier Paolo Pasolini, Italy 1968)

Dyer also suggests that replacing stereotypes with the traditional idea of a 'rounded' character can be an advance of sorts. However, he points out that the 'well-rounded character', as advocated by theorists such as E.M. Forster, is in itself a limiting concept, for, in its strong preoccupation with individuality, it can obscure awareness of the social groups to which that character belongs (Dyer 1985). A really useful study of representa-tion can only take place within an overall awareness of the dominant ideology, the chief component of which, for the purposes of this essay, is the assumption of heterosexu-ality as a dominant, structuring outlook and viewpoint (see Steven 1985).

The Colour of Pomegranates (Tsvet Granata) (Sergei Paradjanov, USSR 1969)
Fox and his Friends (*Faustrecht der Freiheit*) (Rainer Werner Fassbinder, W. Germany 1975)

1 Compare and contrast E.M. Forster's novel *Maurice* with the James Ivory film version (UK 1987) bearing in mind Dyer's ideas about rounded characters.

2 Examine the extent to which the characters and situations of *The Torch Song Trilogy* (Paul Bogart, US 1988) and *La Cage aux Folles* (Eduard Molinaro, US 1978) embody heterosexual ideology.

The following film analyses are intended as sample case studies for an approach which can be applied to other films, to indicate ways in which wider ideological meanings and values can be examined.

☐ CASE STUDY 1: *VICTIM* (BASIL DEARDEN, UK 1961)

Genre, star and theme

Victim has a solidly crafted script in the thriller/detective genre, with the reasons for the suicide of 'Boy' Barrett gradually coming to light through the investigations of barrister Melville Farr, supported by his wife. The black-and-white cinematography recalls film noir in its depiction of urban bedsitters, pubs and clubs, and the key investigator is not the police but a private individual. Tense music evokes mystery and urban spaces. In the tradition of the genre hero, Farr not only uncovers the reasons for the young man's suicide, but makes a heroic stand against injustice.

As well as genre, the film utilised the British star system of the time with Dirk Bogarde, a male sex-symbol of the 1950s, playing the lead. The element which makes this film unusual for its time is not only its main theme of homosexuality, but the fact that some of its character portrayals are relatively sympathetic, given the era and social

Dirk Bogarde was a handsome and well-loved star of the popular *Doctor* comedies in the late 1950s. Starring in *Victim* was a risky prospect that turned out to be a major and constructive turning-point in his career. For further reading, see Bogarde's autobiographical writings.

• Plate 10.9 *Victim* (Basil Dearden, UK 1961) Boy Barrett (right) is a tormented but honourable character driven to suicide, despite the help of the sympathetic Detective Inspector (seated behind).

*See Chapter 11 for
further discussion of
Bristish cinema and
society.*

climate in which the film was made. *Victim* was produced by the Rank studios at a key period of social change in British attitudes towards gay people, and was unique in being specifically seen, at the time of its release in 1961, as a liberal film campaigning against the legal oppression of male homosexuals. In 1957, a government report had recommended a limited reform of the laws that then existed against male homosexual relations. These changes became law in 1967, and the intervening period was one of widespread debate in the British media about homosexuality, a central theme of which was the vulnerability of homosexuals to blackmail, which forms a central theme of *Victim*. A very high proportion of gay men were blackmail victims.

The construction of images

American film noir, the genre which *Victim* echoes, often featured homosexual characters. The insinuatingly weak Cairo in *The Maltese Falcon* and the mean, manipulative Waldo Lydecker in *Laura* are two examples. A major generic element of film noir was its dealings with characters, themes and settings that were considered abnormal, corrupt or deviant in some way, and *Victim* makes use of this tradition in its creation of a secretive, oppressive homosexual underworld whose only solace seems to be the pub with its unsympathetic landlord.

As Farr uncovers more victims of blackmail, we see a succession of nervous, oppressed men paying money to the blackmailers in order to protect their jobs and social standing, which in that era would be destroyed by revelations of then-illegal homosexual relations. The film deliberately depicts a wide social cross-section of men, most leading successful lives. The film's most pathetic minor character is Eddie Henry, the barber. He is jumpy and defensive in conversation with Farr, where he reveals that he has been to prison four times as a result of his homosexuality. Apologetic for his own existence, he is subsequently attacked by the thuggish blackmailer, and dies of a heart attack. Throughout the film minor characters express various types of anti-gay prejudice, and the words 'Farr is queer' are painted on the Farrs' garage door in large letters.

Liberal arguments

So far, the representations dealt with in this film have been predominantly negative in that they indicate secretiveness, oppression and misery. They tie in with an underlying social view at that time of homosexuality as some sort of unfortunate affliction. Critics have pointed out this negativity. In his essay '*Victim*: Hegemonic Project', Richard Dyer (1993) argues that the whole film promotes an attitude of pity for homosexuals as pathetic outsiders. At the same time the film arguably reflects the discrimination and distress experienced by many gay men in the late 1950s and early 1960s. By pointing out these conditions as unjust, the film itself formed part of a wider discourse about the need for change.

A key figure in pointing out legal injustice is the sympathetic, worldly-wise Detective Inspector. The film is punctuated by office discussions which, although over-wordy at times, serve to make the audience aware of the main argument of the film. The Inspector says that it is unjustifiable for the police to interfere in private consensual behaviour between adults and concentrates his anger against blackmailers who make the lives of homosexuals a misery. As the film unfolds and the audience witness this misery, a classic build-up of narrative expectation is brought into play by the Inpector's heartfelt assertion that if only one blackmail victim had the courage to come forward, he could do something.

New attitudes

The film is an important precursor of newer attitudes towards homosexuals, which were to culminate a decade later in the gay movement. The character of Melville Farr epitomises these changes. At the start he is secretive and ashamed, refusing to see Boy or even speak to him on the phone. He later admits: 'I thought he was trying to blackmail me.' It takes the knowledge of Boy's motivations to galvanise him into positive action. Boy has in fact been trying to shield him from blackmail by stealing money from his employers in a brave but futile attempt to pay off the blackmailer for the negative of a photograph of the two of them together. Boy's last action before being apprehended by the police was to attempt to destroy his collection of press cuttings about Farr, which Boy's friend has retrieved and brought to Farr.

Both Boy and his friend are attractive, ordinary-looking young men, a very important point for positive representation. The half-burnt pile of press cuttings attests to Boy's continuing devotion to Farr. Boy's suicide when he thought Farr was rejecting him is yet more evidence of the depth of his feelings, as well as his courage in not betraying the 'secret'.

Once Farr takes the decision to act positively, his character is seen to develop in courage and moral responsibility. Jolted by the injustice of Boy's death, Farr is clearly prepared to risk his career and marriage to expose the blackmailers' injustice. He enlists the help of Boy's friend, saying 'fear is the oxygen of blackmail' and asking the friend to 'watch for signs of fear' among his circle. The friend clearly points out to Farr that his actions will bring him down.

The emotional impact on Farr's wife, Laura, of seeing the newspaper headline about her husband's involvement with the suicide leads to a climactic confrontation where she draws her husband out into declaring his true feelings. The audience, significantly, never see the blackmail photograph so pivotal to the plot. Instead, we see various people's reactions to it, mainly Laura's. On seeing the photo she asks: 'Why is he crying?'; and Farr replies: 'Because I just told him I couldn't see him again.'

The ensuing conversation imbues Laura's character with strength and psychological credibility. She doesn't hesitate to point out the pain and emotion on both men's faces in the photo, and makes her husband come clean and declare: 'I stopped seeing him because I wanted him.' To which she replies: 'You don't call that love?' Her subsequent courageous declaration that she will stand by her husband gives Farr courage to continue his pursuit.

Melville Farr has other supporters in his quest for justice. The Inspector admires and supports him. Boy's friend advises him and makes enquiries on his behalf in London's homosexual community. It is this friend who notices that Eddie Henry is looking harassed and has decided to sell his business and move out, thus enabling Farr to home in on one of the blackmail suspects.

Ambiguous messages

Certain figures in the film are presented in such a way as to reverse conventional audience expectations, a recognised genre tactic in the thriller/detective tradition. The bowler-hatted man in the pub who seems to be trying to pick other men up turns out to be a plain-clothes police officer on the track of the blackmailers. When Doe's secretary and her thuggish accomplice are eventually tracked down, the case is thereby solved and genre expectations are clearly satisfied.

On the other hand, the ending of the film is ambiguous on the level of its homosexual theme, and has been much discussed. Perhaps this ambiguity is a suitable reflection of the era in which the film was made. Farr insists that Laura leave him for the duration of the difficult period ahead, when, as he points out, terrible things will be said

Stephen Bourne (1996) has elicited a fascinating range of personal responses from gay men who saw *Victim* when it was first released in Britain. These, along with contemporary reactions from critics, are collected in the appendices of his book (listed in Further reading). They form a rich portrait of the film's contemporary reception.

about him and he couldn't bear to see her implicated and hurt. This is a brave act on his part, and Laura reluctantly agrees. The audience is left with several questions: will Laura and Mel get back together again, and what kind of relationship might they have if they do? Should Laura pursue her own life? Melville Farr's final act is to tear up the photo of himself and Boy and throw it in the fire. What does this indicate about his attitude towards his own homosexuality, or his relationship with Jack Barrett? The film's final image is of Dirk Bogarde/Melville Farr leaning on the mantelpiece in a pose that conveys despair and dejection. What kind of feeling does this leave the audience with about Farr, and perhaps about homosexuals in general? Does the film as a whole portray homosexual men as sad cases or does a feeling of hope for the future emerge from the brave stand of Melville Farr and his friends?

How do you think audience reactions to *Victim* have changed since the 1960s?

Compare and contrast *Victim* with a similarly liberal-minded American production, *The Detective* (Gordon Douglas, US 1968).

1 How do the narratives reveal contemporary attitudes to homosexuality?
2 How are the main characters portrayed?

□ CASE STUDY 2: *DESERT HEARTS* (DONNA DEITCH, US 1985)

Critical attitudes

Like Andrea Weiss, Richard Dyer sees Donna Deitch's *Desert Hearts* as an example of a feature film which breaks refreshingly free of dominant heterosexual ideology. The film concentrates closely on the psychological world of its two central female characters, and their love is seen to grow and realise itself in a natural progression. Black lesbian film-maker Michelle Parkerson, on the other hand, sees the film as part of what she calls the 'easy heterosexist niches for homosexuality on the silver screen' negotiated by Hollywood (Gever, Greyson and Parmar 1993: 236). The relationship portrayed is easy in the sense of being an idealised one between two beautiful, socially well-placed white women, and the male characters are too good to be true. On the level of the film's production history this comment seems less warranted, since Donna Deitch spent nearly ten years trying to persuade reluctant financial backers to support this film adaptation of Jane Rule's novel. It was eventually made independently on a very small budget by Hollywood standards.

Plot patterns

The opening scene is signalled with a caption, 'Reno, Nevada, 1959' and shows a woman, Vivian Bell, tentatively descending from a train, and welcomed by Frances, in whose house she is staying as a paying guest. Most American viewers know that people come to Reno to gain divorces and we subsequently see Vivian consulting her lawyer. Driving Vivian to the house, Frances talks of her 'wild' daughter who, she says, is just like her dead father. We see the wide-ranging desert scenery glide past.

> **Critically analyse the directors' use of location in *Desert Hearts* and *Salmonberries* (Adlon, Germany 1991). In the latter, consider how the director has used location to illuminate the stages in the relationship between Kotzabue and Roswitha.**

Frances' daughter Cay zooms up in her car, Buddy Holly blasting on her radio. She recklessly drives on the wrong side of the road in order to converse with Frances, who introduces her to 'Professor Bell'. After Cay zooms off, narrowly missing an oncoming car, Vivian reaches for a cigarette, and is portrayed as nervy, shy and tentative. She later starts to get to know Cay, who produces sculpture and works at one of the casinos. The two are soon discussing ambitions and plans.

In keeping with its genre pattern of romance, this film follows a simple plot whereby Vivian and Cay gradually come together, fall for each other and, towards the end, make passionate love. The generic plot complications consist of the very different personalities and backgrounds of the two women, and the neurotically possessive nature of Frances which is gradually revealed. She is not Cay's natural mother but lived for ten years with Cay's father and is the mother of Cay's half-brother Walter. We learn that Cay's father died young, that Frances still loves and adores him, and that she has a voracious need to keep Cay near her as a reminder of him. When she dances with Cay at the engagement party of Cay's friend Silver, Frances talks of how special the memory of Glen, her lover, is to her 'because he reached in and put a string of lights around my heart'. She tells Vivian: 'I got what I wanted. I had a love of my own.' Vivian's reply ('You had more than most people dare hope for') sets up the main dramatic expectations of the plot, as we gradually learn of Vivian's conformist marriage that she is escaping from. She tells her lawyer: 'I want to be free of what I've been.'

Character patterns

The differences between Vivian and Cay are clearly signalled through dress and behaviour. Vivian wears a steel-grey, precisely cut 1950s skirt-suit with a matching cloche hat. Her blonde hair is up in a neat, business-like style which matches her stiff, formal move-

• **Plate 10.10** *Desert Hearts* (Donna Deitch, US 1985)
Cay (left) never loses the support of her friend Silver.

ments. She is ten years older than Cay. She lectures in English literature at Columbia University, and makes frequent references to what she calls her 'circle'. In terms of representation in American films, this brings into play a whole set of stereotypes in the contrast between the more intellectual, snobbish Easterner and the more physical Westerner. Cay shows off her long brown legs in skimpy denim shorts and cowboy boots. Her medium-length black hair flows freely. A representational tradition of associating blonde hair with aloof coolness, and dark hair with a lively, passionate nature, is being brought into play.

Cay is open and positive about her love of women. The first time Vivian visits Cay in her cottage she is disconcerted to glimpse another woman, Gwen, in Cay's bed. Vivian accepts Cay's offer of a lift into town, but is evidently awkward sitting between Gwen and Cay. Cultural differences are underlined when Cay replaces the blaring pop music on the radio with another station playing Prokofiev, whereupon Vivian recognises the music and says she likes it.

Although undeveloped in her education, Cay is open to new ideas and cultural influences, and it is for this reason that Vivian later wants to take her to New York. Cay is strong-minded, and tells Frances firmly: 'One of these days I'm gonna meet somebody that counts.' We see her resisting various social pressures to 'settle down' with Darrell, the male supervisor at the casino. She makes it clear to her friend Silver that she wants to be accepted for what she is, and Silver declares her continued friendship.

Cay tells Silver that she is very much in love with Vivian, but doesn't know whether anything will come of it. Darrell is shown protecting Cay from the unwanted advances of a client at the casino, and is polite and patient with her. His offer to 'look the other way' about Cay's affairs with women evokes her exasperation, and shows his complete misunderstanding of who Cay is.

It is Cay who makes most of the moves in bringing herself and Vivian together. She makes Vivian laugh, offers to go riding with her, takes her to the cowboy clothing shop to equip her with jeans, shirt and boots, and insists, much to Frances' annoyance, on her coming to Silver's engagement party. At the motel, when Vivian, on the opposite side of the door, asks her to go away, Cay replies: 'I can't, honest.' Once she has let Cay into the room, Vivian turns round to find Cay naked in her bed. Cay succeeds, once again, in relaxing Vivian by making her laugh.

Vivian slowly develops a more relaxed outlook. She adopts a looser hairstyle, wears jeans and visits the casino. As she watches a rodeo, we see a close-up of her slipping her wedding ring off her finger, symbolising a new life. When she finally gets her divorce, the lawyer remarks that Vivian has found a 'pen-pal' in Reno. Her reply ('I've found much more than that, Mr Warner') is strong and confident.

Cay's brother Walter, a good-looking, gently understanding, rather idealised figure, offers to accompany Vivian to the engagement party, thereby calming the confrontation with Frances that arose when Cay insisted on Vivian coming along.

Sex and the spectator

A key scene in advancing the couple's intimacy occurs when Cay is driving Vivian home after the party, where Silver's performance of her loving country song is accompanied by shots of the two looking at each other. Cay tells Vivian that she can only find real love with a woman. When Vivian, continuing to wrap her reactions in a cloak of academic tolerance, says: 'Are you trying to shock me?' Cay replies calmly: 'No, I was only telling you the truth.' As Vivian flees to the car Cay makes her wind down the window, bends down and caresses Vivian's cheek with her lips. The romantic convention of the first kiss is made dramatic and memorable through the heavy shower that is drenching Cay, and the unusual positioning of the lovers.

The lovemaking scene at the motel raises the vexed question of erotic voyeurism. We have a woman directing a scene of woman-to-woman lovemaking which generally avoids angles or shots which could echo those traditionally associated with images directed at heterosexual males. Helen Shaver as Vivian conveys pleasurable sexual awakening and a nervousness that is carried into the next scene. In a restaurant, the two declare their love for each other but Vivian is uncomfortable and her lack of 'points of reference' leads to a quarrel and reconciliation with her lover.

Given the 1950s setting, remarkably little **homophobia** is encountered by the two lovers in this film. The prejudice of Lucille, another house guest, and the incomprehension of Darrell are balanced by the tolerant support of Silver and Walter. Frances' attitudes remain ambiguous and perhaps more credible given the era in which the film is set. When they return to find Frances has kicked Vivian out of her house and booked her into a motel, this act is equally aimed at hanging on to Cay, although she says 'at least I'm normal'. The act backfires, and Cay moves out to stay with Silver. In her final conversation with Cay, Frances displays mystified antagonism: 'I just don't understand it. Women together.' Cay uses Frances' words to explain: 'She just reached in … put a string of lights around my heart' and earns a reluctant blessing and a hug, an action marred by Frances' comment that people will be talking about her.

The fragility of this lesbian relationship across the class, regional and educational differences of 1950s America is echoed by the question posed narratively at the end as the train pulls away: will it be to the next station as she claims, or will Cay stay with Vivian on that train journey to New York?

homophobia
Irrational prejudice and hatred against a person because of their homosexuality.

☐ CASE STUDY 3: *THE LIVING END* (GREGG ARAKI, US 1993)

Genre and anarchy

Gregg Araki began his film-making career in 1987 producing quirky short films which directly challenged the conventions of classic narrative. *The Living End*, his first feature-length work, follows more conventional narrative patterns. However, the film uses traditional genre elements of the road movie, with comedy and romance, in unusual, offbeat and sometimes outrageous ways.

In the opening shot of the film we see Luke, a gorgeous young man in torn jeans, leather jacket and Ray Ban sunglasses, spraying 'Fuck The World' on a wall, an image which sets the anarchic tone of the film. We immediately cut to the other main character, Jon, writing 'the first day of the rest of my life' in his diary, an entry explained for us with the mechanical-sounding voiceover of the doctor explaining to Jon that he is HIV+. The film's offbeat attitude to HIV and death is indicated when Jon says: 'Live fast, die young, leave a beautiful corpse – yeah right. Death is weird.'

Jon's friend Doris is seen hugging him, comforting him and offering help. Throughout the film she worries about him, even as she is breaking up with her boyfriend, but we see little indication of her state of mind other than her nervously playing with an executive toy. That, and the scene of her concentrated work on her painting, indicate the similarity of her world and Jon's. Her feelings for Jon are portrayed as warm and concerned, but she has a limited role within the film as foil and support for Jon.

Later, Jon picks Luke up in his car. Their conversation reveals Jon's conventional attitudes and Luke's anger. Jon invites Luke home to his apartment. Andy Warhol posters, a large blow-up dinosaur and the word processor indicate Jon's playfully arty lifestyle. Jon starts clearing his things away and Luke points out that he is being para-

• **Plate 10.11** *The Living End* (Gregg Araki, US 1993)
The characters Luke (left) and Jon form an oddly-matched couple. Here they are, seen with director Araki in the centre.

noid. The differences in personality and outlook between the two young men are further underlined with Luke's lack of interest in the film-maker Derek Jarman and in the way he casually strips before an embarrassed Jon.

When Luke and Jon begin to make love, Luke shows himself to be sensitive to Jon's uptightness. Jon falteringly starts to explain: '…I just found out this afternoon that…'; Luke's tone is firm and affectionate: 'If you're trying to say what I think you are, don't worry about it.' With a kiss, he says: 'It's really no big deal.' He switches off the light and says: 'Welcome to the club, partner.' Being HIV+ is seen as a continuing lifestyle.

Luke goes on to point out that there must be millions of people like them walking 'with this thing inside them', that he, Jon and people like them have nothing to lose, are totally free, and can do whatever they want, whereupon he produces a credit card which he says is his uncle's.

Audience reactions

These scenes evoke conflicting audience reactions of outrage and laughter. Daisy chats Luke up in order to anger her girlfriend, calling him 'a sexy slab of hunk beefcake'. Fern stops the car and threatens to blow Luke's face to smithereens. The script pushes the man-hating lesbian stereotype to comic extremes with Daisy's descriptions of the painful deaths she and Fern have inflicted on previous victims, right to the point where Fern says: 'You got me so agitated with all this talk, I gotta pee.' She tells Daisy not to kill Luke until she gets back 'and no more flirting'. Daisy's line ('I love it when she gets jealous') caps their over-the-top comic dialogue. The two women are strong foils for each other, and Daisy cares enough for Fern to run to her aid when she calls. The ambiguities of queer theory come to the fore here. Tamsin Wilton (see Further reading) points out the misogyny in this portrayal, as Luke abandons the two women in the middle of the desert and symbolically appropriates the phallus in the form of their car and their gun.

The outrageous humour continues as we see the wife of the bisexual man bursting into the bedroom where he is sleeping with Luke. She informs her husband bitterly that: 'It's not the seventies any more, when being married to a bisexual was fashionable.' We see a low-angle shot of her holding a large knife in both hands and producing a Tarzanic scream, then cut to a splash of blood hitting Luke's face and a series of unexpected shots which culminates in Luke leaving the house, chased by the dog. The combination of skilful editing, *Psycho* references and offbeat subject matter make for unsettling comedy.

The scene where Luke shoots the three queer-bashers could well represent a form of wish-fulfilment. He is confronted with three baseball-wielding thugs: 'Prepare to swallow your teeth, faggot, it's cosmetic surgery time.' He stops them in their tracks when he takes out a gun. First, he calmly shoots the one who tries to run away, then the other two. Luke becomes a liberating hero figure through expressing his anger, from spraying graffiti to bashing a skinhead who makes a gross AIDS joke, a kind of queer hero. Jon's life is transformed once he commits himself to Luke, but his commitment only comes gradually. He goes along with the mad credit card spending spree but throws Luke out after the skinhead-bashing incident, only to discover that he can't live without him.

Motivation and character

The motivation for the two lovers hitting the road is typical of the road movie genre: a crime from whose consequences they need to flee. In this case, Luke admits that he has killed a policeman and they set off for San Francisco. The contrasts between the two characters surface comically. As with much comedy, traditional stereotypes lurk near the surface. Jon is the prissy queen and Luke the butch, street-wise hustler. Luke calls Jon a 'princess' because of his precise bathing habits. Jon declares he's fed up with Luke's 'Clint Eastwood act with the gun'. Meanwhile, the familiar genre imagery of open spaces viewed from a speeding car embodies Jon's ever-growing distance from his old life. Doris, checking his apartment back home, finds an ansaphone full of unanswered messages, and a dead goldfish. Luke writes 'Jon and Luke – till death do us part' on a phone box and Jon confides by phone to Doris: 'I don't know how to describe it. Nothing is the same any more. Everything has changed.'

A romantic ending?

The final sequence presents us with images that are both disquieting and romantic. Luke cuts his wrist to examine his own blood, the source of his HIV anxiety. Jon, angry and exasperated, still binds Luke's wound. The gun becomes a sexual toy as Luke caresses Jon with it and places it in his own mouth while rubbing himself between Jon's legs.

The final long-shot is of the two together peacefully on the beach with just the sound of the sea, a shot which implies a peaceful but questionable final equilibrium. The playful waywardness of this film, its gleeful man-killers, unsafe shower sex, amoral attitudes and discomforting treatment of AIDs, make it a central text of the New Queer Cinema.

To what extent do Araki's unusual methods of comic exaggeration make viewers aware of the tensions, anger and survival strategies associated with being young, gay and HIV+?

☐ CASE STUDY 4: *LOOKING FOR LANGSTON* (ISAAC JULIEN, UK 1994)

Compare and contrast *Looking for Langston* with Isaac Julien's feature, *Young Soul Rebels* (UK 1991), in terms of representations of race, sexuality and narrative structure.

Poetic meditation

Subtitled 'A Meditation on Langston Hughes (1902–1967) and the Harlem Renaissance', this film is a tribute to the American poet Langston Hughes, who lived in New York and whose writings formed a key part of the flowering of black culture in that city during the 1920s, known as the 'Harlem Renaissance'. It is less than an hour long and was funded by Britain's Channel Four TV. As the word 'meditation' suggests, the work is structured in a non-narrative way around a collage of visual images and a soundtrack of poetry by Hughes, Essex Hemphill and Bruce Nugent. It is dedicated to another outstanding American writer who was also gay and black, the novelist James Baldwin.

The film opens with newsreel footage of Hughes' funeral. A female voiceover delivers an oration about the struggle of opposition, which no one undertakes easily. Later on, this idea of opposition is underlined when we see a modern article on Hughes entitled 'Black and Gay', and when we see a gang of fierce-looking skinheads attempting violence on the nightclub space occupied by the men. The skinheads are white, and when they invade the space they are seen to do so with white police officers looking on and doing nothing. The funeral footage immediately cuts to a modern recreation, in

• **Plate 10.12** *Looking for Langston* (Isaac Julien, UK 1988) The beauty of this film's images forms a vivid tribute both to Hughes as an artist and to the culture that nurtured him.

sensuously crisp black and white, of the funeral, with large white lilies and the body laid out in its coffin. The black-and-white cinematography continues throughout the film as a homage and reference to famous gay images. The lilies recall the photography of Robert Mapplethorpe.

Male, black and gay

Images of the funeral recur and evoke respectful homage. They are interwoven with images of a nightclub peopled by handsome men dancing, drinking, talking and laughing together, images of enjoyment, sensuality and cultural solidarity. The men are in formal evening clothes and dancing to music which recalls the 1920s. One of the men is white and is later seen in intimate, loving surroundings with his black lover after displaying jealousy in the club. Later, the music and dancing become disco-style in a mix between 1920s and modern styles and scenes, a mix which recurs throughout the film to evoke the continuity of both black and gay culture.

The central figure in the club is a handsome man with a moustache who sees another very good-looking man. The two are attracted to each other, and the middle part of the film presents sensuous fantasy sequences of the two of them together. The man with the moustache is seen reflected in a pond in a spacious moorland setting. He comes across the other man, who is naked. His firm, well-made body is revealed to the viewer from behind, gradually, from the legs up. The poetry on the soundtrack talks of the man's 'dancer's body' and makes clear that this man is the figure of Beauty; 'Beauty's lips touched his…. How much pressure does it take to awaken love?' The shots of Beauty culminate in a scene of him lying naked in bed with the other man, their bodies intertwined. This memorable image recalls a famous photograph by George Platt Lynes, once again paying homage to a major figure of gay culture.

Cultural continuity

Fantasy elements underline the sense of meditation about Hughes and the cultural tradition of which he formed part. The nightclub is first seen with the men in still poses. Male angels watch over the nightclub. At one point, a beautiful young angel is seen holding a large picture of Langston Hughes, then the camera pans slowly to a large picture of James Baldwin. At another point, the camera rises from the nightclub to a scene of funeral mourning situated on the balcony above. This establishes a spatial relationship between the two main movements and moods of the film, and the words of the poem on the soundtrack ('Let my name be spoken without effect, without the ghost of shadow on it') show that we are invited to celebrate with joy, not mourn with sadness, Hughes and the culture he represents. Nightclub images of kissing, dancing and talking are then followed by the slow pan sideways to a young man with a flower.

Archive footage underlines cultural continuity. There is footage of Hughes reading his poetry on a TV programme, literary gatherings, jazz bands in Harlem, a football team, references to poets and anthologies and to the first production of the play *Amen Corner* by James Baldwin. A sequence which evokes the milieu of Harlem in the 1920s is accompanied by a poem on the soundtrack which tells how black artists at the time were expected to produce something called 'black art', a ghetto concept which was supposed to keep such artists in their place. Black artists were not supposed to concern themselves with wider ideas such as modernism. The poem tells how black art later went out of fashion with collectors: 'History as the smiler with the knife under her cloak.'

Throughout the film, Julien juxtaposes image and sound in order to provoke thought and emotion. What both the modern and the 1920s scenes have in common is a sense of danger for gay men in public spaces, outside the safety of places like the club, but at the same time a sense of going out into, of braving those public spaces. As a young man walks into the club, and the song lyric rings out:

> You're such a beautiful black man,
> But you've been made to feel,
> That your beauty's not real.

To accompany this we see footage of a black sculptor working on a sculpture of a naked black man. The lyric, the footage of the sculptor at work, and the preceding homage to Beauty as a black man, provide a critique of sexual and aesthetic attitudes towards black men in a society dominated by ideas of beauty as white. Sound and image in collision are used to provoke questions and thoughts about how black men are sexually used by whites, black men as both objects and users of pornography, and the use of pornography for safe sex.

Strong, positive attitudes

This film takes on several controversial issues, including interracial sex and the questioning of the nature of black masculinity, and deals with them in an accomplished and stylish way. Such glamorously eroticised male images are, as Andrea Weiss points out, very different from the low-key approach taken by lesbian film-making, as in the film she and Greta Schiller made about the black lesbian jazz artist Tiny Davis, *Tiny and Ruby: Hell Drivin' Women* (US 1988).

The final and dominant mood of *Looking for Langston* is elegiac. A male couple is seen to leave the club and walk across Waterloo Bridge in contemporary London. While a train passes and they look at each other the voiceover poem is wistful: 'I love my friend. He went away from me. There's nothing more to say.' But life goes on, the angels overlook scenes of love and celebration, and a poem refers to Hannibal, Toussaint and other strong figures of black history. As the gang of skinheads advances down the street, the club erupts with disco music and we see the dancers enjoying themselves. The editing rhythm increases as it cuts between the skinheads, clubbers and police with truncheons. The expected clash is undercut when we see the police and thugs enter the club only to find it empty, followed by a shot of a laughing black angel. Is this a comment on the invisibility and/or oppression of black gay culture? Is it a demonstration of how prejudice and oppression can and will be deflected and dissipated? The final upbeat note is sounded when footage of the old TV programme is shown, with Hughes reading:

> Sun's a risin'
> This is gonna be my song.

☐ CASE STUDY 5: *GO FISH* (ROSE TROCHE, US 1994)

Lesbian stardom

Guinevere Turner, a leading actor and co-writer of this film, seems set to become a lesbian film star. Her on-screen charisma and the intertextual effects of publicity in lesbian and gay media contain the classic ingredients for the development of the first openly lesbian film star persona. This is a trail already blazed in other media by figures such as k.d. lang (music and film) and Ellen Degeneres (television).

In the tradition of most lesbian productions, *Go Fish* is a small-budget film. The long list of helpers and contributors following the main credits attests to strong community support. Typical of such projects, many of those participating in the making of the film did several jobs: for example, V.S. Brodie is both main actor and co-producer. The film has excellent black-and-white cinematography by Ann T. Rossi, and an attractive, specially-written score. It took two years to complete, a fact which makes the quality and consistency of Turner's performance all the more laudable.

The time was right for the success of this film. Co-producer John Pierson was aware that what he calls 'the low-budget aesthetic' was very much in vogue in 1994 and the success of *Claire of the Moon*, despite very bad reviews, had made him conscious that the lesbian audience was very poorly provided for. The film was an immediate hit at the Sundance Film Festival that year, and Pierson used his considerable negotiating skills to persuade Goldwyn distributors to snap it up, the first such deal to be achieved. Nevertheless, its success with audiences, and its engaging charm, are mainly due to its lively script, direction and performances.

The script: speaking as lesbians

Go Fish has a simple main storyline. A young lesbian student, Max (Turner) is eager to find a girlfriend. Ely (Brodie) is very reserved, nervous of commitment, and sheltering behind her fading long-distance relationship with a lover who has been living far away in Seattle for over two years. They get together with a lot of help from their friends, which include Kia, a black college lecturer in whose apartment Max rents a room, and Evy, Kia's Hispanic lover. Ely shares an apartment with Daria. These room-mates discuss the women's feelings, with each of them separately and between themselves as a group. Max is initially uninterested, but gradually changes her attitude. It emerges that Ely is very attracted to Max. Daria arranges a party in her apartment where all the friends are invited. At the party Max and Ely get to know each other better and, soon after, arrange a big date.

This outline indicates several features that make a refreshing difference in terms of

The screenplay of *Go Fish*, by Rose Troche and Guinevere Turner, with an introduction by Lea Delaria, is available from The Overlook Press in New York (published 1995).

• **Plate 10.13** *Go Fish* (Rose Troche, US 1994) Guinevere Turner as Max and V.S. Brodie as Ely. A shot that indicates the natural-looking, relaxed feel of this film, conveyed through close-ups.

lesbian film. In contrast with the all too frequent portrayal of lesbian relationships as relatively isolated and fragile, dependent on the goodwill of a limited number of (usually straight, usually liberal) friends, Max and Ely are surrounded by a supportive lesbian culture. Daria is constantly pressing Ely to make up her mind. Kia checks through Max's college paper for her, and discusses her well-being with Evy, Daria and other friends. These women work, eat, drink, make love, have sex, play cards and care for their cats. The script is a collaboration between Guinevere Turner and director Rose Troche. During one of their get-togethers the group of friends discuss various woman-positive words for 'vagina', just one notable example of the way the dialogue crackles with lively repartee about their lived experience as lesbians.

A further example of natural-sounding dialogue occurs during the phone conversation where Max and Ely arrange their date. Gently prompted by Max, Ely admits that she considers her relationship with the woman in Seattle to be over. On hearing this admission, Max prompts Ely to ask her out on a date. They agree to meet at Max's apartment. The scene leading up to their lovemaking is underpinned with gentle humour. Max is late in getting ready, then tells Ely that she's having a 'fashion crisis' in deciding what to wear, and remains in her robe. The act of cutting Ely's nails, very odd for a first date as the friends later comment, brings them into close physical intimacy.

The script celebrates lesbian culture but prevents the tone of the film from becoming cosily idealistic. We see Kia fielding insults shouted in the street and hear Ely talking of being called a 'lezzie' at school. There is a scene where Evy goes home and has a major argument with her mother, because her brother has informed the family that he saw her going into a local gay bar. Her mother utters a stream of homophobic insults in Spanish and English. Evy angrily declares that she is leaving home. She flees to Kia's apartment where Max comforts her in her usual clumsy way, saying 'we can be your family'.

Direction: seeing queerly

The film has a distinct visual style based on frequent use of close-ups. The faces of Max and Ely are shot in extreme close-up, for instance, as the two of them talk on the phone, thus underlining their growing intimacy. Close-ups of hair, earrings, lips and hands make the viewer feel part of the group. This sense of intimacy through physical closeness echoes the style of other lesbian film-makers such as Sadie Benning.

There are scenes throughout the film of Kia, Evy, Daria and the latter's various girl-friends talking about their lives and discussing the progress of Max and Ely's relationship. The director presents these shots in a memorable way. We see only the women's heads in various patterns as they are lying, presumably on some kind of large bed, looking up at the ceiling, an amusing physical embodiment of them putting their heads together in order to formulate their plans.

The narrative is punctuated by shots and montage sequences which comment on the main action. Shots of a spinning top reflect the game of pairing and mating that is being played. The song on the soundtrack echoes the theme, with lyrics about love spinning round. Shots of lights being switched off and wringing hands visually embody the initial tensions of the Max/Ely relationship. A montage sequence uses shots of Max and other women looking uncomfortable in white wedding dresses while people congratulate them. Sometimes the women try to pull off the dresses. In parallel, Max's voiceover gives us her thoughts on how to live her lesbian identity, along with comment on the lures and pitfalls of conformity.

Director/scriptwriter Rose Troche uses light touches which bring the characters to life. One longer close-up of Ely's black boot being carefully laced by her, in readiness for her date with Max, embodies this character's care and nervousness. On her way home afterwards, we see Ely leaping in the air with delight and accepting a rose from a stranger. There is a comic sequence towards the end: scenes of Ely being closely questioned by Daria about what went on during the date are cross-cut with Max giving her account to her room-mates, and these in turn are comically underpinned by contrasting scenes of the date as envisaged by Max, Ely and their friends.

> **Compare and contrast the lesbian worlds portrayed in *Go Fish* with those in *Desert Hearts*, *When Night is Falling* and/or *She Must Be Seeing Things*.**

New lesbian images?

The viewer is introduced to a varying array of lesbians, although there are no older women. Ages range from Kia, who is thirty, to Max, in her late teens. Kia's dress and demeanour contain overtones of the traditional butch stereotype. The fact that she is black provokes further debate about racial and sexual imaging.

The women portrayed have a refreshingly realistic, non-glamorised range of bodies and faces. Characters and attitudes also vary. Ely is firmly monogamous while Daria is happily promiscuous. Ely and Max disagree about the gay images in the film they see when they first go out together. After having sex with a male friend, Daria is waylaid by an angry group of lesbians. The ensuing discussion airs a range of views about personal freedom and sexual identity as Daria insists that she is 'a lesbian who has had sex with a man'. A queer lesbian?

Awareness of age and image is foregrounded. Max initially dismisses Ely's looks as 'Seventies hippie' and with typical youthful impetuosity calls her 'ugly', to Kia's annoyance. Max learns to be less rigid in her outlook. Ely undergoes a drastic change of image, having her long hair cut into a dramatically shaved style. On her next meeting with Max, she confides her worry that the new style may be 'too butch' and the two women talk of the constraints and expectations of body-image for lesbians.

The final sequence of the film, which accompanies the credits, contains an uplifting message. It shows various couples we have met during the film, making love. The imagery skilfully avoids hetero titillation and has a convincingly lesbian feel, recalling the photographic images of Della Grace. The voiceover advises viewers to keep an open mind because 'The girl is out there'.

Note the visual contrast between the characters in Go Fish and the more overt use of make-up and high fashion in Desert Hearts and/or When Night is Falling.

For a lively visual exploration around issues of ageing, see Nitrate Kisses (listed in Further viewing).

For a discussion of race and sexual role-play which parallels issues raised in Go Fish, see the chapter in Wilton 1995 on She Must Be Seeing Things.

CONCLUSION: A QUEER DIVERSITY

Critic B. Ruby Rich described 1992 as 'a watershed year for independent gay and lesbian film', not only because of the number of shorts and features being made and shown, but because of the surge in critical interest which has accompanied them (Cook and Dodd 1993: 164). The recent crop of film and video activity is being called the 'New Queer Cinema'. Lesbian and gay activists, critics, film-makers and audiences are imbuing the previously negative term **queer** with a range of new, exciting, positive meanings in politics, literature, art and film-making. This process of an oppressed group reclaiming and reshaping a previously negative word or idea is known as **reappropriation**; it has happened with the word 'black'. Critic Amy Taubin said: 'American queer cinema has achieved critical mass' with the release of features such as *My Own Private*

queer
Originally a negative term for (mainly male) homosexuals, this word has been recently reappropriated by critics, artists and audiences to describe a challenging range of critical work and cultural production among lesbians and gays, with an emphasis on diversity of race, nationality and cultural experience.

reappropriation
The process whereby a
previously oppressed
group takes a negative
term and turns it around
to invest it with new
meanings of power and
liberation. Examples
include 'black', 'virago'
and 'queer'.

Idaho (Gus Van Sant 1991), utilising the Hollywood star system with Keanu Reeves and River Phoenix, and Tom Kalin's *Swoon* (1992).

The key idea behind the New Queer Cinema is diversity: a range of homosexualities manifested through a variety of character, situation, race, gender, sexual practice and film language. Film-makers are questioning the attitude, developed in the 1970s, that one must promote only positive images of lesbian and gay characters and situations. Although debate rages around what many lesbians and gays see as negative images in mainstream Hollywood films such as *The Silence of the Lambs* and *Basic Instinct*, some lesbian and gay film-makers see such ideas as constraints on creativity in an era where a much wider variety of lesbian and gay images is available. Gus Van Sant's *My Own Private Idaho* dramatises the hopeless love of a teenage male hustler for a straight college boy. In *Swoon* Tom Kalin examines the infamous Leopold/Loeb case of 1924, where two rich, Jewish eighteen-year-olds kidnap and murder a fourteen-year-old boy. Unlike previous film versions, such as Hitchcock's *Rope* (US 1948), Kalin concentrates on the homosexual relationship between the two young men, and the hold which the pathological Leopold had over Loeb. In an interview, Kalin stated: 'We're in a sorry state if we can't afford to look at "unwholesome" lesbian and gay people.' Derek Jarman's *Edward II* (UK 1991) doesn't hesitate to portray England's monarch as weak and vacillating while his male lover, Gaveston, is scheming and slimy. What Kalin's and Jarman's

• **Plate 10.14** *Edward II* (Derek Jarman, UK 1991)
The love between Edward (left) and Gaveston evokes mixed audience reactions.

films do, in their very different ways is make the audience aware of the political dimensions of homosexuality.

New techniques of expression

Diversity and experimentation in film language has characterised recent lesbian and gay film. John Greyson mixes history in *Urinal* (Canada 1988) as famous figures of gay culture, including Langston Hughes and the Russian director Sergei Eisenstein, help to investigate police harassment of gays. In *Edward II*, following a style he had already used in *Caravaggio* (UK 1986) to point up the continuing relevance of its sexual and political themes, Derek Jarman deliberately mixes and clashes the fourteenth century and the 1990s. We see Annie Lennox singing a Cole Porter song, vicars in dog-collars spitting on Gaveston after his banishment, and gay activists with placards and the **pink triangle** symbol invading the King's palace. In *Blue* (UK 1993) Jarman's one-colour screen counterpoints the emotional range of the soundtrack's meditation on his life with, and approaching death from, HIV.

Critically analyse the following films by John Greyson in terms of the formal qualities that they have in common. Can these films be classified according to traditional genres?

- *The Making of Monsters*
- *Urinal*
- *Zero Patience*
- *Lilies*

The documentary work of Stuart Marshall is challenging in subject matter and form. *Bright Eyes* (UK 1984) presents the viewer with ever relevant parallels between Nazi treatment of gays, Victorian medical practice and media coverage of the AIDS epidemic. *Desire* (UK 1989) deals with the lives of lesbians and gay men in Germany under the Nazis, building up a picture of fear, oppression and survival through low-key interviews with young historians of lesbian and gay life, paralleled with people who lived through those times, telling their stories. The strength of Marshall's films lies partly in the way he lets the camera linger over a photograph, a building or a woodland scene to allow the viewer to take in and connect the past with the present.

Rosa Von Praunheim's *I Am My Own Woman* (Germany 1993) presents a portrait of Charlotte Von Mahlsdort (born Lothar Berfelde), a famous lifelong transvestite who is also gay. As well as using direct interviews with him, the film dramatises scenes from his life, including his anti-Nazi work during the Second World War. At the end of many of these dramatised scenes, he himself walks on to the set and is questioned by the actors about his thoughts and motivations, a productive distanciation effect and perhaps an example of queer questioning.

Film genre and film style are mixed creatively in New Queer Cinema. Tod Haynes' *Poison* (US 1991) mixes 1950s B-film sci-fi and zombie elements with a homoerotic section styled as a homage to Genet. In *Caught Looking* (UK 1991) Constantine Giannaris takes the viewer on a journey through a spectrum of gay viewpoints with a character participating in an interactive video fantasy. John Greyson's *Zero Patience* (Canada 1993) subverts the conventions of the Hollywood musical to investigate atti-

Derek Jarman
Painter, writer, activist and acclaimed British gay/queer auteur, Derek Jarman was a provocative figure and an inspiration for younger artists and film-makers. Here are some key films:
Sebastiane (1976)
Jubilee (1978)
The Tempest (1979)
The Angelic Conversation (1985)
The Last of England (1987)

pink triangle
A symbol originally worn by homosexual prisoners in Nazi concentration camps which was later taken up by lesbian and gay people as a reminder of past oppression and an icon of liberation.

tudes to AIDS, once again using a figure from the gay past, the Victorian explorer Richard Francis Burton, in creative and amusing ways.

Gender, race and queer cinema

Monika Treut's feature-length *Virgin Machine* (W. Germany 1985) accompanies its heroine on a sexual odyssey in San Francisco, but the inequality of funding for men's and women's work means that many lesbian film-makers continue to produce shorter films and videos. In *The Meeting of Two Queens* Cecilia Barriga has taken images of Garbo and Dietrich and edited them together to produce a provocatively sensual play of eye contact and undressing between two screen goddesses. The video work of Sadie Benning, such as the ten-minute *Jollies*, intimately explores her own body, thoughts, memories and sexuality with a bold use of camerawork intricately interacting with the soundtrack.

Critically analyse *Virgin Machine* to address the following:

1 **How is Dorothee initially portrayed?**
2 **How does she react to her explorations of the San Francisco lesbian scene?**
3 **Comment on the range of sexual situations and relationships, and their portrayal during the film.**

Pratibha Parmar is a British film-maker and critic of Asian origin who helped found the first group in Britain for black lesbians. For her, as for Isaac Julien, race is as important an issue as sexuality, and the intervention of both film-makers contributes to the new kind of diversity within queer cinema, although one only has to compare Julien's feature film, *Young Soul Rebels*, with the short pieces produced by Parmar to be aware once again of the gender inequality in funding. Parmar is concerned to disrupt and change the conventional images of Asians prevalent in British society. Her 1990 documentary, *Flesh and Paper*, on Indian lesbian poet and writer Suniti Namjoshi was, as Parmar herself said, 'the first time that British television audiences saw an Indian woman in a sari talking about being a lesbian and Indian in a way that was not apologetic or explanatory' (in Gever, Greyson and Parmar 1993: 45). *Khush* (UK 1991) is a television film she made for Channel Four about the experience of being Asian and lesbian or gay. In this piece, interviews are interwoven with images of two women in saris relaxing and dancing together, and a classic Indian musical film is provocatively re-edited so that the dancing girl's glances interplay with those of another woman.

With videos such as *Orientations* (Canada 1985), Richard Fung helps give voice to North American lesbians and gays of Chinese origin. Marlon Riggs' feature-length poetic meditation on the lives of black gay men in the United States, *Tongues Untied* (US 1989), is a beautifully constructed work.

The continuing queer cinema debate

Amy Taubin has called *Tongues Untied* and *The Living End* 'heedlessly misogynistic' (Cook and Dodd 1993: 179), the first because of its exclusion of any idea of lesbian presence, and the second for its two-dimensional female characters which appear as

• **Plate 10.15** *Khush* (Pratibha Parmar, UK 1991)
The title of this memorable film is the Urdu word for 'ecstatic pleasure'. In her look at some Asian lesbian and gay lives, Parmar mixed pleasurable dream sequences with interviews which recall oppression.

mere male appendages, echoing Wilton's comments referred to earlier. *Paris is Burning* (US 1990), Jenny Livingstone's documentary about the black gay drag scene in Harlem, New York, is regarded by some as condescending in its viewpoints.

Such criticism and debate is healthy, and is set to continue along with the wide, creative and growing range of lesbian and gay film- and video-making, work which will surely benefit anybody who seeks to enrich their viewing experience.

Queer questions

What constitutes a lesbian or gay film? Do the makers of such films have to be gay or lesbian themselves? Compare the portrayal of same-sex relationships in *Desert Hearts* and *Black Widow* (Bob Rafelson, US 1987). Arguably, both involve homoerotic attraction and a certain gay sensibility in the play of looks on the screen and/or between the viewer and the text. In *Black Widow* same-sex attraction and lesbian sensibility remain subtextual. Is *Desert Hearts* therefore more 'lesbian' because of its direct portrayal of sexuality in character, situation and action? Or is *Black Widow* equally powerful in this context? A similar comparison can be applied to the male-orientated films *Jeffrey* (Christopher Ashley, US 1995) and *Top Gun* (Tony Scott, US 1986).

Consider the use of homoerotic imagery in *Top Gun* in the portrayal of Tom Cruise and his companions.

What about the concept of 'queer'? Federico Fellini and Ken Russell, both hetero-sexuals, made some very queer films. Conversely, although the homosexuality of George Cukor and Dorothy Arzner informs the so-called 'women's films' that they made, can such films be called 'queer' in the sense of consciously challenging, strange, or diverse?

Consider the varying ideas and attitudes associated with the words homo-sexual, gay and queer. To what extent can these terms be used to describe various kinds of film-making?

Consider varying attitudes to positive images of lesbians and gays. Should we condemn the conflation of homosexuality, violence and murder in such films as *Basic Instinct*? Or can we be confident that a wide enough variety of views of lesbian and gay life now circulates in society to balance out negative images, so that we may embrace the new queer aesthetic?

Critically analyse *The Hanging Garden* (Thom Fitzgerald, Canada 1997) to address the following:

How does the director use the family wedding as a source of confrontation and comedy?
What formal elements are used to portray Sweet William's youthful struggles with his sexuality?

The best way I can think of to conclude this chapter is to point the reader in the direction of the Further viewing section, which contains a selection of mainly feature-length narrative and documentary films. To prevent the list from becoming unwieldy, I have concentrated on presenting a cross-section of the range of viewing experiences available in terms of nationality, historical period and sexual viewpoint. Some films mentioned in the chapter have, for this reason, not been included. Foreign-language films are referred to by their recognised title in the English-speaking world. References to a range of other viewing are also made in the comments on the bibliography.

As well as the recent and remarkable growth in feature-length material, there is now a vast range of small-scale and/or video-based lesbian and gay film-making, including specialised documentaries and safer-sex material for both men and women. Those who wish to investigate further, mainstream or alternative, small scale or big budget, should consult Raymond Murray's recently updated, comprehensive guide. The book on docu-mentary, edited by Holmlund and Fuchs, also contains a helpful reference list. Both these publications are listed in the Further reading section.

Use both the Further reading and Further viewing sections to investigate and develop the questions posed in this chapter. Watch and look into the films using the case studies as models. Above all, explore, enjoy and widen your viewing experiences.

 FURTHER READING

Babuscio, J. 'Camp and Gay Sensibility', in R. Dyer (ed.) *Gays and Film* (BFI, London, 1977). An essay which presents pioneering insights.

Bourne, S. *Brief Encounters: Lesbians and Gays in British Cinema 1930–1971* (Cassell, London and Washington, 1996). A useful year-by-year guide, with excellent material on the contemporary reception of *Victim*.

Cook, P. and Dodd, P. *Women and Film: A 'Sight and Sound' Reader* (BFI, London, 1993). An excellent section entitled 'Queer Alternatives' contains B. Ruby Rich's essay on queer cinema, Pratibha Parmar's response, Amy Taubin's lively criticisms and an essay on Monika Treut.

Dyer, R. *Now You See It: Studies on Lesbian and Gay Film* (Routledge, London and New York, 1990). A detailed academic study, best tackled in individual sections, mainly on early German film, Genet and developments in the US.

—— *The Matter of Images: Essays on Representation* (Routledge, London, 1993a). Dyer illustrates the power and complexity of images across a range of films, including film noir, *Victim*, and the 'sad young man' tradition which fed into the star persona of James Dean and others.

—— 'Rock: The last guy you'd have figured?', in P. Kirkham and J. Thurmin (eds) *You Tarzan: Maculinity, Movies and Men* (St Martin's Press, New York, 1993b).

Gever, M., Greyson, J. and Parmer, P. (eds) *Queer Looks: Perspectives on Lesbian and Gay Video* (Between the Lines, Toronto; Routledge, London and New York, 1993). A wealth of new insights, including a look at gay punk video-maker Bruce La Bruce, and new interpretations of Fassbinder's films.

Holmlund, C. and Fuchs, C. *Between the Sheets, In the Streets: Queer, Lesbian and Gay Documentary* (University of Minnesota Press, Minneapolis, 1997). Primarily US-centred, but extremely fruitful exploration of the nature, form and address of documentary. Includes contributions on Marlon Riggs, Su Friedrich, Derek Jarman and Sadie Benning. It also has a wide-ranging and useful list of titles.

Jarman, D. *Dancing Ledge* (Quartet, London, 1984). Britain's foremost gay auteur. The critically-acclaimed artist's account of his formative years, which cover the making of *The Angelic Conversation*, *Sebastiane* and *Jubilee*. The first of a number of fascinating writings he produced, which includes books to accompany *Caravaggio*, *War Requiem* and *Edward II*.

Kabir, S. *Daughters of Desire: Lesbian Representation in Film* (Cassell, London and Washington, 1998). Feminist and psychoanalytic approaches are combined with lesbian history and black subjectivity to examine a range of films from *Queen Christina* to *Go Fish*.

Mulvey, L. 'Visual pleasures and narrative cinema', in *The Sexual Subject: A Screen Reader in Sexuality* (Routledge, London and New York, 1995). Suggests ways in which a viewer of classic Hollywood films is addressed as male by being encouraged to adopt the viewpoint of the male protagonist.

Murray, R. *Images in the Dark: An Encyclopedia of Lesbian and Gay Film and Video* (TLA Publications, Philadelphia, 1996). An ideal sourcebook to make further investigations. International in its breadth, it covers mainstream and independent film, and has separate sections on queer, lesbian, gay male and transgender interest, and on camp.

Russo, V. *The Celluloid Closet: Homosexuality in the Movies* (Harper & Row, New York, 1987). The classic introduction to this area.

Steven, P. (ed.) *Jump Cut: Hollywood, Politics and Counter-Cinema* (Between the Lines, Toronto, 1985). Useful essays include viewpoints on lesbian spectatorship, Richard Dyer on stereotyping, and Jan Oxenberg.

Weiss, A. *Vampires and Violets: Lesbians in Film* (Penguin, Harmondsworth, 1993). Key films and the main debates clearly presented.

Wilton, T. *Immortal Invisible: Lesbians and the Moving Image* (Routledge, London, 1995). A collection of essays which investigates lesbian viewing and production. It includes contributions on *Desert Hearts* and *Salmonberries* along with interpretations of *Aliens* and other mainstream films.

Wood, R. *Hitchcock Revisited* (Faber & Faber, London, 1989). This volume includes Wood's original auteurist essays on Hitchcock with challenging new re-readings in the light of gay critical perspectives.

 **FURTHER VIEWING**

Films

Pandora's Box (G.W. Pabst, Germany 1928)
A beautiful and amoral *femme fatale* has several male lovers, but her lesbian lover proves to be the most devoted of her followers. A classic of early German cinema, and one of the first positive and sustained portrayals of a lesbian character.

Queen Christina (Rouben Mamoulian, US 1933)
Despite all Hollywood could do to suppress it, the lesbian subtext rings clear and true through Garbo's performance and Salka Viertel's script.

The Killing of Sister George (Robert Aldrich, US 1968)
A tragi-comedy about a soap opera actress whose homely on-screen image clashes with her off-screen dyke persona. Oppressive stereotypes or liberating humour? Worth watching to make up your own mind.

Pink Flamingoes (John Waters, US 1972)
A cult classic which uses camp modes of expression to explore and subvert conventional sexual structures. It stars the gay idol Divine.

Je, Tu, Il, Elle (Chantal Akerman, Belgium 1974)
This gently paced first feature by one of Europe's leading avant-garde film-makers is captivating. A young woman hitches a lift to revisit her lover. The film scintillates with woman-centred sensuality.

Madame X (Ulrike Ottinger, Germany 1977)
An avant-garde lesbian feminist pirate adventure. Challenging viewing in its attempts to find new ways of presenting women in film, but rewarding.

We Were One Man (Philippe Valois, France 1981)
A beautifully crafted love story set in rural France during the Second World War, which chronicles the affair between a wounded German pilot and a young French peasant.

Another Way (Karoly Makk, Hungary 1982)
Said to be among Eastern Europe's first films dealing with a lesbian relationship, this is an intelligent and finely observed love story set just after the Hungarian uprising of 1956.

Anne Trister (Lea Pool, Canada/Switzerland 1985)
Pool's style sensitively chronicles her main character's melancholy recovery from the death of her father, her move from Switzerland, her creative processes as a painter and the growing realisation of her feeling for the woman with whom she shares her Montreal apartment.

Before Stonewall (Greta Schiller and Robert Rosenberg, US 1985)
A rich documentary of ordinary lesbian and gay lives in the US in the 1940s and 1950s.

Dona Herlinda and Her Son (Jaime Hermosillo, Mexico 1985)
An entertaining comedy of sexual manners where a perceptive mother arranges her son's love-life to cater for his gay lover and her own desire for a grandchild. One of the first Latin American films to deal positively with a gay theme.

Caravaggio (Derek Jarman, UK 1986)
Jarman's view of this famous painter's life. An eye-catching blend of art, gay history and modern sensibilities.

Parting Glances (Bill Sherwood, US 1986)
A beautifully made depiction of a group of people, gay and straight, in New York City.

Law of Desire (Pedro Almodovar, Spain 1987)
A gripping gay melodrama by one of Spain's leading contemporary directors.

She Must Be Seeing Things (Sheila McLaughlin, US 1987)
This film touches on many uncomfortable aspects of lesbian sex, loving and looking. It does so in a stylish and articulate way.

Macho Dancer (Lino Brocka, The Philippines 1988)
A young man's emotional journey through the gay underworld of Manila. A romantic and sensual film. Through his social realism and sympathy for the oppressed, the director was a leading force in the cinema of his country as well as a noted political dissident.

Virgin Machine (Monika Treut, Germany 1988)
A journey of lesbian self-discovery and exploration for a young German journalist in San Francisco. Wacky and provocative views of that city's lesbian scene.

Salmonberries (Percy Adlon, Germany 1991)
A close emotional involvement between an Eskimo woman, played by k.d. lang, and a teacher fleeing her past. Compulsively watchable performances and locations.

Young Soul Rebels (Isaac Julien, UK 1991)
A gay murder is solved. In the process, two young DJs, one gay and one straight, find romance and promote their brand of music. A vivid evocation of the London club scene of the late 1970s, with a lively soundtrack.

The Crying Game (Neil Jordan, UK 1992)
A political thriller which raises unsettling questions about gender and desire.

Forbidden Love: The Unashamed Stories of Lesbian Lives (Aerlyn Wessman and Lynne Femie, Canada 1992)
Wonderful to watch: a 1950s pulp-fiction style lesbian love story is interwoven with older women talking about their lives.

Nitrate Kisses (Barbara Hammer, US 1992)
A mixture of meditation and documentary, this richly textured film explores lesbian and gay sexuality through history, politics and poetry. Especially noteworthy for its lively portrayal of older lesbians, this is a feast for the eye and the mind.

North of Vortex (Constantine Giannaris, UK 1992)
Two men and a woman, a poet, a crook and a waitress, meet by chance and take off across America together in this evocative, erotic road movie. Winner of the 1992 *Gay Times* Jack Babuscio Award. A troubling text of the New Queer Cinema.

No Skin Off My Ass (Bruce La Bruce, Canada 1992)
New Queer Cinema with all its rough edges and unusual cinematic strategies; a punk hairdresser seduces a skinhead. Available for purchase from video distributor Out On A Limb.

Okoge (Takehiro Nakajima, Japan 1992)
One of the best of the recent gay films from Japan. A social comedy of love and compromise with graphic sex scenes and a background of Tokyo gay life.

Blue (Derek Jarman, UK 1993)
Jarman's most artistically audacious film. The soundtrack explores death, AIDS, Jarman's own fight against blindness, and the many connotations of the vivid blue that fills the screen. This is the third in Jarman's trilogy of autobiographical masterworks

of social and political commentary, after *The Last of England* and *The Garden*.

The Living End (Gregg Araki, US 1993)
A road movie featuring two comically contrasting young men, both HIV positive, who fall for each other. They undertake an anarchic and often hilarious journey, with emotional challenges, odd characters and some bad-taste jokes along the way. A landmark of the New Queer Cinema.

The Wedding Banquet (Ang Lee, Taiwan/China/US 1993)
A cross-cultural comedy full of delightful characters. A Chinese gay man living in New York with his lover puts on a show to keep visiting Mum and Dad happy.

Adventures of Priscilla, Queen of the Desert (Stephen Elliott, Australia 1994)
Lots of fun, lots of drag. Terence Stamp gives a nuanced and engaging performance as a male-to-female transsexual.

Only the Brave (Anna Kokkinos, Australia 1994)
Traces the intense and changing relationship between two daughters of Greek immigrant families in a Melbourne suburb. A grim but compelling view of their love and life.

Jeffrey (Chris Ashley, US 1995)
Two beautiful New York men tread the rocky road to love in the age of AIDS, with the help of memorable supporting performances from Patrick Stewart as the arty older friend, and Sigourney Weaver as a new-age guru.

When Night is Falling (Patricia Rozema, Canada 1995)
A glossy and stylish lesbian romance with circus acts and a plot that closely echoes *Desert Hearts*. For a more quirky and attractively watchable film of lesbian interest see Rozema's *I've Heard the Mermaids Singing*.

Bound (Andy and Larry Wachowski, US 1996)
A post-queer lesbian private-eye film; two consciously stereotyped babes-with-brains in steamy union. This seems set to stir up all the old debates.

Stonewall (Nigel Finch, UK 1996)
A passionate and funny version of the historically crucial gay riot of 1969, this film deserves particular credit for the way it puts drag queens, their music and their culture at the centre of it all in a historically accurate way.

Beautiful Thing (Hettie Macdonald, UK 1997)
Two young men find love and comfort in each other's arms on a Bermondsey council estate and start to explore the local gay scene. Mum is eventually won over, and the young woman next door lends a hand. Liberal clichés redeemed by skilful writing and acting.

Bent (Sean Mathias, UK 1997)
This film about the persecution of gays in Nazi Germany reflects the weaknesses of the stage play on which it is based. It is worth viewing, though, for its powerful performances and historically important subject matter.

The Hanging Garden (Thorn Fitzgerald, Canada 1997)
A gay man revisits his troubled family in rural Nova Scotia after fleeing from it ten years before. Magic realism is brilliantly used to embody his confrontations and interactions. Visually striking contrasts between the mature, balanced adult and the troubled, overweight, suicidal teenage younger self.

Happy Together (Wong Kar Wai, Hong Kong 1997)
The cult Chinese director follows two gay men to Buenos Aires. He tells the story of a crisis in their relationship with his usual pacy and energetic style.

Skin Deep (Midi Onodera, Canada 1997)
A male actor plays a woman passing as a man. This character, a transgender loner, becomes involved with a lesbian film-maker and her long-suffering girlfriend. Overstuffed with incident, but fascinating.

The Watermelon Woman (Cheryl Dunye, US 1997)
Cheryl, an aspiring film-maker who is making a documentary about a beautiful and elusive 1930s black film actress, is coolly seduced by the beautiful Diana. Fans of Dunye should recognise her quirky and attractive style in this feature, which seems set to widen her popularity. Stars Dunye herself and Guinevere Turner.

Wilde (Brian Gilbert, UK/US/Japan/Germany 1997)
At times simplistic in its account of the life and times of this great gay artist, the film offers a moving portrayal of the sexual passion that brought about Wilde's doom.

Compilations

The Best of 'Out' and 'Out On Tuesday'.
A diverse compilation from Channel Four's 'Lesbian and Gay' series, including Pratibha Parmar's 'Khush', a documentary meditation about Asian lesbians and gays in Britain. On Connoisseur Video.

Gay Classics (Genet/Julien/Kwietniowski).
Three major, thought-provoking works by gay men; Genet's *Un chant d'amour*, Julien's *Looking For Langston* and Richard Kwietniowski's stylish drama, *Flames of Passion*. On Connoisseur Video.

Lesbian Lykra Shorts.
A rich international compilation which highlights the diversity of recent lesbian film-making. Contact Dangerous To Know video for information about this one, and about *Lesbian Leather Shorts* and *Lesbian Lace Shorts*.

RESOURCE CENTRES

Video availability is very variable. All the following organisations offer helpful, up-to-the-minute catalogues and brochures of currently available material.

Connoisseur Video
10a Stephen Mews
London W1P 0AX.

Dangerous To Know
17a Newman Street
London W1P 3HB
Tel: 0171 255 1955
Fax: 0171 636 5717
e-mail: mail website: www.dtk.co.uk

Dangerous to Know also have a website at
http://www.dangeroustoknow.com
This video supplier has a lively and up-to-date list of titles and will provide brochures and catalogues.

London Lesbian and Gay Film Festival
www.llgff.org.uk
The festival has a website giving details of their presentations at the National Film Theatre in March. For a few months after that, the same programme of films and videos then tours various regional film theatres. Programme and venue details can be obtained via their website.

Additional websites

http://www.planetout.com
A website that provides lists of gay and lesbian films with distributors' addresses and phone and fax numbers: BFI, Channel Four, ICA Projects, and so on. Includes UK, US, Canada and Germany.

http://www.frameline.org
Frameline Distributions is a comprehensive, non-profit organisation dedicated to the exhibition, distribution, promotion and funding of lesbian and gay film and video. A sponsor of the San Francisco Lesbian and Gay Film Festival.

http://www.feminist.org
A website with information on film, arts and literature of particular interest to women.

http://www.glaad.org
The website of the Gay and Lesbian Alliance Against Defamation, with a movie line.

Part five

National cinemas

Chapter 11

British Cinema

Lez Cooke

PART 1: APPROACHES AND DEFINITIONS 348
■ **What do we mean by 'British Cinema'?** 348
■ **What is a 'British' film?** 349
■ **British Cinema as 'national cinema'?** 350

PART 2: BRITISH FILM CULTURE – A HISTORICAL OVERVIEW 351
■ **From cottage industry to mass entertainment** 351
■ **Government legislation in the 1920s** 352
■ **Class and culture in 1930s British cinema** 353
■ **'Realism and tinsel' in wartime cinema** 356
■ **The postwar period** 359
■ **New films for new audiences: Hammer horror and the 'new wave'** 361
■ **Popular cinema: the *Carry On* and Bond films** 363
■ **British Cinema and Hollywood in the Sixties** 366
■ **The 1970s: mainstream decline and the rise of independent cinema** 366
■ **1980s 'renaissance'** 367
■ **'Heritage' cinema** 368
■ **Channel Four and the new multicultural British Cinema** 369
■ **The 1980s: postscript** 371

PART 3: 1990s RENAISSANCE 371
■ **From art house to mainstream** 372
☐ Case study 1: *Trainspotting* (1996) 373
☐ Case study 2: *The Full Monty* (1997) 375
■ **A brief survey of other 1990s British films** 377
■ **Conclusion** 378
■ **Further reading** 379
■ **Further viewing** 380
■ **Resource centres** 380

■ British Cinema

Part 1: Approaches and definitions

Any discussion of British Cinema as 'national cinema' immediately poses problems of definition, and this chapter will begin by addressing three questions:

1 What do we mean by 'British Cinema'?
2 What is a 'British' film?
3 In what sense is British Cinema a 'national cinema'?

WHAT DO WE MEAN BY 'BRITISH CINEMA'?

There are two ways of approaching and defining British Cinema: (1) *institutionally* and (2) *culturally*.

From an *institutional* point of view British Cinema would be seen as synonymous with the British film industry – the sector responsible for financing, producing, distributing and exhibiting films in Britain. Each of these four branches of the industry could be discussed separately as different aspects of British Cinema, but in practice they are all dependent on each other.

While Britain had a thriving film industry in the 1930s, 1940s and 1950s, and a healthy one in the 1960s thanks to American finance, the British film industry as a **vertically integrated structure** has not really existed since the 1970s. Today the financing of British films often comes from sources outside the UK, except in the case of very low-budget films which may receive all of their funding from British investors (often a consortium in which television companies are prominent). British films may be produced in British studios, but film companies are often in competition with American companies for studio space and for film technicians and other production personnel. The distribution and exhibition sectors in the UK are now dominated by American companies, which make sure that American films have precedence on the cinema circuits, squeezing out the lower profile British product which cannot usually compete with the mega-budgets and high concept marketing of the Hollywood films, except in the case of a few isolated examples which will be discussed later.

In contrast to this institutional emphasis, it is possible to take a *cultural* approach to British Cinema, where the focus would shift towards the representation of British life and culture in British films, and the part that those films play in defining and projecting an image of the nation. With this approach it becomes possible to assess the contribution that cinema makes to the forging of a national identity and a national culture. This raises questions about the concept of 'national identity', and the possibility of a 'national' cinema, which will be considered below.

The first of these two approaches is considered elsewhere in this volume and it is with *British film culture* that this chapter is mainly concerned. Through looking at a wide range of British films, produced at different historical moments, this chapter will consider some of the ways in which British films have represented British national identity and culture through distinctively British film genres and movements, such as the Documentary Film Movement, the realist wartime film, costume melodramas, Ealing comedies, Hammer horror films, the *Carry On* and Bond series, 'kitchen sink' films and the 'heritage' film, concluding with a look at the 1990s 'renaissance' in British Cinema.

By taking a broad historical overview it is possible to see that, rather than British Cinema being a 'national cinema' with a national identity, the disparate films, genres

vertically integrated structure
A structure, as in the 'studio system', where the financing, production, distribution and exhibition of a film is controlled by one company.

See Chapter 2 for discussion of cinema as institution.

and movements that constitute 100 years of British Cinema have portrayed the UK in all its regional, national and cultural diversity, helping to forge a multifaceted identity for Britain, and for Britons, which is at variance with the more one-dimensional cultural stereotypes to be found in many Hollywood films. The history of British Cinema is therefore the history of a 'struggle for identity' in relation to Hollywood, with its ever increasing global dominance.

But before embarking on a survey of the many ways in which British Cinema has attempted to counter the dominance of Hollywood we need to consider the two other questions posed at the beginning of this chapter.

WHAT IS A 'BRITISH' FILM?

An economic/institutional definition of a British film was laid down in the 1927 Cinematograph Films Act. This Act had been designed to revive the flagging British film industry in the 1920s by guaranteeing that a quota of British films should be shown in UK cinemas, at a time when Hollywood's dominance at the box office was so great that British films represented less than 5 per cent of the films being shown in British cinemas. For the purpose of administering this quota, the 1927 Cinematograph Films Act defined a British film as one which conformed to the following criteria:

1 The film had to be made by a British company or by a person who was a British subject.
2 All studio scenes must have been filmed in a studio located in the British Empire.
3 British subjects (excluding one foreign actor or producer) had to receive 75 per cent of the labour costs.
4 The author of the scenario had to be British.

(see Dickinson and Street 1985: 5–6)

This definition, like the size of the quota, has fluctuated over the years. Since 1982, when the screen quota was finally ended, the definition of a British film has tended to vary, according to whether the production personnel or the source of finance are used as the main criteria. Having a British director and British production team made Richard Attenborough's *Chaplin* a British film according to *Screen Finance*, whereas *Screen International* considered it an American film because it was financed by an American company (see Cooke 1996: 295).

In its list of seventy-eight British films produced in 1995, the *BFI Film and Television Handbook 1997* gives four categories of 'British' film:

1 Films where the cultural and financial impetus is from the UK and the majority of the production personnel is British (e.g. *Brassed Off*, *Small Faces*, *Trainspotting*).
2 Majority UK co-productions: films in which, although there are foreign partners, there is a UK cultural content and a significant amount of British finance and personnel (e.g. *Carla's Song*, *Nil By Mouth*, *Secrets and Lies*).
3 Minority UK co-productions: foreign (non-US) films in which there is a small UK involvement in finance or personnel (e.g. *Breaking the Waves*, *Stealing Beauty*).
4 American films with a UK creative and/or part financial involvement (e.g. *Emma*, *GoldenEye*, *The Portrait of a Lady*).

(Dyja 1996: 24–7)

These categories, while acknowledging British 'cultural content' as an important factor, put the main emphasis in classifying a British film on the amount of British finance and personnel involved in the production: the greater the involvement, the more 'British' the film is. 'Wholly' British films, according to this method of classification, are to be found in Category 1 and number only twenty-eight of the seventy-eight UK films produced in 1995, although most of the nine films which fall into Category 2 would be recognised as being British on the basis of their cultural content. Of the remaining forty-one films in Categories 3 and 4 however, British involvement is more limited, in terms of finance and production personnel, and these films are less obviously British in terms of cultural content.

In March 1998, the new Labour government's Film Policy Review Group proposed to rationalise this untidy system by introducing a new statutory definition of a British film, based on a points system:

Under the new system a film will be considered British if it scores 20 points. It will earn three points for a British screenwriter and two for a British producer, director, editor, lead actor, etc. If 75 per cent of production costs are spent in the UK it will receive four points. A film's origin is important in calculating subsidy and taxation.

(*The Guardian*, 26 March 1998)

While this may simplify the process of classifying a film as British the rationale here is still an institutional one, more concerned with economics than with cultural criteria. We need therefore to turn to the 'cultural content' referred to above and ask how we might recognise a British film on the screen. What might enable us to identify and distinguish a British film from a Hollywood film or a European film?

iconography
The visual codes of setting, props and clothing which enable us to recognise a film as belonging to a certain genre or type.

For further discussion of iconography, see Chapter 6, pp. 167–8; for further discussion of visual codes, see Chapter 4, pp. 98–110.

The two most immediate factors here are probably **iconography** and speech. It is the iconography of a film, locating the action in a recognisably British setting with recognisable British ingredients, which can provide one of the first signifiers of 'Britishness' in a film. Speech, and especially accents, whether regional dialects or distinguished by a working- middle- or upper-class intonation, may be another immediate signifier of 'Britishness'. From these initial aspects of iconography and speech we may then proceed to identify typical elements: characters, scenes, situations, stories, to be found in British films, elements which serve to identify a film as 'typically British'.

> **Look at the first five minutes of any British film and make notes on what identifies it as 'British'. Consider the iconography (clothing, props, setting, etc.) and the speech of individual characters.**

BRITISH CINEMA AS 'NATIONAL CINEMA'?

For further reading on British Cinema as national cinema, see Cooke 1996; Crofts 1998; Higson 1989, 1995 and 1998; Hill 1992 and 1997; Hill, McLoone and Hainsworth 1994; Richards 1997.

When we come to the question of the extent to which British Cinema can be said to be a 'national cinema', the economic criteria given above for defining a film as British are less useful than the cultural criteria, which take into consideration the presence of distinctively British 'cultural content'. Clearly, to include a Hollywood blockbuster like *Mission: Impossible*, which comes into the fourth category of 1995 UK Film Production listed in the 1997 *BFI Film and Television Handbook*, is to stretch the definition of a British film to the extent where it is not very useful. *Mission: Impossible* is included in this category because it was filmed in a British studio, using British personnel, and the categorisation is an economic/institutional one, rather than a cultural one. On the other hand, *Sense and Sensibility* (based on the novel by Jane Austen), which also comes into the fourth category because it was financed by an American company, makes more sense in terms of a 'cultural' approach to British Cinema.

The question of a 'national cinema' has always been a difficult one for the UK because of the **hegemony** which Hollywood has maintained in the UK since before the First World War. Throughout virtually its entire existence British Cinema has been living under the shadow of Hollywood (see Murphy 1986) and the situation has worsened in recent years as a result of a combination of government neglect and Hollywood's increasing global domination.

There is another reason however why the concept of a 'national' British Cinema is problematic, and this concerns the increasingly **pluralistic** nature of British national identity and British culture since the 1960s. It is debatable as to whether there has ever been a unified 'national cinema' in the UK (though some might argue this was the case during the Second World War), but it has become increasingly difficult to speak of a 'British' national cinema when the concept of nationhood has fragmented with the growth of Irish, Welsh and Scottish nationalism and with the proliferation of ethnic communities and cultures within the nation-state of the UK. This is evident in the representations of an increasingly diverse community, distinguished by different ethnic, class, regional and cultural identities, and in the production of a diverse range of films from the different nations and regions of the UK.

hegemony
The maintenance of power or control (economic, political or cultural) held by a dominant group or class in society.

pluralistic
Multiple; refers in this instance to the fragmentation of society into different ethnic, social and cultural groups.

Part 2: British film culture – a historical overview

In order to consider the ways in which British Cinema has attempted to define itself as a national cinema, with its own distinct cultural identity, it is instructive to take a historical overview, focusing on some key moments and developments in British Cinema. What follows, therefore, is an attempt to identify some of the important genres, movements and tendencies within British film history: an outline, necessarily schematic, of how British Cinema has struggled to assert its own identity in the face of foreign, especially American, competition. Further reading is indicated in the margins, with the full reference listed at the end of the book.

FROM COTTAGE INDUSTRY TO MASS ENTERTAINMENT

The distinctiveness and originality of some of the earliest British films, made between 1895 and 1907, has been recognised and celebrated in the critical reassessment of British Cinema that has taken place in the last two decades. Film production during these early years was a small-scale artisan activity, a novelty which developed into a cottage industry, producing trick films and short narratives which were screened at fairgrounds and amusement parlours. During the 1910s, as film studios and purpose-built cinemas began to proliferate, cinema in the UK underwent a process of **embourgoisement** as the new cinema owners endeavoured to attract a more upmarket middle-class audience to the new picture houses. By the outbreak of the First World War in 1914 the market for films had polarised along class lines, with the adaptation of literary and theatrical classics for a mainly middle-class audience and the production of lowbrow comedies and crime dramas for the working classes who formed the bulk of the cinema-going audience.

During this period, the pattern of subordination of British films to foreign imports had

embourgoisement
A sociological term describing the adoption of middle-class (bourgeois) values and attributes by members of the working class as a result of increased affluence.

For further reading on
early British Cinema, see
Barr 1997; Burch 1990;
Chanan 1996; Cooke
1993.

already been established, with foreign films comprising 85 per cent of the films being shown in British cinemas in the period leading up to the First World War. In 1913, however, American imports overtook European ones and, with the war having a serious impact upon French, German, Italian and British film production, the American hegemony over British Cinema was established. By the end of the war 80 per cent of the films being shown in British cinemas were American.

GOVERNMENT LEGISLATION IN THE 1920s

With so many of the stars, directors and producers of British films in the 1920s coming from a middle-class background, and the literary/theatrical ethos of British Cinema so well entrenched, the working-class audience turned in ever-increasing numbers to the more 'classless', action-orientated films being produced by Hollywood. As John Caughie notes:

In a country as divided as Britain by class and region, with their separate tastes, preferences and prejudices, American films may have occupied neutral territory for the mass market on which the box office depended, and Jimmy Cagney may have been more recognisable as a working-class hero than Michael Redgrave.

(Caughie 1996: 3)

Cinema had become a mass entertainment business by the 1920s, with twenty million people per week visiting Britain's ever-increasing number of picture houses (4,000 by the end of the decade). However, the vast majority of the films that audiences were seeing at those cinemas were Hollywood films. Such was the hegemony that Hollywood had achieved by the 1920s that British film production virtually collapsed, with the number of British films produced falling from 422 in 1922 to just 26 in 1925, less than 5 per cent of the total box office.

The crisis in the British film industry became the subject of government concern. Stanley Baldwin, the Conservative prime minister, made a speech to Parliament in June 1925 stating:

I think the time has come when the position of that industry in this country should be examined with a view to seeing whether it be not possible, as it is desirable, on national grounds, to see that the larger proportion of the films exhibited in this country are British.

(Quoted in Hartog 1983: 60)

Baldwin's concern was with the 'propaganda' to which British audiences were being subjected, but, with American films comprising the vast majority of the films being shown in British cinemas, these views were clearly not confined to the revolutionary propaganda of Soviet films, like Sergei Eisenstein's *Strike* (1924), which were being produced in Bolshevik Russia at the time. Rather, Baldwin's remarks were symptomatic of a growing concern with the 'Americanisation' of British culture.

Within two years of Baldwin's speech a Cinematograph Films Act was introduced, setting a quota for British films to which exhibitors were obliged to adhere. The quota was fixed at 5 per cent in 1927 with the aim of gradually increasing to 20 per cent by 1936. For this to operate it was necessary to define, for the first time, what a 'British' film was (see p. 348). The Act gave an immediate boost to British film production and numerous small film companies came into existence. But what the Act hadn't anticipated was the arrival of sound, which saw the cost of film production increase significantly. The result was that many of these new companies were forced out of business within three or four years.

The second factor which undermined the attempt of the 1927 Act to counter Hollywood's dominance by boosting British film production was the ingenuity of the Hollywood companies, who responded by investing in low-budget British films ('quota quickies' as they came to be known) which were made quickly and cheaply, lacking the production values of the more stylish Hollywood films. Consequently, the quota films were received unfavourably by the public, and by this means the American companies 'discredited film production and the quota legislation' (Hartog 1983: 68).

That the 1927 Cinematograph Films Act had *cultural* as well as economic objectives was confirmed by a member of the Board of Trade in 1936, when the government was considering new legislation to replace it:

By 1925 the depressed state of the British industry was causing general concern. Apart from the purely industrial aspect of the matter it was felt that from the point of view of British culture and ideals it was unwise to allow the United States to dominate the cinemas of this country. At that time nearly every film shown represented American ideas set in an American atmosphere, and the accessories were American houses, American materials, American manufacturers, etc. Whatever the position today, cinematograph audiences then were made up of the most impressionable sections of the community, and it was felt to be of the utmost importance for our prestige, for our trade and, it was asserted, for our morals, that they should see at least some proportion of British films.

For further reading on the 1930s 'quota quickies', see Napper 1997; Wood 1997.

(R.D. Fennelly, quoted in Hartog 1983: 73)

While there may be some argument about the quality of the films produced in the wake of the Act there is no doubt that it did give a boost to the industry, and the number of British films produced each year steadily increased, rising to 228 in 1937, before a slump resulting from over-investment brought a new crisis to the industry.

CLASS AND CULTURE IN 1930s BRITISH CINEMA

The 1930s saw Alfred Hitchcock consolidate his position as the most creative British film director of the period (see Ryall 1986) and saw the emergence of Alexander Korda as an ambitious producer intent upon playing the Americans at their own game. Korda was a producer/director who established his own film studio following the international success of *The Private Life of Henry VIII* (1933), starring Charles Laughton. Korda's strategy was to compete with Hollywood by producing lavish, big-budget films and he followed the success of *Henry VIII* with prestigious films such as *The Scarlet Pimpernel* (1934), *Things to Come* (1936), *The Man Who Could Work Miracles* (1937) and *The Four Feathers* (1939) – films which projected an image of Britain centred upon the upper classes and the aristocracy, as well as on Britain's status as an imperial power. This was one of the first concerted efforts to create a British national cinema to rival Hollywood, but, like much of the internationally targeted 'heritage' cinema that Britain has produced, it was a national cinema which privileged the ruling class and imperialist ideologies.

See the section on heritage cinema, p. 368.

The Scarlet Pimpernel provides an excellent illustration of the class-bound definition of 'Britishness' in Korda's films, a definition which is centred upon the life and culture of the upper classes and which is unashamedly patriotic, emphasising the extent to which Korda, as a middle-class immigrant, wished to demonstrate his credentials to be British through an identification with the middle and upper classes, and with the upper-class gentleman in particular (Korda became a naturalised British subject in 1936).

For further reading on Korda, see Kulik 1975; Richards 1984.

In *The Scarlet Pimpernel* it is Leslie Howard, so often the on-screen embodiment of the cultured English gentleman, who plays the eponymous hero who undertakes to save

• **Plate 11.1** *The Scarlet Pimpernel* (1934)
Celebrating national identity through images of aristocracy.

French aristocrats from the guillotine during the French Revolution. When he is not disguised as the Pimpernel his real identity is the English nobleman Sir Percy Blakeney who adopts an exaggerated foppishness in order to conceal his identity as the Pimpernel. The 'real' Sir Percy, we are led to believe, is the one who recites the John of Gaunt deathbed speech from *Richard II* – 'this earth, this realm, this England' – when he is about to be taken before a French firing squad. But the firing squad has been taken over by the Pimpernel's own men and he therefore lives to utter the final uplifting patriotic invocation to his wife Marguerite as their ship returns them from France: 'Look, Marguerite … England!', a line which Korda believed was guaranteed to stir the audience's emotions and get them applauding. For Korda, national identity equalled the culture of the upper classes. *The Scarlet Pimpernel* not only allowed this definition of national identity to be given expression but also provided a vehicle for the expression of Korda's own nationalistic patriotism.

In contrast to this, British Cinema in the 1930s was also notable for a series of working-class comedies featuring music-hall stars like Gracie Fields, George Formby and Will Hay. These films proved far more popular with working-class audiences in the industrial heartlands of Britain, which is where they were often set, than the middle-class films being produced by Korda's London Films. They were domestic rather than international in scope, and projected an image of working-class life and culture which was far removed from the high culture iconography and imperial overtones of the dominant, middle-class cinema.

Gracie Fields made her screen début in *Sally in Our Alley* in 1931, a film which is of interest in relation to national identity not only because it provides a sharp contrast to the privileging of the upper classes and the aristocracy in Korda's historical films, but for the way in which it engages with class conflict and emphasises a working-class point of view. One sequence in the film illustrates this well. Sally (Gracie Fields) is invited to sing at a high society party by an upper-class lady who has heard her singing in an East End coffee shop where Sally works as a waitress. At the party, however, Sally is treated as a source of amusement by the society party-goers and is clearly portrayed as a fish out of water. Sympathies are clearly intended to be with Sally in this embarrassing situation and the audience (which would have been predominantly working class) is encouraged to see the upper-class characters as patronising and privileged, something

• **Plate 11.2** *Sally in Our Alley* (1931)
A celebration of working-class identity and culture.

which working-class audiences would have had little difficulty in doing, given the high level of unemployment and poverty which existed at the time.

However, when Sally returns to the coffee shop she makes fun of the low-cut dress she has been given to wear at the party before delivering an emotional rendition of the title song to the working-class clientele. This scene is the obverse of the one at the end of *The Scarlet Pimpernel*, which was also designed to stir the emotions of the audience, but it is easier to imagine working-class audiences at the time identifying, culturally, with Sally (and Gracie Fields) than with the aristocratic Sir Percy Blakeney – no matter how much star appeal Leslie Howard may have had.

Both *Sally in Our Alley* and *The Scarlet Pimpernel* can be seen to be performing an **ideological function** for British audiences in the 1930s, the latter by reinforcing the dominant culture and projecting an image of 'Britishness' which equated it with the culture of the upper classes, the former by offering a view of an alternative working-class culture and identity. At a time when the working classes were experiencing real poverty and deprivation in a way that the upper classes were not, it seems likely that the films of Gracie Fields and George Formby (who took over from Gracie as Britain's top box-office star in 1938) were as important a part of 'national cinema' as the more high profile films of Korda and Hitchcock. In terms of representation they certainly had an ideological role to play in countering the representation of the privileged classes in Korda's films by offering alternative, working-class identities and pleasures for what was, after all, the bulk of the cinema-going audience.

The other important development of the 1930s was the Documentary Film Movement, centred around the figure of John Grierson. While marginal in relation to the commercial film industry, the documentary movement was important in cultural terms for its middle-class concern to portray the reality of working-class life during the Depression. The 'creative treatment of actuality', as Grierson described the realist aesthetic of government-sponsored films like *Coalface* (1935) and *Nightmail* (1936), represented a tradition of realism in British Cinema which entered into mainstream cinema during the Second World War and continued to be an important influence on British film-making well into the postwar period.

> **How do representations of 'Britishness' differ in documentary and feature films of the 1930s?**

'REALISM AND TINSEL' IN WARTIME CINEMA

The driving force for British Cinema during the Second World War was the need for national unity. There was a need for the country to put aside its social divisions and class differences and unite to fight a common enemy, but the Ministry of Information, which took over the responsibility for approving scripts during the war, didn't at first reflect that urgency. Consequently, the most memorable wartime films tend to date from the later years of the conflict: such films as *In Which We Serve* (1942), *Millions Like Us* (1943), *This Happy Breed* (1944), *The Way Ahead* (1944) and *The Way to the Stars* (1945).

Film production was, of course, severely affected by the war and the number of films produced dropped to an average of forty-two feature films per year. However, this falling off in production was matched by a noticeable increase in quality as film-makers rose to the challenge of contributing to the war effort by producing morale-boosting films.

While a variety of genre films were made during the war, what distinguishes the best

---

ideological function
Ideology is the system of ideas, values and beliefs held by individuals or groups within society. Ideological function refers to the way in which ideology is disseminated through films or other cultural forms. Audiences may of course refuse to accept the dominant ideological meaning in a film.

For further reading on 1930s British Cinema, see Aldgate 1983; Richards 1984 and 1998.

For further reading on the British Documentary Film Movement, see Chapter 7 and Chapter 9, p. 269.

Also see Aitken 1990 and 1997; Dodd and Dodd 1996; Hood 1983; Lovell and Hillier 1972.

• **Plate 11.3** *In Which We Serve* (1942) A skilful marriage of realism and melodrama.

of the wartime films is often a skilful marriage of realism and melodrama. No film illustrates this better than *In Which We Serve*, one of the most popular films of the war, both in Britain and in America. Written by Noel Coward, who also co-directed (with David Lean), produced, composed the music and starred in the film, *In Which We Serve* told the story of a group of men who survive the torpedoing and sinking of their ship, the HMS *Torrin*, after it has been seen at the beginning of the film wreaking havoc, apparently single-handedly, among a fleet of German transport ships. While the survivors of the capsized ship cling desperately to a life-raft and wait to be rescued, intermittently being machine-gunned by German planes, a series of flashbacks take place from the point of view of each of the three main characters: Noel Coward's upper-middle-class captain, Bernard Miles' lower-middle-class officer and John Mills' working-class rating, a cross-section of the ship's crew reflecting the hierarchy of the British class system. The flashbacks elaborate on these class differences as the three men recollect aspects of their family lives, giving credence to the idea that national unity extended across classes.

The message is clear: class differences are as natural and essential to the social fabric of British life as the rigid but necessary hierarchy of the navy is essential to the smooth operation of the HMS *Torrin*. This is illustrated very clearly when Coward's captain calmly but authoritatively directs operations from the bridge of the ship while the rest of the crew are shown performing their essential individual functions down below. Only once is the smooth efficiency of this routine disrupted, and that is when Richard Attenborough's frightened young rating deserts his post in the heat of the battle.

On more than one occasion the crew are gathered together and reminded by the captain of the need for 'a happy and efficient ship' in an address which could be Winston Churchill's (or King George's) message to the British people – HMS *Torrin* here a clear metaphor for the country as a whole. The propaganda message of the film is obvious but never crude, the melodrama blending with the realism to sweeten the bitter pill that sacrifice is necessary for the common good. However it is not the captain's house which gets destroyed by a German bomb towards the end of the film but that of the officer, killing his wife and mother-in-law, while both Miles' officer and Mills' rating are wounded when the ship is torpedoed, whereas Coward's captain escapes unscathed. Clearly some members of 'the family' have to be prepared to sacrifice more than others.

It is in the skilful blending of realism and melodrama in wartime feature films that the influence of the pre-war documentary film-makers becomes significant, for while some of the documentarists working with Grierson at the GPO Film Unit in the 1930s directed their energies towards producing propaganda films for the Crown Film Unit (a government organisation which superseded the GPO Film Unit in 1940), others ventured into mainstream feature film production, many of them going to work with Michael Balcon at Ealing Studios.

It was this input from the documentarists that perhaps did more than anything to construct a national cinema and to project an image of national identity for Britons during the war, and it is the carefully contrived documentary realism of these films for which British wartime cinema is now remembered.

The documentary realist tradition has been seen as 'Britain's outstanding contribution to the film' (see Higson 1986), a tradition which distinguishes British Cinema and differentiates it from Hollywood, with its emphasis upon escapism and spectacle. But this dominant aesthetic has tended to obscure and marginalise other traditions within British Cinema, non-realist traditions of fantasy, melodrama and horror, which Julian Petley has described as 'the lost continent' of British film-making (see Petley 1986). At least one of these traditions was operating alongside the realist tradition in the 1940s, emerging to be highly successful at the box office: Gainsborough's popular costume melodramas. For Michael Balcon and the middle-class critics of the time, these films represented the frivolous and artificial 'tinsel' of the commercial cinema, an escapist cinema which lacked the authenticity and seriousness of the realist films (see Murphy 1989: Ch.3).

While Gainsborough costume melodramas like *The Man in Grey* (1943), *Madonna of the Seven Moons* (1944) and *The Wicked Lady* (1945) were very successful at the box office, they are not usually included in any discussion of national cinema, perhaps because they blatantly reject the dominant realist tradition. However, feminist film historians have sought to rescue these films from the cultural dustbin of British Cinema history, arguing for their importance as women's pictures and as transgressive texts.

With their emphasis upon strong, independent female characters, such as the highway robber which Margaret Lockwood plays in *The Wicked Lady*, these films offered their female audiences, already emancipated by their experience of performing 'men's work' during the war, forceful and exciting female characters with whom to identify. While these dangerous heroines were often punished for their temerity in challenging the authority of the male heroes, it has been argued that the conventional resolutions in favour of a restoration of the patriarchal order were less important than the power of the liberating and transgressive images contained in the films:

Audiences leaving a screening of *The Wicked Lady* were more likely to remember the stunning image of a fetishized Margaret Lockwood dressed in highwayman gear astride a stallion than to take on board the moral implications of her punishment by death.

(Cook 1996a: 59)

• **Plate 11.4** *The Wicked Lady* (1945) Redefining the role and identity of women.

Pam Cook has argued, furthermore, that these films, rather than being marginal aberrations, are indeed central to any discussion of a British national cinema because 'they celebrate an itinerant spirit in British Cinema, an urge to move beyond fixed national boundaries to a more hybrid notion of national identity' (Cook 1996a: 64). Cook is attempting to shift the terms of the debate about British national cinema here, to make space for the inclusion of other, previously marginal, identities. This, she argues, is the significance of the Gainsborough melodramas in the 1940s. At a time when gender and class roles were undergoing radical revision, costume melodramas like *Madonna of the Seven Moons* and *The Wicked Lady* played an important part in helping to redefine the role and identity of women in British society.

See Chapter 9, pp. 283–6, for further discussion of how female audiences interpret media texts.

For further reading on Gainsborough and women in wartime, see Cook 1996b and 1998; Gledhill and Swanson 1996; Harper 1994; Landy 1997; Lant 1991.

> **How is 'Britishness' portrayed in *In Which We Serve*? Compare the representation of gender in *In Which We Serve* and *The Wicked Lady*.**

THE POSTWAR PERIOD

Three aspects of the immediate postwar British Cinema are worthy of note in this overview of British film history. First, J. Arthur Rank, like Korda before him, made an attempt to compete with Hollywood, having developed the Rank Organisation as a vertically integrated company, with branches controlling film production, distribution and exhibition, along the lines of the major Hollywood studios. During this period Rank was responsible for financing a number of prestigious adaptations of literary and theatrical classics, films such as David Lean's *Great Expectations* (1945) and Laurence Olivier's *Hamlet* (1948), through production companies like Cineguild and Two Cities which came under the umbrella of Rank's 'Independent Producers' consortium. But, despite the introduction in 1948 of a 45 per cent quota for British films (up from 17.5 per cent) and an ambitious programme of film production, Rank's venture failed to break the Hollywood hegemony (see Macnab 1993).

The second aspect also comes under the Rank umbrella: Powell and Pressburger's Archers film company was responsible for some of the most imaginative films produced within British Cinema during this period. With Michael Powell directing and Emeric Pressburger scriptwriting, their collaboration on such films as *A Matter of Life and Death* (1946), *Black Narcissus* (1947) and *The Red Shoes* (1948) represented a distinct departure from the dominant literary/theatrical/realist tradition of British Cinema, and the films they made together between 1939 and 1957 constitute a body of work unparalleled in British Cinema, providing a poetic and often expressionistic counterbalance to the prevailing realist orthodoxy. While directors like David Lean also used an expressionist *mise en scène* in such films as *Brief Encounter* and *Great Expectations*, Lean was mainly working within a tradition of realism deriving from that of the nineteenth-century novel, which results in his sometimes flamboyant visual style ultimately being subordinate to the literary content of his films. With Powell and Pressburger, however, the style is never subordinate to the subject matter and is often so striking, in the use of colour and unusual camera angles, that it forces itself upon the attention of the viewer. *A Matter of Life and Death*, for example, mixes expressionism and romanticism, colour and black-and-white footage, to tell the story of a Second World War pilot (played by David Niven) who is caught between life and death, heaven and earth, when his plane crashes into the sea – the mixture of styles and forms resulting in a film which is, if anything, anti-realist rather than realist.

The third aspect of postwar British Cinema is in marked contrast to the international ambitions of Rank and the expressionist cinema of Powell and Pressburger. Ealing Studios specialised in the production of small-scale, indigenous British films like *Hue and Cry* (1947), *Passport to Pimlico* (1949) and *The Lavender Hill Mob* (1951). These films were imbued with a realism supplied by the documentary film-makers that Michael Balcon had enlisted when he became Head of Production at Ealing in 1938 – a realism which had distinguished Ealing's wartime films – but the postwar films were, on the whole, gentler, more romantic celebrations of a communal, parochial Britishness.

Passport to Pimlico typifies the eccentricity, humour and communality which is characteristic of the vast majority of postwar Ealing films. The film evokes a wartime spirit with its story of a community which declares itself independent of the rest of the country when the detonation of an unexploded wartime bomb unearths some papers revealing it to be part of the Duchy of Burgundy. Ironically, in creating this whimsical and patriotic narrative, the film was celebrating the austerity and community spirit of wartime at a time when those communities and that consensus were in reality beginning to break up.

Other Ealing films of the period, like *Hue and Cry* (1947) and *Whisky Galore!* (1949), perform a similar ideological function, and while some of the postwar Ealing films did address themselves to the darker undercurrents of British society – films as different as the portmanteau horror film *Dead of Night* (1945), and *The Blue Lamp* (1950), in which friendly neighbourhood policeman George Dixon is shot and killed by Dirk Bogarde's ruthless young villain – the dominant tradition at Ealing was that of benign comedies and comedy-thrillers, films like *The Lavender Hill Mob* (1951) and *The Titfield Thunderbolt* (1953), which present a comfortable and reassuring view of British life far removed from the disturbing realism of *Went the Day Well?*, one of Ealing's wartime films.

---

mise en scène
A theatrical term usually translated as 'staging' or 'what has been put into the scene'. In film, *mise en scène* refers not only to sets, costumes and props but also to how the scene is organised, lit and framed for the camera. *Mise en scène* is one way of producing meaning in films which can be both straightforward and extremely complex, depending upon the intentions and skill of the director (the *metteur en scène*).

For further reading on Powell and Pressburger, see Christie 1994.

For further reading on Ealing, see Barr 1993; Pulleine 1997.

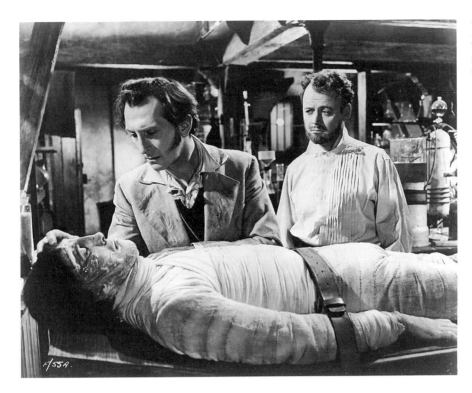

• **Plate 11.5** *The Curse of Frankenstein* (1957) The reaction against realism: Hammer's gothic horror.

NEW FILMS FOR NEW AUDIENCES: HAMMER HORROR AND THE 'NEW WAVE'

When Ealing Studios was sold to the BBC in 1955 it marked the end of an era, both for Ealing and for British Cinema. As Britain moved from postwar austerity into a period of affluence and social change, British Cinema was also about to undergo a transformation. With the rise of television and a boom in consumer goods, leisure was becoming more home-based and the composition of the cinema-going audience was changing. The family audience was declining and a younger audience, reared on television and rock'n'roll, emerged as an important new market for the film industry to target.

Hammer Films was quick to realise the box-office potential of this new audience. Following the low-budget science fiction boom in America in the early 1950s, Hammer produced a film version of the BBC television series *The Quatermass Experiment* in 1955. Then, in the following year, it revived the Gothic horror genre with *The Curse of Frankenstein* (produced 1956, released 1957), followed by *Dracula* (1958). These new films reworked the old Hollywood films of the 1930s, updating them for a new generation and a different social and cultural context. The films cashed in on the new X-certificate, which Hammer used as a marketing device, and offered audiences something new, exciting and daring, a product far removed from what the mainstream cinema had to offer at the time.

Significantly, Hammer's gothic horror films rejected realism, the benchmark by which the middle-class critics evaluated most British films. Consequently, these films were dismissed by these critics as vulgar, distasteful and unworthy of serious consideration. Which of course made them even more attractive to the new youth audience.

In their espousal of any concern with contemporary social reality the Hammer horror

For further reading on
Hammer horror, see
Hutchings 1993; Pirie
1973.

films offered an imaginary escape to late 1950s youth from the conformity of British society at the time. Its 'Cold War' trilogy: *The Quatermass Experiment* (1955), *X – The Unknown* (1956), *Quatermass II* (1957), had already begun this process by exploiting contemporary anxieties about the atomic bomb. The move into the territory of Gothic horror was simply an extension of this, recognising that the threat of 'the monster' resulting from atomic radiation was an important part of the appeal of the science fiction films. In this respect Hammer capitalised on the real fears and concerns of contemporary audiences, especially young people, as well as exploiting (and contributing to) a growing permissiveness in representations of sex and violence.

By the mid-1950s British Cinema, like the society at large, had grown complacent. The excitement and hope of the immediate postwar period, which saw a Labour government elected with a large majority, had worn off. A Conservative government was returned in 1951, beginning a period in office which was to last thirteen years. Social consensus was well established by the mid-1950s and it was against this stultifying complacency and conformity that a new generation raised its voice. In the theatre, John Osborne's *Look Back In Anger* (premièred May 1956) provided a mouthpiece for the new discontent. In British Cinema in the same year, in addition to the turn to horror at Hammer, a new documentary movement emerged under the banner of 'Free Cinema', with a new generation of film-makers wanting to reflect the new developments in popular culture.

In what ways did the Hammer horror films and the 'new wave' films represent a break with the past in British Cinema?

Like Hammer horror, the Free Cinema movement represented a break with tradition in the British Cinema of the 1950s and several of the film-makers involved (Lindsay Anderson, Karel Reisz, Tony Richardson) went on to make feature films in the late 1950s and early 1960s. Films such as *Look Back In Anger* (Tony Richardson's 1959 version of Osborne's play), *Saturday Night and Sunday Morning* (Karel Reisz's 1960 film of Alan Sillitoe's novel), *A Taste of Honey* (Richardson's 1961 film of Shelagh Delaney's play) and *This Sporting Life* (Lindsay Anderson's 1963 film of David Storey's novel) put a new, more realistic image of working-class life and culture on the screen and challenged the stereotypes and caricatures of the working class which had appeared in previous films. In doing so, this 'new wave' of British film-making broke with tradition and introduced a new **social realism** into British Cinema, retaining some features of the documentary realism of the prewar and wartime cinema but revitalising the form by focusing on the new industrial working class of the late 1950s.

However, John Hill (1983; 1986) has questioned the degree to which these films can be seen as a 'breakthrough', arguing that they are far from progressive in their attitude towards women, portraying them as victims and subordinate to the male protagonists. Hill has also questioned the adequacy of the realist form for representing the new subject matter which the films are concerned with, and in relation to the melodramatic excess of Hammer's Gothic horror films they can appear comparatively grim, especially to a present-day audience. While there may be some validity to Hill's criticisms, and some grounds for finding these 'kitchen sink' films bleak and outdated today, it is important to assess them in relation to the conservative, middle-class cinema that had preceded them. To quote John Caughie, writing in a different context:

Under certain conditions ... it may be politically progressive to confirm an identity (of sexuality or

social realism
A form of realism which tries to capture in a 'truthful' way the lives of industrial working-class communities. Also known as 'working-class realism' and often used in relation to the 'new wave' films of late 1950s/early 1960s British Cinema.

• **Plate 11.6** *Saturday Night and Sunday Morning* (1960) New films for new audiences.

class), to recover repressed experience or history, to contest the dominant image with an alternative identity.

(Caughie 1981: 33–4)

In the conservative and conformist context of late 1950s Britain, the 'new wave' films were progressive in confirming an identity for working-class audiences and in putting a more authentic image of working-class culture, and a more explicit sexuality, on to British cinema screens.

POPULAR CINEMA: THE *CARRY ON* AND BOND FILMS

Both Hammer horror and the 'new wave' represented new developments in British Cinema, marginal in some ways (as X-certificate films) but nevertheless proving popular at the box office. The two other new developments in British Cinema in the late 1950s/early 1960s were more mainstream, although they each, in their own way, represented a break with the 'old' British Cinema.

The long-running series of *Carry On* films, starting with *Carry On Sergeant* (1958), could be seen simply as an updating of the *Doctor* series (e.g. *Doctor in the House*, 1954) for a new generation and a more permissive social context. To some extent this is true, and in box-office terms this proved successful, but on another level the *Carry On* films represented a challenge to prevailing standards of decency and social acceptability. In one of the few serious studies of the *Carry On* films, Marion Jordan has summarised their popular appeal:

See Chapter 10, pp. 321–4 , for a case study of Victim *(1961) – not a 'new wave' film as such, but a film which reflected the changing attitudes in Britain towards homosexuality.*

In their day, and despite their denying any place to women in their pantheon – portraying them, indeed, as gaolers, sexual objects, or unnatural predators – they nonetheless asserted by their themes, and by the gusto with which they were presented, a lower-class, masculine resistance to 'refinement'; an insistence on sexuality, physicality, fun; on the need for drink in a kill-joy world, for shiftiness in an impossibly demanding industrial society, for cowardice amid the imposed heroism.

(Jordan 1983: 327)

carnivalesque
Term which refers to an atmosphere or attitude, found at carnivals and similar events, charac- terised by laughter, excess and vulgarity. Seen as a lower-class resistance to the refined tastes of the dominant (upper and middle) classes.

For further discussion of gender and stereotyping, see Chapter 9 and Chapter 10.

For more on the *Carry On* films, see Anderson 1998 and Jordan 1983.

What the *Carry On* films introduced into British Cinema and British culture, along with their negative stereotyping and reactionary elements, was a **carnivalesque** vulgarity and a subversive attitude towards authority and state institutions, contained within a popular comedy format. While Hammer horror and the 'new wave' exerted pressure on the established film culture from more subordinate, marginal positions, the *Carry On* films were busy subverting from *within* the dominant culture. In this respect, even the *Carry On*s, in other ways clearly part of mainstream film culture, can be seen as part of the challenge to conformity and consensus in Britain in the late 1950s and early 1960s and an important part of the redefinition of British national cinema in the period.

The other long-running series of films which, like the *Carry On* series, became an important genre in its own right, is the James Bond series, based on Ian Fleming's Cold War espionage novels. Unlike the *Carry On* series which, with the exception of the retro- spective *Carry On Columbus* (1992), died out in the late 1970s, the Bond films have proved more enduring, with the series continuing into the 1990s. The Bond films of the 1960s, starting with *Dr No* in 1962, seem curiously anachronistic in the context of the radical social and cultural changes taking place at the time, seemingly representing a return to the conservative values of an imperial Britain where gender roles and class relations were more fixed. Despite playing down the Cold War scenarios of the Fleming novels, emphasising instead fantasy and spectacle, the objective of the Bond films seemed to be, on the surface, to project an outdated nationalistic identity at a time when that identity was in the process of being eroded by social, political and cultural changes.

The success of the Bond films however was not simply a result of resurrecting the glory days of imperial Britain, it was a consequence of reworking an old formula and old ideologies for a new era and a new audience. The casting of Sean Connery as James Bond was important here. With his suave but rugged persona, Connery as Bond repre-

• **Plate 11.7** *Carry On Doctor* (1968) Popular culture: the 'carnivalesque' tradition.

sented a new masculinity and a new classlessness which didn't alienate working-class audiences in the way that the middle-class heroes of the 1950s had. Furthermore, in the transition from the novel to the screen, the character of Bond had undergone a significant change which was more in tune with the new 'professional' ethos of the 1960s, rather than the old gentlemanly 'amateurism' of the 1950s:

Functioning as a figure of modernisation, he became the very model of the tough abrasive professionalism that was allegedly destined to lead Britain into the modern, no illusions, no holds-barred post-imperialist age, a hero of rupture rather than one of tradition.

(Bennett and Woollacott 1987: 238–9)

The emphasis in the films on spectacle and new technology was also part of this process of modernisation. With the wartime spectacle of 1950s films like *The Dam Busters* and *The Bridge on the River Kwai* now out-of-date, the huge futuristic sets, exotic locations, and spectacular explosions in the Bond films was simply an updating of old adventures for new times. Similarly, developments in new technology and the role it would play in the modernisation of Britain was very much on the agenda when the first Bond films appeared. In 1963 Harold Wilson had called for a new Britain 'forged in the white heat of a technological revolution' in a rallying cry that was destined to sweep away the old Conservative government which, after twelve years in office, seemed as archaic and outdated as the war films of the 1950s. Hence the significance of the new technology and gadgetry in the Bond films which, like the professionalism embodied in the figure of Bond, helped to define the films as looking forward to a new Britain, while at the same time casting nostalgic glances back to Britain's recent imperial past.

The Bond films, therefore, were by no means simply reactionary, although with the emphasis on the heroic figure of James Bond as a womanising playboy the films were far from progressive in their sexual politics. Their success however revolved around, and depended upon, this combination of the traditional and the modern, providing an

• **Plate 11.8** *Dr No* (1962) Popular culture: redefining patriarchal and nationalistic ideologies.

illustration of patriarchal and nationalistic ideologies being redefined and reproduced for a new, more liberal era.

> **What is 'typically British' about the *Carry On* films and the Bond films? Do they present stereotypical images of 'Britishness'?**

BRITISH CINEMA AND HOLLYWOOD IN THE SIXTIES

For more on British Cinema in the 1960s and the 'Swinging London' films, see Carson 1998; Geraghty 1997; Murphy 1992; Richards 1992; A. Walker 1985; J. Walker 1985.

There was undoubtedly a boom in British film production in the 1960s, but it is ironic that this boom was financially underwritten by Hollywood. Britain, and London in particular, became the focus of a cultural revolution in the arts, fashion and music in the 1960s, and the revival in British Cinema did not go unnoticed by Hollywood. American money had already gone into the production of some of the 'new wave' films and United Artists was quick to realise the international potential of the Bond films. Their lead was soon followed by the other Hollywood companies who set up London offices in 1963–4 to cash in on the revival, in time to capitalise on the 'Swinging London' boom of the mid-1960s. But the boom was short-lived. The pop bubble had burst well before the end of the 1960s and, with the Hollywood studios facing a financial crisis as a result of over-investment at home and abroad, the American money was gradually withdrawn. Deserted by Hollywood, British film production slumped, demonstrating the extent to which the boom in British Cinema in the 1960s was, once again, dependent upon Hollywood.

THE 1970s: MAINSTREAM DECLINE AND THE RISE OF INDEPENDENT CINEMA

See Higson 1994 for a useful summary of British Cinema in the 1970s; also Walker 1986.

The withdrawal of American finance was followed by an exodus of British film talent in the 1970s as directors and actors went to work in Hollywood. Those left behind found themselves working more for television as film production slumped and cinema audiences continued to decline. British Cinema in the 1970s attempted to feed off television by scavenging its successful programmes and turning them into feature films, an indication of how impoverished British film production had become after the highs of the 1960s.

While the mainstream industry went through a relatively uninteresting period, revitalised to some extent by the influence of punk in the late 1970s (see Donnelly 1998), independent cinema emerged as an important practice during the decade, having an influence well beyond its small audiences and often obscure theoretical tracts.

Sylvia Harvey has described independent cinema as:

the forms of cinema that exist outside of a popular or commercial mainstream film industry. Independent films are usually characterized by a rejection of the aesthetic or ideological norms of the dominant industry, and independent cinema is generally thought of as a marginalized, alternative or oppositional cinema within capitalist societies, fighting for a voice in relation to more economically and socially powerful forms of communication.

(Kuhn 1990: 215)

Although it is possible to talk about 'mainstream' independent film production in Britain, in the sense of production companies being independent of the major studios, companies or conglomerates (usually American) which control film production, distribution and exhibition worldwide (and which therefore constitute the 'dominant' cinema), 'indepen-dence' in these terms does not have the *oppositional* connotations which are at the heart of the above definition.

In Harvey's more radical definition, independent cinema constitutes a movement which emerged in the late 1960s, a movement which 'developed in conjunction with movements for social emancipation' (Kuhn 1990: 215). These oppositional movements (the Campaign for Nuclear Disarmament, the campaign against the war in Vietnam, the women's liberation movement, gay liberation and other civil rights campaigns) were all a response to a breakdown in the social-democratic consensus which had existed in Britain since the capitalist boom of the 1950s had ushered in a period of affluence and improved lifestyles for all social classes. This consensus, which had been presided over by successive Conservative and Labour governments in the postwar period, was eroded during the 1960s and came to a head with a series of confrontations between students (largely, but not entirely) and police in 1968, in protests against the Vietnam War. These confrontations, an expression of a growing discontent with the ruling order, were followed, in Britain, by a decade of industrial disputes in the 1970s as the capi-talist boom of the 1950s and 1960s collapsed and an economic recession set in.

It would be wrong, however, to give the impression that the independent cinema which emerged in the late 1960s was born entirely out of, and because of, these circumstances. Even before these political events had given impetus to an oppositional independent cinema there had been moves towards developing an alternative to the mainstream cinema, based upon the example of the 'New American Cinema' of the 1950s and 1960s. This tradition was allied to an **avant-garde** aesthetic in the arts, concerned with formal experimentation and **modernist** aesthetics, and was intent upon developing alternative structures of production, distribution and exhibition based upon the 'co-operative' workshop model. In fact the beginnings of the modern independent cinema movement in Britain can perhaps be dated from the foundation of the London Film-makers' Co-op in 1966 as a centre for film production and exhibition. The develop-ment of alternative structures and spaces for making, viewing and discussing films, outside of the established commercial cinema, was central to both the 'aesthetic' and the 'political' wings of the independent film sector.

1980s 'RENAISSANCE'

In the late 1970s members of the independent sector were very active in campaigning for the fourth television channel as an outlet for independent film and video and, although the 'radical' nature of Channel Four was watered down by the Conservative government that oversaw its introduction, the new channel did, for much of the 1980s, provide a source of finance and an exhibition outlet for film and video work from the independent sector and a wider audience than independent film-makers could ever hope to reach through cinema screenings alone.

With its alternative remit to encourage experiment and innovation and to cater for minority audiences, Channel Four gave a boost to British film production in the 1980s, especially alternative and independent production, and films like *My Beautiful Laundrette* (1985) began to reflect the multiculturalism of Britain in the 1980s, redefining national identity at a time when more traditional, jingoistic concepts of nationalism were being resurrected by Margaret Thatcher's Conservative government, especially in rela-tion to the 1982 Falklands War.

It is one of the ironies of the 1980s that the three consecutive Conservative govern-ments, which did nothing to help the British film industry at a time when it was in desperate need of government support, should have presided over a renaissance in

avant-garde
Literally the 'advanced guard' of experimental film-makers who reject the dominant forms of mainstream cinema in favour of innovation and experiment in film-making, often producing non-narrative, non-illu-sionistic, sometimes abstract films.

modernist
A term used to describe early twentieth-century developments in art, literature, music, film and theatre which rejected realism as the dominant tradition in the arts. Modernist art is characterised by experi-ment and innovation, and modernist artists, because of their avant-garde practices, inevitably constitute a cultural élite.

For further reading on independent cinema, see Blanchard and Harvey 1983; Harvey 1986; O'Pray 1996; Street 1997; Whitaker 1985.

For further reading on
Channel Four and TV
films, see Auty 1985;
Ellis 1982; Giles 1993;
Harvey 1982; Pym 1992.
For more on British
Cinema and
Thatcherism, see
Friedman 1993.

'Thatcherism'
A political ideology
named after Margaret
Thatcher, Conservative
prime minister from
1979–90, involving a
free-market approach to
politics and economics
which rewarded indi-
vidual enterprise over
and above communal
welfare. Led to a huge
rise in unemployment
and a widening of social
divisions between the
'haves' and the 'have
nots' in Britain in the
1980s.

British film-making, a renaissance led mainly by a television channel whose introduction was overseen by the first Thatcher government. Another irony was that many of the films which resulted from this renaissance were either overtly or covertly critical of the political doctrine that became known as **'Thatcherism'**.

'HERITAGE' CINEMA

The standard-bearer of the mainstream film industry renaissance in the 1980s was *Chariots of Fire* (1981). Based on an original screenplay by Colin Welland, produced by David Puttnam, and directed by Hugh Hudson, *Chariots of Fire* did much to initiate a new cycle of 'heritage' cinema with its nostalgic remembrance of a victorious moment in British history when the British athletics team was successful at the 1924 Olympic Games. The film was the first of a series which looked back to the early years of the twentieth century, when the nation was still 'Great', possessing an Empire, and with a hierarchical and well-defined class structure.

With its release coinciding with the Falklands War, which occurred shortly after the film had received four Oscars at the 1982 Academy Awards, *Chariots of Fire* inevitably became caught up in the jingoism of the time, which Thatcher and the Tory press did much to encourage. Consequently, and ironically, the film acquired a reputation as a flag-waving Thatcherite film, despite the fact that it was completed before the outbreak of the Falklands War, that the original version of the script was written before the Thatcher government even came to power, and that the political leanings of the film's writer, producer and director were very much to the left of Thatcher's extreme right-wing government.

The film certainly received no help from the government in getting made, the bulk of its finance coming from American and Egyptian sources, and in its story of 'two main characters fighting against various kinds of bigotry' (Hudson, quoted in Johnston 1985: 100), cultural, racial and religious, it ostensibly champions the underdog and the

• **Plate 11.9** *Chariots of Fire* (1981)
Waving the flag.

outsider against the establishment. But the ideology of Thatcherism was considerably removed from previous versions of Conservatism, and Thatcher held no high regard for the kind of establishment and tradition which the film ostensibly criticises. Ironically therefore, *Chariots of Fire*, with its advocacy of individual achievement and self-enterprise, found itself in accord with the new Conservative philosophy.

One problem which *Chariots of Fire* creates for itself, resides in the contradiction of wanting to present a social critique of a bigoted and hierarchical establishment while employing a visual aesthetic which celebrates the very ethos which it wishes to condemn. The sumptuous iconography of this and other 'heritage' films of the 1980s, such as *Another Country* (1984), *A Passage to India* (1985), and *A Room with a View* (1986), ultimately detracts from any attempt at social criticism, glossing over any contradictions and inequities which the films may be seeking to expose and subordinating them to a visual aesthetic which romanticises the past, 'inviting a nostalgic gaze that resists the ironies and social critiques so often suggested narratively by these films' (Higson 1993: 109).

Several of these 'heritage' films have been adaptations of the novels of E.M. Forster (*A Passage to India, A Room with a View*, *Maurice*, *Where Angels Fear to Tread*, *Howard's End*) but, as Andrew Higson notes, the seductive visual style of the films has tended to take precedence over the social criticism of the novels:

The novels explore what lies beneath the surface of things, satirizing the pretentious and the superficial, and especially those who are overly concerned with keeping up appearances rather than acting according to the passions of the heart. The films, however, construct such a delightfully glossy visual surface that the ironic perspective and the narrative of social criticism diminish in their appeal for the spectator.

(Higson 1993: 120)

What is 'heritage' cinema, and what image of Britain do these films generally present?

CHANNEL FOUR AND THE NEW MULTICULTURAL BRITISH CINEMA

The flip side of this 'heritage' cinema is represented by a number of Channel Four-financed films, of which *My Beautiful Laundrette* was one of the most successful, critically and commercially. Contemporary in subject matter and eschewing the seductive visual style of the heritage films, *My Beautiful Laundrette* offers a multicultural perspective on Thatcher's Britain. Written by Hanif Kureishi, a young British Asian, and directed by Stephen Frears, a leading exponent of indigenous British film-making in the 1980s, *My Beautiful Laundrette* offered an 'ironic salutation to the entrepreneurial spirit in the 1980s that Margaret Thatcher championed' (Barber 1993: 221). Ironic because the entrepreneurs here are an extended Pakistani family who have taken the Thatcherite ideology to heart and turned the tables on the old colonial order.

Omar, a young ambitious member of the family, persuades his uncle to let him run a launderette as a part of the family business, employing his white, male lover Johnny to work for him, while Johnny's unemployed, racist peers hang around outside: the new disenfranchised underclass of Thatcher's two-tier Britain. The film was ironic also in portraying a gay relationship at a time when the Tories were introducing legislation designed to prevent Labour-controlled local authorities from pursuing policies which

See Chapter 10 for further discussion of gay and lesbian cinema.

might be seen to be supportive of gay and lesbian relationships. The unexpected success of *My Beautiful Laundrette* on its cinema release seemed to prove that a substantial number of people disagreed with this particular attempt by Thatcher to turn the clock back to a pre-permissive, more **homophobic** era.

The film ends with the entrepreneurial ambitions of the family in ruins, relationships (apart from that between Omar and Johnny) broken up, and violent conflict between the white and Asian communities, with Johnny taking the side of the Asian family against his old mates. Unlike *Chariots of Fire*, there is no possibility that *My Beautiful Laundrette* could be read as an endorsement of Thatcherism. Instead, it provides a damning critique of the socially divisive policies which the Thatcher government was pursuing.

homophobia
Fear or hatred of homo-sexuals.

For more on black British Cinema in the 1980s and 1990s, see Malik 1996.

• **Plate 11.10** *My Beautiful Laundrette* (1985)
The new multicultural British Cinema.

THE 1980s: POSTSCRIPT

The 1980s 'renaissance' in British Cinema, much hyped following Colin Welland's rallying cry of 'The British are coming!' at the 1982 Academy Awards when *Chariots of Fire* received four Oscars, proved premature. Certainly there were successes (*Gandhi* followed *Chariots of Fire* with eight Oscars in 1983), but there were also failures, culminating in the collapse of Goldcrest Films. Goldcrest had represented a new manifestation of the dream that British Cinema could compete with Hollywood on its own terms: producing big-budget films which could achieve international success. The company's financial collapse in 1986 signalled the end of that dream.

For more on Goldcrest Films, see Eberts and Illott 1990.

In retrospect the success of British Cinema in the 1980s was on a smaller scale and led by television. The impetus which Channel Four gave to the revival of British Cinema in the 1980s cannot be over-estimated and the real achievement of British Cinema in that decade needs to be seen in the ways in which low-budget, indigenous films like *My Beautiful Laundrette*, *The Ploughman's Lunch* (1983), *Dance with a Stranger* (1984), *Defence of the Realm* (1985), *Mona Lisa* (1986), *High Hopes* (1988), *Distant Voices, Still Lives* (1988) and numerous others, revitalised British film culture and set an example for how cinema and television could work together in the UK to produce and exhibit films which were distinctively British, which engaged with contemporary issues, and which affirmed an indigenous cultural identity which was in opposition to the globalising one of Hollywood.

The real problem for British Cinema in the 1980s was the complete absence of government support for the industry. With Hollywood so powerful on the world market, and with American companies controlling most of the distribution and exhibition structure in the UK, British films struggled to compete, even when they did get made. In a free market the richest and the strongest survive and the free-market philosophy of Thatcher's Conservative governments enabled Hollywood to maintain and consolidate its control of the British film industry, ensuring that British Cinema would remain subordinate to it.

For further reading on British Cinema in the 1980s, see Auty and Roddick 1985; Friedman 1993.

Part 3: 1990s renaissance

With the re-election of a Conservative government under the leadership of John Major in 1992, the neglect of the British film industry was set to continue. Critically and commercially successful British films continued to get made, increasingly with co-production finance which sometimes compromised the indigenous cultural identity of the films, but there was no real support or encouragement for British Cinema under the Tories. Despite this, films like *The Crying Game* (1992), a surprise success in America given its mixture of transvestism and Irish Republican politics, and *Four Weddings and a Funeral* (1994), a contemporary 'heritage' film made with one eye on the American market, proved that low/medium-budget films, reflecting very different aspects of the national culture, could become huge commercial and critical successes, in the UK and abroad.

See Chapter 3, pp. 37–9, for a case study of The Crying Game.

The success of these films brought new claims that a renaissance was underway in British Cinema in the 1990s, but with the Conservative government continuing to show no real interest in the British film industry, these claims looked as hollow as the similar claims of the early 1980s. Subsequent developments, however, not least the election of a Labour government in 1997, ending eighteen years of Tory rule, suggested that there were real grounds for optimism about a renaissance in British Cinema, for several reasons.

FROM ART-HOUSE TO MAINSTREAM

For more on auteur and genre theory, see Chapter 6.

In a review of British Cinema published in 1998, Andrew Higson noted how, following the decline of the British film industry and the demise of studio production, British Cinema in the 1980s and 1990s had been promoted increasingly in terms of authorship, films made by individual auteurs, rather than as genre films:

> What the mainstream journalists have considered significant and distinctive about British Cinema in this period has not been a sense of national style, or a coherent movement, or a concern with representing the nation, but the particular styles and world-views of a number of critically successful directors whose allegiance is more to the art-house than to the multiplex mainstream: Nicholas Roeg, Peter Greenaway, Derek Jarman, Stephen Frears, Mike Leigh.... Even realist film-makers, like Ken Loach, are now treated as auteurs.
>
> (Higson 1998: 504)

In the latter half of the decade, however, that suggestion seemed to apply more to the 1980s than the 1990s. While 1980s auteurs like Greenaway, Friers, Leigh and Loach continued to make films in the 1990s, the films made by the new generation of film-makers that emerged in the middle of the decade were more notable for their collaborative nature, producer/director/writer/star often being given equal weighting in the marketing, rather than the film being seen as the work of an individual auteur.

Furthermore, this new generation of film-makers had its eyes more firmly on the popular multiplex audience, rather than the more specialised, minority art-house market. Having grown up on a diet of popular American Cinema these film-makers wanted to make popular mainstream films, not esoteric art films. But, being British (though distinctively English, Irish, Scottish or Welsh), the new generation has also grown up with the strong influence of the realist tradition in British Cinema, a tradition which television (where many of the new generation made their first venture into feature film-making) has inherited as the social realist/social issue TV play of the 1960s and 1970s metamorphosed into the TV film of the 1980s and 1990s.

This combined influence has resulted in a new type of British film emerging, lending credence to the proposition that there really has been a 'renaissance' in British Cinema in the 1990s. The 'new' British film is one which combines the popular appeal of mainstream cinema with the social realism that has been a dominant tradition in British Cinema, from the 1930s documentarists, through the 'kitchen sink' films of the late 1950s and early 1960s, to the naturalistic dramas of Ken Loach and Mike Leigh (different though they are in style and subject matter) in the 1980s and 1990s.

This new hybrid of popular and 'art' cinema, as the documentary realist tradition has been described is not of course unique or particularly new. The skilful blending of realism and melodrama in many of the best wartime films has already been noted (see page p. 356–8) and Peter Wollen has used the term 'riff-raff realism' to describe 'the disturbing and difficult combination of realism with excess and fantasy' in an article on the 1940s 'spiv-cycle', films such as *Waterloo Road* (1945), *It Always Rains on Sunday* (1947) and *Brighton Rock* (1947) (Wollen 1998: 19). Wollen begins his article by referring to Alan Lovell's 1997 critical reassessment of the contrasting attitudes towards realism and fantasy in British Cinema, in which Lovell argues that the abundance of British Cinema scholarship in the period since he delivered his 1969 seminar paper on 'British Cinema: The Unknown Cinema' has tended to counterpose 'realist' and 'anti-realist' film-making, 'posing excess and restraint against each other', whereas 'British Cinema is often most exciting when restraint and excess interact with each other' (Lovell 1997: 239).

See Lovell and Hillier 1972 on the documentary movement as Britain's art cinema; and Hill 1986, Chapter 4, on the 'poetic' realism of the 'new wave' films.

Lovell's examples to illustrate this are David Lean's *Brief Encounter* (1945) and

Powell and Pressburger's *The Small Back Room* (1949), but we might also consider whether some of the British films of the 1990s represent a new manifestation of this hybrid tradition.

☐ CASE STUDY 1: *TRAINSPOTTING* (1996)

Trainspotting, 'from the team that brought us *Shallow Grave*' as the advertising announced, was one of the most successful films of the decade. Andrew Macdonald (producer), Danny Boyle (director) and John Hodge (writer), as the 'team' responsible, are symptomatic of the shift away from individual auteurism in the 1990s, collaborating on several films which have featured prominent representatives of a new generation of British film stars, such actors as Christopher Ecclestone, Robert Carlyle and Ewan McGregor.

Trainspotting is a good example of a 'crossover' film, one which can fit equally comfortably into an art house programme as it can into a multiplex programme. As such it is representative of what might be described as a **postmodern** shift in 1990s film production and consumption: a blurring of the dividing line between the type of film which has traditionally been thought of as popular and mainstream, and the type of alternative, non-commercial film previously screened only in 'art' cinemas.

Despite the fact that *Trainspotting* was financed entirely by Channel Four (for a total of £1.7 million) it was conceived and made very much with the large cinema screen in mind. This had a lot to do with wanting to get away from the tradition of realism with which TV films are associated, as director Danny Boyle explains:

People working in television are always asking themselves: 'What's the real solution to [any given] situation? What would really happen?' That's what television people depend on, and fall back on, and it defines the relationship between the viewers and the makers of television. It's a pact that I've tried to steer away from, firstly in my television work and certainly in *Shallow Grave*. People go to the cinema to see something bigger than yourself, larger than your own life. It can still be about life in some way, but the insane, huge films like *Apocalypse Now*, or Nic Roeg's films are the ones that I longed to be able to do.

(Quoted in Finney 1996: 177)

This rejection of realism is evident in the non-naturalistic, and occasionally surrealistic, style which the film adopts and, together with the contemporary setting and subject matter, is largely responsible for the film's fresh and innovative approach. As writer John Hodge describes it:

Although I quite enjoy watching realist films, I can't write that way myself. I'm always looking for a way out of a realist situation. So when I came to write the scene in the toilet, the idea of seeing that in a totally realistic way was totally off-putting to me. So I just went with the flow.

(Quoted in Finney 1996: 176–7)

The scene which Hodge refers to introduces a surrealistic element into the film which was not in Irvine Welsh's novel and it is indicative of the way in which the film combines moments of escapist fantasy, or 'excess' to use Lovell's term, with a realist aesthetic, derived in part from Welsh's novel but which also shows the influence of the realist tradition in British film and TV drama, especially in the manner in which the film uses naturalistic speech and a realist iconography of city streets and landscapes. In this respect it is interesting to compare *Trainspotting* with Ken Loach's more orthodox, realist approach in the Glasgow-based *My Name is Joe* (1998).

postmodern
A term used to describe many aspects of contemporary cultural production of the 1980s and 1990s. Among its many characteristics are an eclectic borrowing from earlier styles (see **bricolage,** p. 376), an emphasis on stylish surface appearances rather than social realism or psychological depth, and a blurring of the dividing line between cultural forms, products and tastes, such as the division between 'high culture' and 'popular culture'.

• **Plate 11.11** *Trainspotting* (1996)
1990s renaissance: realism or surrealism?

> **Compare and contrast *Trainspotting* and *My Name is Joe* (Loach, 1998), with
> reference to their differences in form, style and subject matter.**

With its focus on youth and drug-taking, and with its trendy 'Britpop' soundtrack,
Trainspotting has been as big an influence on young British film-makers as Quentin
Tarantino's *Reservoir Dogs*. But where both have acquired cult status, *Trainspotting* is
significant for its cultural specificity, not just a distinctively British film, but a Scottish
one. John Hill has identified the extent of its achievement as a new kind of British film
which is helping to redefine ideas of national and cultural identity in the 1990s:

One of the most commercially successful films of 1996, it was fully financed by the public service
broadcaster Channel Four, and combines an interest in social issues (drug-taking, AIDS, poverty)
with a determinedly self-conscious aesthetic style reminiscent of the French and British 'new
waves'. In experimenting with cinematic style, however, it also plays with the inherited imagery of
England and Scotland. Thus when the film's main character, Mark Renton (Ewan McGregor), arrives

in London, the film cheerfully invokes the most clichéd images of London in an ironic inversion of the touristic imagery which commonly accompanies the arrival of an English character in Scotland.

(Hill 1997: 252)

Scottish films, film-makers and stars have been at the cutting edge of the renaissance in British Cinema in the 1990s. In foregrounding 'Scottishness', as distinct from 'Englishness', films like *Trainspotting* have contributed to a debate about national identity and what it really means to be 'British' in the 1990s. Along with Welsh films like *House of America* (1996), Irish films like *The Boxer* (1997), multicultural films like *Bhaji on the Beach* (1993), plus 'regional' English films like *Brassed Off* (1996) and *The Full Monty* (1997), the idea of a unified 'national identity', together with that of a typically 'British' cultural identity, has been put into flux.

How does *Trainspotting* portray Scotland and 'Scottishness', compared to big-budget films like *Braveheart* (1995) and *Rob Roy* (1995)?

Trainspotting was the most successful British film at the box office in 1996, taking over £12 million in the year. It helped to give impetus to the mid-1990s renaissance in British Cinema and, despite its far from glamorous subject matter, contributed to the rebranding of Britain as 'Cool Britannia', a term which became ubiquitous following the landslide election victory of the 'new' Labour Party under Tony Blair's leadership in 1997.

Trainspotting's box-office performance in the UK and around the world was great news for the UK industry. It appeared for a while as if our film industry was able to address a young audience in the way British musicians have done so successfully since the 1960s. The success of *Trainspotting's* cutting-edge soundtrack album, not to mention the presence of several Britpop stars at the *Trainspotting* party in Cannes, suggested a rare creative energy, a moment at which British Cinema became hip again. This was also reflected in the film's distinctive marketing campaign which not only heralded the arrival of the film but also spawned a series of parody advertisements and gave graphic designers the opportunity to use orange wherever possible – an affirmation of what was 'cool'.

(Thomas 1997: 33)

☐ CASE STUDY 2: *THE FULL MONTY* (1997)

An even greater commercial success at the box office was *The Full Monty*. Made for £3.5 million, with money from Fox Searchlight, a division of the American major Twentieth-Century Fox, *The Full Monty* has taken over £50 million worldwide, the most successful British film ever. Produced by Uberto Pasolini, directed by Peter Cattaneo, and written by Simon Beaufoy, with Robbie Carlyle as the lead actor, *The Full Monty*, like *Trainspotting*, was very much a team production rather than an individual auteur's film. And with the full might of Fox Searchlight's distribution division behind it, the film was given a very wide release on the UK multiplex circuit, perhaps the main reason for its phenomenal commercial success.

Set in Sheffield, the film tells the story of a group of unemployed steelworkers who

• **Plate 11.12** *The Full Monty* (1997)
A successful blend of social realism and fantasy.

form a group of male strippers in order to earn some money. The film was seen as a 'feel-good' movie and marketed as a comedy, but there is also a darker side to the film – it is after all about male unemployment in a depressed industrial city – which has made its huge box-office success even more remarkable. It is in this respect that *The Full Monty* can be seen as a hybrid film: combining the social realism of a classic 'kitchen sink' film like *Saturday Night and Sunday Morning* with the carnivalesque humour of a *Carry On* film (see p. 363). In doing so, it combines 'restraint' with 'excess' and can be seen to be in the tradition of the best of British Cinema, combining realism and fantasy, seriousness and humour.

This is a delicate balance to achieve and for screenwriter Simon Beaufoy the success of the film has tended to obscure its serious message:

The marketing, of course, focused on the fact that it's a rip-roaring comedy about a bunch of strippers, when in fact there are only three minutes of stripping in the entire film. I get particularly pleased when people comment on the sadness at the heart of the film. For me, they've got it. It seems that political messages have to be so hidden in films these days that they are almost invisible.

(Beaufoy 1998: 61)

The hybrid approach taken in *The Full Monty*, combining realism with excess, can be compared to the more naturalistic approach taken by Ken Loach in his 1991 film *Riff-Raff*, a film which was also about the effect of Thatcherism on the working class in Britain. Beaufoy's comparison of the two provides a good illustration of the difference between a more orthodox realist film, made by the leading British exponent of a very naturalistic form of realism, and the new hybrid British Cinema, combining realism and melodrama, restraint and excess, mixing forms and genres in a postmodern **bricolage**:

bricolage
The putting together of features from different genres and styles, self-consciously and usually playfully. This is one of the principal characteristics of postmodernism.

Though I love the naturalism of *Riff-Raff*, my writing moves towards moments that break free of those confines, that rise above the reality of the situation into something that no matter how earthy, one could call a sort of poetry. The scene in the dole queue in *The Full Monty*, where the laid-off steel workers, hearing familiar music, break into an involuntary strip-dance, for instance. You wouldn't find that in a Loach film because it breaks the bounds of pure naturalism.

(Beaufoy 1998: 61)

The Full Monty then, in a different manner to *Trainspotting*, which mixes realism with surrealism, shares the latter's concern to break the bounds of a uniform film style, drawing instead from both realism and fantasy in order to popularise and heighten its political message. The mixture has been successful both commercially and critically, and also in cultural terms, in finding new ways to represent aspects of British culture and identity for a popular cinema-going audience to recognise, enjoy and reflect upon.

> **Is *The Full Monty* a comedy, a social issue movie, or both? Does the comedy undermine the film's social message?**

A BRIEF SURVEY OF OTHER 1990s BRITISH FILMS

In addition to *Trainspotting* and *The Full Monty*, a representative sample of other British films of the 1990s worth studying would include:

- Isaac Julien's *Young Soul Rebels* (1991): a black British film set in the late 1970s, exploring issues of race, youth and sexuality – critically panned but a brave attempt on behalf of the British Film Institute to build on the success of multicultural films like *My Beautiful Laundrette*.

  For further reading on *Young Soul Rebels*, see Julien and MacCabe 1991.

- *Howard's End* (1991): another E.M. Forster adaptation by the team of Ismail Merchant and James Ivory, following their 1980s 'heritage' films, critically acclaimed and a big art house success with its predominantly middle-class audiences.

  See pp. 368–9 om 'heritage' cinema

- *Dream On* (1991): a feature film from Amber Films – one of the first film workshops to be set up in Britain and previously known for its documentaries about working-class life in the North East of England, Amber made a successful transition to feature-length dramas in the 1990s, working with extremely limited financial resources.

- Terence Davies' *The Long Day Closes* (1992): a lovingly crafted autobiographical film from one of the most distinctive auteurs of British Cinema – a different kind of 'art cinema' to that of Merchant/Ivory.

  For further reading on Terence Davies, see Williams 1993.

- *Blue* (1993): Derek Jarman's final film, made when he was losing his sight as a result of AIDS, and consisting simply of a blue screen accompanied by a richly poetic and meditative soundtrack; a highly personal film at the extreme modernist/avant-garde end of the film-making spectrum, and an exemplary film for considering the creative use of film sound.

  For further reading on Derek Jarman, see Lippard 1996.

- *Bhaji on the Beach* (1993): directed by Gurinder Chada, one of the new generation of British film-makers, redefining British national identity as multicultural and multiracial.

- Sally Potter's *Orlando* (1993): a visually stunning realisation of the Virginia Woolf novel; and *The Tango Lesson* (1997): a semi-autobiographical portrait of the film-maker as dancer.

  See Chapter 9 for a case study of *Orlando*.

- *Under the Skin* (1997): a powerful film about a young woman's grief and emotional breakdown following the death of her mother, directed by Carine Adler and starring Samantha Morton.

- Several films marking the re-emergence of Ken Loach in the 1990s, following a fairly unproductive time in the 1980s: *Hidden Agenda* (1990), *Riff-Raff* (1991),

• **Plate 11.13** *Brassed Off* (1996)
A lamentation for the industrial working class.

For further reading on Ken Loach, see McKnight 1997, Fuller 1998.

Raining Stones (1993), *Ladybird, Ladybird* (1994), *Land and Freedom* (1995), *Carla's Song* (1996), *My Name is Joe* (1998), proving there was still a market for his brand of radical naturalistic realism, even though his films have been more widely distributed, and won more awards, in Europe than they have in Britain.

For further reading on Mike Leigh, see Coveney 1996.

■ Several films also from Mike Leigh, the other great naturalistic director that Britain has produced: *Life is Sweet* (1990), *Naked* (1993), *Secrets and Lies* (1996) and *Career Girls* (1997), bitter-sweet observations of British life in the 1990s.

■ *Brassed Off* (1996): a companion piece to *The Full Monty*, suggesting the emergence of a new kind of heritage cinema in the 1990s, not the pretty middle-class heritage cinema of Merchant/Ivory but an industrial heritage cinema rooted in the regional working-class heartlands of the industrial Midlands and the North. *Brassed Off*, like *The Full Monty*, is a lamentation for a lost industrial working-class culture which also provides a celebration of the strength of the working class, especially working-class men, to survive in the face of adversity. The final, moving speech by Peter Postlethwaite against Thatcher, and the ruthless way in which Thatcherism decimated the working-class communities of industrial Britain, packs a powerful political and emotional punch.

CONCLUSION

With Hollywood exerting its dominance at the box office with ever more spectacular and expensive blockbusters in the 1990s, British films have had to fight for a share of the market. While many more films could be added to the above list to support the claims for a renaissance in British Cinema, what the above sample illustrates is not only the diversity of British film culture in the 1990s, but also the extent to which British Cinema has, in the last two decades, been engaged in a continuing struggle for identity, seeking to explore and, in many cases, redefine what it means to be 'British' in opposition to a pervasive American culture.

There continue to be two main strategies for countering Hollywood's hegemony: one is to take the route that Korda and Rank took in the 1930s and 1940s, and which Goldcrest attempted in the 1980s, to compete with Hollywood on its own terms. This is a policy which seems even less likely to succeed today than it has in the past, given the strength of Hollywood's hegemony over all aspects of film production, distribution and exhibition. The other strategy is to take the Michael Balcon/Ealing Studios/Channel Four route and develop a popular indigenous cinema, a small-scale low-budget cinema which has more freedom to take risks and which is heterogeneous and diverse in its representations of British culture and society.

Backed by an assortment of investors, including the television companies, this small-scale indigenous cinema does exist, and films as various as *Riff-Raff*, *The Long Day Closes*, *Bhaji on the Beach*, *Secrets and Lies*, *Brassed Off* and *Trainspotting*, plus a host of innovative British animated films which have been reaping awards at film festivals around the world, are testimony to the ability of British Cinema to produce imaginative, quality films, reflecting British society in its multicultural and multiracial diversity, without the government subsidy enjoyed by other European cinemas such as the French cinema. Yet British films in the 1990s have been successful against the odds, and the arguments and debates about the future of British Cinema are more prolific than ever, recently being linked to debates about the future of a pan-European cinema, where the different European national cinemas might band together to counter Hollywood's increasing global domination.

For further reading on European cinema, see Finney 1996; Hill, McLoone and Hainsworth 1994; Petrie 1992b.

While a pan-European route may not be the answer to the dominance of Hollywood, the vitality of British Cinema in the 1990s bodes well for the future, suggesting that for the UK, a national cinema needs to be a pluralistic cinema, reflecting British cultures and British identities in their diversity, rather than conforming to an idea of national cinema that is uniform and nationalistic. With the election of a Labour government in May 1997 and the subsequent introduction of tax concessions for British films costing less than £15 million in the July 1997 budget, plus the allocation of National Lottery money to boost film production, British Cinema seemed at last to be getting the government support that it had been denied since the 1970s. While there are many obstacles to be overcome, not least the perennial problem of a limited distribution and exhibition structure for British films, the prospects for a reinvigorated and diverse British national cinema look better than they have done for a long while.

Note

This chapter is a revised version of a unit on 'British Cinema and Hollywood' written for the University of Leicester's Distance Learning MA in Mass Communication.

FURTHER READING

For a comprehensive bibliography which includes all those works cited in this chapter, see p. 491–3.

Barr, C. (ed.) *All Our Yesterdays: Ninety Years of British Cinema* (British Film Institute, London, 1986)

Curran, J. and Porter, V. (eds) *British Cinema History* (Weidenfeld & Nicolson, London, 1983)

Higson, A., *Waving the Flag: Constructing a National Cinema in Britain* (Oxford University Press, Oxford, 1995)

—— (ed.) *Dissolving Views: Key Writings on British Cinema* (Cassell, London, 1996)

Hill, J. *Sex, Class and Realism: British Cinema 1956–1963* (British Film Institute, London, 1986)

Murphy, R. *The British Cinema Book* (British Film Institute, London, 1997)

Richards, J. *Films and British National Identity* (Manchester University Press, Manchester, 1997)

Street, S. *British National Cinema* (Routledge, London, 1997)

FURTHER VIEWING

For further viewing please refer to the appropriate sections within the chapter. Over 100 films have been referred to altogether, of which eight (including the two 1990s case studies) have been given slightly more attention as representing different aspects of British Cinema in four different periods. Details of the availability of these eight films are given below. At the time of writing not all of these films are available on video, but they may become available in the near future so it's worth checking with your local video retailer. Many of the other films referred to in the chapter, especially the more recent releases, are available on video.

Sally in Our Alley (1931) – available for hire on 16mm film from Filmbank Distributors.

The Scarlet Pimpernel (1934) – available on video from Carlton.

In Which We Serve (1942) – available on video from New Line Home Video Reel.

The Wicked Lady (1945) – available for hire on 16mm film from the British Film Institute.

Chariots of Fire (1981) – available for hire on 16mm film from Filmbank Distributors.

My Beautiful Laundrette (1985) – available for hire on 16mm film from the British Film Institute.

Trainspotting (1996) – available on video from Polygram.

The Full Monty (1997) – available on video from Fox Pathé.

RESOURCE CENTRES

http:// www.bfi.org.uk
Website of the British Film Institute

21 Stephen Street
London W1 1PL
Tel: 0171 255 1444
Fax: 0171 436 7950

http:// www.shu.ac.uk/services/lc/closeup/title.htm
Website for *Close Up* (the Electronic Journal of British Cinema). Produced in association with Sheffield Hallam University and the Bill Douglas Centre for the History of Cinema and Popular Culture. Contains links to other sites of interest on the Internet.

http://www.filmeducation.org
Website for Film Education, which produces teaching packs on the film industry and individual films, and has also produced a number of BBC Learning Zone programmes on aspects of the British film industry. The website is specifically designed for use by teachers and students, featuring original educational material to complement the content of Study Guides and BBC Learning

Zone programmes. It includes the latest film and education news, a special section on curriculum and exam board developments, suggestions for tasks and projects for students and a public site with links to major distributors and cinema chains.

Alhambra House
27–31 Charing Cross Road
London WC2H 0AU
Tel: 0171 976 2291
Fax: 0171 839 5052

Society for the Study of Popular British Cinema
Publishes the *Journal of Popular British Cinema*. Enquiries about membership should be addressed to:

Alan Burton (Secretary SSPBC)
Department of English, Media and Cultural Studies
School of Humanities
De Montfort University
Gateway House
Leicester LE1 9BU
Tel: 0116 255 1551 (ext. 8683)

Chapter 12

An introduction to Indian Cinema

Asha Kasbekar

■ **Introduction** 382

■ **The narrative structure** 382

□ Case study 1: *Dilwale Dulhaniya Le Jayenge* 391

■ **History of the popular Hindi film** 396

□ Case study 2: Mehboob Khan (1904–64) 402

□ Case study 3: Raj Kapoor (1926–88) 403

□ Case study 4: Bimal Roy (1902–66) 403

□ Case study 5: Guru Dutt (1925–64) 403

■ **Colour and the triumph of romance** 405

□ Case study 6: Satyajit Ray (1921–92) 408

■ **The distribution network** 410

■ **Satellite television** 411

■ **The influence of Hollywood** 411

■ **Consumption of popular Hindi films in Britain** 412

■ **Conclusion** 413

■ **Recommended viewing** 413

■ **Further viewing** 414

■ **Resource centres** 414

■ An introduction to Indian Cinema

INTRODUCTION

See Chapter 2 for discussion of film production in the US and the UK.

India produces over 900 films a year, making it the world's largest film producing nation. These films are viewed not just within the country, where they constitute the most important cultural activity, but in all of South Asia (Pakistan, Bangladesh, Sri Lanka), Africa (including the Maghreb countries of North Africa), South America, Eastern Europe and Russia. These films are also imported into all major European cities with a sizeable population of people of Asian and African descent.

The popular Indian film is radically different in narrative form and content to the Hollywood model of entertainment. Consequently, it offers its audiences an alternative to Hollywood, and one that is more in keeping with concerns particular to developing countries. Critical studies on Indian Cinema, both in India and abroad, have been confined to just a handful of books and articles, and most of these have tended to concentrate on the work of 'art' film directors such as the internationally renowned Satyajit Ray. This emphasis on highbrow art films tends to distort the understanding of Indian Cinema, where the bulk of films are low-brow, mass-produced for multicultural audiences from varied linguistic backgrounds within India.

Although there is a tendency to refer to Indian Cinema as if it were a cohesive whole, it is in fact fragmented into many regional film-producing centres, scattered all over the country. India has sixteen official languages and films are made in all the regional languages, with even an occasional film in classical Sanskrit. Hindi, the national language, is spoken in a variety of dialects by about 40 per cent of the population, and is broadly understood in most of the northern and central states. About 200 Hindi films are made each year in Bombay and are distributed throughout the country. Although Madras, the other film-making centre, makes more films a year in the regional languages of Tamil and Telugu, language barriers prevent it from challenging Bombay's national, and international, distribution network.

This chapter on Indian Cinema will concentrate on the popular Hindi film. It will consider its narrative structure and formal conventions, both of which are in fact common to regional films as well, before embarking on a brief account of its historical evolution. This is so that the reader may bear in mind the unique nature of the cinematic experience while understanding the particular historical factors that have moulded it. It will also highlight certain directors, from the popular as well as the élite 'art' cinema, and briefly examine their individual contributions.

THE NARRATIVE STRUCTURE

See Chapter 4, pp. 115–26, for further discussion of narrative in film.

Popular Hindi Cinema incorporated many of the formal conventions of the popular theatres, both rural and urban, that flourished in 1896 when the first foreign films began to be screened in the country. As a result the narrative structure does not follow the classic codes of Hollywood. Instead it has a loose storyline that is fragmented by frequent digressions into sub-plots and song-and-dance sequences. The audience is usually familiar with the main plot because it is often a reworking of a previously successful film. Often it contains deep mythological resonances that are easily accessible to them. The films indulge in highly emotional scenes that are played out with tumescent rhetoric in grand, declamatory style. The comic sub-plots, the overstated emotions and the song-and-dance sequences, all of which are held together by the thin thread of a main storyline, result in films that would be considered 'nightmarishly long' by western audiences. However, for those initiated into the pleasures of the popular Hindi film, the two hours and forty-five minutes that any viewing demands is a very satisfying and cathartic experience, where not only are the anxieties of its audiences clearly identified, but fantasies to escape from those very anxieties are also provided.

Plot

As in Hollywood, the most favoured theme of the Hindi film is that of romance. A handsome man, usually poor, but hard-working and honest, accidentally meets a rich and beautiful young woman. The two fall in love, but the young woman's father refuses to let them entertain any thoughts of marriage (the man's poverty, a prior marriage arrangement with the father's business partner's son or a feud between the two families being the most common reasons), and the two lovers are separated. However, when the young man saves the father's life, or shows the business partner to be a scheming crook intent on defrauding the credulous father, the father acknowledges his error of judgement and the young man is welcomed into the family fold.

Family relationships

Another recurring theme deals with family relationships. In the 1950s it featured the strains and pressures of modern life on the traditional, extended ('joint') family structure, where three generations of the same family usually live under the same roof. In such films, the initial domestic harmony is threatened by the arrival of a new, westernised daughter-in-law who refuses to respect the family hierarchy and nearly causes the family to break up. The crisis is then resolved through some supreme sacrifice on the part of one family member (usually the hero), who makes the young bride see the error of her ways.

By the 1970s, the family relationships theme evolved into 'lost and found' sagas, where two brothers become separated at birth, either because of a natural disaster (floods, tidalwave, earthquake) or an accident (usually involving trains). The two grow up in the same city (invariably Bombay), and one becomes a police officer while the other becomes a good-hearted gangster. When it falls to the police officer to shoot the gangster in the line of duty, kinship is suddenly recognised (a birthmark, a pendant, a long-lost sepia-coloured photograph) and the two brothers are united. Together they then embark on a mission to capture some other arch-criminal.

Family relationships are crucial to popular Hindi film regardless of its genre. Often, it is an individual character's response to family duties and responsibilities that defines his or her virtue or villainy. Thus in the 'lost and found' plot lines it is the gangster brother's longing for his family, in particular his mother – a longing that is expressed with poignant emotion and reiterated at critical dramatic junctures in the narrative – that reassures the audience of his inherent goodness. By the same token, a villain is one who completely disregards the sanctity of family relationships, and, by doing so, ensures that he is morally irredeemable.

Such romantic, family-related plot lines are completely familiar to the audiences. As Ashis Nandy points out:

The Bombay film-story does not generally have an unexpected conclusion, it only has a predictable climax. It bases its appeal not on the linear development of a story line but on the special configuration which the film presents of many known elements or themes derived from other movies, or, as Sudhir Kakar suggests, from familiar traditional tales.

(Nandy 1981: 90)

In the different forms of popular Indian theatre, such as the *Ram Lila*, episodes from the Indian epics are performed to audiences who are completely familiar with the stories, and who take pleasure in the familiarity of these myths and legends as well as in the visual spectacle of these performances. Since the plot is usually familiar to the audience, the interest lies in 'how things will happen rather than what will happen next' (Thomas 1985: 130; emphasis in original). The familiar narrative then serves to provide openings for the exploration of emotions, songs and spectacle.

Whatever the plot, the central conflict involves notions of 'good' and 'evil' in which the Hindu concept of *dharma* (duty), kinship ties and social obligations play a crucial role (Thomas 1985: 125). The action is set in a fictional world that is not governed by spatial and temporal verisimilitude. This does not mean that in the fictional world constructed by the film, time and space relations are completely 'unmotivated', but that the popular Hindi film is not committed to a 'realist aesthetic', and consequently it does not construct the fictional world as an authentic 'slice of life'. Instead it constructs a system that has its own logic, and where 'realism' is sacrificed to the advantage of other considerations, the most of important of all being that of emotion.

Emotion

The affective principle is considered to be of very great importance to the cinematic experience and for a film to succeed at the box office it must be able to 'move' the audience, to reach out and 'touch their hearts'. Such emphasis on emotion finds its origins in the conventions of the classical Indian theatre, as documented in the *Natyashastra* (c. 2nd century AD), a scholarly treatise on the performing arts. According to Bharata, to whom this work is attributed, drama is played for the amusement of the audience through the use of stylised acting methods in order to convey eight basic emotions (***bhava***): love, humour, energy, anger, fear, grief, disgust and astonishment. These emotions are conveyed by playing their causes and their effects, so that the audiences watching the enactment experience the aesthetic essence of the eight corresponding sentiments (***rasa***): the erotic, comic, heroic, furious, apprehensive, compassionate, horrific and marvellous (Warder 1975: 172). Based on the *rasa*, Bharata then outlined an elaborate theory of aesthetics in the performing arts.

Although the classical stage declined many centuries ago, its dramatic codes were inherited and deployed, albeit in a less refined form, by the various regional and folk theatres throughout the land. The same aesthetic traditions were also incorporated into the popular urban theatres in the nineteenth century, such as the Parsi Theatre (so-called because the theatres were often owned by Parsis, a distinct ethnic group of Persian origin) in Bombay and Calcutta, and later were incorporated into the newly arrived form of entertainment – the cinema. By adapting traditional aesthetics to a modern form of entertainment, the Indian Cinema not only maintained an unbroken link with its historical past, but it also made itself immediately accessible to the people as a mass entertainer.

The exploration of many, and sometimes even all, of the eight emotions, identified by Bharata, within a single film has led Bombay film to be referred to as **'*masala* movies'** (*masala* as in Indian spices). However, it is not enough to just convey these emotions through the various sub-plots and songs – they must also be powerfully overstated. Melodramatic overstatement is a 'crucial stylisation of the Bombay film' for it strives to be 'convincing as a spectacle by exaggeration' (Nandy 1981: 90). Nandy also cites (1981: 90) the case of a disgruntled critic who complained that whenever a clock strikes in Indian films, it always strikes twelve!

Song

Even more important than emotion in the popular film is the presence of songs. Each film has about six to eight songs, although one early film, *Indrasabha*, is said to have

bhava
The eight basic emotions – love, humour, energy, anger, fear, grief, disgust, astonishment.

rasa
The eight sentiments which correspond to the emotions – erotic, comic, heroic, furious, apprehensive, compassionate, horrific, marvellous.

'*masala* movie'
Spicy Indian movie overloaded with emotion.

contained seventy-one songs (Kabir 1991: 1)! Critical studies of popular Indian Cinema tend to concentrate on the structural complexities of film plots and often ignore the extra-narrative texts that are provided by the songs. However, the plot of a film is deliberately engineered so as to provide openings for a song-and-dance number at regular intervals.

The use of song and dance was already established in classical theatre, and Bharata in the *Natyashastra* considered **sangeeta** – that is, song, instrumental music and dance – to be an essential feature of the dramatic performance. The tradition has continued in popular theatre, where, even today, the song-and-dance numbers are the only sequences that are composed and rehearsed by the actors, the rest of the performance – the dialogue and witty repartees – often being improvised.

sangeeta
Combination of song, instrumental music and dance.

In popular cinema, attempts by established directors to present 'songless' films resulted in box-office disasters, and the importance accorded to songs in cinematic entertainment can be gauged by the important billing the 'music director' (the composer and arranger of music) and the lyricist are given in the credits. Their names also appear alongside those of the producer and director on billboard hoardings, posters and other film publicity materials.

The first talkie, *Alam Ara* (A. Irani, 1931), was a direct transfer from the stage of the Parsi Theatre and included many songs. The success of *Alam Ara*, and in particular of its songs, meant that the form of the musical drama set the trend for the future of Indian films. According to film historians Barnouw and Krishnaswamy:

The Indian sound film, unlike the sound film of any other land, had from its first moment seized exclusively on music-drama forms. In doing so, the film had tapped a powerful current, one that went back some two thousand years.

(Barnouw and Krishnaswamy 1980: 69)

The development of song and dance

During the silent era, film screenings were accompanied by live music played by a small group of musicians. Imported films had western musical accompaniment (usually on a piano), whereas Indian films had Indian musical accompaniment. In rural areas, special narrators would explain the 'title cards' and elaborate on the intricacies of the plot. Sometimes they even provided their own sound effects (such as the sound of galloping horses or, for the more dramatic scenes, the crash of thunder).

The songs in the early talkies were based on melodies borrowed from folk and classical traditions. Sound technology in the early 1930s was primitive. The microphones used for sound recording had to be stationary in order to reduce noise disturbances, and thus restricted the physical movements of the actors (Skillman 1986: 134). Early sound recordists recall the difficult circumstances under which songs were performed for the camera. One technique was to bury the camera under mattresses and covers in order to muffle its whirring noise. Then a single microphone would be directed at the actor/singer while a small number of musicians sat outside of the camera frame to provide the accompaniment. The placing of the single microphone meant that the actor could not move without upsetting the balance between voice and musical accompaniment, and the scene had to be shot in a single take with the actor/singer standing stiffly, rooted in one spot (Kabir 1991: 1). Musicians and even orchestras were hidden behind the surrounding trees and bushes which soon became crucial fixtures during song-and-dance sequences. Sometimes the musicians were even suspended from branches in order to be close enough for the singer to hear the notes clearly. These sylvan surroundings, which began as a technical necessity, have today become a clichéd convention of the popular film song, even though they have long outlived their usefulness, and the actor's tendency to 'run around trees' during a song is regularly satirised in the élite press.

play-back
Pre-recording of songs
with good singers and
with non-singing actors
lip-synchronising on
screen.

song picturisation
Filming of a song-and-
dance routine.

The overwhelming importance of song resulted in the industry preferring to employ singers, even if they could not act, rather than actors who could not sing. But in 1935, music director R.C. Boral discovered that if he pre-recorded the songs with good singers, then non-singing actors could be made to lip-synchronise on screen during the song (Skillman 1986: 135). The practice became known as **'play-back'** and is today a standard feature of popular Indian Cinema.

'Play-back' liberated the actor's dance movements, and the filming of the song-and-dance routine is referred to as a **'song picturisation'**. Soon singers became celebrities in their own right. Lata Mangeshkar, who recently retired after nearly half a century of 'play-back' singing, has over 25,000 songs to her credit.

Most songs last about five minutes. According to composer Bhaskar Chandavarkar, these songs started out being three and a half minutes long because:

the 78 r.p.m. was the only recording format available till other means of sound recording came to be invented and the film magazine would not allow very lengthy sequences to be filmed without a break. These factors made it necessary to have songs of about 3½ minutes neatly cut into 3 stanzas along with the opening 'mukhra' – the catch words. The three stanzas were again neatly interspersed with musical interludes. These features became so popular that songs which were not recorded for films also emulated them.

(Chandavarkar 1985: 249)

● **Plate 12.1** Raveena Tandon and Akshay Kumar in Rajiv Rai's *Mohra*

The arrival of the 33¾ long-playing disc-recording developed in the 1950s enabled music directors to compose longer songs and by the 1970s the average film song was about five minutes long and in stereo (Skillman 1986: 142).

Today the film song has a life beyond the screen. They are played over loudspeakers on national holidays and religious festivals. At weddings the band invariably belts out the current favourites. Beggars, singing in the streets and on trains, have incorporated them into their repertoire. Even the 'folk' theatres, that once inspired film music, have now abandoned their original songs for the film versions of the same. Radio stations entirely devoted to film songs abound, and television programmes that provided a compilation of song-and-dance sequences from different films were popular in India long before music videos and MTV were devised.

Spectacle

The song-and-dance numbers are devised as visually spectacular sequences. Traditional forms of entertainment placed great emphasis on spectacle and used elaborate masks (or stylised make-up), ornate costumes and decorative head-dresses. Indian Cinema, having incorporated their aesthetic conventions, places similar importance on spectacular visual display, particularly in the song-and-dance sequences, and uses grand settings (palaces or breathtaking landscapes) and glittering costumes which often have little bearing on the actual story. In *Mughal-e-Azam* (K. Asif, 1960), an extravagant

• **Plate 12.2** Madhuri Dixit and Kumar Gaurav in Aryam Films' *Phool*.

historical costume drama that is alleged to have taken fifteen years to complete, the crucial moment of the film is constructed around a song-and-dance number, and choreographed in a specially constructed 'hall of mirrors' (*Sheesh Mahal*), in such a manner that the danceuse is reflected in miniature in every piece of mirror in the hall. Although not every film can afford to achieve such dazzling brilliance, sumptuous visual effects are eagerly sought after by film directors.

Love songs are central to the popular Hindi film and they are often contrived as 'dream sequences'. During such flights into fantasy the unities of time and space are completely disregarded. The song picturisations strive for maximum visual effect, and each stanza of the song reveals a different panoramic setting and yet another gorgeous costume. The film industry's penchant for such opulent pageantry has resulted in it being regularly condemned by the cultural élite as 'dream merchants' peddling 'escapist fantasies'.

Functions of the song

In addition to the aural and visual pleasures that the song offers its public, it also fulfils a more delicate social function. In a conservative society that frowns on romantic liaisons, and where marriages are arranged within caste groupings (*jatis*), any verbal declaration of love and sexual desire between man and woman risks causing embarrassment. By transferring such declarations into song and distancing the emotions by putting them in the realm of fantasy or dream, the family watching the film together (a common practice in India) is spared any possible awkwardness.

The song also links disparate elements of the usually complicated plot and sub-plots, thus ensuring some coherence in the theme. It also offers a commentary on Life, Fate and Destiny, and even provides an escape from an overwrought emotional scene. More importantly, the song functions as a bridge between tradition and modernity (Skillman 1986: 143). Pressure on music directors to come up with six to eight songs for each film has resulted in rampant pilfering from all musical sources and particularly western pop music. While early films drew on Indian classical and folk traditions, by the 1950s music directors began seeking inspiration from western sources. Not only were western instruments incorporated into ever-growing orchestrations, but blatant copies of rock'n'roll, samba and even western classical symphonies set to Indian lyrics became commonplace. A guitar-strumming Elvis, a disco-dancing John Travolta, a break-dancing Michael Jackson and many other icons of western culture have all been reproduced on the Indian screen. Such 'hybridisation' of film music, although distasteful to the purists, has provided a cultural filter through which the latest musical trends have been made accessible to the Indian public.

Stars

See Chapter 6 for discussion of stars in Hollywood cinema.

Along with the spectacular song-and-dance sequences and the emotional excess indulged in during scenes of dramatic intensity, the next most important feature of the popular Indian film are the stars or 'superstars' (as they have been proclaimed by the well-oiled publicity machinery). The stars earn fabulous sums of money that could easily compare with their counterparts in Hollywood. Male stars are always paid more than female stars. So familiar are their faces to the public that they do not need to be identified by name either on the posters or on the huge hand-painted billboards that dominate the skyline of all major Indian cities.

The actors and actresses work several shifts a day on different films, and getting 'dates' for a major star is a serious problem for film-makers. Gossip magazines provide an inexhaustible supply of stories about their extravagant lifestyles and their unconventional sex lives. They are seldom sued by the stars implicated in the gossip, and often the revelations are made to coincide with an important release to help boost attendance in cinemas. Many stars of the 1960s and the 1970s have been successful in pushing their offspring into films, creating a second generation of stars within certain families. A growing number have been able to pursue a successful career in politics after retiring from films. A few have tried to find fame and fortune in Hollywood but with little success.

Double role

Once film stars achieve a certain status within the industry, they sign a film contract that casts them in a double role. The story usually concerns twin brothers or sisters separated at birth. In *Ram Aur Shyam* (Tapi Chanakya, 1967) the bullied Ram is rescued by the ebullient Shyam, both roles played by **Dilip Kumar**. In *Haseena Man Jayegi* (Prakash Mehra, 1968), **Shashi Kapoor** plays both the good and the bad citizen. **Rajesh Khanna** plays the good and the bad in *Sachcha Jhutha* (Manmohan Desai, 1970). Not to be outdone, **Amitabh Bachchan** played triple roles as a father and his two sons in the comedy *Mahaan* (S. Ramanathan, 1983).

Sometimes the two characters are totally unrelated, and it is pure chance that creates the *doppelgänger*. In *Hum Dono* (Amarjeet, 1961), **Dev Anand** plays an army captain who impersonates his superior, a major in the same regiment after the latter's death; **Govinda** played double roles (the city slicker and the country bumpkin) in *Aankhen* (D. Dhawan, 1993), while **Shah Rukh Khan** plays both the innocent cook and the cynical gangster in *Duplicate* (Mahesh Bhatt, 1998).

Among the female stars **Sadhana** played both the good and the bad sisters in *Woh Kaun Thi* (Raj Khosla, 1964) and *Mera Saaya* (Raj Khosla, 1966), while **Hema Malini** played the meek and submissive Seeta as well as the bold and fearless Geeta in *Seeta Aur Geeta* (Ramesh Sippy, 1972). **Sridevi** replayed the similar roles in *Chaalbaaz* (Pankaj Parashar, 1989).

Genre

Hollywood organises the production and marketing of its films around 'genres' which enable it to predict audience expectation and guide their viewing. Indian films have their own genres that do not always correspond with western generic classifications (Thomas 1985: 120). Since the rise of the independent producer in the 1940s, it is an 'omnibus' genre that has dominated the Hindi film industry. Viewing of Hindi films still remains a predominantly family activity with male and female members, of different ages and belonging to the same (often extended) family, watching films or videos together. The omnibus genre incorporates into the same film conventions that would normally belong to different generic traditions. It offers 'romance', 'melodrama', 'comedy', 'action' as well as the indispensable song/dance/spectacle. Different sections of the film are targeted at different sections of the audience. For example, scenes depicting suffering and 'tears' are deliberately targeted at female spectators, slapstick humour at children, and erotic display of women at male spectators. The reason for such a narrative organisation is commercial rather than aesthetic. Instead of *dividing* its audiences (and hence its revenue) as does Hollywood, the Hindi film industry *amalgamates* its audiences and instead divides the film narrative into specific sections destined for specific sections of its amalgamated audiences. The pleasures of what used to be different genres are thus incorporated into the very same film text.

The omnibus film has revealed that its strength lies in its capacity to absorb visual and aural influences from multimedia (e.g. MTV, advertising), and adapt it to its familiar plot. When necessary, it also adapted a variety of generically different conventions e.g. violent spectacle from the action film, devotional songs and/or miracles from the mythological films and so on. The perennial favourite is the *lost and found* theme in which two

See Chapter 6, for discussion of genre in Hollywood cinema.

brothers (or identical twins) are separated at birth, with one becoming an upholder of the law and the other a fugitive from it; it is also part of the omnibus genre.

The other genres in Hindi Cinema remain peripheral to the omnibus genre. There are 'mythological' films that usually recount myths or legends from the two great Hindu epics, the *Ramayana* and the *Mahabharata*. These stories, the mainstay of the pre-modern forms of entertainment, became the primary source for narratives of early Indian Cinema. In fact, almost all the early silent films were of the mythological genre, e.g. Phalke's Raja *Harishchandra* (1913) and Baburao Painter's *Seeta Swayamwara* (1916). A more recent example of the genre, which was an unprecedented success at the box office, is *Jai Santoshi Maa* (V. Sharma, 1975). (For an analysis of the film, see Veena Das 1980.) Since then the genre has successfully transferred to television.

'Devotional' films (both Hindu and Muslim) explore divine interventions and miracles or recount the lives of saints, or involve a pilgrimage to holy shrines and rivers, because such viewings of sacred sites (even on celluloid) are considered to shower blessings on the viewer.

'Historical films' are based on legends and episodes from history. Already popular as a genre on the urban stage (e.g. the Parsee Theatre), it reached its cinematic apogee in the decades before India became independent, when the genre was used to circumvent colonial censorship that banned any glorification of the national struggle. The post-independence historical film is entirely concerned with celebrating historical or legendary romances such as *Mughal-e-Azam* (K.Asif, 1960) and *Razia Sultan* (Kamal Amrohi, 1983) but thereafter the genre has found its greatest success on television.

The 'social' is a comprehensive generic category that includes any film concerned with social reform. Themes such as the evils of the caste system, child marriages, etc. were explored in the studio productions of the 1930s and 1940s such as V. Shantaram's *Padosi* (1941) and *Duniya Na M ane* (1937) or Franz Osten's *Achhut Kanya* (1936). Mehboob's *Mother India* (1957) (analysed in Rosie Thomas 1989) and its predecessor *Aurat* (1940) are also examples of the social that address the 'women's question'. More recent examples of the women's social are *Damini* (Rajkumar Santoshi, 1993) (analysis of the film appears in Madhava Prasad 1995), *Rihaee* (Aruna Raje, 1988) and *Mrtyudand* (Prakash Jha, 1997).

The 'Muslim social' is not a social (in that it does not always have the spirit of social reform) but a romance set in an archly Muslim ethos. A moribund genre today, it reached its pinnacle in the 1960s with films like *Mere Mehboob* (H.S. Rawail, 1963), *Chaudhavin ka Chand* (M. Sadiq, 1960) and *Barsaat ki Raat* (P.L. Santoshi, 1960). The most recent Muslim social was *Bewafa Se Wafaa* (Saawan Kumar, 1992).

There are a few 'horror' films that feature supposedly Tantric rituals and other black magic practices.

Formula

A film that has a familiar plot and contains romance, dramatic family relationships and an epic struggle between the forces of 'good' and 'evil', themselves determined by traditional concepts of 'duty' (*dharma*) and family obligations, and is enacted by stars and embellished by several spectacular song-and-dance numbers, is referred to as a 'formula' film. The director's skill lies not just in deploying the different components of the 'formula' but also in presenting them in innovative ways so that they appear new and different with each film.

It is this elusive perfection of balance between the different components of the 'formula', this magical combination of the emotional, the visual and the musical ingredients, that holds the key to a box-office success so crucial to the industry. The fact that out of the approximately 200 films produced in Hindi each year, only 5 to 10 per cent are commercially successful, shows that Indian audiences are mercilessly discerning in their assessment of the films on offer. Fifteen to twenty per cent of the films manage to break even, while the rest lose money. A successful film can reap huge financial rewards for the distributors, catapult new actors and actresses into instant stardom or double a star's rates and, as approving audiences flock to the cinemas (estimated at 90 million a week throughout India) to view the film not once but several times, can immediately activate a thriving black market for tickets outside the cinemas.

☐ CASE STUDY 1: *DILWALE DULHANIYA LE JAYENGE*

One of the biggest hits of the 1990s has been the film *Dilwale Dulhaniya Le Jayenge* ('Lovers Will Walk Off with the Bride'), a romance set amidst the Indian diaspora and directed by newcomer Aditya Chopra, whose father Yash Chopra remains one of the leading directors of the Hindi screen.

Plot
The basic plot concerns the footloose and fancy-free Raj (Shah Rukh Khan) who meets and falls in love with Simran (Kajol) during a holiday in Europe. Both Simran and Raj are children of Punjabi immigrants to the UK, but while Raj and his father (Anupam Kher) have been assimilated into the consumer culture of Britain, Simran's father (Amrish Puri, who played in Steven Spielberg's *Indiana Jones and the Temple of Doom*) still clings to Indian traditions. In adherence to these feudal traditions, he drags Simran off to marry Kuljeet, son of his dearest friend and neighbour in Punjab, even though the protesting Simran has never set eyes on the young man.

Not one to give up easily, Raj follows Simran to Punjab. Refusing to elope (despite Simran's impassioned entreaties) because he considers it a cowardly way to resolve matters, he is determined to win her hand by acquiring her parents' consent. To that end, he inveigles his way into the hearts of the members of both Simran's and her fiancé's families. However when Simran's father discovers that Raj is the one who romanced his daughter in Europe and has entered the household under false pretences, he chases him all the way to the village railway station. But, as it gradually dawns on him that Raj *truly* loves his daughter, the father has a change of heart and allows Simran to join him. She leaps on to the train and into his arms just as the train begins to pull out.

Formula
Dilwale Dulhaniya Le Jayenge (henceforth *DDLJ*) is constructed following the classic structure of the Hindi film romance: meeting, falling in love, separation/suffering and reunion. It features a new face (Kajol) and the top star of the 1990s (Shah Rukh Khan); it has seven song-and-dance sequences, breathtaking spectacle and a happy ending. An important feature of the film is its emphasis on affect and melodrama.

The pleasures of the plot are predicated on the pleasures of 'sameness' and 'difference'. The narrative journey through meeting, falling in love, separation/suffering and reunion is largely predictable. These provide the comforting pleasures of 'sameness', where the audience is perfectly aware of what will happen next, and there is little margin for suspense. For instance, most romances include an episode where the hero and heroine are forced by circumstances to spend the night in the same room, but abstain from any sexual activity. In *DDLJ*, Raj and Simran, having missed their train in

Switzerland, find that they must spend the night together in the only room available to them.

On the other hand, how these different stages of meeting, falling in love etc. will be addressed is the paradigmatic space provided by the narrative wherein the pleasures of 'difference' will be proposed. While the plot in *DDLJ* is structured in a manner familiar to audiences, it nevertheless includes interesting variations, which helps to keep alive the interest of the audience. The following are four examples of 'difference':

1 In most Hindi films, the moment the leading characters' paths cross, their eyes meet and love happens instantaneously, usually to the accompaniment of thunder, lightning or a rainstorm. In *DDLJ*, the lovers' paths first cross at Leicester Square, but in a deliberate twist to the predictability of the formulaic plot, they *don't* see each other. In fact they are entirely unaware of each other's existence. The variation is further emphasised by showing the crossing of their paths in close-up and slow motion. In fact, the much awaited crucial encounter (meeting of eyes, holding of hands) is delayed until the train for Europe from Victoria Station begins to pull out and Raj offers Simran his hand to help her board the moving train – a gesture that will be repeated with neat symmetry when Raj and Simran escape from the village in Punjab and from parental authority at the end of the film.
2 Unlike most Hindi films, the 'falling in love' process is not instantaneous or dramatic but instead slow and imperceptible.
3 Sometimes 'difference' is used for comic effect. The hero in most films is often shown to be an exemplary student, achieving a 'first class first' in college exams. Here Raj is shown to be a complete academic failure and the latest in a long, ancestral line of academic disasters.
4 Usually, after the initial romance (accompanied by the song-and-dance spectacles), the lovers are physically separated from each other. The separation is then the cause of great emotional distress and suffering, which is then relieved when the lovers are finally reunited. However, in *DDLJ*, the hero sneaks back into the heroine's family fold as a 'friend' and the lovers continue to meet on the rooftop every night.

The plot, like most Hindi films, is predicated on the confrontation between the young Raj and the old father. But it is more than just a generational confrontation between a mischievous youth and an autocratic father. It is also a conflict between modernity (as represented by Raj) and tradition (as epitomised by the father), a fundamental opposition that recurs in almost every Hindi film. The tradition/modernity dichotomy is an opposition of town (London) and village (in Punjab), of the West and India, of the anxieties of rootlessness and the security of fixedness. In the voiceover during the opening scene of the film, the father is shown feeding pigeons in Trafalgar Square, an activity he has engaged in for twenty-two years. But the father confesses that even after twenty-two years he still feels an outsider in this land: 'I am rootless, like these pigeons', he declares, 'who fly to wherever they can find food. But, one day, I shall return to my home in Punjab.'

The generation game

Many actors and directors from the Hindi film industry have tried to promote the careers of their sons or daughters in the film industry. As in Indian politics, a second generation of stars is being groomed. Not all have been successful. Among women actors are Karishma Kapoor, daughter of 1970s star Babita and actor/director Randhir Kapoor, the latter the son of Raj Kapoor and grandson of actor Prithiviraj Kapoor, and Kajol (who leapt to stardom after *Dilwale Dulhaniya Le Jayenge*), daughter of 1960s star Tanuja and niece of the celebrated 1960s star Nutan.

Among male actors, Sanjay Dutt is the son of 1960s and 1970s star Sunil Dutt, and his mother was the late Nargis, who acted in films of Raj Kapoor and ended her career with Mehboob's *Mother India*, while Amitabh Bachchan, the angry young man of the 1970s screen, is currently promoting his son Abhishek. His mother Jaya Bahaduri is a fine actress who retired from films after her marriage to Amitabh. Saif Ali Khan is the son of 1970s star Sharmila Tagore and India's cricket captain the Nawab of Pataudi. Salman Khan is the son of Salim Khan, who formed part of the Salim–Javed duo of screenplay writers who thrilled audiences with their hit films of the 1970s featuring the 'angry young man'. Another star-turned-politician Vinod Khanna successfully launched his son Akshaye Khanna in J.P. Dutta's *Border* (1997) and Nasir Hussain, director of film hits in the 1950s and 1960s launched his nephew, the 1990s star Aamir Khan.

Aditya Chopra, whose début film was *Dilwale Dulhaniya Le Jayenge* (see Case study 1), is the son of veteran film director Yash Chopra (*Deewar* (1975) and *Dil To Pagal Hai* (1997)).

Song/dance/spectacle

DDLJ carries the standard number of songs (seven) that characterise a 'formula' film. The songs in most cases express a desire or an emotion, rather than directly progress the action of the film. The song-and-dance numbers create the space for visual pleasures via spectacular display and aural pleasures via the melody and lyrics. It would be a useful exercise to see how these song-and-dance sequences are slotted into the narrative.

1   The first song-and-dance number, '*Mere Khwabon Mein Jo Aaye*' ('The One Who Enters My Dreams'), takes place soon after Kajol has been introduced to the spectator as a romantic and sensitive soul through excerpts of her diary, wherein she confides her inner dreams and desires. As she reads it aloud, the scene dissolves into a song-and-dance number that is executed in the intimacy of the family garden. Simran dances in the rain, while her gentle mother who is both her friend and confidante, bustles around in the house happily attending to the household chores. The lyrics reveal a longing for the man of her dreams to come and reveal his identity. It testifies to her own 'coming of age', readiness to fall in love and her inchoate sexual desires. Dressed, as she is, in a very short skirt and a brief knotted blouse which cling to her body wet in the rain, she also becomes an erotic spectacle for visual consumption.

2   The second number '*Ruk Ja Oh Dil Diwane*' ('Stop! Oh Crazy Heart') occurs during the holiday in Europe. Raj and Simran have met on the train, where his attempts at flirtation have been firmly rebuffed. Arriving at a smart restaurant where the floor show includes a 'comic' opera, Raj (accompanied by his mates) and Simran (surrounded by hers) meet once again. This time he tries to flirt with her friend, using the same stock phrases he had used with her on the train. Annoyed at how her friends seem to adore his disingenuous flattery, she decides to call his bluff, and, responding to his wild claim that he is a brilliant pianist, she announces to all the diners that he will now entertain them with a recital. Indulging, at first, in some slapstick buffoonery with the piano, he later reveals himself to be a brilliant pianist. What follows is a mock cabaret dance with him as the star performer surrounded by a bevy of beautiful dancers. While the lyrics praise the beauty and magic of an unnamed woman, the spectacular dance, suffused with energy, grace, charm and skill, reveal Raj's own physical desirability. This time, it is male youth and energy that becomes the object of visual pleasure.

3 Raj and Simran have missed the train that is taking their colleagues to Zurich. Rather than spend the night alone in the same room with him, Simran decides to move to an abandoned stable nearby. Raj joins her bringing food and a bottle of cognac to protect against the bitter cold. Simran fortifies herself with some brandy and is soon very drunk. She then bursts into a song and dance 'Zara Sa Jhoom Loon Mein' ('Let Me Sway and Swing a Little') that is choreographed across Switzerland. The locales change rapidly – from shopping districts to coffee houses, from high hills and snowy peaks to verdant pastures – as Simran, with Raj in hot pursuit, races around rural and urban landscapes. The drunkenness allows the woman to assume a new identity and indulge in an uninhibitedly frank expression of joy and exhuberance.

4 Back in the UK after the holidays, Raj, Simran and friends arrive at Victoria Station. As Raj and Simran make their separate ways home, they realise that they are in love. Both are troubled, because Simran has already told Raj that she is going back to India to marry a man her father has chosen for her and whom she has never met. Two songs are then intercut to make one duet: Raj sings 'Na Jane Mere Dil Ko Kya Ho Gaya' ('I Don't Know What Has Happened to My Heart') while she sings 'Ho Gaya Hai Tujhko To Pyar Sajana' ('You Have Fallen in Love'), which give expression to their realisations and their anxieties about the future. The song is 'picturised' by intercutting their respective journeys home with a series of flash-backs of happy moments together in Switzerland e.g. their drunkenness, their visits to churches and so on.

5 Simran's father overhears his daughter confess to her mother that she is in love and he is incensed. He decides that the entire family will leave for India the very next day. Simran is unable to defy her father's authority and besides, as she tells her mother, she doesn't even know Raj where Raj lives or if he loves her. The transition to India, is achieved by the song 'Ghar Aaja Pardes' whose lyrics urge the self-exiled to 'come home'. The song plays in the background as women in traditional Punjabi dress and their scarves raised in the air, dance in the yellow mustard fields. Refrains of the song have already been introduced in the opening scenes when Simran's father, feeding the pigeons in Trafalgar Square, remembers his homeland. Henceforth the song establishes itself as the melodic metaphor for Indian traditions and is introduced when any act of 'tradition' is performed. For example, it is sung (with different lyrics but the same melody) when the womenfolk in the village end the traditional period of fasting undertaken by Hindu women to ensure their husbands' longevity.

6 Raj follows Simran to her village. When the two reunite in the fields, away from the prying eyes of the world, they sing to each other 'Tujhe Dekha To Yeh Jana Sanam' ('When I Saw You, I Understood What Love's Mad Passion Meant'). Once again the song is picturised by counterposing their meeting in the fields with flashbacks of their romance in Switzerland. In addition to the emotion contained within the scene of reunion, and the visual pleasures of green fields, snowy Swiss peaks, as well as the aural pleasures of vocal music, the song performs yet another important function: namely, it substitutes for any overt display of passion (kissing, love-making etc.) that would conventionally be expected in Hollywood films. This is because the Censor Board, having ruled that kissing is a particularly 'un-Indian' activity, excises any scene that depicts a kiss on the lips. Passion must thus be sublimated via the song, and desire sung about rather than acted upon.

7 Simran and Kuljeet are now formally engaged and it is a day of great festivities for the two households. The family members and friends gather on the roof terrace and celebrate the happy occasion with a group song-and-dance number. The song 'Mehndi Lagaa Ke Rakhnaa, Doli Sajaa Ke Rakhna' ('Adorn your Hands with Henna,

Keep the Palanquin Ready') is sung in 'call and response' by the men and women who are arranged in separate camps. Once again the choreography emphasises spectacle (costumes), energy and a general feeling of euphoria. The dance, abruptly suspended when Simran's authoritarian father arrives on the terrace, is quickly resumed when it is discovered that he doesn't really disapprove.

Functions of song/dance/spectacle

Visual spectacle – via sumptuous costumes, indoor sets or sweeping vistas of natural beauty (the Swiss Alps; yellow mustard fields in Punjab, stretching as far as the eye can see), close-up shots of the stars that constantly focus on their beauty, skill and charisma or glamour – is given extensive expression in the song-and-dance sequences. But in addition to the **scopophiliac** attractions, and the aural pleasures (via the lyrics, melodies and the beautiful singing voices), the song-and-dance numbers perform certain crucial textual functions. As seen in the sixth song, by *insinuating* desire in lieu of overt sexual activity on screen, they provide one way of circumventing censorship.

However, it is not just government censorship that is being circumvented, but also the general social disapproval. Since most viewing of Hindi films is a family-oriented activity, any overt or explicit display of sexual activity is frowned upon. The placing of the expression of passion within the song-and-dance numbers remove it from the realm of 'reality' of the film narrative (i.e. the plot and its tensions). In the realm of fantasy and make-believe, emotional restraint can be temporarily abandoned and transgressive desire given a brief release. The energetic and zestful dances also serve to release the emotional tensions that are contained in the melodramatic plot and its unfolding. Finally, in *DDLJ*, the songs also function as melodic metaphors, where certain musical refrains identify specific desires, traditions and states of minds. Thus, each time tradition is evoked, melodic variations from the fifth song and dance are played, while Raj's love or presence is foreshadowed by melodic variations from the fourth.

scopophilia
Freudian term meaning the 'pleasure in looking', introduced to film analysis by Laura Mulvey.

The 'women's question'

DDLJ raises a strident voice against feudal patriarchy. Most Hindi films feature a male protagonist, while the woman mostly serves as the object of male desire. The few 'women's films', where women are the protagonists and not just sexual cynosures, generally address the impossibility of female desire under patriarchy. In Mehboob's *Andaz*, an innocent woman who had dared to be a little too friendly with another man is imprisoned, and eventually deemed unfit to be a mother to her own children; *Mother India* portrays the ideal wife, mother and citizen, who is persistently betrayed by the men that surround her. The recent *Mirch Masala* (Ketan Mehta, 1985) and *Mrityudand* (Prakah Jha, 1997) take a more active stance and even use violence to overcome patriarchal tyranny. While some of these films do use songs and dances in the narrative and may even be spectacularly choreographed (e.g. *Mother India*), women's films usually work outside the formulaic conventions of the popular Hindi film. What makes *DDLJ* an interesting case for study is that the film attempts an anti-patriarchal discourse *within* the conventions of the formula.

Simran's father embodies feudal patriarchy, and it is her mother who is the bearer of a boldly 'feminist' discourse. In a marked difference to most Hindi films where the mother's position usually supports feudal patriarchy, here the mother is shown to be deeply sympathetic to her daughter's desires but unable to help her escape the father's tyranny. Telling Simran how she was forced to stifle her own passions and desires to assume the roles of daughter, sister and wife that society had forced on her, she says that when Simran was born she had promised herself that she would see to it that her child would never have to suffer in the same way. 'But,' she says, 'I had forgotten, that

For further discussion of feminism see Chapter 9 and Chapter 14 pp. 468–71.

women in our society do not even have the *right* to make such promises. Here, women are born to make sacrifices, while men make none.' However, it must be remembered that despite the feminist rhetoric, the film does not resist box-office pressures to present the woman as an erotic spectacle, and, in the song-and-dance spectacles where skimpy skirts, tight bodices and dancing in the rain are featured, fetishise the female body.

For further study, analyse *DDLJ* to address the following:

1 **How is Simran represented?**
2 **How does she react to her father's tyranny?**
3 **How does she react to her mother's 'feminist' exhortations?**
4 **How is Raj represented?**
5 **What is his relationship to feudal patriarchy?**

HISTORY OF THE POPULAR HINDI FILM

For further information on the development of Early Cinema, see Chapters 2 and 3.

The Lumière Brothers opened their cinematograph to the public on 28 December 1895 in Paris. Six months later their emissary Maurice Sestier, *en route* to Australia to exhibit a collection of short films, stopped off in Bombay. The first screenings of these Lumière films took place in Bombay at Watson's Hotel for an audience consisting largely of British residents in India, some Europeans and a few anglicised Indians. The response from the English-language press was so unexpectedly enthusiastic that further screenings were quickly programmed, and later, to accommodate the even bigger crowds that showed up, the screenings were moved to the much larger Novelty Theatre.

A cinema audience had suddenly been created and from 1897 onwards there was a regular inflow of films, imported from Britain, France, the US, Italy, Denmark and Germany. The British residents in India as well as the Indians soon began to import filming equipment and to make their own films. These short features consisted of comic gags, operas, sports events and other documentaries about local events (Barnouw and Krishnaswamy 1980: 8). By 1902, a network for the distribution and exhibition of films within India and South-East Asia had been put in place by several Indian entrepreneurs.

The silent films

The first feature-length Indian feature was called *Raja Harishchandra*. Made in 1912 by D.G. Phalke, it was about a famous king from Hindu mythology, named Harishchandra, who was willing to sacrifice all his worldly possessions in his pursuit of Truth. The film was 3,700 feet long, and when screened with a hand-cranked projector lasted about fifty minutes. It is said that the inspiration for this film came from *Life of Christ* (Gaumont, 1906) that was being screened in Bombay as a Christmas feature in 1910. Phalke was so impressed by the special effects used to show the miracles performed by Christ, that he went to see it again, this time taking his wife with him and borrowing money from his neighbours for the transport and tickets (Barnouw and Krishnaswamy 1980: 11). Film historian B.V. Dharap cites an article written by Phalke in November 1917 in which Phalke states:

While the *Life of Christ* was rolling fast before my physical eyes, I was mentally visualising the

Gods, Shri Krishna, Shri Ramachandra, their Gokul and their Ayodhya. I was gripped by a strange spell. I bought another ticket and saw the film again. This time I felt my imagination taking shape on the screen. Could this really happen? Could we, the sons of India, ever be able to see Indian images on the screen?

(Dharap 1985: 35)

Phalke, a graduate of an art school and one-time draughtsman and photographer at the Archaeological Department, had given up his job to join the struggle for freedom from British colonial rule. After seeing the *Life of Christ*, he liquidated his possessions, journeyed to London and bought himself some film-making equipment. On returning to India he enlisted the help of his wife and made India's first film feature – *Raja Harishchandra*. It met with phenomenal success. Phalke, also an amateur magician, had incorporated the techniques of Georges Méliès, famed for his special effects. These techniques lent themselves easily to the miracles and divine interventions that abound in stories from Hindu mythology. Suddenly the mythological kings and sages that were so familiar came alive before the very eyes of the cinema audiences, and Hindu legends began to acquire an unprecedented allure.

After the success of *Raja Harishchandra*, Phalke moved to Nasik, bought a huge house and set up the nation's first studio. All the actors lived and worked in Phalke's family home. Initially the actors were all male because acting, as a profession, was considered no better than prostitution. Even prostitutes, unsure of the new form of entertainment, declined to participate. (It was only a decade later that women agreed to act in films. At first the actresses were from the Anglo-Indian community, who were despised by 'respectable' society. They assumed Hindu names to make themselves acceptable to the film-going public.)

Phalke's acting team went on to make at least two silent films a year. The stories were usually drawn from Hindu mythology, which made them instantly accessible to a nation familiar with the myths and legends. Phalke had started a national culture and a lucrative industry. Sadly he died in 1944, a destitute and forgotten man. It was only several decades after his death that his contribution was officially recognised and he was hailed as the 'Father of Indian Cinema'.

Meanwhile, others entered the field, and soon historical and social themes began to be introduced to the screen. Audiences seemed to prefer locally made films to the European and American imports. Between 1912 and 1934 1,279 silent films were made in the country (Wadia 1985: 21). Most of these have perished, but the few that have survived are preserved at the Film Archives in Pune.

The age of sound

The arrival of sound was to prove a serious problem for the film industry. India, with its linguistic diversity, would need to make films in different regional languages which would mean the fragmentation of a vast national market into smaller, and consequently commercially less lucrative, regional ones. *Alam Ara* (A. Irani, 1931), the first talkie, was made in Bombay in Hindi, the national language. Ever since, the Bombay-based film industry, which makes films in Hindi, has dominated film production in India.

See Chapter 3, for discussion of the arrival of sound in Hollywood cinema.

The advent of sound necessitated the construction of sound studios and indoor shooting. Several studios were constructed in the major cities of India, and Lahore (now in Pakistan), Bombay, Calcutta and later Madras became important film centres. By the end of the 1930s there were nearly a hundred studios, big and small, involved in film production. Of these there were three that were to greatly influence the future development of the Indian Cinema.

New Theatres

In 1931, B.N. Sircar, an engineer who had completed the construction of a brand new theatre, decided to build a film theatre for himself in Calcutta. He equipped it with a first-class studio and provided the talented group of Bengalis he had gathered around him with all the resources necessary for creative film-making. This was the start of New Theatres. One director to achieve fame and recognition soon after the studio was set up was Debaki Bose. His first success was *Chandidas* (1932), based on the life of the eponymous sixteenth-century poet-saint. Bose's liberal use of music and song blended well with the requirements of the religious theme. His later films for New Theatres were also on religious or mythological themes, the most famous being *Puran Bhagat* (1933) and *Seeta* (1934). *Seeta* was the first ever Indian film to be screened at an international festival.

However, the greatest sensation to emerge from New Theatres was P.C. Barua, an Assamese prince whose production of *Devdas* (1935), based on a novel by the renowned littérateur Sarat Chandra Chatterjee, was to overwhelm the nation. Made in Bengali and in Hindi, it told the tragic tale of Devdas, a man who takes to drink and drowns his sorrows in melancholic songs when the woman he loves is married off to another by her parents. Indeed, so moving were these soulful songs and the tragic resolution that 'virtually a generation wept over Devdas' (Barnouw and Krishnaswamy 1980: 80). P.C. Barua, who directed both versions but starred in only the Bengali version, also died of drink (but not melancholy) at the age of 48.

Most of the later films made by New Theatres were drawn from literary sources, thus the audience began to associate the studio's productions with sophisticated, high calibre and intellectual music-dramas.

Prabhat Studios

Competition to New Theatres in Calcutta was to come from Prabhat Studios in Pune. First established in Kolhapur in Maharashtra State in 1929, the studio shifted to Pune in 1933. Like New Theatres, Prabhat too began by making mythological and devotional films. The most influential personality to emerge from this studio was V. Shantaram. His first film, made in Marathi (the regional language), was *Ayodhyache Raja* in 1932, and it told the story of the same King Harishchandra that had made Phalke famous. In 1936, Shantaram's associates S. Fatehlal and V.G. Damle made a devotional film on Tukaram, a seventeenth-century poet-saint. Called *Sant Tukaram*, it was the first Indian film to win an international award at the Venice Film Festival and it is still considered one of the finest Indian films ever made.

Shantaram, however, moved away from mythological themes and began to explore social issues. His most famous films dealt with the abuses of arranged marriages (*Duniya Na Mane* in 1937) and Hindu–Muslim animosity (*Padosi* in 1941). Soon Prabhat became known nationwide for its 'social' films. Not only were the films ideologically bold for the times, they were also innovative in their use of camera, music and song, and would greatly influence later directors who began as apprentices at the studio.

Bombay Talkies

The other major studio in the 1930s was Bombay Talkies, which was set up by Himansu Rai. Rai had worked in Britain and Germany, but the economic depression and the subsequent rise of Fascism forced him and his actress wife, Devika Rani, to return to India. Devika Rani, who had trained in London, met Rai and worked with him in Germany where she had the opportunity to watch Fritz Lang, G.W. Pabst and Marlene Dietrich at work (Barnouw and Krishnaswamy 1980: 97). Returning to Bombay with a few German technicians, they set up Bombay Talkies, and proceeded to make three films a year. These were usually sophisticated romances in Hindi, and were directed by

Rai with Devika Rani as the leading actress. Occasionally they made a film with a social message that reflected the nationalism of the time. One such film was *Achhut Kanya* (1936) which explored the doomed relationship between a high caste Brahmin man and a woman from an 'untouchable' caste.

Rai ran his studio with an authoritarian paternalism. He would recruit only university graduates, and all recruits were given equal status regardless of whether they were actors or technicians. They received a monthly salary and worked fixed hours. They were provided with a canteen, healthcare facilities and free education for the children. Film historians Barnouw and Krishnaswamy write:

It was known that at Bombay Talkies all company members, of whatever caste, ate together at the company canteen. It was even said that top actors, on occasion, helped clean floors.... All this was part of the legend and role of Bombay Talkies.

(Barnouw and Krishnaswamy 1980: 103)

Many film directors, who were to find fame and fortune in independent India, received their early training at this studio.

In addition to these three major studios, other smaller studios (or 'banners', as they were called) included Minerva Movietone, built around the personality of Sohrab Modi, the Laurence Olivier of India, which specialised in grand productions based on historical subjects; Wadia Movietone which specialised in stunt films starring the female stunt artiste Nadia. Of Welsh and Greek origin, Nadia amazed her audiences with her daring exploits which often included dramatic rescues from moving trains, runaway cars or wild horses, cheaper imitations of which were reproduced by lesser companies.

The end of the studios

The 'studio era' was an exciting period in the development of Indian Cinema. It laid the foundations for a powerful nationwide industry, trained a whole generation of actors, directors and technicians and created a discerning but enthusiastic audience all over the country. The outbreak of the Second World War was to drastically change the film industry. The war, in which India was an unwilling partner, necessitated an expansion of defence-related industries within the country. Rapid industrialisation brought in new money for investment in films. The reduced marine traffic between Britain and India led to a scarcity in essential commodities, and black marketeering flourished. This untaxed (or 'black') money found its way into films and established a covert relationship between money laundering and film finance, a relationship that continues to thrive even today.

See Chapter 2 for comparison with the Hollywood studio system.

With large amounts of extra cash, new independent producers entered the market. Not wishing to be encumbered with the overheads of a studio and staff, they began to entice actors, musicians, singers and technicians away from the studios for large sums of money. Actors discovered that they could command huge fees for a single film and the producers realised that by promoting the image of an actor as a 'star' they could woo large audiences. Within a decade, the studios, with their high overheads including maintenance of the studios as well as monthly salaries to actors regardless of whether they made films or not, ran into financial difficulties and many, like Bombay Talkies, were soon reduced to renting out their studios to the new breed of independent producers, before being forced to close down completely.

The struggle for independence

The late 1930s onwards was a period of intense political activity that continued until India gained independence from Britain on 15 August 1947. The struggle for freedom from colonial rule, led by Mahatma Gandhi, resulted in strict British censorship of Indian films. Political films that overtly reflected the growing nationalist spirit were subject to close scrutiny. Any film that brought into contempt 'soldiers wearing His Majesty's uniform, Ministers of Religion, Ministers of the Crown, Ambassadors and official representatives of foreign nations, the police, the judges or civil servants of Government' was banned (Shah 1981: 234). But films that dealt with social reform did not challenge British authority. In fact, they promoted the 'civilising' role that the British liked to believe they played in India. Concerned about their financial investments, which would suffer if their films were to be banned, film-makers opted to entertain the Indian public with heady romances or social dramas.

Some film-makers, however, responded to these political strictures by deliberately creating an Indian character who caricatured British mannerisms. Wearing a tailored suit and carrying a hat, he was ridiculed as either a villain or a buffoon who constantly berated the Indians as 'damn fools'. The nationalist hero, in traditional Indian attire, usually got the better of him.

As the fervour for independence increased, some directors responded to the mood of the nation by slipping in patriotic images. For instance, in *Anmol Ghadi* (Mehboob, 1945) a character opens a magazine, the cover of which carries the picture of Subhash Chandra Bose, founder of the outlawed Indian National Army. In courtroom dramas, it was a picture of Mahatma Gandhi that hung on the wall, instead of a picture of the British monarch. The censors lost no time in removing these images. Barnouw and Krishnaswamy write:

Film producers now took to the casual introduction of Congress symbols into films. On the wall, in the background, one would see the Gandhian motif, the spinning wheel, signifying defiance of the economic pattern of empire. In a store there would be a calendar with Gandhi's portrait; in a home, a photograph of Nehru; on the sound track, the effect of a passing parade, with few bars of a favourite Congress song. Often such symbols had no plot reference; but in theatres they elicited cheers. As war began, British censors ordered the scissoring of such shots. After 1942, when Gandhi was again imprisoned – along with a number of other Congress leaders – no photograph of Gandhi was allowed on screen, no matter how incidentally.

(ibid.: 124)

In *Kismet* (G. Mukerjee, 1943), a crime thriller, a rousing song asks the Germans and Japanese to leave India alone. However, the 'song picturisation' leaves no one in doubt as to which foreign power is being implied in the lyrics. In Calcutta alone *Kismet* ran for three and a half years at one theatre.

The pre-independence years also saw the revival of historical and mythological themes as metaphors for the political struggle. In *Sikander* (Sohrab Modi, 1941) a brave Indian ruler fights back Alexander the Great's bid to conquer India. In *Ram Rajya* (Vijay Bhatt, 1943) the epic battle between Lord Rama and Ravana, a struggle between 'good' and 'evil', came to signify India's struggle against the British. Having captured the belligerent mood of the nation, these films proved to be box-office hits.

During the Second World War, the British government introduced a quota system to distribute scarce raw film stock. In order to qualify for the quota, film-makers were required to devote at least one film out of every four films made to promoting the 'war effort' (Barnouw and Krishnaswamy 1980: 130). These films were very rarely popular with the Indian public. Director V. Shantaram found that one way to circumvent the requirements of the British government was to make an anti-Japanese film set in China. *Dr. Kotnis Ki Amar Kahani* (1946), about an Indian doctor who helps the Chinese communist forces fight the Japanese, was perhaps the only 'war effort' film to find favour with the public.

Independence and after

India became independent in 1947. The film industry celebrated by immediately making films about those who had martyred themselves for the cause of liberty, such as *Shaheed* (R. Sehgal, 1948). But the celebrations were marred by the nightmare of partitioning the country into a secular India and an Islamic Pakistan. Millions of Hindus and Muslims crossed the new frontiers and arrived as refugees in the country of their choice. Many Punjabi Hindu film-makers, musicians, lyricists and technicians, who had worked at the studios in Lahore (now in Pakistan), made their way to Bombay and within a decade began to influence film-making there. Calcutta lost a substantial proportion of its audience when East Bengal became East Pakistan (today Bangladesh). As the studios in Calcutta began to flounder, many who had worked and trained at New Theatres moved to Bombay. The decline of Lahore and Calcutta as centres of film-making established Bombay as the film capital of India and it was unofficially christened **'Bollywood'**.

If the film producers were expecting a comprehensive liberalisation of censorship after independence, they were sorely disappointed. The Indian censors had begun to show that they were even stricter than their colonial predecessors. 'Sexual immorality' was to be avoided at all costs. Censorship guidelines quoted in the *Journal of the Bengal Motion Picture Association* in May 1949 advised:

'Bollywood'
Bombay, the film capital of India.

• **Plate 12.3** Akshay Kumar and Raveena Tandon in Trimurti Films' *Mohra*, produced by Gulshan Rai and directed by Rajiv Rai.

Illegal forms of sex relationship, such as free love, companionate marriage or virgin motherhood, shall not be permitted. Adultery or illicit sex relationship, if necessary for the plot, shall not be justified nor presented attractively. Kissing or embracing by adults, exhibiting passion repugnant to good taste shall not be shown.

(Cited in Shah 1981: 246)

Denied the chance to explore desire, the songs sang about it and, at the crucial moment when the lovers' lips came close to kiss, the camera turned away abruptly to show a pair of love birds, a garden of roses or a gushing fountain. Recently the ban on kissing was finally lifted by the censors, but directors still prefer to employ the stratagems evolved over the decades to display passion. Besides, the actresses are still reluctant to kiss their male partners on screen.

The 'golden age' of Hindi Cinema

The *formula film* emerged in the 1950s and with its thematic combination of romance and family melodrama, embellished by stars, song, dance and spectacle, it created the *omnibus* genre which continues to dominate the film industry. (*See p. 389.*)

Enthusiasm for the new republic gave fresh impetus to film production in the country. As talented writers, musicians, lyricists, actors, directors and technicians found their way to Bombay, the combination of such varied talent led film historians to refer to the 1950s as the 'golden age' of Hindi Cinema.

Four directors were to dominate the decade: Mehboob Khan, Raj Kapoor, Bimal Roy and Guru Dutt. All four had served their apprenticeship in the major studios and all four showed themselves to be influenced by the major film movements in the West. These influences they managed to incorporate into the conventions of song, dance, melodrama and spectacle that had by now become well-established within the popular Hindi film. Their works also reflect the changes within a country that had now embraced industrialisation, agrarian reforms and Nehru's socialism.

☐ CASE STUDY 2: MEHBOOB KHAN (1904–64)

In a recent biography, Mehboob Khan has been compared to Hollywood's Cecil B. DeMille. However, in his early films Mehboob brought to the screen his own brand of Marxist-Islamic ideology. His two main concerns were poverty and the tragedy of women under patriarchy. His early film, *Roti* (1942), is a stark denunciation of capitalism and man's incurable greed.

Of very humble origins, Mehboob began as an 'extra' before working his way up to direction and production. His early films show Eisenstein's formalist influence, and only in his later films does he reveal the spectacular flourish of Cecil B. DeMille. Mehboob's most famous work is *Mother India* (1957), the status of which has been compared to that of *Gone with the Wind* in Hollywood. A remake of his earlier film *Aurat* (1940), it tells of a peasant woman's struggle to keep alive her children in the face of famine without sacrificing either her virtue or her self-respect. The story takes place against a background of the nation's transition from primitive farming to modern mechanised agriculture. While the denunciation of exploitation of peasants is robust, the production itself is very lavish and extravagant. Some of his other films, *Najma* (1942), *Andaz* (1949) and *Anmol Ghadi* (1945), explore the claustrophobic world of women, and the tragedy of those who try and escape it. An ardent supporter of Nehru's socialistic programmes, Mehboob's own death occurred one day after Nehru died.

☐ CASE STUDY 3: RAJ KAPOOR (1926-88)

The Kapoor family hold a very special place in Indian Cinema and in the hearts of movie-goers. Raj Kapoor, son of the famous stage and film actor Prithviraj Kapoor, trained with the Bombay Talkies before being given the opportunity to direct his first film *Aag* (1948) at the age of 22. Handsome, with unusual blue eyes, he showed his early influences to be Hollywood actors such as Ronald Coleman, Clark Gable and Charlie Chaplin. His early films tackle issues of unemployment and homelessness – serious themes that he presented, not with didacticism, but with entertaining music and audacious love scenes. With the success of *Awara* (1951), which became an instant hit in the USSR and was alleged to be one of Chairman Mao Zedong's favourite films, and *Shri 420* (1955), in which he assumed a tragi-comic Chaplinesque persona, Kapoor established himself as superb entertainer of the masses.

Raj Kapoor acted in over seventy films in his lifetime and produced about seventeen features. He often played the common man seeking to survive the problems of rapid industrialisation and unemployment. In his later films he was to exploit the theme of sexual corruption, but with increasingly erotic imagery, as in *Sangam* (1964), *Satyam Shivam Sundaram* (1978) and *Ram Teri Ganga Maili* (1985). His younger brothers, Shammi Kapoor and Shashi Kapoor, also became highly successful film stars, and his son Rishi Kapoor is still popular with audiences. With granddaughter Karishma Kapoor now established as an actress, the Indian audiences have seen four generations of the Kapoor family in stellar roles.

☐ CASE STUDY 4: BIMAL ROY (1902-66)

Son of a rich landowning family, Bimal Roy moved from New Theatres in Calcutta to the film industry in Bombay. His first film in Hindi, *Do Bigha Zamin* (1953), shows the stylistic influence of the Italian neo-realists, and in particular Vittorio de Sica's classic *Bicycle Thieves* (1948). *Do Bigha Zamin* tells the tragic tale of the small farmer forced off his land by big business and eventually reduced to a migrant worker seeking employment in the city. Roy's most memorable commercial successes were *Madhumati* (1958) and *Sujata* (1959), both of which revealed his ability to integrate his personal political ideology with the requirements of the box office. A committed opponent of the *zamindari* system of landownership, the tyrannical landlord frequently appears as the villain in his films.

☐ CASE STUDY 5: GURU DUTT (1925-64)

No other popular film director has attained the cult status accorded to Guru Dutt. A trained dancer, he served as an apprentice at Prabhat before being given a chance to direct a film. As his repertoire of films reveals, Dutt experimented with a different genre in each new film. What is striking about his art is his unusually dynamic use of camera and his highly innovative style of 'song picturisation'. Like Raj Kapoor, Guru Dutt acted in many of the films that he directed. His greatest film success came in with *Pyaasa* (1957), which told the tale of a neglected poet, traumatised by society's obsession with money and by the moral corruption that lies behind the respectability of the middle classes. The film has a powerful mystical undercurrent, and the material and spiritual are juxtaposed within the poet's world.

In *Kaagaz Ke Phool* (1959), Dutt pays homage to the studios of the 1930s and in particular to P.C. Barua. In the film a respected director finds that his domestic problems begin to take a toll on his work, and he succumbs to drink and degradation. The film flopped at the box office. A disappointed Dutt committed suicide at the age of 39.

All the four directors mentioned above explored new, exciting themes while honouring the conventional demands of the box office. With great actors like Dilip Kumar, Dev Anand, Raj Kapoor, actresses such as Nargis, Meena Kumari and Madhubala, music directors such as Naushad Ali, Salil Chaudhary and Ravi, lyricists like Sahir Ludhianvi, Majrooh Sultanpuri and Shakeel Badayuni, never again was such a glittering array of talent to be assembled at one time in the Hindi film industry.

• **Plate 12.4** Aamir Khan and Neelam in *Afsana Pyar Ka*.

Actors turned directors

While some stars have sought a second career in politics (Nargis, Sunil Dutt, Raj Babbar, Vyjayanthimala, Rajesh Khanna, Shabana Azmi, Vinod Khanna Shatrughan Sinha), others such as Raj Kapoor, Dev Anand and Manoj Kumar turned to directing in their later years. At 24, Raj Kapoor was one of the youngest film directors.

While Guru Dutt began by directing *Baazi* (1951) and only later acting in the films he directed (*Pyaasa*, *Kaagaz ke Phool*), Raj Kapoor first acted in films he directed (*Awara*, *Shri 420*, *Sangam*, *Mera Naam Joker*), and also acted in films directed by others; only in his later years, when he had lost his box-office appeal, did he give up acting and concentrate exclusively on directing (*Bobby*, *Satyam Shivam Sundaram*).

Dev Anand, who in the 1950s and 1960s created the casual, debonair look (*Taxi Driver*, *Munimji*, *CID*, *Nau Do Gyarah*), turned to directing with *Prem Pujari* (1970) and *Hare Rama Hare Krishna* (1971). Now in his late seventies, and determined not to age, he continues to act under his own direction.

The career of Manoj Kumar – popularly known as 'Mr. Bharat' (Bharat being the Hindi name for India) after his stridently nationalistic films such as *Upkaar* (1967) and *Purab Aur Paschim* (1970) that pit India's supposed superior morality against the West's alleged decadence – spanned three decades. Already a popular actor for ten years, he moved to directing and starring in his own films with *Upkaar*. In all, he acted in and directed six 'patriotic' films. Currently the top male stars have already begun to train in directing for an eventual career in film direction, once their appeal at the box office begins to fade.

COLOUR AND THE TRIUMPH OF ROMANCE

Although Mehboob's *Aan* (1952) was the first colour film in India, colour-processing equipment was not imported into India until the early 1960s. Colour photography raised production costs and at first only a few crucial scenes in some major productions were shot in colour. Colour lent itself easily to the need for spectacle and in *Mughal-e-Azam* (1960), the famed dance in the 'hall of mirrors' was one of the few scenes in colour, while the rest of the film was shot in black and white.

Colour also provided tremendous scope for outdoor shooting in scenes of romance. The magnificent landscape in Kashmir, or the 'hill stations' at the foothills of the Himalayas, brought home to the predominantly urban audiences the majestic beauty of certain regions of India. Film plots were accordingly adjusted to provide scope for such visual delights. For example, in *Jungalee* (S. Mukherjee, 1961), a romantic comedy, the protagonist undertakes a trip to Kashmir where he meets a beautiful woman and falls in love, which then provides the excuse for many love songs set in the snow-covered mountains of the region before the two return to Bombay. When most areas of scenic beauty in India were exhausted, producers began to go abroad in search of new and exotic locations. Film titles like *Love in Tokyo* (1966), *Singapore* (1960), and *Around the World on Eight Dollars* (1967), clearly revealed the producers' intentions to the audiences.

The 1960s was a decade of romance. With the memories of colonial rule now dimmed by the passage of time, it became acceptable to present the hero with a veneer of westernisation. The villain, however, continued to be presented as an over-westernised creature, a caricature devised during colonial rule in order to circumvent censorship. The difference is that today he functions as a symbol, not of British colonialism, but of an un-Indian 'unwholesomeness', of an immoral and decadent 'other' against which the Indian identity can be defined.

For further study, analyse the film *Jungalee*.

1 How does it conform to the 'formula'?
2 Analyse the conflict between tradition and modernity.
3 How are the young women represented?
4 How does the mother function as the agent of feudal patriarchy?

Writing on the subject of Indian identity, Thomas states:

Since it first emerged in the context of colonial India's fight for independence, Indian Cinema, for a number of reasons, has been concerned with constructing a notion of Indian cultural and national identity. This has involved drawing on concepts such as 'tradition'. But a chaste and pristine India has also been constructed by opposing it to a decadent and exotic 'other', the licentious and immoral 'West', with the films' villains invariably sporting a clutter of signifiers of 'westernisation': whiskey bottles, bikini-clad escorts, or foreign limousines.

(Thomas 1989: 11)

For a discussion of the images of Elvis in Indian Cinema, see Rai 1994: 51–77.

The westernised (but not over-westernised) hero – for example Shammi Kapoor, star of several lively romances in the 1960s, who in unabashed imitation of Elvis strutted across the screen sporting a quiff and strumming a guitar – came to epitomise 'modernity' as part of a quest for a modern national identity in post-colonial India.

The angry young man

The *stunt films* of the 1930s and the *social* found a curious evolution in the *action films* of the 1970s, which saw the emergence of 'violence as spectacle'. The main themes of the action film genre were urban poverty, corruption and injustice. Adapted from the Hollywood personage of Clint Eastwood in *Dirty Harry*, the angry young man of the Hindi screen found its fullest expression in the person of star actor Amitabh Bachchan.

fight composer
Individual who choreographs spectacular fights in Indian movies.

The romance of the 1960s was to change dramatically with the arrival of a new team of screenwriters. Salim Khan and Javed Akhtar replaced the anodyne romantic hero with a new 'angry young man'. In their first commercial success, *Zanjeer* (Prakash Mehra, 1973), the new hero was inspired by Clint Eastwood in *Dirty Harry* (Don Seigel, 1971). He was lean, mean and angry, more prone to fight than burst into melancholic songs. This image of the introverted avenger, mostly popularised on screen by actor Amitabh Bachchan, was to dominate the hearts and minds of the cinema-going public for the next fifteen years. Although songs were not entirely dispensed with, these films placed less emphasis on songs and dances and, in many instances, substituted them with colourful, bone-crunching fight sequences. The prioritisation of action over romance led inevitably to the presentation of violence as gory 'spectacle'.

Technology borrowed from Hollywood gave cinematographers greater scope to offer 'realistic' violence (blood spurts, neck breaks etc.). A new function, that of the **fight composer**, who choreographed spectacular fights in which incredible acts of valour and heroism were enacted, was created and was given an important billing in the film credits. The romantic heroes of the 1960s found themselves nudged aside by actors who could perform audacious stunts.

One way of cashing in on the new demand for 'violence as spectacle' was to increase the number of 'villains' in a film, which in turn necessitated a proliferation of heroes to combat these villains. 'Multi-starrers' became a generic term in the 1970s, particularly after the unparalleled success of a spectacular multi-starrer 'curry western', *Sholay* (Ramesh Sippy, 1975). The new 'superstars' as they became known, thanks to the film publicists, were paid enormous sums of money, and more importantly began to exercise control over different aspects of the film. Screenplays, songs and dialogues began to be rewritten to suit the whims of the superstars.

Analyse the film *Deewar* (see Recommended Viewing) and address the following issues:

1 What is the function of legality?
2 What does the mother represent?
3 How does it mark a break from 'formula'?

Film journalism

The 1970s also saw a proliferation of new film magazines. Until that time, staid film trade journals such as *Trade Guide* or *Screen* informed the public about new releases and industry figures. In 1971, a new fortnightly called *Stardust* was launched. Its racy style and sleazy revelations about the private lives of the stars met with unprecedented success. Written in irreverent semi-literate English, with frequent and deliberate lapses into colloquial Hindi (transliterated into English), it was to change the face of film journalism. It bred a whole new generation of women gossip writers, and spawned innumerable magazines that tried to copy the subversive style. So successful was this Indian–English style of writing that soon even established journals began to include a page on 'shocking' revelations. Today *Stardust*'s unique idiom has become *de rigueur* in Indian journalism, and is even sometimes used in political reporting.

Associations

In the 1960s the chaotic world of the film industry began to organise itself into unions and associations. Producers formed the Indian Motion Picture Producers Association (IMPPA) to deal with government bureaucracy. The 'extras', too, formed themselves into a union called the Junior Artistes Association, which demanded that they be referred to henceforth as 'junior artistes' and not 'extras'.

There were three main categories of junior artistes – 'ordinary', 'decent' and 'super decent' with a sliding scale of remuneration according to category (Barnouw and Krishnaswamy 1980: 171). The clothes and footwear are provided by the junior artistes themselves, the only exceptions being made in the case of costume dramas. In addition, men in the 'decent' and 'super decent' categories are required to arrive on the sets with decently shaven faces.

'Art' cinema and the 'parallel' film movemen

While many bemoaned the demise of the romance and the rise of violence in the newer films, the 1970s also signalled the establishment of **'art'** or **'parallel' cinema**, that tried to offer an alternative to the commercially driven 'formula' films. Dispensing with stars, songs and spectacle in favour of serious themes, these films adopted the classic codes of western narrative cinema, with a linear narrative set in a fictional world of spatial and temporal verisimilitude. This move towards realism had already been started by Satyajit Ray in 1955.

'art' or 'parallel' cinema
Serious, realistic film with a linear narrative which offers an alternative to the 'formula' film. Pioneered by Satyajit Ray.

☐ CASE STUDY 6: SATYAJIT RAY (1921–92)

See Chapter 4, pp. 121–6, for discussion of alternative narratives.

Satyajit Ray, the most famous Indian director abroad, brought to the Indian Cinema a respectability and status that it had never known before. Born in Calcutta in 1921, he studied for some time under Nobel laureate Rabindranath Tagore at Shanti Niketan. A young copywriter with an advertising firm, Ray had the opportunity to watch Jean Renoir at work on *The River*. Inspired by him, but with no actual experience of film-making, Ray bought the rights to a Bengali novel, *Pather Panchali* by Bibhutibhushan Banerji, and wrote a complete screenplay for it. Finding a producer was to prove very difficult. Dismayed that the film was to have no songs and dances, producers turned it down. In desperation Ray sold most of his belongings and managed to shoot a few scenes. When the money ran out, as it soon did, he turned to the state government of West Bengal who, surprisingly, agreed to finance the film. This, as many historians have declared, was the best investment ever made by a government body in an artistic field.

Shot on a very tight budget and in natural surroundings, and with a musical score by Ravi Shankar, *Pather Panchali* (1955) is a simple document of extreme realism and great visual beauty on the childhood of a young boy named Apu. It met with great success in West Bengal, and when it was entered at the Cannes Film Festival as an official entry from India, it was voted the 'best human document'; this marked the début of a brilliant career. The film also set a new record for the 'longest running film at New York's Fifth Avenue cinema'. Ray followed *Pather Panchali* with two more films, *Aparajito* (1956) and *Apur Sansar* (1959), on Apu, the central character, to complete what has become known as the Apu Trilogy.

The greatest influences on Ray were undoubtedly the Italian neo-realists from whom he learnt to make film on shoestring budgets. Working mostly in Bengali, he kept tight artistic control over his films and with each film experimented with a new genre. Ray even made one foray into the commercial cinema of Bombay with *Shatranj Ke Khilari* (*The Chess Players*, 1977), in Hindi, which used for the first time leading film actors from Bombay. Whatever the genre – comedy, literary adaptations, adventure, musical fantasy – Ray's view of the world would always remain distinctive.

The establishment of the Film and Television Institute of India (FTII) in 1961 and the Film Archives in 1964 encouraged the development of an alternative kind of cinema that had already been started by Satyajit Ray. An institute that provided professional training in the different branches of film-making led to a growing number of qualified actors, directors and technicians, some of whom were absorbed into the mainstream popular cinemas in Hindi and the regional languages. Others wished to experiment with alternative forms of cinematic expression. However, raising funds for such experimental work was nearly impossible. A few opportunities for the financing of films were provided by the government-funded Film Finance Corporation (FFC), which has since been incorporated into the National Film Development Corporation (NFDC). The erstwhile FFC offered financing for low-budget films in order to provide new talent with an opportunity to pursue ideas without the compromises that would have been demanded by the box office.

It was under these circumstances that director Mani Kaul made the experimental film *Uski Roti* in 1970, which tells a simple tale about a young woman, Balo, who walks several kilometres each day to deliver her lorry-driver husband his midday meal. One day she is delayed and she fears that her husband will leave her forever. The film not only challenged the conventional codes of popular film narrative, but it also rejected 'realism' in favour of a more expressionistic style of narration. The success of such experiments by Mani Kaul, Kumar Shahani (*Maya Darpan*, 1972) and other graduates of the Film Institute began the Indian 'new wave', even though their films never found general release and were restricted to the film club circuit.

Directors such as Shyam Benegal, who also eschewed the popular conventions of song, dance and spectacle, pursued a less experimental kind of cinema and chose the western traditions of a linear narrative and the 'realist aesthetic'. Coming to cinema from the world of advertising, Benegal's first film, *Ankur* (1974), treated the theme of rural exploitation by the landed classes. He brought a western sophistication to Indian themes, making his films appealing not just to the western-educated intellectual and cultural élite of India but also to the western critics, who were looking to find a cinema in India that they could appreciate and, more importantly, understand. Benegal's films are regularly screened at film festivals in the UK, France and the US.

Other kinds of films were made by directors such as Basu Chatterji and Basu Bhattacharya, who worked within the constraints of the popular Hindi Cinema using songs and dances, but toned down its emotional and spectacular excesses and replaced the implausible film plots with more realistic stories. Theirs was not a world of separated twins, reunited by chance meetings, but a world of writers, lecturers and retired postmasters coming to terms with life. Even the songs were given 'realistic' motivations (for example, a record, a radio broadcast) and, on the whole, they offered a more refined form of entertainment for the middle classes.

The cinema in the 1970s could thus be divided into four main categories:

1 the mainstream popular film with its songs, dances, spectacle, familiar plot and overwrought emotion;
2 the emotionally restrained and 'sober' stories told with an attempt at a realistic narrative, without dispensing with songs and dances;
3 the 'realist–representational' film with a narrative linearity that completely dispensed with songs and the other ingredients of popular cinema, as in the works of Shyam Benegal, Govind Nihalani and others; and
4 the 'art' films in which directors such as Mani Kaul and Kumar Shahani experimented with the formal devices of cinema itself.

Women directors

According to the *Encyclopaedia of Indian Cinema*, the first woman director of the Hindi screen was Fatma Begum, who began her career in films by acting and later made her directorial début with *Bulbul-e-Paristan* (1926). Jaddanbai, singer and composer, also moved from acting to directing in her later life. She directed four feature films between 1936 and 1937.

Since the 1970s women directors have made their presence felt in the industry. Most of these women directors eschew the popular 'formula film', preferring to address themes of patriarchy and female sexuality. Among the new women directors are:

Aruna Raje who experimented with different genres in the thriller *Shaque* (1976), the semi-horror *Gehrayee* (1980) and the women's film *Rihaee* (1988);

Sai Paranjpye whose skill for comedy spans her work in television, stage, children's films, film shorts and documentaries. Her first film was *Sparsh* (1979), a love story set against the poignant backdrop of a school for blind children, that still finds space for comedy. *Chashme Buddoor* (1981) is a comedy about three students looking for love and was a box-office hit, and *Katha* (1982) is about life in a rumbustious urban tenement. *Disha* (1990) is a poignant tale about the fragmented lives of migrant workers in the city;

Vijaya Mehta's career too spans the theatre, television and cinema. Her major films have been *Rao Saheb* (1986), adapted from a stage play about the plight of widows, and *Pestonjee* (1987), a melodrama set in the minority community of Parsis in India;

Kalpna Lajmi, niece of the renowned director Guru Dutt (see case study 5), began by making documentaries before moving to stridently feminist feature films such as *Ek Pal* (1986), that addresses female sexuality, *Rudaali* (1992), which is set in the world of professional female mourners, and *Darmiyaan* (1997), that explores the lives of eunuchs;

Meera Nair, who works mostly in English, began by making documentaries on Indian topics in the US. Her first feature film was *Salaam Bombay* (1988), which won her great acclaim, followed by *Missippi Masala* (1991), that explores the world of the Indian diaspora. In *Kama Sutra* (1997), she takes a new look at the eponymous treatise on sex;

Deepa Mehta is a Toronto-based director whose first film *Sam and Me* (1990), about an Indian immigrant in Canada, won acclaim at the Cannes Film Festival. She is currently working on *Fire* with leading stars of the Hindi screen.

Aparna Sen, a star of the Bengali screen who turned to film direction, made her directorial début in 1981 with the English language *36, Chowringhee Lane*, starring Hindi Cinema's matinee idol Shashi Kapoor, and his real-life wife Jennifer Kendal (sister of Felicity Kendal). This was followed by the controversial Hindi/Bengali film *Paroma* (1985) and the Bengali language *Sati* (1989), about a mute woman who, because her astrological chart indicates early widowhood, is married off to a tree;

Hema Malini, a major star of the formula films of the Hindi screen during the 1970s and 1980s where she was known as the 'dream girl', directed *Dil Ashna Hai* (1991), about a girl looking for her mother – a story based on Shirley Conran's best-selling novel *Lace*.

THE DISTRIBUTION NETWORK

See Chapter 2 for discussion of production and distribution in the US and the UK.

The Indian 'new wave' could never combat the sheer volume of production and the extensive distribution network of the popular Hindi Cinema. For distribution purposes, the market was, and continues to be, divided into 'territories' which coincide with the provinces that existed in pre-independence India. Each territory has its own distributor, who works in conjunction with the exhibitors, that is, those who own or have access to film theatres within that territory. Unfortunately there are only about 15,000 cinemas in all of India, most of which are concentrated in the major towns and cities, while tents or temporary structures are usually deployed in the rural areas and the more remote villages. The combined annual production of over 900 films in the different regional languages results in a chronic shortage of outlets for exhibition, and some films fail to ever make it to the screen.

The distributors enter into agreements with the different exhibitors. The latter explain to the distributors what has met with approval from the audiences – a particular song, a particular dance sequence or a certain emotional scene, and so on. All this information in based on audience reactions to the film as a whole as well as to individual scenes, as gauged by the exhibitor attending public screenings, and also from the box-office returns. Armed with this information, the distributors in turn contact producers and book future films. Often the booking fee is paid in advance, well before the film has commenced shooting. This means that distributors are able to indicate their preferences for certain stars, music directors and the kind of film that will eventually be made. Sometimes a particular star may be extremely popular with audiences in Calcutta, but less so in Bombay. In this case, the distributors from the Bengal territory must be able to raise enough funds as advance payment to make it attractive enough for producers to cast their preferred actor in a film. Films are thus part-financed by advances paid by distributors.

The scarcity of cinemas gives both exhibitors and distributors the right to dictate the kind of film that is to be produced, and the refusal to produce the kind of film demanded may result in a producer not finding a venue for his film at all. In the 1980s, recording companies also began to finance films and bought up copyrights to the film songs, long before they were even composed. According to trade journals, the growth in the sale of music audio-cassettes, of which film songs alone account for three-quarters of the total sales of a company, has made investment in films a profitable business for the recording companies (Chandra 1993: 52).

Under such financial arrangements, the low-budget 'art' film producers often cannot find a theatre that is willing to exhibit their film. In fact, many films financed by the NFDC or other quasi-government bodies have never been screened, and many directors find it easier to show their work overseas, usually during film festivals, than in India.

SATELLITE TELEVISION

By the 1980s, Hindi Cinema began to feel the effects of the video boom. Big budget productions, in particular, were unable to get a reasonable return on their investment. Besides, the smaller video screen did not do justice to the extravagant spectacle. Video piracy forced producers to release their films in all territories at the same time (whereas earlier they were staggered so as to recover the investment over three to four years), and in some cases to release the film and the video simultaneously.

For discussion of multimedia empires and ownership, see Chapter 2, pp. 42–3.

In January 1991, satellite broadcasting from Hong Kong by STAR (Satellite Transmission for Asian Region), now owned by Rupert Murdoch, began a media revolution. Hitherto Indian television (Doordarshan), controlled by the government of India, measured out the kind of entertainment seen as being suitable by bureaucrats from their offices in the Ministry of Information and Broadcasting. The satellite invasion has forced the government to loosen its hold on the media, and has put considerable pressure on the popular Hindi Cinema too. So far, the flexible structure of the narrative has allowed it to absorb the foreign influences, and the song-and-dance numbers have begun to show the influence of American music videos as seen on the MTV channel.

THE INFLUENCE OF HOLLYWOOD

Although Indian Cinema has a different narrative structure from that of western cinema, the influence of Hollywood and, before that, of European cinema, has always been apparent. As seen in the section on the historical development of Indian Cinema, the first Indian film was inspired by Gaumont's *Life of Christ*. Later, during the studio era, European film movements also had a stylistic effect on Hindi films. Thus German expressionism, Italian neo-realism and Soviet formalism were incorporated into the quintessential Indian popular narrative. As Barnouw and Krishnaswamy point out, many of Wadia Movietone's 'stunt' films in the 1930s, starring 'Fearless Nadia', were inspired by Douglas Fairbanks, Pearl White and Eddie Polo. According to them:

The American Eddie Polo, now almost forgotten in the United States, was among the most popular film heroes in India in the early 1920s. In 1927 a headmaster of a high school in Hyderabad, Sind, told the Indian Cinematograph Committee: 'I once asked my class of 50 boys what was their ambition in life. Five boys wrote, 'To be Eddie Polo'.

(Barnouw and Krishnaswamy 1980: 110)

The most significant influence of Hollywood has been the use of new technologies in sound recording, colour processing and, most important of all, special effects. Mannerisms, sartorial styles and swaggers too, have been endlessly reproduced, even though the content of the Hindi film still remains traditionally Indian. In the 1950s, Raj Kapoor popularised the Charlie Chaplin look, while in the 1960s, Shammi Kapoor brought Elvis to the popular screen. Amitabh Bachchan's 'angry young man' was inspired by Clint Eastwood in *Dirty Harry*.

See Chapter 3 for more information on film and technology.

Sometimes scenes from Hollywood films are copied into a Hindi film, and, on occasion, entire films are 'borrowed' not once but even twice! For example, the Oscar-winning Hollywood film *It Happened One Night* (Frank Capra, 1934) became *Chori Chori* (A. Thakur) in 1956 and *Dil Hai Ke Manta Nahin* (Mahesh Bhatt) in 1991.

However, whenever a Hollywood film is remade in India it has to be recast in the Indian mould, that is, emotions have to be overstated, songs, dances and spectacle have to be added, family relationships have to be introduced if they do not exist in the original, traditional moral values such as *dharma* (duty) must be reiterated and female chastity must be eulogised. Only then will the film find success at the box office.

CONSUMPTION OF POPULAR HINDI FILMS IN BRITAIN

While the pleasures of the Hindi film as consumed by spectators in the 15,000 cinemas in India is increasingly a subject of academic scrutiny, an even more complex issue is the consumption of films *outside* India. In the UK (as in other developed economies) the consumption of popular Hindi films is largely restricted to populations of Indian origin, and clearly under such circumstances, popular Hindi Cinema cannot (unlike in India) challenge the hegemony of Hollywood.

See list of Resource centres (at the end of this chapter) for cinema outlets and video

The popular Hindi film, with its predictable plot and episodic narrative unfolding, allows for flexibility in placing of song/dance/spectacle/affect in its propositions for pleasure-production for its spectator/consumers, and also for the construction of a very broad-based appeal necessary to overcome linguistic, cultural, class and religious affiliations. The Asian immigrant population in the UK is mainly from the provinces of Punjab, Gujarat, Bengal and, since the political troubles in that country, Sri Lanka. The members of this heterogeneous community, while broadly referred to as Asian, have their own different languages or dialects, and religious beliefs.

Hindi films began to be screened in Britain in 1953, and by the 1960s and 1970s the cinemas that screened these films had become a place of social intercourse for the various members of the Asian communities. Then the VCR arrived, with ownership percentages among Asians far higher than the national average. Most Asian families possess large video collections of Hindi films, with 72 per cent of families owning up to fifty, and the viewing of Hindi films has become a weekend ritual that involves family bonding and togetherness (Gillespie 1995).

The consumption of popular Hindi films is problematised by questions of age and gender. Asian girls enjoy watching Hindi films, particularly the song-and-dance sequences, far more than Asian boys (who prefer 'action' scenes). The girls consider the traditional values expounded in Hindi films as educational (an opinion also expressed by Asian women participating in the Channel Four's *On the Other Hand*, screened in 1992). Many see the films as representative of traditional Indian culture, rather than as Hindi Cinema's own patriarchal ideology, and hence worthy of emulation. The manner in which different viewers react to these films/videos also uncovers a generational divide. The older generation, usually born and educated in India, Pakistan or Bangladesh, and with direct knowledge and experience of living in South Asia, tend to watch these videos with nostalgia and longing for the 'home country', which the second generation, more exposed to transnational entertainment on TV (soaps and pop music programmes), video and cinema, does not. Consequently, 'while young people use Indian films to deconstruct "traditional culture", many parents use them to foster cultural and religious traditions. Some remain sceptical of parental attempts to "artificially maintain a culture through film" but, successful or not, it is clear that the VCR is being used for the purposes of reformulating and "translating" cultural traditions in the Indian diaspora' (Gillespie 1995: 87).

CONCLUSION

By evolving its own narrative style, popular Hindi Cinema offers the Indian audiences an alternative to Hollywood. It challenges American cultural hegemony not just in India but, through the export of its films, in developing countries as well. The fragmented narrative structure gives the films great flexibility and allows the integration of new influences while maintaining links with ancient traditions. Images of westernisation allow the films to tackle issues surrounding modernity and national identity. The songs, through their energetic and unabashed dance movements and sometimes bawdy lyrics, provide the audience with emotional and sexual release, while at the same time the plot reinforces society's conservative moral values.

Indian Cinema currently finds itself under threat from satellite television. However, the flexible narrative structure that it has inherited and which has helped it survive foreign competition will undoubtedly help it survive the threat of new technology and maintain its position as the single most important cultural activity in India.

FURTHER READING

Barnouw, E. and Krishnaswamy, S. *Indian Film* (Oxford University Press, New York, 1980)

Chakravarty, S.S. *National Identity in Indian Popular Cinema, 1947–1987*, (University of Texas Press, Austin, 1993)

Krishen, P. (ed.) 'Indian Popular Cinema: Myth, Meaning and Metaphor', *India International Centre Quarterly* (New Delhi) (Vol. 8, No. 1, March 1980)

Pendakur, M. 'India', in J.A. Lent (ed.) *The Asian Film Industry* (Christopher Helm, Bromley, 1990)

Prasad, M.M. *Ideology of Hindi Cinema* (Oxford University Press, New Delhi, 1988)

Ramachandran, T.M. (ed.) *70 Years of Indian Cinema* (Cinema India-International, Bombay, 1985)

Rajadhyaksha, A. and Willemen, P. *Encylopaedia of Indian Cinema* (BFI, London, 1994)

Rangoonwalla, F. *Seventy-Five Years of Indian Cinema* (Indian Book Company, New Delhi, 1975)

Shah, P. *The Indian Film* (Greenwood Press, Westport, CT, 1981)

Thomas, R. 'Indian Cinema: Pleasures and Popularity', *Screen* (Vol. 26, Nos 3–4, 1985)

RECOMMENDED VIEWING

Videos available with English subtitles:

Awaara (*The Vagabond*, 1951). Black and white, 170 minutes. Producer: R.K. Productions. Director: Raj Kapoor. Script: K.A. Abbas and V.P. Sathe. Camera: Radhu Karmarkar. Lyrics: Hasrat Jaipuri. Music: Shankar–Jaikishen. Cast: Raj Kapoor (Raju), Nargis (Rita), Prithviraj Kapoor (Raju's father), Leela Chitnis (Raju's mother), Shashi Kapoor (young Raju), K.N. Singh (Jaggu).

Story: Raju, a crook, does not know that his father is Judge Raghunath. The judge had banished his pregnant wife from his house because she had been abducted by the criminal Jaggu, and although she was returned unharmed, he suspects that she has been 'dishonoured'. Raju's childhood friend Rita (coinciden- tally the judge's protégée) makes Raju give up his life of crime, but Raju kills Jaggu and is sent to prison. A loving Rita and a penitent father await his release.

Deewar (*I'll Die for Mama*, 1975). Colour, 174 minutes. Producer: Gulshan Rai. Director: Yash Chopra. Script: Salim–Javed. Camera: Kay Gee. Lyrics: Sahir Ludhianvi. Music: R.D. Burman. Cast: Shashi Kapoor (Ravi), Amitabh Bachchan (Vijay), Neetu Singh, Nirupa Roy, Parveen Babi.

Story: Ravi and Vijay are two brothers who move to the city with their mother after their father abandons them. In order to provide his mother with a decent life, Vijay takes to a life of crime and very quickly becomes fabulously rich. His brother Ravi prefers the path of righteousness and joins the police force. The two brothers confront each other, and when it becomes Ravi's duty to shoot Vijay, he does so. Vijay dies in his mother's arms.

Madhumati (1958). Black and white, 163 minutes. Producer/director: Bimal Roy. Story: Ritwick Ghatak. Dialogue:

Rajinder Singh Bedi. Camera: Dilip Gupta. Lyrics: Shailendra. Music: Salil Choudhary. Cast: Dilip Kumar (Devendra/Anand), Vyjayanthimala (Madhumati), Johnny Walker, Pran (Ugra Narain), Jayant, Tiwari.

Story: Devendra, an important official, and his colleague are on an official tour of a distant region when they find they have to seek shelter in an abandoned mansion. At night, Devendra awakes and slowly begins to remember a previous incarnation, and his connection with this mansion. In that life he is Anand, a manager of a timber estate who meets and falls in love with a tribal woman called Madhumati. Landowner Ugra Narain, who is also Anand's employer, tries to rape Madhumati, but she kills herself. Anand brings him to justice, but dies soon after. When the flashback ends, Devendra rejoins his family and finds that his wife is none other than the reincarnation of Madhumati.

Mother India (1957). Colour, 190 minutes. Producer: Mehboob

Productions Ltd. Director: Mehboob Khan. Script: V. Mirza, Ali Raza. Camera: Faredoon Irani. Lyrics: Shakeel Badayuni. Music: Naushad. Cast: Nargis (Radha), Sunil Dutt (Birju), Raaj Kumar (Shyamu), Rajendra Kumar (Ramu), Kanhaiyalal (Sukhilala).

Story: Radha is left destitute by her husband Shyamu when he loses his arms in a farming accident. She struggles to bring up her starving children, and fights off the sexual advances of the moneylender Sukhilala, to whom their land is mortgaged and who is willing to write off her debt if she sleeps with him. Driven to do the unthinkable, her virtue is saved in time thanks to divine intervention. She finds they can survive without Sukhilala's financial assistance. Her sons grow up, but the debt still remains unpaid thanks to Sukhilala's fraudulent accounting. One day Birju kills Sukhilala and abducts his daughter, but mother Radha shoots her son dead in order to preserve the honour of all womankind.

The Bollywood Story (1989)
A two-part documentary on the Bombay film industry, produced for Channel Four. It provides a historical study of Indian Cinema and highlights the salient features of its cinematic conventions.

The Peacock Screen (1991)
A four-hour documentary on popular Hindi Cinema, produced for Channel Four, that combines a historical survey of the industry with a debate on the subject. It contains interviews with many important personalities from the Bombay cinema as well as 'art' film world.

Raj Kapoor – The Living Legend (1988)
A documentary on the life and work of Raj Kapoor, directed by

Simi Grewal and co-produced by Channel Four.

In Search of Guru Dutt (1989)
A documentary on Guru Dutt, produced and directed by Nasreen Munni Kabir for Channel Four. It contains interviews with Dutt's family and associates and excerpts from his major works.

Lata in Her Own Voice (1990)
A six-part documentary on the singing legend Lata Mangeshkar, produced and directed by Nasreen Munni Kabir for Channel Four. It provides an insight into the workings of the Hindi film industry.

Videos of Hindi films are available from:

Tip Top Video, 4 Coronet Parade, Ealing Road, Wembley, London HAO 4AY (Tel.: 0181 903 0605);
Eros International, Unit 26, Park Royal Metro Centre, Britannia Way, London NW10 (Tel: 0181 963 0249)
Dostana Video, 35 Blackbird Hill, London NW9 (Tel: 0181 200 7355)
Geet Video, 1–2 Liberty Market, 14 South Road, Southall (Tel: 0181 574 9208)
Meera Pan House, 22 Queensbury Station Parade, London HA8 (Tel: 0181 952 0412)

Cinemas showing Indian films in Britain:

The Odeon, Glasgow (Tel: 0141 418 0111)
Cinecity, Manchester (Tel: 0121 455 881)

UCI, Preston (Tel: 01772 722322)
The Bollywood, Leicester (Tel: 0116 268 1215)
The Piccadilly, Birmingham (Tel: 0121 773 1658)
UCI, Huddersfield (Tel: 01484 542411)
UCI, Cardiff (Tel: 0122 472980)
Bellevue Theatre, Edgeware, London (Tel: 0181 381 2556)
Odeon, Marble Arch, London (Tel: 0171 315 4216)
Bolyen, East Ham, London (Tel: 0181 471 4884)
Safari, in Harrow and Croydon (Tel: 0181 426 0303)

There are also several useful websites:

http://www.filmindia.com
A website with links and information about Indian films, including directors, films, books and events.

http://www.cinemedia.net/NLA/indian.html
A listing of Indian feature films with detailed information. This is a website of the National Library of Australia.

http://www.gadnet.com/movies.htm
A website with information about Indian Cinema.

http://us.imdb.com/Sections/Countries/India
This is the Internet Movie Data Base (US) with a listing of 3,534 Indian films and TV series, including details of producers, distributors, directors, genres, casts, writers, composers of music and other titles by which the film is known.

Chapter 13

The Soviet montage cinema of the 1920s

Mark Joyce

■ **Introduction: why study the Soviet cinema?** 418

■ **Historical background** 418

■ **Pre-revolutionary Russian cinema** 419

■ **Soviet cinema and ideology: film as agent of change** 420

■ **Economics of the Soviet film industry** 421

■ **Form: montage** 422

■ **Other features of the Soviet montage cinema** 425

■ **The key Soviet montage film-makers of the 1920s** 425

☐ Case study 1: Lev Kuleshov, *The Extraordinary Adventures of Mr West in the Land of the Bolsheviks* (1924) 426

☐ Case study 2: Sergei Eisenstein, *Strike* (1924); *Battleship Potemkin* (1925); *October* (1927); *Old and New* (1929) 428

☐ Case study 3: Vsevolod Pudovkin, *The Mother* (1926); *The End of St Petersburg* (1927) 437

☐ Case study 4: Alexander Dovzhenko, *Arsenal* (1929); *Earth* (1930) 441

☐ Case study 5: Esfir Shub, *The Fall of the Romanov Dynasty* (1927) 443

■ **Audience response** 443

■ **Theoretical debates: montage versus realism** 444

■ **Postscript to the 1920s** 445

■ **Notes and references** 446

■ **Further reading** 448

■ **Further viewing** 449

■ **Resource centres** 450

■ The Soviet montage cinema of the 1920s

INTRODUCTION: WHY STUDY THE SOVIET CINEMA?

> As the lights went up at the end an emotion-charged silence reigned, broken
> only when Lunacharsky [the Soviet Union's Commissar for Education] jumped
> on his chair and began an enthusiastic speech: 'We've been witnesses at an
> historic cultural event. A new art has been born....'[1]

*See Chapter 4 for further
discussion of film form.*

Anatoli Lunacharsky's response to Sergei Eisenstein's 1925 film *Battleship Potemkin*
acknowledges the importance of a new wave of film-making. The films made by the
Soviet directors of the 1920s are considered by many as the most innovative and
exciting to have been produced in the history of the cinema. The names of these film-
makers, such as Eisenstein, Pudovkin, Vertov and Kuleshov, are far from forgotten and
a number of the films and directors from this period consistently score highly in *Sight
and Sound*'s critics'/directors' choice of the best ten films and directors.

Soviet cinema
This will refer to films
made in the Soviet Union
between October 1920
and 1991, although for
the purposes of this
chapter most Soviet
films discussed will be
confined to the 1920s.

This decade of intensive experimentation with film form produced techniques that
have subsequently been widely emulated. In addition, the theoretical debates formulated by these film-makers are still relevant today. For these reasons the **Soviet cinema**
of the 1920s merits detailed analysis.

HISTORICAL BACKGROUND

ideology
There are two key defini-
tions of this term, one
provided by the nine-
teenth-century German
philosopher, Karl Marx,
the other by the twen-
tieth-century French
Marxist philosopher,
Louis Althusser, drawing
on Marx's original ideas.
For Marx, ideology was
the dominant set of
beliefs and values exis-
tent within society, which
sustained power rela-
tions. For Althusser,
ideology consisted of the
representations and
images which reflect
society's view of 'reality'.
Ideology thus refers to
'the myths that a society
lives by'.

The Soviet film-makers of the 1920s reflect the **ideology** (the values and beliefs) and
politics of the society in which they were produced. The early 1920s marked the end of
a period of civil unrest, the causes of which lay in the great divide that separated
wealthy land-owning Russians from the peasants and workers.[2] For centuries Russia
had been governed by the single figure of the Tsar who had absolute powers. The
Russian serfs were not granted freedom from slavery until 1861; this liberation, however,
did not mean improved conditions, as they continued to live an existence of appalling
poverty. Attempts had been made prior to the revolution of October 1917 by various
factions to undermine the Tsarist regime, all of which were unsuccessful. A wave of
revolutionary activity in 1905 included a mutiny by Russian sailors at Odessa which
formed the basis for Sergei Eisenstein's 1925 film *Battleship Potemkin*.

The First World War (1914–18) eventually proved to be disastrous for Tsar Nicholas II,
as it consumed vast amounts of money and resources that were sorely needed at
home. It was also unpopular with the Russian people as the reasons for fighting were
unclear. The peasants and the workers were the worst hit by the impact of the war,
either being killed on the front or starving at home as supplies became depleted. The
land-owning rich were protected by their wealth and were able to continue in their
existing lifestyle.

These conditions provided the catalyst for the revolution of 25 February 1917 which
resulted in the formation of a liberal provisional government led by Alexander Kerensky
and later supported by Menshevik and Socialist Revolutionary factions. This caused
Nicholas II to abdicate on 4 March. The provisional government decided to continue the
war, and for many (especially V.I. Lenin who was in hiding in Zurich) it appeared that the
new government was in effect continuing the policies of the Tsarist order.

*See Chapter 5 for
discussion of ideology in
relation to spectatorship.*

On 25 October 1917 the Bolsheviks, taking advantage of a situation of confusion
and competition between the various factions, seized power by storming the Winter
Palace.[3] The new Bolshevik government agreed to Germany's demands for control of

areas of land previously under Russian administration, and pulled out of the war. Almost immediately, however, a fierce civil war broke out between the Bolsheviks (known as the Reds) and those still loyal to the Tsarist regime (known as the Whites).[4]

By 1920 it was clear that the Bolsheviks had seized ultimate control of the country. The new Soviet government under the leadership of V.I. Lenin was faced with the task of convincing the population of Russia of the evils of the Tsarist regime and the positive points of the new Communist one.

Selected historical dates

1905, Jan.	First revolution (abortive)
	Provides the backdrop for Eisenstein's *Battleship Potemkin*
1914, July	General strike organised by the Bolsheviks
	Outbreak of war and the crushing of the political unrest
	The war was a general disaster for the Russians; low morale and food shortages in the following years led to uprisings in 1917
1917, Feb.	Popular uprisings culminating in the overthrow of the Tsar, and the setting up of a provisional government
1917, Oct.	The Bolsheviks overthrow the provisional government and seize political power
1918–21	Civil war between White and Red factions, as well as fighting of hostile troops sent from abroad in an attempt to restore the power of the Tsar. The continued fighting led to the destruction of trade, agriculture, industry and film production
1922–8	NEP (New Economic Policy) adopted by Lenin. A brief return to controlled forms of capitalism to help to rebuild the shattered economy
1922–3	Soviet feature film production resumes
1924	Sergei Eisenstein's *Strike* completed
1927	The tenth anniversary of the October Revolution. A number of films are made to mark the occasion including:
	October (Eisenstein)
	The End of St Petersburg (Vsevolod Pudovkin)
	The Fall of the Romanov Dynasty (Esfir Shub)

PRE-REVOLUTIONARY RUSSIAN CINEMA

The nature of the Russian cinema

When discussing the Soviet cinema it is important to have at least an outline of the form and content of its antecedent, for although the majority of the Soviet directors had not made films prior to 1919, they would certainly have been familiar with the conventions of the pre-revolutionary cinema. Significantly, for a number of the Soviet directors, this cinema was the antithesis of their new approach to film-making. The **Russian cinema** 1907–17 was in fact markedly different from the Soviet cinema of the 1920s. The majority of the films that are available for viewing today[5] are between thirty-five and seventy minutes long and deal predominantly with the lives of the upper classes, quite frequently centring on their relationship with servants and/or the working class. Their subject matter, plot and preoccupations are often melodramatic; unfaithful husbands and wives, psychological states of mind and death predominate. The form of the films is also different, comprising slow-moving scenes containing a limited number of shots, with an emphasis on the ***mise en scène*** and in particular the expressions of the actors.

Russian cinema
This will refer to the body of films made in Tsarist Russia between 1907 and 1919.

mise en scène
This literally means 'placed in the scene', and it includes all elements that are placed before the camera such as props, actors, costume, movement and position of actors, etc.

See Chapter 4 for further discussion of mise en scène.

A key director working in this period is Evgeny Bauer, who produced a large number of films including *After Death* (1915), *A Life for a Life* (1916) and *The King of Paris* (1917).[6]

The Russian Revolution of October 1917 and the civil war that followed had a devastating effect on the Russian film industry, which was almost completely destroyed. Very few of the Russian directors and stars remained in Russia after 1919, the majority having fled to Paris where they continued production.[7] Initially it would seem that the Russian cinema had little in common with the Soviet cinema that followed, and there appears to have been a clear break in terms of style between the two cinemas after the revolution. The figure of Yakov Protazanov, however, provides an interesting example of a film-maker who made films between 1911–43.[8] His key films from the pre-revolutionary era include, *The Queen of Spades* (1916) and *Satan Triumphant* (1917); these conform to the conventions of the Russian cinema outlined earlier. His best-known film of the 1920s is *Aelita* (1924), a fantasy concerning a revolution on Mars. Protazanov was more concerned with *mise en scène* than with creating new meanings by juxtaposing images. A study of his films reveals that the Tsarist cinema continued into the Soviet **montage** era and was by all accounts successful with the public.[9]

montage
From the French word meaning 'to edit', montage means the assembling of bits of footage to form a whole. In film studies it usually refers to the style of fast editing adopted by the Soviet film-makers of the 1920s.

Russian cinema audiences and imported films

That Russian films had moderate success with native audiences is not surprising. What is significant, however, is that before the revolution the most popular films with Russian audiences were imported from America, France and Germany. The first Russian film studio was not set up until 1907[10] and this can partly account for the success of these foreign films as audiences had grown accustomed to watching them. In the 1910s when native films vied for audiences with imported films, foreign ones were clearly the more successful and were perceived by Russian audiences as being more entertaining and having higher production values than Russian films.

SOVIET CINEMA AND IDEOLOGY: FILM AS AGENT OF CHANGE[11]

The October Revolution was the first successful revolution made in the name of Karl Marx (1818–83). For Marx, the key fact about any society was how it produced its livelihood. He saw capitalism as an economic system, which, just like every other previous economic system, was based on exploitation. In capitalism the class with power was the bourgeoisie, the owners of the means of production, and the class subject to their power was the proletariat or working class. In addition, the bourgeoisie's economic strength was protected by the state and sustained by ideology. However, as capitalism developed, the workers, who survived by selling their labour for wages, would be squeezed more and more as competition between capitalists intensified. At the same time they would become aware that they would have everything to gain by replacing an economic system based on the ownership of private property with one based on the non-exploitative communal ownership of productive property. This awareness, or class-consciousness, would eventually produce a revolution. The October Revolution was seen as such a proletarian revolution in Russia and was celebrated as such by the films of the key Soviet film-makers of the 1920s.

The revolution, however, was only the beginning of a process of radical social change, called the era of 'the dictatorship of the proletariat' because it involved the proletariat, or in this case its representatives, the Bolshevik Party, establishing its dominance. V.I. Lenin writing in *Pravda* outlined the situation:

Theoretically, there can be no doubt that between capitalism and communism there lies a definite transition period which must combine the features and properties of both these forms of social economy. This transition period has to be a period of struggle between dying capitalism and nascent communism – or, in other words, between capitalism which has been defeated but not destroyed and communism which has been born but is still very feeble.[12]

The transition to communism referred to by Lenin would have been a monumental task at the best of times, but the Bolsheviks had seized control of a country whose industry and agriculture were relatively underdeveloped. Also they had to confront internal and external opposition, civil war and famine. In such a situation artists and film-makers were perceived as having a special role as proponents of **propaganda cinema**. Lenin declared in 1922 that 'of all the arts, for us the cinema is the most important'.[13] Prior to this, trains highly decorated with Soviet flags and paintings had been sent into the countryside in an attempt to educate and inform the peasants.[14] Short agitational films called *agitki* were made. Pre-revolutionary newsreels and foreign fiction films were also shown, with a Soviet commentator giving a 'new' reading to the material. Later most of the energy went into the making of new feature films that reflected the ideals of the new regime. Anatoli Lunacharsky (the People's Commissar for Education) had stated in 1924:

> **propaganda cinema**
> A terms used pejoratively with reference to any film that consciously attempts to persuade an audience towards certain beliefs and values.
>
> *See Chapter 7, pp. 219–24 for discussion of propaganda and British cinema during the Second World War.*

There is no doubt that cinema art is a first-class and perhaps even an incomparable instrument for the dissemination of all sorts of ideas. Cinema's strength lies in the fact that, like any art, it imbues an idea with feeling and with captivating form but, unlike the other arts, cinema is actually cheap, portable and unusually graphic. Its effects reach where even the book cannot reach and it is, of course, more powerful than any kind of narrow propaganda. The Russian Revolution, which is extremely interested in exercising the broadest possible influence on the masses, should long since have turned its attention to cinema as its natural instrument.[15]

The enthusiastic, young, educated film-makers, who attempted to fulfil Lunacharsky's ideal of revolutionary cinema, responded by making innovative films, revolutionary both in content and in form.

ECONOMICS OF THE SOVIET FILM INDUSTRY

The pre-revolutionary Russian film industry had previously imported its film stock from abroad, and during the civil war most of the Russian film-makers had fled to White-held areas (or abroad) taking their equipment with them. The reality facing the film-makers of the newly formed state was that there was little in the way of film stock or equipment.[16]

The Soviet government initially attempted to ban the showing of all American and European films, as they were concerned about the public being exposed to films that reflected the values of capitalist societies. The Soviets had little option, however, but to show these films as they had no native film industry to produce their own. The cinema was seen by the new government as a means of keeping the public entertained at a time of hardship and general civil unrest.

From a western perspective it is easy to underestimate the importance of imported films in the Soviet Union in the 1920s. Denise Youngblood (1992: 944–71), in *Movies for the Masses*, states that 'Foreign films accounted for almost two-thirds of the titles screened in the twenties.... Nearly as many American as Soviet films were shown in this period'. She continues: 'Sovkino's head, K.M. Shvedchikov, claimed in 1927 that Sovkino would be bankrupt were it not for the success of its import policy.'[17]

The 1920s could be characterised as a period in which American and European narrative films were in effect directly subsidising the dramatic experimentation with film form undertaken by the Soviet film-makers.

Innovation and experimentation frequently come from a lack. In the Soviet Union the lack of film stock (and even film cameras) meant that certain groups of film-makers worked on re-editing existing films (often European/American films and old Russian newsreels) to make them conform to the values of the Soviet state. Other film-makers experimented with creating films from the small amount of negative available, which often only came in short lengths. Out of this experimentation came Soviet montage cinema.

FORM: MONTAGE

The roots of Soviet montage

The innovative use of montage in film by the Soviet film-makers had its roots in art forms such as painting, literature and music from pre-revolutionary Russia. David Bordwell, in 'The Idea of Montage in Soviet Art and Film', states that by 1910 a group of Russian painters had already experimented extensively with 'montage': 'the Russian futurists declared that conventional art must be destroyed and that a new art, appropriate to the machine age, must be created. Hence the futurists took their subjects from modern life and exploited a technique of shocking juxtapositions.'[18] Poetry, in particular that of Mayakovsky,[19] was also 'shattering words and reassembling them into brutal images'.

The question needs to be asked: why didn't the Russian film-makers of the 1910s experiment with montage earlier? This lack of explicit montage experiment in the Russian cinema compared to that taking place in other art forms can perhaps be attributed to economics. The crucial difference between film and many of the other arts at the time was that the small groups of experimental artists, writers and musicians were often privately funded by rich patrons. The film industry, however, was not.[20] The revolution of October 1917 provided the right conditions for experimentation with film to take place. It is ironic that this experimentation had its roots in the élitist art forms of pre-revolutionary Russia.

The Kuleshov effect and its consequences

See Chapter 4, pp. 110–13, for reference to Kuleshov's experiments with editing, and for discussion of editing in mainstream narrative cinema.

The montage technique is based on the theory that when two pieces of film are placed side by side the audience immediately draws the conclusion that the two shots must be directly related in some way. In other words, the audience try to create meaning by combining the two separate images. The experimentation along these lines by Lev Kuleshov, a young Soviet film-maker, culminated in what became known as the Kuleshov effect. Vsevolod Pudovkin outlined the experiment in a lecture given at the London Film Society in February 1929:

Kuleshov and I made an interesting experiment. We took from some film or other several close-ups of the well-known Russian actor Mosjukhin. We chose close-ups which were static and which did not express any feeling at all – quiet close-ups. We joined these close-ups, which were all similar, with other bits of film in three different combinations. In the first combination the close-up of Mosjukhin was immediately followed by a shot of a plate of soup standing on a table. It was obvious and certain that Mosjukhin was looking at this soup. In the second combination the face of Mosjukhin was joined to shots showing a coffin in which lay a dead woman. In the third the close-up was followed by a shot of a little girl playing with a funny toy bear. When we showed the three combinations to an audience which had not been let into the secret the result was terrific. The public raved abut the acting of the artist. They pointed out the heavy pensiveness of his mood over the forgotten soup, were touched and moved by the deep sorrow with which he looked on the dead woman, and admired the light, happy smile with which he surveyed the girl at play. But we knew that in all three cases the face was exactly the same.[21]

Kuleshov carried out further experiments using editing in which he cut together separate shots of a walking man, a waiting woman, a gate, a staircase and a mansion.[22] When the shots were combined the audience assumed that the different elements were present at the same location. Kuleshov had discovered the cinema's ability to link entirely unrelated material into coherent sequences. He termed the technique 'creative geography'.

Kuleshov's discoveries about the nature of the cinema medium provided a number of film-makers with a new set of ideas about how film could manipulate and deceive an audience. Perhaps the most vital consequence of the Kuleshov effect, however, for later directors, was its recognition that the audience were not merely passive recipients.

Soviet montage cinema

In the 1920s a number of the film-makers carried out further experiments with editing techniques along the same lines as Kuleshov. It was discovered that when two shots were joined together meaning could be made by emphasising the difference between shots, that is, instead of trying to cover up graphic dissimilarities between shots, as in the **Hollywood cinema**, the difference could be emphasised and indeed become the main way in which meaning could be created. This 'montage' cinema which demanded that audiences continually searched for the meanings created by the **juxtaposition** of two shots can thus be seen as **alternative** to the continuity editing-based Hollywood cinema. One of the Soviet film-makers who developed this idea into both a theory and a practice of film-making was Sergei Eisenstein.

Eisenstein believed that maximum impact could be achieved if shots in a scene were in conflict. This belief was based on the general philosophical idea that 'existence' can only continue by constant change. In other words, everything surrounding us in the world is as a result of a 'collision' of opposite elements. The existing world is itself only in a temporary state until the next collision of elements produces a completely new state. It is only through this 'collision' that change can be effected. This method of creating meaning from such collision of opposites is termed **dialectical**. When applying this idea to film, Eisenstein proposed the view that when two shots are combined a completely new meaning is formed. For example, shot A combined with shot B does not produce AB but the new meaning C. The formulation can also be presented as: thesis + anti-thesis = synthesis.

Vsevolod Pudovkin, another key Soviet film-maker, was opposed to the theoretical ideas of Eisenstein, although they both used innovative forms of montage in their films. Pudovkin, like Kuleshov, believed that shots could be likened to bricks in the sense that they could be used as building blocks to construct a scene. Pudovkin then did not see his shots as being in conflict. In Pudovkin's formulae shot A + shot B = AB rather than C. Pudovkin aimed at linkage rather than conflict in his scenes.

The montage technique was not only confined to fiction film-making. Soviet documentary film-makers such as Dziga Vertov and Esfir Shub used montage extensively in a range of films in the 1920s, including Vertov's well-known *The Man with a Movie Camera* (1929). For Vertov much of the power of cinema came from its ability to mechanically record events that took place before the camera, but he also ensured that the audience was made aware of the constructed nature of his films. His films are a whirlwind of conflicting shots which disavow conventional ideas of narrative.

Hollywood cinema
In classical Hollywood cinema, the editing is designed to be 'invisible'. It is intended to allow the audience closer views and to see the point of view of different characters. The editing is used essentially to clarify what is taking place in the narrative. This type of editing had become dominant in Hollywood film-making by approximately 1920.

juxtaposition
In film studies, this usually refers to two different shots that have been joined together to make a contrast.

alternative
Alternative cinema is defined with reference to dominant: it is an alternative (both economically and formally) to the dominant form. In any study concerning an 'alternative' cinema, the films would not only have to be examined in their own right, but also compared to contemporary dominant Hollywood cinema.

A number of questions might have to be posed when analysing these alternative films: In what ways is this group of films different to the dominant cinema of the time? What are the possible reasons for the difference: cultural? economic? social? political? Could this 'alternative' way of making films, given the right conditions, have itself turned into the dominant cinema?

The Soviet cinema of the 1920s, when compared to the Hollywood cinema of the same era, certainly could be regarded as alternative.

The montage technique for the majority of the Soviet film-makers could also provide sequences with a sense of rhythm and momentum, which could be used to increase or decrease the speed of the action. Eisenstein, for example, frequently increases his rate of cutting prior to the climax of a scene. Violent actions could also be emphasised by using a succession of short conflicting shots from different viewpoints. Montage, the film-makers discovered, could further be used to either compress or expand time, which could heighten the effect of certain actions or events.

Four different types of film montage[23]

The first two categories of montage outlined below are frequently, although not exclusively, used in Soviet film; the last two categories deal with montage techniques that are often to be found in mainstream films:

- Intellectual montage (also called dialectical montage or discontinuity editing)
- Linkage editing (also known as constructive editing)
- Hollywood montage
- Fast cutting

Intellectual montage

In this type of editing, shots are placed together to emphasise their difference. They are in 'collision' with each other. For example, in *October* a shot of a mechanical golden peacock is placed next to a shot of a man (the peacock does not form part of the world of the film, that is, it is **non-diegetic**). The audience draw the conclusion that the man is vain. In this type of editing the audience are not passive as they play an active part in producing meaning from the film.

Linkage editing

Mainly used by Pudovkin, who proposed a theory of montage based on this principle. In linkage editing individual shots are used to build up scenes. The shots are not in collision with each other, but are used as fragments or parts of a whole scene. The technique can be seen in *The Mother* and *The End of St Petersburg*.

Hollywood montage

Often used to show a quick succession of events over a period of time. For example, in *Raging Bull* (1980) Martin Scorsese shows the successful career of the boxer Jack La Motta by combining shots (mostly still photographs) taken from a number of different fights interspersed with home movie footage of La Motta's home life. The shots are clearly intended to flow into each other rather than to be in conflict. The music played on the soundtrack over the images reinforces the sense of continuity.

Fast cutting

In which editing is used primarily to build suspense or tension. For example, in the gunfight at the climax of *The Good, the Bad and the Ugly* (1966), Sergio Leone creates a dramatic effect by using a combination of music, tighter and tighter close-ups of the three characters and a shortening of shot length.

Statistical analysis of Soviet films

Soviet films, because of the use of the montage technique, contain many more shots than Hollywood films of the same period. David Bordwell[24] claims that the Soviet films of the 1920s contain on average between 600–2,000 shots, whereas the films made in Hollywood between 1917 and 1928 contain on average 500–1,000 shots. He further suggests that Hollywood films had an average shot length of five to six seconds and the Soviet films had an average shot length of two to four seconds. The comparison provides concrete evidence of the unique nature of the editing used in the Soviet films in this period.

OTHER FEATURES OF THE SOVIET MONTAGE CINEMA

Aside from editing, these films have other features which separate them from the **dominant** Hollywood cinema. In keeping with a Marxist analysis of society, plots frequently do not centre on the individual; for example, in Eisenstein's *Strike*, *October* and *Battleship Potemkin*, individual heroes are replaced by a mass of people. The only characters that are individuated are those that wield power or have wealth. Events in the narrative therefore are not motivated by individuals. Films such as Pudovkin's *The Mother* and *The End of St Petersburg* and Dovzhenko's *Earth* do have central characters, but it is made clear that these characters are representative of the masses. The audience is not interested in the details of the heroes, only what they represent. A number of the Soviet film-makers (including Eisenstein and Pudovkin) also used non-actors to play key parts, believing that the external appearance of the character was vital to the performance. This idea is termed 'typage'.

> **dominant**
> Refers to both economic strength and also to the dominant form or convention, which is realism: dominant cinema in film studies is assumed to be Hollywood.

The montage style also means that Soviet cinema relies more heavily on the use of the close-up than Hollywood cinema. Not only are there more shots overall in a scene, but a greater proportion of them are close-ups. A number of Soviet films also rely on high levels of **symbolism** to achieve their aims. The audience must be culturally and politically aware to be able to decode the messages that are being presented. In Eisenstein's *October*, for example, great demands are made on the audience to create a 'reading' of the film which does justice to Eisenstein's political thinking. It may seem that many of the film-makers ran the risk of making films that were not understood by their audience.

> **symbolism**
> The means by which a film-maker can assign additional meanings to objects/characters in a film. For example, in Dovzhenko's *Earth* and Eisenstein's *Old and New*, the tractor is a symbol of progress.

Several of the montage film-makers combined the montage principle with other techniques that they believed would revitalise the cinema. Lev Kuleshov, for example, placed great emphasis on the gestures and movement of actors. FEKS (Factory of the Eccentric Actor), formed by film-makers Grigori Kozintsev and Leonid Trauberg, had similar concerns about the role of the actor, but also paid great attention to *mise en scène*.

THE KEY SOVIET MONTAGE FILM-MAKERS OF THE 1920s

Fiction	*Documentary*
Lev Kuleshov	Dziga Vertov
Sergei Eisenstein	Esfir Shub
Vsevolod Pudovkin	
FEKS (Kozintsev and Trauberg)	
Alexander Dovzhenko	

A film directed by Eisenstein probably provided most viewers' first experience of Soviet montage. The history of the Soviet cinema of the 1920s, however, involves more than the work of this one director. In this section, although the work of Eisenstein is discussed in detail, the vital importance of Eisenstein's contemporaries is recognised by analysing the work of such directors as Kuleshov, Pudovkin, Kozintsev and Trauberg, Dovzhenko, Vertov and Shub.

Lev Kuleshov (1899–1970)

Shortly after the revolution, Kuleshov was recruited as a teacher by the State Film

School where he set up an experimental film workshop. Kuleshov and his students carried out a number of experiments related to editing, partly inspired by a lack of raw film stock. One of these experiments included re-editing D.W. Griffith's *Intolerance* (1916), a film that had impressed Kuleshov because of its innovative use of editing. The experiments resulted in the formation of a number of principles of film-making that the group adopted. The underlying belief for Kuleshov was that 'Film-art begins from the moment when the director begins to combine and join together the various pieces of film'.[25] Kuleshov's ideas about how editing should work are similar to those of Pudovkin in that his shots, rather than being in conflict, can be seen as blocks out of which a scene can be constructed. Significantly, Kuleshov's students included Vsevolod Pudovkin and for a brief time Sergei Eisenstein. In Eisenstein's films and theoretical writing the influence of Kuleshov can clearly be seen.

Kuleshov's experimentation was not confined to editing, however, but also involved acting. He believed that theatre-trained actors, in particular those from the Moscow Arts Theatre[26] were not suitable for the cinema. He also rejected the idea of using non-actors or 'types' chosen for their visual suitability for a role. He set up an acting laboratory dedicated to developing a style of acting tailored specifically to the requirements of the cinema and he carefully recruited would-be film actors who were 'endowed with natural beauty, good health, and the ability to show expediency and purpose on the screen without "acting" or "recreating", unaided by makeup, wigs, and props, of course'.[27]

The techniques that Kuleshov adopted emphasised gesture and movement, the exact nature and timing of which had been practised rigorously in rehearsals. This style of acting was combined with great attention to the composition and framing of each shot to give maximum impact to the action. Kuleshov's opportunity to apply the principles that he had developed came in 1924 when he was assigned valuable imported film stock to direct the first feature film of the film school: *The Extraordinary Adventures of Mr West in the Land of the Bolsheviks*.

Key films
Engineer Prite's Project (1918)
The Extraordinary Adventures of Mr West in the Land of the Bolsheviks (1924)
The Death Ray (1925)
By the Law (1926)

For comparison and contrast see Chapter 6 for a discussion of the star in Hollywood cinema.

☐ CASE STUDY 1: LEV KULESHOV, *THE EXTRAORDINARY ADVENTURES OF MR WEST IN THE LAND OF THE BOLSHEVIKS* (1924)

The film is an action-comedy which uses satire to expose the false attitudes and beliefs about the Soviet Union that many in the West held. The action is centred on the fate of Mr West, an American visitor to the USSR, whose view of the Bolsheviks as savages is formed by reading the *New York Times*. Mr West falls into the hands of a group of petty criminals who frighten him into parting with his dollars by dressing up to look like the Bolsheviks that Mr West had seen in his paper. At the climax he is rescued by a 'real' Bolshevik who uncovers the deception. Mr West's stereotypical views of the Bolsheviks are dismantled and he sends a radio message to his wife telling her to hang Lenin's picture in the study.

The montage technique used in *Mr West* is largely based on a system of close-ups of the actors that emphasise facial expressions. Kuleshov frequently cuts from an action to a close-up reaction shot of a character's face. He starts the film with a separate shot of Mr West juxtaposed with another of his wife; it is only later that we see them together. Later in the film Kuleshov cuts between a shot of the 'real' Bolshevik and Mr West standing on a balcony and another shot of marching Soviet troops taken at a different place and time (the film stock is markedly different).

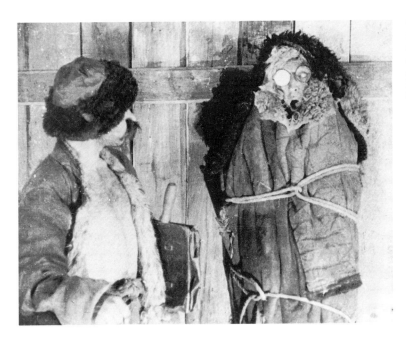

• **Plate 13.1** *The Extraordinary Adventures of Mr West in the Land of the Bolsheviks* (1924) Mr West is duped by the false Bolsheviks.

Kuleshov is here using his technique of creative geography to make the audience construct a location in their minds that does not actually exist. The film also fulfils Kuleshov's ideas concerning acting. The movements of the actors are stylised and precise and it is clear that attention has been paid to even the smallest action. The comical nature of the action and a plot based on individual characters meant that the film was popular with audiences.[28]

Sergei Eisenstein (1898–1948)[29]

Eisenstein, as his age might indicate (he was just 26 when he completed *Strike*), did not emerge from the context of the pre-revolutionary Russian cinema. Prior to his film-making career, he had experimented with a number of different art forms, including the theatre. In this experimentation, the principles of his work in film may be found. In 1923 Eisenstein produced a version of a play by Alexander Ostrovky,[30] in which he attempted to communicate the messages of the play to the audience using a series of shocks which Eisenstein termed 'attractions': 'Emotions were expressed through flamboyant physical stunts ... at the finale, fire-crackers exploded under spectators' seats... [he] explained that the theatre could engage its audience through a calculated assembly of "strong moments" of shock or surprise.'[31]

Eisenstein quickly abandoned experimentation with the theatre and turned to the more popular and accessible medium of film, to which he rigorously applied his theatrical principle of 'montage of attractions'.

key films
Strike (1924)
Battleship Potemkin (1925)
October (1927)
Old and New (1929)

☐ CASE STUDY 2: SERGEI EISENSTEIN, *STRIKE* (1924); *BATTLESHIP POTEMKIN* (1925); *OCTOBER* (1927); *OLD AND NEW* (1929)

Strike (1924)

Strike was the first of a proposed series of eight films[32] made by the Moscow Theatre of the Proletkult, under the general subheading 'Towards the Dictatorship of the Proletariat'. *Strike* is about the repression of a group of factory workers involved in an industrial dispute, which ends with the massacre of the strikers and their families by government forces. The six-part structure of 'Strike' – (1) 'All Quiet at the Factory', (2) 'The Immediate Cause of Strike', (3) 'The Factory Stands Idle', (4) 'The Strike is Protracted', (5) 'Engineering a Massacre', (6) 'Slaughter' – is partly due to Eisenstein's theatrical background, but it would also have been vital for the film to be contained on single reels as many cinemas had only one projector.

The plot of *Strike*, as in Eisenstein's later films *Battleship Potemkin* (1925) and *October* (1927), is not told using individual characters as heroes. Instead, any character that is individuated is deemed to be 'bad' or corrupt. The grotesque factory-owner, for example, is shown completely isolated in a vast office. The workers themselves, however, are seen usually as a group with no one individual standing out to play the role of leader. In Part 3 these ideas are combined. The scenes depicting the four stockholders of the factory carelessly deciding the future of the strikers are intercut with

• **Plate 13.3** *Strike*
(1924)
Mounted police enter
the factory district.

images of strikers being attacked by mounted police; the individual concern of the capitalists contrasts with the collective concern of the masses. The effect of this montage is
dramatic, as parallels can immediately be drawn by the viewer between, for example,
the dishonesty, greed, deviousness and wealth of the management and the poverty and
honesty of the workers. The political implications of this are obvious. Eisenstein,
through montage, is seeking to persuade his audience towards a certain view.

The methods applied by Eisenstein in *Strike* are derived in part from a rebellion
against what Eisenstein termed the 'Bourgeois Cinema' that was still the main form of
entertainment in post-revolutionary cinemas. Eisenstein explains how this cinema was
rejected in favour of his own approach: 'We brought collective and mass action onto the
screen ... our films in this period made an abrupt deviation – insisting on an understanding of the masses as hero.'[33]

In terms of the Hollywood cinema it is not difficult to imagine how the plot of *Strike*
could have been adapted into a mainstream film: the story of one individual's fight
against authority. The comparison may be trite, but it does emphasise the difference in
approach and purpose between the two different modes of representation. Eisenstein's
decision not to use individual heroes is of course deliberate; the film registers a political
ideology that enshrines the notion of collective strength.

In *Strike* Eisenstein applies his principle of 'montage of attractions' to the editing. He
believed that by creating visual 'jolts' between each cut, the viewer would be 'shocked'
into new awarenesses. In most sequences this approach involves juxtaposing shots
that are in conflict with each other in some way, either cutting between different actions
taking place in a scene or emphasising the importance of certain actions or events by
fragmenting them into a number of shots taken from different viewpoints. At various
points in *Strike* Eisenstein juxtaposes shots which need to be interpreted by the audience. One of the best examples of this type of 'intellectual montage' is in the last part of
the film ('Slaughter'), in which Eisenstein juxtaposes a non-diegetic image of a bull
being slaughtered with the shots of the factory workers being systematically butchered
by government forces. The formula mentioned earlier can be applied: shot A (massacre

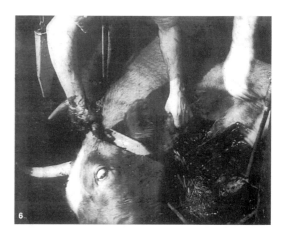

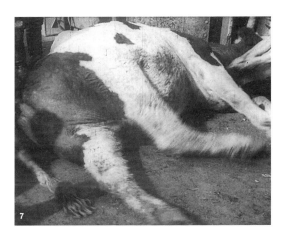

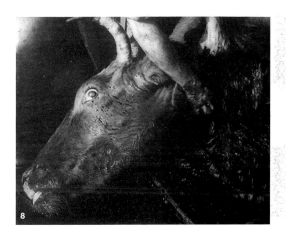

• **Plate 13.4** This sequence from Strike (lasting 25 seconds) illustrates Eisenstein's use of intellectual montage. An inter-title ('Rout')
is inserted between shots 2 and 3.

of the workers) + shot B (bull being slaughtered) = NEW MEANING C (that the workers are being killed cold-bloodedly like animals in a slaughterhouse). It is the audience that is creating meaning here from the juxtaposition of the shots, thus becoming active political interpreters.

Battleship Potemkin (1925)

Eisenstein's second film *Battleship Potemkin* is based on the true story of a mutiny that took place on board the *Potemkin* in 1905.[34] As in *Strike*, *Battleship Potemkin* is split into a number of distinct parts: (1) 'Men and Maggots', (2) 'Drama on the Quarter Deck', (3) 'Appeal from the Dead', (4) 'The Odessa Steps', (5) 'Meeting the Squadron'.

The central scene of the film, 'The Odessa Steps', consisting of parallel lines of soldiers marching down the steps leading to the harbour systematically shooting the onlookers, provides a vivid example of the effectiveness of Eisenstein's montage technique.[35] A close examination of the sequence reveals that Eisenstein, by using montage to repeat certain key events, has expanded time.[36] The effect is to heighten the horrific nature of the slaughter as well as to hold the audience in suspense as the pram finally begins its descent. The furious and shocking climax to the scene demonstrates how Eisenstein is able to use montage to manipulate audience expectations and to shock with violent juxtapositions and graphic images.

In the last part of the film in which the sailors aboard the *Potemkin* are nervously anticipating an attack by the rest of the Russian Fleet, Eisenstein builds up tension by increasing the number of cuts in a montage finale that maintains a consistently high rate of shots per minute. The scene provides an excellent example of the way in which montage could be used to create an event that did not exist as a whole, as according to Eisenstein the shots of the 'Russian' squadron were taken from 'old newsreels of naval manoeuvres – not even of the Russian Fleet'.[37] It also reveals how montage can be used for rhythmic effect, as the fast cutting between the different elements gives the scene a sense of urgency which would be impossible to achieve using any other method.

The opposition of critics at the time ironically stressed the difficulties of understanding *Potemkin*'s experimental form; ironic because it was through film form that Eisenstein hoped to make his political points. It was also declared that *Potemkin* was pitched far above the intellectual level of most peasants, a damning indictment for any propaganda/revolutionary piece. However, although *Potemkin* was not successful as a

• **Plate 13.5** *Battleship Potemkin* (1925) Drama on the quarter-deck (the firing squad).

• **Plate 13.6** *Battleship
Potemkin* (1925)
The Odessa Steps.

• **Plates 13.7, 13.8 and 13.9**
Battleship Potemkin (1925)
Immediately after the massacre on the Odessa Steps, the sailors on the battleship take their revenge by shelling the
headquarters of the generals. As part of this sequence, Eisenstein juxtaposes three images of stone lions in
different stages of awakening as a symbol of the awakening of the Russian people to political ideas and action.

piece of popular propaganda, it did, like *Strike* before it, mark a major step in the
progress of revolutionary cinema. It also represented the first film that gave recognition
and acclaim to Soviet cinema. The claim that the experimental nature of *Potemkin* was
not solely to blame for its unpopularity, and that it was badly let down by Sovkino's
methods of distribution, is a view that should certainly be considered.

October (1927)

October, made for the Tenth Anniversary celebrations of the Russian Revolution, depicts
the build-up to the October Revolution, ending with the storming of the Winter Palace by
the Bolsheviks. It is considered the most experimental of Eisenstein's films, especially in its
increased use of 'intellectual montage', which demands that the audience think critically
and constructively about important political issues. A demonstration of this type of
montage can be found in the scene in which both Kerensky and General Kornilov are
depicted as Napoleons. By intercutting between the two men and the plaster cast figures
of Napoleon, Eisenstein effectively exposes both the vanity and essentially the lack of any

diegetic
The elements of a film
that originate from
directly within the film's
narrative. For example, a
popular song that is
being played on the
soundtrack would be
diegetic if it was clear
that it was coming from
a source within the
world of the film such as
a car radio.

power within the characters themselves to form a separate identity.[38] Eisenstein's 'intellectual montage' also involves **diegetic** material. For example, early in the film, shots of a soldier cowering in a trench are juxtaposed with low-angle shots of a vast cannon being unloaded elsewhere. The combination of shots initially points to the soldier being physically crushed, but then swiftly the assumption is reached that the war is oppressive, degrading and without purpose for the ordinary troops.

Eisenstein also combines montage techniques with visual puns and symbolism for political effect. At one point, in order to degrade the power of the church, he swiftly cuts from the image of one deity to another, starting with a magnificent statue of Christ, and ending up with a primitive wooden idol, demonstrating that all religions essentially worship crude man-made objects. Eisenstein's use of such techniques was considered by many to be obscure, inaccessible in meaning and élitist. Victor Shklovsky, writing in *Novyi Lef* in 1927, records the responses of a man connected with the cinema:

After viewing some Eisenstein sequences a man who is intelligent and conversant with cinema said

• **Plate 13.10** *October*
(1927)
Lenin's arrival at the
Finland Railway Station.

• **Plate 13.11** *October* (1927)

to me, 'That is very good. I like that a lot but what will the masses say? What will the people we are working for say?' What can you say to that?[39]

Indeed, an examination of contemporary criticism of *October* reveals that far from being popular among Soviet audiences, the film was met with derision and apprehension.

Old and New (1929)
The adverse reaction to *October* prompted Eisenstein to produce *Old and New*, a film more readily understood by audiences. Despite employing a number of the techniques

• **Plate 13.12** *Old and New* (1929)
The new tractor is eventually delivered to Martha's co-operative.

used in *October*, Eisenstein presents them in a simplified form. Juxtapositions, for example, are more obvious and on a less symbolic level.

The narrative of *Old and New*, concerned with the collectivisation of agriculture, is, unlike Eisenstein's previous films, bound together by a central character or heroine 'Martha'. Despite its more conventional narrative form, the film contains one of Eisenstein's most effective montage sequences in which a cream separator is delivered to the collective farm. The new machine is eyed suspiciously by the peasants as milk is poured into it. In an ever-quickening flow of images, Eisenstein cuts between the glittering, spinning parts of the machine, the changing faces of the peasants and non-diegetic shots of fountains of water which symbolise the future flow of cream from the separator. The film is fascinating to study in the context of Eisenstein's earlier work and marks an attempt to address problems of understanding associated with *October*.

Vsevolod Pudovkin (1893–1953)

key films
The Mother (1926)
The End of St Petersburg (1927)
Storm Over Asia (1928)

Editing is the language of the film director. Just as in living speech, so, one may say, in editing: there is a word – the piece of exposed film, the image; a phrase – the combination of these pieces.

(Pudovkin)[40]

Pudovkin believed that the power of cinema comes from editing. In the above quotation he claims that a 'shot' (or image) which is the equivalent of the single word in language has very limited meaning. However, when a number of words are combined together they form a 'phrase' which is dense with meaning. Pudovkin's equivalent of a 'phrase' was a number of shots edited together. He went further to support his claim by contending that:

every object, taken from a given viewpoint and shown on the screen to spectators, is a *dead object*, even though it has moved before the camera.... Only if the object be placed together among a number of separate objects, only if it be presented as part of a synthesis of different separate visual images, is it endowed with filmic life.[41]

It would seem initially that Pudovkin's theoretical position regarding the effectiveness of editing was in tandem with his contemporary Eisenstein. There are, however, important differences in the specific way each director thought editing should be used.[42] Pudovkin did not agree with Eisenstein's system of montage, which created visual 'jolts' between cuts. Instead, Pudovkin believed greater impact could be made by linking shots in a constructive way. Shots were to be used as individual building blocks, made to fit together exactly. Though seemingly theoretically opposed to Eisensteinian montage, Pudovkin made extensive use of devices such as 'intellectual montage' in *The Mother* and *The End of St Petersburg*. Pudovkin's juxtapositions, however, are much less symbolic, more clearly related to the diegetic world of the film and less intent on creating conflict than those of Eisenstein. Leon Moussinac, a French historian, summed up the differences between the two directors: 'An Eisenstein film resembles a shout, a Pudovkin film evokes a song.'[43]

Pudovkin, like Eisenstein, cast according to 'type' and was concerned about the problem of 'stagey acting'. He stated:

I want to work only with real material – this is my principle. I maintain that to show, alongside real water and real trees and grass, a property beard pasted on the actor's face, wrinkles traced by means of paint, or stagey acting is impossible. It is opposed to the most elementary ideas of style.[44]

Unlike Eisenstein, however, Pudovkin uses individual characters that are cast in the role of hero or heroine to carry the narrative, and although he discouraged the use of professional actors some of his lead parts were played by professional actors of the Moscow Arts Theatre.[45]

☐ CASE STUDY 3: VSEVOLOD PUDOVKIN, *THE MOTHER* (1926); *THE END OF ST PETERSBURG* (1927)

The Mother (1926)

The scenario for Pudovkin's *The Mother* is based on the earlier play by Gorky of the same name. The plot is concerned with the political awakening of a mother after she betrays her son to the police, in the belief that he will be dealt with justly. The action is set (as in *Battleship Potemkin*) in the revolutionary context of 1905, with strikes, mass protests and a final brutal massacre of the workers.

With its focus on individuals, the film offers an interesting contrast to Eisenstein's approach to revolutionary cinema. In *The Mother*, the role of the individual is reinstated and emphasised. The mass struggle is thus registered through the lives and fates of separate characters involved in that struggle. It is important to note that the individual characters are not highlighted in such a way that the general struggle itself becomes obscured. The audience is encouraged to make connections between individual fate and the fate of the masses. Pudovkin is thus using individual characters to make his political points, believing that the audience would be able to relate better to separate identities than to an anonymous mass.

Pudovkin's use of 'linkage' editing (shot A + shot B = AB) can be illustrated in the trial scene at the mid-point of the film. The scene is composed of a large number of shots which tend to centre on single characters or pairs of characters. The fragmentation allows Pudovkin to draw direct comparisons between, for example, the uninterested and uncaring attitude of the judges, the accused Pavel, his mother and several of the gossiping onlookers. Close shots of the soldiers guarding the courthouse are also inserted in order to demonstrate that 'justice' is being upheld by a substantial force. Pudovkin clearly reveals the judges to be vain and self-interested by highlighting their overriding concern with attire and pictures of horses, rather than the proceedings of the trial. If the same scene had been shot by Eisenstein the vanity of the judges might have been indicated in a similar way to that of Kerensky in *October* (that is, juxtaposing him with a shot of a peacock).

The End of St Petersburg (1927)

Made to celebrate the Tenth Anniversary of the October Revolution, *The End of St Petersburg*, based on André Bely's 1916 symbolist novel *Petersburg*,[46] also uses individual characters to deal with the events preceding the revolution. One is a young peasant boy who has come to St Petersburg to seek work, as his family can no longer support him at home. Despite initial involvement with strikebreakers, the boy quickly becomes aware of the corruption and injustice of the Tsarist regime. His political awakening, however, lands him in prison and then he is forced to volunteer into the Tsar's army, where he is exposed to the horrors of trench warfare.

Using montage, Pudovkin draws a contrast between the suffering of the soldiers who are fighting for the Tsar and the greed of those who are benefiting financially from the war. Horrific images of dying soldiers in mud at the front-line trenches are intercut

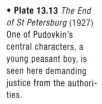

• **Plate 13.13** *The End of St Petersburg* (1927) One of Pudovkin's central characters, a young peasant boy, is seen here demanding justice from the authorities.

with scenes at the St Petersburg stock market. As the fighting gets worse and worse at the front, the higher the value of the shares becomes – thereby enforcing the point that people are making money out of suffering. The old order, by supporting and being supported by the stock market, is seen to be inhumane and preoccupied with the wrong values – the acquisition of wealth at whatever cost. Pudovkin at one point intercuts between the image of a soldier slashing ferociously at an opponent with his bayonet and the image of a stock market figure frenetically dealing at the stock exchange. He thus likens the barbarities of war to the barbarity inherent in the centre of the capitalist structure. Earlier Pudovkin intercut between the images of death at the front and the words 'In the name of the Tsar, the fatherland, and the capital'. This is clearly ironic as the soldiers have no idea what they are fighting for – certainly not for the Tsar.

In the final part of *The End of St Petersburg*, in the storming of the Winter Palace sequences, Pudovkin intercuts the images of the advancing Bolsheviks with both fast-moving clouds and crashing waves. This emphasises the power and inevitability of the revolution – revolution is unstoppable. Earlier in a Bolshevik's speech at the Lebedev factory, images of slowing down machinery are intercut with the speaker to point to the power of his words upon the workers.

Eccentrism of the FEKS: Grigori Kozintsev and Leonid Trauberg

Key films
The Adventures of Oktyabrina (1924)
The Cloak (1926)
The New Babylon (1929)

FEKS (Factory of the Eccentric Actor), formed in December 1921 by a small group of theatre actors and directors, shared the common aim of reforming the traditional theatre and incorporating into their experimental work elements of the circus, music hall and puppet theatre. On 9 July 1922 FEKS published a manifesto which stated their aims as a group.[47] The poster shown on page 439 shows just a small sample of the material contained within the manifesto.

WE

CONSIDER ART AS A TIRELESS RAM SHATTERING THE HIGH WALLS OF HABIT AND DOGMA

But we also have our own ancestors! and lots of them

The brilliant creators of cinema posters, circus posters, music hall posters. Unknown designers of pulp thrillers who exalt the exploits of the King of the detectives or adventurers. In using your art, more magnificent than a clown's red nose, we spring up as if from a trampoline to perform our intripid somersault! Only the poster has escaped the pernicious scalpel of analysis and the intellect. Subject and form are indivisible, but what do they sing of?

Danger, Audacity, Violence, Pursuit, Revolution, Gold, Blood, Laxative pills, Charlie Chaplin, Catastrophes on land, sea and in the air. Fat cigars, Prima donnas of the operettas, Adventures of all sorts, Skating rinks, Tap shoes, Horses, Wrestling, Torch singers, Somersaults on bicycles and all those millions and millions of events which make splendid our Today!

THE 200 VOLUMES OF GERMAN EXPRESSIONISM DO NOT OFFER THE EXPRESSIVITY OF ONE SOLE

CIRCUS POSTER!!!

• **Plate 13.14** *The New Babylon* (1929)

The extract makes it clear that FEKS valued the bold, dynamic and popular elements of circus and cinema posters. It was with these elements that they proposed to revitalise the theatre. Two of the founding members of the group, Grigori Kozintsev and Leonid Trauberg, became interested in the cinema, making a number of short experimental films between 1924 and 1927, including *The Adventures of Oktyabrina* (1924) and *The Cloak* (1926). The films primarily emphasised the artificial nature of the *mise en scène* and the stylised nature of the acting rather than the editing.

Kozintsev and Trauberg are perhaps best known for their 1929 film, *The New Babylon*, based on the events building up to the Paris Commune of 1871. As in their previous films, artificial *mise en scène* combined with stylised acting were employed, but also extensive use was made of camera movement. At one point in the film the camera moves swiftly enough to blur the image, thus conveying the sense of confusion present in the scene. The response to the film was unfavourable, as audiences failed to understand its form.

☐ CASE STUDY 4: ALEXANDER DOVZHENKO, *ARSENAL* (1929); *EARTH* (1930)[48]

Inspired by the creative and political possibilities of film, Dovzhenko had approached the Odessa film studio in 1926. At this point he had little knowledge of cinema, but within a few years he had made an outstanding contribution to Soviet revolutionary cinema with such films as *Arsenal* and *Earth* which, in addition to revolutionary fervour, displayed poetic qualities and provided a demonstration of his love for the Ukraine and its people.

Arsenal surveys the devastating impact of the First World War and the political struggles between the Social Democrats and the Bolsheviks during 1917. The opening sequences of *Arsenal* exemplify Dovzhenko's approach to film-making. There is little camera movement or use of establishing shots and, overall, there is less concern with a conventional rendering of space and time than with the emotional impact of the flow of images. In these opening and further sequences Dovzhenko reveals the loss and impoverishment of the people, as well as the unthinking callousness of the social order.

Arsenal shows that Dovzhenko is not concerned with personalised conflict between individuals, but with the ongoing struggle between opposing social forces. This concern is pursued further in *Earth* which deals with class struggle in the countryside, although like *Arsenal* it features a strong attractive male hero, Vasil. The latter is the operator of the tractor which will allow the collective farm to effectively rid the village of the self-seeking and more prosperous peasants, the kulaks. In the end Vasil is shot by Khoma, the son of a kulak, although what he stands for will not be defeated. Vasil's father, hitherto hostile to the young revolutionaries of the village, commits himself to the cause of collectivisation and rejects a religious burial in favour of the village youth singing songs about the new life to come. The film, then, presents a strong case for the recently instigated policy of the collectivisation of agriculture. Commentators on the film, however,

• **Plate 13.15** *Earth* (1930)

have argued that the formal and poetic qualities of the film actually undermine the political message. Denise J. Youngblood, for example, states that:

Dovzhenko's *Earth* (1930) is a much more curious example of the collectivisation film – the politically correct story of a handsome young village Party activist murdered by an evil and dissolute *kulak* opposed to collectivisation is undercut by a deeply subversive subtext related to its form. The lyrical imagery and slow rhythms of this film, totally unlike Eisenstein's, belie the purported theme and in effect serve as a paean to a way of life soon to be no more.[49]

The opening sequence in which Vasil's grandfather dies would certainly seem to bear out this interpretation. He dies contented, his last act being to enjoy a pear, a product of the fruitful Ukrainian earth. Next to him a baby plays and a boy eats an apple, while the adult members of the family await the inevitable. This portrait of pastoral abundance and peacefulness with its allusions to the cycle of life and death seem to undermine the necessity for revolutionary change, but it is made clear by the old man's friend Petro that his has been a life of hard work – 'Seventy-five years behind a plough'.

Dziga Vertov (1896–1954)

Dziga Vertov[50] (pseudonym of Denis Kaufman) was interested in the idea that the film camera had the potential to capture 'truth'; the camera could be seen simply as a mechanical device that was capable of recording the world without human intervention. Vertov led a group of film-makers called *Kinoki* ('cinema-eye') who stated in their 1923 manifesto:

Key films
Film Truth (Kino-Pravda) (1922)
Kino-Eye (1924)
A Sixth of the World (1926)
The Man with a Movie Camera (1929)
Enthusiasm (1931)

See Chapter 7, pages 215–6, for further discussion of Vertov's contribution to documentary film.

I am the Cine-Eye. I am the mechanical eye.

I the machine show you the world as only I can see it.

I emancipate myself henceforth and forever from human immobility. *I am in constant motion*. I approach objects and move away from them, I creep up on them, I clamber over them, I move alongside the muzzle of a running horse, I tear into a crowd at full tilt, I flee before fleeing soldiers, I turn over on my back, I rise up with aeroplanes, I fall and rise with falling and rising bodies.[51]

Vertov believed that the fiction film could not be used to reveal the 'truth' about a society. His films were based on documenting events around him; nothing should be artificially set up or staged for the camera. In 1922 Vertov had stated: 'WE declare the old films, the romantic, the theatricalised etc., to be leprous.'[52]

Vertov's techniques were based on experimentation caused by the general scarcity of film stock and also, when available, the short lengths of the negative film. His experiments included using old newsreels as part of his films, and he found that new meanings could be created by the conflict produced by the old material and the new. Vertov soon discovered that the conflicts produced by montage were a vital element in the construction of meaning in his films.

Perhaps one of the most interesting features of Vertov's films is that great effort is taken to ensure that the audience is made aware of cameraman, editor and the whole process of producing a film. In *The Man with a Movie Camera*, for example, Vertov shows the cameraman shooting the scenes that we see before us, and later we see shots of this same film being edited. This technique of acknowledging the nature of the film-making process can be linked to documentary film-making practice in the 1970s and 1980s (in the films of Emile de Antonio and Jean-Pierre Gorin, for example) which went against the **fly-on-the-wall** practice and attempted to show the presence of the film-crew and camera and the fact that the audience are watching a manufactured film rather than 'reality'. This style of film-making which draws attention to its own process is often termed 'self-reflexive'.

Esfir Shub (1894–1959)

Esfir Shub is an interesting female figure in a period of film-making dominated by men. She was initially employed by the Soviet government to re-edit foreign films to make them conform to the ideology of communism. Shub also re-edited old Tsarist newsreels to show the corrupt nature of the old order. Shub's practice of reassembling parts of existing films culminated in the adoption of the montage technique.

fly-on-the-wall
A term associated with a style of documentary film-making which attempts to present events as though the presence of the camera and film crew had not influenced them in any way.

Key films
The Fall of the Romanov Dynasty (1927)
The Great Road (1927)
The Russia of Nicholas II and Lev Tolstoy (1928)

☐ **CASE STUDY 5: ESFIR SHUB, *THE FALL OF THE ROMANOV DYNASTY* (1927)**

Shub's first feature-length film, *The Fall of the Romanov Dynasty*, constructed entirely from old newsreels, was made to celebrate the Tenth Anniversary of the October Revolution and it is claimed that 60,000 metres of film had to be examined in order to finish the project.[53] Shub provides new commentary on existing material by inserting intertitles between shots. By juxtaposing sequences of shots from different newsreels she also makes the audience draw new conclusions about the material. For example, she contrasts shots of an aristocratic gathering with shots of workers digging ditches. The intertitle reads 'by the sweat of your brow'. The intertitles and the juxtaposition of the images encourage the audience to assign an aberrant decoding to the original shots. In other words, the audience can deliberately 'misread' the images. Shub uses images which emphasise the pomp and splendour of Tsarist Russia, which in the context of the film look absurd and out of place; the audience is forced to be critical of this obvious display of wealth.

Although the film in principle uses montage in a similar way to Eisenstein or Pudovkin (in particular the way in which the audience are placed as active participants in the text), Shub does not make use of its rhythmic possibilities. Although the pace of the film is on the whole sedate it does put its political messages across in a powerful and convincing way. Recently, there has been a call for a re-evaluation of Esfir Shub by Graham Roberts, who claims that Shub's contribution to the Soviet cinema has been undervalued.[54]

AUDIENCE RESPONSE

Viewers in the West may possibly already have an idea of the nature of the Soviet cinema after seeing extracts from films discussed previously such as Sergei Eisenstein's *Battleship Potemkin* or *October*. They may have wondered how many films such as these were made and how they were received by Soviet audiences that had only a few years previously gone through the upheaval of civil war. They may have pitied or even envied the Soviet cinema-goer – were these the only films that the Soviet cinema-goer could see on a Friday night? How could a largely uneducated population have coped with sophisticated material like this?

Recent research into the Soviet cinema of the 1920s has encouraged new ideas. In the past, attention has focused on a number of key directors such as Pudovkin, Eisenstein and Vertov, whose films in the Soviet Union and later in the West were received with critical acclaim. We must examine, however, new evidence that points to the fact that Russian audiences were far more likely to be watching the Soviet 1920s equivalent of *Jurassic Park* than the likes of *Battleship Potemkin*, *Strike* and *October*.

Richard Stites, in *Russian Popular Culture: Entertainment and Society since 1900*, reveals that the majority of Soviet directors were making mainstream films that were conventional in form and content. The montage film was the exception rather than the rule:

The most popular movie genres of the revolutionary period were the same as the foreign and pre-revolutionary Russian ones: costume drama, action and adventure, literary works adapted for the screen, melodramas, and comedy. Those who patronized them were not merely the *nepmanskaya auditoriya*, that is the bourgeoisie, alleged to be addicted to lurid sex films. Working-class clubs sponsored by the Communist Party also had to show some entertainment films or risk losing their audience.[55]

Soviet audiences also favoured foreign films which were imported in large numbers throughout the 1920s.

But why were the Soviet propaganda films relatively less successful? Why would audiences rather see foreign and conventional Soviet genre films? Were foreign films perceived as being more exciting or exotic? Denise Youngblood, in *Movies for the Masses*, cites an interview conducted in 1929 with a Soviet cinema manager that recorded audience response:

He noted that 'the public watched [Dovzhenko's *Arsenal*] with great difficulty,' and that attendance dropped to 50 percent of normal when his theatre screened *New Babylon*, Kozintsev and Trauberg's famous picture about the Paris Commune. Asked about the reaction to Vertov's *The Man with the Movie Camera*, he replied sarcastically, 'One hardly need say that if *New Babylon* didn't satisfy the spectator's requirements and 'lost' him, then *The Man with the Movie Camera* didn't satisfy him either.'[56]

The problem is clear. The Soviet propaganda films that were intended for the masses, from the illiterate peasant upwards, simply were not being understood by Soviet audiences, whereas the clear hero-led narrative structure of the foreign and Soviet genre films were far more straightforward and appealing. It is well documented that the American version of *Robin Hood* proved more successful in Soviet cinemas on all counts. The film-makers involved in Soviet propaganda production, although committed to the ideals of communism, were also committed to experimenting with film form. The experimentation in this case clearly did not culminate in a popular cinema that appealed to the masses.

THEORETICAL DEBATES: MONTAGE VERSUS REALISM

For further discussion of realism and Bazin, see Chapter 4, p. 106–7.

The montage technique has been widely acknowledged as a powerful means of expression and to many cinema theorists montage is the essence of cinema. The technique, however, does have its opponents, among them the French film critic and theorist André Bazin.[57] Bazin was concerned with the cinema's ability to record 'reality'. He saw in cinema a means of capturing a record of events before the camera with minimum mediation. Bazin regarded the montage cinema of the Soviets (among others) as essentially non-realist because scenes could be manipulated and altered in many different ways. He claimed that the audience of montage cinema was essentially passive,[58] as the director forced the audience towards certain meanings.

Bazin saw montage cinema as being in direct opposition to a style of film-making associated with realism. Realism is a term often associated with the Hollywood cinema, but Bazin used it to refer to a style of film-making adopted by certain film-makers such as Jean Renoir, a French director, who felt that the power of cinema came not from editing, but from *mise en scène*. The realists, unlike the montage film-makers, took great pains to hide the artificial constructed nature of film. The long take, for example, was frequently used as it made editing unnecessary. The use of the long take supported the claim that what was being watched was unmediated and therefore more 'realistic'. Bazin cited further devices that could enhance the 'reality' of a scene, such as the use of deep-focus, wide-angle lenses, the long shot and a highly mobile camera which all meant that the film-maker could preserve real time and space in individual scenes.

POSTSCRIPT TO THE 1920s

The 1930s and after: the decline of experimentation in the Soviet cinema

In the 1930s the Soviet authorities, under the guidance of Stalin, reacted to the unpopularity of many of the Soviet films by issuing strict guidelines on how films should be made. This set of 'rules', essentially demanding hero-led narratives and concerned with realistic subject matter, was termed 'Socialist Realism'. The head of the Soviet film industry outlined why such a policy was necessary in 1933: 'A film and its success are directly linked to the degree of entertainment in the plot ... that is why we are obliged to require our masters [the film-makers] to produce works that have strong plots and are organised around a story-line.'[59]

The policy of 'Socialist Realism' was combined with a complete ban on imported foreign films. By removing these positive representations of capitalism Stalin had also effectively made the Soviet film industry a monopoly; audiences could either see Soviet films or not see any films at all.

The direct interest that the Soviet state took in the film industry reveals its perceived importance, but also had drastic consequences for many of the directors. It was noted by the authorities, for example, that several of these directors were not actually Communist Party members. (This might explain perhaps why they were more interested in form or technique than making positive films about communism that were easy to comprehend.) The film-makers of the 1920s discussed in this chapter were mostly not successful in the 1930s and 1940s. Eisenstein, for example, continued to make films, but the majority were either suppressed or had their funding withdrawn.

However, the decline of montage cinema could possibly be the consequence of another factor: technology. In October 1929 the first Soviet sound films were released and with this advance in cinema technology came the almost immediate downfall of film-making practices that relied on either complex camera movement or rapid editing, as sound cinema initially required non-movable cameras and fixed microphones in order to record dialogue.

The legacy of the Soviet cinema: its influence on modern cinema[60]

The impact of the Soviet films of the 1920s on the analysis of film and film-making itself

For further discussion of realism and documentary film, see Chapter 7, pp. 212–15.

was immediate and continues to this day. The films, however, have not so much provided a model for successive film-makers as been an inspiration for their work. The British Documentary Movement of the 1930s, for example, was influenced by Soviet montage as well as impressed by the idea that films could be a force for education. The film-makers in this movement, however, did not conceive of films having a revolutionary role or even the role of questioning contemporary inequalities. Other film-makers have been inspired by the Soviet cinema because of its rejection of the forms and conventions of the dominant Hollywood entertainment cinema. Jean-Luc Godard, for example, demanded that audiences participate in the construction of meaning in his films and so engage directly with social and political questions. The achievements of Eisenstein continue to impress film editors as well as contemporary film directors. The editor, Ralph Rosenblum, for example, states in his discussion of *Battleship Potemkin* that '[a]lthough the movie is filled with stunning moments, the massacre on the Odessa steps outweighs them all; it remains for editors everywhere the single most intimidating piece of film ever assembled.'[61]

Direct references to Eisenstein's films are numerous, ranging from Bernardo Bertolucci's subtle allusions to *Strike* in his *Tragedy of a Ridiculous Man* (Italy/US 1981) through Brian de Palma's opportunistic reworking of the Odessa Steps sequence in *The Untouchables* (US 1987)[62] to Zbigniew Rybczynski's use of the same sequence in *Steps* (US/UK/Poland 1987)[63] in order to satirise cultural attitudes including the veneration of *Battleship Potemkin* as a work of art.[64] Dovzhenko's influence has not been a direct political one, but the films of Andrei Tarkovsky, at one time a pupil of Dovzhenko, and a film like *My Childhood* by the Scottish film-maker Bill Douglas, exhibit a similar emotional intensity.

NOTES AND REFERENCES

1 Quoted in Yon Barna, *Eisenstein* (Secker & Warburg, London, 1973) p. 102.

2 The term peasants is used to describe those who worked on the land in the country, and the term workers describes those who worked within cities.

3 This was a planned attack by a relatively small force, not a mass uprising as chronicled by Eisenstein in his 1927 film *October*.

4 An unusual account of this period told from the point of view of the White side can be found in Mikhail Bulgakov's 1926 novel, *The White Guard* (available in the UK as a Flamingo paperback).

5 The British Film Institute has released a number of early Russian films on video (in ten volumes).

6 See list of selected Russian films in Further viewing.

7 The history of what happened to the migrant Russian film-makers and stars is an area worthy of study in its own right.

8 Protazanov was not in the Soviet Union for the full duration of this period; he emigrated briefly to Paris in 1920–3.

9 For more information on Protazanov, see Ian Christie and Julian Graffy (eds), *Yakov Protazanov and the Continuity of Russian Cinema* (British Film Institute/NFT, London, 1993). For more information on the Russian cinema, see Jay Leyda, *Kino*, 3rd edn (George Allen & Unwin, London, 1983); and Paolo Usai, Lorenzo Codelli, Carlo Montanaro and David Robinson (eds), *Silent Witnesses* (British Film Institute, London, 1989).

10 The first Russian studio was set up by Drankov in 1907.

11 The first half of 'Soviet Cinema and Ideology: Film as Agent of Change' is by Danny Rivers (Film Studies Lecturer, West Kent College).

12 V.I. Lenin, in *Pravda* (No. 250, 7 November 1919), reprinted in *Lenin: Economics and Politics in the era of the Dictatorship of the Proletariat* (Progress Publishers, Moscow, 1978) p. 3.

13 The context of this remark can be found in Leyda, *Kino*, p. 161.

14 The Museum of the Moving Image (MOMI) has recreated the cinema carriage of an Agit Train complete with commentator, although the Soviet films being shown are from the period 1924–30.

15 Richard Taylor and Ian Christie (eds), *The Film Factory: Russian and Soviet Cinema in Documents, 1896–1939* (Routledge, London, 1988) p. 109.

16 The civil war also resulted in trade barriers being set up which prevented the importation of film stock and cinema equipment into the Soviet Union. This had a dramatic effect on the film industry as the Soviet Union initially had no means of producing its own film stock and lenses.

17 Denise Youngblood, *Movies for the Masses* (Cambridge University Press, Cambridge, 1992) p. 51.

18 *Cinema Journal* (Vol. 11, No. 2, 1972).

19 Vladimir Vladimirovich Mayakovsky (1893–1930).

20 The team effort involved in the production of a feature film would clearly cost a great deal more than an individual artist producing a painting. The Russian film industry, although economically successful, needed to produce films that would appeal to a wide audience. The desire to experiment with film form, when the existing genres were popular, was therefore limited.

21 From Vsevolod Pudovkin, 'Types instead of Actors', in his *Film Technique and Film Acting* (Gollancz, London, 1929).

22 The mansion was in fact the White House.

23 Adapted from Bruce Kawin, *How Movies Work* (Collier Macmillan, London, 1987) pp. 99–101.

24 David Bordwell, *Narration in the Fiction Film* (Routledge, London, 1986). Bordwell uses a technique pioneered by Barry Salt in his article 'Statistical Style Analysis of Motion Pictures', *Film Quarterly* (Vol. 28, No. 2, Winter 1974–5).

25 Quoted by Pudovkin at a lecture given at the London Film School in 1929.

26 The Moscow Arts Theatre under the direction of Konstantin Stanislavski developed a method of acting which required the actor to attempt to 'become' the character.

27 Quoted in Neya Zorkaya, *The Illustrated History of Soviet Cinema* (Hippocrene Books, New York, 1989) p. 52.

28 This can be inferred from the fact that Goskino made thirty-two prints of the film.

29 For fuller details and a chronology of the life of Eisenstein see Bordwell 1993.

30 A well-known Russian playwright (1823–86).

31 David Bordwell, *The Cinema of Eisenstein*, p. 6.

32 The other seven films were never made.

33 Quoted at further length in Leyda's *Kino*, p. 181.

34 Eisenstein bends historical fact in the film as the sailors on board the *Potemkin*, instead of persuading the Russian Fleet to join the struggle, were captured and the mutiny suppressed.

35 The scene has been much copied by recent film-makers: see the section on the 'Legacy of the Soviet cinema: its influence on modern cinema', on pp. 445–6.

36 See Bordwell, *The Cinema of Eisenstein*, p. 74, for an excellent analysis of the sequence.

37 Quotation cited by Leyda in *Kino*, 1983, p. 195. Leyda also points out that the same sequence caused 'an anxious debate in the German Reichstag on the size of the Soviet Navy'.

38 Bordwell, in *The Cinema of Eisenstein*, p. 85, claims that the peacock could be seen as a diegetic image as it forms part of the treasures contained within the Winter Palace. Yuri Tsivian, in 'Eisenstein's *October* and Russian Symbolist Culture' (Christie and Taylor 1993), puts forward the view that 'Eisenstein was hoping to attain the effect of Kerensky entering the peacock's asshole'.

39 Taylor and Christie (eds), *The Film Factory*, p. 182.

40 Quoted in V. Perkins, *Film as Film* (Penguin, London, 1972) p. 21.

41 Ibid., p. 22.

42 Pudovkin's films, like those of Eisenstein, were based on a body of theoretical writing.

43 Quoted by Richard Taylor, *The Politics of the Soviet Cinema, 1917–1929* (Cambridge University Press, Cambridge, 1979) p. 142.

44 Lecture given by Pudovkin at the London Film Society, 1929.

45 The theatre was founded in 1898 by Konstantin Stanislavski and Vladimir Nemirovich-Danchenko.

46 Published in the UK by Penguin (London, 1983).

47 The manifesto was reprinted in 1992 in a limited edition of 500 copies by Aldgate Press, London.

48 Section on Dovzhenko written by Danny Rivers (West Kent College).

49 Youngblood, *Movies for the Masses*, p. 169.

50 Vertov in Russian is derived from the Russian word for 'rotation' and was thus a reflection of his approach to the arts.

51 Quoted in Taylor and Christie (eds), *The Film Factory*, p. 93.

52 Ibid., p. 69.

53 Soviet montage cinema tended to put the stress on the importance of the director (auteur) and work in post-production, rather than scriptwriting and the screenplay. This became a source of dispute in the 1920s when there was greater concern with efficiency and a more elaborate division of labour. See Thompson's 'Early Alternatives to the Hollywood Mode of Production', *Film History: An International Journal* (Vol. 5, No. 4, December 1993).

54 See 'Esfir Shub: A Suitable Case For Treatment', *Historical Journal of Film, Radio and Television* (Vol. 11, No. 2, 1991).

55 Richard Stites, *Russian Popular Culture: Entertainment and Society Since 1900* (Cambridge, Cambridge University Press, 1992) p. 56.

56 Youngblood, *Movies for the Masses*, pp. 18–19.

57 Bazin was also editor of the French film journal *Cahiers du Cinéma*.

58 Eisenstein rigorously opposed this view claiming that the audience for his films played an active part in the text.

59 The head of Sovkino at this time was Boris Shumyatsky. The quotation is taken from Richard Taylor, 'Boris Shumyatsky and the Soviet Cinema in the 1930s: Ideology as Mass Entertainment', *Historical Journal of Film, Radio and Television* (Vol. 6, No.1, 1986) p. 43.

60 This section was written by Danny Rivers (West Kent College).

61 From Ralph Rosenblum and Robert Karen, *When the Shooting Stops...the Cutting Begins: A Film Editor's Story* (Da Capo Press, New York, 1979).

62 A statistical analysis of both scenes in terms of shot length/shot type reveals that they are also very similiar in form.

63 A co-production of KTCA-TV Minneapolis and ZBIG Vision Ltd in association with Channel Four, London.

64 Woody Allen in *Love and Death* (US 1975), also makes reference to this sequence.

FURTHER READING

Key texts

Aumont, J. *Montage Eisenstein* (British Film Institute, London, 1987)

Bordwell, D. *The Cinema of Eisenstein* (Harvard University Press, Cambridge, MA, 1993)

Christie, I. and Taylor, R. (eds) *Eisenstein Rediscovered* (Routledge, London, 1993)

Eisenstein, S. *Notes of a Film Director* (Dover Publications, New York, 1970)

—— *The Film Sense* (Faber & Faber, London, 1986)

(Film scripts of *The Mother*, *Earth* and *Battleship Potemkin* have been published by Simon & Schuster, New York, 1973.)

Kepley, V., Jr *In the Service of the State: The Cinema of Alexander Dovzhenko* (University of Wisconsin Press, Madison, 1986)

Leyda, J. *Kino: A History of the Russian and Soviet Film*, 3rd edn (George Allen & Unwin, London, 1983)

Michelson, A. (ed.) *Kino Eye: The Writings of Dziga Vertov* (University of California Press, Berkeley, 1984)

Taylor, R. *Film Propaganda: Soviet Russia and Nazi Germany* (Croom Helm, London, 1979)

—— *The Politics of the Soviet Cinema, 1917–1929* (Cambridge University Press, Cambridge, 1979)

Taylor, R. and Christie, I. (eds) *The Film Factory: Russian and Soviet Cinema in Documents, 1896–1939* (Routledge, London, 1988)

—— (eds) *Inside the Film Factory: New Approaches to Russian and Soviet Cinema* (Routledge, London, 1991)

Youngblood, D. *Movies for the Masses: Popular Cinema and Soviet Society in the 1920s* (Cambridge University Press, Cambridge, 1992)

Books

Barna, Y. *Eisenstein* (Secker & Warburg, London, 1973)

Barron, S. and Tuchman, M. (eds) *The Avant-Garde in Russia, 1910–1930: New Perspectives* (Los Angeles County Museum of Art, Los Angeles, 1980)

Birkos, A. *Soviet Cinema: Directors and Films* (Archon, Hamden, CT, 1976)

Bordwell, D. *Narration in the Fiction Film* (Routledge & Kegan Paul, London, 1986)

Christie, I. and Gillett, J. (eds) *Futurism/Formalism/FEKS: 'Eccentrism' and Soviet Cinema 1918–1936* (British Film Institute (Film Availability Services), London, 1978)

Christie, I. and Graffy, J. (eds) *Yakov Protazanov and the Continuity of Russian Cinema* (British Film Institute/NFT, London, 1993)

Dickinson, T. and de la Roche, C. *Soviet Cinema* (The Falcon Press, London, 1948)

Goodwin, J. *Eisenstein, Cinema and History* (University of Illinois Press, Urbana and Chicago, 1993)

Kenez, P. *Cinema and Soviet Society, 1917–1953* (Cambridge University Press, Cambridge, 1992)

Lawton, A. *The Red Screen: Politics, Society, Art in Soviet Cinema* (Routledge, London, 1992)

Marshall, H. *Masters of the Soviet Cinema* (Routledge & Kegan Paul, London, 1983)

Petric, V. *Constructivism in Film: The Man with the Movie Camera – A Cinematic Analysis* (Cambridge University Press, Cambridge, 1987)

Rosenblum, R. and Karen, R. *When the Shooting Stops...the Cutting Begins: A Film Editor's Story* (Da Capo Press, New York, 1979)

Schnitzer, J., Schnitzer, L. and Martin, M. (eds) *Cinema in Revolution*, trans. D. Robinson (Secker & Warburg, London, 1973; reprinted by Da Capo Press, New York, 1987)

Stites, R. *Russian Popular Culture: Entertainment and Society Since 1900* (Cambridge University Press, Cambridge, 1992)

Taylor, R. (ed.) *S.M. Eisenstein: Writings 1922–1934 – Selected Works* vol. 1 (British Film Institute, London, 1988)

—— (ed.) *Beyond the Stars: The Memoirs of Sergei Eisenstein – Selected Works* vol. 4 (British Film Institute, London, 1995)

Taylor, R. and Glenny, M. (eds) *S.M. Eisenstein: Towards a Theory of Montage – Selected Works* vol. 2 (British Film Institute, London, 1994)

Tsivian, Y. *Early Cinema in Russia and its Cultural Reception* (Routledge, London, 1994)

Usai, P., Codelli, L., Montanaro, C. and Robinson, D. (eds) *Silent Witnesses: Russian Films 1908–1919* (British Film Institute, London, 1989)

Youngblood, D. *Soviet Cinema in the Silent Era, 1918–1935* (UMI Research Press, Ann Arbor, MI, 1985)

Zorkaya, N. *The Illustrated History of Soviet Cinema* (Hippocrene Books, New York, 1989)

Chapters in books

Bordwell, D. *Narration in the Fiction Film* (Routledge, London, 1990) pp. 234–73.

Cook, P. (ed.) *The Cinema Book* (British Film Institute, London, 1985) pp. 34–6 and 218–19.

Dudley, A. *The Major Film Theories: An Introduction* (Oxford University Press, Oxford, 1976) Chs 3 and 4, pp. 42–101.

Giannetti, L. *Understanding Movies*, 6th edn (Prentice Hall, Englewood Cliffs, NJ, 1993) pp. 135–47 and 373–83.

Giannetti, L. and Eyman, S. *Flashback: A Brief History of Film*, 2nd edn (Prentice Hall, Englewood Cliffs, NJ, 1991) pp. 82–90.

Gomery, D. *Movie History: A Survey* (Wadsworth, Belmont, CA, 1991) pp. 135–60.

Henderson, B. 'Toward a Non-Bourgeois Camera Style', in B. Nichols (ed.) *Movies and Methods* (University of California Press, Berkeley, 1976) pp. 422–38.

Kawin, B. *How Movies Work* (Collier Macmillan, London, 1987) pp. 264–75.

Kenez, P. *The Birth of the Propaganda State: Soviet Methods of Mass Mobilization 1917–1929* (Cambridge University Press, Cambridge, 1985) Ch. 9, pp. 195–219.

Perkins, V. *Film as Film* (Penguin, London, 1972) p. 21.

Robinson, D. *World Cinema 1895–1980* (Methuen, London, 1981) pp. 123–42.

Thompson, K. and Bordwell, D. *Film Art: An Introduction*, 4th edn (McGraw-Hill, New York, 1993) pp. 466–9.

—— *Film History: An Introduction* (McGraw-Hill, New York, 1994) pp. 128–55.

Tudor, A. *Theories of Film* (Viking Press and Secker & Warburg, London, 1973) pp. 25–58.

Articles

Bordwell, D. 'The Idea of Montage in Soviet Art and Film', *Cinema Journal* (Vol. 11, No. 2, 1972)

Christie, I. 'From the Kingdom of Shadows', in the catalogue to *Twilight of the Tsars* (Hayward Gallery, London, 1991)

Hartsough, D. 'Soviet Film Distribution and Exhibition in Germany, 1921–1933', *Historical Journal of Film, Radio and Television* (Vol. 5, No. 2, 1985)

Historical Journal of Film, Radio and Television (Vol. 11, No. 2, 1991) – a special issue centred on new research into Soviet cinema including: Tsivian, Yuri, 'Early Russian Cinema and its Public'; Yangirov, Rashit, 'Soviet Cinema in the Twenties: National Alternatives'; Youngblood, Denise, '"History" on Film'; Yampolsky, Mikhail, 'Reality at Second Hand'; Listov, Viktor, 'Early Soviet Cinema: The Spontaneous and the Planned, 1917–1924'; Roberts, Graham, 'Esfir Shub: A Suitable Case for Treatment'.

Kepley, V., Jr 'The Origins of Soviet Cinema: A Study in Industry Development', *Quarterly Review of Film Studies* (Vol. 10, No. 1, 1985)

Kepley, V., Jr and Kepley, B. 'Foreign Films on Soviet Screens 1922–1931', *Quarterly Review of Film Studies* (Fall 1979)

Screen (Vol. 12, No. 4, Winter 1971–2) – a special issue centred on Soviet film of the 1920s including translations from: LEF, Novy LEF, Brik, Kuleshov, Shklovsky, Vertov, Mayakovsky Film Scenarios.

Stites, R. 'Soviet Movies for the Masses and Historians', *Historical Journal of Film, Radio and Television* (Vol. 11, No. 3, 1991)

Taylor, R. 'Boris Shumyatsky and the Soviet Cinema in the 1930s: Ideology as Mass Entertainment', *Historical Journal of Film, Radio and Television* (Vol. 6, No.1, 1986) p. 43.

Thompson, K. 'Early Alternatives to the Hollywood Mode of Production', *Film History: An International Journal* (Vol. 5, No. 4, December 1993)

 **FURTHER VIEWING**

V = available on video
16mm = available to hire on 16mm
Where neither symbol is listed, the film is not available to buy or rent

Selected Russian films of the 1910s

1908   *Sken'ka Razin*, Drankov (V)
1909   *A Sixteenth-century Russian Wedding*, Goncharov (V)
1910   *The Queen of Spades*, Petr Chardynin (V)
       Rusalka/The Mermaid, Goncharov (V)
       The House in Kolomna, Petr Chardynin (V)
1912   *The Brigand Brothers*, Goncharov (V)
       The Peasants' Lot, Vasilii Goncharov (V)
1913   *Twilight of A Woman's Soul*, Evgeny Bauer
       Merchant Bashkirov's Daughter, Larin (V)
1914   *The Child of the Big City*, Evgeny Bauer (V)
       Silent Witnesses, Evgeny Bauer (V)
1915   *After Death*, Evgeny Bauer
       Daydreams, Evgeny Bauer (V)
       Happiness of Eternal Night, Evgeny Bauer
       Children of the Age, Evgeny Bauer
1916   *The 1002nd Ruse*, Evgeny Bauer (V)
       The Queen of Spades, Yakov Protazanov (V)
       Antosha Ruined by a Corset, Eduard Puchal'ski (V)
       A Life for a Life, Evgeny Bauer (V)
1917   *Satan Triumphant*, Yakov Protazanov
       The King of Paris, Evgeny Bauer
       Grandmother of the Revolution, Svetlov
       The Revolutionary, Evgeny Bauer
       For Luck, Evgeny Bauer (V)
1918   *Jenny the Maid*, Yakov Protazanov
       Still, Sadness, Still, Petr Chardynin
       Little Ellie, Yakov Protazanov

Selected Soviet films of the 1920s–40s

1922–5 *Film-Truth*, Dziga Vertov (a series of newsreels)
1924   *The Extraordinary Adventures of Mr West in the Land of the Bolsheviks*, Lev Kuleshov (16mm)
       Strike, Sergei Eisenstein (V, 16mm)
       Aelita, Yakov Protazanov (16mm)
       Kino-eye, Dziga Vertov
       Cigarette-Girl from Mosselprom, Yuri Zhelyabuzhsky
1925   *Battleship Potemkin*, Sergei Eisenstein (V, 16mm)
       The Death Ray, Lev Kuleshov
1926   *The Mother*, Vsevolod Pudovkin (V, 16mm)
       A Sixth of the World, Dziga Vertov (16mm)
1927   *The End of St. Petersburg*, Vsevolod Pudovkin (V, 16mm)
       October, Sergei Eisenstein (V, 16mm)
       The Fall of the Romanov Dynasty, Esfir Shub (V, 16mm)
       The Great Road, Esfir Shub
1928   *Storm Over Asia*, Vsevolod Pudovkin (V, 16mm)
       The Russia of Nicholas II and Lev Tolstoy, Esfir Shub
1929   *The New Babylon*, Grigori Kozintsev and Leonid Trauberg (V)
       Old and New or *The General Line*, Sergei Eisenstein (V, 16mm)
       The Man with a Movie Camera, Dziga Vertov (16mm)
       Arsenal, Alexander Dovzhenko (V, 16mm)
       Turksib, Victor Turin
       Ranks and People, Yakov Protazanov
1930   *Earth*, Alexander Dovzhenko (V, 16mm)
       Enthusiasm, Dziga Vertov (16mm)
1934   *Chapayev*, Sergei and Georgy Vasiliev (V)
1935   *The Youth of Maxim*, Grigori Kozintsev, and Leonid Trauberg (16mm)
       Aerograd, Alexander Dovzhenko
1936   *We from Krondstadt*, Yefim Dzigan (V)
       Alexander Nevsky, Sergei Eisenstein (16mm)
1945   *Ivan the Terrible: Part I*, Sergei Eisenstein (V, 16mm)
1946   *Ivan the Terrible: Part II*, Sergei Eisenstein (V, 16mm)

RESOURCE CENTRES

Availability of Russian/Soviet films

Soviet/Russian films are easily obtained both on video and for hire on 16mm. Most of the key 1920s Soviet films have been released on video by **Hendring** and can also be hired on 16mm from the BFI at a relatively low cost (on average £25.00 plus delivery). For more information about hiring films see the BFI's films for hire catalogue, *Films on Offer*. A large number of the Russian films of the 1910s are also available (released by the BFI) as a set of ten videos.

http://us.imdb.com/Sections/Countries/SovietUnion
This is the Internet Movie Data Base (US) with a listing of 2,380 Russian films including details of producers, distributors, directors, genres, casts, writers, composers of music, and other titles by which the film is known.

http://www.nd.edu/astrouni/zhiwriter/movies.htm
A Russian cinema/movies website with films, directors, artists, critics, distributors, history, historians and Russian Cinema WWW Server.

Chapter 14

New German Cinema

Julia Knight

■	**Introduction**	452
■	**The American legacy**	452
■	**The development of the film subsidy system**	458
■	**The artisanal mode of production**	461
■	**The quest for alternative images and counter-representations**	463
□	Case study 1: *Yesterday Girl* (1965–66)	463
□	Case study 2: *The American Friend* (1976–77)	474
□	Case study 3: *Germany, Pale Mother* (1979–80)	476
■	**Sponsorship or censorship?**	479
■	**Conclusion**	481
■	**Notes**	482
■	**Further reading**	483
■	**Further viewing**	483
■	**Resource centres**	483

■ New German Cinema

INTRODUCTION

FRG

Before the reunification of Germany in 1990, West Germany was officially known (as the reunified Germany is today) as the Federal Republic of Germany – abbreviated to FRG – while East Germany was called the German Democratic Republic (GDR).

cinéma des auteurs

A term evolved from the *Cahiers du Cinéma*'s approach to the study of French and Hollywood cinema in the 1950s, which attempted to identify directors who brought something personal to their films. It is used to describe particular bodies of film-making which are deemed to be characterised by the distinctive styles and visions of their directors.

art cinema

A term usually applied to films where the director has clearly exercised a high degree of control over the film-making process and thus the films can be viewed as a form of personal expression. This kind of film-making became common in Europe (hence the term, 'European art cinema'), especially from the 1950s onwards, due to the funding structures and nature of the European film industries, which allowed directors greater artistic freedom than was to be found within the US system. In terms of style and content, art cinema is usually characterised by the way it differs from its commercial counterpart,

New German Cinema is the term usually applied to a loose grouping of films that were made in West Germany (**FRG**) during the 1960s, 1970s and early 1980s. Although critics have identified some common elements, these films resist clear generic delineation and can be most easily characterised as a body of work marked by stylistic and thematic diversity. Nevertheless, the New German Cinema was widely heralded as the most promising development in German cinema since German Expressionism, and a handful of its directors – especially Wim Wenders (born 1945), Rainer Werner Fassbinder (1945–82), Werner Herzog (born 1942), and more recently Edgar Reitz (born 1932) – have won international reputations.

In the UK and the US, awareness of the New German Cinema began to grow during the mid-1970s via various magazine and television reports.[1] These early accounts tended to suggest that this new phase in the history of German cinema had been brought into being solely through the endeavours of a small number of talented and dedicated young directors. Consequently many observers focused on the personalities of the new directors, discussing them as creative geniuses, 'artists with something to say' (Eidsvik 1979b: 174), and examined the films almost exclusively in terms of their directors' personal visions. Thus, in the UK and US the New German Cinema was initially discussed predominantly as a ***cinéma des auteurs***. This approach was also adopted in the first major British and American studies of West Germany's new cinema, all of which dealt with no more than six or seven (male) film-makers at most.[2]

To a certain extent this is unsurprising since there is a widespread general acceptance, within mainstream film criticism at least,[3] of the idea of a director as the 'auteur' or 'author' of his or her film – hence we talk about Anthony Minghella's *The English Patient* (1996) or Clint Eastwood's *Absolute Power* (1997), as well as Werner Herzog's *Fitzcarraldo* (1980–1). Furthermore, European cinema in particular has frequently been discussed in this manner since it has been characterised as an **'art' cinema** in order to distinguish it from the more commercially orientated Hollywood product.

However, irrespective of the context, **auteurism** can only ever give us an extremely limited understanding of how and why a particular cinema movement or body of films has come into existence. As the name 'New German Cinema' suggests, the cinema under discussion here is also a **national cinema**, and any consideration of it purely in terms of its directors neglects the specific social, political and economic conditions in West Germany which also helped shape the New German Cinema. This is not to deny that those directors are highly talented, but rather to assert that it is crucial to consider *a range* of factors and issues if we are to achieve a fuller and more adequate understanding of the New German Cinema.[4]

THE AMERICAN LEGACY

West German cinema in the 1950s

For example, it is necessary to examine the way in which the West German film industry developed during the 1950s since this set the essential pre-conditions for the emergence of the New German Cinema. At the end of the Second World War the western Allies felt it was vital to 're-educate' the German people in order both to 'denazify' Germany and to build up the western zones of Germany as a buffer to the Soviet influence in eastern Europe, and American films were quickly identified as an effective way of disseminating western notions of freedom, democracy and capitalist enterprise.[5] Before the American distributors agreed to send their films to the FRG for this purpose, however, they insisted they should be allowed to transfer any profits made in Germany back to America. Since the German market had been closed to America during the war, once this condition had been met, Hollywood had an enormous backlog of films which had already gone into profit and could be made available at prices that undercut any European competitors. This in turn enabled

Hollywood cinema: for instance, a drifting, episodic and open-ended narrative versus the tight cause-and-effect narrative of American cinema with its characteristic closure.

auteurism
A critical approach to the study of film which identifies the director as responsible for whatever the viewer finds of thematic, stylistic or structural interest in a single film or across a body of work by one director.

For further discussion of auteur theory, see Chapter 6.

national cinema
A term commonly used to describe the filmic output of a particular country and to distinguish it from Hollywood film-making. It has also developed as an approach within film studies to explore how films are shaped by nationally prevailing socio-political and economic conditions. This approach to the study of cinema leads on to understanding film as expressing or articulating a sense of national identity. However, defining a national cinema and adopting this approach can be problematic. For instance, rapidly changing national geographies, the increasing trend for pan-European funding for film projects and European co-productions make it increasingly difficult to clearly delineate a single country of origin.

• **Plate 14.1** Wim Wenders (b. 1945)
• **Plate 14.2** Rainer Werner Fassbinder (1945–82)

See Chapter 13 for an analysis of the arrival of the Soviet montage cinema and its attempt to unify the state through film.

See Chapter 2 for discussion of film distribution in the US.

UFA
An abbreviation for Universum Film AG, a large film company initially set up in 1917, consolidated and restructured in the 1920s, and taken over by and centralised under the Nazi regime in the 1930s.

American companies to achieve a position of economic dominance in Germany by the beginning of the 1950s.

The American film industry was keen to protect this lucrative new market. Measures were therefore taken to prevent the imposition of an import quota on American films[6] and American companies remained free to flood the German market with Hollywood films. The Allies also dismantled the remnants of the Nazi film industry which had been centralised and state-controlled through a giant conglomerate, **UFA**. Decartelisation laws were passed which broke up UFA and separated out the various production, distribution and exhibition branches of the industry, and only small independent production companies were licensed. The aim was to permit an indigenous film industry to develop while ensuring it remained on a small scale – making it unable to threaten America's monopoly in the German market.

This pursuit by the Americans of their own political and economic interests had significant consequences for the new West German film industry. As the German industry was forced to remain small-scale, it failed to attract any substantial investment. In countries like the UK and France, American distributors became investors in indigenous film production as their profits had to remain in those countries. But in West

• **Plate 14.3** Werner Herzog (b. 1942)

Germany, as American companies could transfer their profits back to the US, they had little incentive to invest in West German production.

This overall lack of investment meant that German films had to be produced relatively cheaply, making them unable to compete with the expensively produced Hollywood spectacle. As a result, indigenous production was quickly directed towards catering expressly for German audiences and mostly comprised **Heimatfilme** or 'homeland films', which depicted simple country life in a rural Germany, adventure films based on popular German novels, historical films set in imperial Austria, together with romantic adventures and comedies set in picturesque locations. However, this overwhelming orientation towards the home market rendered German films on the whole unsuitable for export. This meant that films had to try and break even on national box-office receipts alone, which ensured production remained low budget and resulted in a national cinema marked by correspondingly low production values. Compared with the Hollywood product, German films looked decidedly provincial and did little for the reputation of West German cinema abroad. Some commentators also noted the cinema's preference for 'escapist' films, and one foreign critic was moved to observe that the 'events of the Thirties and Forties are either ignored or treated as something remote, regrettable, and faintly unmentionable' (quoted in Sandford 1980: 156).

That 1950s German cinema can be characterised by its orientation towards 'escapist' entertainment is hardly surprising. Under the Nazi regime the film industry had been tightly controlled by the Ministry for Propaganda and Popular Enlightenment. Its head, Joseph Goebbels, had quickly identified the propaganda potential of cinema and had informed the industry that he wanted film to be used in support of the new regime. Gradually all film companies came under state control and by 1942 the whole industry had been centralised via UFA. Consequently, for many the cinema had been tainted by Nazism, and this bred a distrust of all but the most innocuous seeming German films.

At the same time, given the traumas and upheaval of the war, followed by the division of Germany which exiled many people from their families and former homes, the 'escapism' of such films proved extremely popular with German audiences, and in fact precipitated a brief boom for the industry during the mid-1950s.

Furthermore, although UFA was dismantled, most of the directors, writers, actors, cameramen and technicians who had worked in the Nazi industry were re-employed after the war. This was partly because those directors who had opposed the Nazi regime – such as Fritz Lang, Billy Wilder, Ernst Lubitsch and Douglas Sirk – had fled the country when the Nazis came to power. But with the escalation of the Cold War, the recruitment of ex-Nazis was also considered preferable to the risk of communist infiltration. Consequently, the new FRG film industry was effectively run by the old UFA generation, limiting any chance of the German cinema experiencing a cultural rebirth in the West after the war.

The fight for survival

There were a few notable exceptions to the general 'escapist' trend,[7] but they could not prevent what became a steady decline in the international standing of West German film. As the 1950s progressed and television gained ground, production figures and box-office receipts also began to decline, and gradually cinemas started to close.

Thus, by the end of the 1950s the Allies' handling of the film industry in Germany had left West German cinema economically vulnerable and artistically impoverished. It had become apparent even in the mid-1950s that, if the German cinema was to survive this American legacy, government intervention would be necessary. Representatives

See Chapter 11 for discussion of Hollywood investment in British films in the 1960s.

Heimatfilme
A German term which can be loosely translated as 'homeland films' and was coined to delineate a film genre which depicted simple country life in a rural Germany.

For further discussion of propaganda in film, see Chapters 7 and 13.

from the industry began to lobby parliament and by the end of the 1950s criticism of West German cinema was being voiced from a number of quarters. In 1959 two young film-makers, Haro Senft and Ferdinand Khittl, campaigned to highlight the need to improve the quality of films and to provide grant aid for film projects. Two years later film critic Joe Hembus condemned the industry's 'factory-like production system where standardised models are turned out on an assembly-line' (quoted in Johnston 1979–80: 72). And in 1961 the organisers of the Venice Film Festival rejected all the FRG entries, while at home the Federal Film Prize given annually by the Federal Ministry of the Interior (**BMI**) went unawarded for best feature film, best director and best screenplay because none were deemed of sufficient quality.

BMI
The Federal Ministry of the Interior which awards the annual Federal Film Prize and was initially responsible for funding the Kuratorium junger deutscher Film.

In 1962 a group of twenty-six film-makers, writers and artists, spearheaded by Alexander Kluge (born 1932) and including Khittl, Senft and Edgar Reitz, added their voices to this escalating condemnation of West German film. They drew up and published the **Oberhausen Manifesto**, in which they argued that given the opportunity they could create a new kind of film which would revive the dying German cinema:

Oberhausen Manifesto
A manifesto drawn up and signed by twenty-six film-makers, writers and artists at the 1962 Oberhausen Film Festival to campaign for access to the means of feature-film production.

The collapse of the conventional German film finally removes the economic justification from a mentality which we reject. The new German film thereby has a chance of coming to life.

In recent years German short films by young authors, directors and producers have received a large number of prizes at international festivals and have won international critical acclaim. These works and their success shows that the future of the German film lies with those who have demonstrated that they speak a new film language.

In Germany, as in other countries, the short film has become a training ground and arena of experimentation for the feature film.

We declare our right to create the new German feature film.

This new film needs new freedoms. Freedom from the usual conventions of the industry. Freedom from the influence of commercial partners. Freedom from the tutelage of other groups with vested interests.

We have concrete ideas about the production of the new German film with regard to its intellectual, formal and economic aspects. We are collectively prepared to take economic risks.

The old film is dead. We believe in the new.

Kuratorium junger deutscher Film
The Board of Young German Film which was the first film subsidy agency, set up by the BMI in 1965. Its brief was and remains to fund first feature films only.

Eventually the government responded to this mounting criticism by setting up the first film subsidy agency, the **Kuratorium junger deutscher Film** (Board of Young German Film). Launched in 1965 by the BMI, the Kuratorium was given a brief to promote the kind of film-making demanded by the Oberhausen Manifesto signatories and to 'stimulate a renewal of the German film in a manner exclusively and directly beneficial to the community' (quoted in Dawson 1981: 16). Kuratorium funding took the form of interest-free production loans for *first* feature films only, which meant that for the first time young, new film-makers who had been unable to gain access to the commercial film industry had a real chance to break into feature film production.

Initially the Kuratorium was very successful in fulfilling its brief. Within two years twenty-five films had been produced with Kuratorium funding. Four of these were the first features of Oberhausen signatories: Alexander Kluge's *Abschied von Gestern* (*Yesterday Girl*, 1965–6), Hans Jürgen Pohland's *Katz und Maus* (*Cat and Mouse*, 1966), Edgar Reitz's *Mahlzeiten* (*Mealtimes*, 1966) and Haro Senft's *Der sanfte Lauf* (*The Gentle Course*, 1967); and a further two were produced by signatory Rob Houwer. In direct contrast to the commercial industry, the contractual arrangements governing the Kuratorium loans allowed film-makers to retain total artistic control, and as a result most of these films broke with the conventions of mainstream cinema, varying from episodic and experimental narratives to highly avant-garde pieces.

Some of these films also enjoyed unprecedented critical acclaim. Kluge's *Yesterday Girl* won several awards, including the Silver Lion at the 1966 Venice Film Festival, while the following year Reitz's *Mealtimes* received the Best First Feature Award. This success also seemed to mark the beginning of a new phase in West German cinema generally. Non-Kuratorium financed films by other new directors were well received at Cannes in 1966, especially Ulrich Schamoni's *Es* (*It*, 1965), Volker Schlöndorff's *Der junge Törless* (*Young Törless*, 1966), and Jean-Marie Straub and Danièle Huillet's *Nicht Versöhnt* (*Not Reconciled*, 1965). Back in Germany Peter Schamoni's *Schonzeit für Füchse* (*Closed Season for Foxes*, 1966) won a Silver Bear at the Berlin Film Festival; and between 1967 and 1969 three Kuratorium films and three further films by new young directors also won Federal Film Prizes.

Not only did these films offer a radical departure from mainstream cinema at a formal level, they also dealt with contemporary concerns in a way that contrasted sharply and refreshingly with the 'escapist' nature of 1950s German cinema. For instance, *It* by Schamoni (born 1939) addressed the question of abortion at a time when it was still illegal in Germany, while *Young Törless* by Schlöndorff (born 1939) used the story – adapted from a Robert Musil novel originally published in 1906 – of a young boy's experience of two fellow pupils at a boarding school torturing a Jewish boy to raise questions about the Nazi past. According to Reitz, 'The press was unbelievably positive. And when the first films came out, there was a degree of public interest which has never been matched since' (quoted in Dawson 1981: 17).

Consequently, the setting up of the Kuratorium and this first batch of critically acclaimed films appeared to many observers to have brought about 'a renewal of the German film' – and this point is often taken to mark the start of what has become known as the New German Cinema. While this may be true in one sense – since that was when the first films were made – the fact that it was possible for those films to be made at all was largely a result of the growing body of criticism that was being directed at West German cinema in the late 1950s and early 1960s. And the origins of this criticism stemmed from the Allies' handling of the film industry after the Second World War, which was motivated by political and economic self-interest.

For a discussion of the British New Wave and its introduction of social realism, see Chapter 11.

• **Plate 14.4** Alexander Kluge (b. 1932)

THE DEVELOPMENT OF THE FILM SUBSIDY SYSTEM

Production funding: problems and solutions

However, this renewal of the German film was almost extremely short-lived. Having made their first feature films, the new directors became ineligible for further Kuratorium funding and were faced with limited possibilities for financing subsequent films. If they had failed to win a Federal Film Prize which carried a cash award for future production work, they had to turn to the diminishing commercial sources. Furthermore, the Kuratorium was dependent on the repayment of its loans from box-office receipts to provide the financing for further film projects. Although the first batch of films had been well received, they did not do well enough in the cinemas to fully repay their loans, leaving the subsidy agency with rapidly diminishing funds.

At the same time the commercial sector viewed Kuratorium-funded films as unfair competition. In a market where it was increasingly difficult to produce films on a commercial basis, young film-makers were being given money to make whatever films they liked. The film industry started to lobby the German government, demanding that any film subsidies should be directed towards revitalising the commercial sector, and was successful in bringing about a more commercially orientated revision of film policy. In December 1967 a new Film Development Act (**FFG**) was passed which raised a levy on every cinema ticket sold in the FRG to provide funding for film production, and the Film Development Board (**FFA**) was set up to administer these funds. In complete contrast to the Kuratorium's promotion of first-time feature film directors, FFA funding was awarded to any film project as long as the producer's *previous* film had grossed a certain amount at the box office during the first two years of its release. Consequently, first-time directors were not eligible for FFA funding, and most of the new films had not done well enough at the box office to trigger the FFA funding mechanism.

As a result, by the beginning of the 1970s Germany's promising new cinema appeared to have almost disappeared. It also quickly became apparent that the FFG was actually failing to stimulate the economic revival of the industry. The retroactive nature of the FFA funding encouraged the production of tried and tested formula films which gave rise to a cinema of 'unparalleled mediocrity' (Phillips 1984: xviii), consisting primarily of sex films and lowbrow classroom comedies. This drove significant segments of the cinema audience away, resulting in further cinema closures.

Ironically, it was television that initially ensured the continuing existence of the new German film. In West Germany there were ten broadcasting companies – nine regional ones which constituted the national network of the first channel (ARD) and the regional networks of the third channel, and Zweites Deutsches Fernsehen (ZDF) which broadcast the second national channel. These were public corporations and produced relatively few programmes themselves, commissioning commercial companies or freelance independents to produce the rest. Consequently, television represented an enormous source of potential funding for the new directors, and by the early 1970s they were increasingly turning to television companies to finance their film projects.

Initially film-makers were commissioned on a fairly arbitrary and ad hoc basis, but in 1974 the role of television within West German cinema was formalised via a **Film and Television Agreement**. This was drawn up between the FFA and the ARD and ZDF television networks, and committed the television corporations to providing DM34 million over a five-year period for film production. Productions funded by this scheme were guaranteed a theatrical release before being broadcast on television, and further funds were given to the FFA to fund the development of film projects.

As the 1970s progressed the film subsidy system was expanded and developed, gradually improving the funding options available. As the shortcomings of the FFG became apparent, the Act underwent successive revisions which, for instance, ensured

FFG
An abbreviation for *Filmförderungsgesetz*, the Film Development Act which was passed in 1967 to raise a levy on every cinema ticket sold in West Germany to provide funding for film production.

FFA
An abbreviation for *Filmförderungsanstalt*, the Film Development Board which was set up to administer the funds raised by the FFG.

To compare to British films' relationship with television, see Chapter 11.

Film and Television Agreement
An agreement made in 1974 between the FFA and the first and second West German television networks which set up a film production fund.

that pornographic and low-quality films could not qualify for subsidies, and permitted the FFA to make discretionary cash awards to 'good entertainment films' which had fulfilled certain audience attendance criteria. The Board also introduced project funding which could be awarded to any project that seemed likely 'to improve the quality and profitability of the German film' (quoted in Pflaum and Prinzler 1983: 99), irrespective of a producer's previous work. In 1977 the *Länder* (states) who had taken over responsibility for the Kuratorium agreed to increase its funding. In the same year the city of Berlin pioneered the idea of regional funding, which was designed both to encourage film-makers to bring work to that region and to promote productions of particular cultural and political interest to the city. Over the next four years Bavaria, Hamburg and North Rhine-Westphalia also introduced regional funding schemes.

Distribution and exhibition

However, it became apparent very early on that if 'a renewal of the German film' was to take place, it was not enough simply to address the production sector: the distribution and exhibition sectors of the industry also needed subsidy support. Since the distribution sector was largely under American control,[8] the new directors had no guarantee that their films would get taken into distribution and hence into cinemas.[9] Thus, as the film subsidy system developed increasing attention was paid to these areas, with the BMI, the FFA and the Kuratorium all channelling some of their funding into distribution and exhibition from 1970 onwards.

See Chapter 2 for a discussion of production, distribution and exhibition in the US and the UK.

For example, in April 1970 the BMI started offering subsidies to cinemas which had screened a so-called 'suitable quota' of 'good' German films. And from December 1976 it introduced awards for companies that had released quality-rated or state subsidised German films.

Kuratorium funding enabled a small production company called Basis-Film to take on the distribution of their first film, *Liebe Mutter, mir geht es gut (Dear Mother, I'm OK,* 1972), when no existing distributor showed any interest in releasing the film. Made by Christian Ziewer (born 1941) and the first in a series of ***Arbeiterfilme*** (worker films), the film is about a mechanic who through losing his job gradually comes to understand the social and political conditions that prevent workers like himself from improving their situation. Filmed in a very detached, static and analytical style, the film proved too demanding for commercial distributors and cinemas. Their experience with this film made Basis recognise the need for a company that specialised in distributing the less commercially orientated, more socially critical films that many of the new young directors were making. They set up their own distribution wing, Basis-Film Verleih, in order to help build up audiences for such films – often among trade union organisations, factories and educational institutions.

Arbeiterfilme
A term used to describe a series of critically acclaimed 'worker films' produced by the television channel WDR in the early 1970s. Made by a predominantly Berlin-based group of film-makers (including Christian Ziewer, Erika Runge, Ingo Kratisch, Marianne Lüdcke and Fassbinder), the films focused on the lives and experiences of the contemporary German working classes.

At the same time a group of thirteen film-makers – among them Wenders and Fassbinder – also took their own initiative and founded Filmverlag der Autoren (Film Publishing House of the Auteurs). Filmverlag was also originally set up as a production company, but it quickly moved into and prioritised distribution. However, in contrast to Basis, Filmverlag identified a need to actively promote the new German films to national and international cinema audiences.

Despite such initiatives few of the films were in fact box-office successes, a fact that elicited some criticism at home. In 1977, for instance, Eckart Schmidt declared: 'Film-makers like Kluge, Herzog, Geissendörfer and Fassbinder, all of whom have collected subsidies more than once, and who despite such public funding are incapable of directing a success, should in future be barred from receiving subsidies' (quoted in Elsaesser 1989: 37). With the dominance of television, the demise of the traditional family audience and the politicisation of the student movement in the late 1960s,

See the discussion of terrorism on p. 467–8.

cinema audiences were highly fragmented: cinema was looked to for both blockbuster spectacles and cult films, as well as for information and education. This, combined with a lack of interest from commercial exhibitors (despite subsidy incentives), the continuing dominance of American distributors and the absence of a film culture in Germany (outside 'centres' like Berlin, Hamburg and Munich), meant that the new German film found it difficult to win a national audience.

A coming of age

Nevertheless, as revisions to the film subsidy system during the 1970s began to substantially improve production opportunities and make some inroads into the distribution and exhibition sectors, the New German Cinema began to reassert itself. By 1977–8 half of the feature films being made were deemed to belong to the new cinema and were winning renewed international acclaim for German cinema. Among those that attracted particular attention were Schlöndorff and Margarethe von Trotta's *Die verlorene Ehre der Katherina Blum* (*The Lost Honour of Katherina Blum*, 1975), Wenders' *Im Lauf der Zeit* (*Kings of the Road*, 1976), *Das zweite Erwachen der Christa Klages* (*The Second Awakening of Christa Klages*, 1977) by von Trotta (born 1942), Fassbinder's *Die Ehe der Maria Braun* (*The Marriage of Maria Braun*, 1978), and Schlöndorff's *Die Blechtrommel* (*The Tin Drum*, 1979). When *The Tin Drum* won the highly coveted American Oscar for the Best Foreign Film in 1980, one British critic was moved to comment that the New German Cinema was 'one of the most remarkable, enduring, and promising developments in the cinema of the 1970s' (Sandford 1980: 6).

Thus, the criticism of the West German cinema in the late 1950s and early 1960s eventually precipitated the development of a whole system of public subsidies which *in turn* facilitated the emergence of a critically acclaimed new cinema by the end of the 1970s. Although the country undoubtedly produced some very talented film-makers, their work would not have been possible without the financial support offered by the various subsidy agencies. And taken together, this complex network of film subsidies can be best understood as a much needed institutional initiative that was designed to promote and develop a national cinema that was both culturally motivated and economically viable.

• **Plate 14.5** Margarethe von Trotta (b. 1942)

• **Plate 14.6** *Die Blechtrommel* (*The Tin Drum*; Volker Schlöndorff, 1979)

THE ARTISANAL MODE OF PRODUCTION

The film subsidy agencies were clearly concerned with promoting the economic revival of German cinema. But in order to stimulate a cinema that was culturally motivated as well, the philosophy behind much of the subsidy system deliberately promoted a mode of production that is more usually associated with the arts, i.e. one that recognises *individual* authorship and creativity. Many of the ideas informing the network of subsidies were most clearly articulated and theorised by Oberhausen Manifesto signatory Alexander Kluge.

In his writings and campaigning work, Kluge developed and promoted the notion of an **Autorenkino**, which roughly translated means 'cinema of auteurs'. Although the German concept of *Autor* differs slightly from the French *auteur*,[10] both terms identify the director as a film's creator and regard a film as an expression of that creator's personality. This approach to cinema was already evident in the Oberhausen Manifesto: since the signatories insisted on freedom from economic and vested interests, they were basically opposing industrial modes of production and demanding the freedom of expression normally associated with 'artistic' production. In subsequent writings, Kluge developed the idea of the director as *Autor* by contrasting the new German film with

Autorenkino
A concept, loosely translated as a 'cinema of authors', promoted by Alexander Kluge while campaigning for the production funding and development of film education necessary to produce a culturally motivated cinema. According to this concept the director is to be regarded as a film's creator and the film can be regarded as an expression of that creator's personality.

what he termed a *Zutatenfilm* (recipe film). The 'recipe film' was a typical industry product, made up of ingredients such as stars, ideas, directors, technicians and scriptwriters which the producer simply went out and purchased according to requirements (Johnston 1979–80: 72). In contrast, the new directors would bring something personal to their films, making the new German film more than just the sum of its parts.

During the 1960s Kluge developed these ideas, together with Edgar Reitz, into a coherent education programme at a private college in Ulm. They developed a course which offered film-makers an all-round film education, familiarising them with all areas of production. Instead of becoming specialists trained in a particular area, such as camera, editing or direction in readiness for an industrial context, students would become *Filmautoren* – that is, directors who exercised a far greater degree of authorial control than industrial production methods normally permitted and who could consequently use film as a medium for personal expression.

See Chapter 6 for discussion of auteur theory.

The lobbying efforts of Kluge and others helped ensure that the concept of an *Autorenkino* informed the framework of the Kuratorium. In his account of its work, Norbert Kückelmann explains that 'according to the fundamental Oberhausen principle the film-maker was to have autonomy in giving shape to his film idea … he was to retain control over the direction and entire production process' (quoted in Knight 1992: 55). Thus the Kuratorium clearly identified the director as a film's author and endeavoured to guarantee his or her independence, implying that film-making is an act of personal expression and hence an art form.

To compare with film production in the US and the UK, see Chapter 2.

However, the institutional sanctioning of the Autorenkino principle was not due solely to the efforts of Kluge and his colleagues. Their campaigning coincided with 'a political will to see film acquire the status of "Kultur"' (Elsaesser 1989: 28) and the desire to use film as a means for promoting German culture as a 'manifestation of national identity' (quoted in ibid.: 29), both at home and abroad. Although the film subsidy system was undeniably shaped by economic considerations, it was equally determined by an institutional belief that just like the fine arts, literature and music, film should also be regarded as an art form. And as the subsidy system evolved most of the agencies identified the director as a film's author.

The concrete result of this was that the contractual arrangements between the funding bodies and directors encouraged film-makers to take on more than just a directorial role, resulting in film-makers often becoming their own scriptwriters and/or producers as well as taking many of the artistic, casting, editing and organisational decisions. Hence, film-makers were not only given institutional recognition as 'artists', but were usually in a position to exercise a large degree of creative control over their films. This, of course, meant that the cinema could be readily discussed as a '*cinéma des auteurs*', which in turn helped obscure the other factors that had contributed to bringing it into existence.

artisanal mode of production
A term used to describe the way in which most New German Cinema films were made with such small budgets and minimal production teams that film-making was considered by some to be more like practising a craft than engaging in a technological process.

At the same time, the subsidy system and the resultant **artisanal mode of production** encouraged the development of a small, team-based 'cottage industry'. Compared to the size of investment normally associated with film production in the commercial sector or even the 'quality' art house cinema, the loans and subsidies granted by the various film promotion agencies were usually extremely small. During the 1970s film-makers were often producing feature films for between DM80,000 and DM200,000 while Italian or French directors might be working with a budget of at least DM800,000. When it was first set up, the *maximum* loan the Kuratorium could offer was DM300,000. As a contemporary writer observed: 'It is like trying to build a Rolls-Royce with money that is just enough to put together a bicycle' (quoted in Elsaesser 1989: 25).

Given the inadequate levels of funding and since the funding agencies actively encouraged film-makers to take on a greater degree of responsibility, directors were more or less forced to work in small teams – without the luxury of, say, a production manager, or extra people for props, costumes and make-up – if they were to realise their projects. However, working in small teams allows the development of much closer collaboration, and film-makers frequently worked with the same people time and again. Wenders often collaborated with writer Peter Handke and cameraman Robby Müller, Fassbinder with actress Hanna Schygulla, and Herzog with editor Beate Mainka-Jellinghaus, while Margarethe von Trotta either co-wrote, co-directed and/or acted in many films made by her then husband Volker Schlöndorff.

Although film-makers argued they needed larger subsidies if they were to produce a 'quality' national cinema, the artisanal and team-based mode of production allowed a far greater degree of experimentation to take place than would have been possible in a conventional commercial context. And this freedom to experiment has, of course, contributed to the enormous stylistic and thematic diversity of the New German Cinema films. But that said, the mode of production – as dictated by the subsidy agencies – nevertheless gave the cinema a clearly identifiable character.

THE QUEST FOR ALTERNATIVE IMAGES AND COUNTER-REPRESENTATIONS

Formal experimentation and contemporary issues

In the early years of the New German Cinema, much of the experimentation that took place was at an extreme formal level. For instance, Straub and Huillet's *Not Reconciled* (1965), which is based on a Heinrich Böll novel entitled *Billiards at Half Past Nine*, completely does away with the book's chronology and instead intermeshes simultaneously the present, the Nazi era and that of the First World War. Indeed, some of the early films have been characterised by the way they seem to operate 'outside any recognisable tradition of film-making either commercial or avant-garde' (Elsaesser 1989: 25). To a certain extent, this kind of experimentation can be viewed as arising out of necessity: small budgets meant it was impossible to make feature films according to the conventions of commercial cinema. Therefore, rather than trying to produce pale imitations, film-makers were forced to try and find completely different ways of working. But as the Oberhausen Manifesto openly declared, many film-makers also *wanted* to break with the 'old cinema' and to develop a new film language in order to inject the German cinema with new life.

See Chapter 4 for discussion of alternatives to mainstream narrative cinema.

Kluge's approach to film-making, for instance, can probably be best described as 'Brechtian' (and his films have also been compared to those of French new wave director Jean-Luc Godard). Like Brecht's epic theatre, Kluge's films are designed to discourage viewers from identifying with the fictional characters, to challenge people's usual forms of perception, and to stimulate a questioning attitude towards their surroundings rather than provide reassurance. This is very evident in his first feature film, *Yesterday Girl* (1965–6).

□ **CASE STUDY 1: *YESTERDAY GIRL* (1965–66)**

This was filmed in black and white and based on the real-life story of a young Jewish woman, Anita G, who comes to West Germany from what was then the GDR (East Germany) in an attempt to make a new life for herself. In a highly episodic and impressionistic narrative, the film follows Anita through a number of unsuccessful jobs, a couple of attempts to steal, and a series of unhappy affairs which end with her becoming pregnant. Unable to support herself, she wanders the streets with her suitcase and finally turns herself over to the police.

In order to break up the narrative, Kluge incorporates intertitles to subdivide the film

• **Plate 14.7** *Abschied von Gestern* (*Yesterday Girl*; Alexander Kluge, 1965–6)

• **Plate 14.7** *Abschied von Gestern* (*Yesterday Girl*; Alexander Kluge, 1965–6)

and comment on events. Verbal commentary, direct address to camera by characters and old photos are also intercut to illustrate and invite reflection upon the narrative sequences. And the events that constitute the narrative are only shown obliquely – we see only the court proceedings against Anita that result from a theft, not the theft itself, nor where it took place or its discovery; we are given only a brief indication that Anita is having an affair, never how or why it started. These filmic devices give the film a very disjointed feel, something that is compounded by the use of music on the soundtrack which is often inappropriate to the visual images it accompanies. This means the viewer has to take a very active role in constructing the film's meaning and can precipitate a more analytical consideration of the issues and ideas raised by *Yesterday Girl*.

Since the filmic devices employed by Kluge discourage us from identifying with Anita as a psychologically-rounded individual, she becomes a powerful signifying element. As a Jew who leaves the GDR, she acts as a reminder both of the Nazi persecution of the Jews and of the communist rejection of capitalism. Thus, through the character of Anita the film links together questions of German history and the contemporary situation of postwar divided Germany, suggesting the inseparability of past and present. Although Anita tries to escape her personal history by moving to West Germany, she fails miserably to make a new life for herself. Just as she would have failed to fit into Nazi Germany and has failed to fit into East Germany, so she fails to integrate into the FRG. In terms of both her past and present, Anita is 'an unwanted outsider' (Sandford 1980: 21) – that is, she cannot escape her past. Her specific situation is, however, peculiarly German, and thus Kluge's film can be understood as a film about Germany, one that suggests that while people may wish to forget the Nazi past, it nevertheless is and will remain an essential precondition of the present socio-political situation.

As is evident from this analysis of *Yesterday Girl*, the desire to develop a new film language extended beyond pure formal experimentation to include questions of content as well. As already discussed, 1950s German cinema had been characterised by its 'escapism', especially in its refusal to address recent history and contemporary concerns. So, for instance, a classic *Heimatfilm* from the mid-1950s, Harald Reinl's *Die Fischerin vom Bodensee* (*The Fisherwoman from Lake Constance*, 1956), shows people living in harmony with their surroundings with no evidence of war damage or postwar reconstruction. For the new generation of film-makers who were all born around the time of the Second World War and grew up in a postwar divided Germany, such films were a blatant denial of the realities of contemporary German life. If there was to be a renewal of German cinema, then its films had necessarily to tackle contemporary issues or demonstrate at least some contemporary relevance.

As the new cinema developed film-makers addressed many issues of contemporary relevance via a number of different styles and genres. Although it is not possible to undertake a comprehensive study here, the films can be characterised as an endeavour to represent a reality that had previously been largely excluded from German cinema – rather than through any shared aesthetic concerns or stylistic similarities – and thus they have been described as 'the quest for alternative images and counter-representations' (Rentschler 1984: 4).

The *Gastarbeiter*

Both Fassbinder and Helma Sanders-Brahms address the presence of **Gastarbeiter** (guest workers) in West Germany in a number of their films: Fassbinder in *Katzelmacher* (1969), *Wildwechsel* (*Wild Game*, 1972) and *Angst essen Seele auf* (*Fear Eats the Soul*, 1973), and Sanders-Brahms in *Die industrielle Reservearmee* (*The Industrial Reserve Army*, 1971) and *Shirins Hochzeit* (*Shirin's Wedding*, 1975).

Gastarbeiter
The term used for the foreign labour that the West German government started to import from Turkey and southern Europe in the 1950s to help sustain its industries.

When the FRG started to enjoy economic prosperity in the 1950s it became necessary to import foreign labour – mostly from Turkey, although also from the former Yugoslavia, Italy and Greece – in order to sustain its industries. These *Gastarbeiter* were regarded by successive German governments as temporary labour and in theory could be sent home if unemployment amongst Germans ever became acute. However, due to the lack of a comprehensively formulated policy, many *Gastarbeiter* remained in West Germany, often establishing their families and raising their children there. Once West Germany's 'economic miracle' began to wane in the 1960s, however, the country was faced with a growing, semi-permanent non-German population who needed education, housing and other resources, but were themselves no longer needed by their host society and thus increasingly prone to racist attack.

The above-mentioned films tackle the *Gastarbeiter* issue in different ways, but they all draw attention to their presence in the FRG. Sanders-Brahms' *Shirin's Wedding*, for example, is the moving story of a young Turkish woman who goes to Germany in search of the man she is betrothed to. By focusing on Shirin's attempts and ultimate inability to survive in the FRG, the film acts as an observation on the meeting of two alien cultures. In contrast, Fassbinder's films are less concerned with exploring the experiences of the *Gastarbeiter* themselves, tending instead to concentrate on exposing the roots of some of the attitudes towards them.

Katzelmacher – a Bavarian term of abuse for immigrant workers – for instance, revolves around a group of directionless young couples who live in a suburban block of flats. With little to interest or motivate them, the arrival of a Greek *Gastarbeiter*, Jorgos, unleashes what critics saw at the time as the Fascist tendencies that were still latent in West German society. As the women gradually become curious about Jorgos it arouses the jealousies of their respective male partners. The situation starts to become antago-

• **Plate 14.8** *Katzelmacher* (Rainer Werner Fassbinder, 1969)

nistic, with the men getting increasingly violent towards 'their' women and eventually beating up Jorgos. A very stylised film, *Katzelmacher* thereby suggests that any perception that the *Gastarbeiter* were unwelcome in West Germany had as much, if not more, to do with attitudes that already existed within German society as with the economic situation that developed after their arrival.

For further study, textually analyse *Shirin's Wedding* to address the following:

1   How is Shirin represented?
2   What effect does life in West Germany have on Shirin?
3   What does the film say about the relationship between German and Turkish cultures?
4   What are the formal characteristics of the film and how do they contribute to the film's meaning?

• **Plate 14.9** *Shirins Hochzeit* (*Shirin's Wedding*; Helma Sanders-Brahms, 1975)

Terrorism

During the 1970s a number of film-makers also turned their attention on the increasing terrorist activity that was disrupting German life. The origins of West German terrorism stem largely from the country's political situation in the late 1960s. In 1966 the FRG's two main political parties had been forced to govern by coalition. The conservative nature of this coalition and the fact that it possessed an overwhelming majority in parliament led to the growth of an extra-parliamentary opposition movement (**APO**). This opposition movement found its most ardent supporters among left-wing students who were disappointed at how little social change had been effected since the end of the war. They were, for instance, extremely critical of the fact that ex-Nazis, such as the then Chancellor, Georg Kiesinger, had been able to attain prominent positions in the

APO
An abbreviation for *außerparlamentarische Oppositionsbewegung*, the extra-parliamentary opposition movement that emerged in Germany in the late 1960s in response to the overwhelmingly conservative nature of the elected parliament. The movement crystallised among left-wing students who were disenchanted with the lack of social change since the end of the Second World War.

new Federal Republic. Student protest of this kind was not confined to Germany, but swept across Europe and America in 1968, opposing in particular America's involvement in Vietnam.

As the 1960s came to a close, however, the student movement in Germany collapsed and a small number of left-wing extremists turned to violence in order to try and bring about concrete changes. Sporadic terrorist acts such as bombings, bank robberies and arson attacks started in 1968. A couple of years later terrorist Andreas Baader met the journalist Ulrike Meinhof, and together they set up the Baader-Meinhof terrorist group which later became known as the **Red Army Faction** (RAF). Although Baader and Meinhof were both arrested in 1972 – together with fellow terrorist Gudrun Ensslin – other RAF members escalated terrorist attacks throughout the 1970s. The government took increasingly repressive action to try and curb the attacks, but largely without success. Events came to a head in Autumn 1977 when, after a spate of terrorist activity involving the kidnapping and killing of prominent industrialist and former Nazi Hans Martin Schleyer, and an airplane hi-jacking, three imprisoned terrorists (Baader, Ensslin and Carl Raspe) were found dead in their prison cells.

Several films were made which directly or indirectly addressed the issues raised by the terrorist activity and the state's response to it. The combined incidents of Autumn 1977 in particular had a profound effect on the new generation of film-makers, and Fassbinder, Kluge, Reitz, Schlöndorff and a few others decided to produce a collectively made film about these events, *Deutschland im Herbst* (*Germany in Autumn*, 1978). Each contributing director made a segment which presented his or her response to the events, and the film is introduced by a short text which states: 'Once atrocity has reached a certain point, it does not matter who committed it, it should just stop.' In his contribution Fassbinder, for instance, reflects on the events in a staged conversation with his mother; Schlöndorff collaborated with writer Heinrich Böll to produce a short drama about the cancellation of a television broadcast of Sophocles' *Antigone* because its themes of violence and resistance would be too inflammatory; while Kluge invented history teacher Gabi Teichert, who uses a spade to literally dig for the roots of German history.

Margarethe von Trotta has also repeatedly returned to terrorist-related themes in her films. In *Die verlorene Ehre der Katherina Blum* (*The Lost Honour of Katherina Blum*, 1975), co-directed with Schlöndorff and based on a Heinrich Böll novel of the same name, she explores what happens to a young woman at the hands of the authorities and the press after she unwittingly becomes involved with a man wanted by the police. Her next feature film, *Das zweite Erwachen der Christa Klages* (*The Second Awakening of Christa Klages*, 1977), is based on the true-life story of a woman who robbed a bank to try and keep open a child-care centre threatened with closure. And the director made *Die bleierne Zeit* (*The German Sisters*, 1981) after she met Christiane Ensslin, the sister of dead terrorist Gudrun Ensslin. The film focuses on the relationship between two sisters, Marianne and Juliane, who are loosely based on the Ensslin sisters. Although we see nothing of Marianne's actual terrorist activities, through the eyes of Juliane we learn how Marianne has left her family to join a terrorist group, is eventually arrested and finally dies in prison. Initially Juliane is unsympathetic to her sister's politics, but on witnessing the inhumane way Marianne is treated in prison and by remembering their childhood together she increasingly comes to understand her sister's actions.

Feminism

The work of Margarethe von Trotta is also part of a vibrant women's cinema that emerged as part of the New German Cinema. In Germany women's film-making was closely connected with the development of the contemporary women's movement, and

Red Army Faction
A West German terrorist group set up by Andreas Baader and Ulrike Meinhof in 1970.

See Chapter 9 for discussion of feminism and films made by women.

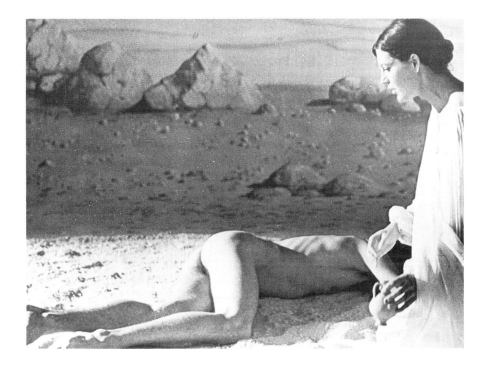

• **Plates 14.10 and 14.11** *Deutschland im Herbst* (*Germany in Autumn*; Fassbinder/ Kluge/Edgar Reitz/Volker Schlöndorff *et al.*, 1978)

• **Plate 14.12** *Das zweite Erwachen der Christa Klages* (*The Second Awakening of Christa Klages*; Margarethe von Trotta, 1977)

the main impetus for the movement came from the student protest movement discussed above. Although the student movement was concerned with bringing about social change, its male leaders failed to acknowledge the oppression of women. Eventually, student film-maker Helke Sander (born 1937) delivered a stinging attack on her male colleagues during the 1968 Socialist German Students Union annual conference, and in the wake of her speech women's groups began to be set up throughout the country to campaign for women's rights. Although it took several years to gain momentum, the growing women's movement gradually raised awareness of such issues as child-care, abortion, violence against women, and discrimination in the workplace.

Some feminist activists also drew attention to the way in which women are so often excluded from the public domain, and thus their stories are rarely told, their experiences rarely acknowledged. Although relatively few women film-makers actively participated in the women's movement, its consciousness-raising aims fostered a new women's cinema that was concerned with representing the authentic experiences of women. The majority of films that made up this cinema explored or were based on the lives of actual women. Several film-makers simply turned their cameras on women in their own circle of friends and acquaintances to produce imaginative and experimental documentaries. For example, in her film *Ein gar und ganz verwahrlostes Mädchen* (*A Thoroughly Demoralised Girl*, 1977) Jutta Brückner (born 1941) documents a day in the life of her friend Rita Rischak and her attempts to improve herself, while Elfi Mikesch (born 1940) made *Ich denke oft an Hawaii* (*I Often Think of Hawaii*, 1978) about her neighbour Ruth, a deserted wife and mother of two. Other films – such as those of von Trotta mentioned above – were based on the documented lives of actual women.

However, some directors turned to their own experiences and produced autobiographical feature films. Among these are Helke Sander's *Die allseitig reduzierte Persönlichkeit – Redupers* (*The All-round Reduced Personality*, 1977), Helma Sanders-Brahms' *Deutschland, bleiche Mutter* (*Germany, Pale Mother*, 1979–80), Jutta Brückner's *Hungerjahre* (*Years of Hunger*, 1980), Jeanine Meerapfel's *Malou* (1980) and Marianne Rosenbaum's *Peppermint Frieden* (*Peppermint Freedom*, 1983). Although

• **Plate 14.13** *Die allseitig reduzierte Persönlichkeit – Redupers* (*The All-round Reduced Personality*; Helke Sander, 1977)

• **Plate 14.14** *Deutschland, bleiche Mutter* (*Germany, Pale Mother*; Helma Sanders-Brahms, 1979–80)

each film adopts a different approach to its subject matter, in many of them the directors look back to their childhoods, their experiences of growing up in the 1950s and the lives of their parents. Others are more contemporary. In *Redupers*, for instance, Sander explores her own experiences of being a working single mother through the fictional character of Edda Chiemnyjewski, a freelance photographer who desperately tries to balance her commitments as a mother with her need to earn a living.

See the case study of The Piano *in Chapter 9, pp. 299–303, for further discussion of mother–daughter relationships in film.*

An important dimension of these films is the desire to put on screen those particular aspects of women's lives that have usually been marginalised by or excluded from mainstream cinema. In the opening scenes of *Redupers*, therefore, we see Edda picking up her young daughter to say goodbye before she leaves for work. The girl clings on to Edda's scarf and refuses to let go. In despair Edda takes off the scarf and rushes out of the flat. This 'tug-of-war' between mother and daughter confronts the viewer with what is so frequently ignored – the difficulties that many women face in trying to combine a career and motherhood.

For further study, textually analyse *The All-round Reduced Personality* to address the following:

1 **What aspects of Edda's life does the film deal with and how are these represented?**
2 **How does the film link Edda's personal situation to the fact of her being German?**
3 **What role does the women's photography project play and how does it comment on the divided city of Berlin?**
4 **What are the formal characteristics of the film and what effect do these have?**

American imperialism and popular culture

A number of other contemporary issues have been addressed within the New German Cinema, but what the cinema has probably become best known for outside Germany has been its exploration of America's role in postwar Germany and its 'remembering' of the Nazi past. As US armed forces took up occupation of West Germany after the war, they brought with them American culture in all shapes and forms. The trappings of American life became so commonplace that film-maker Wim Wenders and others have referred to the 'Americanisation' of West Germany (Sandford 1980: 104). Indeed, in his film *Im Lauf der Zeit* (*Kings of the Road*, 1976) Wenders has one of the characters observe: 'The Yanks have colonised our subconscious.' Initially this seemed to be welcomed by many Germans – when Hollywood films reappeared in the cinemas, for instance, Germans *flocked* to see what they had been missing. Although hardly surprising, Wenders has argued that the reason Germans embraced American culture so readily had more to do with trying to blot out the unpleasant memory of Nazism: 'The need to forget 20 years created a hole, and people tried to cover this ... by assimilating American culture' (quoted in Sandford 1980: 104). But in a postwar *divided* Germany, many Germans also simply lacked any clear sense of what it meant to be German, which compounded the embracing of American culture.

See Chapter 2, pp. 42–3, for discussion of media empires.

Thus, for the new generation of directors who had all grown up in postwar Germany, American culture was very much part of everyday life. Unsurprisingly a number of their films explore the experience of being caught between two cultures. Different film-makers have focused on different aspects of this experience, but several have highlighted the influence of Hollywood cinema by drawing on the conventions of American films while dealing with specifically German subject matter. Fassbinder, for instance, made three films which are all set in the criminal underworld of Munich but which also play with the conventions and plots of the Hollywood gangster genre: *Liebe ist kälter als der Tod* (*Love is Colder Than Death*, 1969), *Götter der Pest* (*Gods of the Plague*, 1970), *Der amerikanische Soldat* (*The American Soldier*, 1970). Later, he also turned his attention to Hollywood melodramas, especially those directed by Douglas Sirk, such as *Written on the Wind* (1956) and *Imitation of Life* (1959). Sirk's films attracted critical praise in the 1970s for the way in which they exposed the underlying tensions present in 1950s American society. During the late 1970s and early 1980s Fassbinder made a number of films, such as *Lili Marleen* (1980) and *Lola* (1981) which drew on the style of Sirk's films and the conventions of melodrama to explore German society.

Although the Americans had been greeted as saviours in 1945, by the time Wenders, Fassbinder and others were starting to make films attitudes towards the American presence in West Germany – particularly among the younger generation – were becoming more ambivalent. As the student movement protested against America's involvement in Vietnam it highlighted what many now began to perceive as America's equally imperialist role in the FRG. This ambivalence towards the 'Americanisation' of West Germany is particularly evident in many of Wenders' films, such as *Der amerikanische Freund* (*The American Friend*, 1976–7).

• **Plate 14.15** *Im Lauf der Zeit* (*Kings of the Road*; Wim Wenders, 1976)

☐ **CASE STUDY 2: *THE AMERICAN FRIEND* (1976–77)**

Based on the Patricia Highsmith novel *Ripley's Game*, the film centres on a friendship that develops between Ripley, a crooked American art-dealer (played by Dennis Hopper) living in Hamburg, and Jonathan, a German picture framer suffering from a terminal illness. When Ripley and Jonathan meet for the first time, Jonathan's clear contempt for him offends Ripley. In retaliation, Ripley suggests Jonathan to a French underworld contact who is looking for an assassin. Initially reluctant, Jonathan is tricked into carrying out two murders in return for a sizeable payment, so that he can leave his family well provided for after his death. His wife, however, wants nothing to do with the money, and due to the stress of his 'adventures' Jonathan dies prematurely.

The ambivalence towards America is expressed narratively in the relationship that develops between Ripley and Jonathan. The latter's dislike of Ripley and his shady dealings results in Ripley tricking Jonathan into thinking his illness is much worse than it is and that he will die in the near future. In order to provide for his family, Jonathan agrees to undertake the two assassinations. This can be read symbolically as signifying an antagonistic relationship between their respective countries. And Ripley's treatment of Jonathan, leading him into a life of crime and to an early death, implies any German dislike of America is totally justified. Other narrative details also suggests a deep mistrust of America's

For further discussion of narrative and mise en scène, see Chapter 4.

• **Plate 14.16** *Der amerikanische Freund* (*The American Friend*; Wim Wenders, 1976–7)

motives for remaining in Europe. Ripley is only in Hamburg in order to use the German art market to circulate forged paintings, and there is a suggestion that the Americans are making money out of the German porn industry. Yet a bond develops between Ripley and Jonathan, to the exclusion of the latter's wife. This is especially evident during the second murder which takes place on a train and with which Ripley unexpectedly helps out. But even when Jonathan eventually finds out why Ripley tricked him he is amused rather than angry and continues to enjoy Ripley's company.

The film also clearly owes much to Hollywood cinema. Ripley dresses, behaves and even talks like the hero from a latter-day Western; in addition to the casting of Dennis Hopper, American directors Samuel Fuller and Nicholas Ray both have cameo roles; and the second murder recalls scenes from two Hitchcock films, *Strangers on a Train* (1951) and *North by Northwest* (1959). All these factors suggest a fascination on Wenders' part with American films. Yet again an ambivalence is apparent. The film makes it clear that both Ripley, as 'a cowboy in Hamburg', and Jonathan, as the reluctant assassin, are acting out roles, roles that are amusing at times, but also ludicrous at others, and that have serious consequences for Jonathan and his family. Thus at a number of levels, the film can be viewed as giving expression to a love–hate relationship with the American role in West German life.

German history

The New German Cinema directors also participated in the country's so-called 'remembering' of its Nazi past. As already mentioned, after the war there had been a desire to forget the Nazi past, and during the 1950s it had simply not been a subject for public discussion. As Margarethe von Trotta has observed: 'We felt that there was a past of which we were guilty as a nation but we weren't told about in school. If you asked questions, you didn't get answers' (quoted in Knight 1992: 141). During the late 1970s, however, for a number of reasons – especially the events of Autumn 1977 and the broadcast of the American television series *Holocaust* on West German television in 1979 – the Germans finally began to 'remember' and deal with their recent history. Unsurprisingly, this act of 'remembering' had an impact on cinema, and by the early 1980s a number of directors had endeavoured to explore the Nazi past in a way that had not been attempted before.

See page 468 for further discussion of Autumn 1977.

Some of the films that have been singled out for attention in this connection are *Hitler – ein Film aus Deutschland* (*Hitler – a Film from Germany*, 1977) by Hans Jürgen Syberberg (born 1935), Rainer Werner Fassbinder's *Die Ehe der Maria Braun* (*The Marriage of Maria Braun*, 1978), Alexander Kluge's *Die Patriotin* (*The Patriot*, 1979), Helma Sanders-Brahms' *Deutschland, bleiche Mutter* (*Germany, Pale Mother*, 1979–80) and Edgar Reitz's sixteen-hour television epic *Heimat* (*Homeland*, 1984). Rather than being about historical events, these stylistically very different films tried to explore how the German people had experienced the Hitler era as a lived reality.

To do this the films tend to concentrate on the telling of personal stories. For instance, Fassbinder's film follows one woman's struggle to survive during the immediate postwar period when her husband at first fails to return from the war and then ends up in prison for murder, while Reitz's *Heimat* traces the lives and fortunes of two families in a small isolated rural village from 1919 to 1982. However, since the films focus on *personal* stories, political events become more of a backdrop to or an intrusive element in people's private lives, or in some cases are virtually excluded. The village in *Heimat*, for instance, seems far removed from the political realities of the twentieth century and, in the episodes that deal with the Nazi era, the persecution of the Jews is barely mentioned. This approach to the representation of German history is particularly evident in the film by Sanders-Brahms (born 1940), *Germany, Pale Mother*.

• **Plate 14.17** *Hitler – ein Film aus Deutschland* (*Hitler – a Film from Germany*; Hans Jürgen Syberberg, 1977)

☐ CASE STUDY 3: *GERMANY, PALE MOTHER* (1979–80)

Filmed using the conventions of art house realism, *Germany, Pale Mother* looks back to the director's own childhood, the lives of her parents and their experiences of the 1950s. Predominantly narrative-based, the film shows her parents (Hans and Lene) meeting in the 1930s, her father's experiences as a drafted soldier during the Second World War, how she and Lene survive on the home front, and the difficulties the family face settling down to a peacetime existence. Unable to adjust to postwar life, Hans becomes increasingly brutal, while Lene develops a facial paralysis and tries to commit suicide.

Although Sanders-Brahms drew on the experiences of other women who lived through the period to develop the film, it is clearly (semi-)autobiographical. Its status as a 'personal story' is also emphasised by the use of an intermittent directorial voiceover.

At the beginning of the film, for instance, the director in voiceover describes her parents' love story as 'happy, perfectly normal', but adds: 'Only it happened at this particular time and in this country.' Although the Nazi regime under which they live is in evidence – via flags, uniformed officers, references to the 'Führer' – it is represented as something in which the young couple have no interest and over which they have no control. Their personal experiences are shaped by historical events but they are not represented as taking part in them.

This is apparent both at the narrative level and in the *mise en scène*. At the narrative level, for instance, the young couple's domestic bliss is torn apart when Hans receives his call-up papers because he is not a party member, while his friend who is a party member is allowed to remain on the home front. In a similar vein, Lene finds herself unable to buy embroidery thread because the local Jewish-owned haberdashery store has been closed down. At the level of the *mise en scène*, an extremely large Nazi flag forms the backdrop at the dance where Hans and Lene meet, but Hans literally only has eyes for Lene and appears oblivious to the political regime under which he lives. Lene's experiences on the home front are also occasionally intercut with archive newsreel footage. The difference in film stock is, however, very noticeable and has the effect of suggesting that Lene is not part of the war. She experiences the effects of war – when, for instance, her house is destroyed in an air raid – but the *mise en scène* positions her as separate from historical events.

• **Plate 14.18** *Die Ehe der Maria Braun* (*The Marriage of Maria Braun*; Rainer Werner Fassbinder, 1978)

• **Plate 14.19** *Heimat*
(*Homeland*; Edgar Reitz,
1984)

For further study, textually analyse *Heimat, Part 1* to address the following:

1   How is the village and community of Schabach represented?
2   Who is represented as not belonging to the community, and how are external elements and foreigners represented?
3   What events outside the Schabach impact on the villagers and how do they experience them?
4   In what ways are the villagers shown as being connected to the outside world?

Helma Sanders-Brahms has stressed she wanted to make a film which dealt with those people like her parents who may not have voted for Hitler, but didn't protest, resist or emigrate either. And the concentration on personal stories to the virtual exclusion of political events means that such films act as a powerful counterbalance to populist representations of German history – such as *Holocaust* – which usually deal *exclusively* with public figures, resistance fighters and the atrocities committed under the Nazi regime. Although such a balance is undoubtedly necessary, and while the films may be a more accurate representation of how many Germans did actually experience Hitler's Third Reich, they conveniently avoid any exploration of who should bear responsibility for the Nazi atrocities. Thus the films have also been viewed as 'revisionist' – that is, it has been suggested that they also attempt to 'rewrite' German history in a manner that is more palatable to the Germans (Kaes 1989: x).

A question of German identity?

As is evident, a consideration of the socio-political context within which the film-makers were working is of crucial importance to an understanding of the films they made. This clearly marks the New German Cinema as a specifically *national* one – that is, one which was shaped at least as much by the nationally prevailing circumstances and conditions as it was by the creative talent of individual film-makers. But the fact that a significant number of the films are effectively exploring the experience of being German in a postwar western society also suggests a deep concern with questions of national identity. Although film and television generally (among other things) help give us or express a sense of national identity, these films are also very much a product of the way in which concerns within West German society shifted during the 1970s from stead-fastly denying the Nazi past, from consuming American culture and allowing others to represent German history for them, to trying to evolve a self-determined German identity.

SPONSORSHIP OR CENSORSHIP?

As the film subsidy system developed, it had quickly become apparent that the new directors were far from free of vested interests. Since the New German Cinema had not achieved wide commercial success, it had remained dependent on public money for its existence. State support may have helped produce an internationally acclaimed cinema, but it had also been responsible for political and artistic censorship.

Although the funding agencies promoted film as an art form, the economic rationale underlying their guidelines often determined whether funds were awarded or not. In 1978 Wilhelm Roth of the FFA Project Commission observed that 'the main discussion that takes place … is always about whether or not the film will be successful at the box-office' (quoted in Knight 1992: 37). Thus, the formal experimentation that characterised many of the early New German Cinema films gradually began to disappear and the cinema became predominantly one of narrative-based feature films.

Projects that addressed politically sensitive issues or were socially critical also often failed to find funding. In 1975, for instance, Fassbinder submitted a proposal to the FFA entitled *Der Müll, die Stadt und der Tod* ('The Garbage, the City and Death'). Based on a Gerhard Zwerenz novel, Fassbinder had originally written it as a play which examined some of the negative aspects of capitalism. However, he was accused of anti-Semitism and the play never staged. The FFA felt that the racist implications persisted in the film project and refused funding. Kluge was even told that he would have to return his subsidy after making *Gelegenheitsarbeit einer Sklavin* (*Occasional Work of a Female Slave*, 1973) because discrepancies were noticed between his original proposal and the finished film. It has been suggested that this was an attempt to censure the film's critical stance on the existing anti-abortion laws (*New German Critique* 1981–2: 23).

Furthermore, representatives of the various political parties in the FRG sat on the boards of all the television corporations and were therefore in a position to exercise censorship powers. In 1980, for instance, members of the right-wing CDU/CSU blacklisted *Der Kandidat* (*The Candidate*), a film about the CSU politician Franz-Josef Strauss made by a group of directors which included Kluge and Schlöndorff. The following year Helga Reidemeister (born 1940) reported that she had received rejections from nine television companies when she was trying to raise funding for a film about Carola Bloch, a Jewish political activist who joined the German Communist Party in the 1930s and lived in East Germany after the war. According to Reidemeister, 'the problem is Carola's past as a CP member, something I can't and don't want to conceal' (in Silberman 1982: 48).

See Chapter 2 for discussion of censorship in the USA and the UK.

Such censorship reached an unprecedented peak in the mid to late 1970s. As terrorist activity had escalated during the 1970s, it resulted in increasing intolerance of dissident viewpoints. Measures were introduced to prevent political extremists from entering the civil service and to prohibit the advocating or approval of criminal deeds in public. And leftist bookshops, printers and news services were subjected to repeated investigations, with arrests and confiscation of material not uncommon. Consequently, by 1977 many people felt West Germany had become a police state in which it was impossible to express oppositional viewpoints.

As a result film funding agencies became even more conservative, avoiding any projects that could be construed as politically radical, controversial or socially critical. This meant that if film-makers wanted to directly address politically sensitive issues such as terrorism they had to seek other sources of funding. And the collectively-made *Germany in Autumn* (1978) was in fact made through private investment.

The effects on state-subsidised film-making were twofold. Firstly, it exacerbated a tendency for German film-makers to draw on literary sources. Since funding agencies demanded that proposals be accompanied by finished scripts, the system already encouraged producers to undertake literature adaptations. However, in 1976–7 political conservatism produced a so-called 'literature adaptation crisis'. In those years there was not only an overwhelming number of literature-based films, but most were adaptations of nineteenth-century classics which appeared to have little or no contemporary relevance.

On the other hand, censorship gave rise to what has been described as a passion for 'oblique approaches and microcosmic case histories' (Dawson 1979: 243). This is particularly evident in such films as von Trotta's *The Second Awakening of Christa Klages* (1977) and *The German Sisters* (1981). Although both films allude to terrorism, they do not overtly examine terrorist politics. Some critics have suggested that the approaches of such films are so oblique that they have little contemporary relevance. According to Charlotte Delormé, 'if *The German Sisters* were really what it purports to be, it would not have received any support, distribution or exhibition' (quoted in Knight 1992: 41). Others, however, have argued that it subtly explores the contemporary social problems and their connections to Germany's past through the experiences of individual protagonists.

Thus, developments during the 1970s appeared to threaten the existence of Germany's new cinema for a second time. Although the apparent crisis had passed by the end of the decade, many film-makers came to view the film subsidy system as something of a mixed blessing. Without doubt it had played an absolutely crucial role in making the New German Cinema possible, but at the same time the subsidy system had limited the scope of that cinema. Not only had the funding agencies promoted one particular mode of production, they had also helped to shape the cinema's narrative-based style and to circumscribe its subject matter.

• **Plate 14.20** *Die bleierne Zeit* (*The German Sisters*; Margarethe von Trotta, 1981)

For further study, textually analyse Margarethe von Trotta's *The German Sisters* to address the following:

1 How are the two sisters, Marianne and Juliane, represented?
2 How does their relationship change during the film?
3 How does the film link the past and the present, and what does it say about the relationship between past and present?
4 To what extent can the film be said to be about terrorism?
5 If the film is not about terrorism, what is it about?

CONCLUSION

By the mid-1980s innumerable critics had pronounced the demise of the New German Cinema. This was partly due to the fact that many of the directors most closely associated with it had moved abroad. Herzog, Schlöndorff, von Trotta, Wenders, Straub and

Huillet had either spent periods working in other countries or emigrated. Furthermore, Fassbinder, who was by far the most prolific of the cinema's directors, had died in 1982.

However, the same year also saw the end of seventeen years of Social Democrat rule, when elections returned the right-wing CDU/CSU union to power. This had far-reaching consequences for the film sector since the ultra-conservative Friedrich Zimmermann became Minister of the Interior. Under his guidance film policy was revised to clearly favour commercial projects over any form of artistic experimentation. Within his own ministry Zimmermann assumed absolute control over how funds were administered, and much of the work that characterised the New German Cinema quickly became a casualty of his approach.

At the same time, the cost of producing films rose so dramatically during the 1980s that national funding initiatives alone were frequently inadequate. As a result film-makers had increasingly to turn to other countries to find co-funding or to apply to the new pan-European agencies to help meet the shortfall. In order to meet the criteria of such funders, however, film projects are often required to demonstrate a broader European appeal. Consequently, it becomes increasingly difficult to view the films funded in such a manner as part of a specifically national cinema.

Thus, just as a set of historically specific circumstances and conditions had brought the New German Cinema into being, another set of historically specific circumstances meant that much of what made the cinema distinctive disappeared. Far from being solely the product of a small number of creative geniuses, the New German Cinema has to be understood as a national and historically specific phenomenon. And in a sense, the reason it was able to establish itself so decisively on the international scene, especially in the UK and the US, is equally historically specific. During the 1970s, the auteurist approach to cinema had gained enormous sway within the field of film studies on both sides of the Atlantic. Since the *Autorenkino* principle informing much of the subsidy system and the cinema's artisanal mode of production meant that the films readily lent themselves to being discussed as the work of creative geniuses, the New German Cinema was easily valued, if inadequately understood, as a '*cinéma des auteurs*'.

See Chapter 13 for a comparison with the Soviet montage cinema of the 1920s.

NOTES

1 In February 1976, for instance, the US magazine *Newsweek* ran an article entitled 'The German Film Renaissance'; a few months later the BBC featured the new cinema in an *Omnibus* report called 'Vigorous Signs of Life'; and by 1978 *Time* magazine described it as 'the liveliest in Europe' (Clarke 1978).

2 See, for instance, *Literature/Film Quarterly* 1979, Sandford 1980, *Wide Angle* 1980, Corrigan 1983, and Franklin 1986.

3 Such as that found in the major daily newspapers, glossy lifestyle magazines and on television film programmes.

4 This chapter will examine some of the key factors that shaped the emergence and form of the New German Cinema. For a more extensive survey (which is beyond the scope of this chapter), see Thomas Elsaesser, *New German Cinema: A History* (Macmillan/BFI, Basingstoke, 1989).

5 In a famous speech Spyros Skouras, head of Twentieth-Century Fox, declared that American films were a potential means of 'indoctrinating people into the free way of life and

instil[ling] in them a compelling desire for freedom' (quoted in Knight 1992: 26).

6 Import quotas were introduced by other European countries after the war as a safeguard to protect their own film industries.

7 Bernard Wicki's *Die Brücke* (*The Bridge*, 1959), for instance, became a classic anti-war film, while Wolfgang Staudte's *Rosen für den Staatsanwalt* (*Roses for the Prosecutor*, 1959) addressed the fact that former Nazi officers had obtained positions of power in the new Federal Republic of Germany.

8 According to Elsaesser (1989: 15), by the early 1970s there was not a single commercial distributor which was not American controlled.

9 According to Rentschler (1984: 46), 'in April 1970 it was reported that nineteen Young German films could not find a distributor'.

10 For a discussion of this difference, see Johnston 1979–80: 67–78.

FURTHER READING

Corrigan, T. *New German Film. The Displaced Image*, revised and expanded edn (Indiana University Press, Bloomington and Indianapolis, 1994)

Elsaesser, T. *New German Cinema: A History* (Macmillan/BFI, Basingstoke:, 1989)

—— *Fassbinder's Germany: History Identity Subject* (Amsterdam University Press, Amsterdam, 1996)

Franklin, J. *New German Cinema* (Columbus, London, 1986)

Frieden, S. *et al.* (eds) *Gender and German Cinema: Feminist Interventions* vols 1 and 2 (Berg, Providence and Oxford, 1993)

Hartnoll, G. and Porter, V. (eds) *Alternative Filmmaking in Television: ZDF – A Helping Hand*, Dossier 14 (BFI, London, 1982)

Kaes, A. *From 'Hitler' to 'Heimat': The Return of History as Film* (Harvard University Press, Cambridge and London, 1989)

Knight, J. *Women and the New German Cinema* (Verso, London and New York, 1992)

McCormick, R. *Politics of the Self* (Princeton University Press, Princeton and Oxford, 1991)

Pflaum, H.G. and Prinzler, H.H. *Cinema in the Federal Republic of Germany*, revised edn (Inter Nationes, Bonn, 1993)

Rentschler, E. *West German Film in the Course of Time* (Redgrave, Bedford Hills, 1984)

—— (ed.) *German Film and Literature: Adaptations and Transformations* (Methuen, New York and London, 1986)

Rentschler, E. and Prinzler, H.H. (eds) *West German Filmmakers on Film* (Holmes & Meier, New York, 1988)

Wenders, W. *Emotion Pictures* (Faber & Faber, London, 1989)

FURTHER VIEWING

Die Artisten in der Zirkuskuppel: Ratlos (*Artists at the Top of the Big Top: Disorientated*; A. Kluge, 1967)

Chronik der Anna Magdalena Bach (*Chronicle of Anna Magdalena Bach*; J.-M. Straub and D. Huillet, 1968)

Die Angst des Tormanns beim Elfmeter (*The Goalie's Fear of the Penalty Kick*; W. Wenders, 1971)

Aguirre, der Zorn Gottes (*Aguirre, Wrath of God*; W. Herzog, 1972)

Die bitteren Tränen der Petra von Kant (*The Bitter Tears of Petra von Kant*; R.W. Fassbinder, 1972)

Ludwig – Requiem für einen jungfräulichen König (*Ludwig – Requiem for a Virgin King*; H.J. Syberberg, 1972)

Strohfeuer (*A Free Woman*; V. Schlöndorff, 1972)

Alice in den Städten (*Alice in the Cities*; W. Wenders, 1973)

Angst essen Seele auf (*Fear Eats the Soul*; R.W. Fassbinder, 1974)

Fontane Effi Briest (*Effi Briest*; R.W. Fassbinder, 1974)

Jeder für sich und Gott gegen alle (*The Enigma of Kaspar Hauser*; W. Herzog, 1974)

Bildnis einer Trinkerin (*Ticket of No Return*; U. Ottinger, 1979)

Die dritte Generation (*The Third Generation*; R.W. Fassbinder, 1979)

Schwestern oder die Balance des Glücks (*Sisters of the Balance of Happiness*; M. von Trotta, 1979)

Der subjektive Faktor (*The Subjective Factor*; H. Sander, 1980)

Die Berührte (*No Mercy No Future*; H. Sanders-Brahms, 1981)

Das Boot (*The Boat*; W. Petersen, 1981)

Stammheim (R. Hauff, 1986)

Himmel über Berlin (*Wings of Desire*; W. Wenders, 1987)

RESOURCE CENTRES

A wide range of New German Cinema films can be hired from Glenbuck Films, British Film Institute, 21 Stephen Street, London, W1P 1PL (tel: 0171 957 8938, fax: 0171 580 5830).

A selection of films by Wenders, Fassbinder and Herzog are also available on video sell-through.

Useful websites include:

http://us.imdb.com

This is the Internet Movie Data Base (US) with a listing of 4,610 German films including details of producers, distributors, directors, genres, casts, writers, composers of the music, and other titles by which the film is known.

http://www.yahoo.com

A website with entries for more than 150 countries and film listings which you can access under Entertainment. It contains genres, film history and film festivals country by country (including Jewish, lesbian and gay, and science fiction).

http://uk.imdb.com/search.html

This is the Internet Movie Data Base (UK) which provides extended searches for German films in the English language using different specified criteria: genre, year, producer, and so on.

http://us.imdb.com/Glossary/

An extensive glossary of movie terms by alphabetical listing.

Glossary

35mm film The measurement of film in millimetres (16mm, 35mm, 70mm) describes the length of the individual film negative frames which are exposed in order to capture an image: the larger the negative, the higher the resolution of the projected image. Larger format film such as 70mm, while superior in quality, is cumbersome to use and comparatively expensive to work with. There are also fewer cinemas able to screen formats other than the now-standard 35mm print.

alternative Alternative cinema is defined with reference to **dominant**: it is an alternative (both economically and formally) to the dominant form. In any study concerning an 'alternative' cinema, the films would not only have to be examined in their own right, but also compared to contemporary dominant **Hollywood cinema**. A number of questions might have to be posed when analysing these alternative films: In what ways is this group of films different to the dominant cinema of the time? What are the possible reasons for the difference: cultural? economic? social? political? Could this 'alternative' way of making films, given the right conditions, have itself turned into the dominant cinema? The **Soviet cinema** of the 1920s, when compared to the Hollywood cinema of the same era, certainly could be regarded as alternative. In other words, it offered a style of film-making that was radically different to the mass of films that was being produced in America.

animation The creation of artificial movement through a variety of techniques. Usually recorded one frame at a time, animation replicates naturalistic movement and creates the illusion of life in objects and images.

anthropomorphism The tendency in **animation** to endow creatures with human attributes, abilities and qualities. This can redefine or merely draw attention to characteristics which are taken for granted in live-action representations of human beings.

APO An abbreviation for *außerparlamentarische Oppositionsbewegung*, the extra-parliamentary opposition movement that emerged in West Germany in the late 1960s in response to the overwhelmingly conservative nature of the elected parliament. The movement crystallised among left-wing students who were disenchanted with the lack of social change since the end of the Second World War.

Arbeiterfilme A term used to describe a series of critically acclaimed 'worker films' produced by the television channel WDR in West Germany in the early 1970s. Made by a predominantly Berlin-based group of film-makers (including Christian Ziewer, Erika Runge, Ingo Kratisch, Marianne Lüdcke and Fassbinder), the films focused on the lives and experiences of the contemporary German working classes.

art cinema A term usually applied to films where the director has clearly exercised a high degree of control over the film-making process and thus the films can be viewed as a form of personal expression. This kind of film-making became common in Europe (hence the term, 'European art cinema'), especially from the 1950s onwards, due to the funding structures and nature of the European film industries, which allowed directors greater artistic freedom than was to be found within the US system. In terms of style and content, art cinema is usually characterised by the way it differs from its commercial counterpart, **Hollywood cinema**: for instance, a drifting, episodic and open-ended narrative versus the tight cause-and-effect narrative of American cinema with its characteristic closure.

art-house A crude shorthand way of referring to films in which artistic ambition and intellectual challenge are more important than the simple motive to provide entertainment. 'Great' art-house directors such as Bergman and Godard are unquestionably considered to be **auteurs**.

artisanal mode of production A term used to describe the way in which most New German Cinema films were made with such small budgets and minimal production teams that film-making was considered by some to be more like practising a craft than engaging in a technological process.

associative mode Approach to **documentary** which attempts to use footage in such a way as to provide the maximum degree of symbolic or metaphorical meaning on top of the literal information available in the image.

auteurism A critical approach to the study of film which identifies the director as responsible for whatever the viewer finds of thematic, stylistic or structural interest in a single film or across a body of work by one director. See also *Autorenkino* and *cinéma des auteurs*.

Autorenkino A concept, loosely translated as a 'cinema of authors', promoted by Alexander Kluge while campaigning for the production funding and development of film education necessary to produce a culturally motivated cinema in Germany. According to this concept the director is to be regarded as a film's creator and the film can be regarded as an expression of that creator's personality.

avant-garde Literally the 'advanced guard' of experimental film-makers who reject the dominant forms of mainstream cinema in favour of innovation and experiment in film-making, often producing non-narrative, non-illusionistic, sometimes abstract films. Avant-garde film is often self-conscious and frequently makes use of devices such as cuts to the camera crew, talking to the camera and scratching on film.

background plates An optical process whereby foreground elements are placed over background artwork, CGI elements or models.

bhava The eight basic emotions in Indian cinema – love, humour, energy, anger, fear, grief, disgust, astonishment.

binary analysis An approach which derives from cultural anthropology and particularly the work of Claude Levi-Strauss. The study of binary opposites is a useful means of identifying structures at work in, for instance, the genre of a film.

bio-pic A film which dramatises the biography of a real or imaginary person. It is usually characterised by a linear narrative. Examples of musical bio-pics range from *The Glenn Miller Story* (Mann, 1954) to *The Doors* (Stone, 1991).

blue screen A process that involves the subject being filmed in front of a blue screen. Optical manipulation of this footage creates imagery of the actor against a black background. Additionally, the actor's silhouette is set against a clear background. Using these two elements as **mattes** it is possible to place the action into any scene required.

BMI The Federal Ministry of the Interior in Germany which awards the annual Federal Film Prize and was initially responsible for funding the **Kuratorium junger deutscher Film**.

'Bollywood' Bombay, the film capital of India.

bricolage The putting together of features from different genres and styles, self-consciously and usually playfully. This is one of the principal characteristics of **postmodernism**.

butch Description of behaviour-patterns – such as aggression, sexual dominance – traditionally associated with masculinity.

camp A critical attitude which involves looking at texts less as reflections of reality than as constructed sets of words, images and sounds at a distance from reality. The attitude often involves irony or detachment when considering this distance.

carnivalesque Term which refers to an atmosphere or attitude, found at carnivals and similar events, characterised by laughter, excess and vulgarity. Seen as a lower-class resistance to the refined tastes of the dominant (upper and middle) classes.

cinema apparatus The power of cinema as a system of communication, controlling and holding the spectator in place.

cinéma des auteurs A term evolved from the *Cahiers du Cinéma*'s approach to the study of French and Hollywood cinema in the 1950s, which attempted to identify directors who brought something personal to their films. It is used to describe particular bodies of film-making which are deemed to be characterised by the distinctive styles and visions of their directors. See also **auteurism**.

cinéma-vérité A phrase often coupled with the concept of 'direct cinema'. Literally 'cinema truth', vérité emerged out of the film-making practices of Jean Rouch in France. Based on Vertov's approach, it acknowledged the impact of the film-making process upon the recording of 'actuality', and more readily recognised the subjectivity of the film-maker in securing filmic evidence of what took place. Rouch essentially suggests that the documentary form must be defined through the integrity and purpose of its author. The value and purpose of 'actuality' footage in regard to its delineation of documentary 'truth' is therefore in direct relationship to the intention of those who produce it.

Cinéorama A large circular structure with a tower in the centre, in which the audience stood. A number of lanterns situated below the audience projected images outwards onto the huge curved screen.

close-up Normally defined as a shot of the head from the neck up.

condensation The compression of a set of narrative or aesthetic agendas within a minimal structural framework. Essentially, achieving the maximum amount of suggested information and implication from the minimum amount of imagery used.

consent decree A court order made with the consent of both parties – the defendant and the plaintiff – which puts to rest the law suit brought against the former by the latter.

conventions Conventions are established procedures within a particular form which are identifiable by both the producer and the reader. The implication of the idea of conventions is that a form does not naturally mean anything, but it is an agreement between producer and user.

deconstruction All media 'texts' are constructed. To understand all the components within each construction it is necessary to deconstruct the text and analyse all its elements. For example, the cartoon is made up of a number of specific aspects which define it as a unique cinematic practice i.e. its frame-by-frame construction; its modes of representation and so on.

dialectical A difficult term to define, as it has many different meanings. The *Collins English Dictionary* (2nd edn, 1986), for example, defines it a 'disputation or debate, esp. intended to resolve differences between two views rather than to establish one of them as true'. The crucial factor to grasp in the context of Eisenstein's thinking, however, is the notion of change and the creation of a new order. Eisenstein would have defined dialectic with reference to **Marxist** philosophy, which believed that society was contradictory and in need of change.

diegetic The elements of a film that originate from directly within the film's narrative. For example, a popular song that is being played on the soundtrack would be diegetic if it was clear that it was coming from a source within the world of the film such as a car radio. See also **non-diegetic**.

Diorama A circular building housing translucent paintings where, through the manipulation of shutters and screens, the transformation of the various scenes was effected.

direct cinema American documentarists of the 1960s and 1970s believed that the advent of light, portable, technically sophisticated camera equipment enabled a breakthrough in the ways that documentary film-making could reveal personal and social 'truth'. The fact that the documentarist could literally film anywhere under any conditions meant that a greater intimacy could be achieved with the subject, heightening the sense that 'reality' was being directly observed, and that the viewer was party to the seemingly unmediated immediacy of the experience. Less controlled, unscripted, apparently spontaneous, the look and feel of 'direct cinema' arguably demonstrated a less deliberately authored approach.

discourse systems A discourse is a mode of speech which has evolved to express the shared human activities of a community of people. Film studies has, like other academic disciplines, developed its own langauge – its own discourse system – to make possible the identificaiton and 'mapping' of that area of human activity and experience with which it is concerned.

Disney dust The term given to the glitter and sparkle that usually accompanies any form of magic or unearthly effect such as the glowing dust trail left by the flying Tinkerbell in Disney's *Peter Pan* (1953) and again in *Hook* (1991).

distribution Division of the film industry concentrating on the marketing of film, connecting the producer with the exhibitor by leasing films from the former and renting them to the latter.

documentary A non-fiction text using 'actuality' footage, which may include the live recording of events and relevant research material (i.e. interviews, statistics etc.). This kind of text is usually informed by a particular point of view, and seeks to address a particular social issue which is related to and potentially affects the audience.

dominant Refers to both economic strength and also to the dominant form or convention, which is **realism**: dominant cinema in film studies is assumed to be **Hollywood**.

drama-documentary   Any format which attempts to re-create historical or typical events using performers, whether actors or not.

dystopia   A world of the future where everything has gone wrong.

economic presentation   All the components are designed to help us read the narrative. An examination of the first few minutes of almost any mainstream fictional film will reveal a considerable amount of information about characters, their social situation and their motivation.

embourgeoisement   A sociological term describing the adoption of middle-class (bourgeois) values and attributes by members of the working class as a result of increased affluence.

establishing shot   A shot using distant framing, allowing the viewer to see the spatial relations between characters and the set.

exclusive run   Where a film is only screened in one movie theatre.

exhibition   Division of the film industry concentrating on the public screening of film.

exposition   The use of voiceover or direct-to-camera address by a figure who is essentially directing the viewer in the reception of information and argument.

fade and mixes   Where one image fades from view to be replaced by a separate image. When this is done with two images simultaneously the effect is known as a 'mix' or a 'dissolve'.

Fauvism   Fauvism literally means 'wild-beastism', and describes the vivid colours and distorted forms in the paintings of artists like Henri Matisse and André Derain, which emerged as part of the first modern art movement at the turn of the century.

feminism   This is based on the belief that we live in a society where women are still unequal to men; that women have lower status than men and have less power, particularly economic power. Feminists argue that the media reinforces the status quo by representing a narrow range of images of women; for instance, woman as carer, as passive object, as an object of desire. Many feminists now argue that the range of representations for both male and female is limited and slow to change. In recent years feminism has become fragmented and it is difficult to argue that feminism is a complete area of study; but gender and power relations in society can be seen as central to feminist thinking.

femme   Description of behaviour-patterns – such as gentleness, sexual passivity, concern with dress and appearance – traditionally associated with femininity.

FFA   An abbreviation for *Filmförderungsanstalt*, the Film Development Board which was set up in West Germany to administer the funds raised by the FFG.

FFG   An abbreviation for *Filmförderungsgesetz*, the Film Development Act which was passed in 1967 to raise a levy on every cinema ticket sold in West Germany to provide funding for film production.

fight composer   Individual who choreographs spectacular fights in Indian movies.

Film and Television Agreement   An agreement made in 1974 between the FFA and the first and second West German television networks which set up a film production fund.

film noir   A term developed by French film critics in the postwar period to describe a number of films produced in the 1940s. It has subsequently become a marketing device used to describe films with some of the lighting and narrative conventions of the period.

first-run   Important movie theatres would show films immediately upon their theatrical release (or their 'first-run'). Smaller, local theatres would show films on subsequent runs, hence the terms second run, third run etc.

flocking routine software   In simple terms this is a computer program whereby the movement of a single designated computer element, for instance an animated bird, influences and determines the nature of movement of a selected group of elements. Animation of the primary element is followed by the subordinate objects. An elaborate form of this process was used to achieve the cavalry charge sequence in Disney's *Mulan* (1998).

fly-on-the-wall   A term associated with a style of documentary film-making which attempts to present events as though the presence of the camera and film crew had not influenced them in any way.

foley stage   Named after the sound editor Jack Foley, the foley stage is a sound recording room equipped with a screen and the necessary items for the creation of sound effects.

free publicity   Free coverage of subjects the media feel newsworthy.

FRG   Before the reunification of Germany in 1990, West Germany was officially known (as the reunified Germany is today) as the Federal Republic of Germany – abbreviated to FRG – while East Germany was called the German Democratic Republic (GDR).

gamelan   An ensemble of musicians playing tuned percussion instruments – mostly gongs, drums, cymbals and metallophones (similar to a xylophone but with metal bars instead of wooden ones).

Gastarbeiter   The term used for the foreign labour that the West German government started to import from Turkey and southern Europe in the 1950s to help sustain its industries.

gay   A description of strong, positive sexual love and attraction between members of the same sex, used by extension to describe cultural products, such as film and video, concerned with similar themes. Mainly referring to males, it can also be used for any person.

gender   A name for the social and cultural construction of a person's sex and sexuality. Gender, sex and sexuality can overlap but are by no means an exact match. It is this 'mismatch' which has generated a fascinating body of film production and criticism.

go-motion   A refinement of **stop motion**. Animated puppets are controlled with motorised rods. Their actions are determined by computer which permits a predetermined amount of motion during the film's exposure. The result is a slight blurring of the image, eliminating the somewhat stiff action associated with traditional model animation.

gramophone   A device similar to the **phonograph**. Initial models utilised wax-covered cardboard cylinders, though later ones used hard rubber disks pressed from a metal master disk. Models were fitted with a sound horn to enhance volume.

hegemony   A set of ideas, attitudes or practices becomes so dominant that we forget they are rooted in choice and the exercise of power. They appear to be 'common sense' because they are so ingrained, any alternative seems 'odd' or potentially threatening by comparison. Hegemony is the **ideological** made invisible.

   In relation to the development of cinema, it can be seen how **Hollywood** developed hegemonic status and power. The Hollywood form of genre-based narrative realist film is considered a 'common sense' use of the medium. Other forms of cinema, by comparison, are more or less 'odd'. In looking at the early history of cinema we can begin to understand how and why Hollywood assumed this position.

Heimatfilme A German term which can be loosely translated as 'homeland films' and was coined to delineate a film genre which depicted simple country life in a rural Germany.

heterosexual A word used to name and describe a person whose main sexual feelings are for people of the opposite sex.

high angle A shot from a camera held above characters or object, looking down at them.

Hollywood cinema In classical Hollywood cinema, the editing is designed to be 'invisible'. It is intended to allow the audience closer views and to see the point of view of different characters. The editing is used essentially to clarify what is taking place in the narrative. This type of editing had become dominant in Hollywood film-making by approximately 1920.

hommage The French word for an act of paying homage, sincere respect.

homoerotic A description of a text – prose, poem, film, painting, photograph etc. – conveying an enjoyable sense of same-sex attraction.

homophobia Irrational prejudice and hatred against a person because of their **homosexuality**.

homosexual A word used to name and describe a person whose main sexual feelings are for people of the same sex. Mainly, but not exclusively, used in reference to males.

iconic The iconic is defined by the dominant signs that signify a particular person or object – Chaplin, for example, would be defined by a bowler hat, a moustache, a cane and some old boots; Hitler would be defined by a short parted hairstyle and a small 'postage stamp' moustache.

iconoclasts Documentarists committed to challenging the received construction and meanings of images, partially through the critique of those images, and mainly through the reconfiguration of imagery in a subjective style.

iconography The visual codes of setting, props and clothing which enable us to recognise a film as belonging to a certain genre or type.

identification The process of identification allows us to place ourselves in the position of particular characters, either throughout or at specific moments in a movie. The devices involved include subjectivity of viewpoint (we see the world through their eyes, a shared knowledge, we know what and only what they know), and a sharing in their moral world, largely through narrative construction.

ideological function Ideology is the system of ideas, values and beliefs held by individuals or groups within society. Ideological function refers to the way in which ideology is disseminated through films or other cultural forms. Audiences may of course refuse to accept the dominant ideological meaning in a film.

ideological Although a complex issue, ideology may be seen as the dominant set of ideas and values which inform any one society or culture, but which are imbued in its social behaviour and representative texts at a level that is not necessarily obvious or conscious. There are two key definitions of this term, one provided by the nineteenth-century German philosopher, Karl Marx, the other by the twentieth-century French Marxist philosopher, Louis Althusser, drawing on Marx's original ideas. For Marx, ideology was the dominant set of beliefs and values existent within society, which sustained power relations. For Althusser, ideology consisted of the representations and images which reflect society's view of 'reality'. Ideology thus refers to 'the myths that a society lives by'. An ideological stance is normally politicised and historically determined.

illustrative mode Approach to **documentary** which attempts to directly illustrate what the commentary/voiceover is saying.

IMR The Institutional Mode of Representation is a broad categorisation of systems of film form and narrative characterising mainstream cinema from around 1915 onwards. It was perceived as replacing the Primitive Mode of Representation (a set of conventions used in early film between 1895 and 1905) as a gradual process in the first twenty years of cinema.

incoherent cinema Influenced by the 'Incoherents', artists working between 1883 and 1891, a movement principally led by Cohl. This kind of animation was often surreal, anarchistic and playful, relating seemingly unrelated forms and events in an often irrational and spontaneous fashion. Lines tumble into shapes and figures in temporary scenarios before evolving into other images.

independent cinema This is a highly problematic term but may be usefully divided into two areas. First, independent mainstream production which aims to compete with the big studios, although without any large financial backing finds it difficult to survive. Palace Films was one such casualty; the success of *The Crying Game* came too late to save its demise. Second, the term is used to describe film-making outside the mainstream sector, for instance, film workshops, **avant-garde** film, feminist film. The boundaries between these two areas are not always clear and may overlap.

Internet A system of interlinking computers in a world wide network (WWW/World Wide Web). Since the Internet was privatised in April 1995 the rise in monthly traffic on the Net has been such that it represents a hundredfold increase in less than three years.

intertextuality This refers to the ways in which a (film) text refers to other films, either explicitly or implicitly, and thereby triggers ideas and associations which might enrich our response.

juxtaposition In film studies, this usually refers to two different shots that have been joined together to make a contrast.

kinetograph Edison's first movie camera.

Kuratorium junger deutscher Film The Board of Young German Film which was the first film subsidy agency, set up by the BMI in 1965. Its brief was and remains to fund first feature films only.

lesbian A word used to name and describe a woman whose main sexual feelings are for other women. Coined as a medical term in the late nineteenth century, the word has been invested post-Stonewall with new ideas of openness and liberation. It can also be used to describe cultural products, such as film and video, dealing with lesbian themes.

liberal humanist A political perspective in which the emphasis is placed upon an openness of democratic discourse and a multiplicity of perspectives which directly relate to the actual experiences of people and the fundamental principles relating to what it is to be 'human'.

low-key image Light from a single source producing light and shade.

magic lantern A projection system comprised of a light source and a lens, used to project an image. Usually oil-lamp fired, though many were later converted to electricity. Earliest known use was by Athanasius Kircher, recorded in a work published in 1646.

mainstream Feature-length narrative films created for entertainment and profit.

Mainstream is usually associated with '**Hollywood**', regardless of where the film is made.

Marxist theory Argues that those who have the means of production have control in a capitalist society. The dominant class have control of the means of production and have an interest in perpetuating the dominant **ideology**. More recently exponents of Althusserian Marxism, particularly post-1968, have argued that mainstream narrative cinema reinforces the capitalist system and that a revolutionary cinema is needed to challenge the dominant ideology.

'*masala* movie' Spicy Indian movie overloaded with emotion.

match-move Shots that have separate elements within them that need to be accurately matched, frame by frame. Usually involves live action elements being coupled to animation or effects elements.

mattes Opaque images that mask out certain areas of the film negative. Subsequent passes through the camera allow the initial matted-out space to be exposed with another image.

mediation A key concept in film and media theory, it implies that there are always structures, whether human or technological, between an object and the viewer, involving inevitably a partial and selective view.

merchandising Where manufacturers pay a film company to use a film title or image on their products.

metamorphosis The ability for a figure, object, shape or form to relinquish its seemingly fixed properties and mutate into an alternative model. This transformation is literally enacted within the animated film, and acts as a model by which the process of change becomes part of the narrative of the film. A form starts as one thing and ends up as something different.

mise en scène A theatrical term usually translated as 'staging' or 'what has been put into the scene'. In film, *mise en scène* refers not only to sets, costumes, props and position of actors, but also to how the scene is organised, lit and framed for the camera. *Mise en scène* is one way of producing meaning in films which can be both straightforward and extremely complex, depending upon the intentions and skill of the director (the *metteur en scène*).

modernist A term used to describe early twentieth-century developments in art, literature, music, film and theatre which rejected **realism** as the dominant tradition in the arts. Modernist art is characterised by experiment and innovation, and modernist artists, because of their **avant-garde** practices, inevitably constitute a cultural élite.

montage From the French word meaning 'to edit', montage means the assembling of bits of footage to form a whole. In film studies it usually refers to the style of fast editing adopted by the **Soviet** film-makers of the 1920s.

Moore's law 'The capacity of processing power of computers doubles every 18 months': this 'law' is named after Gordon E. Moore, the co-founder of Intel, who first described it.

multiple exposures A number of exposures being made on a single frame of film. This usually entails the film being rewound in the camera for subsequent passes and further exposures. Multiple exposures are normally made with the assistance of **mattes**.

multiple run Where a film is shown simultaneously at a number of screens.

myth A key term within media and cultural studies: a myth is something which is not true but which is repeated so frequently that it becomes part of the '**reality**' of the people who share it. In some instances it can become part of a culture's 'common sense'. Myth is a means by which the **ideology** of a culture takes form.

narrative The idea that films have a primary function of telling a story.

national cinema A term commonly used to describe the filmic output of a particular country and to distinguish it from **Hollywood** film-making. It has also developed as an approach within film studies to explore how films are shaped by nationally prevailing socio-political and economic conditions. This approach to the study of cinema leads on to understanding film as expressing or articulating a sense of national identity. However, defining a national cinema and adopting this approach can be problematic. For instance, rapidly changing national geographies, the increasing trend for pan-European funding for film projects and European co-productions make it increasingly difficult to clearly delineate a single country of origin.

noise In the film industry, it refers to any barrier to successful communication.

non-diegetic Refers to any element that remains outside the world of the film, such as voiceovers, credits and mood-setting music, that does not originate from the world of the film.

NRA (National Recovery Administration) programme 1930s government programme designed to rescue the US economy from the Great Depression (commonly known as the 'New Deal').

Oberhausen Manifesto A manifesto drawn up and signed by twenty-six German film-makers, writers and artists at the 1962 Oberhausen Film Festival to campaign for access to the means of feature-film production.

oligopoly Where a state of limited competition exists between a small group of producers or sellers.

overheard exchange The recording of seemingly spontaneous dialogue between two or more participants engaged in conversation/observation.

paid advertising Promotion on TV, radio, billboards, and printed media.

Panorama Created by the painter Robert Barker, the Panorama was first exhibited in 1788. It consisted of a huge cylindrical building fitted out with a 360° painting.

patent pool An association of companies, operating collectively in the marketplace by pooling the patents held by each individual company.

patriarchal society A society in which it is men who have power and control. Women are generally disadvantaged and have lower status.

persistence of vision The phenomenon of persistence of vision is due to the momentary retention of an image on the eye's retina. This retention was found to be approximately one-tenth of a second by Chevalier d'Arcy in 1765 when he successfully carried out one of the first systematic scientific studies and presented his findings to the French Académie des Sciences.

personality/character animation Many cartoons and more sophisticated adult animated films, for example, Japanese *anime*, are still dominated by 'character' or 'personality' animation, which prioritises exaggerated and sometimes caricatured expressions of human traits in order to direct attention to the detail of gesture and the range of human emotion and experience. This kind of animation is related to identifiable aspects of the real world and does not readily correspond with more abstract uses of the animated medium.

Phenakistoscope Invented by the Belgian physicist, Joseph Plateau, in 1832, this is an optical device consisting of a disk with slots cut into its edge. When rotated, images on one side can be viewed with the aid of a mirror. The resulting stroboscopic images give the illusion of movement.

phonograph A mechanical sound-recording device utilising a brass cylinder covered with metal foil. As the cylinder was rotated, vibrations of the sound being recorded would cause a metal stylus to score grooves in the foil. These same grooves would provide the information through which the original recording could be reproduced through ear tubes.

pink triangle A symbol originally worn by **homosexual** prisoners in Nazi concentration camps which was later taken up by **lesbian** and **gay** people as a reminder of past oppression and an icon of liberation.

pixillation The frame-by-frame recording of deliberately staged live action movement to create the illusion of movement impossible to achieve by naturalistic means, i.e. figures spinning in mid-air or skating across grass. This can also be achieved by particular ways of editing material.

play-back Pre-recording of songs with good singers and with non-singing actors lip-synchronising on screen.

pluralistic Multiple; refers in this instance to the fragmentation of society into different ethnic, social and cultural groups.

polysemic Having many meanings – a polysemic text is likely to be less stable, more hotly contested by different sections of an audience.

post-Impressionism After the Impressionist movement had determined pictorialness in a spirit of the felt experience of a context or place, the post-Impressionists re-imposed a more defined sense of structure which was still subject to a sense of dream-like softness and distortion.

postmodern A term used to describe many aspects of contemporary cultural production of the 1980s and 1990s. Among its many characteristics are an eclectic borrowing from earlier styles (see **bricolage**), an emphasis on stylish surface appearances rather than social realism or psychological depth, and a blurring of the dividing line between cultural forms, products and tastes, such as the division between 'high culture' and 'popular culture'.

post-structuralism The critical movement away from an emphasis on the film text and the 'machinery' of cinema to an emphasis on the spectator's decoding of the text in order to create meaning. This represents a rejection of some aspects of the deterministic **Marxist**/Freudian theories at the heart of structuralism while still recognising that the spectator is himself or herself 'determined' by a range of factors (compare with **structuralism**).

Praxinoscope Invented by the Frenchman Emile Raynaud in 1878, the device was a more advanced and sophisticated version of the **Zoetrope**. Utilising mirrors and its own discrete light source, this was the forerunner of Raynaud's spectacular and charming, though ultimately short-lived, Théatre Optique.

proactive observationalism Documentary film-making in which specific choices are made about what material is to be recorded in relation to the previous observation of the camera operator/director.

production Division of the film industry concentrating on the making of film.

propaganda The systematic construction of a text in which the **ideological** principles of a political stance are promoted, endorsed and made attractive to the viewer in order to influence the viewer's beliefs and preferences. Such a text may often include critical and exploitative ideas and imagery about oppositional stances. 'Point of view' in these texts is wholly informed by political bias and a specificity of intention to persuade the viewer of the intrinsic 'rightness' of the authorial position.

proto-animation Early live-action cinema demonstrated certain techniques which preceded their conscious use as a method in creating **animation**. This is largely with regard to **stop-motion**, mixed media and the use of dissolves to create the illusion of metamorphosis in early **trick films**.

psychoanalytic theory Based on the theories of Freud and, more recently, Lacan. Feminists argue that aspects of psychoanalysis are questionable because they are based on patriarchal assumptions that woman is inferior to man. Freud found female sexuality difficult and disturbing. Lacan argues that the mother is seen as lacking by the child because she has no phallus. Uncertainty about the role of the female in psychoanalytic theory has been picked up on by a number of feminists such as Mulvey, De Lauretis and Modleski, who question the inevitability of Freud and Lacan's theories which emphasise the importance of the phallus, penis envy and patriarchal supremacy.

pyrotechnics The description given to effects involving the use of fire, fireworks and explosives.

queer Originally a negative term for (mainly male) **homosexuals**, this word has been recently reappropriated by critics, artists and audiences to describe a challenging range of critical work and cultural production among **lesbians** and **gays**, with an emphasis on diversity of race, nationality and cultural experience.

rasa In India, the eight sentiments which correspond to the emotions – erotic, comic, heroic, furious, apprehensive, compassionate, horrific, marvellous.

reactive observationalism Documentary film-making in which the material recorded is filmed as spontaneously as possible subject to the immediacy of observation by the camera operator/director.

reading a film Although films are viewed and heard, the concept of 'reading' a film implies an active process of making sense of what we are experiencing.

realism or reality The concept of the 'real' is problematic in cinema, and is generally used in two different ways:

First, the extent to which a film attempts to mimic reality so that a fictional film can appear indistinguishable from documentary.

Second, the film can establish its own world and can, by consistently using the same conventions, establish the credibility of this world. In this later sense a science-fiction film such as *RoboCop* can be as realistic as a film set in a contemporary and recognisable world such as *Sleepless in Seattle*.

With regard to **animation**, the animated form in itself most readily accommodates 'the fantastic', but Disney preferred to create a hyper-realism which located his characters in plausibly 'real' worlds which also included fantasy elements in the narrative.

reappropriation The process whereby a previously oppressed group takes a negative term and turns it around to invest it with new meanings of power and liberation. Examples include 'black', 'virago' and '**queer**'.

Red Army Faction A West German terrorist group set up by Andreas Baader and Ulrike Meinhof in 1970.

reduced animation Animation may be literally the movement of one line which, in operating through time and space, may take on characteristics which an audience may perceive as expressive and symbolic. This form of minimalism constitutes reduced animation, which takes as its premise 'less is more'. Literally an eye movement or the shift of a body posture becomes enough to connote a particular feeling or meaning. This enables the films to work in a mode which has an intensity of suggestion.

reflexive/performative documentary   Documentary which is much more subjective and self-reflexive in its construction, foregrounding the arbitrariness and relativity of 'objectivity', '**reality**' and 'truth'.

representation   The media *re*-presents information to its audience, who are encouraged by the mainstream media to see its output as a 'window on the world', as reflecting reality. Yet the process of representing information is highly complex and highly selective. Many feminists argue that the way notions of gender are represented by the media perpetuates and reinforces the values of **patriarchal society**; for instance, men tend to take on strong, active roles, while women are shown as passive and relying on their attractiveness. There are exceptions to such narrow stereotyping, the 'strong' woman shown by Ripley in the *Alien* trilogy and the two heroines in *Thelma and Louise* could be seen as positive, although rather more cynically they could be seen merely as 'role reversal' films and thus as having purely novelty value. Representations often make use of **stereotypes** because they are a shorthand, quick and easy way of using information. It could be argued that the media production process encourages the use of stereotypes because of the pressure of time and budget. Many feminists point out that because so few women hold key positions in the media hierarchies representations of women are bound to be from a male perspective.

Russian cinema   The body of films made in Tsarist Russia between 1907 and 1919.

sangeeta   Combination of song, instrumental music and dance.

saturation run   Where a film is shown simultaneously at an enormous number of screens (usually a minimum of 1,000 in the US/Canadian market), accompanied by heavy media promotion.

scopophilia   Freudian term meaning the 'pleasure in looking', introduced to film analysis by Laura Mulvey.

sex   A word used to denote and describe a person's physical type according to their genital make-up. In academic discourse, this is primarily a scientific term.

sexuality   A name for the sexual feelings and behaviour of a person. When applied to groups of people (e.g. **heterosexuals**) ideas of social attitude and organisation are implied.

social realism   A form of **realism** which tries to capture in a 'truthful' way the lives of industrial working-class communities. Also known as 'working-class realism' and often used in relation to the 'new wave' films of late 1950s/early 1960s British cinema.

song picturisation   Filming of a song-and-dance routine.

Soviet cinema   Films made in the Soviet Union between October 1920 and 1991, although for the purposes of the chapter in this book most Soviet films discussed will be confined to the 1920s.

spectator   The individual responding to a film, as distinct from the collective response of an audience. Spectator study concentrates on the consumption of films that are 'popular' and are geared towards providing typical forms of cinematic pleasure – spectacle, emotion, plot, resolution – with conventional narrative and generic forms.

squash and stretch   Many cartoon characters are constructed in a way that resembles a set of malleable and attached circles that may be elongated or compressed to achieve an effect of dynamic movement. When animators 'squash and stretch' these circles they effectively create the physical space of the character and a particular design structure within the overall pattern of the film. Interestingly, early Disney shorts had characters based on 'ropes' rather than circles and this significantly changes the look of the films.

Steadicam A technical development from the late 1970s which permits the use of a camera held by hand which walks with the action, but with the steadiness of a camera moving on rails.

stereotyping A quick and easy way of labelling or categorising the world around us and making it understandable. Stereotypes are learned but are by no means fixed, yet are often resistant to change. They tend to restrict our understanding of the world and perpetuate beliefs that are often untrue or narrow. For instance, the concept that only thin women are attractive is a stereotype promoted by much of the media in the late twentieth century (though there are some exceptions like comediennes Dawn French and Roseanne); yet in other eras the opposite has been true. Stereotyping is not always negative, but tends to be very much concerned with preserving and perpetuating power relations in society. It is in the interests of those in power to continue to stereotype those with lower status in a negative light, thus preserving the status quo.

stop motion An animation technique whereby a 3D model is filmed a single frame at a time, the model being moved by the animator between exposures.

structuralism This was founded on the belief that the study of society could be scientifically based and that there are structures in society that follow certain patterns or rules. Initially, most interest was centred on the use of language; Saussure, the founder of linguistics, argued that language was essential in communicating the **ideology**, the beliefs, of a culture. Structuralists have applied these theories to film, which uses both visual and verbal communication, and pointed out that the text conveys an illusion of **reality**, so conveying the ideology of a society even more effectively.

substitution technique An early **trick film** technique used by George Méliès. It involved one object being filmed, the camera being stopped during filming and the object being replaced by a second object before filming recommenced. This was the basis of his famous vanishing lady effect, used in many of his films.

surplus of meaning Meaning in excess of what is required to fulfil the functional requirements of the narrative; a 'surplus' will include ambiguity, complexity rather than clarity and simplicity.

suspending disbelief This refers to the ability a person has when engaging with a constructed object – film, play, novel – to repress their knowledge that the object is in fact just a 'construct', and respond to it as though it is real.

symbolism The means by which a film-maker can assign additional meanings to objects/characters in a film. For example, in Dovzhenko's *Earth* and Eisenstein's *Old and New*, the tractor is a symbol of progress.

symmetry Direct balance of imagery in the composition of the frame using parallel or mirrored forms.

synecdoche The idea that a 'part' of a person, an object, a machine, etc. can be used to represent the 'whole', and work as an emotive or suggestive shorthand for the viewer, who invests the 'part' with symbolic associations.

synergy strategy Combined or related action by a group of individuals or corporations towards a common goal, the combined effect of which exceeds the sum of the individual efforts.

Technicolor The first successful Technicolor process was introduced in 1922. This involved the use of a two-colour camera with a beam splitter, which recorded red and green images of the scene. The three-colour Technicolor process developed in 1929 used three separate negatives. However this was replaced in 1932 by a prism beam splitter.

testimony The recording of solicited observation, opinion or information by witnesses, experts or other relevant participants in relation to the **documentary** subject. The primary purpose of the interview.

'Thatcherism' A political ideology named after Margaret Thatcher, Conservative prime minister from 1979–90, involving a free-market approach to politics and economics which rewarded individual enterprise over and above communal welfare. Led to a huge rise in unemployment and a widening of social divisions between the 'haves' and the 'have nots' in Britain in the 1980s.

Thaumatrope Attributed to the London physician Dr John Ayrton, this was first made in Paris in 1826. It consists of a disk of card on either side of which are printed two separate images, such as a bird and a cage. With the use of twisted threads attached to opposite edges of the disk, a spinning motion is achieved which enables both images to be viewed simultaneously due to the phenomenon of **persistence of vision**.

THX A designation of sound reproduction quality in cinemas. The standards established necessitate the installation and maintenance of sound equipment to the specifications and according to the guidelines laid down by Lucasfilm Limited.

tie-ins Mutually beneficial promotional liaisons between films and other consumer products and/or personalities.

trick film The generic term for the development of cinematic special effects using such techniques as **mattes**, **multiple exposures**, **proto-animation** and **substitution techniques**. Generally attributed to the pioneering French film-maker George Méliès.

trust A group of companies operating together to control the market for a commodity. This is illegal practice in the US.

UFA An abbreviation for Universum Film AG, a large film company initially set up in Germany in 1917, consolidated and restructured in the 1920s, and taken over by and centralised under the Nazi regime in the 1930s.

'uses and gratifications' A specific approach to the study of audiences. It considers how individuals and groups may consume a film or some other media product to satisfy their particular needs.

vaudeville A type of variety entertainment popular in the early part of the twentieth century, chiefly in the US, consisting of short acts such as song and dance routines, acrobats and animal acts.

vertical integration Where a company is organised so that it oversees a product from the planning/development stage, through production, through market distribution, through to the end-user – the retail consumer. In the case of the film industry, this translates to a company controlling **production**, **distribution** and **exhibition** of its films.

Vitaphone A synchronised sound system based on the use of **gramophone** disks. This system could be fitted to any make of projector and was relatively easy to use, unlike earlier systems such as the cinematophone and the cinephone.

wire frame Three-dimensional shapes, with neither surface colour nor texture, illustrated through a pattern of interconnecting lines, literally a framework of 'wires' on a two dimensional surface – the computer screen.

wire removal The process of digitally removing any unwanted elements within a shot, such as a support for an animated object, puppet or prop. Used in the flying motorbike shot in *Terminator 2*.

Zoetrope The forerunner of the **Praxinoscope**, this consists of a drum with vertical slots cut into the top edge. As the drum is rotated, the images on the inner surfaces, when viewed through the slots, achieve the same illusion of movement as with the **Phenakistoscope**.

zoom A technique whereby the image appears to advance towards or recedes away from the viewer.

Bibliography

For those chapters not listed in this bibliography, please see Notes and Further Reading at the end of each chapter.

CHAPTER 2: CINEMA AS INSTITUTION

Algate, A. and Richards, J. *Britain Can Take It* (Basil Blackwell, London, 1986)

R. Allen and Gomery, D. *Film History: Theory and Practice* (Newbery Award Records, New York, 1985)

Altman, R. (ed.) *Genre: The Musical* (BFI/Routledge & Kegan Paul, London, 1981)

Andrew, N. 'The Censors Who Are Fighting a Losing Battle', *The Financial Times* (5 September 1993)

Austin, B. *Immediate Seating: A Look at Movie Audiences* (Wadsworth Publishing Company, Belmont, California, 1989)

Balio, T. (ed.) *The American Film Industry* (University of Wisconsin Press, Madison, 1976)

—— (ed.) *Hollywood in the Age of Television* (Unwin Hyman, Boston, 1990)

Barr, C. (ed.) *All Our Yesterdays* (British Film Institute, London, 1986)

British Board of Film Classification *A Student's Guide to Film Classification and Censorship in Britain*

—— *Memorandum on the Work of the British Board of Film Classification*

Bernstein, I. *Hollywood at the Crossroads: An Economic Study of the Motion Picture Industry* (Hollywood Film Council, LA, 1957)

Biskind, P. 'Going For Broke', *Sight and Sound* (October 1991)

Bordwell, D., Staiger, J. and Thompson, K. *The Classical Hollywood Cinema* (Routledge & Kegan Paul, London, 1985)

Campbell, R. 'Warner Bros. in the 1930s: Some Tentative Notes', *The Velvet Light Trap* (No. 1, June 1971)

Champlin, C. 'What Will H. Hays Begat', *American Film* (Vol. 6, No. 1, October 1980)

Christie, I. (ed.) *Powell Pressburger and Others* (British Film Institute, London, 1978)

Daly, D. *A Comparison of Exhibition and Distribution Patterns in 3 Recent Feature Motion Pictures* (Arno Press, New York, 1980)

Deschner, D. 'Anton Grot: Warners Art Director 1927–1948', *The Velvet Light Trap* (Vol. 15, 1975)

'Dialogue on Film', an interview with Richard Zanuck and David Brown, *American Film* (Vol. 1, No. 1, October 1975)

Dibie, J. *Aid for Cinematographic and Audio-Visual Production in Europe* (John Libbey & Company, London, 1993)

Dickinson, M. and Street, S. *Cinema and State* (British Film Institute, London, 1985)

Docherty, D. Morrison, D. and Tracey, M. *The Last Picture Show?* (British Film Institute, London, 1987)

Eckert, C. 'The Carole Lombard in Macy's Window', *Quarterly Review of Film Studies* (Vol. 3, No. 1, 1978) pp. 1–12

Elsaesser, T. (ed.) *Early Cinema* (British Film Institute, London, 1990)

Falcon, R. *Classified! A Teacher's Guide to Film and Video Censorship and Classification* (British Film Institute, London, 1994)

Finney, A. *The Egos Have Landed* (Mandarin, London, 1997)

Fleming, M. and Klady, L. '"Crying" All the Way to the Bank', in *Variety* (22 March 1993)

Giles, J. *The Crying Game* (BFI Publishing, London, 1997)

Gomery, D. *The Hollywood Studio System* (Macmillan Publishers, London, 1986)

—— *Shared Pleasures* (British Film Institute, London, 1992)

Gottlieb, C. *The Jaws Log* (Dell Publishing, New York, 1975)

Handel, L. *Hollywood Looks at its Audience* (University of Illinois Press, Urbana, 1950)

Hardy, P. (ed.) *Raoul Walsh* (Edinburgh Film Festival, 1974)

Jowett, G. and Linton, J. *Movies as Mass Communication* (Sage Publications, Newbury Park, California, 1989)

Kent, N. *Naked Hollywood* (BBC Books, London, 1991)

Koenig, P. 'Steve's World, and Our Own', *The Independent on Sunday* (21 February 1993)

Leff, L. and Simmons, J. *The Dame in the Kimono* (Grove Weidenfeld, New York, 1990)

Perry, N. 'Will Sony Make it in Hollywood', *Fortune* (9 September 1991)

Robertson, J. *The British Board of Film Censors: Film Censorship in Britain, 1896–1950* (Croom Helm, Kent, 1985)

Roddick, N. *A New Deal in Entertainment* (British Film Institute, London, 1983)

Sheinfeld, L. 'The Big Chill', *Film Comment* (Vol. 22, No. 3, May/June 1986)

Squire, J. (ed.) *The Movie Business Book* (Columbus Books, Bromley, Kent, 1986)

Stevenson, W. 'Film Jackpot Solves Nothing', in *The Daily Telegraph* (15 May 1997)

Taylor, C. 'Marks the Spot', *Sight and Sound* (Vol. 60, No. 1, Winter 1990/1)

Wall, I. *et al. Film Industry Pack* (Film Education, London, 1997)

Woolley, S. 'Last Palace Picture Show', in *The Guardian* (30 October 1992)

CHAPTER 6: GENRE, STAR AND AUTEUR – CRITICAL APPROACHES TO HOLLYWOOD CINEMA

Overview

Belton, J. *American Cinema/American Culture* (McGraw Hill, New York, 1994)

Collins, J., Radner, H., Preacher, A. and Collins, S. (eds) *Film Theory Goes to the Movies* (AFI/Routledge, New York, 1993) – see particularly ch. 4, Dudley Andrews, 'The Unauthorized Auteur Today' and ch. 16, Jim Collins 'Genericity in the Nineties'.

Maltby, R. and Craven, I. *Hollywood Cinema* (Blackwell, Oxford, 1995)

Four books which provide excellent contextual accounts of the studio system and the 'new' Hollywood are:

Hillier, J. *The New Hollywood* (Studio Vista, London, 1993)

Neal, S. and Smith, M. (eds) *Contemporary Hollywood Cinema* (Routledge, London, 1998)

Ray, R.B. *A Certain Tendency of Hollywood Cinema, 1930–1980* (Princeton University Press, Princeton, NJ, 1985)

Schatz, T. *The Genius of the System: Hollywood Filmmaking in the Studio System* (Pantheon, New York, 1988)

Strongly recommended as an introduction to the theories referred to in this chapter is a book focusing not on film but on television:

Fiske, J. *Television Culture* (Routledge, London, 1987)

A very much less theoretical book which communicates the conventions and formulae of popular cinema 'construction' is:

Vogler, C. *The Writer's Journey – Mythic Structures for Storytellers and Screenwriters* (Boxtree, London, 1996)

Other well-known books which offer a theoretical overview of the principal topics of this chapter include:

Cook, P. (ed.) *The Cinema Book* (BFI, London, 1986)

Hill, J. and Church Gibson, P. (eds) *The Oxford Guide to Film Studies* (Oxford University Press, 1998)

Hollows, J. and Jancovich, M. (eds) *Approaches to Popular Film* (Manchester University Press, Manchester, 1995)

Fiske, J. *Television Culture* (Routledge, London, 1987)

Lapsley, R. and Westlake, M. *Film Theory: An Introduction* (Manchester University Press, Manchester, 1988)

Turner, G. *Film as Social Practice*, 2nd edn (Routledge, London, 1993)

A very good example of the kind of study which takes the study of Hollywood cinema from textual to cultural analysis is:

Traube, E.G. *Dreaming Identities: Class, Gender and Generation in 1980's Hollywood Movies* (Westview Press, Boulder, CO, 1992)

Structuralism and semiotics
Useful introductions:
Fiske, J. *Introduction to Communication Studies*, 2nd edn (Routledge, London, 1990) Chs 3–7
Morgan, J. and Welton, P. *See What I Mean – An Introduction to Visual Communication* (Edward Arnold, London, 1986) Ch. 3

For more advanced discussion see:
Gaines, J. (ed.) *Classical Hollywood Narrative: The Paradigm Wars* (Duke University Press, Durham, NC, 1992)
Stam, R., Burgoyne, R. and Flitterman-Lewis, S. *New Vocabularies in Film Semiotics* (Routledge, London, 1992)
Wollen, P. *Signs and Meaning in the Cinema* (Secker & Warburg, London, 1972)

And for an eloquent (and sometimes persuasive) rejection of much of the standard film theory of the last twenty-five years:
Carroll, N. *Mystifying Movies* (Columbia University Press, New York, 1988)

Genre
Altman, R. (ed.) *Genre – The Musical* (Routledge, London, 1981) – see particularly Richard Dyer, 'Entertainment and Utopia'.
—— *The American Film Musical* (BFI, London, 1989)
Cawelti, J.G. *Adventure, Mystery and Romance* (University of Chicago Press, Chicago, IL, 1976)
Feuer, J. *The Hollywood Musical*, 2nd edn (Macmillan, London, 1993)
Kitses, J. *Horizons West: Studies of Authorship Within the Western* (Thames & Hudson, London, 1969)
McConnell, F. *Storytelling and Mythmaking* (Oxford University Press, New York, 1979)
Neale, S. *Genre* (BFI, London, 1980)
Schatz, T. *Hollywood Genres: Formulas, Filmmaking and the Studio System* (McGraw Hill, New York, 1981)

Stars
Dyer, R. *Stars* (BFI, London, 1979; 2nd edn, 1998)
—— *Heavenly Bodies – Film Stars and Society* (BFI/Macmillan, London, 1987)
Gledhill, C. (ed.), *Stardom – Industry of Desire* (Routledge, London, 1991) – see particularly ch. 13, Barry King, 'Articulating Stardom', ch. 15, Andrew Britton, 'Stars and Genre', and ch. 16, Christine Gledhill, 'Signs of Melodrama'.
Hinson, H. 'Some Notes on Method Actors', *Sight and Sound* (vol. 53, no. 3, Summer 1984) – worth seeking out for the comparative study of Brando and De Niro.

A very witty and wide-ranging study of the relationship between stars and movie-goers is:
Basinger, J. *A Woman's View – How Hollywood Spoke to Women, 1930–1960* (Chatto & Windus, London, 1994)

Biographies
For practical use as well as for entertainment value, all students of popular cinema should have access to David Thomson's *A Biographical Dictionary of Film*, new edn (Andre Deutsch, London, 1994).

There are many popular biographies available; the following are indicative rather than particularly recommended:
Agan, P. *Robert De Niro – the Man, the Myth and the Movies* (Hale, London, 1989)
Anderson, C. *Citizen Jane – The Turbulent Life of Jane Fonda* (Virgin Books, London, 1990)
Leigh, W. *Liza Minnelli* (New English Library, London, 1993)

Auteur
Caughie, J. (ed.) *Theories of Authorship, A Reader* (Routledge, London, 1981)

Kolker, R. *A Cinema of Loneliness: Penn, Kubrick, Scorsese, Spielberg, Altman*, revised edn (Oxford University Press, Oxford, 1988)
Sarris, A. *The American Cinema: Directors and Directions 1928–1968* (Dutton, New York, 1968)
Thompson, D. and Christie, I. (eds) *Scorsese on Scorsese* (Faber, London, 1989)

New York, New York
Particularly useful are two articles in *Movie* (Vol. 31–2, Winter 1986):
Cooke, L. '*New York, New York* – Looking at De Niro'
Lippe, R. '*New York, New York* and the Hollywood Musical'

CHAPTER 9: WOMEN AND FILM

Agosterios, V. 'An Interview with Sally Potter', *Framework* (No. 14, 1979)
Arthur, J., 'Technology and Gender', *Screen* (Vol. 30, 1989) pp. 40–59
Auty, M. and Roddick, N. (eds) *British Cinema Now* (British Film Institute, London, 1985)
Banner, L. *Women in Modern America* (Harcourt, Brace, Jovanovich, New York, 1984)
Berger, J. *Ways of Seeing* (Penguin, London, 1972)
Bergstrom, J. 'Rereading the work of Claire Johnston', in C. Penley (ed.) *Feminism and Film Theory* (Routledge/British Film Institute, London, 1988)
Betterton, R. *Looking On: Images of Femininity in the Visual Arts and the Media* (Pandora, London, 1987)
Bobo, J. '*The Color Purple*: Black Women as Cultural Readers', in E.D. Pribram (ed.) *Female Spectator: Looking at Film and Television* (Verso, London and New York, 1988)
Brundsen, C. (ed.) *Films for Women* (British Film Institute, London, 1986)
Bruzzi, S. 'Tempestuous Petticoats: Costume and Desire in *The Piano*', *Screen* (Vol. 36, No. 3, Autumn 1995) pp. 257–66
Burns, M., 'Women in Focus', *In Camera* (Spring 1992) pp. 3–5, 17–19.
Byars, J. *All That Heaven Allows: Re-reading Gender in 1950s Melodrama* (University of North Carolina Press, Chapel Hill, 1991)
Cook, P. *The Gold Diggers*, *Framework* (Vol. 24, 1981)
—— (ed.) *The Cinema Book* (British Film Institute, London, 1985)
Cook, P. and Dodd, P. (eds) *Women and Film: A 'Sight and Sound' Reader* (Scarlet Press, London, 1993)
De Lauretis, T. 'Guerrilla in the Midst – Women's Cinema in the 1980s', *Screen* (Vol. 31, No. 1, 1990)
Donald, L. and Scanlon, S. 'Hollywood Feminism? Get Real!!', *Trouble and Strife* (Vol. 25, Winter 1992) pp. 11–16
Dove, L. 'Feminist and Left Independent Filmmaking in England', *Jump Cut* (Vol. 10–11, 1976)
Dyson, L. 'The Return of the Repressed? Whiteness, Feminity and Colonialism in *The Piano*', *Screen* (Vol. 36, No. 3, Autumn 1995) pp. 269–76
Ehrenstein, D. 'Out of the Wilderness', *Film Quarterly* (Vol. 47, No. 1, 1993) pp. 2–7
Fitzgerald, T. 'Now About These Women', *Sight and Sound* (Summer 1989)
Florence, P. 'A Conversation With Sally Potter', *Screen* (Vol. 34, No. 3, Autumn 1993) pp. 275–84.
Francke, L. *Script Girls* (British Film Institute, London, 1994)
Friedan, B. *The Feminine Mystique* (Penguin, London, 1963)
Gledhill, C. 'Some Recent Developments in Feminist Criticism', in S. Mast and M. Cohen (eds) *Film Theory and Criticism* (Oxford University Press, Oxford, 1985)
—— 'Pleasurable Negotiations', in D. Pribram (ed.) *Female Spectators: Looking at Film and Television* (Verso, London and New York, 1988)
Greer, G. *The Female Eunuch* (Flamingo, London, 1971)
Hall, S. 'Encoding/Decoding', in S. Hall, D. Hobson, A. Lowe and P. Willis (eds) *Culture, Media, Language* (Hutchinson, London, 1980)
Haskell, M. *From Reverence to Rape* (New English Library, London, 1973)
Heck-Rabi, L. *Women Filmmakers – A Critical Reception* (Scarecrow Press, Metuchen, New Jersey, 1984)
hooks, b. *Black Looks : Race and Representation* (Turnaround, London, 1992)
Johnston, C. 'Women's Cinema as Counter-cinema', *Screen Pamphlet* (No. 2, 1973)
—— 'The Subject of Feminist Film Theory/Practice', *Screen* (Vol. 21, No. 2, 1980)
Kaplan, E.A. *Women and Film: Both Sides of the Camera* (Methuen, London, 1983)
Kuhn, A. *Women's Pictures* (British Film Institute/Routledge & Kegan Paul, London, 1982)
Lapsley, R. and Westlake, M. *Film Theory: An Introduction* (Manchester University Press, Manchester, 1988)
Lehman, P. and Maynes, J. 'An Interview with Susan Clayton', *Wide Angle* (Vol. 6, No. 3, 1981) p. 72
Lovell, A. 'That Was the Workshop That Was', *Screen* (Vol. 31, No. 1, 1990) pp. 102–8

Lovell, T. *Pictures of Reality: Aesthetics, Politics and Pleasure* (British Film Institute, London, 1983)

Mast, S. and Cohen, M. (eds) *Film Theory and Criticism* (Oxford University Press, Oxford, 1985)

Maynard, M. 'Current Trends in Feminist Theory', *Social Studies Review* (Vol. 2, No. 3, 1987)

Millet, K. *Sexual Politics* (Virago, London, 1977)

Modleski, T. *The Women Who Knew Too Much* (Methuen, London, 1988)

Muir, A.R. 'The Status of Women Working in Film and Television', in L. Gammon (ed.) *The Female Gaze* (The Women's Press, London, 1988)

Mulvey, L. 'Visual Pleasure and Narrative Cinema', *Screen* (Vol. 16, No. 3, 1975)

—— *Framework* (Vol. 10, Nos 6–7, 1977) p. 7

—— 'Afterthoughts on Visual Pleasure and Narrative Cinema', *Framework* (Vol. 6, Nos 15–17, 1981)

—— *Visual and Other Pleasures* (Macmillan, London, 1989)

Murphy, J. 'A Question of Silence', in C. Brundsen (ed.) *Films for Women* (British Film Institute, London, 1986)

Nicholls, B. (ed.) *Movies and Methods*, Vol. 1 (University of California Press, Berkeley, 1976)

Penley, C. (ed.) *Feminism and Film Theory* (Routledge/British Film Institute, London, 1988)

Pilcher, J. 'I'm Not a Feminist, but…', *Sociology Review* (November 1993) p. 4

Pilling, J. (ed.) *Women and Animation: A Compendium* (British Film Institute, London, 1992)

Pollock, G. *Vision and Difference* (Routledge, London, 1988)

Pollock, G. and Parker, R. *Old Mistresses* (Routledge & Kegan Paul, London, 1981)

Pribram, E. (ed.), *Female Spectators: Looking at Film and Television* (Verso, London and New York, 1988)

Radway, J. *Reading the Romance* (Verso, London, 1987)

Slide, A. *Early Women Directors* (A.S. Barnes, South Brunswick, 1976)

Smith, S. *Women Who Make Movies* (Hopkinson and Blake, New York, 1975)

Stacey, J. 'Desperately Seeking Difference' in *The Sexual Subject: A 'Screen' Reader in Sexuality* (Routledge, London and New York, 1992)

Tasker, Y. *Working Girls* (Routledge, London, 1998)

Thornhan, S. *Passionate Detachments* (Arnold, London, 1997)

Walters, S. *Material Girls* (University of California Press, Berkeley, 1995)

Zoonen, L. van *Feminist Media Studies* (Sage, London, 1994)

CHAPTER 10: LESBIAN AND GAY CINEMA

Babuscio, J. 'Camp and gay sensibility', in R. Dyer (ed.) *Gays and Film* (British Film Institute, London, 1977). An essay which presents pioneering insights.

Bad Object Choices (ed.) *How Do I Look?: Queer Film And Video* (Bay Press, Seattle, 1991). Queer theory investigates the process of looking: at Asians in pornography, Dorothy Arzner, skinheads, safe sex, history, and photo images of blacks.

Benshoff, H.M. *Monsters in the Closet: Homosexuality and the Horror Film* (Manchester University Press, Manchester, 1997). Benshoff investigates ways in which homosexuality and homophobia have manifested themselves in this genre, from classic Hollywood to the modern slasher film.

Bourne, S. *Brief Encounters: Lesbians and Gays in British Cinema 1930–1971* (Cassell, London, 1996). An illuminating year-by-year list of critical readings of relevant films. See especially the fascinating appendices containing contemporary reactions to *Victim*.

Burston, P. and Richardson, C. (eds) *A Queer Romance*: *Gay Men, Lesbians and Popular Culture* (Routledge, London, 1995). Freud, Lacan, Barthes and Foucault are brought together to make things queer. Thought-provoking essays on the mechanisms of gay and lesbian spectatorship; includes a section on German film-maker Monika Treut, notes by Canada's Bruce LaBruce, and an in-depth look at the appeal of the lesbian vampire.

Cook, P. and Dodd, P. *Women and Film*: *A Sight and Sound Reader* (British Film Institute, London, 1993). An excellent section entitled 'Queer Alternatives' contains B Ruby Rich's essay on queer cinema, Pratibha Parmar's response, Amy Taubin's lively criticisms and an essay on Monika Treut.

Dyer, R. 'Pasolini and homosexuality', in P. Willemen (ed.) *Pier Paolo Pasolini* (British Film Institute, London, 1977). A key perspective on this major twentieth-century film-maker and writer.

—— 'Resistance through charisma: Rita Hayworth and Gilda', in E. Ann Kaplan (ed.) *Women in Film Noir* (British Film Institute, London, 1980). A case-study in homoerotic sub-text.

—— 'Judy Garland and gay men', in R. Dyer *Heavenly Bodies – Film Stars and Society* (Macmillan, Basingstoke, 1987). This essay on gay spectatorship includes a lucid application of camp as a critical concept.

—— *Now You See It: Studies on Lesbian And Gay Film* (Routledge, London and New York, 1990). A detailed, rewarding academic study, mainly of early German film, Genet and developments in America.

—— *The Matter of Images*: *Essays on Representation* (Routledge, London, 1993). Dyer illustrates the power and complexity of images across a range of films, including film noir, *Victim*, *Papillon* and *A Passage to India*.

Fuss, D. (ed.) *Inside/Out: Lesbian Theories, Gay Theories* (Routledge, New York and London, 1991). A stimulating source of academic ideas. Contributions on lesbian spectatorship, gay authorship, Hitchcock's *Rope*, and a semiotic exploration of Rock Hudson's body.

Gever, M., Greyson, J. and Parmar, P. (eds) *Queer Looks*: *Perspectives on Lesbian and Gay Video* (Between The Lines/Routledge, Toronto, 1993). A wealth of new insights, including a look at gay punk videomaker Bruce La Bruce, new interpretations of Fassbinder's films, and a superb essay by Thomas Waugh on gay spectatorship.

Giles, J. *The Cinema of Jean Genet*: *Un chant d'amour* (British Film Institute, London, 1991). This look at Genet's production and influence in film includes an illustrated script of 'Un chant d'amour'.

Hadleigh, B. *The Lavender Screen*: *The Gay and Lesbian Films* (Citadel Press, New York, 1993). Good illustrations and some lively insights.

Hamer, D. and Budge, B. *The Good, the Bad and the Gorgeous: Popular Culture's Romance with Lesbianism* (Pandora, London, 1994). Contains a reading of *Basic Instinct* that contrasts with that of Hoogland, entitled *Basic Instinct: Damning Dykes* by Angela Gavin.

Holmlund, C. and Fuchs, C. (eds) *Between the Sheets, in the Streets: Queer, Lesbian and Gay Documentary* (University of Minnesota Press, Minneapolis 1997). Chapters on the history of postwar documentary in the US, the lesbian documentary styles of Su Friedrich and Sadie Bening, and Derek Jarman as documentarist.

Hoogland, R.C. *Lesbian Configurations* (University of Columbia Press, New York, 1997). This book explores a variety of cultural forms to tease out the contradictory meanings of lesbian sexuality in western culture. Chapters on *The Color Purple*, *Basic Instinct* and Polanski's *Bitter Moon*.

Jarman, D. *Dancing Ledge* (Quartet, London, 1984). The critically acclaimed artist's account of his formative years, which cover the making of *The Angelic Conversation*, *Sebastiane* and *Jubilee*. The first of a number of fascinating writings he has produced, which includes books to accompany *Caravaggio*, *War Requiem* and *Edward II*.

Julien, I. and MacCabe, C. *Diary of a Young Soul Rebel* (British Film Institute, London, 1991). Includes the script of this lively film, along with an introduction and interview which throws light on its director's fascinating insights into race and sexuality.

Kabir, S. *Lesbian Representations in Film* (Cassell, London and Washington, 1998). Lesbian history, black subjectivity, feminist film criticism and the insights of psychoanalysis applied to a range of films from *Queen Christina* to *Go Fish* via *Desperately Seeking Susan* and *The Hunger*.

Kirkham, P. and Thumin, J. (eds) *You Tarzan: Masculinity, Movies And Men* (Lawrence & Wishart/St Martin's Press, London, 1993). Contains Richard Dyer's essay on the star image of Rock Hudson. An inspiring set of essays to investigate the construction of masculinity in, for example, Clarke Gable's films.

Kureishi, H. *My Beautiful Laundrette and the Rainbow Sign* (Faber & Faber, London, 1986). The script of this noted film, along with scriptwriter Kureishi's articulate essay on its themes of sexuality, race and Britishness.

Mayne, J. 'The Critical Audience', in her *Cinema and Spectatorship* (Routledge, London and New York, 1993). An informed critical overview of lesbian spectatorship.

—— *Directed by Dorothy Arzner* (University of Indiana Press, Bloomington, 1994). The first detailed critical work on the life and films of this neglected Hollywood auteur.

Merck, M. '"Lianna" and the lesbians of art cinema', in C. Brunsden (ed.) *Films for Women* (British Film Institute, London, 1986). See also Mandy Merck's essay on 'Desert Hearts' in the *Queer Looks* anthology cited above.

Meyer, M. (ed.) *The Politics and Poetics of Camp* (Routledge, London, 1994). Various contributors discuss the concept of camp, and use it for textual exploration.

Murray, R. *Images in the Dark*: *An Encyclopedia of Gay and Lesbian Film and Video* (TLA Publications, Philadelphia, 1996). A comprehensive and illuminating book. It has a refreshingly international outlook, covering mainstream and independent film. There are separate sections on queer, lesbian, gay male and transgender interest, and on camp.

Pierson, J. *Spike, Mike, Slackers and Dykes: A Guided Tour Across a Decade of Independent American Cinema* (Faber, London, 1996). Pierson is a skilled and perceptive producer. A chapter entitled 'Parting Glances and the New Queer Cinema' gives his first-hand account of the production and marketing of that film. Another chapter explains vividly how he steered *Go Fish* at the Sundance Film Festival towards a valuable distribution deal with the Goldwyn company.

Pilling, J. and O'Pray, M. (eds) *Into the Pleasure Dome*: *The Films of Kenneth Anger* (British Film Institute, London, 1989). A useful set of essays on this influential talent.

Russo, V. *The Celluloid Closet*: *Homosexuality in the Movies* (Harper & Row, New York and London, 1987). The classic introduction to this area.

Sontag, S. 'Notes on Camp', in *A Susan Sontag Reader* (Penguin, London, 1982)

Steven, P. (ed.) *Jump Cut: Hollywood, Politics and Counter Cinema* (Between The Lines, Toronto, 1985). Useful essays include viewpoints on lesbian spectatorship, Richard Dyer on stereotyping, and Jan Oxenberg.

Tyler, P. *Screening The Sexes: Homosexuality in the Movies* (DeCapo, New York, 1993). The original pioneering survey, with a new introduction by Andrew Sarris. The breadth and richness of the material Tyler covers, and the insights he presents, make this 1972 text of continuing value.

Weiss, A. 'A queer feeling when I look at you: Hollywood stars and lesbian spectatorship in the 1930's', in C. Gledhill (ed.) *Stardom: Industry of Desire* (Routledge, London and New York, 1991). A valuable contribution to star study.

—— *Vampires and Violets – Lesbians in Film* (Penguin, London, 1993). Key films and the main debates clearly presented.

Whatling, C. *Screen Dreams: Fantasising Lesbians in Film* (Manchester University Press, Manchester 1997). Critical appraisal and meditation around such films as *Maidens in Uniform* and *Heavenly Creatures*, as well as the star images of such figures as Meryl Streep and Jodie Foster.

Wilton, T. *Immortal Invisible: Lesbians and the Moving Image* (Routledge, London, 1995). A collection of essays which investigates lesbian viewing and production. It includes contributions on *Desert Hearts* and *Salmonberries* along with interperations of *Aliens* and other mainstream films.

Wood, R. 'Responsibilities of a gay film critic', in B. Nichols (ed.) *Movies and Methods*, Vol. II (University of California Press, Berkeley, 1985). Wood's seminal essay of the late 1970s outlines his critical stance and provides re-readings of some of his work on Renoir, Bergman and Hawks.

—— *Hitchcock Revisited* (Faber & Faber, London, 1989). This volume includes Wood's original auteurist essays on Hitchcock, with challenging new reinterpretations in the light of gay critical perspectives.

CHAPTER 11: BRITISH CINEMA

Aitken, I. *Film and Reform* (Routledge, London, 1990)

—— 'The British documentary film movement', in R. Murphy (ed.) *The British Cinema Book* (British Film Institute, London, 1997)

Aldgate, A. 'Comedy, class and containment: the British Domestic cinema of the 1930s', in J. Curran, and V. Porter (eds) *British Cinema History* (Weidenfeld & Nicolson, London, 1983)

Anderson, M. '"Stop messing about": the gay fool of the *Carry On* films', *Journal of Popular British Cinema* (1, 1998)

Armes, R. *A Critical History of the British Cinema* (Secker & Warburg, London, 1978)

Auty, M. 'But is it cinema?', in M. Auty, and N. Roddick (eds) *British Cinema Now* (British Film Institute, London, 1985)

Auty, M. and Roddick, N. (eds) *British Cinema Now* (British Film Institute, London, 1985)

Barber, S.T. 'Insurmountable difficulties and moments of ecstasy: crossing class, ethnic, and sexual barriers in the films of Stephen Frears', in L. Friedman (ed.) *British Cinema and Thatcherism* (UCL Press, London, 1993)

Barr, C. *Ealing Studios*, 2nd edn (Studio Vista, London, 1993)

—— 'Before *Blackmail*: silent British Cinema', in R. Murphy (ed.) *The British Cinema Book* (British Film Institute, London, 1997)

Beaufoy S. 'Hidden agendas', *Sight and Sound* (Vol. 8, No. 3, 1998)

Bennett, T. and Woollacott, J. *Bond and Beyond: the Political Career of a Popular Hero* (Macmillan, London, 1987)

Blanchard, S. and Harvey, S. 'The post-war independent cinema – structure and organization', in J. Curran, and V. Porter (eds) *British Cinema History* (Weidenfeld & Nicolson, London, 1983)

Burch, N. *Life to Those Shadows* (British Film Institute, London, 1990)

Burton, A., O'Sullivan, T. and Wells, P. (eds) *Liberal Directions: Basil Dearden and Postwar British Film Culture* (Flicks Books, Trowbridge, 1997)

Carson, B. 'Comedy, sexuality and "swinging London" films', *Journal of Popular British Cinema* (1, 1998)

Caughie, J. 'Progressive television and documentary drama', in T. Bennett *et al.* (eds) *Popular Television and Film* (British Film Institute/Open University, London, 1981)

—— 'Great Britain: an historical overview', in J. Caughie with K. Rockett *The Companion to British and Irish Cinema* (Cassell/British Film Institute, London, 1996)

Chanan, M. *The Dream That Kicks: The Prehistory and Early Years of Cinema in Britain* (Routledge, London, 1996; first published 1980)

Christie, I. *Arrows of Desire: The Films of Michael Powell and Emeric Pressburger* (Faber & Faber, London, 1994)

Cook, P. 'Neither here nor there: national identity in Gainsborough costume drama', in A. Higson (ed.) *Dissolving Views: Key Writings on British Cinema* (Cassell, London, 1996a)

—— (ed.) *Fashioning the Nation: Costume and Identity in British Cinema* (British Film Institute, London, 1996b).

—— (ed.) *Gainsborough Pictures* (Cassell, London, 1998)

Cooke, L. 'British Cinema: from cottage industry to mass entertainment', in C. Bloom (ed.) *Literature and Culture in Modern Britain, Volume One: 1900–1929* (Longman, London, 1993)

Coveney, M. *The World According to Mike Leigh* (Harper Collins, London, 1996)

Crofts, S. 'Concepts of national cinema' in J. Hill and Church P. Gibson (eds) *The Oxford Guide to Film Studies* (Oxford University Press, Oxford, 1998)

Dickinson, M. and Street, S. *Cinema and State: The Film Industry and the British Government 1927–84* (British Film Institute, London, 1985)

Dixon, W.W. (ed.) *Re-Viewing British Cinema, 1900–1992* (State University of New York Press, New York, 1994)

Dodd, C. and Dodd, P. 'Engineering the nation: British documentary film, 1930–1939', in A. Higson (ed.) *Dissolving Views: Key Writing on British Cinema* (Cassel, 1996)

Donnelly, K. 'British punk films: rebellion into money, nihilism into innovation', *Journal of Popular British Cinema* (1, 1998)

Drazin, C. *The Finest Years: British Cinema of the 1940s* (Andre Deutsch, London, 1998)

Durgnat, R. *A Mirror for England: British Movies from Austerity to Affluence* (Faber & Faber, London, 1970)

Dyja, E. *BFI Film and Television Handbook 1997* (British Film Institute, London, 1996)

—— *BFI Film and Television Handbook 1998* (British Film Institute, London, 1997)

Eberts, J. and Illott, T. *My Indecision is Final: The Rise and Fall of Goldcrest Films* (Faber & Faber, London, 1990)

Ellis, J. 'Television, video and independent cinema', in S. Blanchard and D. Morley (eds) *What's This Channel Four?* (Comedia, London, 1982)

Finney, A. *The State of European Cinema* (Cassell, London, 1996)

Friedman, L. (ed.) *British Cinema and Thatcherism* (UCL Press, London, 1993)

Geraghty, C. 'Women and sixties British Cinema: the development of the "darling" girl', in R. Murphy (ed.) *The British Cinema Book* (British Film Institute, London, 1997)

Giles, P. 'History with Holes: Channel Four Television Films of the 1980s', in L. Friedman (ed.) *British Cinema and Thatcherism* (UCL Press, London, 1993)

Gledhill, C. and Swanson, G. (eds) *Nationalising Femininity: Culture, Sexuality and British Cinema in the Second World War* (Manchester University Press, Manchester, 1996)

Harper, S. *Picturing the Past: The Rise and Fall of the British Costume Film* (British Film Institute, London, 1994)

Hartog, S. 'State protection of a beleaguered industry', in J. Curran and V. Porter (eds) *British Cinema History* (Weidenfeld & Nicolson, London, 1983)

Harvey, S. 'New images for old? Channel Four and independent film', in S. Blanchard and D. Morley (eds) *What's This Channel Four?* (Comedia, London, 1982)

—— 'The "other cinema" in Britain: unfinished business in oppositional and independent film, 1929–1984', in C. Barr. (ed.) *All Our Yesterdays: 90 Years of British Cinema* (British Film Institute, London, 1986)

Higson, A. 'Britain's outstanding contribution to the film: the documentary-realist tradition', in C. Barr. (ed.) *All Our Yesterdays: 90 Years of British Cinema* (British Film Institute, London, 1986)

—— 'The concept of national cinema', *Screen* (Vol. 30, No. 4, 1989)

—— 'Re-presenting the national past: nostalgia and pastiche in the heritage film', in *Waving the Flag: Constructing a National Cinema in Britain* (Oxford University Press, Oxford, 1993)

—— 'A diversity of film practices: renewing British Cinema in the 1970s', in B. Moore-Gilbert *The Arts in the 1970s: Cultural Closure?* (Routledge, London, 1994)

—— 'British Cinema', in J. Hill and P. Church Gibson (eds) *The Oxford Guide to Film Studies* (Oxford University Press, Oxford, 1998)

Hill, J. 'The Issue of National Cinema in Britain', in D. Petrie (ed.) *New Questions of British Cinema* (British Film Institute, London, 1992)

—— 'British Cinema as national cinema: production, audience and representation', in R. Murphy (ed.) *The British Cinema Book* (British Film Institute, London, 1997)

Hill, J. and McLoone, M. (eds) *Big Picture, Small Screen: The Relations Between Film and Television* (John Libbey Media/University of Luton Press, Luton, 1996)

Hill, J., McLoone, M. and Hainsworth, P. (eds) *Border Crossing: Film in Ireland, Britain and Europe* (Institute of Irish Studies/University of Ulster/British Film Institute, Belfast, 1994)

Hood, S. 'John Grierson and the Documentary Film Movement', in J. Curran, and V. Porter (eds) *British Cinema History* (Weidenfeld & Nicolson, London, 1983)

Hutchings, P. *Hammer and Beyond: The British Horror Film* (Manchester University Press, Manchester, 1993)

Johnston, S. 'Charioteers and ploughmen', in M. Auty and N. Roddick (eds) *British Cinema Now* (British Film Institute, London, 1985)

Jones, G. and Johnson, L. *Talking Pictures: Interviews with Contemporary British Film-makers* (British Film Institute, London, 1997)

Jordan, M. 'Carry On...follow that stereotype', in J. Curran and V. Porter (eds) *British Cinema History* (Weidenfeld & Nicolson, London, 1983)

Julien, I. and MacCabe, C. *Diary of a Young Soul Rebel* (British Film Institute, London, 1991)

Kuhn, A. (ed.) *The Women's Companion to International Film* (Virago, London, 1990)

Kulik, K. *Alexander Korda: The Man Who Could Work Miracles* (W.H. Allen, London, 1975)

Landy, M. 'Melodrama and femininity in World War Two British Cinema', in R. Murphy (ed.) *The British Cinema Book* (British Film Institute, London, 1997)

Lant, A. *Blackout: Reinventing Women for Wartime British Cinema* (Princeton University Press, New Jersey, 1991)

Lippard, C. *By Angels Driven: The Films of Derek Jarman* (Flicks Books, Trowbridge, 1996)

Lovell, A. 'British Cinema: the known cinema?', in R. Murphy (ed.) *The British Cinema Book* (British Film Institute, London, 1997)

Lovell, A. and Hillier, J. *Studies in Documentary* (Secker & Warburg, London, 1972)

McKnight, G. (ed.) *Agent of Challenge and Defiance: The Films of Ken Loach* (Flicks Books, Trowbridge, 1997)

Macnab, G. *J. Arthur Rank and the British Film Industry* (Routledge, London, 1993)

Murphy, R. 'Under the shadow of Hollywood', in C. Barr (ed.) *All Our Yesterdays: 90 Years of British Cinema* (British Film Institute, London, 1986)

—— *Realism and Tinsel: Cinema and Society in Britain 1939–49* (Routledge, London, 1989)

—— *Sixties British Cinema* (British Film Institute, London, 1992)

Napper, L. 'A despicable tradition? Quota quickies in the 1930s', in R. Murphy *The British Cinema Book* (British Film Institute, London, 1997)

O'Pray, M. (ed.) *The British Avant Garde Film 1926 to 1995* (The Arts Council of England/John Libbey Media/University of Luton Press, Luton, 1996)

Petley, J. 'The lost continent', in C. Barr (ed.) *All Our Yesterdays: 90 Years of British Cinema* (British Film Institute, London, 1986)

Petrie, D. (ed.) *New Questions of British Cinema* (British Film Institute, London, 1992a)

—— (ed.) *Screening Europe: Image and Identity in Contemporary European Cinema* (British Film Institute, London, 1992b)

—— (ed.) *Inside Stories: Diaries of British Film-makers at Work* (British Film Institute, London, 1996)

Pirie, D. *A Heritage of Horror: The English Gothic Cinema 1946–72* (Gordon Fraser, London, 1973)

Pulleine, T. 'A song and dance at the local: thoughts on Ealing', in R. Murphy (ed.) *The British Cinema Book* (British Film Institute, London, 1997)

Pym, J. *Film On Four* (British Film Institute, London, 1992)

Richards, J. *The Age of the Dream Palace: Cinema and Society 1930–1939* (Routledge & Kegan Paul, London, 1984)

—— 'New waves and old myths: British Cinema in the 1960s', in B. Moore-Gilbert and J. Seed (eds) *Cultural Revolution? The Challenge of the Arts in the 1960s* (Routledge, London, 1992)

—— *Films and British National Identity* (Manchester University Press, Manchester, 1997)

—— (ed.) *The Unknown 1930s: An Alternative History of the British Cinema* (I.B.Tauris, London, 1998)

Ryall, T. *Alfred Hitchcock and the British Cinema* (Croom Helm, London, 1986)

Thomas, N. 'UK film, television and video: overview', in E. Dyja *BFI Film and Television Handbook 1998* (British Film Institute, London, 1997)

Walker, A. *National Heros: British Cinema in the Seventies and Eighties* (Harrap, London, 1985)

—— *Hollywood, England: The British Film Industry in the Sixties* (Harrap, London, 1986; first published 1974)

Walker, J. *The Once and Future Film: British Cinema in the Seventies and Eighties* (Methuen, London, 1985)

Whitaker, S. 'Declarations of independence', in M. Auty and N. Roddick (eds) *British Cinema Now* (BFI, London, 1985)

Williams, T. 'The masochistic fix: gender oppression in the films of Terence Davies', in L. Friedman (ed.) *British Cinema and Thatcherism* (UCL Press, London, 1993)

Wollen, P. 'Riff-raff realism', *Sight and Sound* (Vol. 8, No. 4, 1998)

Wood, L. 'Low-Budget British Films in the 1930s', in Murphy, R. (ed.) *The British Cinema Book* (British Film Institute, London, 1997)

CHAPTER 12: AN INTRODUCTION TO INDIAN CINEMA

Armes, R. *Third World Film-Making and the West* (University of California Press, Berkeley, 1987)

Basu, S., Kak, S., and Krishen, P. 'Cinema and society: a search for meaning in a new genre', *India International Centre Quarterly*, New Delhi (Vol. 8, No. 1, March 1980)

Bhattacharya, R. *Bimal Roy – A Man of Silence* (Indus, New Delhi, 1994)

Chakravarty, S. 'National identity and the realist aesthetic: Indian Cinema of the fifties', *Quarterly Review of Film and Video* (Vol. 11, 1989) pp. 31–48.

—— *National Identity in Indian Popular Cinema 1947–1987* (University of Texas Press, Austin, 1993)

Chandavarkar, B. 'Indian film song', in T.M. Ramachandran (ed.) *70 Years of Indian Cinema* (CINEMA India-International, Bombay, 1985)

Chandra, A. with Shetty, K. 'Hitting the Right Notes', *India Today* (30 November 1993) p. 52–3

CinemaIndia: An Introductory Guide (MOMI Education, 1991)

Das, V. 'The mythological film and its framework of meaning: an analysis of *Jai Santoshi Maa*', in *India International Centre Quarterly*, New Delhi (Vol. 8, No. 1, March 1980)

Dharap, B.V., 'Dadasaheb Phalke: father of Indian Cinema', in T.M. Ramachandran (ed.) *70 Years of Indian Cinema* (CINEMA India-International, Bombay, 1985)

Dissanayake, W. and Sahai, M. *Raj Kapoor's Films: Harmony of Discourses* (Vikas, New Delhi, 1988)

George, T.J.S. *The Life and Times of Nargis* (Indus, New Delhi, 1994)

Gillespie, M. *Television, Ethnicity and Cultural Change* (Routledge, London, 1995)

Kabir, N.M. 'Indian Film Music' (unpublished monograph, 1991)

Krishen P. (ed.) 'Indian popular cinema: myth meaning and metaphor' *India International Centre Quarterly*, New Delhi (Vol. 8, No. 1, March 1980)

—— 'Knocking on the doors of public culture: India's parallel cinema', *Public Culture*, Philadelphia (Vol. 4, No.1, Fall 1991)

Micciollo, H. *Guru Dutt* (L'Avant-Scene du Cinéma, Paris, 1979)

Mishra, V. 'Towards a theoretical critique of Bombay cinema', *Screen* (Vol. 26, Nos 3–4, 1985) p. 133–46.

—— 'The actor as parallel text in Bombay cinema', *Quarterly Review of Film and Video* (Vol. 11, 1989) pp. 49–67

Nandy, A. 'The popular Hindi film: ideology and first principles', *India International Centre Quarterly* (Vol. 8, No. 1, 1981) pp. 89–96

Passek, J.-L. (ed.) *Le Cinéma Indien* (Centre Georges Pompidou/l'Equerre, Paris, 1983)

Pendakur, M. 'India', in J.A. Lent (ed.) *The Asian Film Industry* (Christopher Helm, Bromley, 1990)

Pfleiderer, B. and Lutze, L. *The Hindi Film: Agent and Re-Agent of Cultural Change* (Manohar, New Delhi, 1985)

Prasad, M. 'Cinema and the Desire for Modernity', *Journal of Arts and Ideas*, New Delhi (Nos 25–6, 1993)

—— 'Signs of Ideological re-form in two recent films', *Journal of Arts and Ideas*, New Delhi (No. 29, 1995)

—— *Ideology of Hindi Cinema* (Oxford University Press, New Delhi, 1998)

Rai, A. 'An American Raj in Filmistan: images of Elvis in Indian films', *Screen* (Vol. 35, No. 1, 1994) pp. 51–77

Rajadhyaksha, A. 'Neo-traditionalism', *Framework*, London (Nos 32–3, 1986)

Rajadhyaksha, A. and Willemen, P. *Encyclopaedia of Indian Cinema* (BFI, London, 1994)

Rangoonwalla, F. *Indian Cinema: Past and Present* (Clarion, New Delhi, 1982)

Ray, S. *Our Films, Their Films* (Orient Longman, Bombay, 1976)

Rueben, B. *Mehboob – India's De Mille* (Indus, New Delhi, 1994)

Robinson, A. *Satyajit Ray: The Inner Eye* (André Deutsch, London, 1989)

Shah, P. *The Indian Film* (Greenwood Press, Westport, CT, 1981)

Skillman, T. 'The Bombay Hindi film song', in *Yearbook for Traditional Music 1986* (International Council for Traditional Music, New York, 1986) pp. 133–44

Thomas, R. 'Indian Cinema: pleasures and popularity', *Screen* (Vol. 26, Nos 3–4, 1985) pp. 116–31

—— 'Sanctity and scandal in Mother India', *Quarterly Review of Film and Video* (Vol. 11, 1989) pp. 11–30

Vasudev, A. *The New Indian Cinema* (Macmillan, Delhi, 1986)

Vasudevan, R. 'The melodramatic mode and commercial Hindi cinema', *Screen* (Vol. 30, No. 3, 1989) pp. 29–50

—— 'Shifting codes, dissolving identities: the Hindi social film of the 1950s as popular culture', *Journal of Arts & Ideas*, New Delhi (Nos 23–4, 1993)

—— 'Bombay and its public', *Journal of Arts & Ideas*, New Delhi (No. 29, 1995)

Wadia, J.B.H. 'The Indian silent film', in T.M. Ramachandran (ed.) *70 Years of Indian Cinema* (CINEMA India-International, Bombay, 1985)

Warder, A.K. 'Classical literature', in A.L. Basham (ed.) *A Cultural History of India* (Oxford University Press, Oxford, 1975)

Books published in India can be ordered from:
Books from India, 45 Museum Street, London WC1A 1LR. Tel.: 0171 405 3784.

CHAPTER 14: NEW GERMAN CINEMA

Clarke, G. 'Seeking planets that do not exist: the New German Cinema is the liveliest in Europe', *Time* (20 March 1978)

Collins, R. and Porter, V. *WDR and the Arbeiterfilm: Fassbinder, Ziewer and Others* (BFI, London, 1981)

Corrigan, T. *New German Film. The Displaced Image* (University of Texas Press, Austin; Indiana University Press, Bloomington and Indianapolis; 1983; revised and expanded edition, 1994)

Dawson, J. 'The sacred terror', *Sight and Sound* (Vol. 48, No. 4, 1979) pp. 242–5

—— 'A labyrinth of subsidies', *Sight and Sound* (Vol. 50, No. 1, 1981) pp. 14–20

Eidsvik, C. 'The state as movie mogul', *Film Comment* (15, March–April 1979a) pp. 60–6

—— 'Behind the crest of the wave: an overview of the New German Cinema', *Literature/Film Quarterly* (Vol. 7, No. 3, 1979b)

Elsaesser, T. *New German Cinema: A History* (Macmillan/BFI, Basingstoke, 1989)

—— *Fassbinder's Germany: History Identity Subject* (Amsterdam University Press, Amsterdam, 1996)

Fehrenbach, H. *Cinema in Democratizing Germany: Reconstructing National Identity after Hitler* (University of North Carolina Press, Chapel Hill and London, 1995)

Franklin, J. *New German Cinema* (Columbus, London, 1986)

Frieden, S. *et al.* (eds) *Gender and German Cinema: Feminist Interventions* Vols 1 and 2 (Berg, Providence and Oxford, 1993)

Hartnoll, G. and Porter, V. (eds) *Alternative Filmmaking in Television: ZDF – A Helping Hand,* Dossier 14 (BFI, London, 1982)

Horak, J.C. 'West German film politics – from A to Zimmerman', *Afterimage* (Vol. 11, No. 9, 1984)

Johnston, S. 'The author as public institution. The 'new' cinema in the Federal Republic of Germany', *Screen Education* (Vol. 32, No. 3, 1979–80) pp. 67–78

Johnston, S. and Ellis, J. 'The radical film funding of ZDF', *Screen* (Vol. 23, No. 1, 1982) pp. 60–73

Kaes, A. *From 'Hitler' to 'Heimat'. The Return of History as Film* (Harvard University Press, Cambridge and London, 1989)

Knight, J. *Women and the New German Cinema* (Verso, London and New York, 1992)

McCormick, R. *Politics of the Self* (Princeton University Press, Princeton and Oxford, 1991)

Pflaum, H.G. and Prinzler, H.H. *Cinema in the Federal Republic of Germany* (Inter Nationes, Bonn, 1983; revised edn, 1993)

Phillips, K. (ed.) *New German Filmmakers* (Frederick Ungar, New York, 1984)

Rentschler, E. *West German Film in the Course of Time* (Redgrave, Bedford Hills, 1984)

—— (ed.) *German Film and Literature. Adaptations and Transformations* (Methuen, New York and London, 1986)

Rentschler, E. and Prinzler, H.H. (eds) *West German Filmmakers on Film* (Holmes & Meier, New York, 1988)

—— *The Ministry of Illusion: Nazi Cinema and its Afterlife* (Harvard University Press, Cambridge, MA, and London, 1996)

Sandford, J. *The New German Cinema* (Eyre Methuen, London, 1980)

Silberman, M. (ed.) 'Film and feminism in Germany today', *Jump Cut* (No. 27, 1982) pp. 41–53

—— (ed.) 'German film women', *Jump Cut* (No. 29, 1984) pp. 49–64

—— (ed.) 'German women's film culture', *Jump Cut* (No. 30, 1985) pp. 63–9

Wenders, W. *Emotion Pictures* (London, Faber & Faber, 1989)

Journals

Discourse (No. 6, Fall 1983)
Literature/Film Quarterly (Vol. 7, No. 3, 1979)
Literature/Film Quarterly (Vol. 13, No. 4, 1985)
New German Critique (Nos 24–5, Fall/Winter 1981–2)
Persistence of Vision (No. 2, Fall 1985)
Quarterly Review of Film Studies (Vol. 5, No. 2, 1980)
Wide Angle (Vol. 3, No. 4, 1980)

Index

A Bout de souffle (Godard) 112
aberrant reading 139
acting/actors 105–6, 187, 188, 194
action genres 118–19
actuality 212, 213–14, 223, 225; *see also* documentary; realism
Adventures of Andre and Walley B. (Lassetter) 76
Adventures of Robin Hood, The (Korngold) 26
advertising 31
Age of Innocence (Scorsese) 205
agents/agencies 32–3
agitki 421
Aladdin (Disney) 76, 260
Alam Ara (Irani) 385, 397
Ali Baba (Méliès) 95, 98
Alice Doesn't Live There Anymore (Scorsese) 202
Alice in Cartoonland (Disney) 241
Alien 74
All that Heaven Allows (Sirk) 101–2, 120, 284, 317
All-round Reduced Personality, The (Sander) 470–2
alternative cinema 29, 121–4, 274, 367, 407–9, 423–4
Althusser, Louis 137, 418
Altman, Robert 114, 120
Amazing Equal Pay Show (London Women's Film Group) 275
Amber Films 274, 377
American film industry 14–27, 38–9, 41; domination of 14, 371, 454; 'New American Cinema' 367; origins of 14–17; studio era 17–21
American Friend, The (Wenders) 474–5
Americanisation 352–3, 472–3
Andaz (Mehboob) 395, 403
Anderson, David 258
Anderson, Lindsay 124, 362
Andrews, Dudley 199
Anger, Kenneth 274, 309
Animal Farm (Batchelor) 269
animation 238–61; and avant-garde cinema 240, 250, 255–6; cartoons 68, 239–53; cel 240, 245; character

240, 244, 248–9; computer aided 62, 73, 76, 85, 259–60; condensation 249; configuration 246; developmental 245, 250–1; dialogue 243–4, 247, 251–2; experimental 245, 255–7; gendered 248–9; and live action 241, 253, 258; metamorphosis 247; as mock documentary 251–2; narrative 239, 246; orthodox 245–7, 252; paint and trace 84–5; pencil test 241, 245; pixillation 252; protoanimation 239; puppets/models 240, 250, 251, 258; realism 241–2, 259; reduced 250; sound/music 70, 241, 243–4, 245–6, 247, 257; squash and stretch 250; symmetry 253
anthropomorphism 240, 251
Araki, Gregg 327–30
Arbeiterfilme 459
Arsenal (Dovzhenko) 441, 444
Arrivée d'un train en gare à la Ciotat (Lumière) 155–6, 215
art cinema 377, 407, 452–3
art-house 195, 372; *see also* art cinema
Arthu, P. 231
artisanal mode of production 461–3
Artist's Dream, The (Bray) 240
Arzner, Dorothy 269, 276, 317–8, 340
associative mode 214
audience 44–7; attendance 1, 14, 16, 45–6; class 14, 16, 28, 135, 351–2, 363; gay 310–11; as interpreters 285, 422, 424, 429, 432; pre-knowledge 95, 98, 148; psychological testing 46–7; *see also* spectator
auteur/auteurism 162, 164, 195–203, 453; house style 22, 199; insurance value 196; 'signature'/identity 165, 196–9; spectator-as-auteur 200; staras-auteur 199; structure 196, 203; theory 195–6, 199; Warner Bros. 22, 199
Autorenkino 461; *see also* auteur
avant-garde cinema 255–6, 274–5, 278, 367, 377
Avery, Tex 242, 245

Babuscio, Jack 313
background plates 78
Back, Frederick 238
Back Street 51
Back to the Future 3 168
Baker, Aaron 231
Balazs, Bela 213
Balcon, Michael 358, 360, 379
Barnouw 385, 399, 411
Baron, Zelda 286
Barrett, Lezli-Ann 286
Barriga, Cecilia 338
Barsam, Richard 213–14
Barthes, Roland 146
Barton Fink (Coen) 176
Barua, P.C. 398
Baseball (Burns) 231
Basic Instinct 336, 340
Basic Training (Wiseman) 229
Basis-Film 459
Batchelor, Joy 238, 269
Battacharya, Basu 409
Battleship Potemkin (Eisenstein) 51, 62, 219, 418, 432–3, 443
Batman 30
Bauer, Evgeny 420
Bazin, André 106, 444–5
Beauty and the Beast (Disney) 76
Beaufroy, Simon 376, 377
Beddington, Jack 52
Before Stonewall (Schiller and Rosenberg) 230, 311, 317
Begum, Fatma 409
Belton, John 176
Benchley, Peter 34–5
Benegal, Shyam 409
Benning, Sadie 338
Bergman, Ingmar 122
Bergstrom, Janet 280
Berlin, Symphony of a Great City (Ruttman) 216
Bertolucci, Bernardo 446
Betty Boop (Fleischer) 240, 246
Bhaji on the Beach (Chada) 287
bhava 384
Big Five/Little Three 17–18, 19, 21, 26–7
binary analysis 169–70, 174

biopics 22, 23, 163, 206
Birds, The (Hitchcock) 109
Birth of a Nation, The (Griffith) 110
Blaché, Alice Guy 268–9
Black Widow (Rafelson) 339
Blackmail (Hitchcock) 282
Blackton, J. Stuart 68, 238, 239
Blade Runner (Ridley Scott) 101, 198–9
Blue (Jarman) 277
Blue Light, The (Riefenstahl) 222
Blue Scar (Craigie) 270
blue screen 78–9, 81
Bobo, Jacqueline 285
body language 97, 106
Bodyguard, The (Costner) 200
Bogarde, Dirk 321
Bollywood 401
Bond films 364–6
Boral, R.C. 386
Borden, Lizzie 281, 319
Born in Flames (Borden) 281, 319
Bordwell, David 422, 424
Bose, Debaki 398
Boulting, Roy 316
Bourne, Stephen 323
Box, Muriel 270–3
Boxcar Bertha (Scorsese) 202
Boyd, Todd 231
Boys in the Band, The (Friedkin) 314, 316
Bram Stoker's Dracula (Coppola) 177
Brando, Marlon 186, 188, 227
Brassed Off 375, 378
Braveheart (Gibson) 172
Bray, John R. 240
bricolage 176, 373, 376
Bright Eyes (Marshall) 337
Bringing up Baby 119
British Board of Film Censors 51
British Board of Film Classification
    (BBFC) 49, 52
British cinema 348–79; art-house 372,
    373; categories 349–50; class and
    culture 353–56; cultural approach
    348–9, 350, 351; documentary
    movement 293, 348, 358, 362–3,
    446; financing/support 4, 33, 38,
    39–40, 348, 371; mainstream 366–7,
    372–3; media conglomerates 42;
    multiculturalism 367, 369–70, 377;
    national identity 348–50, 351, 354,
    358, 367, 375, 378; 'new wave' 363,
    364, 366; popular cinema 363–6;
    postwar 359–60; renaissance 367–8,
    371–3; Soviet influences 446;
    wartime 356–9; women 269–73;
    working class comedies 354–5
Britton, Andrew 212
Brocka, Lino 311
Broomfield, Nick 231
Brophy, Philip 247
Brückner, Jutta 470
BSkyB 42
Bugs 86
Bugs Bunny 247
Bugsy Malone 168

Buñuel, Luis 116
Burch, Noel 108, 132
Burness, Pete 250
Burns, Ken 231
Burns, Moya 288
Buscombe, Ed 113
Busustow, Stephen 250
butch/femme role playing 311
Bwana Devil (Paramount) 73
Byars, Jackie 284

Cabaret 165
Cabin in the Sky (Minnelli) 165
Cabinet of Doctor Caligari, The 101
Caine, Michael 106
camera: angle of shot 109; lighting
    106–7; movement 108–10, 133, 247,
    252–4; and truth 441–2
camera crew: visual styles 25; women
    286, 288
cameraman system of production 16, 17
Cameraman's Revenge, The (Starawicz)
    240
camp 313
Campion, Jane 290, 299–303
Cannon, Bob 250
Cape Fear (Scorsese) 118, 176
Capra, Frank 101
Cardinal, Roger 238
Carpenter, John 110
carnivalesque 364
Carrey, Jim 86
Carry On films 363
cartoons *see* animation
Caughie, John 352, 362–3
Caught Looking (Giannaris) 337
Cavalcanti, Alberto 216
censorship 14, 48–52, 81, 158, 159
central producer system 17, 20
central/a-central imagining 157, 158
Chada, Gurinda 287
Chandavarkar, Bhaskar 386
Chandidas (Bose) 398
Chang (Cooper and Schoedsack) 217
Channel 4 television 37, 287–9, 291–2,
    367, 369–70, 371, 379
Chant d'Amour, Un (Genet) 309
character animation 240
Chariots of Fire (Puttnam) 368–9, 371
Chatterji, Basu 409
Chien andalou, Un (Buñuel and Dali) 116
Chienne, La 51
children 49, 52–3
Children's Hour, The (Wyler) 318
Chopra, Aditya 391–6
Christopher Strong (Arzner) 269
Churchill, Winston 52
Cinema Action 274
cinéma des auteurs 452; *see also* auteur
cinema runs 29
cinéma vérité 213, 216, 225–6
cinemas: location 18, 28, 45, 46; multi-
    plex theatre 28–9, 30, 372, 373
CinemaScope 72
cinematic codes 98–115

Cinematograph Films Act (1927) 349,
    352–3
cinematography 66
Cinéorama 72
Cineplex 28–9
Citizen Kane (Welles) 106, 107, 109, 112,
    114
Citron, Michelle 230
City Symphony documentaries 216
Clampett, Bob 242
classical narrative cinema *see* narrative
classification 48–9, 349–50; *see also*
    censorship
Clayton, Sue 280
Clockwork Orange, A (Kubrick) 274
close-up 26, 95, 108–9, 112, 133, 334,
    425
closure 122–4
Clueless 172
Coen brothers 176
Cohl, Émile 68, 238, 239–40
Collins, Jim 176, 178
Colonel Heeza Liar (Bray) 240
Color Purple, The (Spielberg) 285, 319
colour 28, 62, 63, 69, 71
Colour Box, A (Lye) 258
Comedy in Six Unnatural Acts
    (Oxenberg) 311
commutation test 185
computer-generated images 63, 73–7,
    77–9, 79, 85, 259
condensation 249
Connery, Sean 364
consent decrees 26, 28, 30, 32
contracts 20–1
conventions 93; *see also* narrative
Cook, Pam 359
Cooper, Budge 270
Cooper, Merian C. 216–7
Coppola, Francis Ford 197, 198
Corner, John 214
Correction Please (Burch) 108, 132
Costner, Kevin 178, 191, 200
costume 25, 103–5, 358
counter-cinema *see* alternative cinema
Countryman and the Cinematograph
    (Paul) 155
Coward, Noel 357
Craigie, Jill 270
Creative Artists Agency (CAA) 32–3
creative geography 423
Creature Comforts (Park) 251–2
Criminal, The (Toccafondo) 254–5
Cronenberg, David 314
cross-dressing 104
Crow, The 79
Cruising (Friedkin) 314
Crying Game, The 14, 34, 37–9, 104, 371
Cukor, George 340
cultural studies 157, 283–6
Curse of Frankenstein, The (Hammer)
    361
Curtiz, Michael 25
Cutler, J. 231
'cybercam' 260

Dali, Salvador 116
Damle, V.G. 398
Dance Girl Dance (Arzner) 269
Dances with Wolves (Costner) 177, 200
Daughter Rite (Citron) 230
De Antonio, Émile 229–30
De Niro, Robert 187, 188, 194
de Palma, Brian 446
Dead Ringers (Cronenberg) 314
Deadsy (Anderson) 258–9
Deans, Marjorie 270
Dearden, Basil 313
decoding 284
deconstruction 242
Deitch, Donna 230, 324–7, 339
Delegates at the Photographic Congress (Lumière) 66
Delormé, Charlotte 481
Demme, Jonathan 314
Derrida, Jacques 146
Desert Hearts (Deitch) 324–7, 339
desire (in spectatorship) 143–4
Desire (Marshall) 337
Desperately Seeking Susan 104–5, 284
Devdas (Barua) 398
dialectics 423, 424
Diary for Timothy, A (Jennings) 221
DiCaprio, Leonardo 185
diegesis 122, 434
Different from the Others 309
Dilwale Dulhaniya Le Jayenge (Aditya Chopra) 391–6
Dineen, Molly 231
Diorama 71–2
direct cinema 225, 229
director 195–9, 200, 205, 299, 405
director-unit system 17
'Director's Cut' 198, 199
Dirty Harry 117
Disney 69, 70, 72, 76, 85, 240–5; Disney dust 77
dissolves and fades 65, 110, 239, 247
distribution industry 14–15, 17, 19, 21, 27, 31–2, 36–9, 41, 81
Do the Right Thing (Lee) 139
documentary films 212–33, 293, 348, 358, 362–3, 446; blacks 225, 230, 231–2; constructedness 212; drama-documentary 92; and education 219–20, 224, 224–5; fly-on-the-wall 225; institutional life 219, 228–9; lesbian and gay 230; reflexive/performative 230; relativity 227; subjectivity 227; and truth/reality 213, 214, 216, 217–18, 219, 224, 232
dominant cinema 425; *see also* Hollywood
Don Juan (Warner Bros.) 21, 69
Don't Look Back (Pennebaker) 255
Don'ts and Be Carefuls, The 50
Douglas, Bill 446
Douglas, Michael 184
Dove, Linda 275
Dover Front Line (Watt) 220
Dovzhenko, Alexander 441–2, 446

Dr No 364
Dr. Strangelove 171
Dr Zhivago 115
Drabinsky, Garth 30
Dracula (Hammer) 361
Dracula (Whale) 102
Dream On (Amber films) 287, 377
Drew, Robert 225
Drifters (Grierson) 219–20
Duck Amuck (Jones) 242–5
Dutt, Guru 402, 403–4, 405
Dyer, Richard 180, 182–3, 192, 313, 317, 320, 322
dystopia 101

Ealing Studios 360–1, 379
Earth (Dovzhenko) 425, 441–2
Eastman, George 66
Eastwood, Clint 79, 171, 178, 453
Eaton, Michael 39–40
economic presentation 97
Edinburgh Film Festival 41
Edison Company 15, 16, 215
Edison, T.A. 69
editing 110–13, 133–4, 134; continuity 16, 111, 112; cross-cut 110; cutting speeds 113; establishing shot 93, 111, 119; eye-line match 97, 111; Hollywood 423; jump-cut 111; montage editing 112–13; and narrative 116; non-diegetic insert 113, 424, 429; 180 rule 110, 112; Pudovkin 422–3, 436; styles 111–12, 422–3; 30 rule 111
Edward II (Jarman) 336–7
Ehrenstein, David 290, 298
Eisenstein, Sergei 219, 337, 423, 427–36, 445, 446; *Battleship Potemkin* 62, 418, 425; *October* 425; *Old and New* 435–6; *Strike* 112, 425
embourgeoisement 351
Enchanted Drawing, The (Blackton) 239
encoding 284
End of St Petersburg, The (Pudovkin) 425, 436, 437–8
English Patient (Minghella) 141, 177, 453
Epstein, Robert 230, 312
Eraserhead (Lynch) 115
establishing shot 93
ethnographic research 285
Eurotrustees 37
exclusive run 29
exhibition industry 14–15, 16, 18–19, 26, 28–9, 35–6; development of 135–6; UK 28, 30, 38, 41
exposition 215
expressionism 101–2, 107, 360
Extraordinary Adventures of Mr West in the Land of the Bolsheviks, The (Kuleshov) 426–7
Eyes on the Prize (Hampton) 230

fabula 116
fade and mixes 65
Fall of the Romanov Dynasty (Shub) 443

Fallen Champ (Kopple) 231
Falling Down (Schumacher) 206
'false consciousness' (Marxist theory) 144, 149
Family Way, The (Boulting) 316
Fantasia (Disney) 70
Fantasmagorie (Cohl) 68, 239–40
Fassbinder, Rainer Werner 452, 459, 460, 463, 465, 468, 475
Fatehlal, S. 398
Fauvist art 254
Feeding the Baby (Lumière) 84
FEKS (Factory of the Eccentric Actor) 425, 438–40
Fellini, Federico 340
Fellow Traveller 14, 39–41
feminism 268
feminist film: accessibility 280–1; avant-garde 274, 278; black feminist film theory 284, 285; and documentary 230, 274, 275, 280, 292–3; film groups 274–5; fragmentation 289–91; German cinema 468, 470–2; lesbian feminist film theory 284, 285–6; Marxist theory 276–7, 280, 296; melodrama 282, 284, 358; need for audience 278; pleasure 276–7, 281; Red Flannel 289, 291–92; separatism 294; theory 276, 283–6
femme 311
Field, Connie 230
Field, Mary 269
Fields, Gracie 355, 356
Fifth Element, The 101
fight composer 406
film: agent of change 420–1; language of 95; and politics 224–5, 229–30; reading of 93, 94–5, 97, 116, 138–9, 162; theory 131–2, 136–41, 137
film exchange 15, 17
film form: alternatives 135; evolution of 132–5
film journalism 407
film noir 22, 23, 102, 107
Film and Television Agreement (Germany) 458
Film and Television Institute of India 408
film theatres *see* cinemas
film-making: co-operative enterprise 197; German courses 461; public funding 31, 33
financier-distributor, power of 31
Fires were Started (Jennings) 221
Fireworks (Anger) 309
Firm, The 46
First Days, The (Jennings) 220
First National 18, 21
first run 18, 19
Fischinger, Oskar 240
Fisher King, The 101
Fistful of Dollars, A 100
Flaherty, Robert 216–19
Fleischer brothers 240, 246
Flesh and Paper (Parmar) 338
Fletcher, Yvonne 270

flocking routine software 78
Flowers and Trees (Disney) 62, 71, 242
Flubber 86
fly-on-the-wall 443
focus 106–7, 108, 109
Foldes, Peter 259
foley stage 70
Fonda, Jane 192
Footlight Parade (Warner Bros.) 22
Formby, George 354–5, 356
formula film 390–1, 402
Forrest Gump 79, 86, 106, 172
Forster, E.M. 320, 369, 377
Foucault, Michel 146
Four Weddings and a Funeral 34, 119, 371
Frankenstein (Whale) 101
Frankfurt School 136
Free Cinema 362
Freed, Arthur 20, 199
Freedman, Jeffrey 312
French Lieutenant's Woman, The (Reisz) 121–2
Freud, Sigmund 276–7, 282, 284
Friedan, Betty 273
Friedkin, William 314, 316
Friedrich, Su 311
Fugitive, The 46
Full Metal Jacket (Kubrick) 229
Full Monty, The (Catteneo) 86, 141, 375–7
Fung, Richard 338

Gainsborough costume melodramas 358
Gallopin' Gaucho (Disney) 70
gamelan orchestra 69
gangster cycle 23
Gardner, Robert 231
Garland, Judy 190, 206, 317
Gast, Leon 232
Gastarbeiter 465
Gaudio, Tony 25
gay cinema *see* lesbian and gay cinema
Gay Liberation 310
gaze: male camera 134; male/female 276–7, 283, 284, 300–1, 308
gender 274, 279, 299, 300, 301, 308
General, The (Keaton) 95–8
General Film Company 16, 17
generic identity 164–5, 179–80; signifiers 176, 180
Genet, Jean 309
genre films 118–19, 162, 164, 166–81; and anarchy 328; classifying 170–4, 179–80; construction 169–70; crossover 168, 174; culture 169; hybrids 176, 178; iconography 167–8; identity 164–5; Indian cinema 389–90; inherited 175; narrative structures 169–70; order/integration 171–2, 174, 190; paradigms 167, 168, 205, 206; playing with 175–8; production units 20; props 167; reality shaping 166; romance 118; signifiers 167–8, 173; and stars 192

Gerald McBoing Boing (Cannon) 250
German cinema 452–82; alternative images 463–4; American influence/culture 453–5, 472–5; *Arbeiterfilme* 459; artisanal production 460–3; *Autorenkino* 460–1, 482; censorship 479–81; *cinéma des auteurs* 452, 462, 482; decartelisation laws 454; directors emigrated 455, 481–2; distribution and exhibition 459–60; escapism 455, 465; feminism 468, 470–1; FFA 458; Filmverlag der Autoren 459; *Gastarbeiter* 465–7; *Heimatfilme* 455, 465; Kuratorium junger deutscher Film 456, 457, 458, 459, 461, 462; national identity 461, 472, 479; Nazism 455, 472, 475, 477, 479; New Cinema 452–3, 457, 458, 460, 463, 481–2; Oberhausen Manifesto 456, 460, 461, 464; social issues 479–80, 481; sponsorship 479–81; subsidy system 458–63, 481, 482; survival 455–6; television 458; terrorism 467–8, 480–1; *Zutatenfilm* 460–1
German Sisters, The (von Trotta) 468, 480–1
Germany in Autumn 468, 480
Germany, Pale Mother (Sanders–Brahms) 470, 475, 476–7, 479
Gertie the Dinosaur, The (McCay) 68, 240
Giannaris, Constantine 337
Gilda (Vidor) 146, 317
Gimme Shelter (Maysles brothers) 226, 227
Girls in Uniform (Sagan) 309
Girls Night Out (Quinn) 248–9
Gish, Lillian 268
Gledhill, Christine 277–8, 285
Glynn, Elinor 269
Go Fish (Troche) 332–5
go-motion 76
Godard, Jean-Luc 112, 121, 123, 274, 446
Godfather, The 102–3, 112
Godzilla 86
Gold Diggers, The (Potter) 281, 287, 297
Goldcrest Films 371, 379
Gone with the Wind 53, 109
Good Fairy in the Cabbage Patch, The (Blaché) 268
Goodbye Columbus 112
GoodFellas (Scorsese) 109, 112, 114, 120, 205
Gordon, Clive 231
Gorris, Marlene 293–5, 319
Gottlieb, Carl 35
Graef, Roger 225
gramophone 69
Gramsci, Antonio 144–5, 285
Granton Trawler (Anstey) 220
Grass (Cooper and Schoedsack) 216–7
Great Depression 19, 21

Great Mouse Detective, The (Disney) 76
Great Train Robbery (Edison Company) 16
Greyson, John 311, 337, 337–8
Grierson, John 213, 219–20, 269
Grierson, Ruby 269
Griffith, D.W. 95, 110, 426
Grot, Anton 25
Guns in the Afternoon (Peckinpah) 168

Hackford, Taylor 232
Halas, John 238
Hale, George C. 216
Hall, Stuart 285
Haller, Ernest 25
Halloween (Carpenter) 110
Hammer, Barbara 311
Hammer horror 361–2, 364
Hampton, Henry 230
Handsworth Songs (Akomfrah) 230
Hampton, Henry 230
Harman and Ising 246
Harryhausen, Ray 63
Haunted Hotel, The (Blackton) 239
Hay, Will 354
Haynes, Tod 337
Hays Code 49–51
Hays, Will 50
HBO 30, 39–40, 41
Heart of Britain (Jennings) 220
Heaven's Gate (Cimino) 163
hegemony 135, 285, 351
Heimatfilme 455
Hembus, Joe 456
heritage cinema 348, 368–9, 371, 378
Herzog, Werner 452, 463
heterosexism 313, 324
heterosexual 308
high angle shot 93–4
High School (Wiseman) 229
Higson, Andrew 369, 372
Hill, John 362, 374
Hiller, Arthur 314
Hindi films *see* Indian cinema
Hirschfield, Dr Magnus 309
Hitchcock, Alfred 101, 109, 112, 269, 277, 282, 353
Hitler, Adolf 222, 224
HIV/AIDS 311–12, 328–30, 337
Hodge, John 374
Hollywood 351, 352, 353, 378, 379, 423; New Hollywood 163, 197–8
Homeland (Reitz) 475
hommage 178
homoeroticism 309, 318
homophobia 327, 370
homosexuality 309
Hoop Dreams (James, Marx, Gilbert) 231
horror films 119, 361–2
House of Wax (Warner Bros.) 73
Housing Problems (Anstey/Elton) 220
Houston, Whitney 191
Houwer, Rob 456
Howard's End (Merchant and Ivory) 377
Hubley, John and Faith 250
Hudson, Rock 317

Hughes, Langston 330–2, 337
Huillet, Daniele 457, 463
Humorous Phases of Funny Faces (Blackton) 68, 239
Hurtz, Bill 250
hyper-realism 76

Ice Storm, The (Ang Lee) 116
Ichikawa, Kon 231
iconic 243
iconoclasts 231
iconography 167–8, 350
identification 97, 148–9
identification *v.* estrangement 121
ideology 144–6, 244, 313, 418
If... (Anderson) 124–6
illustrative mode 214
image: computer-generated 63, 73–7, 77–9, 79, 85, 259; persistence of vision theory 62, 239; sound 113–14
IMAX 82–3, 155
Imperator Films 21
impersonation 186, 188
IMR (Institutional Mode of Representation) 95–6
In the Company of Men (Labute) 139
In the Line of Fire 46, 79
In Which We Serve (Coward) 357
In the Year of the Pig (De Antonio) 229
In the Year 2000 (Blaché) 269
incoherent cinema 240
Independence Day (Emmerich) 86, 172
independent films 27, 31, 32, 274–5, 366–7, 399
Indian cinema 382–413; actors 397, 399, 405, 406; actors-turned-directors 405; angry young man 406, 411; 'art' films 382, 407–9, 411; associations 407; *bhava* 384; Bollywood 401; Bombay Talkies 385, 398–9; censorship 395, 399–400, 401–2; colour 405, 411; comedy 382, 389; commercial success 412; costume 387–8; devotional films 390; *dharma* 384, 412; dialogue 385; distribution network 410–11; erotic imagery 403; family relationships 383; fantasy 383, 388; and feminism 395–6, 410; fight composer 406; Film Archives 408; film stock quotas 400; Film and Television Institute of India 408; financing 408; formula film 390–1, 402; genre 389–90; Hindi films 382–91, 396–402; historical films 390, 399; history of 396–402; Hollywood influence 411–12; independence from Britain 390, 399–402; 'lost and found' sagas 383, 390; *masala* movie 384; melodrama 384, 389; 'multi-starrers' 406–7; multicultural audiences 382; mythological films 390, 396–7; narrative structure 382–4, 411; national identity 406; New Theatres 398; parallel film movement 407; Parsi theatre 384, 385; and patriarchy 395; *play-back* 386; plot 383–4, 391; popular theatre 382, 383, 384; Prabhat Studios 398; *Ram Lila* 383–4; *rasa* 384; realism 384, 407, 408–9; romance 383, 389, 390, 391, 405; *sangeeta* 385; satellite television 411; silent era 385, 397; social films 390, 398, 399, 402–3; song 384–5, 388, 395, 411; song picturisation 386, 388, 404; song-and-dance 382, 385–7, 389, 391, 393–5; sound 385, 397, 411; spectacle 387–8, 393–5, 395, 405; stars 388–9, 391, 406–7; studio era 397–9; stunt films 399, 406, 411; and war effort 400; western influence 388, 402–3, 406, 408, 411; and women 395–6, 397, 403; women directors 409–10
intellectual montage 424, 433, 436
International Creative Management (ICM) 32
Internet 60–1, 81–2, 82
interpellation 134, 135, 137, 143, 150
intertextuality 178, 206
Intolerance (Griffith) 106, 426
Italian neo-realists 408
It's a Wonderful Life (Capra) 101
Ivens, Joris 222, 224

Jarman, Derek 337, 377
Jason and the Argonauts 63
Jaws (Universal) 14, 34–7, 117
Jazz Singer, The (Warner Bros.) 21, 62, 69
Jennings, Humphrey 220–1, 293
Johnny Guitar 100
Johnston, Claire 276, 279–80
Jones, Chuck 242–5
Jordan, Marion 363–4
Jordan, Neil 37
Julien, Isaac 330–2, 338
Jumanji 63, 259
Jungalee (Mukherjee) 405
Jungle Fever (Lee) 139
Jurassic Park (Spielberg) 30–1, 47, 62, 76, 169, 259
Just Another Girl on the IRT 146–7
juxtaposition 423, 429–32, 436, 443

Kaagaz Ke Phool (Dutt) 404
Kalin, Tom 336
Kaplan, Ann 281, 296
Kapoor, Raj 402, 403, 404, 411
Katzelmacher (Fassbinder) 465–6
Kaul, Mani 408–9
Kawaguchi, Yoichiro 260
Keaton, Buster 95–8, 254
Keighley, William 25
Khan, Salim 406
Khittl, Ferdinand 456
Khush (Parmar) 338
Kidron, Beeban 286–7
Killing of Sister George, The (Aldrich) 316, 318

Kinematascope 239
kinetograph 15
Kinetoscope 14, 95
King of Comedy (Scorsese) 202
King Kong (Cooper and Schoedsack) 62, 63, 83, 217
King's Row (Korngold) 26
Kircher, Athanasius 65
Kismet (Mukerjee) 400
Kiss Me Deadly 120
Kitses, Jim 100
Kleist, Solveig von 238
Kluge, Alexander 456, 457, 461, 463–5, 468, 475, 479–80
Knick Knack 259
knowingness 176, 177, 178
Kopple, Barbara 231
Korda, Alexander 354, 378
Korngold, Erich Wolfgang 25–6
Kostelac, Nikola 250
Kozintsev, Grigori 440
Krishnaswamy 385, 399, 411
Kubrick, Stanley 229, 273
Kuchar, George 309
Kückelmann, Norbert 461
Kuhn, Annette 281
Kuleshov, Lev 110, 422–3, 425–7
Kundun (Scorsese) 205
Kuratorium junger deutscher Film 456–7

L-shaped Room, The (Forbes) 316
Lacan, Jacques 137, 143–4, 146, 276, 281, 282, 284
Lang, Fritz 73, 101, 455
language 143; feminist film 278–9; and genre 175; and meaning 258
Lantz, Walter 246
Lanzmann, Claude 230
Lasseter, J. 76, 238, 259
Last Action Hero, The 33
Last Seduction, The (Dahl) 107–8, 177
Last Tango in Paris 188
Last Temptation of Christ (Scorsese) 205
Last Year in Marienbad 110
Lathan, James 260
Laura (Lydecker) 322
Lauretis, Teresa De 283
Lawnmower Man, The 74–6
Le Roy, Mervyn 25
Leacock, Richard 216, 225
Lean, David 359, 360, 372
Leather Boys, The (Furie) 316
Lee, Brandon 79
Lee, Spike 82
Legion of Decency 50
Leigh, Mike 378
Leone, Sergio 107, 108, 109–10, 115
lesbian and gay cinema 308–40; analysis 315–20; audiences 310–11; and black culture 331–2; documentary 337, 338, 339; and feminist film 284, 285–6; film clubs 310–11; film festivals 311–12; gay sensibility 313–14; new attitudes 323; new images 335; 'New Queer Cinema' 335–6, 337;

and race 338–9; representation 308–9, 315, 318, 320–1; sex and spectator 326–7; stereotypes 320–1, 328–9; *see also My Beautiful Launderette*
lesbian/gay: definitions 309–10; identification 318; and race 338–9
Lévi-Strauss, Claude 169
Lewton, Val 199
L'Homme à la Tête de Caoutchouc (Méliès) 62
liberal humanism 229
licensing, projection equipment 16
Liebe Mutter, mir geht es gut (Ziewer) 459
Life of an American Fireman (Porter) 113
Life and Death of Col. Blimp, The 52
Life and Times of Grizzly Adams, The 47
Life and Times of Rosie the Riveter, The (Field) 230
Lift to the Scaffold 115
lightening cartoonists 239
lighting 25, 63, 106–8
lightning cartoonist 239
linguistic theory 137
linkage editing 437
Lion King, The (Disney) 76, 260
Lippmann, Walter 219
Listen to Britain (Jennings) 221, 293
literary classics 16, 359
Little Caesar 92, 184
Little Nemo in Slumberland (McCay) 92, 239
Littlewood, Joan 272
Living End (Araki) 327–30
Livingstone, Jenny 339
Loach, Ken 372, 373–4, 377–8
Logan, Jacqueline 269
Lolita (Kubrick) 273
London Can Take It (Jennings) 220
London Electronic Arts 29
London Film-makers' Co-op 29, 274
London Films 21
London Women's Film Group 275, 293
Long Day Closes, The (Davies) 277
Long Kiss Goodnight, The 146
look, the 134, 137, 318; *see also* gaze
Look Back in Anger (Richardson) 63, 362
Look Who's Talking 171
Looking for Langston (Julien) 330–2
Lorentz, Pare 224–5
Lost Honour of Katherina Blum, The (von Trotta and Schlöndorff) 460, 468
Lost in Space 86
Lost World, The (Spielberg) 76
Lovell, Alan 372
Lovell, Terry 282
low-key image 107
Lubitsch, Ernst 455
Lucas, George 70
Lumière brothers 66–7, 83, 155, 215, 396
Lunacharsky, Anatoli 418, 421
Lupino, Ida 276
Lye, Len 258
Lynch, David 115

MacCabe, Colin 145
McCay, Winsor 68, 238, 239–40
McClaren, Norman 238, 252–3
McConnell, Frank 171, 175, 180, 189
McKimson, Robert 242
McLaughlin, Sheila 320
Madonna 190
magic lantern 65
Magnificent Ambersons, The (Welles) 198
mainstream films 92, 121–4
Making Love (Hiller) 314
Malini, Hema 410
Maltese Falcon 111, 322
Mam (Red Flannel) 292–3
Man of Aran (Flaherty) 218–19
Man with a Movie Camera, The (Vertov) 216, 423, 442, 444
Man Who Shot Liberty Valance, The (Ford) 171
Mander, Kay 270
Mangeshkar, Lata 386
March of Time, The 224
Marey, Etienne Jules 66
marginalisation 230, 268, 281, 310
marketing 31, 35–6, 38–9, 47
Marnie (Hitchcock) 109, 277, 282
Mars Attacks! 77–9, 171
Marsh, Mary 270
Marshall, Stuart 337
Marxist theory 144–5, 276–7, 280, 296
'masala' movies 384
Mask, The 86
match-move 78
mattes 67
Maxwell, James Clerk 71
Maysles brothers 225–6, 227
Mean Streets (Scorsese) 114, 202
meaning: cultural 206; film-maker/audience 275; music 114–15; surplus of 194, 205; *see also* language; reading of film
Media II programme 31, 34
mediation 94
Meerapfel, Jeanine 470
Meet Me in St Louis (Minnelli) 20, 165
Meeting of Two Queens, The (Barriga) 338
Mehboob Khan 402, 405
Mehra, Prakash 406
Mehta, Deepa 410
Mehta, Vijaya 409
Méliès, Georges 61, 62, 67, 94, 95, 97, 238, 239, 397
melodrama 22, 23, 201, 299, 358
Men in Black 86
merchandising 31, 36–7
Merrie England 22, 23
metamorphosis 247
Method acting 187, 188, 194
Metropolis (Lang) 73
metteur-en-scène 195, 198
Mickey Mouse 70, 85, 241
Mikesch, Elfi 470

Mildred Pierce (Steiner) 20, 25, 103–4, 107–8, 114, 115, 118, 174
Millett, Kate 230
Millhouse: A Whitehouse Comedy (De Antonio) 229
Minnelli, Liza 165–6, 194
Minnelli, Vincente 165–6
Minghella, Anthony 178, 452–3
Minh-ha, Trinh T. 231
minimalism 106
Miramax 38–9
Mirch Masala (Ketan Mehta) 395
'mirror phase' 144
mise-en-scène 98–9, 105, 110, 116, 133, 360, 419–20, 440, 445
misrecognition 144
Moana (Flaherty) 213, 218
modernism 97, 367, 377
Modi, Sohrab 399
Modleski, Tania 282
monopolistic practice 14, 16, 17, 26
Monroe, Marilyn 181–2
montage 25, 62, 112–13, 420, 422–4, 434, 436, 444–5
montage of attractions 429
Monterey Pop (Pennebake) 225
Moore, Michael 230–1
Moore, Peter 212
Moore's Law 81
moral/ideological rules 158
Morris, Errol 230
Mother India (Mehboob) 395, 402–3
Mother, The (Pudovkin) 51, 425, 436, 437
Motion Picture Association of America (MPAA) 48
Motion Picture Patents Company (MPPC) 16–17; anti-trust violation 17, 18
Motion Picture Producers and Distributors of America (MPPDA) 50
mountain movies 222
Moussinac, Leon 436
movie theatres 16, 18, 21, 29; *see also* cinemas
Mr Magoo 250
Mrityudand (Prakah Jha) 395
Mughal-e-Azam (Asif) 387–8, 390, 405
Mukerjee, G. 400
Mukherjee, S. 405
Mulazinni, Simona 254
multi-media empires 14, 42–3
multi-plane camera 85, 242
multi-reel feature films 16, 17
multimedia conglomerates 28, 42–3
multiple exposures 62, 67
multiple run 29
Mulvey, Laura 134, 145, 276–80, 281, 282, 285, 308, 317
Murdoch, Rupert 42
Murphy, Jeanette 294
music 113, 115; dynamics of musicality 257; non-diegetic 114, 115; as signifier 168, 300
musicals 23, 179–80; binary analysis 170; integrated 20

Muybridge, Edward 66, 215
My Beautiful Launderette 34, 367, 369–70
My Darling Clementine 100
My Name is Joe (Loach) 373–4, 378
myth 169, 171

Nair, Meera 410
Nandy, Ashis 383
Nanook of the North 217–18
narrative 115–26; alternative 121–6; analysis 116–17, 169–70; cartoons 239, 246; cause-effect 117–18; characters 120; closure 123; and commentary 96; complexity 17; compressed 25; disruption 118–19, 124; endings 119–20, 124; equilibrium 118–19, 169, 170; fabula 116; fractured style 116, 124; framing device 120; plot/sub-plot 116; Proppean analysis 120; silent films 95–8; stylistic practices 124–6; transivity v. intransivity 123; villain/hero 119
national cinema 348, 453
national identity: British 348–50, 351, 354, 358, 367, 375, 378; German 461, 472, 479; Indian 406
National Lottery 29, 33, 379
Natural Born Killers (Stone) 121, 149, 176
Natyashastra (Bharata) 384, 385
Nazism 222–3, 455, 472, 477, 479
negotiated reading 139, 285
Neighbours (McClaren) 252–3
New Babylon (Kozintsev and Trauberg) 440, 444
New Hollywood 163, 197–8
New Queer Cinema 335–6, 337
New Wave 110, 112
New York, New York (Scorsese) 162–4, 178–81, 193–5, 202–3
newsreels 70, 214, 216
Nichols, Bill 230
nickelodeons 14, 16
Night Cleaners (Berwick Street Collective) 275
Nightmail (Wright/Watt) 220, 356
Nightmare on Elm Street 115, 117
Nippon Development and Finance 37
noir-melodrama 20
noise 92
non-diegetic 112, 424
non-fiction films: aesthetics 214; authored 217; categories 213–14; developments 215–16; as records 225–6; sociological dimensions 214; travelogue 216–17
North by Northwest (Hitchcock) 112, 117, 282
North Sea (Watt) 220
nostalgia 219, 368, 369, 378, 412
Notorious (Hitchcock) 282
Now Voyage (Steiner) 25
NRA programme 23

Nykino 224

Oberhausen Manifesto 456, 463
O'Brian, Will 63
obscenity 48–9, 52–3
October (Eisenstein) 425, 433–5
Old Mill, The (Disney) 85, 242
Old and New (Eisenstein) 435–6
oligopoly 18, 21, 43
Olympia (Riefenstahl) 231
OMNIMAX 82–3
On the Town 179
On the Waterfront 186
Once upon a Time in the West (Leone) 107, 108, 109–10, 115
oppositional cinema *see* alternative cinema
oppositional reading 138, 285
optical experiments 65
optical sound 70
Orlando (Potter) 287, 290, 296, 298–9, 377
Other Cinema, The 274
Out of the Inkwell (Fleischer) 240, 260
Outlaw Josey Wales, The (Eastwood) 171
overheard exchange 214
Oxenberg, Jan 311

pack-of-cards financing 34, 37
package-unit system 32, 35
Panorama 71
Pantopticon 14
parallel cinema 407
Paramount 18, 28, 29, 30, 72, 124; antitrust case 21, 26
Paranjpye, Sai 409
Parenthood 171
Paris is Burning (Livingstone) 339
Park, Nick 238, 251–2
Parmar, Pratibha 338
Parting Glances (Sherwood) 311
Passport to Pimlico (Ealing Studios) 360
patent pool 16
Pathé 71
Pather Panchali (Ray) 408
patriarchy 274, 276, 277, 278, 283, 294–6, 300, 301, 303, 395
Paul, Robert 155
pay-TV 30
Peckinpah, Sam 168, 274
Penley, C. 282
Pennebaker, Don 225–6
Penny Journey (Jennings) 220
performative documentary 230
persistence of vision theory 62, 239
Persona (Bergman) 122
personality animation 240
personification 186, 188
Petley, Julian 51, 358
Pett and Pott (Cavalcanti) 220
Phalke, D.G. 396–7
phallocentrism 277, 281
Phantasmagoria (Robertson) 65, 83
Phenakistoscope 65, 239

Philadelphia (Demme) 172, 314
Phonofilm 70
phonograph 69
photography 66
Piano, The (Campion) 284, 290, 299–303
Pickford, Mary 268
Pierson, John 333
pink triangle 337
Pitt, Brad 185
PIXAR company 259
pixillation 252
Plane Crazy (Disney) 70
Platoon 52
play-back 386
Player, The (Altman) 198
playfulness 178
pleasure (in film narrative) 141–3, 206, 277
plot (syuzhet) 116
Plow that Broke the Plains, The (Lorentz) 224
pluralism 351
Pohland, Hans Jurgen 456
Point (Milton Keynes) 30
Point of Order (De Antonio) 229
Poison (Haynes) 337
political-cultural theories 137
Polito, Sol 25
polysemy 190, 285
Popeye (Fleischer) 240, 246
popular culture 132, 136
Porter, Edwin 16
Post Haste and Locomotives (Jennings) 220
post-Impressionism 254
postmodernism 156, 162, 171, 175–8, 189, 373
post-structuralism 146
Potter, Sally 276, 278, 281, 287, 289, 290, 296–9, 377
Powell, Michael 360
Praxinoscope 65, 66, 239
preferred reading 138
Pressburger, Emeric 360
Pretty Woman 118, 183
Primary (Drew) 225
proactive observationalism 214
producer, as auteur 199
producer-unit system 20, 199
production 14–16, 17, 32–4, 35–6, 38, 41; artisanal 461–3; director system of 17; finance 30, 84–5; hierarchical system 17, 20; world economics 84–5
Production Code 49–51
propaganda: americanisation 352; censorship 51–2; documentary 220–2, 269–70; in Soviet cinema 421; wartime 357–8
Propp, Vladimir 120, 169
props 101–3
Prospero's Books (Greenaway) 85
Protazanov, Yakov 420
proto-animation 239
Psycho (Hitchcock) 113, 114

psychoanalytic theory 136, 137, 143–4, 148, 276, 282, 284
Public Enemy, The (Warner Bros.) 50, 51, 184
publicity 31
Pudovkin, Vsevolod 422–3, 425, 426, 436–8
Pulp Fiction (Tarantino) 120, 148–57, 157, 177, 199
Puttnam, David 368–9, 371
Pyaasa (Dutt) 404
pyrotechnics 79

Quatermass Experiment, The 361, 362
queer 335
Question of Silence, A (Gorris) 293–5, 319
Quick and the Dead, The 168
Quinn, Joanna 248–9
quota legislation 352–3

Radio-Keith-Orpheum (RKO) 18, 21, 26
Radway, Janice 285
Rafelson, Bob 339
Raging Bull (Scorsese) 187, 188, 202, 231
Rai, Himansu 398–9
Raiders of the Lost Ark 117
Rain Man 106
Raising Arizona (Coen Bros) 176
Raja Harishchandra (Phalke) 396
Raje, Aruna 409
Ram Rajya (Vijay Bhatt) 400
Rani, Deviki 398–9
Rank, J. Arthur 359–60, 378
Rank Organisation 21
rasa 384
Rashomon (Kurasawa) 122–3
ratings system 48; *see also* classification
Ray, Satyajit 382, 407–8
Raynaud, Émile 61, 65, 69, 86, 239
Razia Sultan (Kamal Amrohi) 390
reactive observationalism 214, 216
reading of film 93, 94–5, 97, 116, 138–9, 162; oppositional 138; preferred 138
real person/role persona 182–3
realism 363, 372, 384, 407, 408–9; animation 241–2, 259; cinéma vérité 213, 216, 225–6; dramatic 106–7; and fantasy 126, 372, 376–7; Hollywood classical 111; ideology 418; montage 444–5; Socialist 445; wartime cinema 356–9; *see also* actuality; documentary; surrealism
reality, illusory 92–4, 156, 189
reality status 126
RealVideo 81
reappropriation 335–6
Rear Window (Hitchcock) 277, 282
Rebecca (Hitchcock) 282
Rebel Without a Cause (Ray) 109, 315–6
recipe films 460–1
recognition 149, 150
Red Skirts on Clydeside 281
reduced animation 250

reflexive documentary 230
regional arts councils 29
regional film theatres (RFTs) 29
Reidemeister, Helga 480
Reinl, Harald 465
Reisz, Karel 123, 362
Reitz, Edgar 452, 456, 461, 468, 475
religion, and films 50
Renoir, Jean 445
representation: class 353–6; and ideology 319; IMR 95–6; lesbians/gays 308–9, 315, 318, 320–1; questioned 279; women 273–4, 277, 279, 281
Rescuers, The (Disney) 76
Rescuers Down Under, The (Disney) 76
responses 138, 139, 150, 154, 285
Reville, Alma 269
Rich, B. Ruby 335
Richardson, Tony 362
Riefenstahl, Leni 222–4, 231
Rien que les heures (Cavalcanti) 216
Riff Raff (Loach) 376, 377
Riggs, Marlon 338
Rising Sun 46
River, The (Lorentz) 224–5
Roaring 'Twenties, The 103
Robert, Étienne Gaspard 65
Roberts, Graham 443
Roberts, Julia 182–3
RoboCop (Verhoeven) 92–4
Roger and Me (Moore) 230–1
Roget, Peter Mark 239
romance genre 118
Rosenbaum, Marianne 470
Rosenberg, Robert 230, 311
Roth, Wilhelm 479
Roy, Bimal 402, 403
running time, increased 16
Rush to Judgement (De Antonio) 229
Russell, Erica 238
Russell, Ken 340
Russian cinema 419–20; *see also* Soviet cinema
Russo, Vito 315–16
Ruttman, Walter 216, 240
Rybczynski, Zbigniew 446

Sagan, Leontine 309
Salesman (Maysles brothers) 226–7
Sally in our Alley 355, 356
Sander, Helke 470, 471
Sanders-Brahms, Helma 465, 470, 475, 476–7, 479
sangeeta 385
Sant Tukaram (Fatehlal and Damle) 398
Sarris, Andrew 201
saturation run 29
Saturday Night and Sunday Morning (Reisz) 362
Saturday Night Fever 156
Saussure, Ferdinand de 143
Scagliotti, John 230
Scarface 103

Scarlet Pimpernel, The (Korda) 353–4, 356
Scorpio Rising (Anger) 274
Schamoni, Peter 457
Schamoni, Ulrich 457
Schatz, Thomas 171–3, 175, 180, 189, 190
Schiller, Greta 230, 311, 332
Schlesinger, Leon 260
Schlöndorff, Volker 457, 460, 463, 468
Schmidt, Eckart 459
Schoedsack, Ernest 216–7
Schwartz, Lillian 259
Schwartz, Zack 242
Schwarzenegger, Arnold 33, 189, 200
scientific management methods 17, 18–20
scopophilia 276–7, 301, 395
Scorsese, Martin 96, 165–6, 194, 200, 226; *Cape Fear* 177; *GoodFellas* 109, 112, 114; *Mean Streets* 114, 202; *New York, New York* 180, 194, 202–3; *Who's that Knocking at my Door?* 112, 202; *see also* Taxi Driver
Scott, Ridley 101, 198–9
script content 64
script development, finance 40
Searchers, The 118, 119
Second Awakening of Christa Klages, The (von Trotta) 468, 480
Seeta (Bose) 398
self-regulation 48
Sen, Aparna 410
Senft, Haro 456
Sense and Sensibility 172, 351
Sestier, Maurice 396
setting 99–101
Seventh Veil, The (Box) 270–2
sex and censorship 50–1
sexuality 299, 309
sexual ideology 313–14, 317
sexual immorality 401
shadow puppets 64, 69
shadows 107
Shaheed (R. Sehgal) 401
Shane (Stevens) 100, 101, 119
Shantaram, V. 398, 400
Sharma, V. 390
She Must Be Seeing Things (McLaughlin) 320
Sheffield Film Co-op 280
Sherwood, Bill 311
Singin' in the Rain 169
Shirin's Wedding (Sanders-Brahms) 465
Shklovsky, Victor 434–5
Shoah (Lanzmann) 230
Shootist, The 168
Shortcuts (Altman) 120
shot: high/low angle 109; point of view 134, 152; point-of-view 133; side-on 152
shot-reverse-shot dialogue 151
Shub, Esfir 423, 443
Shurey, Dinah 269

signifiers 176, 180; props 103; stars 106, 181, 184, 190, 192
Sikander (Sohrab Modi) 400
Silence of the Lambs 102, 336
Silkwood (Nichols) 318–19
single-reel films 14, 16, 17
Sinkin' in the Bathtub (Harman and Ising) 246
Sircar, B.N. 398
Sirk, Douglas 101, 200–1, 317, 455, 473
Sklar, Robert 245
Sleeping with the Enemy 183
Sleepless in Seattle 46
Sliding Doors 124
Smith, George A. 71
Snow White and the Seven Dwarfs (Disney) 242
social commentary 219–20
social conscience film 23
social films 390, 398, 399, 402–3
social issues: abortion 457; anti-semitism 457; guest workers 465–7; terrorism 467–8, 480–1
social realism 362
Some Like it Hot 104, 119
Song of Ceylon (Wright) 220
Song of the Shirt (Clayton and Curling) 281
song picturisation 386, 404
Sontag, Susan 222–3, 313
Sony Corporation 30–1, 42
sound 62, 63, 69–70, 85, 113–15; and continuity 114; diegetic 113; Dolby 70; effects 70, 114; and narrative 116, 126; peripheral 115; stereophonic 28, 70; voiceovers 111–14, 120
sound-synch systems 69
Soviet cinema 418–46; acting/actors 425, 426, 436–7, 440; audience reponse 443–4; documentary 423; economics of film industry 421–2; FEKS 425, 438–40; historical background 418–19; ideology 418, 420–1; imported films 420, 421, 444, 445; Kuleshov effect 422–3; legacy 445–6; mainstream films 444; montage 420, 422–4, 426, 432, 433–4, 436, 437–8, 443; 1930s and after 445; narrative 425; pre-revolutionary 419–20, 421; propaganda 421, 444; re-editing films 422, 426, 443; Socialist Realism 445; statistical analysis of films 424; women film-makers 443
Space Jam (Warner Bros.) 260
Spaghetti Westerns 100
Spanish Earth 51
Spare Time (Jennings) 220
special effects 63–4, 66–7, 76, 78, 239, 411; *see also* technology
specialisms, and production units 20
spectator/spectatorship 130–59; and auteur identity 201; and character 148–57; cine-literateness 150, 153; competence 154–5; complicity with

genre 175; and desire 144, 148; evaluative judgement 154–5; imagination 155; interventionism 159; passivity 132, 137, 139, 143, 155, 285; political positions 158–9; and regulation 158–9; schemas 162, 175, 179; as subject 137–8, 143; *see also* audience; reading of film; responses
Spielberg, Steven 35, 201, 285, 319
sport 231–3
Spring Offensive (Jennings) 220
Squadron 992 (Watt) 220
squash and stretch 250
Stacey, Jackie 284
Stagecoach (Ford) 112, 167
Stallone, Sylvester 200
Stanislavski, 188
Stanley Company 21
Star Wars (Lucas) 70, 169
Starawicz, Ladislaw 238, 240
Starr, Cecile 252
stars 162, 164, 181–95; actor stars 186–9, 205; analysis 181–6; as auteurs 199; casting 185; charisma 183; commutation test 185, 192; fantasy role models 190; and genre 24, 184, 192; identity 165; and ideology 189–91; image 149, 181, 181–2, 183, 190–1; maximised types 191; meaning systems/structures 185, 188, 189, 195; paradigms 184–6, 188; persona 149, 181, 184; and popularity 192, 206; sexuality 318; signature 199; as signifiers 106, 181, 184, 190, 192; star moment 182, 183; as structure 184–6; study of 165; value of 33, 182
Starship Troopers (Verhoeven) 93, 259
Steadicam 93, 108, 109, 110
Steamboat Willy (Disney) 70, 85, 241
Steiger, Rod 186
Stein, Jules 32
Steiner, Max 25–6
Stephenson, Ralph 250
stereotyping: gender roles 274, 279; lesbian and gay cinema 314–15, 320–1, 328–9, 334; women 273, 276, 279
Stites, Richard 444
Stone, Oliver 202
stop-motion techniques 68, 77–8
Storck, Henri 51
Story of a Mosquito, The (McCay) 240
Strangers on a Train (Hitchcock) 101–3
Strasberg, Lee 186, 188
Straub, Jean-Marie 457, 463
Strike (Eisenstein) 112, 425, 428–32
structuralist approach 136, 139, 184, 205, 206, 276
studio era 17–20, 22–6
studio system 199
stunt films 399, 406, 411
subscription TV 30
substitution technique 67
Sulivan, Pat 61

Sunset Boulevard 120
Superman (Fleischer) 240
surplus of meaning 194, 204, 206
surrealism 238, 250, 374
Survage, Leopold 256
suspension of disbelief 92, 156, 189
suture 137, 138, 150
Svankmajer, Jan 238
Sweetie (Campion) 299
Swept from the Sea (Kidron) 288
Syberberg, Hans Jürgen 475
symbolism 144, 425
symmetry 253
synecdoche 243
synergy strategy 42
syuzhet (plot) 116

'tableau' films 95, 98
talkie shorts 19
Tango, The (Toccafondo) 254
Tango Lesson, The (Potter) 287, 296, 377
Target for Tonight (Watt) 220
Tarkovsky, Andrei 446
Taste of Honey, A (Richardson) 316, 362
Taubin, Amy 338
Taxi Driver (Scorsese) 119, 120, 181, 202, 205
Taylor, F.W. 17
Technicolor 71, 242
technology 60–86; high-definition 42; of illusion 62–5; impact of 60–2; innovations 62–3; revolution 365
television: BBC 39–40, 41; Channel 4 37, 289, 291–2, 367, 369–70, 371, 379; co-production 33–4, 37–8, 39–41, 371; distribution of film 30–1; documentary films 229–30; effect on cinema audiences 28, 44–5; and film production 28, 31–2, 33; film promotion 42; German films 458; and Internet 81–2; letterboxing 82; network 30; syndicated 30, 31; women film-makers 289, 291
Terminator (Cameron) 60, 167
Termintor 2 (Cameron) 102, 259
terrorism (and German cinema) 467–8
testimony 214
Thatcherism 368–9, 369, 376, 378
Thaumatrope 65
Théâtre Optique 65, 69, 239
theatre ownership 28
Thelma and Louise (Ridley Scott) 174, 199, 290
Thin Blue Line, The (Morris) 230
35mm film 72
39 Steps, The (Hitchcock) 269
This Sporting Life (Anderson) 362
Thompson, Richard 242, 244
Thread of Life, The (Wollheim) 155
3-D 28, 73
Three Lives (Millett) 230
Thriller (Potter) 280, 296, 297
THX 70
tie-ins 31, 36–7
Time-Warner 42

Times of Harvey Milk, The (Epstein) 230, 311
Tin Drum, The (Schlöndorff) 460
Tirez sur le pianiste (Truffaut) 110
Titanic 64, 86, 141, 185
Titicut Follies (Wiseman) 228–9
To Be a Woman (Craigie) 270
Toccafondo, Gianluigi 238, 254–5
Todorov, 120, 169, 170
Tokyo Olympiad (Ichikawa) 231
Tongues Untied (Riggs) 338
Tootsie 104
Tours and Scenes of the World (Hale) 216
Toy Story (Lasseter) 68, 76, 259
Toye, Wendy 270
Trainspotting (Macdonald) 34, 116, 373–5
transparency *v.* foregrounding 122
Trauberg, Leonid 440
travelogue 216–17
Treut, Monika 338
trick film 66–7
Triumph of the Will (Riefenstahl) 222–3
Troche, Rose 332–5
Tron (Boxleitner) 74
Truffaut, François 110, 274
trust companies 17; anti-trust case 21, 26
truth 213, 217, 274, 275, 441–2; *see also* documentary; realism
Turner, Guinevere 332–3
Twentieth-Century Fox 29, 30, 72
Twister 86, 259
2001: A Space Odyssey (Kubrick) 73–4
Tyler, Parker 315
typage 425
Tyrell, Lord 51

UFA (Universum Film Ag) 454, 455
Under the Skin (Adler) 377
Unforgiven, The (Eastwood) 100, 177, 289–90
United Artists 18, 21, 27, 163
United Productions of America 250
unity of style 247
Universal 18, 21, 28, 29, 30, 35–7
Urinal (Greyson) 337
'uses and gratifications' 190
Uski Roti (Kaul) 408
Usual Suspects, The 117

Vanderbeek, Stan 259
Vanishing, The (Sluitzer) 198
Vanishing Lady, The (Blackton) 239
vaudeville acts 18, 19, 68
vertical integration 14, 17, 21, 348

Vertigo (Hitchcock) 117–8, 277
Vertov, Dziga 215–16, 422–3, 442–3
Victim (Dearden) 313, 321–4
Victory of Faith (Rieferstahl) 222
videos 30–1
Vidor, Charles 318
Virgin Machine (Treut) 338
virtual reality 73, 83–4
vision, wrap-around 82
Visit to the Spiritualist, A (Blackton) 239
visual signifiers 167
Vitaphone sound system 21, 69
voiceovers 120
Von Praunheim, Rosa 311, 337
von Trotta, Margarethe 460, 463, 468, 480–1
Voyage dans la lune, Le (Méliès) 62, 68, 95
voyeurism 134, 277, 300–1, 327
Vukotic, Dusan 250

Waiting to Exhale 146–7
Wald, Jerry 20
Walsh, Raoul 25
Walters, Susan 284
War of the Worlds (Welles) 83
Warhol, Andy 274, 309
Warner Bros. 18, 21–6, 29, 30; animation 246, 247; art direction 25; as auteur 22, 199; background music 25–6; contract directors 25; 'fast' editing style 25; genre films 20, 21, 23–4; studio bound style 21, 25; style 22–6; theatre ownership 28
Warner Village 29
Wasserman, Lew 32
Waterworld (Costner) 200
Watson, Paul 225
Watt, Harry 220
Way We Live, The (Craigie) 270
Weber, Lois 269
Weiss, Andrea 317–20, 332
Welles, Orson 106, 107, 109, 112–13, 114
Wenders, Wim 452, 459, 460, 463, 472, 473–5
Western Electric sound equipment 21
Westerns, binary analysis 170
Westworld 168
Whale, James 315
What's Up Doc? 119
When Harry Met Sally 118, 119
When We Were Kings (Gast and Hackford) 231, 232
Whitney, James 259
Who Framed Roger Rabbit? 260

Who's that Knocking at my Door? (Scorsese) 112, 202
Wicked Lady, The (Gainsborough) 358
widescreen 28, 72
Wild Party, The (Arzner) 317
William Morris agency 32
Williams, Robin 86
wire frame shapes 74
wire removal 78
Wiseman, Frederick 227–9
Wolder, Billy 455
Wollen, Peter 124, 372
Woman to Woman (Deitch) 230
women 268–303, 443; alternative films 274; documentary film 230, 269–71; erotic object 277; film crew 286, 288, 297; film groups 274–3, 280–1; film-makers 268–73, 288, 289–90; Indian cinema 395–6, 397, 403, 409–10; mainstream films 286, 288; representation 273–4, 277, 279, 281; stereotyping 273, 276, 279; television 289, 291
Women of the Rhondda (London Women's Film Group) 275, 293
Woodstock (Wadleigh) 226–7
Wooley, Steve 37
word-of-mouth 29, 47
Words for Battle (Jennings) 220–1
Workers' Film and Photo League of America 224
Workers Leaving the Lumière Factory (Lumière) 66, 215
workers' unions 20
workshops 274
World Today, The (Nykino) 224
Written on the Wind (Sirk) 201
Wrong Arm of the Law 104

xerography 258

Yesterday Girl (Kluge) 456, 457, 463–5
You Oughta Be in Pictures 260
Young Soul Rebels (Julien) 377
Young Törless (Schlöndorff) 457
Youngblood, Denise 422, 440

Zagreb school/Studios 238, 250
Zanjeer (Mehra) 406
Zanuck, Richard 35
Zero Patience (Greyson) 337–8
Zetterling, Mai 272
Ziewer, Christian 459
Zoetrope 65, 66
zoom 65